*Czechoslovakia between
Stalin and Hitler*

Czechoslovakia between Stalin and Hitler

The Diplomacy of Edvard Beneš in the 1930s

IGOR LUKES

New York   Oxford
OXFORD UNIVERSITY PRESS
1996

Oxford University Press

Oxford   New York
Athens   Auckland   Bangkok   Bombay
Calcutta   Cape Town   Dar es Salaam   Delhi
Florence   Hong Kong   Istanbul   Karachi
Kuala Lumpur   Madras   Madrid   Melbourne
Mexico City   Nairobi   Paris   Singapore
Taipei   Tokyo   Toronto

and associated companies in
Berlin   Ibadan

Library of Congress Cataloging-in-Publication Data
Lukes, Igor.
Czechoslovakia between Stalin and Hitler : the diplomacy of
Edvard Beneš in the 1930s / Igor Lukes.
p.   cm.
Includes bibliographical references and index.
ISBN 0-19-510266-5; ISBN 0-19-510267-3 (pbk.)
1. Beneš, Edvard, 1884–1948.   2. Czechoslovakia—Foreign
relations—Germany.   3. Germany—Foreign relations—Czechoslovakia.
4. Czechoslovakia—Foreign relations—Soviet Union.   5. Soviet
Union—Foreign relations—Czechoslovakia.   6. Czechoslovakia—
Foreign relations. I. Title.
DB2078.G3L85   1996
327.437043'09'043—dc20   95-9284

1 3 5 7 9 8 6 4 2

Printed in the United States of America
on acid-free paper

PREFACE

Edvard Beneš (1884–1948) was a major European politician, foreign policy strate-gist, and important actor in the Czechoslovak-German drama of the 1930s. This volume studies the first two decades of his diplomacy and analyzes the Prague government's attempts to secure the existence of the Republic of Czechoslovakia in the treacherous space between the millstones of East and West.

The crisis of the 1930s, especially the Four Power Agreement signed at Munich in September 1938, provoked a vast amount of writing. To be sure, some important questions still remain to be answered. But it is safe to say that we now have a high-resolution picture of the British, French, German, Hungarian, and Polish dimen-sions of the crisis. This cannot be said about the roles played by the Prague govern-ment and the Kremlin.

Czechoslovak territory in the Sudetenland was one of the main points of con-tention in 1938, yet historians have often downplayed the activities of President Beneš and his colleagues in the escalating European conflict. And no wonder: until the fall of the Berlin Wall, it was difficult for researchers unaffiliated with official Czechoslovak institutions to gain complete access to the relevant archival collections in Prague. Under such circumstances, one had to treat as evidence politically slanted memoirs, official pronouncements, and collections of arbitrarily selected docu-ments. Because of this limitation, the Prague government was frequently treated as the passive object of a Franco-British deal with Hitler, an entity without options and incapable of initiatives. The scarcity of Czechoslovak primary sources concerning the crisis of the 1930s closely paralleled the dearth of Soviet documentation. This—and Stalin's absence at Munich—led many historians to treat the Soviet role in the Czechoslovak-German crisis as marginal at most. Others chose to give an approving account of the Soviet leader's behavior in Central Europe prior to World War II.

This book deals with the European crisis of the 1930s by focusing on the hitherto neglected Czechoslovak and Soviet perspectives. Chapter 1 analyzes Czechoslovak-Soviet relations from the end of World War I to the beginning of the Nazi rule in Germany. Thomas G. Masaryk, Edvard Beneš, and other policy-makers in Prague held the view that Russia—under whatever regime—would not be able to develop without strong ties with Europe and that the European political scene needed active Russian participation to become stable. Therefore, Prague was at first cau-tiously inclined to respond positively to signals from the Kremlin that the Soviets were ready to enter into full diplomatic relations. But Masaryk and Beneš refused to ignore the cruelty of Bolshevism; they maintained the hope that a new and more tolerant Russia would eventually reappear. Consequently, by the time Adolf Hitler came to power, most European countries had granted the Bolsheviks de jure recognition while diplomatic contacts between Czechoslovakia and the Soviet Union were almost nonexistent. It seems in retrospect that until the beginning of the Nazi era in Germany, the Prague government was guided by a rather pessimistic view of Bolshevism. More so than other European politicians who had rushed to do business with the Kremlin already in the 1920s. Paradoxically, this did not prevent them a decade later from showing off their anti-Communist credentials by dismissing Czechoslovakia as a Bolshevik outpost in the heart of Europe.

Chapter 2 studies the impact of Hitler's *Machtergreifung* in 1933 on Prague's relations with Moscow and shows how Nazism helped to legitimize the Soviets in the eyes of Edvard Beneš. Henceforth, he would devote much of his energy to bringing Stalin's Soviet Union into Central European politics in order to compensate for the spectacular growth of the Third Reich. Prague entered into full diplomatic relations with the Kremlin in 1934 and proceeded the next year to negotiate the Czechoslovak-Soviet agreement. This chapter analyzes the stipulation that made Soviet action on behalf of Czechoslovakia in case of war with Germany dependent on the prior involvement of France. It shows that the stipulation was put into the text by Prague.

The role assigned to Czechoslovak communists by the 7th Congress of the Communist International and western attitudes toward Central Europe in 1935–37 are analyzed in Chapter 3. Moscow's early efforts to become an active participant in the crisis-laden political scene are contrasted with the passive acceptance of the decline and collapse of the Versailles system by Great Britain and France. In addition, just when the Nazis began kicking at the doors of Czechoslovakia, at a time when Prague would have needed signs of firm support from the Kremlin, the Soviet Union's value on the international scene declined dramatically. This was the result of a variety of factors among which the most important was the Stalinist terror. The latter's roots were extraordinarily long, and some reached even as far as Prague and Paris.

Chapter 4 delves into Prague's secret negotiations with Berlin and Beneš's role in the famous Tukhachevsky affair. It identifies early signs of Stalin's campaign against the Red Army leadership: in 1935 a Prague-based Russian newspaper began publishing a series of articles designed by the Stalinist secret police to plant seeds of doubt about the loyalty of large numbers of Red Army officers. By early 1937, Beneš started receiving clear indications that a Soviet-German *rapprochement* was in the cards. This would have meant the immediate collapse of one of Prague's main security arrangements, the Czechoslovak-Soviet agreement of 1935. Hence Beneš's relief when he learned in the summer of 1937 that Tukhachevsky had been shot for his treasonous schemes with various German personalities and agents. Importantly, however, this chapter shows that, Beneš's own claims notwithstanding, the Prague government did not pass to the Kremlin the rumors implicating Marshal Tukhachevsky and others in acts of high treason.

Chapter 5 studies the *Anschluß* of Austria and the so-called partial mobilization of the Czechoslovak army in May 1938. Documents from the Second Bureau of the Czechoslovak army's General Staff are analyzed to disprove Prague's assertion that reservists and military specialists had to be called up in response to hostile strategic military concentrations by the *Wehrmacht*. Hitler did not intend to attack in May 1938, but the Prague government had been deliberately misled into thinking that he did. Given the relatively high quality of the intelligence reports that the Second Bureau received during the May crisis, it is safe to assume that it came from a professional espionage organization. Alas, only speculation can be offered regarding the identity of the source of this daring deception which brought Europe to the brink of war.

Chapter 6 deals with the crisis during the summer and fall of 1938, and sheds new light on Stalin's strategic thinking on the eve of World War II. Soviet assumptions at this time regarding the shape of future developments were rooted in the analytical framework of the 7th Congress of the Communist International, and they were reaffirmed in Prague by Andrei Zhdanov in August 1938. The evidence presented here shows that in 1938 Stalin was not bent on avoiding war. His objective was for the conflict to break out at the right time and place so that opportunities for the growth of Soviet power in postwar Europe would be maximized. This in itself did not make him the main villain of international politics at the time: he would have failed to project his influence throughout Central Europe but for the war uleashed by the Third Reich of Adolf Hitler. As it happened, some assumptions made by the Soviet policy-makers turned out to be quite inaccurate; nevertheless, the strategy designed in the Kremlin at the height of the crisis proved to be considerably more sophisticated than such poorly thought-out tactical schemes as the mission of Lord Runciman.

Chapter 7 traces the paths that led the participants in the Czechoslovak-German drama to the Munich solution. Properly, the focus is on the tragic figure of Edvard Beneš and his agonizing decision to capitulate. The president has been sometimes portrayed as a man who had mistaken deal-making in the League of Nations for a viable foreign policy. He has been criticized for his failure to come to terms with Czechoslovakia's neighbors and the numerous Sudeten German population. Some have seen in him a man who spoke with toughness when he could hide behind the backs of his French and Soviet allies but who ultimately lacked the necessary resolve to lead his people to war against the *Wehrmacht*. It is suggested throughout that Beneš was a flawed man, and so was his foreign policy, but this chapter offers evidence that the president lacked neither courage nor the capacity for greatness. He had in fact hoped for a military conflict to break out in September 1938, and it appears that the moments during the crisis when he was optimistic corresponded with those occasions when war seemed inevitable. The president did not give up hope that war would break out even after it had become quite clear that no assistance could be expected from France: on 28 September 1938 the Prague government requested "immediate air support" from the Soviet Union and an inquiry concerning the availability of Soviet assistance to Czechoslovakia was made even after the Munich agreement had been signed. A recently uncovered document presents definitive evidence regarding the possibility of Soviet aid to Czechoslovakia in the fall of 1938. Beneš stated that Moscow's failure to respond to his repeated inquiries regarding Soviet help against the Third Reich "was the main reason why I capitulated." Specialists in Beneš studies will note that this is a new dimension of the crisis, and it leads us to reconsider previously held opinions. Notable, too, is the evidence that the Kremlin attacked the leader of the Communist party of Czechoslovakia, Klement Gottwald, for his failure to use the crisis in September 1938 as a convenient catalyst for carrying out a revolution.

This book deals with the escalating crisis of the 1930s mainly on the basis of original primary sources from the recently opened archives in Prague. It would be presumptuous and naive to think that such a method could result in a product that sheds light of equal intensity on all the many layers of the decade. Instead, the book emphasizes those questions and themes on which the archives yielded the most interesting and significant new information. This, as well as the enormity of the topic, necessitated that several important components of the Munich affair had to be ignored or merely sketched. Prominent in this category is the important French role in the Czechoslovak-German crisis: it is merely touched on in this volume, and the reader will have to turn to *Documents diplomatiques français* and some of the specialized studies of the topic to gain a more complete picture. Prague's complicated relations with the Sudeten German population, the Slovak question, Soviet global maneuvers, details of politics in the Kremlin, the Spanish civil war, the brewing troubles in the Far East, and the roles played by Czechoslovakia's neighbors Hungary and Poland also deserve a more extensive treatment than is given here. Volumes dealing with such issues, old and new, can be found in the bibliography attached at the end. My main goal has been to demonstrate how the developing crisis that resulted in the Munich Agreement appeared from the perspective of Prague. This approach may seem somewhat narrow, but it allows for the hitherto missing Czechoslovak perspective to be added to what we already know, thanks to Walter Laqueur, Robert C. Tucker, Adam B. Ulam, Piotr S. Wandycz, Donald Cameron Watt, and Gerhard L. Weinberg.

The collapse of the Soviet Union has resulted in greater access to Moscow archives than ever before. Consequently, it has become possible to uncover evidence regarding many important topics in Soviet history. Unexpectedly, the greatest advances have been achieved in what would appear to be some of the most sensitive areas: Stalin's murder of more than fifteen thousand Polish army officers in 1940, Soviet atomic research and diplomacy, the Cuban missile crisis, and the 1968 Warsaw Pact invasion of Czechoslovakia, to name only a few examples. Except for several sets of documents released to the Ministry of Foreign Affairs in Prague, cited in this book, much less evidence has been made available on Soviet behavior in the 1930s. Regarding Moscow's role in the Czechoslovak-German crisis, some interesting documents can indeed be found in the archives of the Soviet Ministry of Foreign Affairs, especially when it comes to personalities—the Soviet Minister in Prague, Sergei S. Aleksandrovsky; his Czechoslovak colleague, Minister Zdeněk Fierlinger; political journalist and future Czechoslovak diplomat and politician, Hubert Ripka; and others. But these documents add relatively little to what had been made gradually available—albeit in an edited form—from the 1950s onward. There is every reason to think that crucial documentation on some of the central topics of this book (Beneš and the Tukhachevsky affair or the Soviet role in the May partial mobilization) is hidden in the so-called Presidential Archives in the Kremlin and in the archives of the KGB. My own vain attempts to obtain a research permit from those quarters suggest that we will have to await yet another miracle in Moscow. In the meantime, the Czechoslovak-German drama and the role played by Stalin can be narrated from the perspective of Prague archives.

Acknowledgments

It gives me pleasure to acknowledge that this project was made possible by the generous support I received from various foundations. My research in Prague was conducted while I was a Fulbright Research Fellow and an IREX (International Research and Exchanges Board) Fellow; I could later return to Prague for a shorter time with travel grants from the National Endowment for the Humanities and IREX. The writing of this volume was accelerated thanks to the John M. Olin Faculty Fellowship in History and a fellowship in the Society of Fellows at my professional home, Boston University, both of which released me from teaching duties.

Some of the themes explored in this book were dealt with in previously published articles, which appeared in *Diplomacy & Statecraft, Slavic Review,* and *Vierteljahrshefte für Zeitgeschichte.*

I am most grateful to Gioia Stevens, my Oxford University Press editor, for her support and guidance. Special mention must be made of Professor Hsi-Huey Liang, Vassar College; Dr. Eva Jonas, Harvard University; and Dr. Antonín Klimek of the Historical Institute of the Czech Army in Prague, all of whom allowed me to use photographs from their private collections. Dr. Klimek, moreover, helped me selflessly, and often at the expense of his own writing and other academic obligations, to orient myself in the Prague archives.

My mother, Milena Lukesova, an author of dozens of books, is also an outstanding editor. She patiently read through the manuscript and pointed out numerous ways of improving it. I wish I knew as much about history as she does about the art of writing. My father, Professor Dr. Zdeněk Lukes, assisted me with archival research at a time when I could not travel to Prague. He was one of many Czechoslovak army reserve officers who never fully recovered from the humiliation of their retreat in early October 1938. It is from him that I inherited my interest in this topic.

Wellesley, Massachusetts   I.L.
Choceň, the Czech Republic
July 1995

CONTENTS

ABBREVIATIONS

ACC CPC	Archives of the Central Committee of the Communist Party of Czechoslovakia, Prague
AMFA	Archives of the Ministry of Foreign Affairs, Prague
AMI	Archives of the Ministry of Interior, Prague
ANM-D	Archives of Prokop Drtina at the Archives of the National Museum, Prague
ANM-F	Archives of Zdeněk Fierlinger at the Archives of the National Museum, Prague
ANM-M	Archives of Vojtěch Mastný at the Archives of the National Museum, Prague
ANM-S	Archives of Jaromír Smutný at the Archives of the National Museum, Prague
HI-CA	Historical Institute of the Czech Army, Prague
MHA-B	Archives of President Edvard Beneš at the Military Historical Archives, Invalidovna, Prague
MHA-OP	Military Office of the President of the Republic at the Military Historical Archives, Invalidovna, Prague
OP	Office of the President of the Republic of Czechoslovakia at the Castle, Prague
NA	National Archives, Washington, D.C.
NA RG-165	National Archives, Records of the War Department, Research and Analysis Branch, Army Intelligence, Suitland, MD
PRO	Public Record Office, London
SCA	State Central Archives at Loreta, Prague

Czechoslovakia between
Stalin and Hitler

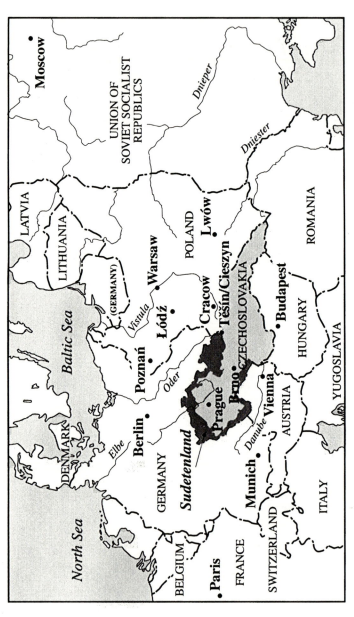

**Czechoslovakia and Its Neighbors
1918–1938**

Czechoslovakia's Sudetenland region is shown here only approximately.

1

Czechoslovak-Soviet Contacts from the End of World War I to Adolf Hitler's *Machtergreifung,* 1918–1933

"You hooligan, you'll never make it," burst out Professor František Hrdlička at Eduard Beneš, his student at the Imperial and Royal Gymnasium in Prague. The professor quickly calmed down, but he remained serious. He advised Beneš to resign from the prestigious school and join the Hapsburg army. The year was 1902, and Vienna needed soldiers to deal with the latest crisis in the Balkans. After twelve years in uniform, Beneš should be able to secure a position in the Austrian civil service; a post office job would be suitable, Hrdlička thought. But the eighteen-year-old rebel laughed in his face.[1] Beneš knew he would never be a clerk. He was preparing for a more spectacular career, and he was not an idle dreamer. A year ago he had already established contact with Thomas Garrigue Masaryk, professor of philosophy at Charles University and a prominent personality on the Prague political scene. Their friendship grew, and so did their anti-Hapsburg sentiments. When the Great War broke out in 1914, Masaryk and Beneš were ready to assume prominent roles in the campaign to create a new state, the Republic of Czechoslovakia. Beneš did not excel in Professor Hrdlička's subject, Latin, but he had a great talent for politics and diplomacy.

With the war in progress, the sixty-four-year-old Masaryk went abroad to work for independence in December 1914.[2] Beneš followed him in September 1915. After three more years of intensive work, the two achieved their main objective: on 14 October 1918, the allies granted recognition to a provisional Czechoslovak government. It was headed by Masaryk, and Beneš fulfilled the roles of minister of foreign affairs and minister of interior. Just two weeks later, at seven o'clock in the evening, the newly formed National Committee in Prague issued its first law. Its preamble stated: "The independent Czechoslovak State has come into existence."[3] The Hapsburg political and military authorities on the scene were not able, and in no

3

mood, to object. Beneš later boasted that he and Masaryk had been in a position to determine the future of the Hapsburg empire and that they had decided to do away with it.[4]

Beneš did not take time off to celebrate the declaration of Czechoslovak independence. He was ascetically inclined, and there was still a lot to be done. The astonishing news from Prague found him at the Beau-Rivage Hotel in Geneva, where he was conducting negotiations with a delegation from home.[5] On 31 October 1918, the thirty-four-year-old man packed up his small suitcase and headed for Paris. Four days later, a messenger from the French Foreign Ministry appeared at his door to invite him to a session of the Supreme War Council. In the afternoon, Beneš was in an official automobile adorned with the new Czechoslovak flag. Only three years earlier, he had escaped from Vienna's jurisdiction with a borrowed passport to join Masaryk's action abroad.[6] Now, that same Beneš whom Professor Hrdlička wanted to throw out of high school was sitting next to the representatives of France, Great Britain, the United States, Italy, Japan, Serbia, Greece, Belgium, and Portugal.

The achievements of the Czechoslovak team in Paris and at other postwar conferences were impressive. Its *spiritus agens* was Beneš. There were few signs in his youth indicating that Eduard (he would later adopt the more exotic spelling "Edvard") Beneš would for most of his life play such a prominent role on the twentieth-century international scene.[7] Beneš—his mother called him Edek—was the tenth and last child, born on 28 May 1884 to a poor family in central Bohemia. He was short and somewhat overweight and offered an easy target for the local toughs. Thus he was often alone, accompanied only by his books and his ambition. From the beginning, he was endowed with an abnormal capacity for hard, concentrated intellectual work. Many authors would later attempt to draw a portrait of Edvard Beneš, but few succeeded as well as one of his teachers who captured the youth's essence in a few sentences. "Beneš," he wrote, "deserved his good grades more because of his limitless and patient industry than because of any special talent. He studies very hard, but what he has once learned he remembers forever. He is motivated and driven to excel. . . . He is still a child and cannot know well in what field to succeed and how. But the ambition is in him and it works like an inner engine."[8] This ambition and his tremendous discipline would stay with Beneš to the very end of his life.

The results became obvious once he was released from the suffocating atmosphere of the Gymnasium. Beneš quickly discovered that in the freedom of the university he could unleash his powerful intellect and succeed far beyond the expectations of his teachers. He abandoned his rebelliousness and started clawing his way up and away from the poverty of his birthplace. In 1908, by the time he turned twenty-four, he was awarded a doctorate in law by the University of Dijon, France, and a year later a Ph.D. from Charles University in Prague. He had also studied at the University of Berlin and at the Sorbonne. In order to appreciate Beneš's work ethic, one must realize that his parents were unable to assist their youngest child financially, and so Beneš had to work full time to support himself throughout his studies. He did so mainly as a journalist, and he was very productive. In 1907 alone, Beneš published almost a hundred articles, mostly in the social democratic press in Prague.[9]

Given such a background, it is hardly surprising that Edvard Beneš believed in himself. According to a colleague, Beneš's self-confidence had the aura of "a mystical faith in his mission." Even when he was merely an exile in Paris, Beneš became convinced that he was "indispensable" for the future of Czechoslovakia.[10] Some of these sentiments were justified, for Beneš and his team achieved almost all of their objectives while negotiating Czechoslovakia's position on the Central European map. The young foreign minister argued that Czechoslovakia was the only state in Central Europe capable of stabilizing a region that was sinking dangerously into anarchy and revolution. Beneš claimed that only the Czechs could stop Bolshevism, and the French supported him without much hesitation. Although the British and the Americans were not so sure, once the former indicated they were ready to endorse some of Beneš's arguments, the latter quickly followed suit and accepted— provisionally, it was thought—Beneš's demand for the historical boundaries of Bohemia, Moravia, and Bohemian Silesia to be maintained. But Beneš had another card up his sleeve: when Slovakia was under discussion, he argued somewhat inconsistently that borders ought to be marked in such a manner that the carved-out territory would form a viable economic unit. Thus, Czechoslovakia's borders in the west were drawn in accordance with the historical principle, while in the Slovak east the diplomats at Versailles applied the more pragmatic, economic principle of demarcation. His strategy worked: the Czechoslovak delegation did not get everything it had asked for, but it was successful nevertheless.

Beneš flourished in the busy and heady atmosphere of the Paris Peace Conference and at other postwar conferences. He made a good impression on many of his colleagues at these meetings.[11] The doyen of Czechoslovak politicians, Václav Klofáč, normally a hard-headed realist, lost all sense of proportion when he reported to friends in Prague upon returning from meeting with Beneš in Switzerland, "Wilson and all the others never say anything that they have not received in writing from Masaryk and Beneš. The authority of those two is simply incredible."[12]

Beneš returned to Prague from exile only on 24 September 1919, and wherever he went he was greeted by enthusiastic, patriotic crowds. He had every reason to feel good about himself. Although he was only thirty-five, he was a co-founder of a brand-new country, a foreign minister, and one of the best known diplomatic personalities in Europe.

Minister Beneš soon established his reputation as a cautious, rational, and cool-headed politician. He also made clear at the very beginning of his diplomatic career that he was incorruptible. While he was still in Paris, Beneš had been approached by an old friend who proposed to establish for him a special fund—created from contributions of anonymous "patriots"—from which the foreign minister would be free to draw whenever he needed to conduct public relations campaigns abroad. The thirty-five-year-old man sensed that the offer was irregular, and he had his tempter arrested.[13] After he had acquired enough wealth (the main source of which was his wife's fortune) to guarantee the security of his family, Beneš lost interest in money and devoted himself to his work.

His colleagues thought of him as an intellectual dynamo.[14] They admired his intellect, toughness of character, and limitless capacity for work, and such a man was badly needed in Prague. There was much to be done. For all the successes of Czechoslovak diplomats, even a quick look at a map showed that the new republic would find it difficult to fit properly within its assigned place. Its border was 4,113 kilometers long. Of this, the border with Germany and Austria was 2,097 kilometers; that with Hungary, 832 kilometers; that with Poland, 984 kilometers; and that with Romania, 200 kilometers.[15] Only Romania reacted sympathetically to the emergence of Czechoslovakia. Other countries looked on the new democratic state with considerable hostility. Consequently, Prague politicians had to operate in a difficult political environment.[16]

How did the map of the Czechoslovak Republic appear to professional soldiers? A secret strategic analysis of the country's position in Europe, written in 1921 by the Ministry of Defense, pointed out that Czechoslovakia was vulnerable militarily because of its length and lack of depth. The report stressed the importance of preparing an infrastructure for organizing a new Czechoslovak army abroad from recruits of Czech and Slovak origin because it was impossible to guarantee that the home army would not be eliminated in toto in a possible German blitzkrieg.[17] This prescient analysis, we must remember, was written in 1921.

The ethnic composition of Czechoslovakia was so complicated that it represented an even greater challenge to national security than the geographic factor. The Prague government had a hard time gaining acceptance and legitimacy in the eyes of minorities. From the beginning, many Germans from the Czechoslovak Sudetenland and some other minority groups were unhappy about their position within the new state. Pessimists could begin to argue that Czechoslovakia was too large to be a Czechoslovak national state and too small to play the role of a multinational state successfully.

Despite its problems, Czechoslovakia soon emerged from its difficult beginning and—surprising all skeptics—commenced its march toward political stability and a considerable degree of economic prosperity. The main reason for this was simple: while some in Europe began toying with one authoritarian ideology or another, the Prague government stayed the course of liberal democracy. That was no small achievement. President Masaryk dismissed fascism as the product of the pathological dregs of society, and his critical view of Bolshevism was a matter of published record. He warned against the pseudo-scientific nature of Russian communism and pointed out that, although it had achieved nothing positive, Lenin's experiment had already cost thousands of innocent lives. Bolshevism, he concluded, was "an orgy of ignorance, violence and corruption."[18] During the two decades of Czechoslovak history between the wars, neither Masaryk nor Beneš and their collaborators strayed from the path of democracy. A broad spectrum of politicians and citizens accepted President Masaryk's authority despite differences in social and economic status. During the two decades between the wars, Czechoslovakia had only two presidents and two foreign ministers.[19]

From the beginning, Masaryk and Beneš conceived of Czechoslovakia as a country that would be woven tightly into the fabric of Western Europe. But they knew that their dislike of the Bolshevik regime in Russia would not license them to ignore it, and they studied developments in the East with great attention.

The Hillerson Red Cross Mission in Prague

It is not easy to assign a specific date to the commencement of Czechoslovak-Soviet relations. Because of the existence of the Czechoslovak legions in Russia since 1917, there had been contacts between Prague and the Bolsheviks even before there was a Czechoslovakia and before Lenin and his colleagues established themselves as the new rulers of Russia. But it makes sense to choose 25 February 1920, the day when the Soviet commissar for foreign affairs, G. V. Chicherin, sent his first note to the Prague government expressing hope that Czechoslovakia would refuse to play any role in an anti-Bolshevik coalition. He suggested that there was no reason for Moscow and Prague not to establish diplomatic relations.[20] Soviet Russia formally proposed to commence negotiations in order to form mutually profitable and friendly relations. Please tell us, wrote Chicherin invitingly, when and where you would like to meet our delegation.[21]

Foreign Minister Beneš responded on 10 April 1920—after a month and a half—with an oblique and evasive statement. He rejected the ideological premises of Chicherin's note and concluded by merely affirming his readiness to establish contacts with Moscow in order to help repatriate Czechoslovak citizens from Soviet Russia and to prepare for future commercial contacts.[22] Twelve days later, Moscow responded by formally offering to establish "absolutely normal" diplomatic relations between the two countries.[23] This was too fast for Prague. It was not prepared to go beyond its first offer, which was to put in place some means for dealing with humanitarian causes. That position prevailed, and on 8 July 1920 the Soviet Red Cross mission arrived in Prague via Berlin.[24] The Prague Foreign Ministry would refer to it in internal correspondence as the "Hillerson mission," so named after the chief of the Soviet delegation, S. I. Hillerson.[25]

Negotiations between Prague and Moscow regarding the Red Cross mission were problematic. On the day of the group's arrival, Miss Alice Masaryk, chairwoman of the Czechoslovak Red Cross and the president's daughter, published an open letter to Chicherin. She pointed out that Red Cross missions had come to be abused as tools of political propaganda or for base commercial reasons. This was true. Soviet Red Cross missions had already caused scandal by becoming involved in political machinations in Germany and Hungary, and a serious incident had taken place in Poland at the end of 1918. A Soviet Red Cross mission had arrived in Warsaw, unannounced as well as uninvited; nevertheless, it promptly made itself at home. It contacted the Polish Communist party but paid no attention to local Red Cross institutions. This was too much, and the mission was for a brief time put in isolation. When Polish authorities attempted to deport the so-called Soviet Red Cross mission, its members were murdered while under an escort of Polish state police. The affair was never properly clarified.[26]

Given this record, it is little wonder that Miss Alice Masaryk was apprehensive. She stated forcefully that she disapproved of any misuse of the Red Cross symbol and insisted that the Bolshevik Red Cross in Prague deal strictly with matters properly within its jurisdiction. She would watch closely, she wrote, whether the

Hillerson team devoted itself exclusively to its mission—that is, the welfare of Russian citizens displaced by the war.[27] In expressing her skepticism regarding the Hillerson mission in Prague, Miss Masaryk spoke for a significant segment of public opinion in Czechoslovakia. The press was particularly hostile to the idea of allowing a Bolshevik organization, under whatever cover, to establish itself in Prague.[28]

After much public debate and weighing of the danger of Bolshevik propaganda on the one hand and the plight of Czechoslovak and Russian refugees on the other, Prague officially agreed to receive the Soviet Red Cross mission. But Miss Masaryk was not alone as she kept an eye on the Hillerson group. The Prague police surrounded the seven members of the team with agents who submitted detailed reports on the Soviet mission's day-to-day business, the persons visiting the mission, and some of the mission's correspondence. Several employees Hillerson hired in Prague were, conveniently, police agents.[29]

Chicherin chose not to respond to Miss Masaryk or to attacks in the Czechoslovak press, and Hillerson and his people quietly set up shop at Prague's Hotel Imperial, a reassuringly bourgeois address. Gradually, however, it became clear that Alice Masaryk's worst fears had come true. Police agents' reports left little doubt that Hillerson, under the cover of the Red Cross, ran a large intelligence network in Prague.

It so happened that Prague authorities did not rely only on reports of their agents and informers for an accurate view of Hillerson and his activities. Incredibly, they also had access to all of his top secret communications with Moscow. The Soviet Red Cross mission in Czechoslovakia lacked diplomatic standing, and therefore it could not operate its own communications equipment for sending encoded messages and receiving secret instructions from Moscow. But it was allowed to encode its telegrams and hand them, encoded, to the Foreign Ministry's Third Section, which dealt, in part, with communications.[30] The Third Section, as promised, sent out Hillerson's messages (and received coded telegrams from Moscow addressed to Hillerson), but all such texts were passed immediately on to a cipher-cracking squad. The code-breakers eventually produced a plain Russian text for all the Hillerson messages.[31] Moscow was mistakenly confident that its communications were entirely secure; on one occasion, Chicherin and Hillerson even reassured each other on the safety of their ciphers.[32] Therefore, both sides were open, and their telegrams offer a unique glimpse into the functioning of a Soviet network.

It was no coincidence that the Hillerson team came to Prague in the summer of 1920; its arrival coincided with the Soviet-Polish war. The Bolsheviks were winning, and the team's mission had a lot to do with the Soviet drive against the "corpse of White Poland," as General Mikhail Tukhachevsky put it.[33] In the summer of 1920, just as Hillerson was establishing himself in Prague, the Red Army smashed through the Polish lines, and by early August Soviet troops were approaching the Warsaw suburbs. Foreign diplomats, except for the papal nuncio Achile Ratti, who chose to stay, were evacuated. Prague began to worry that the Bolsheviks might not stop at the Polish border, and the Ministry of Defense quickly prepared "Plan B" to resist a Bolshevik military offensive against Czechoslovakia.[34] Then, miraculously, a reversal occurred.[35] With a series of swift and daring maneuvers, the Poles encircled and nearly trapped the overconfident Bolshevik troops, and at the end of

September 1920 the Red Army started to fall apart. The armistice and Preliminaries of Peace were signed in mid-October 1920, and the final peace treaty in March 1921.[36] It is against this background that one must interpret the machinations of the Soviet Red Cross in Prague.

A study of the Hillerson file shows that the Bolshevik Red Cross in Prague devoted almost no time to settling the affairs of Russians stranded in Central Europe. It had two related missions: one was diplomatic; the other had to do with espionage.

Chicherin informed Hillerson that his main job was to keep Czechoslovakia neutral in the conflict between Soviet Russia and Poland. Moscow was particularly concerned about a rumor, which it had picked up in Paris, that Poland would like to create a bloc of states in Central Europe with one French-controled general staff. The Soviet commissar urged Hillerson to see Beneš in order to assure him that Soviet Russia had no claims on Czechoslovak territory and represented no threat to it. Prague should therefore remain strictly neutral. Hillerson duly brought up the issue of Czechoslovakia's neutrality in the Polish-Soviet conflict with the minister and was glad to report his assurances in this regard. Beneš "begged me," he wrote "to believe him that he had not violated one letter of the commitment to maintain neutrality. I told him that, in the absence of evidence to the contrary, I accepted his assurances."[37]

A large component of Hillerson's diplomatic job in Prague was to secure diplomatic recognition of the Bolshevik regime by President Masaryk. Chicherin stressed to Hillerson that contacts with Prague were vital for Moscow and that the Kremlin was prepared to upgrade its representation. "We have to take care to maintain good relations with Czechoslovakia," he radioed to the Red Cross mission in Prague.[38] Hillerson succeeded in keeping Czechoslovakia neutral during the Polish-Soviet war, but, despite much cajoling, he failed to obtain Prague's recognition of the Bolsheviks. The Hillerson file contains a transcript of one attempt made on 27 November 1920. The chief of the Soviet mission stated at the Prague Foreign Ministry that Czechoslovakia could derive numerous advantages from entering into diplomatic relations with Soviet Russia, but those would be available only if Masaryk and Beneš were to act sooner than others in Europe. It was vital for Czechoslovakia, Hillerson lectured Václav Girsa, a high official of the Prague foreign ministry, to liberate itself from French influence. After all, France was not the most reliable ally, Hillerson stated pointedly. Paris was "ready to hand Czechoslovakia over to the Poles, Hungarians or anybody else," he warned.[39] Girsa listened politely but remained unpersuaded. Beneš confirmed Prague's refusal to enter into diplomatic relations with the Kremlin at this stage in early January 1921. The minister said that he was against foreign intervention in Russian affairs but went on to say that any official relations with the Bolshevik government were out of the question.[40]

Hillerson drew a bleak picture of the French attitude toward Central Europe. The whole area, especially Poland, he suggested, was regarded with pessimism in Paris. Even the victory of the Poles over the Red Army was to be explained, according to French military specialists, by Bolshevik errors rather than as a sign of Poland's long-term viability.[41] The French, according to a Hillerson report of 24 February 1921, demanded of Beneš that Czechoslovakia involve itself with greater vigor in the anti-Soviet effort. To this the cautious foreign minister was said to have replied that he could put the Czechoslovak arms industry at the disposal of any French-sponsored campaign, but he could not afford to be openly involved in an anti-Bolshevik front for serious domestic reasons.[42] As we will see, he was in no way exaggerating the strength of his opposition at home.

But Hillerson's main mission in Prague had to do with espionage, sabotage, and money and weapons transfers. The Soviet-Polish war underlined the importance of his activities. Only a few weeks after its arrival in Prague, the Soviet Red Cross team was engaged in financing unconventional warfare in eastern Galicia in support of Red Army operations. On 10 August 1920, Hillerson informed Moscow that preparations for an uprising had been completed and could commence within two weeks.[43] On 28 August 1920 he wrote to Chicherin that he had just paid 40,000 Czechoslovak crowns (Kc) to provide a military communist organization in eastern Galicia with weapons and that his people on the scene now demanded an additional 200,000 Kc to escalate their efforts. Hillerson asked whether he should pay this sum from the coffers of the Red Cross mission or wait for money from Moscow. Reacting to recent reversals on the battlefield, Chicherin cabled that further military actions and uprisings in Galicia were unwelcome. "Be on your guard against provocation," Moscow wrote to Hillerson, but that was not to be the end of his activities. "How much money do you need?" Chicherin inquired.[44]

In late 1920 Hillerson reported unconfirmed rumors that Austria, Czechoslovakia, and Poland had arrived at a secret agreement to ship weapons from Vienna to Bratislava on the Danube and then by train across Czechoslovakia to Poland via the Bohumin station on the Czechoslovak-Polish border.[45] Hillerson's task was to continue whipping up pro-Soviet, anti-Polish sentiments among the railroad personnel in Czechoslovakia with the purpose of undermining efforts to supply Poland with badly needed weapons and ammunition. The Hillerson organization was successful in this regard: the Prague government had failed to prevent agents from sabotaging the supply trains.[46]

The extent of Hillerson's involvement in unconventional warfare is evident from a message sent to Moscow in November 1920 requesting money to pay an agent who had been blowing up bridges in Galicia.[47] On another occasion, in December 1920, Hillerson radioed Moscow about an intelligence operation inside Czechoslovakia:

> Both couriers have arrived and I have everything. I understand my task and am working on it. It is not easy to get into the [Czechoslovak] General Staff, as I have mentioned before. . . . However, I already have a lead and if all works well I will soon receive the documents. . . . As you know, the first step is the most important. I sent a courier to Warsaw, but without a result. It takes a local person (*rezident*). . . . I have at my disposal an officer of the former Russian General Staff; he is a specialist with a perspective.[48]

In the early 1920s, Czechoslovakia had no serious counterintelligence capability, and cases of espionage were uncovered only when agents or their bosses conducted themselves with recklessness. Had the Hillerson team not had to use communications equipment of the Ministry of Foreign Affairs, its real mission in Czechoslovakia would have remained unknown.

By 1921 Hillerson's activities in Czechoslovakia angered Minister Beneš so much that he worked to get rid of the man. He pointed out that the chief of the Soviet Red Cross mission had done nothing in the area of humanitarian relief and repatriation of Czechoslovak citizens from Soviet Russia or on behalf of Russian citizens in Czechoslovakia. The minister instructed Major Josef Skála, Czechoslovakia's temporary representative in Moscow, to secure Hillerson's recall. If this were not successful, Beneš warned, Prague would have to declare Hillerson persona non grata.[49] The involvement of the Prague-based Soviet Red Cross mission in guerrilla warfare in the Ukraine and intelligence operations did not go unnoticed in Warsaw, and, as a result, it contributed to a poisoned atmosphere between Czechoslovakia and Poland; this would have tragic consequences for both countries.[50] Furthermore, Hillerson failed on the diplomatic front. His behavior in Prague set back the formation of regular diplomatic relations between Czechoslovakia and the Soviet Union.

Prague's Attitude toward the Bolsheviks

Czechoslovakia's early view of Soviet Russia was, to a great extent, determined by the views of its president. Masaryk had been in Russia in 1887 and 1890, he spent nearly a year there in 1917, and he wrote volumes on Russian politics and philosophy.[51] He was horrified by the brutality of the Bolsheviks, but he did not care for their predecessors, either. Lenin, he wrote, "was a logical consequence of Russian illogiciality." Communism was, in his view, essentially a Russian phenomenon, and the Bolsheviks were children of tsarism.[52]

Masaryk's thoughts regarding the group around Lenin were complex. In a memorandum on Russia for the U.S. government, he wrote in April 1918 that he was well aware of the "weak points of the Bolshevists," but he also knew the other parties involved in the Russian civil war, who were "neither better nor abler." He went on to say that the forces behind the drive to restore monarchy in Russia were hopelessly weak and should not be supported by the West. The Bolsheviks would stay in power for a longer period than their adversaries typically assumed. Masaryk advised the Allies that they should quickly recognize the Bolsheviks de facto, although there was no need, for the time being, to discuss de jure recognition.[53]

Beneš was torn when it came to contemporary Russian affairs. On the one hand, he was a lifelong socialist. As far as he was concerned, *égalité* and *fraternité* were the two most important attributes of humanity. *Liberté* was secondary because it was merely derived from these other two "philosophical presuppositions."[54] Therefore, Beneš had little trouble accepting the social component of the Bolshevik ideology as he understood it. He believed that real democrats were, *ipso facto*, radical socialists. Indeed, they were "often more radical than many of those who have by now reached the state of Bolshevism."[55] These were strong, almost provocative words, coming as they did from the mouth of a democratic foreign minister at a time when Europe was just discovering the Soviet threat. But for all his theoretical sympathy with socialist methods in economic planning and distribution of wealth, Beneš most definitely rejected the Bolshevik methods; he abhorred disorder, anarchy, and the Bolshevik terror.[56] The real question was, By what means should the Bolsheviks be opposed? Naked force against Lenin and the Bolsheviks would not do.[57] The Allies had failed to understand, Beneš argued, that to intervene in Russia would have required not only armies with millions of soldiers but also a huge and expensive administrative and logistical apparatus.[58] It was one thing to dislike Bolshevik violence; it would have been quite another thing to want to do something about it. Beneš was dead set against any kind of hostile involvement in Russian affairs by foreign powers.

Masaryk and Beneš held the view that Europe would be best served by the emergence of a strong and democratic Russia.[59] The two needed each other. Russia could not fully develop without Europe, which could not peacefully develop without Russia.[60] This would be brought about only by a concerted effort of all the major European countries and America. Beneš believed that the edge of Bolshevik revolutionary ideology could be blunted by the development of commercial ties between Soviet Russia and the rest of the world.[61] Naturally, this line of thinking was looked on with much sympathy in the Czechoslovak business community, whose leading personalities had said for quite some time that there could be no peace in Europe without a stable and peaceful Russia and that only economic forces were strong enough to carve out a path leading in that direction. Jaroslav Preiss, director of one of Prague's most powerful banks and a member of the conservative National Democratic party, had suggested in late 1919 that Czechoslovakia could become a bridge between East and West.[62] At a Prague meeting of representatives of the business community in the spring of 1921, various speakers suggested that the vast Russian market was too important to be ignored.[63]

Beneš would have been inclined to respond positively to signals indicating Lenin's desire to enter into diplomatic relations with Prague—primarily because he believed that not extending full recognition was in itself not going to do away with the Bolsheviks. But he was not prepared to act without consulting others, especially France. The minister was also not eager to antagonize Poland any further; it was already upset by Czechoslovakia's behavior during attempts at finding a solution for the dispute involving the Teschen area.[64] It would have seemed cruel to strike a diplomatic deal with Moscow when the Bolsheviks were engaged in military activities against Poland. Although Warsaw recognized the Soviets de facto in 1921 and would follow with de jure recognition two years later, Polish diplomats remained very sensitive when it came to signs of Czechoslovakia's cooperation with the Kremlin. They tended to see any strengthening of ties between Prague and Moscow as an indirect attack on Poland's national security. Beneš tried to explain to his Polish colleagues that it was vital for Central Europeans to stop quarreling with each other before the Soviets entered the political arena.[65] But the Teschen issue and Prague's failure to accommodate Polish sensitivity as far as Russia was concerned made it impossible for tensions to decline between the two countries. Reasonable people in Warsaw, Prague, and Paris could see the importance of improving Czechoslovak-Polish relations, and the pact signed in November 1921 by Beneš and Konstanty Skirmunt, the Polish foreign minister, was a step in the right direction.

But a trivial territorial issue involving the Javorina region brought about the failure of the Beneš-Skirmunt experiment.[66]

In addition to the Polish concerns, Beneš had to pay attention to his allies in the Little Entente, the political and military alliance he had formed in 1920 and 1921 with Romania and Yugoslavia to guard the Versailles status quo in Central Europe, since Bucharest and Belgrade were unable to grant recognition to Moscow.[67] Romania's relations with Moscow were almost paralyzed by the divisive territorial quarrel involving Bessarabia, and Yugoslavia was unprepared to grant the Soviets de jure recognition because of personal factors involving royal family connections between Serbia and Tsarist Russia. Beneš thought highly of the Little Entente, and he treated the Romanian and Yugoslav reasons for not recognizing the Bolsheviks with the utmost seriousness.[68]

Beneš's hands were also tied by forces on the domestic front. By the 1920s, he and Masaryk had lost their once nearly absolute control over Czechoslovak foreign policy. They had to consider the views of several important and very anti-Soviet politicians. Among the most prominent was Karel Kramář, the first prime minister (1918–19) and chairman of the National Democratic party, who hated the Bolsheviks with zeal.[69] Even the moderate Czechoslovak National Socialist party actively supported the anti-Bolshevik cause. One of its founders, Václav Klofáč, stated in September 1922 that he and his party would never shake hands with the Bolsheviks.[70] Masaryk and Beneš also had to pay attention to Czechoslovak Catholic political circles, which were radically anti-Bolshevik, especially in Slovakia. And the Social Democratic party was not prepared to stay in the background: it demanded of Beneš sharp diplomatic interventions with the Moscow government on behalf of social democratic victims of Bolshevik terror.

Furthermore, the plan to upgrade Prague's relations with the Bolsheviks was hampered by reports from Czechoslovak representatives in Russia. For the sake of reciprocity, there was a Czechoslovak Red Cross mission in Soviet Russia.[71] It was busy organizing the repatriation of thousands of Czechoslovak citizens: soldiers of the Masaryk legions, prisoners of war, and ethnic Czechs and Slovaks who had settled in Russia under the old regime and who were now eager to escape the Bolsheviks.[72] To some extent, like the Hillerson team in Prague, the Czechoslovak Red Cross in Russia also gathered political information for the benefit of the Prague government.[73] The reports, combined with debriefing records of persons returning from the war-torn country to Czechoslovakia, offer a view of Russia shortly after the Bolshevik victory. The overall picture was neither soothing nor romantic.[74] One report from the Czechoslovak Red Cross mission, dated 4 April 1921, stated that the cities and the countryside under Bolshevik control were relatively peaceful, but it was the "peace of famine and slow dying."[75] The report noted that the authorities sought to win the support of workers at the expense of everybody else, but where there was any sign of resistance Lenin responded with detachments of the security forces, the Cheka, under the command of Felix Dzerzhinsky. Its sentences were "draconian." Suffering was in the air. Another report, of 8 June 1921, described the famine conditions observable in large parts of the Ukraine and local uprisings against Bolshevik rule caused by despair.[76] Half a year later, Czechoslovak observers reported dreadful traces of famine in Kharkov, where corpses could be found scattered around the city.[77] President Masaryk organized several support actions on behalf of children and starving Russian intellectuals and commented that the famine conditions in Russia amply showed that "a crowd" could not administer a state.[78]

The reports of the Czechoslovak Red Cross in Russia speculated that Lenin and his colleagues were in a situation so critical that they themselves expected to fall. This was confirmed in the summer of 1921, when the Prague authorities intercepted a letter from the Executive of the Communist International addressed to a Czechoslovak communist. The letter stated explicitly that the Bolshevik government could collapse unless revolutions in Western and Southeastern Europe erupted.[79] Without exerting any special effort, the police in Prague began to arrest large numbers of Bolshevik agents traveling furiously in and out of Czechoslovakia in pursuit of their secret missions.[80] Several scandals involving Soviet spies were reported in the Prague press, and journalists began to criticize Moscow for attempting to interfere in the domestic affairs of a sovereign state.[81] This ultimately strengthened the stance of those politicians in Prague who opposed any rapprochement with the Bolsheviks.

The pragmatic Beneš was apparently ready to flow with the anti-Soviet current in Prague and have only limited contacts with Moscow. When a communist deputy heckled him in the National Assembly over the recognition of the Kremlin, Beneš exploded, "The Soviet government has not been recognized, it is not recognized, and it won't be recognized."[82] On this occasion, the minister overstated his position, but he certainly knew that he would have to move with caution and without fanfare concerning the Bolsheviks. He explained his attitude toward the issue of de jure recognition of Soviet Russia in a circular memorandum to Czechoslovak legations. It was important, he said, to move slowly. The key to the strategy he envisioned was to operate on the basis of quid pro quo. Step by step, the international community should grant "political, diplomatic, legal and commercial concessions to the present Russian regime" in exchange for a gradual dismantling of its Bolshevik character.[83] Beneš hoped—in vain—that the world community would orchestrate its strategy toward the Kremlin.

In March 1921 Czechoslovak diplomats traveled to the Soviet Union for talks with Maxim Litvinov, a top Soviet diplomat. Their purpose was to upgrade the channels of communication between Prague and Moscow. As had happened before when the Hillerson mission was discussed, the negotiations were problematic. One obstacle was a demand by Litvinov that Czechoslovakia recognize the future Soviet mission in Prague as the only legitimate representative of Russia. This was tricky because a Russian legation already existed in Prague with an officially accredited chargé d'affaires, M. Rafalovich, who represented the short-lived provisional government of Russia between the tsar's resignation and the Bolshevik revolution. Since 1918 the Masaryk government had treated him as the sole legitimate Russian representative in Czechoslovakia. It was clear that the legation could not remain in Prague for long because by 1921 it represented a nonexistent government. But the whole affair was made problematic by the fact that the post-Tsarist and pre-Bolshevik Russian government, seated in Omsk at the time, had granted full recognition to Czechoslovakia.[84] Beneš was disinclined to accept Litvinov's demand because he thought that it came too close to de jure recognition. He was prepared only to state that the Soviet mission was "authorized" to represent Soviet Russia.[85] Neither

Masaryk nor Beneš was willing to give up on the possibility—remote as it appeared in 1921—that a democratic alternative to the Bolsheviks might still emerge.[86]

Another obstacle in the Czechoslovak-Soviet negotiations was Litvinov's request that Soviet representation be many times bigger than its Czechoslovak counterpart.[87] The Prague negotiators were taken aback. Given the vastness of Soviet Russia on the one hand and the small size of Czechoslovakia on the other, this seemed absurd. Prague was determined not to become a center for Bolshevik ideological or intelligence activities—for the sake of its own security and out of comity to its neighbors—and demanded an explanation. Litvinov could offer only excuses. He argued that the Soviet economy was centralized and that Prague's representatives in the Soviet Union could talk directly to top decision makers, whereas the Czechoslovak economy was capitalist and Soviet commercial specialists posted in Prague would have to deal with owners of individual enterprises.[88]

It is unlikely that such arguments could have persuaded the Czechoslovak government. But the pressures from Prague's business community, tempted more than ever by the vision of the vast Russian markets, proved too strong, and the negotiations were brought to a conclusion. Ultimately, Minister Beneš had to accept the Soviet demand that the missions be described as the exclusive representative institutions of the two countries.[89] Nevertheless, the so-called Provisional Treaty, signed by representatives of the Soviet Union and Czechoslovakia in Prague on 5 June 1922, stated that it constituted no precedent for the issue of de jure recognition.[90] It stressed that Prague and Moscow would observe the principles of neutrality toward each other if either were in a conflict with a third party.[91] Perhaps in response to the extradiplomatic activities of the Hillerson mission, Prague insisted on including Article 5 of the treaty, which stated that both parties could use couriers only once a week with no more than ten kilograms of diplomatically protected cargo.

The Provisional Treaty was ratified in August 1922 and provided a basis for official dealings between Czechoslovakia and the Soviet Union. Henceforth, in addition to the already existing commercial offices opened in the summer of 1921, the two governments would have diplomatic missions in Prague and Moscow plus a Czechoslovak mission in Kharkov.[92] A group of Soviet diplomats, headed by K. K. Yurienev, arrived in Prague on 30 August 1923.[93] The Soviet mission was in Villa Tereza on Žižka Street in Prague-Vinohrady; its telephone number was 1027. Czechoslovakia's chief diplomat in the Soviet Union was Josef Girsa.[94] This was definitely a step above Red Cross missions.

Gradually, the Soviets increased the number of their representatives in Prague. Although the two countries had not recognized each other de jure, Prague agreed to grant up to six Soviet citizens limited diplomatic status.[95] This was motivated by the desire of the Czechoslovak Ministry of Foreign Affairs to protect its personnel in the Soviet Union. By the mid-1920s, arrests, often quite random, were in full swing in large Soviet cities. Prague worried that if Czechoslovak diplomats serving in the Soviet Union were not shielded by diplomatic identification cards they would be vulnerable to abuse at the hands of Soviet security, the GPU.[96] These were not groundless fears.[97]

By late 1926 the Soviet mission employed four diplomats who had full diplomatic status (the famous Vladimir Antonov-Ovseenko, N. M. Kaliuzhnii,

S. P. Kalina, and N. G. Golst) and fourteen others with official passports.[98] It also hired on the spot eight Czechoslovak citizens. In addition, there was the commercial section, with one Soviet citizen bearing a diplomatic passport (I. V. Lenskii), twenty-nine Soviet officials, one Austrian, one Bulgarian, and nineteen Czechoslovak citizens.[99] Full diplomatic recognition was still far away, however.

In April 1922, while the Prague government was contemplating the best course of action regarding Soviet Russia, Chicherin and the German foreign minister, Walter Rathenau, signed the Treaty of Rapallo. This provided the Bolsheviks with de jure recognition as rulers of Soviet Russia and allowed the two countries to escape their isolation. The treaty improved the Bolsheviks' international position significantly. Following Rapallo, in less than two years the Kremlin received a bucketful of de jure recognition documents. Many countries, large and small, wanted to have official relations with the Soviet government, and Beneš was understandably eager to join this trend. He told the National Assembly in early February 1924, soon after the Soviet Union had received full recognition documents from Great Britain, that establishing de jure relations with the Kremlin leaders would help "introduce Russia again as a political agent into European politics because without Russia there will be no peace in Europe." De jure recognition from Prague would mean support for the progressive, less ideological elements in the Kremlin. Beneš argued that Czechoslovakia should recognize the Bolsheviks de jure "whether the Soviet regime stays or falls,"[100] and the diplomatic community in Moscow expected him soon to offer de jure recognition to the Soviets.[101] Other sources indicate that recognition documents had already been drafted and that plans had been made for an official exchange of these papers. At the last moment, however, all was canceled by Beneš.[102]

As it happened, Lenin died in January 1924, and his departure from the scene brought to the surface an ongoing succession struggle among his colleagues. There had been few historical antecedents for the brutality with which Lenin's colleagues fought each other. Czechoslovak observers in Moscow predicted the victory of Stalin, Zinoviev, and Kameniev over Trotsky and warned that the triumvirate seriously believed in communism. Beneš now hesitated. Should he risk a domestic struggle with the anti-Bolshevik forces in Prague when the scene in Moscow had become so difficult to understand? By March 1924 Beneš's hesitation was made public by Chicherin. Czechoslovakia, he said, made an effort to maintain good and diplomatically correct relations with the Soviet Union, but it kept hoping for the emergence of a "'democratic' Russia" the commissar complained. Moscow also expressed its bitterness over existing contacts between White Russian émigrés and leading politicians in Prague.[103]

In this regard, Chicherin was not exaggerating. Twenty thousand Russian émigrés were in Prague, and they formed more than ten vibrant organizations. Some were openly supported by President Masaryk, others by the lord mayor of Prague, Karel Baxa, who was in charge of the Russian Aid Committee, and by the Czechoslovak Social Democratic party. It was Masaryk's intention to turn Prague into the center of all "progressive Russians."[104] Prague provided food, shelter, clothing, and legal assistance to some one hundred Russian refugees daily.[105] Masaryk believed that supporting the Russian émigré community represented an investment that might come in handy in the future, and Beneš refused to rule out the possibility that the Bolsheviks could still fall because "they committed errors and crimes which will be their curse."[106] Even in 1924 the Prague government believed that a new political system could emerge in Russia.

Chicherin found it hard to believe. When all the great powers of Europe had already recognized the Soviet Union, why was Czechoslovakia still doubting the Bolsheviks' ability to remain in control of Russia? The commissar focused on this question in the fall of 1924. Everything on the international scene, he said, was in a state of a flux. Only one aspect remained unchanged: the attitude of Masaryk and Beneš toward Bolshevism. They stubbornly believed, Chicherin complained, that the Soviet government would collapse or that it would abandon its revolutionary ideology and embrace capitalism. The Prague government continued working with anti-Bolshevik émigrés in the hope that one day they would return to Moscow and overthrow the Kremlin rulers. Beneš, Chicherin concluded, was a "keeper of a den of state criminals."[107] Human memory is short. Within a decade, tensions between Prague and Moscow in the 1920s would be forgotten, and many in Europe would begin to take seriously Berlin's propaganda picturing Beneš and Czechoslovakia as agents of Stalin's Soviet Union.

Despite Chicherin's hints, Czechoslovak politicians held onto the opinion that "recognition of communism and Bolshevik methods . . . *de jure* recognition would be a great error."[108] This had become a minority viewpoint on the international scene. Most other governments in Europe had made up their minds and had begun, or would soon begin, to treat the Bolsheviks as legitimate and sovereign successors to the tsars. In 1920 Prague had proposed to civilize the Bolsheviks by bringing them into Europe, hoping that Europe could also be stabilized by doing so. This approach seemed natural to Masaryk and Beneš. By the end of 1924, the Bolsheviks had been recognized de jure by such powers as Germany, Great Britain, Italy, China, Mexico, and France, yet Czechoslovakia still held out. Moscow warned in May 1929 that Prague's refusal to recognize the Soviet Union "cannot lead to any good."[109] President Masaryk's Czechoslovakia remained among the few European countries that had failed to establish proper diplomatic relations with the Soviet Union.

The Kremlin found it difficult to believe that this abnormal state of affairs could last, and it tried probing the situation, mostly with threats and undiplomatic talk. In January 1925 Grigori Zinoviev said that Czechs were "Chekhosobaki" (Czecho-dogs).[110] Five months later, Josef Girsa reported on his meeting with Antonov-Ovseenko. Girsa's Soviet colleague opened the conversation by praising the beauties of Prague and the Czech democratic tradition and then launched into a tirade about Czechoslovakia's failure to grant de jure recognition to the Soviets. He raised the possibility that Moscow would tire of waiting; it could close down its mission in Prague. The Czechoslovak diplomat said as little as possible.[111]

Antonín Hobza, a respected Prague jurist, outlined the reasons for Czecho-slovakia's distance from the Bolsheviks. New regimes were routinely granted de jure recognition, he said, even if they came to power as a result of a violent coup d'état. But the Bolsheviks were an unprecedented lot. They refused to fulfill the obligations of their predecessors, they did not recognize the concept of private property, they engaged in large-scale expropriations, and they declared as their objective the destabilization of existing governments on a global scale.[112] Under such circumstances, there was reason for prudence and caution before full recognition was offered.

From Diplomacy to Confrontation

It was clear by the end of 1924 that, for the time being, de jure recognition was not obtainable from the Masaryk government. The atmosphere between Moscow and Prague quickly started to thicken as the Soviets initiated hostile actions to escalate the crisis. As a result, from 1924 to 1933 Czechoslovak-Soviet relations were covered by a layer of ice. Some episodes from the period seem so violent and unbefitting to the world of diplomacy that only the original signatures on the official stationery, now deposited in the Prague archives, prompt the contemporary reader to trust the dry language of diplomatic communications.

In 1925 Josef Girsa found that he was being summoned more frequently than others in the diplomatic community to the Commissariat for Foreign Affairs for stern lectures by Soviet bureaucrats on the alleged transgressions of Czechoslovak policy-makers. At the same time, the personnel of the Soviet mission in Prague developed the habit of presenting at the Foreign Ministry sharp protests against such banalities as newspaper cartoons.

Disturbed by this course of affairs, the Prague Foreign Ministry sent a briefing paper to its mission in Moscow. It summed up the situation, and Czechoslovak diplomats were advised to use it in future contacts with the Foreign Commissariat. The Soviets liked to complain about trivialities, the document stated, but Czechoslovak diplomats had more serious matters to take up with their counterparts. The memorandum then presented an impressively long list of Soviet violations of international law and diplomatic customs regarding the Czechoslovak mission. For instance, there had been "three armed attacks upon the premises of our Mission in Moscow." On one occasion, a Czechoslovak diplomat was wounded, and the mission frequently received threats that mass demonstrations would occur in front of the building to protest capitalist oppression in Czechoslovakia. It should be clear who had the most reason to complain concluded the tersely written paper.[113]

On 10 August 1925 Girsa was again summoned to the Foreign Commissariat. As was to be expected, he was treated very coldly. The complaints dealt primarily with articles in the Czechoslovak press that were, or were perceived to be, hostile to the Soviet Union. Girsa attempted to explain that because Czechoslovakia was a democracy, its government was in no position to dictate the ideological spin of newspaper articles and hardly anything published expressed the official opinion. In contrast, he pointed out, the Soviet press was controlled—and how was one to understand the vicious articles about the Czechoslovak President Thomas Masaryk one found so frequently in it?[114]

Matters had become critical by the end of 1925, and Girsa requested that Prague authorities supply him with two large revolvers and five smaller ones. Was he overreacting? Hardly. The premises of the Czechoslovak mission had been again burglarized. It was impossible to tell whether Soviet authorities were behind each attack, but there was reason to be suspicious. In one case, the attackers included a Soviet security officer whom the Commissariat for Foreign Affairs had previously supplied to guard the mission. On another occasion, goods taken from the mission were found displayed for sale in the market the next day. When a Czechoslovak diplomat demanded of a security officer that he confiscate the items as stolen property, the militiaman, in a scene taken from Gogol, spent so much time verifying the identity of the diplomat that the thieves were able to pack up and leave the bazaar with their loot. At that point Girsa and his staff decided to take matters into their own hands, and a diplomat was posted to guard the mission at night. When yet another group of thieves appeared, he fired and killed one of the attackers.

The Soviet authorities responded swiftly. The official car equipped with diplomatic license plates and the Czechoslovak flag, carrying Chief of Mission Girsa, Deputy Consul Hejny, and the consul's wife, all with diplomatic status, was stopped, and the three occupants were forced out and marched under heavy guard and at a brisk pace to a distant police station. Passersby were led to believe that the three were criminals arrested by the vigilant Soviet authorities. The diplomats were released, but their protests were ignored.[115] This kind of behavior could no longer be considered acceptable, and it was unprecedented in the short history of Czechoslovak foreign relations. Moscow seemed more interested in open confrontation than in diplomatic schemes.

Josef Girsa was able to keep cool in the bizarre and dangerous atmosphere surrounding the Czechoslovak mission. Despite the dramatic events that characterized his tenure in the Soviet Union, his reports were balanced and designed to inform the Prague Foreign Ministry objectively. But conducting regular diplomacy had become, at least for the Czechoslovak mission, nearly impossible. Writing a year after his arrest by Soviet security, Girsa attempted to put Soviet behavior toward Czechoslovakia in perspective. His brief statement pointed out that diplomacy and espionage, from the Bolshevik perspective, were but two sides of the same coin. Activities of the Communist International or GPU operations were always carried out from Soviet legations and embassies abroad. Even in countries like Czechoslovakia, which had not established de jure relations with the Moscow government, the Soviet Union set up other operations—missions or commercial firms—that also served subversive intelligence purposes.[116] Of his own difficulties in Moscow Girsa made no mention.

At about the time the Czechoslovak mission was a target for Soviet security, the police in Prague began noticing an increase in activities by the GPU. The government was well informed about this organization. In April 1923 the Ministry of Foreign Affairs obtained a detailed document describing the GPU's organizational structure, both domestic and international, names of important GPU officers, their posts, and the existing chain of command.[117] The ministry circulated this unique document throughout the government in Prague, as well as to several exposed regional police command posts. The papers obtained by the Foreign Ministry included as an attachment a circular note signed by Yan Unschlicht. It ordered GPU personnel abroad to seek out Russian émigrés and lure them back to the Soviet Union; to place Soviet agents in anti-Bolshevik organizations; to recruit among prominent émigrés, especially among those who had been tsarist officials or army officers; to cause and maintain conflict and dissent inside the émigré community; and to focus on seeking out Russian women who lived in the loneliness and poverty of exile to help perform these tasks.

The Czechoslovak government was sensitive to signs of hostile operations by the GPU among the émigré community because President Masaryk had established himself as one of the most prominent protectors of Russian refugees. But from Prague's perspective, the most serious revelation was that Czechoslovakia had become an important operational zone for the GPU. The document revealed that the organization's Third or Foreign Section (its chief was Comrade Meshcheriakov) was divided into eight special regions. Czechoslovakia, together with Austria and Switzerland, was subordinated to GPU commanders in Region I, with headquarters in Germany. A note from the Ministry of Interior to the Ministry of Defense stated that the GPU's Czechoslovak section was in room 128, Lubyanka 2, Moscow. Its chief was Jaroslav Pil, a Czech lawyer who was last seen in Prague in 1920 organizing intelligence for the procommunist elements in the Social Democratic party.[118]

The document also described the structure of the Soviet military intelligence, the GRU. Berlin was listed as the "central office for espionage abroad." Its chief was Miron Yakovlevich Abovich. The second post was in Paris; Prague was listed as number three. In addition to the GPU and the GRU, Moscow operated a third network in Czechoslovakia that was subordinated to the Communist International. According to a document obtained from a source in Moscow, Czechoslovakia was subsumed under Section XI (Western Europe), Department I (Central Europe), Group f. The Comintern's Division XI/I/f had its headquarters in Kladno, an industrial and coal-mining town some forty kilometers outside Prague. Its staff consisted of Comrades Sonnenschein, Hůla, Malířová, Goldenberg, Vaněk, and Kreibich. The post's commander was a Comrade Neurath.[119]

Prague authorities had virtually no counterintelligence capability, even by 1933 when Adolf Hitler came to power.[120] If the police were already able to arrest scores of Soviet spies in the mid-1920s, one must assume that the GPU and GRU were quite active in Czechoslovakia. This became especially true as governments in neighboring countries turned progressively authoritarian. Czechoslovak military intelligence had several indications that Moscow had started using Prague to the hilt. Doing so made sense: in Germany, Poland, Hungary, and Yugoslavia those found guilty of espionage on behalf of the Soviet Union risked being executed. In Romania they would be sentenced to drastic terms in prison. Austria had recently closed down an important GPU central in Baden.[121] Therefore, Czechoslovakia was for the Soviets and their underground networks the only country in Central Europe where they could work relatively undisturbed.[122]

Various Soviet agents behaved with complete brazenness, and the Czechoslovak police, probably the one organization in Central Europe most restrained by legal concerns, had its hands full. Some agents appeared over and over again. Consider the case of Boris Lago-Kolpakov. A former Wrangel army officer, Lago-Kolpakov retreated in 1920 with his unit into Turkey, where he was granted political asylum. He soon showed up in Prague and was recruited for espionage on behalf of the Bolshevik regime by the top Soviet agent, the *rezident,* who was posing as an employee of the Soviet Commercial Mission. The *rezident* equipped Lago-

Kolpakov with a false Czechoslovak passport issued to "František Kelber." In 1924, after he had carried out various tasks in the Balkans, especially in Romania, Lago-Kolpakov returned, this time using a false Austrian passport issued to "Oskar Spatczek."[123] Most agents carried out tasks designed to gather military intelligence that was deemed useful in Moscow. In such cases, they were detained briefly and expelled.[124]

But not all Soviet agents sought industrial or military secrets. One Ivan Piotrovski had primarily a political mission. This former White Russian officer found himself in Prague after the victory of the Lenin government. He approached the Czechoslovak Ministry of Defense with offers involving military information and was turned down. At that point, desperate and vulnerable, Piotrovski was recruited by the Soviet *rezident* in Prague. His main mission was to penetrate some of the most prestigious Russian émigré organizations in Prague, particularly the ones that acted as advisors to Czechoslovak policymakers. Piotrovski was to learn as much as possible about the preparations of the Czechoslovak government for de jure recognition of the Soviet Union. He was arrested by Czechoslovak police, tried, and sentenced to five years in jail.[125]

Given Moscow's confrontational behavior and the freeze in Czechoslovak-Soviet relations, Prague was taken aback in late 1926 by yet another Soviet maneuver designed to obtain de jure diplomatic recognition. The Czechoslovak mission in Moscow received a note—on Christmas Eve—from the Foreign Commissariat. The message could only be read as an ultimatum. Prague had one month to declare its mission in Kharkov a consulate and grant a corresponding "consulate patent" to the Soviet mission in Bratislava, Czechoslovakia, or the Kharkov mission would be shut down.[126] Prague's response was sharp. It was a gross violation of the principles of basic comity for Moscow to resort to ultimatums and threats, the Foreign Ministry stated. After all, the status of the Czechoslovak mission in Kharkov had been determined by the agreement of 5 October 1923, while the Soviet mission in Bratislava was treated in accordance with the agreement of 15 December 1926. It was unheard of in normal diplomacy for one party to demand something to which it was not entitled under existing agreements and then resort to threats to obtain it nevertheless. The Soviet government "did not have the slightest right," wrote the Prague Foreign Ministry, to redefine the legal status of the missions in Kharkov and Bratislava—and just days after it had signed a binding agreement pertaining to one of the two missions. For internal use, the ministry warned that the latest Soviet demand was an attempt to trap Czechoslovakia. If the two countries had had "consulates" rather than "missions" it would have created the appearance that Czechoslovakia had granted de jure recognition to the Soviet Union.[127]

Prague's determined rejection of the Soviet ploy brought about a further freezing of Czechoslovak-Soviet relations. Henceforth, Moscow reduced its diplomatic activities in Czechoslovakia to almost nothing. It focused instead on intelligence operations and on deliberate provocations against Czechoslovak diplomatic personnel in Moscow.

On occasion, the Soviet mission in Prague carried out brazen espionage operations designed to provoke an open confrontation. For instance, in early 1931 various Czech engineers began receiving letters from the Soviet mission. The letters implied that the engineers had contacted a Soviet diplomat and inquired about job opportunities in the Soviet Union. Many jobs were available for qualified technicians, said the letter, and it suggested that the addressee send the Soviet mission four copies of his curriculum vitae. In its analysis of this case, the Ministry of Interior pointed out that foreigners were being either wiped out by the secret police or driven out of the Soviet Union. Therefore, the incident was not an attempt to recruit engineers. It was the beginning of an intelligence operation. Those who responded would have been subsequently open to blackmail. Some engineers reported having been approached by the Soviet mission in Prague.[128] Others, curious to explore the unexpected opportunity, responded and were subsequently invited to the Soviet mission. Those who showed up were subjected to an aggressive interrogation by a German engineer who demanded a detailed description ("Draw it!") of their professional activities.[129] Prague authorities knew that intelligence-gathering was as old as diplomacy itself, but such behavior was deliberately provocative and went significantly beyond the line of what was tolerable.

By the early 1930s the Stalinist Soviet Union seemed to have lost all sense of proportion concerning its conduct on the international scene. A new low was reached in December 1931. The authoritative *Izvestia* brought a TASS release that gave pause to personnel of the Czechoslovak mission in Moscow, now armed with revolvers. It stated that a Soviet citizen, identified only as G., surrendered to the authorities. He had worked for some time as a spy for a foreign diplomat, whom he supplied with reports regarding new railroads in the Soviet Union. Unexpectedly, the diplomat told G. that it was necessary to drive Japan into a war against the Soviet state. One way of achieving this objective was for G. to assassinate the Japanese ambassador in Moscow. It was at this point that G. saw what an appalling game was being played, wrote *Izvestia,* and decided to trust the Soviet authorities and reveal the plot. When the security organs fully verified G.'s testimony, the Foreign Commissariat declared the diplomat persona non grata. The mysterious diplomat turned out to be Karel Vaněk from the Czechoslovak legation. He left the Soviet Union on the day the article appeared. He was completely innocent.[130]

When Adolf Hitler came to power in Germany in January 1933, serious diplomatic contacts between Czechoslovakia and the Soviet Union were almost nonexistent. The Prague government had concluded that the Soviet Union was a police regime and that it was futile to conduct normal diplomacy with it. Telling was an analysis of the nature of the Bolshevik regime by Czechoslovak military intelligence. It stated that the whole Soviet system rested on its security apparatus, the OGPU, the recently renamed GPU. It was, the report stressed, a uniquely perfect and utterly brutal apparatus of Soviet administration and the main source of its strength. Although many countries had tried to fight the OGPU, Czechoslovak intelligence analysts wrote, one could see almost no positive results. The Bolshevik adversary proved to be far too ruthless as well as sophisticated for the obsolete methods of European police organizations engaged in resisting the spread of Soviet power.[131]

IN THE EARLY 1920s, Masaryk and Beneš had tried to bring Russia back to Europe. They had hoped to form a common front of states that would weave the country into the European fabric by exchanging commercial ties and diplomatic recognition for the gradual deconstruction of Bolshevism. Their plan failed utterly. More than a decade later, most European countries had granted full recognition to the Kremlin while Czechoslovakia and the Soviet Union were not even on speaking terms. On occasion, tensions escalated into break-ins and shootings and arrests of Czechoslovak diplomats in Moscow. In 1933, however, Adolf Hitler's *Machtergreifung* would serve as a reminder to Prague that a dramatic improvement in its relations with the Soviet Union was absolutely necessary. It would have to be obtained at almost any cost.

Notes

1. Karel Amerling, "Vzpomínka z gymnásia," in *50 let Dra Edvarda Beneše* (Prague: Pokrok, 1934), 40. Amerling later became a professor of medicine at Charles University and remained Beneš's friend. Beneš attended the gymnasium at Vinohrady, a district of Prague.

2. An Austrian border police officer was uncertain whether he should let Professor Masaryk board the train into neutral Italy, and he therefore decided to seek guidance by telegraph from the police in Prague. But the train for Venice would have left before an answer could be received; moreover, there was no telling what the reply would have been. Therefore, Masaryk produced his identification card as a member of parliament, claimed immunity, frightened the policeman, and took his place on the train. Masaryk, *The Making of a State: Memoirs and Observations, 1914–1918* (New York: Frederick A. Stokes, 1923), 35.

3. František Soukup, *28. říjen 1918: Předpoklady a vývoj našeho odboje domácího v československé revoluci za státní samostatnost národa* (Prague: Ústřední Dělnické Knihkupectví a Nakladatelství Antonín Zasvěcený a Orbis, 1928), 2: 1006.

4. Arthur Werner, *Eduard Beneš: Der Mensch und der Staatsmann* (Prague: Verlag Roland Morawitz, n.d. [perhaps 1935]), 136.

5. The Beau-Rivage Hotel in Geneva was associated in the minds of Central Europeans with the stabbing of Elisabeth of Austria in 1898.

6. Beneš liked to say that he had to crawl "through the thickets" to avoid getting caught by the Austrian and Bavarian border police on his way to exile in 1915; see Edward B. Hitchcock, *"I Built a Temple for Peace": The Life of Edvard Beneš* (London: Harper, 1940), 161. Alas, a passport deposited in the MHA-B, personal matters, box 1, leaves no doubt about it: Beneš left the country on 2 September 1915 with a passport no. 90 RP 106 issued to a traveling salesman Miroslav Šícha, Vertreter der Firma Hruby, Lehrapparatenfabrik. Interestingly, Beneš used the passport without any change; it had Šícha's name, photograph, and description.

7. I am grateful to Dr. Antonín Klimek, senior researcher of the Historical Institute of the Czech Army, Prague, for his guidance regarding archival documents on Edvard Beneš's youth.

8. MHA-B, box: Articles about Beneš, 1. The quotation is from an unpublished manuscript of Ladislav Kunte, "Do třiceti let," 22–23. The manuscript is undated but it makes a reference to President Beneš; therefore, it must have been written after 18 December 1935 and before 5 October 1938. Most likely, Kunte wrote the article in 1936 or 1937. Kunte (b. 22 April 1874), formerly a Catholic priest, was not a historian by training. But as a collaborator of Masaryk—he was an editor of *Čas*—and later of Beneš, Kunte had access to an impressive array of information regarding Edvard Beneš's youth. Some of the documents he quotes came from Beneš's family archives.

9. Antonín Klimek, *Zrození státníka, Edvard Beneš, 28.5.1884–24.9.1919* (Prague: Melantrich, 1992), 4.

10. MHA-B, Personalities, box 8, file General Štefánik. The opinions come from an

unfinished letter by Lev Sychrava, Beneš's "most intimate" collaborator in Paris, to President Masaryk of 8 December 1918. Sychrava did not mail the letter at the time, but he handed it to President Masaryk in the early 1920s as a historical document.

11. Jan Opočenský (ed.), *Edward Beneš: Essays and Reflections Presented on the Occasion of His Sixtieth Birthday* (London: Allen & Unwin, 1945).

12. Soukup, *28. říjen 1918*, 1094. Klofáč claimed further that Masaryk and Beneš succeeded because they were knowledgable and well prepared—in contrast to the other diplomats "who had no understanding" of the complicated problems before the Paris Peace Conference. Therefore, they had to accept the views of the Czechoslovak delegation.

13. The affair began in January 1919 in Paris and involved Professor Alois Jirák, one of Beneš's best friends and one of his few confidants. After Beneš returned to Prague in 1919, he invited Jirák to his office and asked him to describe once again the whole scheme. Jirák, convinced that the two were alone, described it in detail, hinting, perhaps, that nobody would know how the minister chose to spend the money. At that point two detectives emerged from an adjacent room and put Jirák under arrest for an alleged attempt to corrupt an official. Jirák proclaimed his innocence in letters to President Masaryk and to others in the government. Nevertheless, he was sent to jail on the strength of Minister Beneš's testimony. Some information on this is from Klimek, *Zrození státníka*, 30.

14. Pierre Crebites, *Beneš: Statesman of Central Europe* (London: Routledge, 1935), 232.

15. AMFA, Second Section, box 502. In 1921 the Czechoslovak Ministry of Defense already considered Austria to be part of Germany in case of Czechoslovak-German hostilities.

16. D. Perman, *The Shaping of the Czechoslovak State* (Leiden: E. J. Brill, 1962), 275. Perman continues to say that this "encirclement . . . was never successfully broken by Czech foreign policy."

17. AMFA, Second Section, box 502, the Ministry of Defense to the Ministry of Foreign Affairs, 12 June 1921, secret.

18. Thomas G. Masaryk, "Pomoc Rusku Evropou a Amerikou" (Prague: H & H, 1992), 11: "The Bolsheviks claim to be Marxists, but Marx and Engels demanded of the proletariat education, science, and philosophy. The Russian workers are not educated and they have neither science nor philosophy." (This is a reprint of the original text written in early 1922.)

19. Technically, Czechoslovakia had three foreign ministers. Prime Minister Milan Hodža was the Czechoslovak foreign minister from 20 December 1935 to 29 February 1936. But only Edvard Beneš and Kamil Krofta served long enough at the Černín Palace in Prague to deserve mention as foreign ministers.

20. Chicherin had employed remarkably similar arguments at least once before, in late 1918, in an effort to entice or, if necessary, force Poland into diplomatic relations with Moscow. Piotr S. Wandycz, *Soviet-Polish Relations, 1917–1921* (Cambridge, Mass.: Harvard University Press, 1969), 82–84.

21. *Sborník zahraniční politiky*, 15 April 1920.

22. Ibid.

23. *Sborník zahraniční politiky*, 29 April 1920.

24. Dated according to archival sources; a secondary source has the Hillerson team arriving in Prague on 10 July 1920; see *Přehled dějin československo-sovětských vztahů v údobí 1917–1939* (Prague: Academia, 1975), 116.

25. Office of the President of the Republic of Czechoslovakia, T 48/21. Hillerson is identified as Dr. S. Hillerson, Représentant de la Croix Rouge Russe. His name is sometimes spelled "Gillerson." The arrival of the Hillerson mission was discussed in the Prague press;

see *Národní listy,* 9 July 1920. Hillerson's presence in Prague was first noted in Alfred L. P. Dennis, *The Foreign Policies of Soviet Russia* (New York: Dutton, 1924), 398. Dennis mistakenly claims that Hillerson came to Prague in 1919, but he correctly suspects Hillerson's involvement in intelligence operations.

26. Wandycz, *Soviet-Polish Relations,* 85–89.

27. Alice Masaryk's letter is in SCA, Presidium of the Ministry of Interior, IV R/I, box 214.

28. SCA. See, for instance, *České slovo,* 30 September 1920; *Národní politika,* 1 October 1920; and *Venkov,* 6 October 1920. Clippings are in SCA, Presidium of the Ministry of Interior, IV R/12, box 212.

29. SCA, Presidium of the Ministry of Interior, IV R/1, box 209.

30. The Third Section of the Ministry of Foreign Affairs was, in addition to being a communications center, one of Czechoslovakia's intelligence services. Its chief, Section Chief Jan Hájek, was born in 1883 in the small village of Přepychy (near Nové Město nad Metují). At the beginning of World War I, he was already involved in the Czechoslovak patriotic movement organized around Masaryk and Beneš. While those two had chosen exile, Hájek stayed in Prague, where he helped maintain channels of communication between the home front and the exiles. Although he was directly involved in the anti-Hapsburg conspiracy, Austrian authorities determined that the charge of high treason could not be proven in a court of law, and Hájek was granted amnesty, along with other political prisoners, by Emperor Charles. Once the war ended, Hájek joined the Ministry of Foreign Affairs, where he built up an efficient intelligence organization. The main activities of the Third Section were directed at Western public opinion. Jan Hájek gradually developed a worldwide network of journalists who on a regular or an intermittent basis accepted money in exchange for articles sympathetic to the viewpoint of Prague. In France alone, Hájek's checks (which sometimes had to be co-signed by Foreign Minister Beneš or by his successor, Kamil Krofta) went regularly to twenty-eight dailies, journals, and press agencies. The Third Section was just as active in London, Vienna, and Geneva. Hájek also extended covert financial support to the anti-Hitler democratic media in Germany. Some of Hájek's archives were published by the Germans during World War II in a tendetious but interesting volume by Rudolf Urban, *Tajné fondy III. sekce: Z archívu MZ Republiky Československé* (Prague: Orbis, 1943).

31. AMFA. I have found the whole Hillerson collection in the Ministry for Foreign Affairs in Prague; it has no archival number, and all the papers are in a black, three-ring binder. Frequently, one section of a message was encoded according to one key and then, abruptly, another code was used. The code specialists commented that on such occasions Hillerson was merely passing along messages from Bolshevik agents in Europe, which he had already received encoded. By the time the cipher squad had done its job, Hillerson had disappeared from Prague into the whirlwind of Soviet Russia.

32. AMFA, Hillerson File, 37/1920 Rus., 9 September 1920: "Rozshifrovanie nashikh depesh bez kliuchei predstavliaetsia malo veroiatnym primite vse mery k nailuchshemu khraneniu kliuchei i rasshifronvannych depesh osobo sekretnye depeshi noebkhodimo pereshifrovyvat" (Chicherin assures Hillerson: It is unlikely that, without the key, Prague could break the code and urges him to be extra careful).

33. Norman Davies, *God's Playground* (New York: Columbia University Press, 1982), 396.

34. MHA, Ministry of National Defense, General Staff, box 423, no. 2, "Plan B."

35. The miraculous nature of the reversal was stressed by some; others, more pragmatically inclined, pointed out that the Red Army had overextended its command and communications, as well as its supply lines.

36. Beneš welcomed the Treaty of Riga between the Bolsheviks and Poland, but he

pointed out that it was not signed in Paris and that "none of the Great Powers has attached its signature to this peace arrangement." It therefore concerned only the Bolsheviks and Poland. Prague was neither for nor against any of the treaty's specific points. Edvard Beneš, *Problémy nové Evropy a zahraniční politika Československa: Projevy a úvahy z r. 1919–1924* (Prague: Melantrich, 1924), 120. Even as late as in 1924, Polish diplomats were trying to secure Beneš's approval of the terms agreed on at Riga, but Beneš would not cooperate. "C'est votre affaire," he told K. Bader, the Polish chargé d'affairs in Prague on 5 January 1924. Polish-Soviet affairs and the Treaty of Riga did not interest him, he said. The Warsaw Foreign Ministry promptly circulated this memorandum to its embassies and legations. Archiwum Akt Nowych, AAN, Poselstwo R.P. v Paryżu, t. 284, k. 7. As quoted by Radko Břach, " 'Ruský problém' v čs. zahraniční politice na počátku roku 1924," *Československý časopis historický* 15, no. 1 (1968): 6.

37. AMFA, Hillerson File, 60/20 Rus.

38. Ibid., 64/21 Rus.

39. Ibid., 124/20 Rus.

40. Ibid., 65/21, 7 February 1921. Hillerson was later able to report that anti-intervention sentiments had prevailed also in France. He wrote that, according to his source in Paris, French military circles had given up on the idea of direct armed intervention against the Lenin government. This news must have been welcomed in the Kremlin. Ibid., 5 January 1921.

41. Ibid., 65/21 Rus and 66/21 Rus. The French, wrote Hillerson, "look at Poland with pessimism."

42. Ibid., 98/21 Rus.

43. Ibid., 12 c/20 Rus. Hillerson claimed that he had at his disposal five hundred cossacks and weapons; now he needed 200,000 Czechoslovak crowns (Kc).

44. Ibid., 28/20 Rus and 146 a/20. There was a good reason for Chicherin's warning against provocations. In March 1921 Hillerson had been approached by a sergeant of the Czechoslovak army who proposed to sell him the latest Czech-made machine-gun and other military secrets for 20,000 Kc. Hillerson had him arrested immediately. SCA, Presidium of the Ministry of Interior, IV R/12, box 212. The case reached the press; see *Národní politika*, 18 March 1921. On 31 December 1920, Hillerson radioed Moscow via the Foreign Ministry's Third Section that Prague security spied on the Soviet Red Cross mission in Czechoslovakia as much as was possible, but nothing was done in a vulgar or diplomatically "incorrect" manner.

45. AMFA, Hillerson File, Rus 154/1920.

46. W. G. Krivitsky, *In Stalin's Secret Service* (New York: Harper, 1939), 30. Krivitsky shows that during the Soviet-Polish war the Soviet military intelligence was active throughout the region—Danzig, Warsaw, Kracow, Lwow, German and Bohemian Silesia, and Vienna—in conducting acts of sabotage and preventing arms shipments to Polish troops. Krivitsky was attached to the military intelligence of the Western Front, and his mission was to operate behind Polish lines and elsewhere as needed. He claims to have organized strikes— some in Czechoslovakia—to stop trains with ammunition and weapons for the Polish army.

47. AMFA, Hillerson File, 113/20.

48. Ibid., 137/20 Rus.

49. AMFA, Minister Edvard Beneš, Prague, to Major Josef Skála, chief of the Czechoslovak mission, Moscow, 3 January 1921, radiogram 4465/27, Moscow 1921.

50. For the rest of the period between the wars, Czechoslovak-Polish relations declined whenever Czechoslovak-Soviet relations improved. See František Moravec, *Špión, jemuž nevěřili* (Prague: Rozmluvy, 1990), 100.

51. *Slovanské studie: Slavjanofilství Ivana V. Kirejevského* (Prague: Bursík a Kohout,

1893); *Natsionalizm i internatsionalizm sotsial' demokratii* (Moscow: Izd. Viktora Kugel' [1906?]); *The Spirit of Russia* (1919, rpt. London: Allen & Unwin, 1961). The latter was originally published in German in 1913.

52. Masaryk, *Making of a State,* 183. "Of Russia, the Bolshevists know little . . . [but it] is wrong to charge Lenin and his experiment with not being Russian. They are entirely Russian" (182–83). "In my eyes, Lenin was no less Russian than the Tsar Nicholas; nay, despite his Mongolian descent, there was more Russian blood in his veins than in those of the Tsar" (192).

53. Ibid., 201–2.

54. Edvard Beneš, *Nesnáze demokracie* (Prague: Nákladem Svazu Národního Osvobození, 1924), 6–7.

55. Beneš, *Nesnáze demokracie,* 20.

56. Beneš, *Problémy nové Evropy,* 50: "We reject forcefully the cruelty and terror which now exist in Russia."

57. Ibid., 48.

58. Ibid., 47.

59. Beneš's views on this are in "Politika rekonstrukce Ruska" (Prague: H & H, 1992). This originally appeared in German in the semiofficial *Prager Presse* on 25 December 1921. Masaryk expressed his views in "Pomoc Rusku."

60. Beneš, *Problémy nové Evropy,* 161: "The only way to reconstruct Russia is for Europe to be present in Moscow." See also Masaryk, "Pomoc Rusku," 20. The view that there could be no peace in Europe without a stable Russia was, of course, fully supported by the Bolshevik government. Its note to the Allies of 11 May 1922 stated: "The place of Russia can be taken by nobody else but by Russia itself. The political isolation of Russia had consequences that are as serious as those of Russia's economic isolation." The full text is in *Zahraniční politika* 1, nos. 11–12 (1922): 903–8.

61. Beneš, *Problémy nové Evropy,* 51.

62. Zdeněk Sládek, "Československá politika a Rusko 1918–1920," *Československý časopis historický* 16, no. 6 (1968): 865.

63. AMFA, Hillerson File, 220/21 Rus.

64. Teschen (Těšín in Czech, Cieszyn in Polish) was an area of 350 square miles inhabited, according to the latest Austrian census in 1910, by 227,000 people. Of the region's four districts, three (Teschen, Bielsko, and Frysztat) were predominantly Polish, and one (Frýdek) was Czech. Altogether, 69 percent of the Teschen population was Polish. The duchy of Teschen had been part of Poland; in the fourteenth century it went to Bohemia. It stayed under the Czech crown until the dissolution of the independent kingdom in the seventeenth century, when it fell to the Hapsburgs. It remained part of the Hapsburg possessions until 1918.

While the Great War was still in progress, Czech and Polish politicians in exile (for instance, Masaryk, Władysław Grabski, and Ignacy Jan Paderewski) discussed the Teschen question. The Czechs felt then, and they argued subsequently in Paris, that the Karviná coal basin and the important Bohumín railroad junction were vital for Czechoslovak economic development. Although they claimed title to Teschen on the basis of historic rights, their main objectives were utterly pragmatic. The practical perspective was stressed by Masaryk in his letters to Beneš during the Paris Peace Conference. See Zdeněk Šolle, *Masaryk a Beneš ve svých dopisech z doby pařížských mírových jednání* (Prague: Studia Historiae Academiae Scientiarum Bohemicae, 1993).

The Poles were also interested in the Karviná coal and the Bohumín railroad link, but their main interest was not economic. It had to do with national honor and domestic political concerns. Czechoslovakia occupied the area militarily in January 1919, when the Poles were engaged in armed conflicts on different fronts with the Germans, Ukrainians, and Russians.

As a consequence of the Czechoslovak military action, Poland was briefly isolated from the West, and its economic life was seriously affected.

The Conference of Ambassadors in 1920 rejected the Czechoslovak occupation, but it largely followed Beneš's position paper. It divided the territory. Czechoslovakia got the western section, which included the Karviná coal basin as well as Bohumín. Poland was never satisfied with the solution of the Teschen dispute. The conflict had been mishandled by the two rivals as well as the Allies, and it tragically marred the relations between Czechoslovakia and Poland for the next decades. See Piotr S. Wandycz, *France and Her Eastern Allies, 1919–1925: French-Czechoslovak-Polish Relations from the Paris Peace Conference to Locarno* (Minneapolis: University of Minnesota Press, 1962), 75–103; Jaroslav Valenta, "Vyvrcholení národně osvobozeneckého hnutí a utvoření samostatných států (1918–1920)," and "Pokusy o československo-polské sblížení a spolupráci (1921–1925)," in *Češi a Poláci v minulosti: Období kapitalismu a imperialismu* (Prague: Academia, 1967), 431–518; Victor S. Mamatey, "The Establishment of the Republic," in *A History of the Czechoslovak Republic, 1918–1948*, ed. Victor S. Mamatey and Radomír Luža (Princeton: Princeton University Press, 1973), 33–34; Perman, *Shaping of the Czechoslovak State*, 228–57; Beneš, *Problémy nové Evropy*, 61–82. The Czechoslovak consul at Lille reported to Prague on 10 March 1939 regarding a discussion with his colleague, the Polish consul general. The latter told him that the most divisive issue between Poland and Beneš was not Teschen, which could have waited for another fifty or a hundred years for a solution. The most divisive issue was the perception that Beneš was anti-Polish, if not pro-Soviet, during the Soviet-Polish war of 1920. AMFA, Second Section, box 470.

65. Brach, "Ruský problém," 25.

66. Wandycz, *France and Her Eastern Allies*, 238–64; Piotr S. Wandycz, *The Twilight of French Eastern Alliances, 1926–36: French-Czechoslovak-Polish Relations from Locarno to the Remilitarization of the Rhineland* (Princeton: Princeton University Press, 1988), 9.

67. For a recent analysis of the Little Entente's origins, see Magda Ádám, *The Little Entente and Europe, 1920–1929* (Budapest: Akadémiai Kiadó, 1993), 47–192.

68. AMFA. Beneš wrote to Prague from Genoa: "The main principle of our policy will be to maintain the Little Entente's unity at all cost." Telegrams received, Dr. Edvard Beneš from Genoa to the Ministry of Foreign Affairs, 11 May 1922, number 617/1922.

69. Karel Kramář's wife belonged to Russian aristocracy. Her property, especially a beautiful villa in Crimea, had been confiscated by the Bolsheviks.

70. Věra Olivová, "Postoj československé buržoazie k Sovětskému svazu v době jednání o prozatimní smlouvu z roku 1922," *Československý časopis historický* 1, no. 3 (1953): 314.

71. The Czechoslovak Red Cross mission was headed by Major Josef Skála.

72. Czechs started migrating to Tsarist Russia around 1870, and by the beginning of World War I some sixty-five thousand ethnic Czechs lived in all parts of the Russian empire. See Rowan A. Williams, "The Czech Legion Revisited," *East Central Europe* 6, no. 1 (1979): 20. Jan Šeba, "Naše obchodní posice v Rusku," *Zahraniční politika* 1, no. 2 (1922): 15, states that there were twenty-five thousand Czechs in Southern Russia alone.

73. The intelligence component of the Czechoslovak Red Cross activities is underlined by the fact that the organization reported both to the Czechoslovak Ministry of Foreign Affairs and the Ministry of Interior.

74. SCA, Presidium of the Ministry of Interior, IV R/1, box 211.

75. Ibid.

76. Ibid.

77. SCA, Presidium of the Ministry of Interior, 1922/12.

78. Věra Olivová, *Politika Československa v ruské krizi roku 1921 a 1922* (Prague: H & H, 1992), 38–39; *Československá republika*, 5 March 1922.

79. SCA, Presidium of the Ministry of Interior, IV R/1, box 211. Letter is dated 8 August 1921 and was mailed in Berlin.

80. Ibid., R/12, box 212. For instance, a security report of 13 October 1921 dealt with the case of František Toman, who had come back from Russia in 1920 only to return there a few weeks later. He was back in Czechoslovakia in December 1920 but returned to Russia in March 1921 and then went to and from Russia yet again in July and September. He arrived in Czechoslovakia on 5 October 1921, posing as Herr Max Behrendt, a businessman with a German passport. When arrested, "Behrendt" carried 50,000 Kc.

81. See, for instance, *Národní politika*, 25 February 1921, which describes cases of various persons who, posing as refugees from the Bolshevik rule, were found to be traveling with significant sums of money (100,000 Kc).

82. Archives of the National Assembly, Prague; Beneš spoke on 25 January 1921. Quoted from Olivová, "Postoj československé buržoazie," 318.

83. AMFA, telegrams sent, 13 January 1922, number 45/1922.

84. V. Vochoč, "Uznání sovětského Ruska," in *Pocta k šedesátým narozeninám Univ. Prof. Dr. Ant. Hobzy,* ed. T. Saturník et al. (Prague: Bursík & Kohout, 1936), 115.

85. Olivová, "Politika Československa," 36–37.

86. Chicherin complained to the Berlin correspondent of the *Prager Tagblatt,* 4 April 1922, that Prague could not make up its mind whether to recognize the Bolsheviks as the sole representatives of Russia and was unwilling to sever its ties with the White Russian community.

87. AMFA, Second Section, box 562a. This was not unusual for the Soviets. The Czechoslovak legation in Berlin reported on 16 June 1924 that the Soviet commercial mission on Lindenstrasse, Berlin, had a thousand employees, 700 of whom were Soviet citizens. Originally, Moscow demanded extraterritoriality for the whole building and diplomatic status for all Soviet citizens. This was an audacious request, not least because there was also a fully staffed Soviet embassy in Berlin. The final compromise was to grant extraterritoriality to three-quarters of the building and diplomatic status to all "important" Soviet citizens.

88. SCA, Presidium of the Ministry of Interior, IV R/1, box 209. The report from Moscow on the negotiations with Maxim Litvinov is of 2 April 1921.

89. This provision was expressed in a note attached to Article I of the treaty; both parties agreed to sever all contacts with organizations and individuals whose mission it was to struggle against either of the two signatories.

90. The document was signed by Dr. Václav Girsa and Jan Dvořáček for Czechoslovakia and by Pavel Nikolayevich Mostovenko for the Soviet Union. The Provisional Treaty was analyzed by Jan Dvořáček. See *Zahraniční politika* 1, no. 13 (1922): 1010–13 and "Naše prozatimní smlouvy s RSFSR a USSR" (928–29).

91. SCA, Presidium of the Ministerial Council, Secretariat, PMR-S, 1918–1942, 781, vol. 1, box 279. The Czechoslovak Ministry of Defense protested against this clause, pointing out that it would be perceived as hostile in Warsaw and Bucharest. The Ministry for Foreign Affairs, however, prevailed.

92. AMFA, Second Section, box 564. The status of the Czechoslovak mission in Kharkov was established on 5 October 1923, when Prague and Moscow signed the so-called Provisional Agreement.

93. Ibid. The first mention of the Soviet mission in the official diplomatic record, *Úřední list,* was on 25 September 1923.

94. Josef Girsa is not to be confused with Václav Girsa, another (and high-ranking) official of the Czechoslovak Ministry of Foreign Affairs.

95. AMFA, Second Section, box 562a. A legal analysis of the status of employees of the Soviet mission in Prague stated that they enjoyed an extraterritorial status; however, they were not real diplomats. As such, they had to testify in a court of law if summoned, and they did. The identification card issued by the Ministry of Foreign Affairs differed slightly from cards issued to diplomats from other countries.

96. Ibid., secret, 5 October 1925.

97. Ibid. As Josef Girsa reported in 1926, Soviet security entered the Czechoslovak mission and arrested a secretary, Miss Náprstková. She was ultimately released, but others were not so lucky. A Latvian secretary to the Latvian military attaché was arrested and sentenced to death for espionage and then exchanged for a Soviet spy arrested in Latvia; similarly brutal treatment was visited on Polish, Greek, and Estonian diplomats who had full diplomatic status. Soviet citizens fared worse, of course. A Russian lawyer for the Finnish embassy was sent to the Solovyev Island concentration camp without any trial, and a friend of the Norwegian minister was arrested and executed, despite protests from the Norwegian legation. Josef Girsa, Czechoslovak Mission, Moscow, to the Ministry for Foreign Affairs, Prague, 2 September 1926.

98. AMFA, Second Section, box 562a. Josef Girsa of the Czechoslovak legation reported on 24 July 1924 that Antonov-Ovseenko had come to introduce himself in the company of an official of the Commissariat for Foreign Affairs. This probably indicated, wrote Girsa, that Antonov-Ovseenko was not fully trusted, because all his predecessors (Mostovenko, Levitskii, Yurienev, and Aleksandrovsky) had come alone. Girsa felt that the Soviets had decided to send Antonov-Ovseenko to Prague in order to get him out of opposition politics. Another report, dated 4 October 1926, stated that Antonov-Ovseenko was a Trotskyite. If Trotsky had won in the power struggle to succeed Lenin, Antonov-Ovseenko would have become the new commissar of defense.

99. Ibid., box 562.

100. Beneš, *Problémy nové Europy*, 293–94.

101. AMFA, the Czechoslovak Mission, Moscow, to the Foreign Ministry, Prague, 14 February 1924.

102. Vochoč, "Uznání sovětského Ruska," 105.

103. AMFA, J. E. Šrom, the Czechoslovak Mission, Moscow, to the Foreign Minister, Prague, 2 March 1924.

104. Olivová, "Politika Československa," 34.

105. MHA-B, box marked "USSR: 1937–1938."

106. Beneš, *Problémy nové Evropy*, 51.

107. G. V. Chicherin's reply to the discussion on his report to the Central Executive Committee, 19 October 1924, quoted from Jane Degras, *Soviet Documents on Foreign Policy* (London: Oxford University Press, 1951), 1:469–70.

108. Office of the President of the Republic of Czechoslovakia, the Castle, T 232/22.

109. A. I. Rykov's speech at the Fifth Soviet Congress, 20 May 1929, in Jane Degras, *Soviet Documents on Foreign Policy* (London: Oxford University Press, 1952), 2:379.

110. AMFA, Second Section, box 562a, Josef Girsa, Czechoslovak Mission, Moscow, to the Ministry of Foreign Affairs, Prague, 24 August 1925. Zinoviev spoke on 13 January 1925 at the Soviet Teachers' Congress.

111. Ibid., 25 May 1925.

112. Vochoč, "Uznání sovětského Ruska," 117.

113. AMFA, Second Section, box 562a, the Prague Foreign Ministry to the Czechoslovak Mission in Moscow, 6 August 1925.

114. Ibid., Josef Girsa, the Czechoslovak Mission, Moscow, to the Ministry for Foreign Affairs, Prague, 10 August 1925.

115. Ibid., 17 December 1925.

116. Ibid., box 572. Josef Girsa, the Czechoslovak Mission, Moscow, to the Ministry of Foreign Affairs, Prague, 7 December 1926.

117. SCA, Presidium of the Ministry of Interior, 1919–1924, signature IV R/12, archival number 225–215–3/16–32. The cover letter is dated 5 April 1923. The document is analyzed in Igor Lukes, "The GPU and GRU in Pre-World War II Czechoslovakia," *International Journal of Intelligence and Counterintelligence* 8 (spring 1995): 91–104.

118. SCA, Presidium of the Ministry of Interior, 1919–1924, signature IV-R/12, box 215.

119. Ibid. The document was dated 15 February 1924. Its authenticity was affirmed by specialists in the two embassies.

120. Ibid., X/V/31/1, archival number 225–970–1. The Presidium points out in a statement of 4 July 1933 that Czechoslovakia needed to develop a serious counterintelligence capability, particularly against industrial espionage.

121. SCA, Police Directorate, PP-1931–1940, box 1517. The closing down of the GPU central in Baden, Austria, in late 1931 is mentioned in a memorandum from the Presidium of the Ministry of Interior to the Police President, Prague, 19 August 1932.

122. SCA, Presidium of the Ministry of Interior, 1931–1935, X/R/24/21, archival number 225–902–2, box 902. General Chalupa's letter is dated 17 August 1932. Chalupa stated that the top Soviet agent, the *rezident,* was Aleksandr Arkadiyevich Polocki, the first secretary of the Soviet mission in Prague.

123. Ibid., 1919–24, signature R/27/2, archival number 225–578–1. This whole file is called "Bolshevik Couriers: Border Crossings." File SCA, PMV, R/27/2, archival number 225–577–6 contains other cases involving Soviet spies who had false passports and attempted illegal border crossings.

124. AMFA, Second Section, box 271. Before they were expelled, agents were photographed and immediately put on a list of persons suspected of being Soviet agents. The list was distributed throughout Europe. Czechoslovakia had bilateral agreements with almost all European countries regarding information-sharing on Soviet and Comintern agents. In the Prague archives, especially in AMFA, are files with names and photographs of agents from British, French, Dutch, German, Austrian, Italian, Romanian, Yugoslav, and several other police organizations. Only Poland and Czechoslovakia did not seem to cooperate directly; they exchanged information via Paris or London.

125. SCA, Presidium of the Ministry of Interior, 1919–1924, signature R/27/2, archival number 225–578–2. This trial was followed extensively by the press. See *Národní osvobození,* 22 August 1925, 28 March 1925; *Deutsche Zeitung Bohemia,* 31 July 1925; *Rudé právo,* 2 July 1925; *Právo Lidu,* 2 July 1925; *Venkov,* 28 April 1925; *Národní listy,* 13 March 1925; and *České slovo,* 31 March 1925.

126. AMFA, Second Section, box 564, the Czechoslovak Mission, Moscow, to the Ministry of Foreign Affairs, Prague, 24 December 1926, reports received, number 1221/26.

127. AMFA, Second Section, box 564.

128. SCA, Presidium of the Ministry of Interior, 1931–1935, X/R/24/21, archival number 225–902–2, box 902. The case was opened when František Kratochvíl of the Military Technical Institute in Prague reported that he had received an unsolicited letter from the Soviet mission.

129. Ibid. Based on Prague police interviews of Alois Mottl, 2 January 1932, and Alexandr Němec, 2 January 1932.

130. AMFA, Second Section, box 553. Czechoslovak Mission, Moscow, to the Ministry of Foreign Affairs, Prague, 25 December 1931.

131. SCA, Presidium of the Ministry of Interior, 1931–1935, X/K/28, 225–787. Second Bureau of the General Staff, Ministry of Defense, to the Ministry of Interior, 7 February 1933.

2

Dangerous Relations:
Beneš and Stalin in Hitler's
Shadow, 1933–1935

Edvard Beneš had no illusion that his country could rely on its own strength alone. He fully shared Masaryk's view that Czechoslovakia needed an ally on which it could always depend. That role was to belong to Paris. In the early 1920s France was the most important, and the mightiest, European power, and policymakers in Prague should have been delighted by clear signals that the French were ready to sign a diplomatic treaty with Czechoslovakia that would contain a firm military component.

Others would have gladly seized the opportunity to tie their fate to that of the French superpower. But Masaryk and Beneš saw that there were problems. They wanted French protection, but they were not at all eager for Czechoslovakia to become a pawn in a French militaristic scheme against Germany; they feared that Paris intended for Prague to play the role of a needle that was to cause discomfort, if not pain, in Berlin. This made no sense to them. After all, Czechoslovakia enjoyed good political relations with Weimar Germany in the early 1920s, and the two countries had strong economic ties as well.[1] Masaryk and Beneš saw no reason to sacrifice this situation in order to diminish French fears of German revenge. Moreover, Prague was worried that an agreement with Paris directed against Germany would only drive Berlin closer to Hungary, the source, from Prague's perspective, of real danger. Although Germany had no claim on Czechoslovak territory, Hungary did.

Finally, a military arrangement with France was likely to end Prague's good relations with Italy because of tensions between Rome and Paris. Thus, when Marshal Ferdinand Foch proposed a Czechoslovak-French agreement on political and military cooperation during his visit to Prague in 1921, Beneš refused.[2] Paris did not give up, however, and it brought up the offer again two years later. Still the problem remained unchanged. The proposed treaty was to bring together two parties with dissimilar objectives and different sources of concern: Prague wanted help against Hungary while Paris needed assistance against Germany; at the same time, Czechoslovakia had little reason to fear Berlin, and France had no reason to worry about Hungary. Therefore, Masaryk and Beneš responded evasively to a French draft of the treaty that included an article on military cooperation of June 1923. Their counterproposal, presented after much hesitation only in November 1923, made no reference to the military dimension of Czechoslovak-French friendship; it was a straightforward political treaty. Even at the end of 1923, Beneš informed Lewis Einstein, the U.S. minister in Prague, that he had been exposed to a "very strong French pressure" to sign a military agreement with Paris and that he declined the offer.[3]

But only month later, on 25 January 1924, the French-Czechoslovak Treaty of Alliance and Friendship was signed. It seemed to be a political agreement along the lines Prague suggested; the military component was only vaguely implied. The treaty stated that the two parties would act in concert in foreign policy matters, particularly those relating to national security, and it committed them to guarding the status quo in Central Europe. Despite appearances, the French had in fact prevailed in their desire for the alliance to have a military element. This was expressed in secret letters exchanged between the two foreign ministers, Raymond Poincaré (on 26 January 1924) and Beneš (on 31 January). The letters stated that French and Czechoslovak general staffs would work together to develop a plan to resist aggression against either of the two parties by a common enemy.[4] It seemed to be a compromise. It delivered what France wanted without committing Prague to taking part in adventures not in its interest and without unnecessarily antagonizing Czechoslovakia's neighbors and allies.[5]

In October 1925, however, came the Treaty of Locarno.[6] Under its terms, guaranteed by Great Britain and Italy, Germany concluded binding agreements with France and Belgium which stipulated that its borders in the west were inviolable. In contrast, Germany's agreements with Poland, represented by Alexander Skrzynski, and Czechoslovakia, represented by Beneš, were not part of the treaty, which had thus failed to guarantee Germany's eastern borders.[7] Moreover, the participants treated Skrzynski and Beneš as low-level petitioners who could be kept waiting in the antechamber while representatives of Germany, Belgium, France, Great Britain, and Italy negotiated. "Herren Beneš and Skrzynski had to sit in a neighboring room until we let them in," boasted the German representative Gustav Stresemann.[8]

In response, Prague abandoned its previous caution and embraced its French ally without reservation. The Franco-Czechoslovak Treaty of Mutual Assistance, which contained an explicit military commitment that the two come to each other's assistance if either were a victim of an unprovoked German aggression, was signed at Locarno on 16 October 1925. Once the Nazi threat fully blossomed in Germany (by 1933 Hitler was looming menacingly over the whole of Central Europe), Masaryk and Beneš must have looked back at their hesitation to accept a military treaty with France and shuddered. What if their initial hesitation for Czechoslovakia to become a military partner of France had prevailed? What if Prague had not entered into a military agreement with Paris? But the 1925 treaty had been signed, and Czechoslovakia seemed completely safe, protected by mighty France. Of course, one could always look for an additional security guarantee, and Beneš was inclined to do precisely that. The reason was to be found in the emergence and rapid growth of the Third Reich.

Early on, in July 1933, Vojtěch Mastný, the Czechoslovak minister in Berlin, went to see the new German chancellor to complain about the mistreatment of scores of Czechoslovak citizens at the hands of the Nazis.[9] He pointed out that racism was unbecoming to the high German culture. Hitler retorted rather weakly that Germany was in the midst of a revolution, and he invited Czechoslovakia to join him in a crusade against communism. But he turned silent when Mastný pointed out that democracy was the best protection against extremism.[10] Masaryk and Beneš read this and other such reports carefully. They could see that recent developments in Germany represented a serious threat to Czechoslovakia and that the normalization of diplomatic relations between Moscow and Prague had become necessary.

Even when the Nazis' victorious songs were ringing from all quarters in Germany, the Prague government was not rushing into a deal with Stalin's Soviet Union incautiously. For the moment, it was satisfied with the existing commercial ties with Moscow. Leading politicians in Prague had been saying for years that Western Europe should use its economic leverage to civilize the Bolsheviks and to dissolve their communist ideology in the acid of economic benefits. Although there were few indications that Soviet leaders were ready seriously to modify their behavior as a result of Western economic pressures, Beneš hard-headedly maintained his belief in the miracle weapon of commerce.

Business activities between Moscow and Prague had been developing with the ups and downs that could be expected given the drastic social and economic changes in the Soviet Union. In response to the great economic crisis, various countries competed during the period from 1930 to 1933 for access to the seemingly vast and promising Soviet markets, and Czechoslovakia tried to avoid being left behind. Its exports to the Soviet Union reached a peak in 1931 but began declining radically from 1932 through 1933 and reached bottom in 1934.[11] Some of the decline was caused by political factors: Moscow was deliberately making it difficult for Czechoslovak firms to access Soviet markets in order to signal Prague that there could be no commerce without de jure recognition. Czechoslovak businessmen sensed they were being discriminated against but had no evidence to prove it. The Soviet Union finally spelled out its policy in explicit terms in April 1934. N. N. Krestinskii, the deputy commissar for foreign affairs, told a Czechoslovak diplomat in Moscow that there would be no normal commercial relations without full recognition. Moscow informed its representative in Prague that this would henceforth be the official Soviet policy.[12] Thus, Soviet leaders were the first to resurrect the issue of de jure relations, which had been buried from late 1924 until early 1933 under the ice covering Prague's relations with the Moscow government.

V. M. Molotov spoke about Soviet relations with Czechoslovakia before the Central Committee in Moscow in early 1933. He poked fun at "certain Czechoslovak ministers" who felt the need to study the Soviet Union.[13] He seemed to be asking, What is the matter with Czechoslovakia, what do we have to do to persuade President Masaryk and Minister Beneš that we exist? These questions were justified. The shadow of Hitler, his racist doctrine, and his nationalistic claims gave pause to European democracies and autocracies alike. As a consequence, many countries started paying court to the Kremlin. In November 1933 the United States, that bastion of capitalism, recognized the Soviet Union de jure. From then on, few were willing to be left behind. Various European countries started to indicate their willingness to commence a new era of friendship with the Soviet regime. Romania even started to turn over to OGPU (soon to be renamed NKVD) refugees who, taking tremendous risks, had tried to escape from the famine by crossing the red border.[14] Beneš was most certainly not sending White Russian refugees to the Lubyanka prison, but in early 1933 he wanted to take the final step and offer de jure recognition to the Soviet Union as soon as possible.

At Last: De Jure Recognition and Its Consequences

The first sign that an improvement in relations between Moscow and Prague was in the cards occurred in early March 1933. The Czechoslovak mission in Moscow received a request from the Foreign Commissariat to obtain Prague's agreement for Sergei S. Aleksandrovsky as the next Soviet representative in Czechoslovakia. At the same time, the Czechoslovak Foreign Ministry was informed that Aleksandr Yakovlevich Arosev, the current chief of the Soviet mission, had asked to be relieved of his duties in Prague and return to the Soviet Union.[15] Moscow stressed that Arosev was departing on his own request, but the Prague police department in charge of foreign diplomats did not believe it. Arosev had just married a Czechoslovak citizen, and he had said publicly on more than one occasion that he enjoyed his life in Prague immensely. The policemen were right. Arosev was arrested after he returned to Moscow and both he and his Czech wife, Gertruda Aroseva (née Freund) formerly an official of KOSTUFRA, disappeared in the murderous Stalinist GULAG.[16]

Having secured Prague's agreement, Moscow officially announced in early June that Aleksandrovsky was going to be the next chief of the Soviet mission in Prague.[17] The Czechoslovak foreign service establishment knew him quite well, partly because he had already served in Prague as chief of the Soviet mission in 1923–24.[18] More important, Aleksandrovsky had been quite visible to the Prague authorities as a member of the young Soviet diplomatic corps. In fact, he had made quite a name for himself within a decade and a half of service as a Soviet diplomat. He was a formidable personality whose arrival in Prague was the prelude to a dramatic increase in the quality of contacts between the Soviet Union and Czechoslovakia.

The new Soviet diplomat made clear from the beginning of his tenure in Prague that his main mission was to bring about Czechoslovakia's de jure recognition of the Soviet regime. He had been following parliamentary debates regarding the recognition issue, Aleksandrovsky stated at the Ministry of Foreign Affairs in late 1933, and he could not understand why so many deputies worried about the possibility that, if fully recognized, Soviet diplomats would come to Prague to carry out communist activities under the protective umbrella of extraterritoriality. Aleksandrovsky pointed out that the Soviet mission had had extraterritorial status since 1922, and it did not do anything illegal.[19] It is not clear whether Dr. Blahož, the foreign service officer who conducted the interview with Minister Aleksandrovsky, had seen the Hillerson file. But he had definitely consulted at least some of the many documents regarding Aleksandrovsky's extradiplomatic exploits in Germany and, therefore, the most diplomatic response Blahož could offer to such assurances by the Soviet representative was a polite silence.

The Soviet minister returned to the Foreign Ministry again in January 1934. This time, he was received by Deputy Foreign Minister Kamil Krofta. Aleksandrovsky started obliquely—with a description of the Far Eastern crisis—and then he approached the matter itself. It would help Moscow if Prague, together with the rest of the Little Entente (Romania and Yugoslavia), finally extended de jure recognition to the Soviet government as soon as possible. Aleksandrovsky inquired why Beneš had stated during a recent interview that Prague's negotiations with the Kremlin leadership would focus exclusively on economic matters. He wanted to know why the two parties could not discuss political matters as well. It seemed that Aleksandrovsky was determined not to leave without giving the discussion a positive spin; he told Krofta that when he had been stationed in Prague for the first time, in 1923 and 1924, Czechoslovak-Soviet relations were so bad that he had had no desire to take up the Czech language. Now he had his own language tutor, and he studied with diligence.[20] Throughout the interview, the top Soviet diplomat in Prague attempted to signal that Moscow was ready to end the decade-long era of tensions and confrontation and return to regular diplomacy. Prague felt, naturally, that this would be a welcome development, and Beneš's activities on the domestic front and in the League of Nations soon indicated why Krofta concluded by asking Aleksandrovsky for a little patience.

In preparing the final move toward a full recognition of the Soviet regime, Beneš was encouraged by signs of growing Franco-Soviet cooperation under the French Foreign minister Louis Barthou. For its own reasons, Paris was greatly concerned about the reemergence of the German threat, and it had started to explore the Soviet option independent of Beneš's prompting. The Czechoslovak mission in Moscow analyzed Franco-Soviet relations in a report which found that the two former opponents had been drawn together by the need to respond to the Nazi threat.[21] This was very welcome from Prague's perspective as it prepared the final move. On 6 June 1934, Beneš telephoned the Prague government from the League of Nations in Geneva and requested the authority to grant de jure recognition to the Soviet Union.[22] He could afford to demand a quick response: it seemed possible at the time that the Franco-Soviet negotiations would result in the so-called Eastern pact, the formation of a large bloc of states tied together by political and security agreements on mutual assistance. Within that organization, Czechoslovakia would have had a binding arrangement with the Soviet Union, a state it did not recognize officially. Such an absurdity had to be prevented at all costs, and Beneš promptly received from Prague what he had requested.

On 9 June 1934, a year and a half after Hitler had come to power, Czechoslovakia extended de jure recognition to the Soviet Union—a dozen years after Germany had recognized the Bolsheviks; a decade after Great Britain, France, Austria, Greece, Denmark, Italy, Norway, and Sweden had followed suit; and a year after the United States had joined them. Only a handful of European states still held out.[23] The recognition document was signed in Geneva by Beneš and Litvinov, and the final text stated that the Czechoslovak government resumed "normal" diplomatic relations with the Soviet Union. The Russian version also talked merely of "normal" relations and made no mention of de jure recognition. It may have been so formulated in order not to offend Czechoslovakia's ally from the Little Entente, Yugoslavia.[24] Romania, the third partner to the Little Entente, joined Prague and extended de jure recognition to the Soviet Union on the same day as Czechoslovakia.

As could have been expected, Masaryk and Beneš were immediately attacked by the conservative National Democrats. One of their leaders, Karel Kramář, predicted in *Národní listy,* a major Czechoslovak newspaper, that "the nation will pay dearly for the recognition of the Bolsheviks." But his was a minority position. Other periodicals, such as *Národní osvobození,* which traditionally expressed the view of veterans of the Czechoslovak legions who had fought against the Bolsheviks in Russia, regretted that the recognition was not accorded sooner. The voices of the Czechoslovak business, financial, and industrial circles spoke in a similar vein.[25] The official journal of the Prague Foreign Ministry summed up the situation in Europe after the emergence of the Third Reich and the apparent dissolution of the Rapallo friendship between Germany and Russia. When Hitler came to power, observed *Zahraniční politika,* the Soviet Union found itself in the first line of countries directly threatened by the Third Reich. It was under pressure in the East from Japan and in the West from Germany, and so it naturally moved closer toward France and sought to negotiate friendly arrangements with its neighbors. To achieve this, Moscow had embraced the cause of defending the status quo.[26] And this kind of Russia, implied the article, was a welcome ally for the Prague government, which needed to strengthen its security arrangement with France by another protective layer. So why not Moscow, the defender of the status quo on which Czechoslovakia depended for its existence? As foreign service officers, the editors of *Zahraniční politika* were not naive regarding the nature of the Stalinist regime. They knew—in rough terms—that Joseph Stalin was extraordinarily brutal. But Beneš and his colleagues did not intend to live in the Soviet Union; they only wanted to develop a security arrangement with it. They reasoned that a strong hand at the top of the Kremlin pyramid of power made it more stable, and this made Moscow a reliable partner for Paris and Prague.

In the 1920s Beneš thought it likely that the Bolshevik regime would collapse or change so radically that it would lose its communist component. A decade and a half later it was obvious that such expectations were for naught and that the Soviet Union was there to stay. From Prague's perspective, Adolf Hitler made the existence of the Soviet card welcome. As Beneš saw the situation, the Versailles system had been created at a time when Germany was weak and Russia was absent. The first condition ceased to hold with the appearance of the Third Reich, and to protect the whole structure from collapsing an equilibrium of power in Europe had to be reestablished. It was necessary to compensate for the German threat by bringing Moscow westward and giving it a real presence on the scales of power in Europe.[27] This policy, Beneš believed, was dictated by common sense. It was, as far as he was concerned, what the traditional concept of balance of power was all about. Beneš did not mind helping to bring Russia to Europe as long as the job was to be done together with others, especially with France. He knew that certain circles, both at home and abroad, would attack him for any kind of diplomatic scheme involving the Soviet Union, and he was prepared to absorb their criticism, but only if it was at the same time directed against France. It would become Beneš's policy to deal with Moscow via Paris. Only during the very last days of the Czechoslovak-German crisis in 1938 would Beneš permit himself to approach the Soviet Union directly without having first secured agreement from the French.

Minister Beneš felt energized by the normalization of relations between Prague and Moscow. He was optimistic that the emergence of the Soviet Union on the international scene, despite its otherwise disagreeable Bolshevik government, was going to improve the overall situation significantly. Shortly after de jure recognition of the Soviet Union, he drafted a circular note for Czechoslovak legations. It predicted that the return of Russia to European politics, which happened to coincide with Prague's recognition of the Kremlin, was going to produce a new constellation, a new balance of power. France would no longer have to choose in each conflict with Germany between two arbiters, England and Italy. Historically, this had driven France to accept compromises, sometimes at the expense of Central Europe. Not any longer: France would in times of danger have an additional, Russian card. Paris and Moscow would be able to maneuver together against Berlin without the annoying interference of London and Rome.[28] These in essence were Beneš's diplomatic desiderata for the 1930s. His main task was to see to it that Czechoslovakia would belong to the strongest alliance in Europe. Regarding Prague's growing crisis with Hitler's Third Reich, the issue was, Who was going to isolate whom? Beneš would repeat the question even at the end of September 1938. So far, there was no reason to despair.

Having finally achieved de jure relations with the Soviet Union, Beneš immediately started using his considerable influence in Geneva to bring about Moscow's admission into the League of Nations. He succeeded on 18 September 1934. With Beneš's prompting, the Fifteenth Assembly of the League even went so far as to *invite* the Soviets to join. In his first speech at the League's assembly, Litvinov recorded "with gratitude the initiative taken by the French Government . . . and the President of the Council, Dr. Beneš, in the furtherance of this initiative."[29] This was not mere persiflage. Beneš wielded real influence in the League, and he used it to help the Soviet case.

There seemed every reason to try to bring the Soviet Union into the equation of power in Central Europe; the Third Reich worried all clear-headed observers. To make matters worse, President Paul von Hindenburg, the German field marshal, died during the summer of 1934, and his successor was, of course, Hitler, who became chancellor and then Führer. His elevation to the position of a virtual dictator was confirmed by a national referendum in August. Prague watched these signs with increasing concern. In November 1934 Czechoslovak military intelligence organized in Prague a conference of its partners from Romania, Yugoslavia, and France. Analysts took note of recently acquired evidence documenting the dramatic pace of the military buildup in Germany. They agreed that the first strike of the German armed forces was probably going to be directed at Czechoslovakia.[30] This conclusion was communicated directly to President Masaryk in December 1934. The president's military adjutant noted that for some time Germany had been building certain types of fortifications along its borders with France and Poland but none against Czechoslovakia. This probably meant that Germany was planning to attack Czechoslovakia while assuming a defensive posture against France and Poland. It was to be expected that the Luftwaffe was going to bomb vital political and economic centers; the aerial attack would be followed by an invasion of the fast-moving Wehrmacht.[31]

How could Czechoslovakia respond to such a threat? Of course, one response was to do nothing. After all, there were the Franco-Czechoslovak agreements. But France had failed to act decisively on behalf of Poland during the Bolshevik invasion in 1920 when Germany was weak. Could the French be relied on when Germany's armed forces might soon become stronger than their own? Beneš did not doubt France. He was completely confident of the value of his French card, and he would maintain this conviction until September 1938. But the French alliance could now be ensured and strengthened by a security arrangement with Moscow, which was, in turn, dependent on Prague's primary ally, Paris.

Beneš's *Ostpolitik*

The first Czechoslovak minister in the Soviet Union, Bohdan Pavlů, was an unassuming man who tried his best to understand the Bolshevik rulers of Russia. He was happy to take note of the first signs of improving relations between Prague and Moscow and reported on them with pedantic detail.[32] He was officially received in the Kremlin in August 1934, although his opposite number in Prague, Aleksandrovsky, had presented his credentials to President Masaryk in July.[33] When he served with the Czechoslovak legions in Russia, Pavlů had the reputation of being anti-Bolshevik, but as the Czechoslovak minister in Moscow, he would turn out to be a sympathetic observer of the Soviet Union in the 1930s.[34]

The Czechoslovak legation continued the work of its predecessor, the mission, in trying to repatriate Czechoslovak citizens or ethnic Czechs and Slovaks who found themselves for whatever reason in the Soviet Union. It was sometimes successful. Foreign Ministry Archives in Prague contain boxes filled with protocols based on interviews with Czechoslovaks who had managed to enter the legation in Moscow. Of those, only a small number were subsequently able to leave the Soviet Union. In rural areas, the interviewees testified, life had become unbearable in 1929 primarily because of enforced collectivization of land and famine. Since then, living had become "slow dying." By early 1934 corpses were often ignored for days along rural roads as well as in some cities. The OGPU was in total control of the entire country.[35] The language of these protocols is so dry, the tone so free of emotion, that the message these wretched people tried to communicate is all the more powerful.

But Minister Pavlů came to Moscow to improve Czechoslovak-Soviet relations, not to humanize the Bolshevik system. He did not like the Stalinist terror, but he always sought to explain even the most shocking signs of ruthlessness by some higher, strategic good that Stalinism allegedly presented to Czechoslovakia. Pavlů was a professional foreign service officer, and he focused on his task of strengthening the Soviet connection for the policymakers in Prague. Similarly, Krofta, who only four years before had declared that the Soviet Union represented a threat to all of Europe, saw the situation differently just two days after the Soviet entry into the League.[36] It was true, he said, that communists sought to expand and to proliferate their ideology, but so did the Roman Catholic Church, and it was still possible to maintain good relations with it. Having contacts with the capitalist world was bound to blunt the edge of Bolshevism, stated Krofta, repeating an early theme of Czechoslovak politicians. In conclusion he quoted Beneš: "We have to have good relations with Russia, no matter what regime they have there."[37] This was accepted by diplomats and soldiers alike. Czechoslovak military leaders were eager to establish contacts with their Soviet colleagues. The first Czechoslovak military attaché in the Soviet Union, Lt. Colonel František Dastich, one of the founders of the Czechoslovak Military Intelligence, arrived in Moscow on 27 October 1934, together with his deputy, Staff Captain Alexandr Kühnel.[38]

Two days after his arrival in Moscow, Lt. Colonel Dastich was introduced to officials of the Soviet General Staff. Commander Gekker of the department for international relations told him that the Red Army was ready for close cooperation with Czechoslovakia. On 5 November 1934, Dastich was received by the commissar for defense, Kliment Voroshilov, who instantly brought up the anti-Bolshevik activities of the Czechoslovak legions in Russia. "I am glad that the tough Czechoslovak army has finally sent its representatives to us," said the commissar with what Dastich described as a knowing smile. "It has left here many memories." The Czechoslovak officer tried to play the role of a diplomat and suggested that all that was "unpleasant" had been forgotten. "Of course," laughed Voroshilov.[39] What a development! Czechoslovak and Soviet soldiers who had not too long ago fought against each other were now—only weeks after the de jure recognition papers had been signed—exchanging diplomatic pleasantries.

Meanwhile, Czechoslovak and Soviet politicians had begun designing ever more ambitious schemes of political and commercial cooperation. In late September 1934 Beneš spoke with Litvinov in Geneva. Their most recent agreement summed up the objectives of what almost began to look like a Czechoslovak-Soviet alliance. The two foreign ministers affirmed that Prague and Moscow would sign a commercial treaty and create a fund of 500 million Kc, to be serviced by both governments, from which credits would be made available to deserving business ventures. They agreed further that Czechoslovakia would send its "people," that is, military and intelligence service technicians, to Moscow for consultations. The culmination of all of this was to be a *traité d'amitié* (treaty of friendship).[40] It is important to note that although the idea of a treaty with the Soviet Union appealed to Beneš, he was not the one who requested it. He merely allowed for it to grow naturally from discussions between himself and Litvinov.

Apparently, the Kremlin had learned that it would have to take the initiative when dealing with Beneš, and it went all out in a true *stakhanovite* manner. On 29 December 1934 *Izvestia* published a very friendly article about Czechoslovakia that praised the Prague government for its peace-loving policy and assistance in securing the League of Nation's invitation for the Soviet Union to join. In January 1935 Litvinov received a group of twelve Czechoslovak journalists who had arrived in

Moscow before the end of 1934 and would stay for another two weeks. He told them that both Prague and Moscow had every reason to develop their mutual relations fully.[41] On the same day, the journalists also heard from Nikolai I. Bukharin and Karl Radek. The two Bolsheviks offered a toast at the Czechoslovak legation to Czechoslovakia and the Soviet Union "standing firmly shoulder to shoulder, in peace and in war."[42] Hubert Ripka, a well-connected Prague political journalist who traveled with the group, wrote later that their Soviet hosts had told them repeatedly about Moscow's desire for a collective agreement of all states threatened by Germany. The journalists' hearts were filled with joy, wrote Ripka, when they heard from Litvinov that the Soviet government "without any doubt whatsoever" was committed to resisting any German territorial advance. The delegation was so pleased to hear these words that Dr. Jína of the Czechoslovak legation in Moscow stated that Czechoslovakia was glad to serve as a bridge "between the old West and the new East."[43] Surely this went beyond the original intention of Beneš, who had envisioned Czechoslovakia, a Western country, helping to strengthen the role of the Soviet Union in Central Europe in order to counterbalance the rise of Germany.

Finally, on 29 January 1935, the chief of the Red Army's General Staff, Yegorov, received Lt. Colonel Dastich and "several times" suggested that the two countries should sign a comprehensive military treaty "right now." Dastich reported it to Prague and added that negotiating with the present regime in the Kremlin was quite safe because Joseph Stalin had nearly run out of enemies. Consequently, there was no force anywhere in the Soviet Union that could overthrow or even challenge him. There were three sources of this phenomenon: emigration, executions, and concentration camps.[44] The Czechoslovak military attaché seemed to be saying that Prague could not afford to hesitate and should accept the Soviet offer.

The officer corps of the Czechoslovak army studied Hitler's impact on the European scene with understandable attention. By 1935, it no longer believed in a peaceful future. *Důstojnické listy,* the newspaper of army officers, wrote: "Take off your rose-colored glasses. Reject all those attempts at inoculating us with optimism which have been going on since the present regime took power in Germany." In the Third Reich if one shouted the word "Germany" the echo brought back the sound "Hitler," warned the article.[45] The army had little political influence in Czechoslovakia, but without its active cooperation Minister Beneš would have been seriously handicapped in launching his Soviet initiative. The armed forces' recognition of the German threat played into Beneš's hands as he sat down to design a security structure that would tie Czechoslovakia, via France, with the Soviet Union.

There was no time to be spared. The eventful month of January 1935 ended on a sobering note: Beneš received a secret memorandum from the Czechoslovak legation in Berlin that reported information obtained from "a completely reliable source" who had attended a dinner party hosted by Hitler. Speaking before a small, intimate circle of friends, the Führer stated that he had two main enemies in Europe, Russia and Czechoslovakia, and he was going to destroy them both. His liquidation of Bolshevism in Russia would make him "immortal" in the eyes of the world, and a "national-socialist renewal of Russia" would bring about the victory of national socialism in the whole of Europe. The main obstacle in his path, Hitler stated, was Czechoslovakia.[46] It was an open "ulcer of Central Europe and a nest of Jewish-émigré plotting'' against the Third Reich. Hitler concluded by asserting that his responsibility to wipe out Czechoslovakia was even greater than his duty to ''renew'' Russia.[47] Such reports made Beneš ever more determined to boost Czechoslovakia's security arrangement with France by a similar agreement with the Soviet Union.

In March 1935 Minister Pavlů informed Prague that the Soviet government was willing to open a permanent air connection from Prague to Kiev to Moscow.[48] This was a revolutionary proposal. Few civilians had experienced air travel at that time—even such prominent personalities as Neville Chamberlain and Edvard Beneš would fly for the first time in 1938. Therefore, the whole project had clear military implications. A few days later, Czechoslovakia and the Soviet Union signed a commercial agreement which was praised in *Izvestia* as a victory of Soviet peace-loving policy and a sign of growing ties between Prague and Moscow.[49] It was welcome in official Czechoslovak circles with no less enthusiasm.[50] Litvinov's proclamations during the journalists' visit, the commercial agreement, and then the prospect of regular flights between Prague and Moscow—these were quite obviously preparatory steps for a more substantial development. One wonders whether any of the policymakers in Moscow or Prague involved in setting the feverish pace of growing contacts still remembered the events of ten years before when there had been shootings in the Czechoslovak mission or even just four years before when a Czechoslovak diplomat had been falsely charged with having plotted an act of terrorism in Moscow. All of this seemed to have been put aside as each new achievement of the Führer increased the pressure on Germany's neighbors either to reach a modus vivendi with the Third Reich or to seek alliances for the future war. From Beneš's diplomatic initiatives aimed at Moscow, one can see that Czechoslovakia was getting ready to resist the Nazis and not appease them. Beneš took Hitler seriously from the beginning and did his best to act in accordance with the nature of the threat the new lord of Germany presented to the rest of Europe.

From Prague's perspective, the completion of a Franco-Soviet alliance acquired great importance once the Soviet Union had accepted a seat in the League of Nations.[51] An agreement between Paris and Moscow was meant to have two advantages. First, French involvement with the Soviet Union would stretch the field of the Quai d'Orsay's operations so as to cover Czechoslovakia, thus reaffirming the existing Franco-Czechoslovak agreements. Second, a French alliance with the Soviet Union would legitimize Beneš's own *Ostpolitik* with regard to his opposition at home. It would protect him he thought, against the charge from Berlin, Budapest, and Warsaw of being an advocate of the Soviet regime. Beneš was, naturally, not influential enough to cause either Russia's return to Europe or to bring about the Franco-Soviet alliance. But in his characteristic way, he worked ceaselessly to contribute to other forces already pushing in those two directions. His expectations were fulfilled. As a first step, on 5 December 1934, Litvinov and Pierre Laval signed a protocol in Geneva committing France to fulfilling what was in effect the legacy of Foreign Minister Louis Barthou. The French and Soviet foreign ministers agreed to continue working toward the Eastern Pact and to abstain from entering into any bilateral or multilateral arrangements that would compromise it. The statement also vaguely celebrated Franco-Soviet diplomatic collaboration.[52]

Beneš sprang into action on 7 December 1934 when he fired off a letter to Litvinov containing a declaration that Czechoslovakia accepted all provisions of the Franco-Soviet protocol and would adhere to them. Litvinov responded the same day, acknowledging the statement from Beneš and stating that, henceforth, the Geneva protocol would "reciprocally bind all three Governments."[53] This daring diplomatic maneuver changed a bilateral arrangement into a de facto trilateral one. Litvinov and Beneš presented Laval with a fait accompli, and he would have had to take the initiative to disassociate France from it. He was not ready to go so openly against the legacy of Barthou, his predecessor in office. Therefore, he did nothing, and Beneš had thus managed to lay the foundations for a Franco-Czechoslovak-Soviet mutual security arrangement.

The Czechoslovak-Soviet Treaty of 1935 and Its Mysterious Stipulation

Of the three parties, Prague was by far the most vulnerable to the growing German threat, and Beneš had every reason to think that a security pact involving Paris, Prague, and Moscow could give him all the advantages of French and Soviet protection with few corresponding responsibilities. It was unlikely in late 1934 or even in 1935 that Hitler would dare to attack France. Attacking the Soviet Union, given the limits imposed by geography, seemed out of the question. The Geneva protocols of December 1934 were the stepping-stone to what Beneš had described to Litvinov in September: *traité d'amitié*. It was now apparent that Beneš and Litvinov, if not Czechoslovakia and the Soviet Union, had become partners. A lot had changed in a short time! *Izvestia* celebrated this new, still informal, alliance in terms that were more than diplomatically warm. An article on 29 December 1934 praised Prague's peace-loving policy, as well as its closeness to Moscow. The paper stated that Czechoslovakia had recently taken a number of steps to stabilize the European scene. It made clear that Moscow was grateful for Beneš's assistance with membership in the League, and it identified the Laval-Litvinov-Beneš Geneva protocol of December 1934 as another positive step taken by Czechoslovak diplomacy.[54]

A tense moment came when Pierre Laval went to London in February 1935. Prague feared the British could threaten to limit their responsibility for French security unless the French foreign minister renounced or limited the scope of the Geneva protocols. But, according to Prague's envoy in London, Jan Masaryk, Laval stood his ground. He was bound by what was agreed on and it could not be changed, he told the British.[55] The final communiqué did not renounce the Geneva protocols, and Laval's negotiations in London had therefore reaffirmed them. Beneš, always the realist, was satisfied with his achievements so far, and there was more progress in early April 1935 when Laval made a formal promise at a meeting of the Little Entente that he would enter into a bilateral agreement with the Soviet Union before the beginning of May 1935.[56] That was not exactly what Beneš and Litvinov had hoped for. They would have preferred a trilateral pact among France, the Soviet Union, and Czechoslovakia—that is, an Eastern pact without Germany, Poland, and the Baltic countries. But Laval made clear that his regard for the feelings of British,

German, and Polish politicians made it impossible for him to sign a trilateral pact. The Czechoslovak minister in Paris cabled Prague in April 1935 that Litvinov had worked hard to achieve a trilateral arrangement, but that Laval rejected it out of hand because it would unnecessarily provoke Germany and create the impression in Poland that France was now plotting against it.[57] Laval's worries were justified. It was bad enough that Germany was bound to complain about "encirclement" by its neighbors, but a trilateral pact involving Russia, Poland's historic enemy, would have been just as unwelcome in Warsaw. Hence the French concern. Kremlin leaders had no such consideration for Polish feelings. Strengthened by the prospect of an alliance with France, the Soviet Union fired a few propaganda rounds at Warsaw. *Izvestia* carried a series of articles informing the Polish foreign minister, Colonel Józef Beck, that Soviet-Polish relations were not "good enough." The paper also reminded the colonel that the situation in Eastern Europe was not quite as peaceful as he was wont to portray it.[58]

This was a specifically Polish problem, and Beneš was determined to stay away from any arrangements binding Warsaw and Prague closely together. He warned his colleagues that military or even strong political ties with Poland could prove dangerous for Czechoslovakia.[59] The Poles, as far as Beneš was concerned, were free to play the role of a big European power, but they would have to do so on their own, without Prague's backing. The most he would do for Czechoslovak-Polish relations was to assure Warsaw in a perfunctory manner that Prague's future arrangements with Moscow would not be directed against Poland.[60] The Foreign Ministry in Prague was not going to pretend that Czechoslovakia was a European or even regional power; it would secure the country's existence through alliances with real players: France and the Soviet Union.

The Franco-Soviet Treaty of Mutual Assistance was signed on 2 May 1935. The final text contained provisions that tied French assistance to the Soviet Union with both the League of Nations and the Locarno pact. If, for instance, Great Britain and Italy determined that a German attack on the Soviet Union had been provoked, France was under no obligation to provide Moscow with military assistance. Some of the pact's centrally important provisions were left vague. This may have been, at least to some extent, deliberate. As Laval observed, the Franco-Soviet pact was designed "to prevent war and not to make it."[61] Article IV of the protocol of signature stated that the negotiations which had led to the signing of the treaty had originally been undertaken to produce a security agreement involving, in addition to France and the Soviet Union, Germany, Czechoslovakia, Poland, and the Baltic States, but that "circumstances" had made it impossible for such agreements to come to life. This statement was meant, perhaps, to remind Berlin and Warsaw that the existing bilateral arrangement between Paris and Moscow was expandable, but such an open admission of failure in the text of a treaty was unusual in diplomatic practice. The Franco-Soviet pact was also encumbered with various complicated provisions that would have allowed an aggressor to come close to victory before Paris and Moscow could come to each other's assistance. In short, the impression was formed that France was still unsure whether or not to oppose Hitler with a collective of like-minded states.

For all its imperfections, the pact was good enough for Beneš. He was kept in the dark during the final stages of negotiations between France and the Soviet Union, and he found out about the signing ceremony on 2 May 1935 only half an hour before it was to take place in Paris.[62] This was unpleasant, for he had started thinking of himself as an important communicator between Moscow and Paris. But Beneš had one important gift in life: he never wasted time brooding. He was a realist. He always worked as hard as he could, and then he lived with whatever result he achieved. Therefore, he called Aleksandrovsky to his office at the ministry, and the two started preparing a repeat of the maneuver Beneš had performed in December 1934. This time he was going to sign with the Soviet Union, not with France, but the outcome would be the same: a bilateral arrangement between Paris and Moscow would be turned into a de facto trilateral one involving Prague.

Shortly after the Franco-Soviet pact had been signed, European capitals were abuzz with rumors about a similar arrangement between Czechoslovakia and the Soviet Union. Although intensive negotiations involving the final text had gone on ever since Beneš received the text of the Franco-Soviet pact in Prague, Litvinov chose to be secretive about his dealings with Czechoslovakia. When the U.S. ambassador in Moscow, William C. Bullitt, asked him in early May 1935 whether it was true that the signing of a pact with Prague was imminent, the Soviet commissar replied that "his discussions with the Czechoslovaks had not yet assumed any definite form."[63] This was true only technically because the final text had not been agreed on, but there was no question that Moscow's agreement with Prague was going to be nearly identical with the Franco-Soviet one. The problem was exactly how it was going to differ from it.

Beneš, the chiefs of all the relevant departments of the Prague Foreign Ministry, legal specialists, and linguists worked around the clock preparing various versions of the text. Diplomats and lawyers studied all imaginable, even some farfetched, scenarios that could arise under the terms of the Franco-Soviet and Czechoslovak-Soviet agreements on the increasingly volatile European scene. Their main concern was to strengthen Czechoslovakia's security without allowing a situation to emerge in which Prague would have to provide the Soviet Union with military assistance while Paris would be allowed, or would choose, to remain neutral. From the beginning, Beneš was prepared to sign a pact with Moscow only if it would require him to act in concert with France, never on his own. He described his policy frankly to the Austrian foreign minister, who asked him in April "how far" he intended to go with Moscow. "I won't go any further than France," replied Beneš. "Our policy is and always will be with Western Europe."[64] Undoubtedly, Beneš meant exactly what he said. He was convinced that nothing would dislodge the Western mooring of his strategic visions.

Had it not been for the requirements dictated by political necessity, specialists of the Prague Foreign Ministry would probably have continued toying with ever more creative versions of the final text for several weeks to come. But the Czechoslovak parliamentary elections scheduled for 19 May 1935 quickened the pace considerably. It appeared, moreover, that for health reasons President Masaryk would soon resign from office. In that case his successor would be elected by the new parliament. It was known that Beneš was Masaryk's choice to be the second president of Czechoslovakia, but no one could predict whether the parliament would accept him. Beneš therefore badly needed a major diplomatic success to strengthen his chances for election.

To accelerate their negotiations, Prague and Moscow agreed to attach to the text of the Czechoslovak-Soviet treaty a Protocol of Signature. Article II contained the statement that "the two Governments recognize that the undertakings to render mutual assistance will operate between them only in so far as . . . assistance may be rendered by France to the Party who is victim of aggression." Thus the Franco-Soviet and the Czechoslovak-Soviet treaties became closely intertwined. Politicians, historians, and also the general public have debated exactly who wrote the stipulation that would become crucially important during the Czechoslovak-German crisis of 1938. Prague seemed the most natural choice because, for pragmatic reasons, Czechoslovakia could insist on the stipulation in order to protect itself from having to march on behalf of the Soviet Union in circumstances in which France declared itself neutral under the Franco-Soviet pact.

This explanation was widely accepted in 1938 and was propagated at the height of the Czechoslovak-German crisis by Czechoslovak communists and others on the left. A brochure published by the Society for Friendship with the Soviet Union stated that Moscow had wanted to sign treaties with Paris and Prague that would have included the principle of "automatic mutual assistance," but the French objected and so did Beneš.[65] This interpretation was strengthened when Litvinov presented it at the League of Nations on 23 September 1938. It was, he said, "the Czechoslovak Government that had at the time [in May 1935] insisted that Soviet-Czechoslovak mutual assistance should be conditional upon assistance by France: that was reflected in the treaty in question."[66] Because neither Beneš nor anyone around him challenged this view in 1938 or subsequently, the debate seemed to have been closed.

But the problem reemerged soon after the end of World War II. The authoritative *Istoria diplomatii* stated that the stipulation linking the Czechoslovak-Soviet pact with the Franco-Soviet one was put in the text because Moscow had to make sure it would not be drawn into a conflict under unfavorable conditions since it was "aware of the danger that France could have placed the burden of military assistance to Czechoslovakia on the Soviet Union, if the Soviet aid had not been directly related to assistance by France." *Istoriia diplomatii* viewed the stipulation as "a wise reservation of Soviet diplomacy."[67] To make matters more difficult, *Istoria mezhdunarodnykh otnoshenii* (1967) expressed an altogether different theme.[68] Its argument was similar with the original position of Litvinov and the Czechoslovak left in 1938: Beneš so mistrusted the socialist Soviet state that, guided by his bourgeois background, he used the stipulation as a security fence preventing closer cooperation between Czechoslovakia and the Soviet Union.[69] Such disunity of opinion was unusual for official chroniclers of the former Soviet Union, and it indicated that Moscow had a hard time determining which version was going to be more advantageous. The confusion attracted interest among historians. Most accepted the view that the stipulation was put in the final text by Beneš who distrusted the Soviet Union; others accused Soviet diplomacy.[70]

The truth regarding the stipulation is quite simple: it was put in the text because both parties profited from it and because Paris and London supported it. It was formulated by Prague diplomats. Arnošt Heidrich, the chief of the Fourth Department of the Political Section of the Foreign Ministry, described in writing how the Czechoslovak side put the stipulation into the text. It was Heidrich's task to present it to the Soviet minister in Prague. This was a job Heidrich dreaded because he knew the Kremlin was sensitive to "the slightest hint of discrimination." He was genuinely worried when he laid the latest draft of the Czechoslovak-Soviet treaty before Aleksandrovsky. But instead of a diplomatic fit and loud declarations that the Soviet Union was offended by the stipulation, the Soviet minister was completely blasé about it. "The phrase," wrote Heidrich, "was accepted without the least reaction from either Aleksandrovsky or the Kremlin."[71] Finally, the most important witness in support of the argument that the stipulation was written by Prague was Edvard Beneš. During a dinner conversation on 30 March 1938, the president told a group of ministers that he had deliberately made Czechoslovakia's agreement with the Soviet Union dependent on the assistance being rendered first by France. Thus, he argued, it was Paris that had a treaty with the Kremlin, not Prague.[72]

Beneš, Heidrich, and others in the Prague ministry saw in the stipulation a protection from becoming entangled in circumstances that had nothing to do with Czechoslovak security interests. The ongoing Soviet-Japanese skirmishes could have escalated into a full-scale war at any moment, and it would have been absurd for the Prague government to agree to mobilize in order to help the Soviet Union in the Far East. There is direct evidence that Prague worried about the possibility of having to come to Moscow's assistance in a conflict unrelated to Czechoslovak interests. Krofta stated at a meeting of high-level officials of the Foreign Ministry of 16 May 1935 that, as far as Prague was concerned, the most important provision of the Czechoslovak-Soviet treaty was that "we are obligated to assist Russia only if France does so as well."[73] Furthermore, the Franco-Soviet pact had not yet been ratified when the Czechoslovak-Soviet pact was signed, and Prague needed to protect itself against the eventuality that a ratification would become unobtainable in France because of domestic political developments.[74] In that case, Beneš wanted to be free from any treaty arrangements with the Soviet Union, and that is what the stipulation actually achieved.

It is likely, furthermore, that Paris was happy about the stipulation because it was "justifiably anxious to avoid a position in which Russia could set off a war by her own motion."[75] There is also firsthand evidence that Great Britain had indicated to the Czechoslovak Foreign Ministry its support for the stipulation because without it, "Soviet Russia might [at] some time in the future use her treaty with Czechoslovakia to penetrate deep into Central Europe."[76] Czechoslovakia, France, and Great Britain were happy to see Article II in the Protocol of Signature.[77]

The stipulation in Article II also made a great deal of sense from Joseph Stalin's perspective. The Soviet Union needed to delay its military engagement with the capitalist world until it would be strong and its opponents weakened by a lengthy and bloody conflict among themselves. To achieve that, Moscow was prepared to enter into temporary alliances but not to allow itself to be dragged into a war not in its interest.[78] By applying this general strategy to the situation in 1935, one can see that the Kremlin would not want to march on behalf of the bourgeois Czechoslovak government unless France had already absorbed the blows of Hitler's Wehrmacht.

The Soviet Union did not have common borders with either Germany or Czechoslovakia, and it was next to impossible that Hitler's aggression against Czechoslovakia could spill over onto the Soviet territory. Under such circumstances, Moscow would not have to fight at all once Paris, Berlin, and Prague began a shooting war—save perhaps for dispatching to Czechoslovakia a few pilots, parachutists, or guerrilla instructors whose mission would be to keep the flames of war from being extinguished too soon by a rapid German victory. The Kremlin had to welcome the fact that France was committed to getting itself into a war with Germany before anything was expected from the Soviet Union. It was Article II that safeguarded Stalin from becoming entangled in a military conflict in which the French would not be the earlier and—because of the absence of a Soviet-German border—also the primary and the more direct opponent of the Third Reich. This is why Soviet diplomacy did not object when Heidrich brought up the stipulation with Aleksandrovsky.

In short, Czechoslovakia liked Article II in the Protocol of Signature because it protected the state against becoming involved in causes not in its interest and far from its security zone. Moscow was happy to accept Article II because it pushed France to the position of a shield between Germany and the Soviet Union. Stalin, naturally, knew only as much as the other players involved, and he could not have anticipated the Franco-British behavior in the summer of 1938, the Munich agreement, or Czechoslovakia's surrender to Hitler. But there was no reason for him to oppose a provision in the treaty that put the obligation for military defense of Czechoslovakia, a country located in an area vital for Soviet security interests, upon the shoulders of bourgeois France. As early as 1935 the stipulation made complete sense from Stalin's standpoint. Three years later, with all Europe on the brink of another conflagration, it would prove precious. France would be able to weasel out of its obligations toward Czechoslovakia only by dishonorably breaking its legal commitment. The Kremlin, on the other hand, would use the stipulation to maintain complete freedom of action throughout the crisis.

The Czechoslovak-Soviet Treaty of 1935 offered a great deal of comfort to Beneš, but was advantageous for the Kremlin. Its immediate achievement was that it strengthened Prague's resolve to resist the Third Reich. This was important. It was no longer impossible to imagine that London's pressure could cause Paris to abandon its Czechoslovak ally. Prague's subsequent capitulation or military defeat would put Czechoslovakia under German occupation. This would bring the Third Reich dangerously close to the borders of the Soviet Union itself. Beneš's alliance with Moscow was likely to make him more confident and less inclined to seek a rapprochement with Berlin. Reacting to rumors about secret talks between Berlin and Prague, Moscow expressed its concern about such a development in no uncertain terms. Aleksandrovsky in Prague was instructed to ask a journalist with well-known political connections whether Czechoslovakia had become so afraid of Germany that it was thinking of establishing a modus vivendi with Hitler.[79] This would have been the worst possible development from the Kremlin's perspective because it would have brought the Third Reich, unharmed by a war with France and Czechoslovakia but strengthened by the latter's weapons and industry, near the Soviet doorstep.

Prague's Pact with Moscow

On 9 May 1935, after days of round-the-clock activity in the Foreign Ministry, Beneš could proudly cable the Czechoslovak legation in Moscow that Prague's treaty with the Soviet Union would be signed next week and that its text would be identical with the Franco-Soviet pact, omitting only those passages pertaining exclusively to France.[80] The Czechoslovak-Soviet treaty of mutual assistance was signed on 16 May 1935 at 1 P.M. by Beneš and Aleksandrovsky.

Immediately after the official ceremony, Beneš sent a telegram to Litvinov which implied the de facto trilateral character of the treaties of May 1935: "At a time when Your Excellency and other members of the Soviet Government discussed peaceful projects with the representatives of allied France, I concluded . . . an agreement on mutual assistance with the Soviet representative in Prague."[81] Beneš also gave an interview to *Pravda* on 17 May 1935, during which he surprised the journalist by speaking Russian, and his effusive statements were no less astonishing. The treaty, said Beneš, was something he had dreamed about for a long time. It had always been one of the unchanging principles of his political thinking that the Soviet Union had to be brought into Europe. It was impossible to secure world peace and a balance of power without the active participation of Soviet policymakers. He went on to declare that Stalin's Soviet Union was "a mighty shield of peace in Europe." Beneš then turned to the October revolution of 1917, losing all proportion when he compared the Bolshevik coup d'état with Czechoslovakia's birth on 28 October 1918. "These two great revolutions," *Pravda* quoted Beneš, "serve as the new and firm foundation for a new and firm friendship among our nations." This was an unwise, absurd statement. The interview was promptly translated by foreign diplomats in Moscow and reported within the next few days to Berlin, London, Paris, Warsaw, and Budapest, and it contributed to the emerging diplomatic isolation of Czechoslovakia. Signs of isolation drew Beneš into a vicious circle: the Soviet alliance would weaken his ties with Western Europe, so the only rational reaction, given that Beneš was not prepared to appease Hitler and that Hitler was ultimately not appeasable, was to strengthen his ties with Moscow.

On the surface it appeared that a new era had dawned. Beneš and some of his colleagues gradually seemed to have convinced themselves that the Kremlin under Stalin's rule had abandoned revolutionary Marxism-Leninism and began a return to Russia's national needs. Not everyone shared this opinion. For one, the French were not quite as convinced as Beneš that one could do business with Stalin. They signed the treaty, but it contained no proper military arrangement and this suggested that Paris was satisfied with the political impact it would make on its neighbors in Europe. It did not seriously anticipate that a Franco-Soviet military action against German aggression would ever take place. The Czechoslovak legation in Moscow reported a rumor that French military leaders were expressing doubts about the value of the treaty, and even the French embassy in Moscow was said to be divided over the question of its desirability.[82] This was quite true. The French General Staff believed the Red Army could perhaps put up stiff resistance if Germany invaded the Soviet Union, but an offensive in support of France was out of the question.[83]

In contrast to the French, who had Great Britain on their side to say nothing of their own military might, Czechoslovakia was far more vulnerable. In addition to international factors, and they were serious enough, the Prague government also had to consider the domestic situation. President Masaryk understood that the viability of Czechoslovakia depended to a great extent on Prague's ability to win the loyalty of the Sudeten Germans, and he repeatedly spoke out against manifestations of Czech chauvinism.[84] Nevertheless, most attempts to lure the Sudeten Germans to the position of unconditional acceptance of the new republic remained half-baked, and, although they were better off in Czechoslovakia than in other countries, they never ceased feeling that they were a minority in a state that belonged to others. The Czech landlord was friendly and tolerant but he made sure his Sudeten tenants knew who owned the house.[85]

In the 1930s the voice of the German community in Czechoslovakia was getting stronger and more critical every day. Although some of its representatives had worked for several years within the constitutional framework of the democratic institutions in Prague, the emergence of Hitler, combined with the world economic crisis that hit the Sudetenland especially hard, gave a new impetus to anti-Czechoslovak sentiments. These were at first wrapped up as issues pertaining to job distribution and social policy, and some of these complaints were legitimate. But from the mid-1930s on, unbridled Nazi propaganda began to find more and more converts in the Sudetenland. Especially worrisome was the electoral victory of the Sudeten German party (SdP) in May 1935. It won the plurality in statewide elections with 15.2 percent (more than 62 percent in the German-speaking districts).[86] The Czechoslovak Republican party came in second with 14.3 percent, and the Social Democratic party was third with 12.6 percent.[87] So far, the SdP's leader, Konrad Henlein, had disguised his loyalty to Nazism—he would not declare it openly until April 1938—but it was impossible to miss hints that his party's political philosophy and methods would put the Sudeten Germans on a collision course with the Republic of Czechoslovakia, of which they were citizens.

All such developments, international and domestic alike, put pressure on Beneš. His French colleague, Laval, could remain level-headed in his dealings with the Kremlin, but the Czechoslovak foreign minister did not have that comfort. And when he became anxious, like many people, he started to make mistakes; typically, he talked too much. It is a small handicap for most, but for a statesman like Beneš it was a dangerous habit. His interview in *Pravda* (17 May 1935) and his apparent enthusiasm for all things Soviet further stigmatized Beneš as an ally of Stalin. And that perception would cause a great deal of harm to the Czechoslovak cause, as well as to Beneš's standing in the community of world-class politicians.

The Aftermath of Czechoslovakia's Agreement with the Soviet Union

The Czechoslovak-Soviet agreement was very warmly received by all Soviet media. Never inclined toward understatement, they held little back when praising the foresight and statesmanship of Foreign Minister Beneš. On 17 May 1935 both *Pravda* and *Izvestia* hailed the agreement between Prague and Moscow with superlatives. On the same day, the Red Army paper *Krasnaya Zvezda* editorialized that Czechoslovakia's national security was threatened but—as opposed to others in Europe—the Prague government actively sought to do something about it. Moreover, "it can see clearly that without the Soviet Union any struggle for peace is unthinkable." On 18 May the official *Journal de Moscou* praised the treaty and attacked the racist component of the Nazi ideology.

As was to be expected, Berlin reacted to Prague's security arrangement with Moscow with barely concealed anger displayed in the highly controlled German press; Hitler personally contributed to the campaign with his speech on 21 May 1935. But the fury (things would get considerably worse three years later) of the German propaganda machine could simply indicate that Beneš had made the right move when he entered into a mutual assistance alliance with the Soviet Union. By the spring of 1935, it was no longer possible for him to conduct foreign policy that would avoid displeasing the Third Reich.

Czechoslovak communists under the leadership of Klement Gottwald were not at all sure how to react to Prague's pact with Moscow. They had been saying for years that Czechoslovakia should seek security via an alliance with the Soviet Union. Now they were taken aback by the unexpected fulfillment of their political slogans. Was it a trick of their bourgeois enemy? Was Stalin merely bluffing? Reports of large-scale executions in Moscow were trickling down to Prague and contributed further to the uncertainty felt by Gottwald and others in his circles.

While the communists hesitated and waited for the latest instructions from the Communist International, other Czechoslovaks felt energized by Prague's new alliance with Moscow. František Machník, the new defense minister, assumed his post in the early summer of 1935.[88] He soon captured the essence of public opinion when he declared solemnly, "If necessary, all of us will be soldiers."[89] *Důstojnické listy* spoke on behalf of the Czechoslovak army when it welcomed the agreement. The paper pointed out that just recently Germany had reintroduced obligatory military service, thus escalating tensions on the international scene. On 23 May it invited members of the Communist party of Czechoslovakia to follow the example of their French comrades and embrace the cause of national defense. Even the most conservative elements on the political scene in Prague caught the spirit. Rudolf Beran of the Republican party reiterated the need to seek peaceful solutions. But the country had to be ready for any eventuality; there could be no negotiation when it came to state sovereignty, stated Beran.[90] In the context of the recently signed Czechoslovak-Soviet treaty, Beran seemed to be implying in 1935 what Winston Churchill would famously declare after Hitler's attack on the Soviet Union in June 1941: there are times when one must be ready to look even at the devil from a new angle if it is necessary to find an ally in a life-or-death struggle for national existence.

Stalin's Wooing of Edvard Beneš: The 1935 Trip to Moscow

"Everybody asks me here: 'When is Beneš going to come?' " cabled the Czechoslovak minister from Moscow on 17 May 1935.[91] This kind of informal warmth was quite atypical for Soviet foreign affairs specialists in the mid-1930s. That it was afforded to Beneš was a loud and clear signal, and it was, therefore, in a heady atmosphere that the foreign minister and his advisors prepared for their first visit to the Soviet Union. Just before his departure, he gave a friendly interview to TASS.[92] Undoubtedly, Beneš looked forward to his trip to Moscow, for he sensed that he was regarded there as an important ally. He enjoyed that thought.

Beneš arrived in Moscow on 8 June 1935 at 11:35 A.M.[93] His reception was almost royal. At the end of a red carpet, stood Beneš's old friend from Geneva, Maxim Litvinov, and several other dignitaries of the Soviet state. In his brief statement at the train station, decorated with a sea of Soviet and Czechoslovak flags, Beneš attempted to anchor his visit to the Soviet Union in the concept of collective security. All in Europe, he stated, should realize that cooperation between Prague and Moscow was motivated by only one objective: "the maintenance and strengthening of peace." But most of the subsequent developments, and his declarations during the next several days, made it impossible for the rest of Europe to believe that restrictions had been imposed on the newly developing alliance between Czechoslovakia and the Soviet Union.

Edvard Beneš's Soviet hosts knew how to make an impression on their guest. At the train station he was swept up in a propaganda machine that took him through all the famous spots of the Bolshevik capital. The Czechoslovak legation later analyzed the visit and found that Soviet protocol specialists had given Beneš a more respectful reception at the train station, as well as outside it, than was accorded Anthony Eden and Pierre Laval, who had preceded him in Moscow. The number of flags, noted the legation, was doubled for Beneš in comparison with his British and French colleagues. Outside the station, he was received by a crowd of several tens of thousands—many times more than the number of greeters produced for the British and French ministers. Mounted police and building supervisors were called on to form a cordon separating the convoy of official cars from Muscovites crowding the sidewalks. Moscow, the analysis concluded, had not seen many such visits under the Bolshevik regime.[94] Beneš was taken through the Soviet capital from the solemn mausoleum of Vladimir Lenin, through the colorful new Moscow subway, to the opera, and on to see the treasures of the Kremlin. The wooing of the Czechoslovak minister was under way.

Beneš, whom no one would accuse of being immune to flattery, was impressed. He liked what he saw. At a reception that evening, Litvinov welcomed him to the Kremlin "as an outstanding champion of international collaboration and of reinforcing universal peace." From here on, Litvinov proceeded to praise his guest in the most generous manner imaginable. Undiplomatically making no reference to the founder of Czechoslovakia and its sitting president, Masaryk, the Soviet commissar painted a positive portrait of his guest. He stressed that "the community of interests" of the two countries resulted in a series of substantial developments that had taken place in a short time: the establishment of normal diplomatic relations, an air travel convention, a credit agreement, and, finally, the mutual assistance pact.[95] The Czechoslovak side reciprocated with a reception at the legation the next day, 9 June 1935. Pilsner Urquell beer and Bohemian sausages were plentiful, to the complete satisfaction of many foreign diplomats. The guests promptly formed orderly lines and, despite the long wait for each item, the atmosphere at the legation was merry. A British diplomat overheard Karl Radek remark that "on a foundation of such beer any kind of treaty could be negotiated."[96] But the reception did have a serious aspect. An expert on Soviet affairs would have recognized among the Soviet guests the chief of the Soviet air force, Y. I. Alksnis. Because Czechoslovakia had no common borders with the Soviet Union, the building of an "air bridge" was vitally important for the military component of the recently signed treaty. Alksnis's presence among the guests was the first sign of emerging Czechoslovak-Soviet military cooperation.

The best was still to come. Soviet attempts to seduce Minister Beneš into believing the promise embedded—with the French reservation—in the Czechoslovak-Soviet agreement culminated in the evening of 9 June 1935. He received an exciting introduction to the military consequences of the treaty from Voroshilov. Their one-on-one conversation must have been unusual in the Kremlin practice at the time; the purge had made it vital for each official to have a witness at all meetings, especially for those involving a capitalist foreigner. In the beginning, Voroshilov tried jokingly to educate the Czechoslovak minister about the virtues of alcohol and smoking. Beneš, who despised both throughout his life, refused to touch the offered glass and tried to laugh at the whole episode together with the hard-drinking Soviet soldier. Nevertheless, the two quickly agreed that there was a need for close contacts between Czechoslovak and Soviet soldiers. Beneš tried to lecture Voroshilov about the strategic importance of Czechoslovakia both for France and the Soviet Union. The Soviet soldier quickly agreed with all his points, and then he took the floor himself. "We don't want war," he said several times, "but we aren't afraid and if we're attacked by anybody we'll fight and terribly too; we'll rip the enemy apart!" This soldiery toughness must have warmed Beneš's heart, but it was only the beginning. Voroshilov proceeded to be specific. "We're not afraid of Hitler. If he attacks you, we'll attack him because if you fall Hitler would go further and attack Romania." These words were more potent than Voroshilov's vodka. Beneš asked his host how this would be done, given that Czechoslovakia and the Soviet Union were not neighbors. In order to reach the Czechoslovak-German battlefield would Soviet troops cross the territory of other countries? "Konechno" (of course), replied Voroshilov. "Whether there's an agreement regarding this [a corridor for Soviet troops] or not, we take it for granted." This was so astonishing that Beneš, who must have feared that the red-faced Voroshilov had exceeded his official instructions, brought up the conversation later with Litvinov. But there was no need to worry. Litvinov assured him that Voroshilov had expressed the opinion of the Soviet government.[97]

Beneš could not have known at the time that this was but one of many conflicting pieces of information he would receive about Soviet intentions in the growing Czechoslovak-German crisis. During the next three years there would be many more declarations of Soviet willingness to help Prague should it come to a shooting war with Germany. From the perspective of Czechoslovakia in 1935, a country that had just started to feel the threat posed by its powerful German neighbor, the words of Commissar Voroshilov were important, and Beneš must have felt energized when he left for Leningrad on 11 June 1935. When he returned to Moscow two days later, he went to see the American Ambassador William Bullitt. Beneš explained that Germany's rearmament had so altered the balance of power in Central Europe that it would be necessary to establish "the most intimate possible relations with the Soviet Union." He went on to say that the kernel of his entire policy was not to make the Soviet Union dominant in the region but to produce a balance of power between the Soviet Union, Germany, and Italy.[98] There was nothing wrong with such a plan in Bullitt's view, and he passed it on to Washington without any criticism of the Czechoslovak minister.

The problem was that Beneš, whose tendency to talk too much and to overstate his arguments was getting the better of him, made himself freely available to the press in Moscow.[99] He began by presenting views on the balance of power after the emergence of Nazism that he had already shared with Bullitt. He brought up Hitler and showed why the participation of the Soviet Union in European politics had become crucially important. That was the reason he considered his visit "to the Soviet Union to be the culmination of my sixteen or seventeen years in politics." Beneš suggested that it was natural for him to cooperate with the Soviet Union. "Just look at a map of Europe. We're at the heart of it." He left the Soviet Union on 16 June 1935. With Commissar Voroshilov's words still ringing in his ears, Beneš felt satisfied with his achievements.

Czechoslovakia was a small country but he, its foreign minister, had managed to secure it by weaving it into a sophisticated network of alliances that appeared reliable, first and foremost with France and now with the rapidly growing Soviet power. Of course Stalin's cruelty made Beneš uneasy; of course a regime that based its existence on the brutality of the secret police was not to his liking. Had Great Britain been Czechoslovakia's neighbor, Beneš would have worked ceaselessly to establish an alliance with it. He would have been more comfortable dealing with a Laborite prime minister than with Stalin. But England was far away, its politicians were at best reserved, Hitler was very close to Prague, and the Soviet Union extended its helping hand. Beneš could not ignore it.

Stalin Was "Gracious, Thoughtful, and Accommodating"

Upon returning to Prague, Beneš tried to soften somewhat the perception that he had gotten too close to the Soviet regime. A foreign service officer who had traveled with the delegation was dispatched "confidentially" to brief the U.S. minister in Prague on the visit. The delegation was given no opportunity to meet Russians, reported the Czechoslovak diplomat. Wherever the delegation went it was shadowed by NKVD agents. Members of the Czechoslovak delegation felt "as if they were living in prison."[100] There was, of course, nothing new or confidential about any of this, but the U.S. legation in Prague appreciated the gesture.

Unfortunately, Beneš chose to brief the British by himself and thus demonstrated that he could be his own worst enemy. On 24 June 1935 he received Sir Joseph Addison, the British minister in Prague, and gave him a detailed outline of his trip to the Soviet Union. Under the best of circumstances this would have been a difficult task. Never quite sure what they thought of the dissolution of the Hapsburg empire, British diplomats in Prague were unfriendly toward Czechoslovakia. Some of the hostility was hidden, but some of it was allowed to surface on occasion. Robert Hadow, the British chargé d'affaires in Prague, was of the opinion that "Austria and Czechoslovakia had no right to separate existence" and that German hegemony in southeastern Europe was not only inevitable but desirable.[101] (British diplomats in Berlin had an even worse record.)[102] Sir Joseph and his successor in Prague, Basil Newton, were not much different. Moreover, they both disliked Beneš's personality. Unfortunately, on occasion the minister confirmed their prejudices.

As the skeptical Englishman listened, Beneš took one hour and forty minutes to paint a rosy portrait of the Soviet Union. He talked of prosperous collective farms and factories with happy peasants and industrial workers who were well paid, very well fed (better than in Czechoslovakia itself). It was common, he said, for them to spend six weeks every year by the sea in Crimea with the whole family. The population was well supplied, Beneš claimed. After all, his own wife had gone shopping and found no shortages anywhere. Most important, communism as an ideology was disappearing. Stalin was "gracious, thoughtful, and accommodating," and he recognized the futility of communist propaganda abroad. Regarding the strategic framework for his trip to Moscow, Beneš offered, yet again, his opinion that after the rise of Hitlerism it "had been necessary to attract Russia westwards, in order to reestablish equilibrium in Europe (*de façon a rétablir l'equilibre europeen*)." The Englishman dismissed most of what Beneš had to say as "the usual platitudes."[103]

Sir Joseph deliberately wrote his report in a form that allowed him to show between the lines his contempt for Beneš and his optimistic views of Stalinist Russia. He portrayed him as a naïf who had fallen for the simplest tricks of the public relations specialists in Moscow. Worse still, he indicated that Beneš may have become a fellow-traveler who had already decided before his trip that Czechoslovakia's future would be better secured via an alliance with the Soviet Union than with the West.[104] It is not easy to understand why Sir Joseph and some other high-ranking British civil servants felt more sympathy (at least until March 1939) for the Henlein movement in Czechoslovakia than for the democratic government in Prague. But Beneš was partly responsible for his own lack of popularity among the British. Obviously, there was no merit in what he had said regarding life in Stalin's Soviet Union in the mid-1930s. Suspicion of communism in general and of Stalin's Russia specifically was justified, and Beneš's effort to portray Stalin as a trustworthy politician who should be drawn toward the center of power to make up for the emergence of Hitler proved naive. It further increased the gap between Czechoslovakia and its neighbors (especially Poland and Hungary) and also London and even Paris.

The style with which Beneš presented his political theories was just as poor. Perhaps to make up for his uncharismatic personality, he tended to lecture at great length to experienced foreign diplomats who soon resented being treated as students of international affairs. Although Beneš's analyses were always interesting and often correct, his high-pitched voice managed at best to persuade but hardly ever to convince his audience. In the League of Nations and among his colleagues in

Prague, Beneš was respected for his intellect and for his command of facts. But his diplomatic partners often failed to be impressed by "that machine for thinking and working."[105]

If only Beneš had been satisfied with his recent diplomatic achievements. They were very real. If only he had kept what he had been shown by his Soviet hosts to himself. There was no need for him to brief anybody, save for President Masaryk, the government, and parliament. He could have sent others to inform Czechoslovakia's allies through normal diplomatic channels. The charming Jan Masaryk in London and the well-connected professional Štefan Osuský in Paris would have done the job well. But Beneš knew only one place for himself in politics: next to Masaryk or at the very center. It was understandable that he was excited by what he heard from Commissar Voroshilov, but it was an error for him to attempt to educate the British about the virtues of Stalinism.

THE FRANCO-SOVIET AND the Czechoslovak-Soviet agreements appeared to be triumphs of pragmatic diplomacy. In reality they were handicapped from the beginning by three factors. First, Joseph Stalin and his colleagues did not enter into their obligations toward France and Czechoslovakia out of a desire to protect the Versailles system, peace in Europe, or the democratic government in Prague. They saw in their arrangements with Paris and Prague a tool that could be used to keep the next war, or at least its initial stage, away from Soviet territory. Second, Great Britain was so suspicious of any alliance with the Kremlin that it would pressure France to choose between itself and the Soviet Union. Naturally, any rational French politician would stay with Great Britain for reasons of proximity, history, and ideology—to say nothing of the ethical dimension of seeking alliances with Joseph Stalin. The resulting French coolness toward the Soviet connection had an immediate and direct impact on the value of the Czechoslovak-Soviet agreement. Third, the injudicious statements of Edvard Beneš regarding the Soviet Union put a distance between Czechoslovakia and others in Europe. Prague's agreement with Moscow would become a potent weapon in the hands of German, Polish, and Hungarian propagandists. In a more subtle way, it would have a negative impact on the public in Great Britain and elsewhere.[106] Soon, many in Europe would begin thinking of Beneš not as a victim of Hitler's brutal threats but as a hard-headed bully of the Sudeten German minority who had come to believe that there was no need to accommodate its reasonable demands, because of his strong Russian bodyguard. This line of thinking was flawed, but Czechoslovak diplomacy had failed to explain the real state of affairs.

In retrospect, it seems that Edvard Beneš could have properly explored the potential of the Soviet connection through diplomatic contacts in Geneva, signed the Mutual Assistance Treaty, and visited the Soviet Union. He should have done so without comparing the Bolshevik coup d'état with the birth of democratic Czechoslovakia, without talking about the peaceful intentions of the Stalinist Soviet Union, and without declaring that his trip to Moscow represented the culmination of his life. Such exaggerations were unnecessary and gained him nothing. The Kremlin chose to deal with Czechoslovakia because it saw, more clearly and sooner than many others in Europe, the danger Adolf Hitler's Third Reich represented to Europe—not because of Edvard Beneš's geopolitical arguments. At the same time, the minister's overstatements fueled hostility and suspicion toward the Prague government abroad.

Edvard Beneš convinced himself that his *Ostpolitik* was safe because he would conduct it in the footprints of his French allies. The French were to be the umbrella that would protect him from charges of being a Soviet sympathizer. This strategy never worked properly. First, Laval, as opposed to Beneš, distanced himself from the Kremlin master, and it was Czechoslovakia that stood out in 1935 among the Western European countries for being the least anti-Stalinist. Second, France had a committed, powerful ally across the English Channel, and, for all its dealings with Moscow, it was firmly embedded in the fabric of Western Europe. Czechoslovakia, on the other hand, was a Central European country, sitting astride the mythical fence between East and West. Moreover, it was surrounded with neighbors, of whom several had a claim on its territory.[107] Some took joy in adding to the flames of anti-Czechoslovak propaganda by portraying Prague as an outpost of the Communist International. Thus, from about 1936 onward, Beneš would have to live with the public image of an ally of Stalin's Russia, and Czechoslovakia's neighbors would exploit this perception without mercy. It would hang like a millstone around Edvard Beneš's neck until the Munich Conference.

By 1936 Beneš was no longer a mere foreign minister. Thomas G. Masaryk resigned as Czechoslovak president on 14 December 1935, and four days later, after a sharp, intensive campaign, the National Assembly elected Edvard Beneš as his successor. After some political posturing the Communist party representatives voted for Beneš. Henceforth, all his actions would reflect even more directly on Czechoslovakia than had been the case so far. Significantly, TASS in Moscow was the first among foreign press agencies to report on the changes at the top of the political scene in Prague. Gone were the cartoons of Masaryk and Beneš as lackeys of capitalist powerbrokers, images served to Soviet readers for more than a decade. Instead, the two founders of Czechoslovakia were portrayed as senior European statesmen.[108]

It is said that whenever Beneš's political opponents or friendly critics approached President Masaryk to complain about his foreign minister's latest faux pas, the old man always listened carefully before posing the same question: ''Gentlemen, and if not Beneš, who?'' On occasion, attacks on Beneš would be carried out in public and gain in intensity. Masaryk would then abandon caution and defend his partner to the hilt. ''Without Beneš—and I say it quite seriously—there would have been no Republic,'' wrote Masaryk to a vocal critic, and he went on to defend Beneš and to endorse his foreign policy decisions without reservation.[109] With such support it was not surprising that Beneš's career continued to flourish. But would he be able as president and without Masaryk's counsel to steer the Czechoslovak state through the stormy seas that lay ahead?

Notes

1. Gerhard L. Weinberg, *The Foreign Policy of Hitler's Germany: Diplomatic Revolution in Europe, 1933–36* (Chicago: University of Chicago Press, 1970), 107. See also the work by Karl Bosl (ed.), *Die deutsch-tschechoslowakischen Beziehungen von ihren Anfängen bis zum Ausgang der Ära Stresemann, 1918–1929* (Munich: Oldenbourg, 1975).

2. This is described in Magda Ádám, *The Little Entente and Europe, 1920–1929* (Budapest: Akadémiai Kiadó, 1993), 193–204.

3. NA 751.60f.11/3, Lewis Einstein, U.S. Legation, Prague, 19 December 1923, to the Secretary of State, Washington, D.C., quoted from Piotr S. Wandycz, *France and Her Eastern Allies, 1919–1925* (Minneapolis: University of Minnesota Press, 1962), 299. This work deals with the French-Czechoslovak alliance on pages 292–311.

4. The full text is in Piotr S. Wandycz, "L'Alliance franco-tchécoslovaque de 1924: Un échange de lettres Poincaré-Beneš," *Revue d'Histoire Diplomatique* 3–4 (1984): 328–33. Wandycz discovered copies of the two letters in Papiers d'Agents (Papiers Millerand, volume 56, pages 157–60) and in Archives de Service Historique de L'Armée de Terre à Vincennes (7 N 3105, carton 12, dossier 1).

5. In February 1937 the French General Staff attempted to reinterpret the agreement. It claimed that France was obligated to assist Czechoslovakia against Berlin only if it had been itself a target of German aggression. Wandycz showed, however, that this interpretation was without foundation. See "L'Alliance franco-tchécoslovaque de 1924," 330–31.

6. See Radko Břach, "Locarno a československá diplomacie," *Československý časopis historický* 8 (1960): 662–95.

7. The French, British, and German texts are well known; for the Czech rendition, see *Zahraniční politika* 1 (1925): 819–36 and *Zahraniční politika* 2 (1925): 1460–68.

8. Eric Sutton (ed. and trans.), *Gustav Stresemann: His Diaries, Letters, and Papers* (New York: Macmillan, 1937), 228.

9. ANM-M, Dr. Vojtěch Mastný, the Czechoslovak Legation, Berlin, to the Ministry of Foreign Affairs, Prague, 17 May 1933. Mastný wrote that, within only four and a half months, 125 Czechoslovak citizens had been abused by the German justice system. Poland, Mastný stated, officially listed 600 cases of this kind, although the real number was probably much higher.

10. Ibid., 17 July 1933.

11. Stanislav Brandejs, "Význam československo-sovětské obchodní smlouvy," *Zahraniční politika* 14, no. 3 (1935): 186. NA 760F.61/42. Chargé d'Affaires S. Pinkney, the U.S. Legation, Prague, to the Secretary of State, Washington, D.C., 22 August 1932, offers an entirely different picture of Czechoslovak-Soviet commercial relations for the given period: he claims that the commercial ties between Prague and Moscow were dramatically improving. But this claim is at variance with other sources. See, for instance, B. R. Mitchell, *European Historical Statistics, 1750–1970* (New York: Columbia University Press, 1975), 513; Mitchell's numbers fully agree with information provided by Brandejs. According to Mitchell:

Czechoslovak Exports (in million Kc)

	Germany	Russia	U.K	U.S.
1920	3,331	126	813	544
1921	3.061	133	2,104	771
1922	4,118	93	1,347	932
1923	3,205	9*	1,219	557
1924	4,131	73*	1,586	719
1925	5,347	404*	1,535	756
1926	4,780	156*	1,540	845
1927	5,721	190*	1,520	1,012
1928	5,670	279*	1,148	1,170

(Continued)

Czechoslovak Exports (in million Kc)(*Continued*)

	Germany	Russia	U.K	U.S.
1929	4,691	259*	1,423	1,472
1930	3,527	328*	1,378	977
1931	2,493	489*	1,356	805
1932	1,454	121*	406	507
1933	1,170	77	360	428
1934	1,618	32	466	494
1935	1,224	104	547	615
1936	1,230	181	723	729
1937	1,801	94	1,039	1,112

*Data available only for the European parts of the Soviet Union.

12. AMFA, Second Section, Moscow, no. 25, 5 April 1934.

13. Jane Degras, *Soviet Documents on Foreign Policy* (London: Oxford University Press, 1952), 3:1–2.

14. NA 751.61/144, B. Reath Riggs, the U.S. Legation, Berne, to the Secretary of State, Washington, D.C., 24 October 1933. Riggs quotes from an article which appeared in *Journal de Genève* on 17 October 1933. The article singles out Italy, Poland, and Romania as being the most eager to start a new, positive chapter in their relations with the Soviet Union.

15. AMFA, Second Section, the Safe, Ministry for Foreign Affairs, 18 March 1933, no. 33727.

16. AMFA, telegrams received, Bohdan Pavlů to the Ministry of Foreign Affairs, no. 361/37 and 311/37. The first telegram, dated 3 August 1937, stated that, according to a Soviet official, Arosev and his wife were on vacation. With the next one, dated 7 August 1937, Pavlů reported that Arosev and his wife had been arrested. KOSTUFRA (Communist student fraction) was a small student organization under the control of Moscow-oriented elements in the Communist party of Czechoslovakia. AMFA, Second Section, the Safe, Zdeněk Fierlinger, Czechoslovak Legation, Moscow, to the Ministry for Foreign Affairs, 7 March 1938, secret. Minister Arosev was charged with being a Trotskyite, and his wife was accused of being a Czechoslovak spy. Her disappearance caused problems in Czechoslovak-Soviet relations. Prague argued that Freund-Aroseva did not give up her Czechoslovak citizenship after she had married Arosev in April 1932, and she had not become a Soviet citizen. But even heartbreaking letters from her parents to President Beneš and many others, including Franklin D. Roosevelt, did not help. Neither Aroseva nor her husband were ever heard from again. Bohdan Pavlů and his successor in Moscow, Zdeněk Fierlinger, brought up Aroseva's case with Soviet authorities but were unsuccessful, although the case was still alive in the summer of 1938.

17. AMFA, Second Section, the Safe. The agreement for Aleksandrovsky was granted on 31 March 1933. Ibid., the Czechoslovak Mission, Moscow, to the Ministry of Foreign Affairs, 6 June 1933. The announcement appeared in *Izvestia*. AMFA, Second Section, box 564a, the Czechoslovak Mission, Moscow, to the Ministry of Foreign Affairs, 6 June 1933.

18. Ibid. A Foreign Ministry note pro domo, no date, states that Aleksandrovsky in 1924 replaced Antonov-Ovseenko as chief of the Soviet mission in Prague. Aleksandrovsky's first audience with President Thomas Masaryk was on 12 April 1924; his title at the time was "Représentant Plénipotentiaire de l'Union des Républiques Sovietistes Socialistes, *ad interim.*" A record of the audience is in the Office of the President of the Republic of Czechoslovakia, the Castle, A 1109, Audiences of Representatives of the USSR.

19. AMFA, Second Section, the Safe, pro domo note of the Ministry of Foreign Affairs, number 134.846/1933, signed Dr. Blahož, 11 December 1933. Minister Aleksandrovsky commented on the speech by Senator Havlín, a member of the conservative National Democratic party. Havlín's speech against de jure recognition is in *Národní listy,* 16 November 1933.

20. AMFA, Second Section, the Safe, Kamil Krofta's note pro domo number 9846/1934, 20 January 1934. The interview had taken place a day before.

21. AMFA, Second Section, reports from Moscow, 1934, no. 40, 29 May 1934.

22. AMFA, the Cabinet, 1934, no. 2999, 6 June 1934.

23. Czechoslovak de jure recognition of the Soviet Union in 1934 was followed, for instance, by Bulgaria, Belgium, Luxemburg, Yugoslavia, Switzerland, and Ireland. A. A. Gromyko, *Diplomaticheskii Slovar'* (Moscow: Izdatel'stvo Nauka, 1985).

24. NA 760F.61/50, J. Webb Benton, the U.S. Legation, Prague, to the Secretary of State, 14 June 1934.

25. Ibid.

26. "Mezinárodní politika," *Zahraniční politika* 13, no. 7 (1934): 408–9.

27. There were many occasions on which Beneš spoke in this vein. On 26 June 1935, he talked along these lines with the Bulgarian minister in Prague, M. Karadzhovov, and on 3 July 1935 he outlined his views before the Presidium of the Executive Council of the Czechoslovak National Socialist party in Prague. Both statements are in Sergei I. Prasolov, "Česko-slovensko-sovětská smlouva o vzájemné pomoci z roku 1935," *Studie z dějin českoslo-vensko-sovětských vztahů 1917–1938* (Prague: Academia, 1967), 102–3. He said much the same to Sir Joseph Addison, the British minister in Prague, and to J. Butler Wright, the U.S. minister in Prague, and to William C. Bullitt, the U.S. ambassador in Moscow.

28. AMFA, telegrams sent, 1934, numbers 370, 371/34, 17 June 1934.

29. Degras, *Soviet Documents,* 3:89.

30. Jaroslav Kokoška-Malíř, "Organizace československého vojenského ofenzivního zpravodajství v letech 1934–1939," *Historie a vojenství* 6 (1989): 52.

31. MHA-MOP, secret, 1935–39, 20 December 1934, no. 32.

32. AMFA, Second Section, box 553. As a result of the improvement in relations between Moscow and Prague, the official *Le Corps Diplomatique á Moscou* abandoned its practice of listing Czechoslovakia dead last and began listing it in accordance with its alphabetical place.

33. *Zahraniční politika* (1935): 97.

34. Čestmír Amort et al., *Přehled československo-sovětských vztahů* (Prague: Academia, 1975), 35–37.

35. AMFA, Second Section, box 471.

36. Amort, *Přehled československo-sovětských vztahů,* 232.

37. AMFA, Fond Krofta, box 6, no. 22/34, 20 September 1934.

38. MHA-MOP, 1936, secret, no. 174. František Dastich was born 18 September 1895 in Olomouc. He became an officer of the Second Bureau of the General Staff of the Czechoslovak army, that is, military intelligence, and served in Moscow as the Czechoslovak military attaché until 19 November 1938. Dastich was promoted to brigadier general as of 1 May 1945 and worked again as a Czechoslovak military diplomat in Budapest and Berlin. He resigned on 31 December 1948 in protest against the communist coup d'état in Prague and moved to the United States, where he died in Astoria, New York, on 16 February 1964. See his "Armáda čekala na rozkaz?" *Čas,* no. 4 (January 1958). *Čas* was an émigré paper published in New York. See also "Klátilova odpověd gen. Dastichovi," *Čas* (January 1959).

39. AMFA, Second Section, box 523, Lt. Colonel František Dastich, the Czechoslovak Legation, Moscow, to the Ministry of Defense, Prague, 13 November 1934.

40. Ibid., box 471, no. 37147/35, 27 September 1934.

41. AMFA, telegrams received, secret, Bohdan Pavlů, the Czechoslovak Legation, Moscow, to the Foreign Ministry, Prague, 24 April 1935.

42. AMFA, telegrams received, Bohdan Pavlů, the Czechoslovak Legation, Moscow, to the Foreign Ministry, 3/35, 4 January 1935.

43. Hubert Ripka, "Českoslovenští novináři v Sovětském svazu," *Zahraniční politika* 14, no. 1 (1935): 14, 16. Both parties deemed the visit a great success, and it was agreed that a Soviet team should reciprocate the visit in a near future. The Soviets would stay in Czechoslovakia from 5 to 19 October 1935.

44. MHA-MOP, secret, no. 75, 1938.

45. "Odložte brýle mámení," *Důstojnické listy,* 31 January 1935.

46. "Hitler's antagonism toward the Czechs was profound and long-standing; it included the view that it was their presence in Bohemia and Moravia that constituted the key nationality problem of the area, and that their expulsion was the appropriate solution." See Gerhard L. Weinberg, *The Foreign Policy of Hitler's Germany: Starting World War II, 1937–1939* (Chicago: University of Chicago Press, 1980), 314.

47. ANM-M, Dr. Vojtěch Mastný, the Czechoslovak Legation, Berlin, to the Ministry of Foreign Affairs, Prague, 27 January 1935.

48. AMFA, telegrams received, Bohdan Pavlů, the Czechoslovak Legation, Moscow, to the Foreign Ministry, 129/35, 15 March 1935.

49. AMFA, telegrams received, secret, Bohdan Pavlů, the Czechoslovak Legation, Moscow, to the Foreign Ministry, 27 March 1935; the article appeared in *Izvestia* on 26 March.

50. Brandejs, "Význam československo-sovětské obchodní smlouvy," 186–88.

51. The classic treatment of the French-Soviet relations is in William Evans Scott, *Alliance against Hitler: The Origins of the Franco-Soviet Pact* (Durham, N.C.: Duke University Press, 1962), passim and 56–73.

52. Degras, *Soviet Documents,* 3:96–97.

53. Ibid., 3:97.

54. AMFA, Bohdan Pavlů, the Czechoslovak Legation, Moscow, to the Foreign Ministry, secret, 24 April 1935.

55. AMFA, Jan Masaryk, the Czechoslovak Legation, London, to the Foreign Ministry, Prague, 4 February 1935.

56. AMFA, Štefan Osuský, the Czechoslovak Legation, Paris, to the Foreign Ministry, Prague, telegrams received, 9 April 1935.

57. Ibid., telegrams received, no. 201/35, 10 April 1935.

58. AMFA, Bohdan Pavlů, the Czechoslovak Legation, Moscow, to the Foreign Ministry, Prague, secret, 16 March 1935; the *Izvestia* articles appeared on 4 and 5 February 1935.

59. SCA, Ministry of National Security, 109–4–227, statement by Rudolf Beran to K. H. Frank, Hitler's *Staatsminister* in the Protectorate of Bohemia and Moravia.

60. AMFA, telegrams sent, no. 253/35, 9 May 1935.

61. Quoted from Piotr S. Wandycz, *The Twilight of French Eastern Alliances 1926–36: French-Czechoslovak-Polish Relations from Locarno to the Remilitarization of the Rhineland* (Princeton: Princeton University Press, 1988), 398.

62. Prasolov, "Československo-sovětská smlouva," 81.

63. NA 760F.6111/4, William C. Bullitt, U.S. Embassy, Moscow, to the Secretary of State, Washington, D.C., 4 May 1935.

64. Quoted from Prasolov, "Československo-sovětská smlouva," 85.

65. *Dokumenty k otázce spojenectví s SSSR* (Prague: Společnost pro kulturní a hospodářské styky s SSSR, 1938).

66. Degras, *Soviet Documents*, 3:304.

67. V. P. Potemkin (ed.), *Istoria diplomatii, 1919–1939* (Moscow: OGIZ, 1945), 3:389.

68. The first sign that Moscow was going to disassociate itself from authorship of the stipulation, and Potemkin's *Istoria diplomatii*, was registered in 1953, but only in articles. See S. I. Prasolov, "Chekhoslovakia v period ugrozy fashizma i gitlerovskoy agressii (1933–1937 gg.)," *Uchenye zapiski Instituta slavianovedenia AN SSSR* 7 (Moscow, 1953); S. Grachev, *Pomoshch SSSR narodam Chekhoslovakii v ikh borbe za svobodu i nezavisimost'* (Moscow, 1953). The problem with both sources is that they offer no real evidence; see Prasolov, "Československo-sovětská smlouva," 105. The author refers to Litvinov's well-known statement in Geneva of 23 September 1938, and Grachev quotes the unreliable Klement Gottwald. Neither article tries to explain why Potemkin's *Istoria diplomatii* chose to argue the opposite.

69. V. G. Trukhanovsky (ed.), *Istoria mezhdunarodnykh otnoshenii i vneshnei politiki CCCP, 1917–1939* (Moscow: Institut Mezhdunarodnykh Otnoshenii, 1967), 1:316.

70. Prasolov, "Československo-sovětská smlouva," 79–125; Ivan Pfaff, "Jak tomu opravdu bylo," *Svědectví* (1978): 573.

71. ANM-D, Arnošt Heidrich, "International Political Causes of the Czechoslovak Tragedies of 1938 and 1948," 11–12. The manuscript is deposited in the archive of Prokop Drtina, Archives of the National Museum, Prague. It was written in the United States in 1962.

72. František Ježek, "Z pamětí o mnichovské krizi roku 1938," *Historie a vojenství* 4 (1969): 674–701; the quotation is on page 680.

73. AMFA, Fond Krofta, 16 May 1935, as quoted by Prasolov, "Československo-sovětská smlouva," 106.

74. The treaty between Paris and Moscow was ratified by the French on 27 February 1936, some ten months after the signing.

75. Henri Noguères, *Munich: "Peace for Our Time"* (New York: McGraw-Hill, 1965), 358. The author goes so far as to suggest, in italics, that the stipulation was inserted into the text "at the express request of the French government." But there is no evidence for such a strong claim.

76. ANM-D. The quotation is from the manuscript version of Heidrich, "International Political Causes of the Czechoslovak Tragedies of 1938 and 1948," 11–12.

77. It is possible that the controversy regarding the stipulation might continue in the future. See, for instance, Ivan Pfaff, *Ruská zrada: 1938* (Prague: BEA, 1993), 22–27.

78. Stalin dealt with the question of future war in a speech before the Central Committee of the Russian Communist party in January 1925. "Our banner is still the banner of peace. But if war breaks out we shall not sit with folded arms. We will have to undertake action, but we will be the last to act. And we will do so in order to throw the decisive weight in the scales, the weight that can turn the scales." See *Works* (Moscow: Foreign Languages Publishing House, 1954), 7:14. The Soviet leader returned to the issue of future armed conflicts in Europe at the Fifteenth Congress of the CPSU in December 1927. Looking at the next decade or two, Stalin observed that war with the capitalist world was inevitable, but it could be postponed. Either "until the moment when the proletarian revolution in Europe is ripe. . . or until the moment when the capitalists come to blows over the division of the colonies." See *Works* (Moscow: Foreign Languages Publishing House, 1954), 10:296.

79. MHA-B, Fond Munich: Soviet Union, box 1, record of journalist Jan Münzer's conversation with Minister Aleksandrovsky, 20 August 1936, 11 A.M. to 12:30 P.M.

80. AMFA, Minister Beneš, Prague, to the Czechoslovak Legation, Moscow, 9 May 1935, telegrams sent, 252/35.

81. *Lidové noviny*, 17 May 1935.

82. AMFA, Bohdan Pavlů, the Czechoslovak Legation, Moscow, to the Ministry of Foreign Affairs, Prague, 26 October 1935. See also Wandycz, *Twilight*, 404.

83. Robert J. Young, *In Command of France: French Foreign Policy and Military Planning, 1933–1940* (Cambridge: Harvard University Press, 1978), 93.

84. See Masaryk's letter to Viktor Dyk of 6 June 1929: "Our policy toward the Germans must not be guided by chauvinism. . . . It follows for all reasonable politicians from our geographic location, from history and naturally also from . . . the strength of Germany." Jaroslav Pecháček, *Masaryk, Beneš, Hrad: Masarykovy dopisy Benešovi* (Munich: České Slovo, 1984), 23.

85. The important Sudeten German issue is not dealt with in this volume. A good introduction into the historical background is Eugenie Trützschler von Falkenstein, *Der Kampf der Tschechen um die historischen Rechte der böhmischen Krone im Spiegel der Presse 1861–1879* (Wiesbaden: Otto Harrasowitz, 1982). Czechoslovak-German relations between the wars are dealt with, for instance, in Ronald M. Smelser, *The Sudeten Problem, 1933–1939: Volkstumspolitik and the Formulation of Nazi Foreign Policy* (Middletown, Conn.: Wesleyan University Press, 1975); Johann W. Brügel, *Tschechen und Deutsche, 1918–1938* (Munich: Nymphenburger Verlagshandlung, 1967); Francesco Leoncini, *I Sudeti e l'autodeterminazione, 1918–1919: Aspetti internazionali* (Padua: Centro Studi Europa Orientale, 1973); Elisabeth Wiskemann, *Czechs and Germans: A Study of the Struggle in the Historic Provinces Bohemia and Moravia* (London: Oxford University Press, 1938); Radomír Luža, *The Transfer of the Sudeten Germans: A Study of Czech-German Relations, 1933–1962* (New York: New York University Press, 1964); F. Gregory Campbell, *Confrontation in Central Europe: Weimar Germany and Czechoslovakia* (Chicago: University of Chicago Press, 1975); Rudolf Jaworski, *Vorposten oder Minderheit? Der sudetendeutsche Volkstumskampf in den Beziehungen zwischen der Weimarer Republik und der CSR* (Stuttgart: Deutsche Verlagsanstalt, 1977); Koloman Gajan and Robert Kvaček (eds.), *Deutschland und die Tschechoslowakei, 1919–1945: Dokumente über die Deutsche Politik* (Prague: Orbis, 1965); Jaroslav César and Bohumil Černý, *Politika německých buržoazních stran v létech 1918–1938* (Prague: Nakladatelství Československé Akamedie Věd, 1962); Václav Král, *Die Deutschen in der Tschechoslowakei, 1933–1947: Dokumentensammlung* (Prague: Nakladatelství Československé Akademie Věd, 1964); Henryk Batowski (ed.), *Irredenta Niemecka w Europie Śródkowej i Południowo-Wschodniej przed II Wojną Światową* (Cracow: Państwowe Wydawnictwo Naukowe, 1991); Gotthold Rhode, "La situation en Allemagne en 1938 et la question des nationalités en Tchécoslovaquie," *Revue des Études Slaves* 1–2 (1979): 99–108; Jiří Veselý, "Ein Deutscher unter uns: Fritz Walter Nielsen in der Tschechoslowakei, 1933–1939," *Philologica Pragensia* 59, no. 3 (1977): 133–48; Jaroslav César and Bohumil Černý, "Německá irredenta a henleinovci v ČSR v létech 1930–1938," *Československý časopis historický* 10 (1962): 1–17.

86. The SdP enjoyed a real following in 1935 among the Sudeten German population, but to be on the safe side it received "large financial subsidies from Berlin for the campaign preceding the May 1935 elections." Weinberg, *Foreign Policy of Hitler's Germany*, 225.

87. *Lidové noviny*, 21 May 1935.

88. *Důstojnické listy*, 6 June 1935. Machník, who replaced Bohumír Bradáč, was a deputy representing the Republican party. According to his file in the Archives of the Ministry of Interior, he was a man of considerable personal courage. In July 1943 he was arrested by the Gestapo after three members of a resistance group identified him during Gestapo interrogations. After his arrest, Machník was given a simple choice—to become a Gestapo informer or to face death. The former defense minister chose the latter, and in December 1943 he was transferred to a German court in Dresden. He was found guilty and sentenced to death. The

sentence was changed in September 1944 to ten years in a concentration camp. Machník survived Dachau, took part in a death march, and was liberated by the U.S. Army in late April 1945. AMI, 12434.

89. *Důstojnické listy,* 29 August 1935.

90. *Důstojnické listy,* 18 July 1935.

91. AMFA, Bohdan Pavlů, the Czechoslovak Legation, Moscow, to the Ministry of Foreign Affairs, Prague, telegrams received 261/35, 17 May 1935.

92. AMFA, Bohdan Pavlů, the Czechoslovak Legation, Moscow, to the Ministry of Foreign Affairs, Prague, 20 June 1935. The whole report is marked secret.

93. AMFA. The following description of Beneš's trip to the Soviet Union is taken from Bohdan Pavlů, the Czechoslovak Legation, Moscow, to the Ministry of Foreign Affairs, Prague, 20 June 1938.

94. AMFA, Bohdan Pavlů, the Czechoslovak Legation, Moscow, to the Ministry of Foreign Affairs, Prague, 26 October 1935.

95. Statements by Litvinov quoted from Degras, *Soviet Documents on Foreign Policy,* 3:134–35.

96. PRO, FO 371/19461 N 3140, 13 June 1935; quoted by Harry Hanak, "The Visit of the Czechoslovak Foreign Minister Dr Edvard Beneš to Moscow in 1935 as Seen by the British Minister in Prague, Sir Joseph Addison," *Slavonic and East European Review* 54 (October 1976): 592.

97. MHA-B, Fond 39, Soviet Union, box 5.

98. NA 760F.6111/10, William C. Bullitt, U.S. Embassy in Moscow, to the Secretary of State, Washington, D.C., 14 June 1935.

99. AMFA. The rest of Beneš's trip to Moscow is in Josef Šust, chargé d'affaires, the Czechoslovak Legation, Moscow, to the Ministry of Foreign Affairs, secret, 22 June 1935.

100. NA 760F.6127/3, J. Butler Wright, the U.S. Legation, Prague, to the Secretary of State, Washington, D.C., 19 June 1935.

101. NA 760F.62/353, George S. Messersmith, the U.S. Legation, Vienna, to the Secretary of State, Washington, D.C., 4 June 1938.

102. MHA-B, box 3, Hubert Ripka's record of his conversation with Miss Grant-Duff of 2 December 1937. Grant-Duff told Ripka she found it hard to believe how the British embassy in Berlin was biased in favor of Germany. The ambassador had said openly that Great Britain would not move to assist Czechoslovakia and that it would prevent France from acting on behalf of its ally as well. Grant-Duff alleged that, except for three people, the whole staff were Nazi admirers.

103. PRO, FO 371/19461 N 3240, 27 June 1935; quoted by Hanak, "The Visit of Dr Edvard Beneš to Moscow," 588–91.

104. Such was certainly the view of Robert Hadow, the British chargé d'affaires, who wrote on 11 June 1935 that "Dr Beneš had made up his mind that in Russia, and not France lies Czechoslovakia's main hope of active assistance against German danger which the victory of Henlein at the polls has magnified out of all proportion in the imagination of the Czech electorate." Hanak, "The Visit of Dr Edvard Beneš to Moscow," 587.

105. Chancellor Jaromír Smutny's characteristics of Edvard Beneš, 22 March 1940, England; published as document no. 69 in Libuše Otáhalová and Milada Červinková, *Dokumenty z historie československé politiky,* 91. Pierre Crabites, a sympathetic biographer of Beneš, called him "an intellectual dynamo insulated from the nation he helped to bring into being." *Beneš: Statesman of Central Europe* (London: George Routledge and Sons, 1935), 232.

106. NA RG 59, Department of State, Decimal file 1930–39, box 4307, J. Butler Wright, the U.S. Legation, Prague, to the Secretary of State, Washington, D.C., 8 May

1935. Even Minister Wright, a rather friendly observer of the Czechoslovak political scene in the 1930s, seemed to believe the rumors regarding Czechoslovak-Soviet military cooperation. He reported to Washington that "the Czechoslovak military authorities have been more than usually active in the province of Moravia where, I understand, large underground tanks for the storage of gasoline are now under construction." It follows from his report that the tanks were to be made available eventually "for Russian military operations." No such underground gasoline tanks ever existed.

107. AMFA, Second Section, box 471, the Czechoslovak Legation, Warsaw, to the Ministry for Foreign Affairs, Prague, 16 July 1935. Beneš's trip to Moscow, and his new Soviet orientation, was especially unwelcome in Warsaw, and some periodicals reacted with brutal scorn. The official *Gazeta Polska* (10 July 1935) was restrained, however. It merely observed that Beneš had made too many promises to his new allies in the Kremlin. In the end, he would fail to deliver, the paper predicted.

108. AMFA, Bohdan Pavlů, the Czechoslovak Legation, Moscow, to the Czechoslovak Ministry of Foreign Affairs, Prague, 28 December 1935.

109. Jaroslav Pecháček, *Masaryk, Beneš, Hrad* (Munich: České Slovo, 1984), 25. Masaryk's letter to Viktor Dyk, 6 June 1929.

3

Between the Agile East and the Apathetic West: Central Europe, 1935–1937

In the spring of 1935 Joseph Stalin's Kremlin had established itself as one of the busiest centers of power in Europe. Anthony Eden visited the Soviet Union in late March, Pierre Laval followed him in May, then came the Czechoslovak delegation. Minister Edvard Beneš's entourage had barely left Moscow when an altogether different group of foreign visitors arrived on official business. Some five hundred foreign communists representing sixty-five parties descended on the city to attend the 7th Congress of the Communist International (Comintern).

The meeting was long overdue. Despite enormous organizational endeavors orchestrated from Moscow, the international communist movement was adrift. Intuitively, communists were inclined to resist the growth of Nazi power, but the Kremlin was playing a high-stakes strategic game in which the rules tended to change quite abruptly. Even the most weathered members of the international movement found Moscow's instructions, as well as the periods of its occasional silence, unfathomable. The Kremlin's orders to the foot soldiers of organized communism in Europe seemed sometimes so counterintuitive that many parties were broken into factions, a serious violation in the eyes of the Moscow center. It was not hard to understand why Moscow had failed to instruct its legions regarding Nazism. Stalin and his colleagues could not make up their minds: Was Hitler a mortal enemy? Was he a potential ally? Or could he be used to prepare the ground for a communist offensive? For a long time, no one had an answer.

In the mid-1930s, the Comintern was a highly centralized institution instilled with military discipline. Without clear instructions from the top, the lower echelons did not dare to act on their own; even a temporary hesitation in the Kremlin could immobilize the organization. This was no time for disruptions. In Germany, Hitler was firmly in power and the communist organization had been partly eradicated and partly coopted by the Nazis. Nevertheless, the Comintern continued maintaining that the communists' main effort was to be directed against the social democrats. As

Heinrich Himmler's Gestapo was efficiently flushing out the remnants of underground communist networks, the helpless social democracy was singled out as
communism's main enemy. This made no sense, and many German communists
knew it. Hitler had already banned the Social Democratic party in June 1933, only
months after he had outlawed the Communist party. The result was that the remaining German communists were supposed to be fighting a nonexisting rival while
ignoring the murderous Nazis. Finally, in 1935, it became painfully obvious even to
the most hard-line Comintern apparatchiks that Moscow's existing policy was di-
vorced from reality. By that time, the Communist party of Germany had lost its
struggle and communists elsewhere were dispirited, hence the need for a new Comintern congress.

The CPC and the 7th Congress of the Comintern

Central Europe between the world wars was not a particularly friendly milieu for
communism. The Communist party of Germany was born in December 1918 amid
violence, and violence would characterize much of its existence until it was outmaneuvered and defeated by Hitler in 1933. Communist parties in Poland and Hungary
had never managed to shed the appearance of being antipatriotic. This relegated
them from the beginning to the political margin, where they had to compete with
other political extremists.

    The Communist party of Czechoslovakia (CPC) shared its origins with other
communist parties in Central Europe. It emerged as a revolutionary branch of the
Social Democratic party in May 1921 and was formed officially on 30 October
1921.[1] After the victory of the Bolshevik faction under the leadership of Klement
Gottwald in February 1929 the CPC had given up on pursuing its own path and
oriented itself to Moscow.[2] Alongside its open (i.e., public) structure, it also maintained an illegal apparatus that was to take over the party's administration in the
event of revolution, civil conflict, or war.[3] However, the CPC was planted into a soil
unlike that of Poland and Hungary. In contrast to communists in other Central
European countries, the party was able (with varying degree of plausibility) to link
its rhetoric, ideology, and agenda with genuine antecedents in Czech history—from
the fifteenth-century rebellious Hussites to the late-nineteenth-century Marxist (but
also patriotic) currents in the social democratic movement. Furthermore, the loss of
their national elite in the early seventeenth century rendered many Czechs, including
Beneš, vulnerable to the seductive appeal of egalitarianism, more so than was the
case with the Poles and Hungarians, whose natural ties with their nobles and aristo-
crats had been strengthened by centuries of wars against foreign enemies. But the
main advantage the CPC enjoyed over communist parties in Poland and Hungary
was the absence of conflicts, or even direct contacts, between Czechs and Russians.
After 1917 Central Europeans came to think of communism as a Russian phenomenon. The tsars' attempts to stamp out or Russify partitioned Poland throughout the
nineteenth century and Russia's bloody action against Hungary's quest for independence in 1848 and 1849 made it hardly surprising that Poles and Hungarians were
wary of ideologies imported from the Russian east. Most Poles and Hungarians

rejected Lenin without much reflection: he was a Russian. The Czechs who looked askance at Bolshevism had to think about it. Those who rejected it did so because Lenin was antidemocratic and, therefore, anti-Masaryk.

Because there was nothing in Czech history to cause an automatic anti-Russian reaction, one would expect that Gottwald had a constituency that was considerably less skeptical than in other Central European countries. Nevertheless, the party moved only slowly toward its revolutionary goals. The openness of Czechoslovakia's political system, its stability, and the social-mindedness of the country's founders had deprived the communists of a well-defined political platform. There were simply too many other political parties at the center of the Czechoslovak political spectrum seeking to advance the cause of social decency, and they did so within the framework of a patriotic and democratic Czechoslovakia and without the radicalism of communist revolutionary slogans.[4] According to a confidential police report, during the 1920s and 1930s the CPC could boast only some sixty thousand registered members, of whom just one-sixth paid dues.[5] This seemed hardly significant in the context of Czechoslovak politics. As the threat of Adolf Hitler's Third Reich became ominous, the CPC increased its visibility on the Czechoslovak political scene, but the percentage of voters who had cast their ballots for the party of Gottwald changed little between 1929 (10.2 percent) and 1935 (10.3 percent).[6] The party's share of votes remained frozen at around 10 percent of the general vote until the CPC was driven underground on 27 December 1938.

In the 1930s the party was primarily a tool in the hands of the Kremlin leaders. First, they controlled the physical existence of the CPC leadership. One must only look at the fate of Polish and Hungarian communist leaders, many of whom were executed in the Soviet Union on Stalin's direct orders, to realize that this fact of life had to be taken seriously. Second, they also controlled the CPC's finances. Prague police estimated in the 1930s that the party's monthly income was 114,000 Kc, of which only 4,000 Kc came from dues-paying members.[7] The rest was made up from salaries paid to various communist politicians, mainly members of parliament, by the bourgeois Czechoslovak state. In accordance with the requirements of party discipline, all such salaries had to be turned over to the party, which then paid its representatives a small fraction as stipends. The party needed considerably more than the 114,000 Kc that fell into its coffers regularly each month. According to the police report, the party's monthly expenses totaled 289,000 Kc: 100,000 Kc went to support the central party apparatus; 10,000 Kc was for electricity, telephone, mail, and heat; 20,000 Kc went to official travel; 9,000 Kc was needed to pay medical insurance for party employees; 120,000 Kc was pumped into various party newspapers; 5,000 Kc was spent on propaganda; 15,000 Kc was needed to support small regional party secretariats; and 10,000 Kc had to be set aside for unexpected expenditures. All in all, the CPC needed an additional 175,000 Kc to supplement its income from dues and salaries. Some money could be raised from gifts or random fund-raising. Still, at a minimum there was a monthly deficit of 125,000 Kc, and that was covered by the Comintern. Every month the CPC received $5,000 from Moscow, a large sum at the time. Of the Comintern's overall financial commitments to revolutionary movements abroad, Czechoslovak communists received a considerable portion.[8] They would have been unable to operate without it.

Given all this, it is hardly surprising that the CPC leaders tried to follow the meandering line of the Comintern to the letter. For instance, in a 1931 statement for internal purposes, the party rejected the idea that there existed "the duty to defend one's homeland," a notion advanced by the democratic parties throughout Czechoslovakia in response to the growth of tensions in Europe. The proletariat had no homeland, stressed the document, as long as it had not won political power. Communists were instructed to arm the workers with weapons, which would then be directed against their class enemies. This was because communists opposed imperialist wars but were in favor of civil wars.[9] It was a daringly bellicose statement for the democratic atmosphere of Czechoslovakia, and it showed how close Gottwald was to the decision-making center in the Comintern and how far he was from the popular Czechoslovak democratic playing field. There was no threat of civil war whatever in the republic of Masaryk and Beneš.

In the early 1930s, acting against its own inclinations, the party obediently followed the official line and treated social democracy as its main enemy. For instance, the Central Committee's plenum of March 1933 found that there was no significant difference among the capitalist bourgeoisie, the social democrats, and Nazism.[10] Even in late October, ten months after Hitler had become chancellor, the party's evening paper asserted that the social democrats in Germany had produced Nazism.[11] The CPC went so far as to declare a state of alert for its members. It claimed that Czechoslovak social democrats were about to deliver the country into the clutches of fascism, and it instructed party members regarding political life under the conditions of illegality.[12] Even in early 1934, the Communist party warned— absurdly—against the threat of fascism in Czechoslovakia, and it denied the seriousness of Nazism in Germany. Speaking before the Central Committee of the CPC, Gottwald asserted that the so-called Nazi threat in Germany had been invented by the Czechoslovak capitalists who needed it as a pretext for building up the army to be used to impose a fascist dictatorship. The crisis in Europe had been manufactured, continued Gottwald, by the bourgeoisie who wished to drive Czech workers against German workers for capitalists' profits. Gottwald concluded: "Down with the [Prague] government implementing a fascist dictatorship. Long live the Soviet power."[13] Because the fascist movement in Czechoslovakia was minuscule, if not grotesque, there was little connection between the CPC alerts and reality.

But even if the CPC appeared to follow its Soviet marching orders quite obediently, not all was well from the Comintern's perspective. Moscow knew that although the party's General Secretary Gottwald attacked the Czechoslovak social democrats, other leaders did so only pro forma, and many party members did not like it. A statement by the Comintern's Executive (ECCI) of November 1933 singled out Czechoslovakia for especially harsh criticism. Many communists there did not understand, said the ECCI, "that social democracy . . . is not only the conductor but also the bearer of fascism." The ECCI focused on a group of Czechoslovak communists led by Joseph Guttmann as the main villains within the ranks of the CPC.[14] This was one of the first signs of a serious split in the ranks of the party. Guttmann, a member of the CPC's politburo and editor-in-chief of the party's daily *Rudé právo,* was not intimidated by Moscow's attack.[15] In December 1933, he prepared a long statement to the Central Committee dealing with the Nazi regime in

Germany. He wanted to know why all criticism was to be directed at social democrats now that Hitler was in power, in part as a result of an unseemly collaboration of communists and Nazis. Guttmann demanded: Should not some criticism be directed at the Communist party of Germany? After all, Nazism represented a threat to all in Europe. The Gottwald leadership reacted swiftly to this breach of discipline in its own ranks. Guttmann was subjected to a critical party resolution, and he was, quite innocently, invited to travel to Moscow in order to defend his views before the leaders of the Comintern. In contrast to thousands of other foreign communists, Guttmann apparently understood the nature of Stalinism. He sensed the danger hidden at the end of such a seemingly innocuous trip to Moscow, and he refused to go, saying that he was far too ill to be able to travel. He resigned from his position as editor-in-chief of *Rudé právo* and stayed put in the safety of bourgeois Prague.[16]

Guttmann's followers responded with a memorandum "The Party's Fate Is at Stake," criticizing the Comintern for its failure to accept at least some responsibility for Hitler's victory in January 1933.[17] The memorandum pointed out that the CPC, under Moscow's guidance, had at first denied that Nazism represented a threat. It now behaved as if the victory of Nazism everywhere, including Czechoslovakia, was inevitable. Gottwald responded in the well-tested Bolshevik manner by expelling Joseph Guttmann from the party. This triggered a series of statements that went back and forth between the CPC leadership and the rebellious group. Guttmann's memorandum of 17 March 1934 no longer hid its ironic tone, but the main question posed by the dissidents gathered around Guttmann was deadly serious: Why had the Comintern prevented the Communist party of Germany from fighting the Nazis with all its might? Is it that Hitler's success was not supposed to be Moscow's loss?

The party leadership had to put a great deal of pressure on rank-and-file members before it could respond to Guttmann's latest missive in accordance with the Comintern's wishes. In doing so, Gottwald confirmed some of the central suspicions voiced in the dissidents' memorandum of March 1934. The CPC statement attacked Guttmann and his followers for claiming that the arrival of Hitler to power was a defeat for the proletariat:

> It is obvious that fascism means the growth of terror and bloody wounds on the body of the proletariat. But renegades, Trotskyites and cowardly capitulationists see only the growth of terror, hear only the cracking of the whip. They do not see that simultaneously there grows a new revolutionary wave. They do not hear the thundering of the coming revolutionary clashes.

The CPC asserted that the world communist movement was on the threshold of a new round of revolutions and that the coming wars and general crises would shake the foundations of capitalism. Only violence could bring about a solution of the crisis in Europe. The document concluded that Guttmann was mistaken in criticizing the Comintern, the Communist party of Germany, and the CPC for their view that Hitler's dictatorship was an inevitable stage on the road toward the victory of the proletariat in all countries.[18] (It will be noticed that the ideas and some of the language of Gottwald's resolution are strongly reminiscent of the documents that would come out of the 7th Congress of the Comintern.)

It was thus amid much confusion within the sections of the Comintern that the 7th Congress met in Moscow during the summer of 1935. It lasted for twenty-seven days and was attended by 371 voting and 139 nonvoting delegates. Joseph Stalin had chosen to remain in the shadows for most of the proceedings, but his presence could be felt everywhere. He was known to be the main conductor of this event, and that alone made the result predictable: every single resolution put before the diverse plenum was adopted unanimously—for the first time in the history of the movement.

The congress is best known for the policy of "popular front" that was formulated by D. Z. Manuilsky, the outgoing general secretary of the Comintern, and by Georgii Dimitrov, who was elected to replace him. Manuilsky repeated the Marxist premise that the capitalist world necessarily produced wars. But at the moment, he said, some capitalist countries would like to avoid having to fight a costly war, and this had to be exploited. Dimitrov described how to do that. First, it was necessary to form a "single mass political party of the working class," consisting of all of the anti-Nazi parties. Second, "the political split in the ranks of the proletariat," had to be brought to an end.[19] This was a complete reversal of the Comintern's dogma that the main enemy was not Nazism but social democracy. In his long speech on 20 August 1935, the last day of the Congress, Dimitrov admitted that the communists had underestimated Nazism. Henceforth, they would have to "secure joint action with the social democratic parties, reformist trade unions and other organizations."[20]

That the Soviet organizers of the congress had bothered to announce such a reversal of the original line was unusual. The Kremlin realized the growing seriousness of the situation in Europe. It decided to stabilize European democracies because a strong France and a strong Czechoslovakia meant that, at least temporarily, the energy of the Third Reich would be contained or in any case diverted from the Soviet Union. There was a need for a degree of social tranquillity and political unity among the antifascist parties, hence the popular front of all against Hitler.

But the strategy laid down by the 7th Congress had a second component that has often been overlooked. It was assumed that in the near future there would be a "period of sharp clashes" among various capitalist countries, and it was anticipated that the forces of the popular front, under communist control, would prepare the ground "for the forthcoming great battles of the second round of proletarian revolutions." Thus, Dimitrov predicted, popular fronts in various European countries would ensure a defeat not only of Nazism but also of capitalism, and they would usher Europe into an era of "the dictatorship of the proletariat and the power of the Soviets."[21] This second aspect of the 7th Congress was hardly ever stressed by official historians in the Soviet Union and Eastern Europe, who typically focused on the popular front—antifascist—component and ignored the second dimension of the Comintern's strategic guidelines of August 1935.

In the summer of 1935 Stalin must have decided that Hitler did not represent a threat so overwhelming that it would force him to abandon his revolutionary schemes for Western Europe. But Hitler was also not a potential collaborator who could be seduced or coopted. Henceforth, the Hitler movement would be treated as a catalyst for Soviet-style revolutions throughout Europe. The 7th Congress resolved that a new generation of "genuinely Bolshevik leaders" had to be trained who would be able "at sharp turns of events" to follow and implement the instructions of the Comintern.[22] Off the main platform of the congress, Manuilsky criticized the view that fighting Nazism meant not fighting capitalism, and he reaffirmed the theory (he called it "Stalin's theory") that Nazism and social democracy were "not antipodes but twins." Therefore, the 7th Congress did not mean that the Soviet Union had extended its hand to Great Britain, France, Czechoslovakia, and the rest of the democratic Europe in order to resist further growth of the Third Reich. Rather, it viewed opposition to Hitler as a means to accelerate the growth of civil conflicts latent within capitalism in order to bring about the revolution the communists could not provoke on their own. In short, the 7th Congress wrote a crude how-to manual on communist power acquisition.

The year 1935 turned out to be a difficult one for the CPC. Czechoslovakia's mutual assistance treaty with the Soviet Union and Beneš's trip to Moscow caused a great deal of confusion in the communist ranks. During the seventeen years it had taken for Czechoslovakia to grant the Soviet Union de jure recognition, the CPC had a well-defined political platform. It denounced Prague's relations with the West and demanded close cooperation with the Soviet Union. Beneš's agreement with the Soviet Union encroached on the political terrain that had been hitherto under complete control of the CPC. A Czechoslovak police report on the situation inside the CPC from confidential sources stated that Gottwald and others in the leadership were confused and depressed. The report listed four causes of this situation. First, the new instructions from the Comintern calling for communist cooperation with other groups of the left and center were contrary to the previous dogma. Given the suddenness of change, party leaders were scared to act. What if the next day were to bring yet another radically different policy? Second, friendly relations between Stalin and Beneš deprived the CPC leaders of their most familiar rhetorical themes. Third, the party suffered enormous losses in the Sudetenland, where the German-speaking proletariat ignored its class brothers in the rest of Czechoslovakia and moved to join the Sudeten German party of Konrad Henlein. The CPC lost as much as 35 percent among the Sudeten Germans. Fourth, the CPC had realized that the increase in its popular appeal during the severe economic crisis of the late 1920s and early 1930s had been motivated by economic factors, not by faith in socialism or communism.[23]

There was no good time at which a party's leaders could afford the kind of "panic and immobilization" that Czechoslovak police informers detected among the leaders of the CPC, but 1935 was absolutely the worst time for it.[24] A secret meeting of Czechoslovak and Comintern activists stressed that the CPC had a great responsibility to maintain functioning underground networks. It was from Czechoslovak territory that communist activities directed at Germany and other countries, perhaps Poland and Hungary, would have to be organized. A Comintern representative then proceeded to give the CPC leadership a serious warning regarding the Henlein movement in Czechoslovakia's Sudetenland. It was no longer interested in advancing the position of the German-speaking minority within the democratic republic: it was now after "strategic objectives." That meant Henlein had chosen the path of Nazism, and he would seek to rip the Sudetenland from Czechoslovakia and attach it to the Third Reich.

The anonymous speaker who briefed the secret meeting proceeded to show on a large map of Czechoslovakia how in case of a Czechoslovak-German war the mechanized columns of the German army would cut the republic in half by simultaneous attacks, one from Silesia aiming south and the other from Austria leading north. This information proved to be astonishingly accurate. The officer of the Comintern who conducted the briefing concluded that it "was necessary to act like the fascists when it comes to dealing with the masses."[25] One can easily imagine how Gottwald and his colleagues must have felt at hearing this. Yes, they thought, but the Hitler movement could rely on well-oiled machinery that followed clear instructions, and those changed only rarely. In contrast, the CPC's leadership was having a difficult time trying to discern Moscow's true wishes within the Hegelian complexities of its communiqués.

The 7th Congress of the Comintern only added to the many difficulties of the CPC. Gottwald had every right to think of himself as an insider within the Comintern. In the summer of 1935, he enjoyed a unique position in the international communist movement because he was a member of the Comintern's Executive Committee, its Presidium, as well as its Secretariat. He took it to be his duty to demonstrate complete obedience to Moscow. Therefore, he followed the rhetoric of the popular front tactics and called intermittently for a period of cooperation with social democrats and all others who could join the struggle against Nazism. At the same time, he understood the complex nature of the strategic instructions laid down at the 7th Congress. But was he or was he not supposed to be preparing for a civil war, a war among classes?

Gottwald attempted to outline the two-pronged strategy in his speech at the end of February 1936. He dealt with the two components of the congressional platform in a manner that was deliberately disproportionate. Regarding the popular front, he simply admitted that, after Hitler had come to power, the party was not "flexible" enough to oppose him, and he left it at that. The communist leader rediscovered his eloquence concerning the likely consequences of Hitler's rise and the proper party strategy within this new political environment. He suggested that the CPC should turn the fear that many Czechoslovaks felt regarding their country's security into a tool and use it "to bring the masses to the position of class struggle." Some comrades had thought, said Gottwald, that the CPC should respond to the rise of Hitler by supporting the institutions of the Czechoslovak Republic. In fact, the CPC had made a great mistake in casting pro-defense votes in the Parliament recently. It was also a mistake for it to portray Beneš as an antifascist. The party had further erred when it acted on its belief that the fear of Hitler and the recent treaty with the Soviet Union would open a new chapter in its relations with social democrats and others. The opposite had to be done, cried Gottwald. He then offered a summary of the 7th Congress hardly ever found in those traditional accounts of the event that stress its popular front directive: "No class peace, no appeasement of the bourgeoisie. On the contrary, we must intensify the class struggle." And just to be sure his audience, the Central Committee, knew on whose authority he spoke before them, Gottwald concluded: "Here is your lesson: listen to the voice of Moscow and take it seriously. There is no one there who would put pressure on our party for frivolous reasons."[26]

There was an element of desperation in this final plea. Gottwald traveled frequently to the Soviet Union—he sometimes stayed for six months or more—and he knew better than most of his colleagues in the communist circles of Prague what had happened to some foreign communists who had gone to live in Moscow. Especially in 1937 and 1938, he must have reflected frequently on the very real possibility that he might one day have to follow in the footsteps of German, Polish, Hungarian, and other communists who were shot during the Stalinist purge in the cellars of various prisons in Moscow or elsewhere in the Soviet Union.

In the spring of 1936, the Communist party of Czechoslovakia devoted its own full congress to analyzing the platform of the 7th Congress of the Comintern.[27] Various speakers called for a popular front against Nazism and in defense of peace. Nevertheless, even official party historians observed that at that time the "CPC took the popular front policy to be a means for further class struggles directed at the imposition of the dictatorship of the proletariat."[28] This CPC gathering took place only some five weeks after Germany had occupied the fifty kilomeer-wide zone in the Rhineland that had been demilitarized under the terms of the Paris Peace Treaty following the end of World War I. On 7 March 1936, the day Hitler reoccupied the Rhineland, Beneš told the French that Prague stood ready to synchronize its policy with Paris and that Czechoslovakia would "follow France if it chooses to react to Hitler's action."[29] Although Beneš spoke toughly (he knew in all likelihood that the French would not move) Czechoslovak communists ignored the occupation of the Rhineland.[30] Instead, the delegates voted in favor of a resolution stating that if the Soviet Union were to come under attack, all Czechoslovak communists would offer their lives, side by side with the invincible Red Army, to defend the birthplace of socialism.[31] Given the realities of geography in 1936, there was no way for Hitler to attack Stalin while the likelihood that the Wehrmacht could be unleashed against Czechoslovakia was increasing day by day. In light of this, it is interesting that the resolution was silent on Soviet obligations toward Czechoslovakia under the terms of the 1935 agreement.

Undoubtedly, Gottwald and his colleagues thought they were on safe ground when they continued using the tough Bolshevik language. Alas, life in Stalin's Comintern in the 1930s was a dangerous affair. The received wisdom of today could tomorrow be unmasked as a deviation or as sabotage. The growth of Nazi Germany and signs of the British abandonment of the Versailles system increased the likelihood of Hitler's future aggression against Central Europe. And this was as terrible a prospect as Voroshilov had explained to Beneš during their conversation in the Kremlin in the summer of 1935. If communist parties were to continue, much like the CPC, to mumble phrases about the popular front while preparing revolutionary actions, what was there to stop Adolf Hitler from taking over one destabilized country after another and getting closer to Soviet territory? France, Czechoslovakia, and other countries, weakened by internal communist subversion, could fall into Hitler's lap without much effort. This had to be prevented. Regarding Czechoslovakia, the Kremlin decided that someone would have to explain to President Beneš that the threat of German aggression was real, as the Comintern had already explained to the CPC leadership in late March 1935. Czechoslovakia would have to be stabilized, its ability to resist the Third Reich would have to be built up, and local communists would have to be put on a shorter leash. These operations were launched immediately.

First came the task of warning the Prague government about the German threat. Stalin chose an unusual messenger on this occasion. Nikolai Bukharin, whose own fall into the pit of Stalinist terror was imminent, was tempted to escape during his authorized trips to Paris and Prague. But like Socrates and Ovid, he could not conceive of being an eternal exile.[32] Although he had come to understand the cruel nature of Stalinism, he fulfilled his mission in Prague with complete loyalty to Stalin, his present as well as future torturer. Bukharin was received at the Castle in Prague by Beneš on 29 February 1936. He told the president with Bolshevik direct-ness that Czechoslovakia's situation was "strategically catastrophic."[33] The presi-dent, who was known in diplomatic circles for his "facile optimism," must have been taken by surprise.[34] Had Bukharin gone mad? Was he a provocateur? wondered Beneš, completely unpersuaded by his claims. Bukharin's warning words fell on deaf ears at the Castle. Therefore, Moscow dispatched its Minister Aleksandrovsky to make the usual round of important personalities in Prague with a similar message, but all he could do was repeat what the Czechoslovaks had already heard from Bukharin. When Aleksandrovsky had explained the Soviet view to Jan Münzer, a well-connected political journalist, Münzer took the unusual step of asking the Soviet minister to stop threatening Prague with Nazi Germany. Czechoslovakia, Münzer stated, had nothing to fear. "I don't know," responded Aleksandrovsky, his voice trailing off.

All the talk about the Nazi threat to Czechoslovakia provoked Münzer to ask Aleksandrovsky a direct question: What would the Soviet Union do if Hitler attacked Czechoslovakia? "It depends," responded the minister, developing for the first time a theme that would characterize much of Moscow's behavior during the Czecho-slovak-German crisis of 1938. If it were a localized conflict between Prague and Berlin, Moscow would be unable to do much. But if it were to be a "global" conflict, then "the Soviets would disregard everything and march [to Czechoslo-vakia's assistance] through Romania as well as through Poland."[35]

It was unlikely that Aleksandrovsky succeeded in persuading Münzer about the immediacy of the German danger any more than Bukharin had done with Beneš. But his interview with Münzer made one aspect clear: the Soviet Union hoped that in case of war between the Third Reich and Czechoslovakia, France and, hopefully, other Western European countries would become involved. By contrast, an isolated Czechoslovak-German conflict would represent a danger from the Soviet perspec-tive. It so happens that this was a view shared by everyone around President Beneš at the Castle.

It seems that the Kremlin saw the German threat to Czechoslovakia and to itself at least as realistically as Prague did, and possibly even more so. Moscow decided to increase pressure on Klement Gottwald and his colleagues in the CPC. There were indications that Gottwald found it exceedingly hard to build bridges with the Czecho-slovak social democrats. It was also clear from his speeches that he had failed to change his vocabulary enough to make Czechoslovak communists viable political partners for social democrats and others who were supposed to have been lured into a popular front several months ago. He enjoyed the revolutionary component of the 7th

Congress platform too much to be able to suppress it in public and replace it with some mush about cooperation between the communists and other political parties. The result was that the CPC had nothing to show in the area of organizing a popular front.

What happened next could have been predicted. Prague police informers inside the CPC soon alerted the authorities that Gottwald had been unceremoniously called to Moscow for urgent consultations. The man must have had nerves of steel to withstand this sort of pressure. He had seen it many times in his circles in Moscow: one day you were an important comrade, a dignitary of the Comintern; the next day you were unmasked as a traitor and shot. Yet Gottwald always faithfully obeyed whenever summoned to Moscow. On this occasion, he left Prague on 18 May 1936.[36] When he returned on 7 June, his head must have been abuzz. According to police sources in the CPC, he had been treated quite harshly by his bosses in the Comintern. He was "severely criticized" for his failure to adopt the popular front line of the 7th Congress with appropriate energy. "Change, or else," Gottwald heard in Moscow. He was to work with all his might toward strengthening that same democratic bourgeois Czechoslovakia he had been told repeatedly to destroy. This time, things were different. After all, Beneš and Czechoslovakia pursued the same "peace policy" as Stalin and the Soviet Union.

The CPC was also ordered to support all measures to build the Czechoslovak armed forces.[37] Czechoslovak communists would now support the army? Gottwald and his colleagues used to speak eloquently against the "militaristic orgies" of Czechoslovak capitalists, and they fought tooth and nail against any increase of the military budget. "Not a man, not a dime!" Gottwald used to shout from the floor of the National Assembly in Prague. Just four months before, at the end of February 1936, he had stated before the plenum of the CPC Central Committee that the party had to insist on democracy in the military so that it would be able "at the crucial revolutionary moment to explode it from within. This is our main objective, not a mere technique."[38] He had spoken in a similar vein on 28 April 1936 before the National Assembly in Prague. There he said that the Bill for the Defense of the Republic number 131 of 1936, which was drafted to strengthen Czechoslovakia's ability to defend itself against the Third Reich, had been designed to enslave people and that both the Prague government and the Czechoslovak army were run by fascists.[39] Gottwald's attacks on the armed forces took place within a volatile and dangerous political context in Czechoslovakia. The Berlin government had issued a travel advisory warning German citizens against trips to Czechoslovakia and accused the country of committing vile crimes against German-speaking travelers, and Joseph Goebbels had begun the campaign to portray Czechoslovakia as but a Soviet military base.[40] Under such circumstances, Gottwald's approach had become unacceptable and—on Moscow's orders—he would have to change. The CPC would have to help strengthen Czechoslovakia's ability to defend itself against Hitler, thereby erecting a protective shield in front of the Soviet Union.

Three weeks after he had come back from his trip to the Soviet Union, on 28–29 June 1936, Gottwald stood before the Central Committee of the CPC. He now fully embraced the policy of building a popular front "from above," the policy he had opposed.[41] Naturally, such public reversals did not help the party. Police informers reported that the leadership had been weakened by "sharp divisions." In addition to the confusion caused by the two-pronged nature of the 7th Congress, there were also the ongoing trials with Lenin's former colleagues. Many had been popular in Prague, and Stalin's attack on them caused dissent among the top of the party hierarchy. Prague police analysts wrote that party bosses, including Gottwald, had stopped leading; most were simply hiding behind official instructions. The party was facing a serious internal crisis.[42] It was said to be divided into three factions. The top group, consisting of Klement Gottwald, Václav Kopecký, and Viliam Široký, was most eager to follow whatever instructions came from the Comintern. The other faction, built around Antonín Zápotocký, Jan Šverma, and Bohumír Šmeral, wanted the party to commence an aggressive bridge-building effort with the social democratic camp. This group wanted a true "popular front from above." Finally, the faction of Bruno Köhler rejected any compromise with social democrats, even if it meant going against the philosophy of the 7th Congress of the Comintern. Köhler insisted on preparing a violent revolution against the Czechoslovak bourgeoisie.[43]

The Kremlin could not tolerate factionalism in the CPC for long. It decided that party leaders did not know how to apply the popular front system and that they needed more indoctrination. Jacques Duclos, a high-ranking French communist and a deputy of the parliament, was dispatched to Prague. In his speech of 10 November 1936, Duclos was open about his contempt for the popular front business, but it had to be done, whether one liked it or not, he told Gottwald.[44] In the final analysis, the popular front meant the strengthening of France, Czechoslovakia, and, perhaps, other countries so that they could withstand the pressure of the Third Reich. In practice, the main objective was not so much to work hand in hand with social democrats but to build up the bourgeios state. Duclos explained how French communists had supported various economic measures, such as the recent devaluation of the French franc, and how they even accepted the French declaration of neutrality in the Spanish civil war. The popular front meant expanding the Communist party's appeal to the center and right. In fact, Duclos advised Gottwald, even religious issues were not allowed to be divisive.[45]

Gottwald and his colleagues in the Communist party circles in Prague finally understood what was expected of them, but no popular front would ever emerge in Czechoslovakia. For all the camouflage and deceitful rhetoric of the 7th Congress of the Comintern, the CPC remained a marginal force in Prague. If Gottwald had originally found it difficult to cooperate with the social democrats, they continued to regard the communists as agents of a foreign power. Most social democrats would have no difficulty working with parties of the right—as long as they were patriotic and committed to the defense of the Masaryk-Beneš Czechoslovak democracy. But communists? Out of the question! Therefore, even when the CPC leadership—after Moscow's prodding—started signaling its willingness to form a common platform with the Social Democratic party, the results were minuscule.

That does not mean, however, that the Kremlin had given up on the plan to carry out a "second wave of proletarian revolutions," as proposed by the 7th Congress of the Comintern. It will be shown that Moscow would certainly attempt to use the crisis of 1938 to escalate the Czechoslovak-German conflict into a revolution fueled not by national but by class concerns. However, it would find that the CPC before World War II was not a worthwhile partner for the schemes of Soviet foreign policy strategists.

Czechoslovakia and the Frigid West

In contrast to France, Great Britain had no legal obligations toward the Prague government, and it took upon itself the role of referee in the Czechoslovak-German crisis in the 1930s. As a consequence of the German naval buildup, Hitler's drive into the demilitarized zone on the Franco-German border along the Rhine, and the introduction of obligatory two-year military service, the British political scene was quite stormy in 1936. The main reason for that was the growing fear of Germany.[46]

The British became nervous when they heard of tensions in the German-speaking districts of Czechoslovakia. Soon, influential politicians in London and much of the British press began expressing impatience with President Beneš and the democratic government in Prague. Despite the obvious excesses of the Nazi regime, the British found the German interpretation of the causes of tensions between Prague and Berlin to be the more plausible one. Konrad Henlein, leader of the Sudeten German party, made a favorable impression on a number of prominent personalities in London who came to believe that the conflict was caused primarily by stubborn Czechs who had failed to respect the Sudeten Germans' legitimate needs. Czechoslovak diplomats, especially Minister Masaryk in London and Minister Mastný in Berlin, found that it was next to impossible to argue with this view by bringing up facts and statistical evidence on the situation of the Sudeten German minority. The British had made up their minds, and no additional amount of data would undo that fact. Beneš's successor in the Foreign Ministry, Kamil Krofta, attempted to explain to British Foreign Secretary Anthony Eden, who brought up the topic, that Czechoslovak Germans were not a homogenous group. He tried to show that a significant segment of the population in the Sudetenland was loyal to Czechoslovakia and that the social democrats among the Sudetens were committed anti-Nazis. Eden impatiently interrupted Krofta's analyses by pointing out that all he wanted to communicate to the Prague government was that it should offer the Sudeten politicians large scale concessions for tactical reasons in order to placate Hitler. He made clear that he was not interested in details.[47]

This sort of treatment was in stark contrast to the sympathetic attitude and support that the Czechoslovak cause (and Beneš personally) was getting from Moscow. Prague's primary ties were with Paris, and the recently developed Soviet connection was secondary. But the disparity between the frigid reaction to Prague's difficult situation by the democratic West and the eager encouragement it received from Moscow threatened to dislodge Czechoslovakia's western moorings. President Beneš saw this and tried to set the developing problem right. This would prove to be difficult. The sympathy British politicians and soldiers (especially those politicians who had served as junior officers in World War I) felt for Germany predated the Czechoslovak-German crisis. It stemmed, at least in part, from the sense of shared loss that was born in the trenches in France during the Great War. Captain John C. MacArthur, the assistant U.S. military attaché in London, spoke with a group of British soldiers in the early 1930s. The American soldier-diplomat listened in disbelief as his British colleagues freely expressed their sympathy for all things German. Hitler was aware of such sentiments and cleverly exploited them.[48]

But Great Britain could not remain blind in the face of Hitler's successes. By the mid-1930s, most had to do with the domestic German scene, but some had already begun encroaching on British interests. Czechoslovak diplomats in London were encouraged by the abdication of Edward VIII in December 1936. Masaryk wrote to Prague that the former king felt "closer to fascism and nazism than to democracy, which he found slow and boring." The minister reported that the king's fiancée loved Budapest and Vienna and felt no sympathy for the hopelessly middle-class Prague. The German ambassador in London, Joachim von Ribbentrop, "lost in Mrs. Simpson a dangerous ally."[49]

A few days after the abdication, Jan Masaryk had an unusual opportunity: he was to address a small, elite group of members of Parliament. His presentation was designed to respond to German and Hungarian propaganda that had saturated political circles in London. He also attempted to explain that Czechoslovakia had performed a service for Europe by trying to bring Russia out of its isolation. It was high time that other countries, especially Great Britain, stopped calling the Prague government names for acts that had benefited the European democracies. "If we treat Russia as a pariah," warned Masaryk, "it cannot be excluded that Russia and Germany could once again get together." After Masaryk's speech, there followed a two-hour period reserved for questions. Sir Austen Chamberlain and Winston Churchill asked Masaryk to pay the greatest possible attention to Sudeten German affairs. They expressed the opinion that the German question was the one weapon that Berlin "would be able to use against us."[50] It remained unclear whom they meant by "us."

In early 1937 Anthony Eden officially introduced Masaryk to George VI. Eden said to the new king on that occasion, "The political and economic situation in Czechoslovakia, Sir, is good and firm." But Masaryk was able to observe the introduction of von Ribbentrop, who greeted the king with the Hitler salute to which the king responded with a smile. Masaryk summed up the signals in a message to Prague: it would be a mistake to rely too much on English friendship and possible assistance. The Prague government and its conflict with Berlin were but unpleasant burdens for the British. Neither sympathy for Czechoslovakia nor regard for the truth would move London to become involved in the crisis.[51]

By 1937 the British did not hesitate to approach top German leaders directly with ideas that ran contrary to existing diplomatic and security arrangements in Europe. In May, Lord Lothian had extensive conversations with Hitler, Göring, and others in Berlin. He expressed his regret that Germany would be unlikely to regain access to its former colonies in Africa, which it had lost after the end of the Great War. However, he saw no reason why Germany should not extend its influence over Central and Eastern Europe. Lothian assured the Nazis that the British would fight only to defend the Empire, the Low Countries, France, and British shipping. Specifically, Great Britain would not go to war in defense of causes related to the League of Nations or to some "hazy ideas" or "anything else that did not directly concern" the British people.[52]

In addition to Lord Lothian, Hitler conferred with Lord Mount Temple, president of the Anglo-German Fellowship; T. P. Conwell Evans, secretary of the fellowship; Oliver Vaughan Gurney Hoare (Sir Samuel Hoare's younger brother); and others. He was also familiar with the views of Sir Robert Vansittart, one of the most influential personalities in the British foreign service. Sir Robert had told Konrad Henlein that "no serious intervention in favor of the Czechs was to be feared from Great Britain and probably also from France." The German legation in Prague learned of the conversation and promptly informed Berlin.[53] Any information from Vansittart had to be taken seriously, not only because of his position in the British foreign service establishment but also because he had developed a real friendship with Konrad Henlein and would not deliberately mislead him.[54] It is likely that Vansittart's statement had strengthened Hitler's conviction regarding Franco-British inaction in case of his attack upon Czechoslovakia. Hence, he relied on firsthand information rather than intuition when it came to predicting British intentions. It is against this background that one must evaluate Hitler's so-called genius in foreseeing British behavior in case of a Czechoslovak-German conflict.

Reassurances from London were always welcome, although it is unclear how much encouragement the Führer needed. Polyps recently discovered in his throat reminded him of his mortality, and this drove him forward with an increased sense of urgency. It is a matter of historical record that his views and his plans for the next world war had been developed by November 1937. Speaking before a select audience, he outlined his views on the political, economic, and military dimensions of his plan covering the period until 1945. Czechoslovakia played a prominent role both in Hitler's presentation and in the debate that followed. It was at the top of the list of his future victims: "For the improvement of our politico-military position our first objective . . . must be to overthrow Czechoslovakia and Austria." Hitler's audience inquired about the West and its reaction to such German aggression. "Actually, the Führer believed that almost certainly Britain and probably France as well, had already tacitly written off the Czechs and were reconciled to the fact that this question would be cleared up in due course by Germany."[55] Hitler's audience was astonished by the strength of his convictions. By early October 1938 British behavior would confirm his predictions, but far from providing proof of unusual acumen in political matters, it took no more than common sense on Hitler's part for him to discern that the champions of British-German rapprochement had told him the truth.

"Lord Halalifax"

President Edvard Beneš did not know about most of these important developments as he awaited with apprehension the imminent meeting between Lord Halifax, a close associate of the prime minister, and Hitler scheduled for November 1937.[56] It had been in the works for some time; the German invitation to Halifax had been secured by Lord Londonderry in September 1937. As the meeting between Hitler and Halifax approached, the rumor started to circulate in European capitals that in return for Germany's renewed commitment to respect existing borders in the West, Great Britain would give Hitler complete freedom of action in Central Europe. The British embassy in Berlin vigorously denied the rumors.[57] But Ambassador Henderson told the Czechoslovak Minister Mastný at that time that there was only one way to maintain peace in Europe: through the unity of Great Britain, France, Germany, and

Italy and the exclusion of Russia. The main obstacle to European peace, Henderson stated to Mastný, was the Franco-Czechoslovak-Soviet pact, and Czechoslovakia had to abandon it. He went on to observe that the Czechs were as hard-headed as the Serbs had been on the eve of the Great War. Such an uncompromising attitude could lead only to a catastrophe, and Prague would simply have to give up its orientation toward France and the Soviet Union. At the end of their encounter, Henderson told Mastný matter-of-factly that Lord Halifax was expected to arrive in Berlin on 17 November 1937 for "general discussions with the Reich Chancellor."[58]

While Mastný spoke with Henderson, the Prague government received information from its intelligence source in the Abwehr that Hitler would offer Lord Halifax a deal: Germany would commit itself to respecting British colonial possessions in exchange for a free hand against Czechoslovakia.[59] This idea seemed so dangerous that Prague tried to preempt it. Foreign Minister Krofta said he was in the position to state that all rumors to the effect that Great Britain was prepared to abandon Central Europe to Germany were absolutely untrue.[60] Unfortunately, Krofta was unable to offer any evidence to support his categorical statement, and it soon transpired that he was wrong.

Officially, Halifax came to attend a hunting exhibition in Germany, hence the playful nickname "Halalifax" he received from Berliners: *Halali* is the German for "tally-ho."[61] In reality, his trip to Germany was undertaken with great seriousness. The meeting between Hitler and Halifax had been preceded by a diplomatic tug-of-war: Germany proposed that the two should meet at the Berghof, Hitler's mountain villa at Berchtesgaden. Although the British preferred Berlin, the Berghof it would be. The Foreign Office would have liked for Halifax to meet Hitler accompanied by other British diplomats. But Hitler determined that he would receive his guest in a small study, and he would have been "cramped" were additional British personalities included. Therefore, Halifax would be alone, facing Hitler, Konstantin Baron von Neurath, the Reich's foreign minister, and Hitler's interpreter, Paul Schmidt.

Lord Halifax arrived in Berlin on 17 November 1937 and, after some sightseeing and two dinner parties, left in the evening of the 18th by train for Berchtesgaden. He traveled in comfort; his special coach consisted of a large sitting room and several bedrooms. The sitting room was equipped with a radio, a speedometer, a luminous clock, and even a photograph of Adolf Hitler. Three large Mercedes cars awaited the guest and his entourage at the station. After a short drive, they arrived safely at Hitler's villa. The view was spectacular.[62] But it was a cold morning when the Führer and Halifax met. The Englishman shivered visibly, and the host led him quickly to his small study on the second floor. Hitler then indicated for the British negotiator to begin. This he did by stating that he had come to find out whether Great Britain and Germany "were both prepared to work together for the cause of peace." Halifax offered a list of possible trouble spots: Danzig, Austria, and Czechoslovakia. "On all these matters we were not necessarily concerned to stand for the status quo as today," Halifax said to the delighted Hitler, for whom this was an official confirmation of information he had received before, "but we were concerned to avoid such treatment of them as would be likely to cause trouble." On at least two occasions Hitler heard from his British guest that no one in London expected that "the world could stay as it was forever." Throughout the meeting, Hitler seemed reserved but friendly and courteous.[63] Halifax noted with sympathy, after a friendly chat with members of Hitler's staff, that Germans wanted to be treated with respect by other Europeans and that they had surrendered their individual liberties to Nazism in order to achieve that objective. Halifax's conversation with the Führer lasted for more than three hours.[64] In the evening, the Englishman was taken to Munich, where he was shown Nazi headquarters, the Brown House; this was followed by a dinner that featured a lot of Bavarian beer. Lord Halifax was glad when he was finally able to retire to the luxurious train coach that took him back to Berlin.

The next day, 20 November, Halifax met Hermann Göring at his hunting headquarters at Schorfheide. The general wore "brown breeches and boots all in one, with green leather jerkin and fur-collared short coat on top—the green jerkin surrounded with a green leather belt, to which was hung a dagger in a red leather sheath . . . [and] a green hat and large chamois tuft." Nevertheless, he managed to make a good impression on Halifax, who reported he found him attractive, "like a great schoolboy, full of life and pride in all he was doing." They spoke for two hours.[65] The English visitor also met Hjalmar Schacht, Germany's chief economist, whom he found entertaining. He had expected to dislike the propagandist Joseph Goebbels but did not, which made him wonder whether this was a sign of "some moral defect." Finally, Lord Halifax met Field Marshal von Blomberg, the Reich's war minister and commander-in-chief of the Wehrmacht. The German soldier expressed curiosity over why France, the country that exercised its authority in Western Europe and the Mediterranean, failed to realize that Germany was entitled to do the same in Central Europe. Von Blomberg assured Halifax that Czechoslovakia was an outpost of Russia.[66] He returned to this theme a few days later with a written note sent to Lord Halifax via the British embassy in London. The Germans, he said, "passionately desired good relations with England," had no interest in quarreling with France, and had no aggressive designs in the West. But von Blomberg could not understand why "France so bitterly opposed the satisfaction of Germany's vital needs"—that is, Germany's needs for territory in Central Europe.[67]

Throughout his trip to Germany, Lord Halifax was especially keen on preventing any leaks by the press; his own statement to the press merely praised Hitler's and Göring's love of nature, as well as the hunting exhibition in Berlin.[68] Halifax even refused to brief the French ambassador in Berlin, André François-Poncet, who came to see him in Berlin on his return from Berchtesgaden.[69] Although Prague followed the encounter in Berchtesgaden with concern, there are no indications in the Prague archives that President Beneš and Czechoslovak diplomacy were aware, except in broad terms, of what had transpired at Berchtesgaden on that cold, foggy day in November 1937. Basil Newton, the British minister in Prague, noticed a great deal of nervousness in local political circles because the Czechs feared that Lord Halifax was about to throw them "to the German wolf." That tension largely dissipated in December 1937, when Beneš and his colleagues convinced themselves that they could still rely on the effective support of a loyal and powerful France—working in close cooperation with Great Britain—and also on their Romanian and Yugoslav allies from the Little Entente. "Beneš has strong nerves," Newton wrote to London, "and the Czechs are tough, obstinate and mistrustful of the Germans. The President

professes to believe, and very likely does believe, that the authoritarian States
. . . will be faced with increasing difficulties in the future while the democratic
Powers are beginning to make up leeway.''[70] Nothing could sway Beneš from his
conviction that what he called the "dynamic regimes," such as those in Germany,
Italy, and the Soviet Union, could not last. They would, in his view, eventually
either sink in competition with the democratic world or, like Stalin's Soviet Russia,
gradually abandon their aggression. In the long term, Edvard Beneš saw no alternative to liberal bourgeois democracy.

In retrospect, it is tempting to accuse Beneš of unwarranted optimism, but his
conviction that France, with its powerful army and British support, remained
Czechoslovakia's ally in late 1937 was not based on mere speculation or wishful
thinking. Yvon Delbos, the French minister of foreign affairs, came to Prague on 15
December 1937, a month after Halifax had spoken with Hitler at Berchtesgaden.[71]
The Prague government intended to turn the visit into a demonstration of Czechoslovak-French friendship and unity.[72] Delbos did not disappoint. He stated solemnly
before a large audience at the six-hundred-year-old Town Hall in Prague that France
and Czechoslovakia were bound by existing treaties to which they would remain
completely loyal. After all, there would be no civilization without respect for written
agreements.[73] The audience, naturally, was in full agreement. On another occasion
the French foreign minister became poetic. He observed that ''Czechoslovakia is like an extension [*un prolongement*] of France. We are united by so many ties,
we feel things in such a similar way, and our régimes are so similar that a Frenchman
in Czechoslovakia feels as though he were in France, and a Czechoslovak in France
feels as though he were in Czechoslovakia.''[74]

Delbos met Beneš on three separate occasions, and their meetings lasted for six
hours. The president explained that autonomy for the German minority in Czechoslovakia was out of the question. After all, a large percentage of Sudeten Germans
were loyal to the republic, and they should not be forced to live under a Henlein
regime. Nevertheless, Beneš was willing to hear what others, even Berlin, thought
should be done to improve Prague's relations with the Sudetenland. For the moment,
Prague would further increase the quality of German schools and see to it that more
local government officials were recruited from among the Sudeten Germans. Delbos
specifically stated that the measures the president proposed were satisfactory and
would be received well, not only in Paris but also in London. Beneš did not fail to
remind his French guest that Czechoslovakia was militarily strong and ready.[75] The
final communiqué mentioned the need of all countries to improve relations with their
neighbors—this was directed at Beneš—but it stressed that peace in Europe could be
maintained only in an atmosphere of respect for the rights of all states.[76]

When Delbos boarded his special train for Paris at the Wilson station in Prague,
Beneš had no reason to doubt the reliability of his French ally. On the contrary, he
felt powerfully reassured. At Cheb, just before the French delegation was to leave
Czechoslovak territory, Delbos was treated to the Marseillaise and the Czechoslovak
anthem. Touched, he stated before the official party at the train station that Paris and
Prague were united by ''indissoluble bonds.''[77] On his arrival in Paris, Delbos
emerged from the train smiling as he told the press, ''J'ai fait un excellent voyage.''
A few days later, however, he informed the Foreign Affairs Committee of the

Chamber that France remained popular among the peoples of Poland, Yugoslavia, and Romania, but the official circles in Warsaw, Belgrade, and Bucharest did not share the pro-French sentiments of their subjects. Only in Prague did Delbos find a true idyll. France was popular not only among the people but also at the highest level of the government.[78]

AFTER HE HAD RETURNED from his trip to the Soviet Union in the summer of 1935, Beneš found that for every bit of friendship he had gained in the Kremlin he automatically lost a comparable amount of support in the West. As a result of the crisis between Berlin and Prague concerning the Sudetenland and Beneš's diplomatic endeavors in Moscow, Czechoslovakia came to represent a liability to Western democracies. The British had convinced themselves that the Hitler phenomenon could be managed through a frank and absolutely pragmatic dialog with Berlin and a few concessions as far away from the British empire as possible, perhaps in Central Europe. That would be acceptable as long as the changes were achieved without untoward violence. This is what had led Prague to fear at the time of Halifax's meeting with Hitler in November 1937 that Great Britain might decide to sacrifice Czechoslovakia on the altar of peaceful relations with Hitler. Prague's defensive agreements with Paris and Moscow represented an unpleasant obstacle to a British rapprochement with Berlin.

As the year 1937 came to an end, the shape and contours of the post-Versailles system were clearly visible. The system's main characteristic was France's inability to maintain the status quo in Europe on its own. By failing to protect Central Europe against Germany, France revealed its weakness. Second, Great Britain no longer wanted to uphold the Versailles system crumbling under the vigorous blows of the Third Reich. In fact, Lord Halifax told Hitler that, as long as the Third Reich managed to advance its interests in Central Europe without a shooting war, Great Britain would remain disinterested and would, moreover, pressure France to follow suit, notwithstanding its legal commitments. Finally, the Soviet Union's value on the international scene declined precipitously in late 1937. It had reached its peak in the summer of 1935 when the 7th Congress of the Comintern gave its members the ambitious task of forming a popular front against Nazism and at the same time prepared to transform the war against Hitler into socialist revolutions. Most communist parties attempted to obey their orders from Moscow, but it proved difficult to work for a Soviet-style revolution while the Soviet Union sank ever deeper into the mire of purges and executions that followed the murder, arranged by Stalin, of Sergei Mironovich Kirov on 1 December 1934 at the Smolny Palace in Leningrad. Once the machinery of terror, perfect in its combination of precision and randomness, systematic thoroughness and unpredictability, was put into motion, it brought normal domestic developments to a near halt. Anthony Eden approached Maxim Litvinov in the summer of 1937 to complain that foreign observers found it difficult to follow internal events in the Soviet Union. The Soviet commissar responded arrogantly that "there were no events to follow." Only a few supporters of Trotskyism had to be neutralized, he said.[79] Litvinov had no choice but to sound blasé about the purge. Who could tell, after all, what fate Stalin had in mind for him? But no diplomatic denials were able to do away with the fact that Soviet Russia's value as an ally had declined significantly since the heady days of May 1935.

President Beneš had a good understanding of the situation. He could tell that the foundations of Czechoslovakia's security system had started to crack. Although it remained firmly committed to help maintain Czechoslovak national security, France was afraid of Germany; Great Britain was officially disinterested in the Czecho-slovak-German crisis, privately hostile to Prague, and cautiously sympathetic to the Konrad Henlein movement; and to top it off, Moscow's stock in Prague, as Newton observed, had sunk to a new low.[80] It was hard to imagine a worse scenario. Yet there was one. What if behind the facade of hostile rhetoric between Berlin and Moscow there lurked the possibility of a rapprochement? In that case, the infor-mation Beneš started receiving from Berlin would put the show trials in Moscow in an altogether different light. He had a reason to fear precisely that develop-ment.

Notes

1. ACC CPC, Fond 19, inventory no. 5.

2. The Klement Gottwald faction won over the so-called opportunists at the party's 5th Congress in Prague, from 18 to 23 February 1929. Thereafter, the CPC attempted—with minor exceptions—to follow Moscow's instruction with complete obedience.

3. ACC CPC, archival number 66062. This is an undated and unsigned forty-three-page analysis of the CPC. The document was written in the 1930s, possibly by someone from the counterintelligence section of the Ministry of Interior.

4. Before World War II, Bruce Lockhart wrote, "Czechoslovakia had been the Euro-pean democracy with the least contrast between wealth and poverty." See R. H. Bruce Lockhart, *My Europe* (London: Putnam, 1952), 123.

5. ACC CPC, Fond 19, inventory no. 5, signature 1223; the intelligence report is dated 13 November 1936. Ibid., signature 1063. A top-secret Communist party of Czechoslovakia report on party membership up to 1 July 1935 states: October 1932 (59,405), October 1933 (50,647), January 1934 (27,367), January 1935 (32,051), June 1935 (43,491), and July 1935 (48,000). From another report (ACC CPC, Fond 19, inventory no. 5, signature 1223), the Intelligence Central of the Police Directorate, 2 July 1937, reported to the Police Presidium that at the end of 1936 the CPC had about 75,000 members; as a result of a large-scale campaign to recruit new members, the party had about 90,000 by June 1937. The number of the party's elected representatives in the two houses of the Czechoslovak parliament remained unchanged between 1929 and 1935 (30 members in the house, 16 members in the senate). The ups and downs in party membership are explainable, at least partly, by intermittent purges.

6. ACC CPC, Fond 19, inventory no. 5, signature 1223. The report of the Intelligence Central of the Presidium of the Police Directorate is dated 2 July 1937.

7. Ibid. The confidential report on CPC finances was dated 13 November 1936.

8. According to an official publication of the Comintern's Executive Committee, *Thesen und Beschlüsse* (Basel: Prometheus, 1933), 24, the Comintern spent $650,000 annually in support of communist movements worldwide.

9. ACC CPC, Fond 19, inventory no. 5, signature 530.

10. Ibid., signature 67, Central Committee plenum of 11–13 March 1933. The resolu-tion was published as *Rozviňme veliký zápas za sjednocení dělnictva proti hladu, fašismu a válce* (Prague: Nakladatelství Senátora J. Hakena, 1933).

11. Ibid., signature 69. "Proti jednotné frontě fašismu, jednotnou frontu komunismu!" *Rudý večerník*, 27 October 1933.

12. Ibid., signature 70; Central Committee Resolution of 29 October 1933, *Proti fašistické diktatuře, za diktaturu proletariátu* (Prague: Max Forejt, 1933).

13. Ibid., signature 703. This is a Central Committee document called "The Soviets: Our Only Hope." It is dated February 1934.

14. Degras, *Communist International*, 3:274.

15. ACC CPC, Fond 19, inventory no. 5, signature 74. Guttmann's statement was dated 21 December 1933.

16. Josef Guttmann survived Stalin as well as Hitler and died peacefully in the United States in 1962. Jaroslav Bouček, "Odhalené tajemství moskevského procesu," *Slovanský přehled* 78, no. 1 (1992): 61.

17. ACC CPC, Fond 19, inventory no. 5, signature 185. Josef Guttmann was joined, among others, by Štefan Budín who was expelled from the CPC on 15 February 1936. The Central Committee letter bearing the news accused him of "guttmanniáda." Another person who joined the Guttmann group was Záviš Kalandra, who was sharply critical of the trials in Moscow, see "Odhalené tajemství moskevského procesu," *Slovanský přehled* 78, no. 1 (1992): 61–66. After the communist coup d'état in February 1948, Kalandra was tried together with Milada Horáková of the Czechoslovak National Socialist party. They were both hanged.

18. ACC CPC, Fond 19, inventory no. 5, signature 74. The CPC resolution on the Guttmann case is undated but must be either spring or summer 1934.

19. Degras, *Communist International*, 3:346–47.

20. Ibid., 3:362.

21. Ibid., 3:369–70.

22. Ibid., 3:354.

23. ACC CPC, Fond 19, inventory no. 5, signature 1222. This report by the Ministry of Interior is dated 1 June 1935.

24. SCA, Presidium of the Ministerial Council, 225–1055, (Prague) Police Directorate to the Ministry of Interior, 24 October 1936.

25. ACC CPC, Fond 19, inventory no. 5, signature 1222. The meeting took place on 18 March 1935; the police report is dated 27 March 1935.

26. Ibid., signature 79. Gottwald spoke before the plenum of the Central committee of the CPC, which lasted from 24 to 26 February 1936.

27. The CPC congress met in Prague between 14 and 16 April 1936.

28. Čestmír Amort et al., *Přehled československo-sovětských vztahů v údobí 1917/1939* (Prague: Academia, 1975), 290–91.

29. Edvard Beneš, *Paměti* (Prague: Orbis, 1947), 21. Of course, whether Beneš would have followed up his words with action is anyone's guess.

30. Gauleiter Warner expressed his view of the Rhineland occupation with a variation on Leninist logic: "We have not broken any treaty. But even if we have, we deny others the right to condemn us. What Hitler declares to be right is and will remain right for all time. What Hitler did on March 7 benefitted the German people. Anything that benefits the German people is right; anything that harms the German people is wrong." Raoul de Roussy de Sales (ed.), *Adolf Hitler: My New Order* (New York: Reynal & Hitchcock, 1941), 356.

31. Amort, *Přehled*, 291.

32. Bukharin, one of the six Bolsheviks who were, according to Lenin's testament, to determine the future of the Bolshevik revolution, was arrested on 27 February 1937 and subjected to some twelve months of the most innovative tortures. He was executed on 15 March 1938 on his fiftieth birthday. He was fully rehabilitated fifty years later on his 100th birthday in 1988.

33. Office of the President of the Republic, A 472/34.

34. NA, Record Group 165, Military Intelligence Division, Correspondence, 1917–41.

Major J. S. Winslow, U.S. Military Attaché, Warsaw, 29 June 1937, report no. 2898, G-2 2657–II–92, box 1704.

35. MHA-B, box marked "The USSR, 1937–38 [*sic*]." Jan Münzer's conversation with Minister Aleksandrovsky took place on 20 August 1936. They talked for an hour and a half.

36. ACC CPC, Fond 57, signature 16. This contains three Gottwald's passports. One other passport, his first, was reported to the Czechoslovak legation in Moscow as stolen in late November 1935. On 3 February 1935, Gottwald, the professional revolutionary, had a brand-new passport no. 64/757/36 from the legation, valid until 2 February 1941, for all European countries and the USSR.

37. ACC CPC, Fond 19, inventory no. 5, signature 1223. The confidential report is dated 19 June 1936.

38. Ibid., signature 79. The meeting took place on 24–26 February 1936.

39. Zdeněk Procházka et al., *Vojenské dějiny Československa* (Prague: Naše Vojsko, 1987), 3:372–75; ACC CPC, Fond 57, signature 565. Gottwald consistently put inverted commas around the word defense.

40. AMFA, Second Section, box 458. This is an undated official manuscript, one hundred pages long, from either late 1937 or early 1938. It provides a record of German claims against Czechoslovakia and official protests by the Czechoslovak Foreign Ministry or by Mastný, the Czechoslovak minister in Berlin.

41. ACC CPC, Fond 19, inventory no. 5, signature 1223. The confidential report is dated 30 June 1936. The Central Committee meeting took place on 28–29 June 1936.

42. Ibid. The confidential report from the Police Directorate is dated 10 September 1936.

43. SCA, Presidium of the Ministerial Council, 225–1055, K/26, the Police Directorate to the Ministry of Interior, 24 October 1936.

44. SCA, Police Directorate to the Ministry of Interior, 1936–1940, X/K/26/22–1, no. 11837/1938 [*sic*]. This report indicates that just when Gottwald had to go to Moscow to receive additional instruction on the popular front policy, the French activist Marcel Cachin was there for similar reasons.

45. ACC CPC, Fond 19, inventory no. 5, signature 1223. The confidential report on Duclos's speech is dated 10 November 1936.

46. AMFA, Jan Masaryk, the Czechoslovak Legation, London, to the Ministry of Foreign Affairs, Prague, 6 January 1936.

47. MHA-B, box 3, Record of Minister Kamil Krofta's conversation with Anthony Eden during a meeting of the League of Nations at Geneva, 29 September 1936.

48. NA, Record Group 165, G–2/2657–D–997–1, Capt. John C. MacArthur, assistant military attaché, London, report no. 30066, 28 February 1931. The conversation took place on 25 February 1931. "It is too bad we ever had to fight them," said an English colonel. Norman H. Baynes (ed.), *The Speeches of Adolf Hitler, April 1922–August 1939* (London: Oxford University Press, 1942), 1105–6.

49. MHA-B, box 3, Jan Masaryk, the Czechoslovak Legation, London, to the Ministry of Foreign Affairs, Prague, 14 December 1936.

50. Ibid., 19 December 1936. Masaryk included in this report an interesting anecdote: he sat twice within one week next to Mrs. von Ribbentrop during various diplomatic affairs. On one occasion, Masaryk pointed out that it was the hundredth anniversary of the birth of a certain German artist. "Das interessiert mich nicht," responded Mrs. von Ribbentrop, a good Nazi. "Die deutsche Kunst fängt mit dem Jahre 1933 an." Masaryk did not comment on her view that German art only began in 1933.

51. MHA-B, box 3, Jan Masaryk, the Czechoslovak Legation, London, to the Ministry of Foreign Affairs, Prague, 5 February 1937, 22 January 1937, 28 June 1937.

52. *Documents on British Foreign Policy, 1919–1939* (henceforth *DBFP*), 2d series, vol. 18 (London: Her Majesty's Stationery Office, 1980), document no. 480, Letter from Sir Nevile Henderson, Berlin, to Sir Robert Vansittart, 10 May 1937. Lord Lothian was a flexible man; see his speeches delivered in the United States in the early stages of World War II in *The American Speeches of Lord Lothian, July 1939 to December 1940* (London: Oxford University Press, 1941).

53. *Documents on German Foreign Policy, 1918–1945* (henceforth *DGFP*), series D (1937–45) (Washington, D.C.: United States Government Printing Office, 1949), 2:22–23. Minister Ernst Eisenlohr's report to the German Foreign Ministry is dated 22 October 1937.

54. After the war, Vansittart's closeness to Henlein during the late 1930s had become an embarrassment, and so an effort was made to cover it up. For instance, Appendix 2, "Herr Henlein's conversations in London, May 1938, Note of a Conversation with Sir R. Vansittart," which appeared in *DBFP*, 3d series (London: His Majesty's Stationery Office, 1949), 1:630, was published without its crucially important first sentence, although no omission was indicated. The sentence reads: "I have been on very friendly terms with Herr Henlein for some years past and have seen him frequently during his visits to London." This discrepancy was pointed out by J. W. Bruegel, *Czechoslovakia before Munich* (Cambridge: Cambridge University Press, 1973), 212, and in "Remarks on the Roundtable 'Munich from the Czech Perspective,'" *East Central Europe/L'Europe du Centre-Est* 10, nos. 1–2 (1983): 158–59.

55. *DGFP*, series D, 1:29–39. This is, of course, the famous Hossbach memorandum; see also Friedrich Hossbach, *Zwischen Wehrmacht und Hitler, 1934–1938* (Göttingen: Vandenhoeck & Ruprecht, 1965).

56. See Earl of Birkenhead, *Halifax: The Life of Lord Halifax* (Boston: Houghton Mifflin, 1966), and Andrew Roberts, *The Holy Fox: A Biography of Lord Halifax* (London: Weidenfeld & Nicolson, 1991).

57. *Evening Standard*, 13 November 1937; *DBFP*, 2d series, vol. 19 (London: Her Majesty's Stationery Office, 1982), no. 321, 525.

58. ANM-M, Vojtěch Mastný, the Czechoslovak Legation, Berlin, to the Minister of Foreign Affairs, Prague, 13 November 1937, no. 963/37, secret.

59. The agent was Paul Thümmel, service no. A-54, who worked for the Second Bureau of the Czechoslovak army's General Staff (military intelligence). His information on the imminent encounter between Halifax and Hitler came in a letter dated 13 November 1937 and was based on discussions among Abwehr officers. Jaroslav Kokoška and Stanislav Kokoška, *Spor o agenta A-54* (Prague: Naše Vojsko, 1994), 65.

60. NA 760F.00/56, Wilbur J. Carr, U.S. Legation, Prague, to the Secretary of State, Washington, D.C., 17 November 1937.

61. Paul Schmidt, *Hitler's Interpreter* (New York: Macmillan, 1951), 76.

62. *DBFP*, 2d series, vol. 19 (London: Her Majesty's Stationery Office, 1982), document no. 338, 557.

63. The German record of the meeting is in *DGFP*, series D, vol. 1 (Washington, D.C.: United States Government Printing Office, 1949), document no. 31, 54–67. The British record of the meeting is in *DBFP*, 2d series, vol. 19 (London: Her Majesty's Stationery Office, 1982), document no. 336, 540–55.

64. AMFA, the Czechoslovak Minister, Berlin, Vojtěch Mastný, to the Ministry of Foreign Affairs, Prague, 24 November 1937. Mastný reported that Halifax spent five hours in Hitler's house—from 10 A.M. to 3 P.M.—but some of the time was devoted to sightseeing.

Moreover, everything had to be translated, and that was also likely to cut into the time devoted to politics.

65. AMFA. This is from Mastný's analysis of the visit mentioned above.

66. *DBFP,* 2d series, vol. 19 (London: Her Majesty's Stationery Office, 1982), document no. 336, 552.

67. Ibid., 554–55.

68. AMFA. This is from Mastný's memorandum, quoted earlier.

69. *DBFP,* document no. 336, 553.

70. PRO, FO 408/68.r802/385/12, Mr. Newton to Mr. Eden, Prague, 22 January 1938.

71. John E. Dreifort, *Yvon Delbos at the Quai d'Orsay: French Foreign Policy during the Popular Front, 1936–1938* (Lawrence: University Press of Kansas, 1973), 143–47.

72. The trip to Prague was part of a large sweep through Poland, Romania, Yugoslavia, and Czechoslovakia. Delbos also met with von Neurath during a brief stop in Berlin. See Robert Kvaček, *Obtížné spojenectví: politicko-diplomatické vztahy mezi Československem a Francií, 1937–1938* (Prague: Acta Universitatis Carolinae, 1989), 30.

73. Robert Kvaček et al., *Československý rok 1938* (Prague: Panoráma, 1988), 29.

74. The quotation is from Alexander Werth, *The Twilight of France, 1933–1940* (New York: Harper, 1942), 138.

75. AMFA, telegrams sent, 1937, Kamil Krofta to various Czechoslovak legations, 18 December 1937. Krofta summed up the Delbos-Beneš meetings in a circular telegram.

76. *Zahraniční politika* (December 1937): 783.

77. Werth, *Twilight of France,* 138.

78. Ibid., 133.

79. PRO, FO 418/83.N2608/255/38. The meeting took place on 11 May 1937.

80. PRO, FO 408/68.R802/385/12, Mr. Newton to Mr. Eden, Prague, 22 January 1938.

4

Beneš and the Tukhachevsky Affair: New Evidence from the Archives in Prague and Moscow

In September 1936 military diplomats and invited specialists from around the world watched large-scale Red Army maneuvers in Byelorussia. They were favorably impressed. The climax of the war games involved a parachute deployment and the reassembly, in battle formation, of more than a thousand men armed with machine guns and equipped with light artillery pieces.[1] This was received as a sensation by the large group of foreign military observers.[2] Even at the height of World War II the event was still viewed as groundbreaking.[3]

If the Red Army was found to be a considerable fighting force in the fall of 1936, Western specialists' views changed dramatically within eight months. Between 1937 and 1938, the officer corps of the Soviet armed forces was more than decimated in a gigantic purge. One by one, the leaders of the Red Army confessed, according to laconically formulated newspaper articles, to high treason; they were spies for Nazi Germany. The purge weakened the Red Army and caused its perceived importance in European affairs to decline sharply. When measured by its sheer destructiveness, the purge had few historical antecedents.[4] The most famous victim was the dashing Marshal Mikhail Tukhachevsky, who had a creative military mind that was open to innovations. His career in the Red Army spanned service in the civil war, the Bolshevik invasion of Poland, the ruthless suppression of the rebellion in Kronstadt, and then a meteoric rise through the ranks to the very top; he was among the first to attain the rank of marshal of the Soviet Union. Tukhachevsky's career came to a cruel end, however, when he was charged with plotting against the Kremlin and espionage on behalf of Germany. His execution took place on 12 June 1937 after a brief and secret trial on the previous day.[5]

The charge against Tukhachevsky seemed like a dramatic replay of the Wallenstein affair that had captured Europe's attention some three hundred years before the news of the Soviet marshal's fall was made public.[6] But the similarities between the Hapsburg generalissimo and the Soviet marshal were only superficial. Unlike

Wallenstein, Tukhachevsky was innocent of the charge of plotting with the enemy. The purge of the Red Army and Marshal Tukhachevsky's execution were part of Stalin's general attack on the whole Soviet society.

Znamia Rossii and Other Tremors before the Earthquake

It is a little-known fact that the opening act of Stalin's assault on the Red Army leaders was played out during the winter of 1935, or perhaps even a year earlier, and that the stage was in the editorial rooms of *Znamia Rossii,* a Russian monthly published in Prague.[7] It occupied a prestigious address off Wenceslas Square (8 Krakovská St.) at the heart of the bustling city. Only a close look behind the flashy facade of the building with modern, tall windows would have revealed that the newspaper was a shoestring émigré publication. It had been in business since 1929, the year Stalin consolidated his power base in the Kremlin, and its leaders were among the tens of thousands of Russian refugees who had fled from the Bolsheviks and settled in Czechoslovakia. It claimed to speak on behalf of a Russian peasant party, and it showed global ambitions by advertising its price in seven different currencies. Readers had to pay a steep 15 cents a copy when the *New York Times* cost only 2 cents. *Znamia Rossii* seemed destined to remain an obscure newspaper with a loyal audience.

The newspaper stepped out of its provincial role and into the world of international politics unexpectedly but with resolve. The editors announced in December 1935 that they had received "about a year ago" through secret channels materials pertaining to KRASKOMOV, a large underground organization in the Soviet Union. Having waited for a year, they were finally authorized by the organization's emissary, "a person very close to us," to make the information public. Indeed, they had received authoritative and firm assurances that the materials from Russia would be published at the request of the leading representatives of the underground organization.[8] Even a cursory look at the materials revealed that KRASKOMOV was not just another of the many illegal organizations that the émigré press alleged to exist in the Soviet Union. It stood out because of its ambitious program, and especially because of its unusual composition. Most of its members were commanders of the Red Army, and their objective was the overthrow of the Stalinist regime.[9]

The first installment in December 1935 provided the historical background of the organization and discussed its composition and the political profiles of its leaders. The initial discussions that subsequently resulted in the emergence of KRASKOMOV, the article asserted, took place in May 1929, but it did not become a full-fledged underground organization until March 1931, when the horrors of Stalin's collectivization became apparent. The organization's leaders were ideologically close to the right deviation in the Soviet Communist party. But unlike Bukharin, Tomsky, and Rykov, KRASKOMOV never believed in giving public speeches and it did not hope to outmaneuver Stalin on the floor of the Central Committee. From the beginning, it was designed as an underground conspiracy. Nine-tenths of its members belonged to the party, but they were men of action not words. The core of the organization, perhaps as many as three-fourths, were senior

Red Army leaders. It had no enlisted men or junior officers. KRASKOMOV had one leader, a general staff, and primary organizations at all the crucial posts of state and party apparatuses in the Soviet Union. At first, the organization had planned to strike in the fall of 1935 or during the winter of 1935–36. A coup d'état, *Znamia Rossii* predicted, could also take place in the near future, for instance, in the winter of 1936–37. KRASKOMOV was determined to overthrow the whole Stalinist system before the outbreak of the next world war.

The February 1936 issue of *Znamia Rossii* presented an analysis of the organization's political philosophy. Neither capitalism, with its rule by a few and naked self-interest as the fuel of progress, nor communism, with its violence against all, was acceptable to the leaders of KRASKOMOV, who were portrayed as Russian isolationists, unwilling to take pride in Russia's wars with Napoleon, the Russian army's action against Hungary in 1849, or Russia's involvement in global communist activities. On the domestic front, the organization was supposed to aim at the development of a modern state with social democratic tendencies. Some components of the Stalinist system would be maintained but without the unproductive egalitarianism. The conspirators were supposed to have a high regard for intellectuals: the fountain pen was to be added to the hammer and sickle as a token of their respect for science, technological progress, and the arts.

In March 1936 *Znamia Rossii* outlined the steps KRASKOMOV intended to take once in power. Its program was remarkably liberal. The new regime would be neither a savior nor a destructive revolutionary. It planned to become a reorganizer. Its guiding principle would be Russia's welfare. All could stay in their present posts, many Soviet innovations would be maintained, but the Communist party, Komsomol, and the Communist International would be outlawed. Freedom of religion would be restored and free elections organized. Political prisoners, especially the kulaks, would be released and rehabilitated. The new government would encourage the return of émigrés and exiles, but each case would have to be evaluated on its merits. Educated people with experience abroad would be invited to join the new foreign service, but monarchists, reactionaries, or fascists inclined to trample on the human rights of others would be prevented from returning. ''The new Russia which will be built for the people and the nation, through the people and by the people, will have no use for such elements,'' concluded *Znamia Rossii* in the fourth installment of the materials it had allegedly obtained from the secret organization in the Soviet Union.

The final segment of the whole series appeared in April 1936. It was the most cunning component of all. The editors tried to deal with the many letters they had received from their readers. They confessed that scores of the letters were quite critical. Did KRASKOMOV exist at all? they asked. If it did, why would *Znamia Rossii* expose it to the blows of Stalin's security apparatus by revealing its existence? Some readers suggested that the published materials had been manufactured by Soviet security organs. Had *Znamia Rossii* fallen for a trick? Had the whole story been designed to serve Stalin's interests? The editors admitted that those were reasonable questions. They reaffirmed their absolute trust in the person who had delivered the documents in December 1934 and suggested that the leaders of KRASKOMOV may have decided to make certain information public in order to weaken the image of Stalin's security organs as being omniscient. It could be a useful recruiting device for the organization, offered the editors. Whatever the reasons behind the conspiracy leaders' decision to seek publicity, they wrote, the very existence of the organization should bring joy to all Russian patriots, and it would have been wrong to remain silent. The series concluded with a statement that read like a prophecy of the dark night about to fall on the Red Army officer corps: "The dangers awaiting Russia are great and frightening."

Even before the opening of the KGB and presidential archives in Moscow, it is possible to surmise that the articles in *Znamia Rossii* were a deception operation carried out by the Stalinist secret police.[10] Their objective was to plant seeds of doubt about the loyalty of the Red Army leaders and prepare the ground for the purge. There was little risk involved in publishing the series in an émigré newspaper that was either owned by Soviet security or whose editors had been duped into believing the fictitious scheme.

The second, more visible stage of the plot against the armed forces' leaders unfolded a year later. From 23 to 30 January 1937, various Soviet party leaders, including Karl Radek, stood accused of having organized an opposition, "parallel center" on the instructions of Lev Trotsky. As had already become the standard procedure in such trials, all the accused pleaded guilty to all the charges. But something unexpected happened on 24 January 1937. During his interrogation, Radek mentioned the name of Marshal Tukhachevsky. He stressed that he knew the marshal as a man who was "absolutely devoted" to the party and the government (that is, devoted to Stalin). Nevertheless, he fully implicated his colleague and subordinate General Vitaly Putna. The following exchange was crucial:

> *Vyshinsky:* So Putna came to you, having been sent by Tukhachevsky on official business having no bearing whatever on your affair since he, Tukhachevsky, had no relations with them whatsoever?
>
> *Radek:* Tukhachevsky never had any relations with them.
>
> *Vyshinsky:* He sent Putna on official business.
>
> *Radek:* Yes.[11]

Since Soviet officials were held fully responsible for actions of their subordinates, Marshal Tukhachevsky was marked for liquidation as of late January 1937 while he still had his rank and his job.[12]

The third stage was reached in May 1937. After weeks of dark rumors, Tukhachevsky was relieved of his duties as deputy people's commissar of defense, and less than two weeks later he was arrested, viciously tortured, tried, and executed in mid-June 1937. Contemporaries such as Edvard Beneš and Winston Churchill believed (Beneš more than Churchill) that Tukhachevsky and other officers had been involved in some kind of conspiracy against the Kremlin and that Stalin was justified in taking action against them.[13] Others in the West rejected this view and maintained that Tukhachevsky and his colleagues were innocent. This opinion was at first most vocally advanced by the anti-Stalinist European Left and also by German diplomats in Moscow. After the war, however, as more information about Stalin's methods became available, all but one author accepted the view that there had been no Red Army conspiracy against Stalin.[14]

By the mid-1950s, a new and intriguing interpretation began to emerge. A former officer of German intelligence, the Sicherheitsdienst (SD), claimed that Stalin had been deceived into thinking that the leaders of the Red Army had conspired against him by SS Obergruppenführer Reinhard Heydrich.[15] Working together with the Gestapo and a Russian émigré, Nikolai Skoblin, Heydrich was said to have forged documents falsely implicating Tukhachevsky and others in treasonous activities. It was alleged that the forgeries were then passed on to Beneš in Prague, who forwarded them to the Kremlin. Beneš, the deceived middleman, played a central role. Czechoslovakia had reasonably good relations with the Soviet Union, and false evidence against Tukhachevsky and others from Prague was more plausible and therefore likely to trigger Stalin's destructive response than if it had come from Great Britain or France. This interpretation seemed especially convincing because it was supported by information contained in Beneš's memoirs. The president asserted that he had received advance warning of a plot to overthrow Stalin involving Red Army officers with pro-German sympathies, whereupon he at once informed the Kremlin.[16] According to this interpretation, Moscow and Prague were victims of a disinformation scheme, and Berlin was the *tertius gaudens;* it stood only to profit from the instability it had caused in the Soviet Union.

By the late 1950s Tukhachevsky's innocence was generally taken for granted, but the extent of the German disinformation scheme as the explanation of Stalin's assault on the armed forces was still unclear. Was Stalin acting entirely as a pawn in a script written by the Germans? A complex view of the Tukhachevsky affair emerged in the 1980s, when new evidence became available in the Soviet Union. Research confirmed the existing suspicion that the impetus for the purge had actually come from Stalin, who had decided to ensnare Marshal Tukhachevsky and other high-ranking military commanders in a fictitious plot against himself. He used Skoblin, who was a Soviet agent (his service number in the NKVD was YeZh/13), to contact Heydrich and perhaps others from the Gestapo.[17] The Germans, who probably considered Skoblin to be an anti-Stalinist émigré, were duped into taking part in a scheme which—they were convinced—would weaken the Stalinist regime.[18] Heydrich believed he would play on Stalin's paranoia by supplying him with forged documents indicating that Tukhachevsky was a German agent. He thought he had designed the ultimate deception scheme. In reality, he played a role assigned to him by Stalin and the NKVD.[19]

As far as Beneš's role in the affair was concerned, there seemed to be no reason not to accept the president's own claim that he had wasted no time and warned the Kremlin as soon as he found out about the possiblity of an anti-Stalinist military coup d'état in Moscow. This perception has been strengthened from time to time by books and scholarly articles. Many authors portrayed the Czechoslovak president as an active, perhaps eager, participant in the Tukhachevsky drama. One has claimed that when Beneš came into contact with the forgeries from Berlin he held a series of four meetings with the Soviet minister and, as a result of information obtained from Prague, the Tukhachevsky drama was set into motion. The author chastised Beneš for not being more careful in handling the forged documents and charged that the Politburo of the Soviet Communist party had been so impressed with Beneš's action in support of Stalin that it passed a resolution expressing its official gratitude.[20] Such claims were made on the basis of dubious or even fictitious sources, and they obscured rather than clarified Beneš's role in the Tukhachevsky affair.[21] The topic can now be approached with the help of documentary evidence.

Tukhachevsky and the Secret Negotiations between Prague and Berlin

The Czechoslovak government became aware of the possibility of treasonous contacts between the Red Army and the German armed forces during the winter of 1937 within the context of the secret negotiations between Prague and Berlin. On 14 August 1936, during a reception at the French embassy, Maximilian Karl Graf zu Trauttmansdorff asked Ambassador André François-Poncet to introduce him to the Czechoslovak minister in Berlin, Vojtěch Mastný.[22] In a brief conversation after their formal introduction, zu Trauttmansdorff told Mastný that he had been authorized to discuss issues of mutual interest and asked for an interview at the legation.[23] He stressed that he desired to bring about an improvement in the relations between Prague and Berlin and added that Hitler shared his desire. Much emphasis was put on the nondiplomatic nature of his mission; nothing was to be conducted through the established foreign service on either side. This was the first stage of what would soon develop into a diplomatic effort known as the secret negotiations between Prague and Berlin.[24] Three days after his first encounter with zu Trauttmansdorff, Mastný had dinner with Beneš and Jan Masaryk, the Czechoslovak minister in London. All agreed that the German initiative should be taken seriously.[25]

As it turned out, zu Trauttmansdorff had been instructed to make the first contact, but the idea to hold the talks with Prague was proposed by Georg Albrecht Haushofer, a former lecturer at the Hochschule für Politik, who was loosely associated with a group of foreign affairs specialists around Joachim von Ribbentrop.[26] Haushofer produced a secret memorandum on new political opportunities for Germany and presented it to von Ribbentrop in the spring of 1936. The paper noted that the growing unlikelihood of Franco-Soviet involvement on behalf of Czechoslovakia in its conflict with the Third Reich, and the rise of German strength, had made the Prague government realize that Czechoslovakia was vulnerable. Therefore, the time had come to break through the encirclement of Germany via an agreement with Prague, which Haushofer envisioned, primarily, as a ten-year nonaggression pact.[27]

Haushofer brought up his ideas first with Mastný in Berlin on 18 October 1936 during a meeting prearranged by zu Trauttmansdorff.[28] Mastný listened to Haushofer attentively and decided to deliver the offer of secret talks to President Beneš in person. He went to Prague and discussed the matter on two occasions, on 22 October 1936 and again two days later.[29] It is not hard to imagine that Beneš was greatly relieved when he heard of the Haushofer initiative. Despite the secrecy that characterized the preliminary contacts, he had for the first time in many months a reason to breathe freely. It seemed unlikely that Hitler would be planning an assault on Czechoslovakia while he extended his invitation to negotiate a nonaggression pact. Therefore, Prague, its enthusiasm barely concealed, accepted Berlin's invitation.

Traveling incognito, Haushofer and zu Trauttmansdorff went to Prague in mid-November 1936. They were expressly forbidden to seek any contact with the German legation in Prague in order to keep the project secret from the German diplomatic service, especially from Minister of Foreign Affairs Baron von Neurath.[30] The two emissaries took rooms in the Esplanade Hotel, just a block or two off Wenceslas Square and not far from the editorial office of *Znamia Rossii*. Their two meetings with President Beneš and Foreign Minister Kamil Krofta on 13 and 14 November 1936 went well, and the Führer subsequently authorized the two negotiators to make another trip to Prague.[31]

The next meeting took place at the Castle in Prague on 18 December 1936 and lasted for six hours.[32] Zu Trauttmansdorff returned to Prague for yet another two-day visit on 3–4 January 1937, and Mastný traveled to Czechoslovakia a day later to be briefed on this latest development.[33] He met the president at Sezimovo Ústí, at his country villa near Tábor in southern Bohemia. On 6 January 1937, Beneš and Mastný spent seven hours discussing the prospects for a nonaggression pact between Berlin and Prague and Beneš's draft of the future Czechoslovak-German agreement.[34] The next day, Mastný devoted another five and a half hours to the same topic with Krofta. As he returned to Berlin on 8 January 1937, the diplomat had reason to feel satisfied.[35] He had assumed his post determined to improve Czechoslovakia's relations with Germany, and at last, after long years of tension and propaganda wars, he seemed to be near the end of the tunnel. Three days after Mastný had returned from Prague, zu Trauttmansdorff sent Haushofer a report on his last solo trip and also a draft of the proposed treaty, which he had apparently received from Beneš. Haushofer passed the text to Hitler on 14 January 1937.[36] The Führer, however, told the two German negotiators to drop the whole project. It would never be resurrected.

President Beneš did not want to appear too eager, but soon the silence from Berlin became deafening. At long last, Mastný was instructed to approach zu Trauttmansdorff and inquire about the status of the talks. Prague demanded an explanation for the unexpected breakdown, and Mastný did his best to get to the bottom of the mystery. He met with zu Trauttmansdorff on 9 February 1937 and then immediately summed up their conversation in a top secret message exclusively for the president. According to Mastný's record, the German aristocrat suggested diplomatically that in the Führer's opinion the time was not right for Berlin and Prague to proceed any further. Then, as if searching for a plausible explanation, zu Trauttmansdorff made a statement that linked the failure of the secret negotiations with the Tukhachevsky affair. Swearing the Czechoslovak minister to secrecy, he told him that

> the real reason behind the Chancellor's hesitation is his assumption, based on certain information which he received from Russia, that in the near future there may be a possibility for an imminent reversal in Moscow, the fall of Stalin and Litvinov and the imposition of a military dictatorship. Should that happen the Chancellor would substantially change his Russian policy; he would be ready to deal simultaneously with both east and west—albeit only by means of bilateral agreements.[37]

Mastný did not entrust this record of his meeting with zu Trauttmansdorff to the diplomatic courier who traveled the distance between Berlin and Prague with great frequency. Instead, he took the train to Prague and personally hand-delivered the memorandum to Beneš and Krofta on 11 February 1937. For the next two days he was caught in a feverish cycle of meetings at the Prague Castle. He returned to Berlin on 13 February 1937 and, exhausted, fell ill. He stayed in bed more than a week.[38]

President Beneš responded to the news from Berlin on 13 March 1937. His letter to Mastný, which bypassed Foreign Minister Krofta, took note of the rumor that "something was going to happen in Russia."[39] This note constitutes the first written evidence of Beneš's knowledge of (although not involvement in) the affair that would gradually escalate into the purge of the Soviet armed forces. Mastný's reply of 21 March 1937 further underlined Prague's awareness of the allegations regarding a coup d'état in Moscow. He reminded Beneš that

> the Reich Chancellor was said to have accepted the possibility of a sudden reversal in Russia in the near future, of the fall of Stalin and Litvinov, and [the imposition of] a military dictatorship in Moscow. This could result in a fundamental reversal of German policy toward Russia for which, as is well known, there is still much sympathy in the German army even under the present circumstances.[40]

Mastný then went on to explain that many in the Third Reich would welcome such a reversal, and he concluded, "Thoughts regarding the possibility of some fundamental reversal in [Germany's] policy toward Russia must have an impact also on the question of [Germany's] attitude toward Czechoslovakia and *in concreto* on the question of a possible agreement with us." This in a nutshell is how the aborted secret negotiations between Prague and Berlin were linked with the purge of the Soviet armed forces.

For Beneš, the prospect of a military coup d'état in Moscow that would turn Russia into an ally of Nazi Germany was a nightmare. The thought of Central Europe sandwiched between two powerful evils strained his innate tendency for optimism to the breaking point. The president could quite reasonably have inferred that the whole Haushofer initiative had been abandoned because Hitler had realized he would not need a rapprochement with the Prague government after all; it would have only imposed unnecessary legal limits on his ability to act. Those Red Army leaders, who were said to have conspired against the Stalinist regime, were about to strike, seize power throughout the country, and impose a pro-German military dictatorship. Under these new circumstances, the Czechoslovak-Soviet agreement of 1935, if not also the Franco-Soviet agreement of 1935, were going to be abandoned. This would strengthen Germany and drive France away from its commitments in Central Europe. Deprived of both of its allies, Czechoslovakia would fall into Hitler's lap like a piece of ripe fruit. No one, it seemed, would be able to stop the Führer. Who could? Obviously, not "president" Tukhachevsky, who would have reached the top post in the Kremlin as a result of a pro-German coup. Edvard Beneš was in a rotten mood, and he no longer minded if his subordinates could tell.[41]

President Edvard Beneš and the Tukhachevsky Affair

We have seen how the Tukhachevsky affair was woven into the fabric of the aborted talks between Prague and Berlin. Let us now look at it from the perspective of Edvard Beneš. The first question that must be answered is when the president initially came into contact with reports regarding a possible military coup d'état in Moscow. According to Mastný, Beneš received the first signal on 11 February 1937, but the president recalled in his memoirs that his involvement in the Tukhachevsky affair started "in the second half of January 1937." He learned that Hitler was "engaged in other negotiations, which, if successful, would probably also affect us considerably, and that the resumption of our talks must therefore be postponed till later."[42] The president was quite specific regarding the exact date with his English biographer Compton Mackenzie. According to this source, Beneš had learned on 12 January 1937 from zu Trauttmansdorff via Mastný that the Führer was engaged in "extremely important" negotiations with another party and the outcome could affect the final text of the agreement between Prague and Berlin. "Whether deliberately or by indiscretion Count Trauttmansdorff let out that these negotiations were with Moscow."[43]

Did Beneš first learn about the possibility of a military coup d'état in Moscow in January 1937, as he stated to Compton Mackenzie, or in February, when he met Minister Mastný and read his memorandum? The answer can be found in Beneš's conversation with the Soviet minister in Prague, Sergei Aleksandrovsky. According to the Soviet diplomat, Beneš stated that he had been receiving indirect signals about suspicious contacts between the Reichswehr and the Red Army "from January 1937."[44] There is yet another confirmation of January 1937 as the beginning of Beneš's awareness of the affair that would soon destroy Tukhachevsky and some forty thousand other officers of the Red Army. Arnošt Heidrich, a high-ranking official of the Ministry of Foreign Affairs, recalled that on 11 January 1937 Beneš learned from Berlin that Hitler had canceled the secret talks. This shows, the president immediately told Heidrich, that "Germany found a different way in which to weaken the Soviets and it therefore no longer needs to secure Czechoslovakia's neutrality."[45] On the basis of this evidence, it is likely that Beneš came across the first reference to a possible military coup d'état in Moscow in the middle of January 1937 and that Minister Mastný's memorandum of 9 February 1937 from Berlin was not the first occasion on which he heard the allegation that an anti-Stalinist takeover in the Kremlin was imminent.

The second question to be answered concerns who told the president in January 1937 about the possibility of a military coup d'état in Moscow. Beneš wrote in his *Memoirs* that the source of his information was Minister Mastný in Berlin. He said the same to his English biographer and to Heidrich. However, there is not the slightest indication in Mastný's archives, or any other archival collection in Prague, that such a communication took place in January 1937. On the contrary, Mastný's memorandum dated 9 February 1937 recorded zu Trauttmansdorff's information regarding the military plot in the Soviet Union with the urgency of a new, stunning development, not as something that would have been a month old. Furthermore, the Czechoslovak minister wrote to Beneš on 21 March 1937: "I remind you that more than a month ago I reported" regarding Hitler's expectation that Stalin and Litvinov would fall as a result of a military conspiracy against the Kremlin. "More than a month ago" could refer to 9 February but not to mid-January 1937. Therefore, Edvard Beneš must have heard of the imminent reversal in Moscow for the first time not from Mastný, although he subsequently named him as his source, perhaps in order to protect the real informant. Who was he?

Major Josef Bartík, a retired Czechoslovak intelligence officer, testified that Beneš had received the information from the German industrialist Fritz Thyssen, who communicated this intelligence to Prague via an emissary to Jaroslav Preiss, one of the most prominent Prague bankers.[46] Preiss then brought it directly to the president. Bartík, a credible source, stated that he had heard this directly from Beneš at the time.[47] There may have been other couriers, for example, Karl Wittig, but those were at best the necessary backups designed to strengthen the credibility of information from Thyssen/Preiss and, a month later, from zu Trauttmansdorff/ Mastný.[48]

According to Aleksandrovsky's record of his conversation with Beneš on 3 July 1937, the president stated that the source of Mastný's original report had been certain German military personalities:

> Mastný had in Berlin two discussions with important representatives of the Reichswehr. He "photographed" the conversations, apparently not understanding what they meant. Beneš even doubts that the Reichswehr representatives realized that they were revealing a secret. But on the basis of these discussions Beneš grasped that there was a close contact between the Reichswehr and the Red Army and that it was a contact with traitors.[49]

Mastný was reasonably well connected in the diplomatic community in Berlin, but the military was one lacuna in German society in which he was unlikely to have contacts. He was an old-fashioned diplomat, a gentleman who would have felt more comfortable in Victorian England than in Nazi Germany, and he was appalled by the growing interdependency of diplomacy and espionage. His relations with the military attaché, Colonel Antonín Hron, were strained because the diplomat disliked the intelligence officer's line of work.[50] Furthermore, Mastný was in 1945 unjustly accused of collaboration, and many documents found in his archive were produced to rebuff the charge. Had he had intelligence assets in the Reichswehr, or had he been able to ferret out the intelligence on Tukhachevsky during the course of a conversation with German officers, Mastný would not have hesitated to bring up such efforts on behalf of Prague and Moscow in his defense. But he made no reference to a German military source while he wrote at length about his interview with zu Trauttmansdorff on 9 February 1937. Finally, the notion that "important" officers of the Reichswehr would have revealed, unwittingly or otherwise, secret information to a minister of a hostile country is more than far-fetched. Therefore, Beneš's claim that the first hints of a plot against Stalin came from a German military source is unconvincing. How is one to understand his statement to Aleksandrovsky? One explanation is that Beneš simply made up the Reichswehr connection in order to protect the identity of Thyssen and zu Trauttmansdorff, whom he did not wish to identify. The president anticipated that Aleksandrovsky would inquire regarding the source of his information on the Red Army plotters, and so to preempt it he made a vague mention of the Reichswehr. This interpretation seems all the more plausible because there is a neat similarity between zu Trauttmansdorff and the Reichswehr sources: they both, according to Beneš, revealed the information unwittingly; it was said to be a slip of the tongue. Finally, according to the official indictment of the plotters, Tukhachevsky and his colleagues were supposed to have maintained secret ties with the German military. Therefore, Beneš's choice of the Reichswehr as a cover for Thyssen and Graf zu Trauttmansdorff made sense.

It seems evident that Edvard Beneš was exposed to the disinformation regarding treasonous contacts of Soviet military leaders with their German colleagues in January 1937 and that, in all likelihood, the information came to him from Thyssen via Preiss. The next month, the president was led further into error by a memorandum from Mastný, who passed on information he had obtained from zu Trauttmansdorff. It remains a mystery why Thyssen and zu Trauttmansdorff told Beneš about the nonexistent conspiracy. Did they know they were disinforming him? Did they act in good faith? Who had told Thyssen what he then passed on to Preiss, and who had told zu Trauttmansdorff what he shared with Mastný? Were those sources German, Russian, or a mixture of the two?

Thyssen remained silent about the Tukhachevsky affair. Zu Trauttmansdorff, by contrast, spoke out. For the first time, in 1954, he denied that he had even played any role in the Tukhachevsky affair, and he denied it again in early 1962.[51] On the latter occasion, he pointed out, truthfully, that he had been merely an employee of the Reichsarbeitsministerium (Ministry of Labor), not a professional diplomat subsumed in the hierarchy of the Foreign Ministry. But a central component of the Haushofer initiative was bypassing the traditional foreign service structure. Zu Trauttmansdorff stressed further that his encounters with Minister Mastný had a purely social character. The two had known each other for years and he had been many times a guest in Mastný's home, he wrote. This is not a credible statement. Mastný told Beneš and Jan Masaryk on 18 August 1936 that zu Trauttmansdorff had been introduced to him for the first time only four days earlier. All their subsequent meetings were devoted to the Haushofer initiative, and they stopped seeing each other right after the breakdown of the secret talks had become evident. Furthermore, Mastný's diary lists both professional and social engagements, and zu Trauttmansdorff's name does not appear in events unrelated to the negotiations. The aristocrat also vigorously denied ever having passed any forged documents from Berlin to Prague. The first time he heard of the forgeries was during his interrogation by American intelligence (CIC) in 1947. In making this claim, zu Trauttmansdorff was setting up a straw man since neither Beneš nor Mastný had ever claimed that he had anything to do with the forged documents. In fact, Mastný did not mention them at all. But the most suspicious aspect of zu Trauttmansdorff's denials is his complete silence regarding the substance of his meeting with Mastný on 9 February 1937 and Beneš's reference to Trauttmansdorff's "slip of the tongue" in his *Memoirs*. The aristocrat made no reference to this crucial point, although he speculated on various unrelated themes.[52] It can be ruled out that both Beneš and Mastný would have invented zu Trauttmansdorff's statement, and the existence of Mastný's original memorandum of 9 February 1937 in the archives speaks for itself. However, the origin of zu Trauttmansdorff's information remains unknown. We also do not know on whose behalf he passed it on and whether he knew he was not telling the truth.

The third question is, What did Beneš do with the information he received from Berlin in January 1937? In dealing with this problem, we move from his *awareness* of rumors suggesting an imminent military coup d'état in Moscow to his possible *involvement* in the Tukhachevsky affair. Beneš had no control over what Thyssen or zu Trauttmansdorff had chosen to tell him, but he was responsible for whatever information he may have passed on to Stalin. This question is therefore central. Beneš wrote in his memoirs that after he had learned from Mastný of the plotting of the anti-Stalin clique he "at once informed the Soviet Minister at Prague, Aleksandrovsky."[53] He made a similar claim to Winston Churchill, with whom he discussed his role in the Tukhachevsky affair in January 1944. Once he became aware of the Soviet military plot, Churchill recalled their conversation, "President Beneš lost no time in communicating all he could find out to Stalin." The story that President Beneš "at once" reported to Moscow what he had been fed from Berlin was also supported by Walter Schellenberg.[54]

It can now be proven—with the assistance of Soviet diplomatic documents— that this was a fabrication. It may seem bizarre that anyone would like to claim credit for having played any role in the bloody purge of the Soviet armed forces. But it must be remembered that Stalin's reputation in 1944 was much better than it would be later during the cold war. Moreover, Beneš, Churchill, and others continued to believe that Tukhachevsky had been involved in some sort of plotting with the Germans, and the president did not mind claiming credit for bringing the scheme to Stalin's attention. Alas, the reality of Beneš's involvement in the Red Army affair had little in common with the picture he painted.

The president received Minister Aleksandrovsky on 22 April 1937 for an afternoon tea, their only meeting during that month.[55] During the course of the discussion Beneš made mysterious hints without ever spelling out what was on his mind. At one point, he told Aleksandrovsky that no German threats could drive him away from his Soviet partner. Czechoslovakia would remain loyal to its treaties with Moscow and Paris, "no matter what changes could influence Soviet foreign policy." What was the president talking about? asked the Soviet minister, who was unable to follow the esoteric hints. According to Aleksandrovsky, Beneš responded by observing that

> the Soviet Union is a gigantic country with a multitude of interests in Europe as well as in Asia. Beneš imagines the theoretical possibility that these diverse interests would force the USSR to change its foreign policy, for instance, vis-à-vis Germany and England. He means nothing concrete; he merely wants to say that Czechoslovakia will remain friendly toward the USSR under any circumstances.[56]

The Soviet minister, obviously confused, twice assured the president that it was impossible to talk about any kind of Soviet-German rapprochement. It is important that this record of Aleksandrovsky's conversation with Beneš on 22 April 1937 makes it unmistakably clear that, all other assertions notwithstanding, the president who had known at that point of the alleged Tukhachevsky plot for three months told the Soviet minister nothing.

Beneš and Aleksandrovsky returned to the Tukhachevsky affair in their next conversation, on 3 July 1937, some three weeks *after* the marshal's execution. This time there were no vague allusions. The president was beaming with satisfaction, and he took joy in being quite specific. Because of his information from Berlin, Aleksandrovsky recorded, Beneš had been expecting the developments that had recently taken place in Moscow—that is, Tukhachevsky's execution. He was glad that Stalin was able to liquidate the conspiracy, the Soviet minister reported.[57] Furthermore,

> Beneš reminded me [wrote Aleksandrovsky] that in our conversation of 22 April he had stated that, after all, why could not the USSR and Germany come to an agreement. I told him that I remembered and I admitted that I had been greatly surprised by that part of our conversation because it completely failed to fit the pattern of Beneš's thinking. The president gave me a cunning smile and stated that he could now finally explain to me the hidden meaning of our previous discussion. He asked me to treat the following as top secret information, whereupon he told me that he had been receiving since January 1937 indirect signals about very close relations between the Reichswehr and the Red Army. Since then he had been waiting to see how the whole affair might end.[58]

And there we have it. Twenty-one days after the execution of Marshal Tukhachevsky, President Beneš revealed to Aleksandrovsky as a great secret the false information regarding the contacts between Soviet and German generals.

Aleksandrovsky analyzed Prague's perspective on the whole affair in his next report to Litvinov, dated 15 July 1937. The Czechs, he wrote, had obviously been getting hints from Berlin regarding some secret contacts between the Reichswehr and the Red Army. Although Beneš had had no details, it made sense for him to prepare his next moves on the assumption that a Soviet-German rapprochement would come out of the secret ploy, hence his hints that Prague would remain loyal to its commitments arising out of the Czechoslovak-Soviet agreement of May 1935 under any circumstances. But would the same have applied to Moscow? Beneš had been worried and confused by such prospects. All the president's fears and doubts, concluded Aleksandrovsky, disappeared "after the execution of the Tukhachevsky gang."[59] The Soviet minister was right: Beneš was relieved when he discovered that the responsibility for having engaged in secret contacts with Berlin was pinned on the traitor Tukhachevsky, whose execution, he thought mistakenly, marked the ultimate refutation of the spirit of Rapallo.

But what if Beneš communicated with the Kremlin through channels to which Aleksandrovsky had no access? It is true that a permanent Soviet intelligence central had been operational in Prague since the spring of 1936.[60] But its mission had to do with the rough-and-tumble of regular Soviet espionage in Western Europe, and NKVD officers assigned to Prague never came close to Beneš. Furthermore, a close reading of Aleksandrovsky's memoranda of April and July 1937 shows Beneš maneuvering in a manner which rules out the possibility that he communicated with Stalin via some other channel. Therefore, Beneš's and Aleksandrovsky's memoranda capture the accurate and complete state of affairs between Czechoslovakia and the Soviet Union at the time. The president, moreover, wrote in his memoirs and said to Churchill that he had communicated the information from Berlin to Moscow via Aleksandrovsky. We can now tell from the Soviet Minister's record that this claim goes against reliable archival evidence.

The false allegation that Tukhachevsky had conspired with the Reichswehr against Stalin was delivered to Prague with the expectation that it would be soon forwarded to Moscow in the form of evidence usable in a court of law, or at least inside the Lubyanka prison. But the whole complicated operation aimed at President Beneš had failed to produce tangible results. Stalin, however, was too experienced to put all his eggs into one basket. While the NKVD had tried to involve Beneš in the anti-Tukhachevsky scheme, it did the same in Paris with Édouard Daladier, the French minister of war. Unlike the Czechoslovak connection, the one involving France was successful. The scheme played out in Paris can be discerned from a top-secret memorandum by the Soviet ambassador in Paris, Vladimir P. Potemkin, exclusively for Stalin, Molotov, and Litvinov. On 16 March 1937, the ambassador reported on his meeting with Daladier, who told him he had learned "from a serious French source" (read: Deuxième Bureau) and "from Russian émigré circles" (read: Stalin's agent Skoblin) that

> certain Germans, in cooperation with elements from among the commanders of the Red Army who are hostile to the current Soviet regime, are preparing a coup d'état in the USSR. After the new regime in the USSR has been installed, Germany and Russia will sign a military pact against France. . . . Daladier explained to me that, so far, he did not have at his disposal more specific information, but he considered it his "friendly duty" to share with us information which cannot but be of use. I thanked Daladier [wrote Potemkin], but I expressed my definite doubts regarding the seriousness of his source which claimed that leaders of the Red Army took part in a German conspiracy directed against the USSR and indirectly also against France. I observed that lack of concrete information only increased my doubts. Daladier responded by saying that should he receive more specific information he would pass it on without delay. He would not rule out the possibility that remnants of Trotskyites existed in the Red Army.[61]

Beneš informed the Soviet minister about the alleged Red Army treason only after the Tukhachevsky trial and execution. But Daladier spoke with Potemkin in mid-March 1937, in time for the Soviet ambassador's memorandum to reach Soviet leaders and NKVD security officers in Lubyanka. With this in hand, there was plenty of time to arrange for Tukhachevsky's arrest, interrogation, and trial, that is, had "evidence," "proof," and the like come into play at all once the marshal was arrested.

The disinformation, designed to help in the destruction of Tukhachevsky and other Red Army commanders, returned to Moscow via Paris and not via Prague. This disproves the interpretation of the Tukhachevsky affair that has predominated since the mid-1950s—namely, that Beneš in Prague was the unwitting middleman in the affair. The link with Paris was subsequently reaffirmed by V. P. Potemkin in June 1937 to the French Ambassador Robert Coulondre.[62] It was soon—in August 1937—confirmed to Czechoslovak Minister Pavlů. Potemkin noted that members of the anti-Stalinist conspiracy had begun working with the Germans, that this was brought to Stalin's attention "by the West," and that the warning was subsequently found accurate.[63]

But what about the forged documents incriminating Marshal Tukhachevsky and his colleagues that were discussed in the memoirs of Walter Krivitsky, brought up by at least two German intelligence officers, and mentioned in scores of books and scholarly articles?[64] These documents were supposed to have been manufactured in April 1937—presumably by the NKVD agent Skoblin and Heydrich of the Sicherheitsdienst—in the basement of the Gestapo headquarters on Prinz Albert Straße in Berlin.[65] They were brought to Beneš's attention, according to Schellenberg, by an agent who posed as a German émigré in Prague, and the president was then supposed to have sent them to Stalin at once.[66] It is possible that some forgeries may have been passed from Berlin to Prague (the identity of the courier remains a mystery), but it is certain that nothing went on to Moscow. Furthermore, the director of the archives of the Russian Foreign Ministry examined all the relevant files and found no trace of the forged documents, and General Nikolai Pavlenko, a Soviet military historian, testified that his colleague, who had attended the trial of Tukhachevsky, had told him that no documents were ever introduced as evidence.[67] Finally, General František Moravec of the Czechoslovak military intelligence service, the Second Bureau, denied in his memoirs quite vigorously that the organization had been ever exposed to the forgeries.[68]

Naturally, the absence of the documents in the archives of the Ministry of Foreign Affairs in Moscow, a secondhand testimony that they had not been brought up in the courtroom, or denials of a professional intelligence officer, in and of themselves, prove nothing. In fact, two officers of the Czechoslovak Second Bureau, General Oldřich Tichý and Colonel Emil Strankmüller, stated on record—albeit half a century after the affair—that Beneš had asked Colonel Moravec to examine some documents relating to Marshal Tukhachevsky's treasonous contacts with the Reichswehr. The president, Tichý testified, had obtained the documents from Mastný in Berlin.[69] This, of course, is an intriguing testimony, but it is not unproblematic. First, Tichý claimed that Moravec had already told him about the documents in 1936, but as we have established, Beneš was first exposed to the Tukhachevsky affair only in the middle of January 1937 and the documents were manufactured three months later, in April 1937. Second, we know from Aleksandrovsky that the president did not mention the forged documents, even in July 1937 after Tukhachevsky's execution. Third, Moravec had been always distinctly unpopular with his colleagues in the Second Bureau; they questioned his character and disliked his unbridled ambition.[70] It would not be difficult to imagine that Tichý, who had stayed in Prague after the communist coup d'état in 1948, resented his former colleague, now safely ensconced in Washington, D.C., and that he deliberately placed the burden of involvement in the purge of the Soviet military leaders at his feet.

By stressing that Moravec had always acted on his own and with great secrecy, Tichý may have also wanted to protect the reputation of the Second Bureau. The reasoning could be as follows: had Moravec followed service regulations and consulted the appropriate specialists, the trick would have been detected. But Moravec, always ready to bend the rules in order to advance his career, kept the job of verifying the documents for himself, made the wrong judgment, and gave the president erroneous advice. Finally, it is possible that Beneš had received the forgeries from Berlin and that he had asked, as Tichý testified, Moravec for an opinion regarding their authenticity. Under this scenario, either Moravec warned the president that the materials had been forged or he failed to detect the Skoblin-Heydrich trap. In either case, President Beneš chose not to pass the documents to Moscow, and that is the most important point.

IN 1937 JOSEPH STALIN could have ordered that Tukhachevsky be poisoned or arrested at high noon and killed without a trial. That, however, was not his style, in part because he was a cautious man and knew that such a reckless, "lawless" style would cost him sooner or later. The elaborate preparations had also given him satisfaction. Writing the script for KRASKOMOV in 1934–35, determining exactly what the prosecutor A. J. Vyshinski would say about Tukhachevsky during the January 1937 trial, weaving Beneš and Daladier into the scheme, and then observing the marshal's growing isolation and fear during the next five months gave Stalin a sense of power and control. There was also an element of dark humor in his methods: he must have enjoyed a chuckle or two when he received a timely warning against his domestic enemies from the French minister of war. And his cunning and finesse were not lost on his colleagues in the Kremlin. Only the Great Stalin could play such a high-level game.

But a taste for dark humor does not characterize Stalin as well as does his ruthless cruelty in pursuit of political objectives. There is evidence that one of the goals of the Tukhachevsky episode was to cover up Stalin's secret negotiations with Hitler. Beneš and others in European politics had begun to receive indications of secret diplomatic activities between Berlin and Moscow around 1935.[71] The rumors intensified in the spring of 1937. Naturally, the Prague government had been paying close attention to such signs. Suddenly, in early March and throughout April 1937, the Soviet capital was swept by speculation that some kind of secret German-Soviet agreement was imminent. There was something profoundly ironic about it: Soviet diplomats repeatedly warned Prague against seeking any arrangements with the Third Reich, yet the Czechoslovak legation kept reporting from Moscow that Soviet politicians were doing what they had preached against with such zeal.[72] On 7 April 1937 the Czechoslovak minister reported from Moscow that, although nothing could be confirmed, something was definitely afoot between Germany and the Soviet Union.[73] Soon, more of the same. Minister Pavlů wrote from Moscow, "Negotiations are taking place between the Soviets and the Germans. Their objective is not a specific treaty, but a general verbal agreement aiming at some form of détente."[74] Eventually, nothing concrete would emerge from the rumors. Although Stalin was interested, Hitler was not, at least not before 1938–39.

But one can imagine that Beneš, who had been hearing stories about a Soviet-German rapprochement since January 1937, was desperate. There was something he could not understand, and it worried him. Exactly who were the Soviet officials conducting these secret negotiations with Berlin? Was it Stalin and his emissaries, as the Czechoslovak legation in Moscow automatically assumed? Or was it the anti-Stalinist conspiracy led by Tukhachevsky, of which Beneš had been hearing since mid-January 1937? He must have been relieved when he learned in June 1937 that the traitor Tukhachevsky had been shot. Soviet secret initiatives in the Third Reich gave the executions of Marshal Mikhail Tukhachevsky and the forty thousand Red Army officers a new dimension: these men were killed for alleged policies that Stalin himself had tried to pursue.

With all potential rivals shot, Stalin felt satisfied.[75] When the dispirited and poorly led units of the Red Army found themselves consistently outmaneuvered by the German onslaught during the summer of 1941, however, the Kremlin tyrant must have realized that his purge might well have been one of the most notorious Pyrrhic victories in modern history.

Notes

1. NA 861.20/376, Loy W. Henderson, the U.S. Embassy, Moscow, to the Secretary of State, 21 September 1936. See also *Pravda,* 10 September 1936.

2. MHA-MOP. The Czechoslovak delegation included the talented General Vojtěch Luža and other high-ranking officers. On 19 September 1936, at a reception for foreign observers hosted by the Commissar of Defense Kliment Voroshilov, General Luža sat next to Marshal Tukhachevsky. Luža personally briefed President Beneš upon returning from the maneuvers. See MHA-MOP, 1936, no. 4460. In attending the Soviet maneuvers, the Czechoslovaks reciprocated a previous visit by a Soviet delegation, led by Generals Shaposhnikov, Ragovski, and Kutiakov. It had attended the Czechoslovak army maneuvers in the summer of 1935. The Soviet guests were received by President Beneš on 13 August 1935. See MHA-MOP, 1935, no. 3743. Not all observers were unconditionally impressed with the Soviet airborne deployment. One Czechoslovak officer, Lt. Colonel A. R. Hartman, expressed his doubts regarding the real military value of the troops dropped to the enemy's rear in *Důstojnické listy,* 24 October 1935. What would happen to them in a real war? he asked. "In Russia, however, nobody is unnecessarily sentimental about such questions. On the contrary. Heroic self-sacrifice is supposed to be automatic duty for all citizens of new Russia." Nevertheless, the Red Army seemed very impressive to Czechoslovak officers. General Ludvík Krejčí wrote a highly complimentary article on the topic in 1935, after his return from the first official visit. See *Důstojnické listy,* 19 September 1935.

3. See F. O. Miksche, *Paratroops* (New York: Random House, 1943), 9.

4. The purge devoured 3 out of 5 Soviet marshals, 15 out of 16 army commanders, 60 out of 67 corps commanders, and 136 out of 199 divisional commanders. All but 5 of the 80 members of the Soviet Supreme Military Council were shot. Executed were also all 11 vice-commissars of war, 90 percent of Red Army generals, and 80 percent of colonels. Within only sixteen months, 36,761 officers were purged from the army and more than 3,000 from the navy. On the eve of the war with Hitler, only about 7 percent of the Red Army officers had received any higher military education.

5. D. A. Volkoganov, *Stalin: Triumph and Tragedy* (New York: Grove Weidenfeld, 1991), 318–29.

6. The Wallenstein tale had all the ingredients of the Tukhachevsky drama: power, secrecy, immodest ambition, intrigue, betrayal, and the hero's death. Albrecht Wallenstein was a Bohemian soldier who rose through the ranks to become in 1623 the generalissimo of the imperial forces in the Holy Roman Empire and the Low Countries. After many military successes, the Emperor Ferdinand II rewarded his talented commanding general with titles and wealth. Suddenly, in August 1630, at the first indication that Wallenstein had become too independent, the emperor dismissed him. Within three months, Wallenstein was engaged in secret talks with the king of Sweden, one of the emperor's sworn enemies. During negotia-

tions Wallenstein suggested that he would lead his armies over to the Swedish camp and in exchange would be installed by the Swedes as the king of a restored realm of Bohemia. Soon his secret contacts with the enemy became known in Vienna, and the emperor determined that the traitor had to die. Wallenstein was murdered in February 1634 by an English mercenary in Ferdinand's service.

7. It is mentioned in Walter Laqueur, *Stalin: The Glasnost Revelations* (New York: Scribner's, 1990), 86.

8. *Znamia Rossii,* December 1935.

9. Ibid.

10. It may be the case that the NKVD had not written the *Znamia Rossii* articles by itself but in cooperation with Russian émigrés residing in the West. Such coauthors may have been either Soviet double agents or bona fide White Russian activists recruited for Operation KRASKOMOV under a false flag.

11. *Report of Court Proceedings in the Case of the Anti-Soviet Trotskyite Centre* (Moscow: People's Commissariat of Justice of the U.S.S.R., 1937), 146.

12. This was perfectly clear to the diplomatic community in Moscow. Czechoslovak diplomats reported unconfirmed rumors that Tukhachevsky had been arrested on 10 February 1937. AMFA, Bohdan Pavlů, the Czechoslovak Legation, Moscow, to the Ministry of Foreign Affairs, Prague, 11 February 1937, telegrams received no. 64/37. As it turned out, the report was groundless and the legation later corrected it. Ibid., 26 February 1937, telegrams received no. 105/37. But speculation regarding Tukhachevsky continued until his dismissal and arrest.

13. Edvard Beneš, *Memoirs of Dr. Eduard Beneš* (New York: Arno Press, 1972), 47, 151; Compton Mackenzie, *Dr Beneš* (London: G. G. Harrap, 1946), 184–85; Winston Churchill, *The Gathering Storm* (Boston: Houghton Mifflin, 1948), 289.

14. Isaac Deutscher, *Stalin: A Political Biography* (New York: Oxford University Press, 1949).

15. Walter Schellenberg, *The Schellenberg Memoirs* (London: Andre Deutsch, 1956), 46–49. Also interesting is the testimony of Wilhelm Höttl, *The Secret Front: The Story of Nazi Political Espionage* (New York: Praeger, 1954), 77–85.

16. Beneš, *Memoirs,* 47.

17. Leonid Mlechin, "A Minister in Emigration: Hitherto Unknown Pages from the History of the Soviet Intelligence Service," *New Times,* 18 (1990): 39.

18. Walter Laqueur, "The Strange Lives of Nikolai Skoblin," *Encounter* 72 (March 1989): 11–20; Jaroslav Valenta, "Praha ve zpravodajské hře o M. N. Tuchačevského na jaře 1937," *Studie Muzea Kroměřížska* (1990): 155–72; Jaroslav Valenta, "Addenda et Corrigenda: Zur Rolle Prags im Falle Tuchatschewski," *Vierteljahrshefte für Zeitgeschichte* 3 (1991): 437–45.

19. Laqueur, *Stalin,* 85–100.

20. Ivan Pfaff, "Prag und der Fall Tuchatschewski," *Vierteljahrshefte für Zeitgeschichte* 35, no. 1 (1987): 95–134. The alleged resolution of the CPSU Politburo is published in its entirety in the appendix to the article.

21. See Michal Reiman and Ingmar Sütterlin, "Sowjetische 'Politbüro-Beschlüsse' der Jahre 1931–1937 in staatlichen deutschen Archiven," *Jahrbücher für Geschichte Osteuropas,* 37 (1989): 196–216.

22. ANM-M, Mastný, the Manuscript, 35–36. Beneš's account of the secret negotiations between Prague and Berlin ignores this event; the president claims that the first contact took place "in autumn 1936" (Beneš, *Memoirs,* 15). Zu Trauttmansdorff was born in 1900 in Kalksbrug, near Vienna. His mother was Princess Schwarzenberg of the Orlik line. After the Great War, zu Trauttmansdorff studied law and economics in Munich. He then worked for the

Ministry of Labor. He was not a member of the Nazi party, but he considered Hitler to be a stabilizing force in Germany. He believed that the Führer was open to rational arguments and that he desired peace with Czechoslovakia. Zu Trauttmansdorff's brother was a Czechoslovak citizen and owned large property at Hrochův Týn.

23. ANM-M, Mastný, the Manuscript, 35.

24. See Gerhard L. Weinberg, "Secret Hitler-Beneš Negotiations in 1936–37," *Journal of Central European Affairs* 19 (1960): 366–74. For a Czechoslovak perspective see Robert Kvaček, "Československo-německá jednání v roce 1936," *Historie a vojenství* (1965): 721–54 and A. Šnejdárek, "Tajné rozhovory Beneše s Německem v létech 1936/37," *Československý časopis historický*, 9, no. 1 (1961): 112–16.

25. ANM-M, Mastný, the Manuscript, 36.

26. Georg Albrecht Haushofer was born in 1903 in Munich. He acquired a doctorate in history and geography and carried out sensitive missions during naval negotiations between Berlin and London. If he was a member of the Nazi party, observed Mastný, it was not obvious. Georg Albrecht was hanged after the attempt on Hitler's life in 1944; his father, Karl, a general, professor, and president of the Society for Geopolitics, committed suicide in 1946. Both Georg Albrecht and Karl were close to Rudolf Hess, Karl Haushofer's student at the University of Munich, who introduced them to Hitler. See Donald H. Norton, "Karl Haushofer and the German Academy, 1925–1945," *Central European History* 1 (March 1968): 80–97.

27. Weinberg, "Hitler-Beneš Negotiations," 366–67.

28. ANM-M. Mastný met Trauttmansdorff on 16 October and again on 17 October 1936. Haushofer was mentioned as the *spiritus agens* of the initiative for the first time during the second meeting.

29. PO, Book of Presidential Audiences for 1936.

30. Dr. Graf zu Trauttmansdorff, "Die Mission des Grafen Trauttmansdorff," *Frankfurter Allgemeine*, 15 January 1962.

31. ANM-M. According to Mastný, Beneš met with the two German negotiators for the first time on 13 November 1936 at 4 P.M.

32. ANM-M. Mastný's chronology of the Haushofer initiative.

33. Weinberg, "Hitler-Beneš Negotiations." 372.

34. ANM-M, Mastný, the Manuscript, 42. Beneš's draft of the Czechoslovak-German agreement is published in Beneš, *Memoirs,* 46–47.

35. The timing of Mastný's travels to and within Czechoslovakia is from ANM-M, Mastný's diary for 1937.

36. ANM-M, Mastný's chronology of the Haushofer initiative.

37. ANM-M, Mastný, the Czechoslovak Legation, Berlin, for the President, 9 February 1937.

38. ANM-M, Mastný's diary for 1937.

39. ANM-M, President Beneš, Prague, 13 March 1937, to Minister Mastný, Berlin.

40. ANM-M, Mastný's record of his meeting with the Minister for Foreign Affairs, von Neurath of 21 March 1937.

41. Arnošt Heidrich, an official of the Czechoslovak Ministry for Foreign Affairs, recalled that the president was in a foul mood when he got the news from Berlin that Hitler had canceled the Haushofer initiative. See E. C. Koeppl, "Byl Dr. Beneš vinen smrtí maršála Tuchačevského?" *Proměny* 13, no. 2 (1976): 23.

42. Beneš, *Memoirs,* 19–20.

43. Mackenzie, *Dr. Beneš,* 184–85.

44. Aleksandrovsky's telegrams and memoranda from Prague dealing with the Tukhachevsky affair have been released by the Russian Ministry of Foreign Affairs to the Archives

of the Ministry of Foreign Affairs in Prague (AMFA). They have also appeared in print in the Czech Foreign Ministry's journal as Milada Polišenská and Robert Kvaček, "Archivní dokumenty hovoří: Beneš a 'případ Tuchačevskij,'" *Mezinárodní politika* 8 (1991): 28–30.

45. Koeppl, "Byl Dr. Beneš vinen?" 23.

46. Bartík, subsequently promoted to general, was an officer of the Second Bureau of the General Staff. In the late 1930s he was one of seven full-time professionals who ran the Defensive and Counterintelligence Section (Major Bartík, Major Dítě, Staff Captains Fořt, Sláma, Cigna, Taur, Vlček). A detailed organizational chart can be found in an unpublished manuscript by Col. František Havel, "Agent A-54 a Moravcovo zpravodajství bez legend: Příspěvek k historii naší vojenské agentury před Mnichovem a za německé okupace," deposited in the Archives of the Historical Institute of the Czech Army, Prague.

The interview of Bartík was conducted by General Ludvík Svoboda, who was at the time employed as a research fellow of the Historical Institute of the Czechoslovak Army in Prague. He became Czechoslovakia's president in 1968.

Fritz Thyssen (1873–1951) was the son of August Thyssen (1842–1926), the founder of the famous steel works. The senior Thyssen acquired prominence and wealth during the Franco-Prussian war of 1870–71. Fritz Thyssen was originally close to personalities around Adolf Hitler, but he subsequently broke with them and emigrated to Switzerland in 1939. Two years later, he was arrested in France and sent, together with his wife, to a concentration camp. The Austrian Kurt von Schuschnigg ran into Thyssen in the Flossenburg and, later, in the Buchenwald concentration camps. See von Schuschnigg, *Austrian Requiem* (New York: Putnam's, 1946), 266, 274. Thyssen died in Buenos Aires, Argentina. Fritz Thyssen's *I Paid Hitler* (New York: Farrar & Rinehart, 1941) is a work that reveals Thyssen's unsteady character.

47. Valenta, "Praha ve zpravodajské hře," 164.

48. Ladislav Bittman, until 1968 an officer of the Czechoslovak intelligence service (StB), learned in the early 1960s intriguing details regarding Karl Wittig, who worked at the time as a communist spy for Prague in West Germany. It was common knowledge in the StB that Wittig had been a Czechoslovak agent already before World War II; he worked for the intelligence service run from the Ministry of Foreign Affairs by section chief Jan Hájek. What Prague did not know was that Wittig worked at the same time for German intelligence, the SD (Sicherheitsdienst) and that the Germans may have used the versatile agent Wittig to disinform Beneš. Bittman was told by the East Germans: "Wittig is the key to the fate of Marshal Tukhachevsky." See Ladislav Bittman, *Špionážní oprátky* (Prague: Mladá Fronta, 1992), 89. Whether Wittig delivered any material relating to Marshal Tukhachevsky to Prague remains unclear. If he did, it would have reached the president via Jan Hájek. It should be remembered that any information from Wittig or any written materials from him could have come from a variety of sources, not only the SD. For instance, Heydrich of the SD could have cooperated with the Gestapo and also with various White Russians, some of whom, like Skoblin, were agents of the Soviet security. After World War II, Wittig continued his activities in international espionage. In addition to his work for the Czechoslovak StB, he picked up employment with the West German *Verfassungschutz*, the Central Intelligence Agency, and the East German *Stasi*. Ladislav Bittman, *Špionážní oprátky*, 88–92.

49. Milada Polišenská, Robert Kvaček, "Beneš a 'případ Tuchačevskij" *Mezinárodní politika* 8(1991): 29.

50. ANM-M, "Tajná zpráva o činnosti Dr. Ladislava Szathmáryho v Berlíně, Bratislavě a ve Varšavě v létech 1936 až 1939," report submitted to Edvard Beneš in London, no date; written after 27 March 1941 and before the end of the war.

51. The first denial is printed in Boris Celovsky, *Das Münchener Abkommen 1938*

(Stuttgart: Deutsche Verlagsanstalt, 1958), 95–97; the second denial is in zu Trauttmansdorff, "Die Mission des Grafen Trauttmansdorff," *Frankfurter Allgemeine,* 15 January 1962.

52. For instance, zu Trauttmansdorff wrote that Hitler had decided to abandon the secret talks with Prague because he had been encouraged by the sympathetic attitude of the British toward the Sudeten cause and, second, because General Heydrich brought zu Trauttmansdorff's Gestapo file—presumably showing that the aristocrat had a less than friendly view of Nazism—to Hitler's attention.

53. Beneš, *Memoirs,* 20, 47.

54. Churchill, *Gathering Storm,* 288; Schellenberg, *Schellenberg Memoirs,* 48.

55. PO, Book of Presidential Audiences, 1937. This is à-propos one of several erroneous claims in Pfaff, "Prag und der Fall Tuchatschewski."

56. Polišenská and Kvaček, "Beneš," 29.

57. AMFA, Bohdan Pavlů, the Czechoslovak Legation, Moscow, to the Ministry of Foreign Affairs, 2 August 1937. According to Pavlů, Litvinov was of the opinion (on the basis of reports by Aleksandrovsky) that Beneš "understands the present situation in the Soviet Union correctly."

58. Polišenská and Kvaček, "Beneš," 29.

59. Ibid., 30.

60. The Czechoslovak-Soviet intelligence central opened in Prague on 27 May 1936. See Jaroslav Kokoška and Stanislav Kokoška, *Spor o agenta A-54: Kapitoly z dějin československé zpravodajské služby* (Prague: Naše Vojsko, 1994), 53. Also see František Moravec, *Špión, jemuž nevěřili* (Prague: Rozmluvy Alexandra Tomského, 1990) 154–61. The central was located in a villa owned by Major Karel Paleček of the Second Bureau. It was located in Střešovice, a Prague district. František Havel, "Konflikt s Německem," unpublished ms., Military Historical Institute of the Czech Army, Prague, 23.

61. Polišenská and Kvaček, "Beneš," 28.

62. Ministère des Affaires Étrangères, *Documents Diplomatiques Français 1932–1939,* 2e Série, VI (Paris: Imprimerie Nationale, 1970), document no. 144, 225–228. French Ambassador Robert Coulondre reported to Paris on 28 June 1937 on his recent conversations with Litvinov and Potemkin. While Litvinov was evasive when Coulondre demanded an explanation regarding the recent dramatic arrests and executions in Moscow, Potemkin was happy to oblige. According to Coulondre, Potemkin stated: "Je vais, m'a-t-il dit, rappeler tout d'abord un fait qui a peut-être été porté à votre connaissance. Au mois de février dernier, au cours d'une soirée, un membre de votre gouvernement, me prenant à part, et déclarant me parler d'homme à homme m'a dit ce qui suit: 'Suivant des renseignements recueillis par le 2e bureau de notre état-major, le haut-commandement allemand a des contacts secrets avec certains chefs de l-armée rouge. L'objet des transactions serait la préparation d'un coup d'État militaire en U.R.S.S. et la conclusion ultérieure d'une alliance germano-soviétique.'" At the end of his statement, Potemkin added: "Eh bien, êtes-vous satisfait?"

63. AMFA, Bohdan Pavlů, the Czechoslovak Legation, Moscow, to the Ministry of Foreign Affairs, Prague, 2 August 1937.

64. Krivitsky, *I Was Stalin's Agent,* 233–66; Schellenberg, *Schellenberg Memoirs,* 48; Höttl, *Secret Front,* 81–83; Christopher Andrew and Oleg Gordievsky, *KGB: The Inside Story,* (New York: HarperCollins, 1990), 139; Valenta, "Praha ve zpravodajské hře," 165–69.

65. Höttl, *Secret Front,* 81–82.

66. Schellenberg, *Schellenberg Memoirs,* 48.

67. Laqueur, *Stalin,* 90, 347.

68. Moravec, *Špión,* 157–58.

69. Jaroslav Valenta, "Praha ve zpravodajské hře," 169; Jaroslav Valenta, "Zur Rolle Prags im Falle Tuchatschewski," *Vierteljahrshefte für Zeitgeschichte* 3 (1991): 439.

70. See, for instance, the scathing critique of František Moravec by Colonel František Hájek, deposited in the Historical Institute of the Czechoslovak Army, Prague.

71. This is analyzed in Gerhard L. Weinberg, *The Foreign Policy of Hitler's Germany: Starting World War II, 1937–1939* (Chicago: University of Chicago Press, 1980), 211–15; see also Gustav Hilger and Alfred G. Meyer, *The Incompatible Allies: A Memoir-History of German-Soviet Relations, 1918–1941* (New York: Macmillan, 1953), 250–87.

72. AMFA, Bohdan Pavlů, the Czechoslovak Legation, Moscow, to the Ministry of Foreign Affairs, 20 March 1937, political reports, 216, secret.

73. Ibid., 7 April 1937, telegrams received no. 190/37.

74. Ibid., 16 April 1937, telegrams received no. 207/37.

75. Professor Robert C. Tucker summed up Stalin's personality in a short introductory essay. Stalin's mind, wrote Tucker, "worked conspiratorially and was at its most creative, so to speak, in so functioning." Furthermore, "Stalin was totally devoid of the most elementary human feeling for those who fell victim to one or another of his political designs." See Lars T. Lih, Oleg V. Naumov, and Oleg V. Khlevniuk, *Stalin's Letters to Molotov 1925–1936* (New Haven: Yale University Press, 1995), xi–xii.

A view of the Castle (Hrad) and Charles Bridge in Prague. Edvard Beneš lived and worked at the Hrad as president from 1935 to 1938 and 1945 to 1948. From Erich Tylinek, *Prague* (London: Spring Books, 1962).

Steeples of the Old Town. From Václav Jírů, *Praha město fotogenické* (Prague: Orbis, 1968).

A view of the third courtyard of the Hrad where the large demonstration against the Franco-British ultimatum discussed in chapter 7 took place on 21–22 September 1938. On the left is St. Vitus's Cathedral; on the right are the presidential offices. It was from the balcony on the right that General Jan Syrový unsuccessfully tried to appease the hostile demonstrators. From Josef Sudek, *Pražský hrad* (Prague: Sfinx, 1945).

The Czechoslovak Ministry of Foreign Affairs at the Černín Palace. This impressive structure was originally built between 1669 and 1692 for Humprecht Černín of Chudenice. It was converted by the Hapsburgs into a barracks in 1851 and rebuilt and enlarged in 1928–34 to serve the needs of the Czechoslovak foreign policy establishment. From Alois Kubíček, *The Palaces of Prague* (Prague: V. Poláček, 1946).

President Thomas G. Masaryk in his library at the Hrad in 1925. From *Masaryk ve fotografii* (Prague: Orbis, 1947); photograph by Tomáš Vojta.

President Masaryk (*right front*) attending army maneuvers in the 1920s. On the left is Gen. Mittelhauser, chief of the French mission in Czechoslovakia. From *Masaryk ve fotografii* (Prague: Orbis, 1947); photograph by ČTK, the Czechoslovak press agency.

President Masaryk. From the private collection of Dr. Eva Jonas, Harvard University.

President Masaryk being briefed during army maneuvers. From the private collection of Dr. Eva Jonas, Harvard University.

President Masaryk attending a military parade. On the far left is Gen. Jan Syrový, the Czechoslovak prime minister during the Munich crisis. From the private collection of Dr. Eva Jonas, Harvard University.

Gymnasium student Edvard Beneš wearing the uniform of S. K. Slavia, a well-known soccer team in Prague. The game was strictly forbidden to all students, and young Beneš's disregard for the rule had contributed to Professor Hrdlička's outburst mentioned at the beginning of chapter 1. From the private collection of Dr. Antonín Klimek, Prague.

The thirty-four-year-old Beneš and representatives of the National Council at the Beau-Rivage Hotel, Geneva, meeting at the end of October 1918; see chapter 1. *Sitting, from left:* Přemysl Šámal, Václav Klofáč, Edvard Beneš, Karel Kramář, František Staněk, and Gustav Habrman. *Standing, from left:* Jaroslav Preiss, Ludvík Štrimpl, Štefan Osuský, Antonín Kalina, Karel Svoboda, and Ivan Markovič. From the private collection of Dr. Antonín Klimek, Prague.

Foreign minister Edvard Beneš. The photograph was taken soon
after his return to Czechoslovakia on 24 September 1919. From the
private collection of Dr. Antonín Klimek, Prague.

The first and second presidents of Czechoslovakia. Masaryk and Beneš on 18
December 1935 at the Lány presidential estate outside Prague. From *Masaryk ve
fotografii* (Prague: Orbis, 1947); photograph by ČTK, the Czechoslovak press agency.

President Edvard
Beneš in 1937.
From the private
collection of
Dr. Antonín
Klimek, Prague.

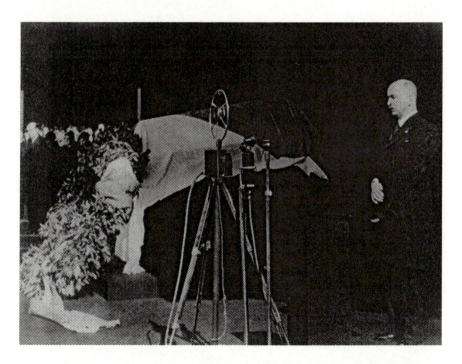

Beneš delivering the oration at Masaryk's funeral in September 1937. From *Masaryk ve fotografii* (Prague: Orbis, 1947); photograph by ČTK, the Czechoslovak press agency.

President Beneš (*center front*) and the Diplomatic Corps in 1937. From the private collection of Professor Hsi-Huey Liang, Vassar College.

Foreign Minister Kamil Krofta (*center front*) and the Diplomatic Corps in 1937. From the private collection of Professor Hsi-Huey Liang, Vassar College.

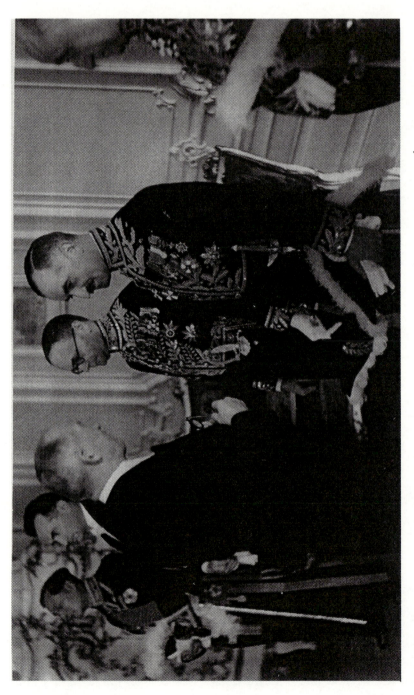

President Beneš (*left*) receiving foreign diplomats on 1 January 1938, upon his return from Sezimovo Ústí. From the private collection of Professor Hsi-Huey Liang, Vassar College.

The signing of the Czechoslovak-Soviet agreement in Prague on 16 May 1935. Sitting is the Soviet minister Aleksandrovsky; Beneš is on the far right. From the private collection of Dr. Antonín Klimek, Prague.

President and Mrs. Beneš in the Soviet Union, June 1935. From the private collection of Dr. Antonín Klimek, Prague.

President and Mrs. Beneš in the Soviet Union, June 1935. From the private collection of Dr. Antonín Klimek, Prague.

President Beneš and Commissar Voroshilov, June 1935. From the
private collection of Dr. Antonín Klimek, Prague.

President Beneš in the Kremlin, June 1935. On the left is Commissar Voroshilov. From
the private collection of Dr. Antonín Klimek, Prague.

Beneš's return to Prague from the Soviet Union on 18 June 1935. Mrs. Beneš is on the right; Lord Mayor Baxa is on the left. From the private collection of Dr. Antonín Klimek, Prague.

5

The Fateful Spring of 1938: Austrian *Anschluß* and the May Crisis

Joseph Stalin's purge of Red Army officers continued for many months after the execution of Marshal Tukhachevsky, and by the late summer of 1937 the terror had spread to envelop large segments of Soviet society. When the Czechoslovak minister Bohdan Pavlů returned to Moscow after a brief vacation he reported that the atmosphere in the country reminded him of the calm after a hailstorm. In Moscow, so many officials had disappeared that foreign diplomats could not find anyone with enough authority to make decisions. Normal diplomatic life had become almost impossible. Only the highest-ranking bureaucrats were trusted to repeat the official clichés.[1]

President Beneš had hoped in June 1937 that "unmasking" the so-called Tukhachevsky conspiracy would stabilize the Soviet Union. But by the fall the purge had spread from the armed forces to undermine other pillars of Soviet society. There seemed to be no prospect for consolidation. Beneš for the moment abandoned the hope that the Soviet Union, a country in such a deep crisis, would be in a position to come to Czechoslovakia's assistance against Adolf Hitler, and he said so openly to the U.S. minister in Prague.[2] As 1937 came to a close, many diplomats posted in the Soviet Union thought that the country had ceased to be a military power; some argued that the Red Army could not even mobilize.[3] Moscow's image as a potential partner in an alliance of antifascist states in Europe had been damaged.

The weaker the Soviet system appeared domestically, the louder it demanded that others stand up to Hitler. On 22 December 1937 *Izvestia* warned Great Britain that the time when one could afford the policy of splendid isolation was over. The paper predicted that the London government's effort to appease the Third Reich by sacrificing small European states to it would fail. *Pravda* presented Soviet desiderata even more openly on 24 December: it encouraged Western democracies to confront Hitler. The leading article counseled that it was in France's vital interest to conduct a policy of determined resistance against the German aggressor; it had to reject any compromise in the future. To guarantee Czechoslovakia's independence was a "task for all true friends of peace." But since the Soviet state seemed to be in no positon to commit itself to any particular course of action abroad, these admonitions left the Kremlin's own future behavior impossible to predict.

Prague had come to realize that the value of anti-Hitler statements from a country in such turmoil was doubtful. For everyone in Czechoslovak society— outside the disciplined but small Communist party—the stock of Stalin's Soviet Union had dropped to its lowest point.[4] And the distrust was mutual: the Czechoslovak legation in Moscow reported, for instance, that a recently opened exhibition of contemporary Czechoslovak art had received no publicity. Since all the leading art critics in Moscow and Leningrad had been arrested with their families, no one was prepared to make any statements regarding abstract paintings from Prague. And Czech books, already translated, remained unpublished because either the translator or the author of the introduction, or both, had been unmasked as "followers of Trotsky."[5]

Edvard Beneš lived under tremendous strain throughout 1937. The collapse of the Haushofer-Trauttmansdorff initiative at the beginning of the year had signaled that the Hitler threat and the internal Sudeten German problem could probably not be solved by diplomatic maneuvers alone. Moreover, in the face of pressure from Germany, Czechoslovakia was now dangerously isolated. The British had convinced themselves that Beneš's hard-headedness and inflexibility regarding the Sudeten Germans were the main if not the sole reason for Czechoslovakia's problems with the Third Reich.[6] The *Times* expressed such views on 29 November 1937. Hubert Ripka, a friend of the president and a talented journalist, attempted to respond to this campaign in the same newspaper by linking Czechoslovakia's continued independence with British interests. He explained that it was vitally important for London to prevent any further growth in Hitler's power, and he emphasized the traditional British policy of resisting the emergence of any power on the Continent that could dictate to all others. But such voices were either ignored or drowned in the cacophony of the Goebbels propaganda machinery. The position of France was complicated. Its officials firmly asserted that France would fulfill its obligations toward Czechoslovakia to the letter. But it was becoming likely that at some point in the future Paris might have to choose between its legal commitment to Prague and the main component of its national security system—its alliance with the isolationist Great Britain.

By the end of 1937 the Little Entente—the alliance of Czechoslovakia, Romania, and Yugoslavia—had given too many signs of disunity for Prague to be able to rely on it.[7] Its main objective was always to resist Hungarian territorial revisionism and Hapsburg restoration in Austria, not Hitler's Third Reich. It did not help Czechoslovakia that the entente, the emergence of which was credited to Beneš's diplomatic skills, was now an alliance only on paper. Yugoslavia seemed to be drifting away from Prague and Bucharest toward Rome and even Berlin. German diplomats repeated a statement of Baron von Neurath's: "Es kracht in der kleinen Entente" (the Little Entente is cracking). German officials liked to imply that the breakup of the Little Entente was but a prelude for the problems awaiting Czechoslovakia.[8]

Others did not yet share the tension and anxiety over Czechoslovakia's future that the president and a handful of his closest political and military collaborators experienced. On the contrary. In the summer of 1937 Czechoslovak citizens knew more about Rosencranz and Guildenstern than about Haushofer and Trauttmansdorff, and the Stalinist purge in the Soviet Union seemed too far away to be of pressing concern. They paid attention mainly to what was happening at home, and on that front most signs were surprisingly good. Czechoslovaks were encouraged by indications of economic recovery in 1937. The country's balance of trade for that year was positive, and the governor of the National Bank in Prague, Karel Engliš, stated at the end of the year that, despite enormous military expenditures, fiscal discipline had been maintained and the budget had a surplus.[9] By the end of 1937 the unemployment rate dropped below 250,000, one-third of its level at the beginning of the year. The city of Prague began preliminary excavations in preparation for the building of a new subway system, and an imposing bank, Živnobanka, was built in the heart of the city.[10] Its tall, thick walls covered with ornaments and marble seemed to augur a peaceful and prosperous future. All was well even in the important realm of sports. The Czechoslovaks were among the best in the world in soccer and ice hockey. In the previous soccer World Cup in Italy, Czechoslovakia had been stopped only in the finals, and the Czechoslovak hockey team was among the top three in the world.

After several years of economic austerity, the citizens of Czechoslovakia could also try to catch up with life's small daily pleasures. Concert halls, cinemas, and theaters in Prague were sold out night after night, and the mesmerized public followed gossip about popular actors and their never-ending affairs on the pages of specialized magazines. Among the most influential theaters was Osvobozené divadlo run by Jiří Voskovec and Jan Werich (V + W). One of their most successful productions, *Těžká Barbora,* involved a struggle between two mythical countries, Eidam and Yberland. Although a comedy, it was understood by all to be a serious warning regarding the dangers of Nazism: nobody in the audience could miss the connection between the Nazi *Übermensch* (superman) and the Yberland created by V + V[11] Coincidentally, the sold-out Osvobozené divadlo was roaring with laughter on 5 November 1937, just as the Führer of the real-life "Yberland" was summing up a conference with a small group of German political and military leaders recorded in the so-called Hossbach memorandum.[12]

No one in Prague knew about Hitler's specific plans and, briefly, life was good. Even a cool-headed observer such as the U.S. military attaché, Major J. S. Winslow, was struck in the summer of 1937 by signs of prosperity among all classes and the feeling of optimism regarding the country's future. While Czechoslovakia's neighbors had been collapsing into militaristic authoritarianism, the Prague government continued to preside over what looked like an island of good manners and sanity. The improved economy in the Sudeten German districts of the country had deprived, at least for the moment, the anti-Czechoslovak leaders of the Konrad Henlein movement of one of their main arguments, that life in Czechoslovakia meant economic misery. As Winslow summed up the situation, "Czechoslovakia is enjoying real economic prosperity; internal political discontent has decreased; and the army has made some progress. . . . At the present time the Czechs do not fear any of their neighbors except Germany, and they have fair grounds to believe that the latter will not attack this summer."[13] Alas, the optimistic summer of 1937 was only a brief anomaly within the context of the European crisis of the 1930s.

From the Death of Thomas G. Masaryk to New Year's Day 1938

The break came on 14 September 1937 with the death of Czechoslovakia's first president, Thomas G. Masaryk. Until then, the country's political and military elites had worried about the future of Czechoslovakia almost in secret among themselves. Masaryk's death jolted the rest of the population out of its complacency, and his funeral caused a sense of bereavement that cut across all ideological and class divisions and touched virtually every household, extending even to the German districts. On the day of the funeral, 22 September, almost a million people came from the countryside to join the inhabitants of Prague in forming a large but highly disciplined crowd.

The death of Thomas Masaryk was noted by the world press, but no one, save for Czechoslovak newspapers, had as much to say as Soviet journalists.[14] Although the *Small Soviet Encyclopedia* of 1930 had dismissed Masaryk with a few lines as the author of a book attacking Marxism, *Izvestia* on 15 September reacted to his death with a long, flattering article depicting him as an early opponent of the tsarist regime and a statesman who later in his life came to appreciate the importance of the Soviet Union and the Communist party led by Lenin and Stalin. The article offered no evidence in support of this claim. Similarly, *Pravda,* also on 15 September, praised Masaryk as a statesman who fought for the system of collective security and as an advocate of the policy of rapprochement between Prague and Moscow. The weekly *Journal de Moscou* added on 21 September that Masaryk's legacy should serve as the rallying point of those who now wished to fight for democracy, freedom, peace, and against fascism. Outright sycophantic was *Deutsche Zentral-Zeitung,* a German-language daily published in Moscow, which claimed on 15 September that Masaryk belonged in the same category as Presidents Woodrow Wilson and Abraham Lincoln. Forgotten seemed to be the years 1917 to 1934 during which Czechoslovakia, under Masaryk's guidance, and the Soviet Union were hardly on speaking terms. Such flattery from the Soviet press shows the depth of Moscow's anxiety at the end of 1937. The Kremlin must have decided that it needed a strong and determined Czechoslovakia because that country by its mere existence kept the unpredictable Hitler away from Soviet borders.

The sorrow displayed on the streets of Prague was not only a reaction to Masaryk's death but also an expression of uncertainty over the future. For all his achievements, Czechoslovakia's second president, Edvard Beneš, had never managed to become a second Masaryk. In the words of Major Winslow:

> As far as the country at large is concerned, President Beneš does not fit into the shoes of his predecessor. His reputation is based on a long and successful career as a foreign minister, but to the people of the villages he has become too much of the

cosmopolitan, at ease with the great in the world's capitals, the diplomat who has
forgotten the prosaic and homely needs of the interior countryside. This is probably
an unfair judgment. . . . Nevertheless, provincial prejudices remain and though
there is no indication that Beneš has many bitter enemies it cannot be said that he is
a popular figure.[15]

It is interesting that Winslow should have taken note of Beneš's alleged reputation for being cosmopolitan. In reality, the president was firmly and unmistakably
rooted in Czech patriotic tradition. His political enemies dismissed him as a simple
deal-maker, but as president of a small country caught between two countries that
gave birth to Nazism and Bolshevism he needed to maneuver. Therefore he was
often—although not always—ready to compromise.[16] But he was also a man of
tremendous personal and professional integrity.[17] He was a pragmatist who applied
with considerable skill the principles of Western rationalism to advance Czechoslovakia's state interests. Moreover, by the end of 1935 Beneš had overcome all his
rivals on the domestic front, and his seat at the Castle in Prague was not seriously
challenged until the first days of October 1938, and then with profound apologies
and regrets from those of his colleagues who would gently urge the president to
resign in the face of dark threats from Berlin. At the same time, Winslow said
nothing about the president's problems on the international scene. Far from being
"at ease with the great in the world's capitals" Beneš had many problems abroad.
He had stopped worrying about his image in Berlin because there was nothing he
could do about it, but his inability to communicate the Czechoslovak point of view in
Great Britain had to be of major concern. Even Clement Attlee, who seemed close to
Beneš ideologically, found in 1934 and again two years later that Beneš had too
much confidence in his diplomatic skills and cleverness. "He did not seem to realize
how long a spoon was needed," wrote Attlee famously, "to sup with the devil."[18]
Although Attlee commented on Beneš's handling of the threat posed by Hitler, the
observation referred also to the president's dealings with Stalin.

Soon after the death of Masaryk, Beneš had to endure the tense days leading up
to the meeting between the Führer and Lord Halifax in November 1937. Then,
before Christmas 1937, the president lost perhaps the last of his few close friends,
Minister Ludvík Štrimpl, who died unexpectedly after a minor operation.[19] The two
had met in Paris during the Great War, and they remained loyal friends for the next
two decades. They even became neighbors when they bought in the 1930s (with
another colleague) a large and richly forested estate in Sezimovo Ústí in southern
Bohemia.[20] The property was defined partly by a meandering brook and a romantic
river, the Lužnice. Strimpl, the chief of protocol at the Prague Castle, had organized
Masaryk's funeral.

But neither temporary political reversals nor permanent personal losses could
divert Beneš from work. He believed that history was guided by certain laws that a
trained professional could uncover and apply with scientific precision to specific
political problems.[21] He thought that Czechoslovak history, and history in general,
moved in a determined direction, and he was meant to play an important role as its
guide. The fantasies and wishes of individuals without discipline—presumably like
Hitler—would ultimately fail to divert the course of international affairs from its

correct, natural path.[22] As winter 1937 approached (it would be one of the hardest in recent memory), the president was acutely aware of Czechoslovakia's difficulties, but he faced them with patience and long-term optimism.

In December 1937 Edvard Beneš was immersed in politics. He saw Minister Mastný from Berlin, he received Wilbur J. Carr, the U.S. minister in Prague, and also Minister Aleksandrovsky. On 24 December 1937, as others in Czechoslovakia were preparing to sit down to the traditional Christmas dinner featuring carp and potato salad, Beneš had four important political events scheduled between 9:30 A.M. and 3:30 P.M.[23] In the afternoon, the president and his wife drove to the Lány estate outside Prague, where they bowed their heads in front of Thomas Masaryk's grave. In late evening, when others were already exchanging presents under their brightly lit Christmas trees, the presidential party arrived at the country villa in Sezimovo Ústí.

Although he was not a religious man, Beneš liked Christmas, and he enjoyed himself in his country house.[24] His schedule shows that he went there as frequently as possible. He must have felt at home in its middle-class comfort, more so than amid the majesty and splendor of the Prague Castle. The house fully satisfied the needs of his loving, childless marriage. But as a man addicted to work, Beneš had become restless after a week in the country, away from politics. He was scheduled to return to Prague on Friday, the last day of December 1937. The new year was about to start, and many wondered whether Czechoslovakia was going to survive it. Much depended on Beneš himself. As it happened, a huge snowstorm on 31 December 1937 made it impossible for the presidential automobiles to negotiate the straight, flat terrain from Tábor in southern Bohemia to Prague. Normally this was an easy, one-hour drive on a new concrete road that had been modernized not too long before for Beneš's convenience. The departure had to be postponed, and Beneš was to return to the many diplomatic duties awaiting him a day later, on 1 January 1938, by a special train.

He did not like trains. As a life-long sufferer from Ménière's disease, an inner-ear problem resulting in vertigo, he never felt well while traveling. The rhythmic motion of a train, boat, or car could cause him unbearable pain. His first audience for 1938 at the Castle was scheduled for 10:30 A.M., and the special train had to leave Tábor quite early. The station was almost deserted. Most of Beneš's compatriots had celebrated the feast of Saint Silvester the night before and were in no hurry to start the following day. It was a state holiday, and only church-goers had a reason to get up early. By contrast, Beneš, who disliked liquor and even nicotine in an era that associated smoking with youthful vigor and sophistication, was perfectly alert.[25] It was snowing heavily as the train headed north toward Prague.

The president was only fifty-three, and for the past two decades he had lived in the heady atmosphere of high-level politics. He had traveled far from the poverty of his birthplace and much higher than his teachers had expected. Now, however, after seventeen years as Czechoslovakia's foreign minister and two years as president, Beneš had to see that the country's position in Central Europe was precarious. Was he going to be able to deal with the crisis awaiting him in Prague? He often impressed his political colleagues at home and abroad as a good organizer and negotiator. Like all human beings, he had character flaws. But his determined climb from Kožlany via Paris to the Prague Castle had shown that he did not lack greatness. The year 1938 had started, and it was up to Beneš to fulfill the tremendous promise he had shown in his early political career. The problem was that it was one thing to conspire against the lethargic Hapsburg police or make deals with polite diplomats in the League of Nations and it was quite another to stand up—possibly alone—to the Third Reich. Yet, that was exactly what would be expected of the president in 1938. But nothing was lost in advance. A close collaborator pointed out that Beneš "struggled through life with incredible energy, industry, patience, and self-discipline." He fought, believed in himself, and succeeded.[26] Beneš was no weakling who would cut and run at the sight of a Nazi. As 1938 started, most Czechoslovak citizens believed that Beneš, who had left the Hapsburg empire in September 1915 with a small handbag only to return triumphant as the Czechoslovak foreign minister four years later, would find a solution for any obstacle that might be thrown into their country's path.

When Beneš's train entered the Woodrow Wilson train station in Prague on Saturday morning, 1 January 1938, it was still snowing heavily. Cleaning crews had to struggle to keep the slippery platforms safe for the official party. The mercurial station chief, eager to give the president the flawless red-carpet treatment that protocol required, ran about in his formal uniform and black dress shoes, checking on the last details. As the train came to a stop, the station chief fell and broke his arm. Prokop Drtina, one of the president's secretaries, was standing among the welcoming entourage on the platform. The sight of the station chief being carried away on an army litter made Drtina reflect on the events of the last few months, and the thought flashed through his mind that the new year had begun in a strange manner.[27] It could not have been more prophetic. In 1938 Czechoslovakia would not spend much time celebrating the twentieth anniversary of its founding. It was going to fight for its survival.

The *Anschluß* of Austria: "This will be very inconvenient to the Czechs"[28]

In the summer of 1933 the Czechoslovak Military Institute in Prague organized a short conference on military fortifications. Brigadier General Hanák briefly summed up Czechoslovakia's geographic problems for an audience of specialists. The country's length and lack of depth (only 150 kilometters in the middle) gave it disproportionally long borders. It looked like a crocodile. Those borders would have to be fortified. The general understood, naturally, that no one could hope to win a war by hiding behind fortified objects. Military strategists in Prague knew that the course of the next war would be characterized by mobility and surprise, and they anticipated that to prevail in any future armed conflict one "would have to win in the air during the first hours and days of mobilization."[29]

Nevertheless, there was good reason to build fortifications in the border areas. They should, at a minimum, allow the Czechoslovak army to win enough time to carry out a complete mobilization. An energetic defense of the borders by troops in well-positioned fortresses would prevent a surprise enemy attack from overrunning the army's strategic centers, and it would also channel enemy forces to areas where the defenders had a comparative advantage. It was impossible to fortify the entire long border, General Hanák stated, and maybe it was unnecessary, because in some areas mountainous terrain gave the entrenched defenders enough natural assistance. But it was vital to fortify the southern Moravian border, the area of Znojmo, Brno, and Hodonín. It was here that an enemy force could drive north from Austria to meet a simultaneous enemy attack moving south from Prussian Silesia. "If successful, such an operation would result in cutting Czechoslovakia into two separate halves, which would mean a total military catastrophe."[30] In one of their greatest blunders, military planners would disregard General Hanák's suggestion.[31]

The decision to build up a complex system of fortified objects along the Czechoslovak border and defensive lines within the country was taken in the fall of 1934, and construction began early the following year. The project's chief, General Karel Husárek, divided the area the Czechoslovak army would have to defend into four fronts. The highest priority was assigned to the northern front, from Ústí nad Labem to the Moravian-Slovak border east of Ostrava, where fortifications of the highest quality were to be concentrated. It was along this line that the German attack was most likely to take place. If attacked, the army's mission was to absorb, punish, and repel the enemy's aggression. The western front, from Ústí to České Budějovice in southern Bohemia, was given the second priority, and it was to be less fortified. In this zone, the army was to conduct an orderly retreat, protecting the course of general mobilization in progress throughout the country. The southern front, facing Austria, and the Slovak front, facing Hungary and Poland, were to be only lightly fortified because it was assumed that those countries would remain neutral. The whole project was divided into several phases, of which the first was to be completed in 1942, the last in 1946. The budget, prepared by the project's director in November 1937, was for 8,562,874,040 Kc. (For illustration, the hourly wage of a construction worker building the fortifications was .80 Kc.)[32]

It may well be that the Wehrmacht would have overrun the Czechoslovak fortifications, even when fully constructed, armed, and vigorously defended, within days. It is quite possible that tanks, moving behind a shield of artillery fire, closely supported by the Luftwaffe and followed by disciplined infantry, would have quickly punched holes in the fortified lines while airborne troops and dive-bombers paralyzed the rear areas. This would have thrown the whole strategy Husárek envisioned into disarray. It will never be known what might have happened.[33] But fortifying the border area was a logical attempt to deal with the fact that in the summer of 1938 the Czechoslovak army had only 73,635 soldiers in the peace-time army, only half of whom had completed basic training, to defend 2,940 kilometers of hostile borders. This worked out to just 12.5 soldiers a kilometer.[34] Under such circumstances, it made sense to give the defenders the advantage of facing the aggressor from behind fortified positions. For all the weaknesses of the defensive system in Czechoslovakia, it could be said that the army had prepared for the crisis as well as it could have. It is noteworthy that Czechoslovakia was possibly more ready 1938 for an armed conflict with the Third Reich than others in Western Europe would be even two years later.[35]

Although still unfinished in the fall of 1938, the project had advanced well and with surprising swiftness on the northern and western fronts: Colonel František Havel, a high-ranking intelligence officer, estimated that some 10,000 small fortified bunkers and 280 heavy fortresses had been finished.[36] But little had been accomplished in the south. The Czechoslovak-Austrian border was protected only by lightly fortified positions that were on rare occasions strengthened by medium-sized forts. The defensive line was doubled in the area of Znojmo and Mikulov, but in comparative terms the defenses along the Austrian border were weaker than other sections of the country's border with Germany proper.[37] Thus the country's soft underbelly was exposed to the very maneuver against which General Hanák warned in 1933. Of course, the Czechoslovak-German border was assigned the highest priority because it was Germany, after all, that threatened Czechoslovakia's national security. In contrast, Austria was small and militarily weak. Most important, it was a neutral country—but for how long? Hilter was a master of surprise.

On 12 February 1938 the Führer had summoned Kurt von Schuschnigg, the Austrian chancellor, to his mountain villa, the Berghof, outside Berchtesgaden. The roads were so icy that the Austrian party had to be driven from the train station up the mountain in military vehicles on caterpillars (one wonders how this added to the Austrians' feeling that they were at the mercy of their host). Three German generals just happened to be visiting, von Schuschnigg was told at the last moment. Franz von Papen, the German ambassador to Austria, asked him if he minded. (No, he did not. What was the poor man supposed to say?) Finally, Hitler and von Schuschnigg sat down in the same room where the Führer had heard two and a half months earlier from Lord Halifax that Great Britain would not defend the status quo in Central Europe as long as Germany managed to achieve its objectives without unseemly violence. Fortified by this certainty, the Führer bullied and threatened the isolated chancellor. The entire history of Austria, stated Hilter, was but one act of high treason. "And I can tell you right now, Herr Schuschnigg, that I am absolutely determined to put an end to all this." At one point the Austrian warned that a German invasion would mean bloodshed and war. Nobody, nobody was going to help Austria, Hitler exploded. Certainly not Mussolini. "And England? England will not move one finger for Austria. Not long ago an English diplomat sat in the very chair you are now sitting. . . . No you can't expect any help from England."[38] One wonders how Lord Halifax felt reading after the war in von Schuschnigg's memoirs the reference to "an English diplomat" whose assurances of British disinterest in Austria had made Adolf Hitler's decision to carry out the *Anschluß* of Austria considerably easier.

Later, in the afternoon, Hitler demanded that von Schuschnigg sign a document "without changing one iota" of its text. The Austrian reviewed it and observed that he was prohibited by the Austrian constitution from appointing ministers—only the president could do that—and so he could not guarantee that the Austrian Nazi Artur Seyss-Inquart would become minister of public security with unlimited control over the police forces in Austria.[39] Hitler exploded with rage and ran to the door, shouting "General Keitel!" Von Schuschnigg was ordered to leave the room. The Viennese guests instinctively gathered in a corner, expecting to be arrested on the spot. This was definitely a new style of diplomacy. Eventually, a compromise solution of sorts was found and, as the Austrians drove home, von Papen remarked: "You know the Führer can be quite charming."[40]

The final agreement, the so-called *Berchtesgadener Abkommen,* covered up the violent scenes. Its text seemed like a relatively mild solution of the tensions between Vienna and Berlin. Under its terms, von Schuschnigg agreed to open his cabinet to several Nazi ministers and to assert that national socialism was compatible with conditions in Austria. This was only a small sample of bigger things to come.

When the agreement was made public three days later at an official dinner for diplomats stationed in Berlin, Hitler approached Czechoslovak Minister Mastný and told him that Germany's agreement with Austria was a step toward European peace. As far as Czechoslovakia was concerned, Hitler stated explicitly that he did not wish to harm the country or even to interfere in its affairs; Berlin had no hostile intentions toward its neighbor. A day later, on 16 February 1938, Mastný learned that the Führer had also repeated his assurances of good will toward Czechoslovakia to the French ambassador in Berlin.[41] This would prove to be but the first of Hitler's false assurances to President Beneš during the winter of 1938.

On the same day, the German minister in Prague, Ernst Eisenlohr, spoke with Beneš. The German diplomat, just like the Führer in Berlin, struck a reassuring note: Czechoslovakia had nothing to fear from Germany. The president, thinking that Berlin would probably renew the Haushofer-Trauttmansdorff initiative, felt energized. He told Eisenlohr he was not prepared to haggle with Hitler.[42] If Germany did not like what was happening in Czechoslovakia, then the president was happy to authorize Eisenlohr to report to Berlin that "he did not care." Beneš did not like the Nazi ideology, and he was unwilling to make flattering remarks about Germany. But he was prepared to make a straightforward deal—on the condition that anything upon which he agreed with Hitler could be immediately reported to Paris and London.[43] Few European politicians had enough courage to speak to an envoy of Adolf Hitler in such blunt terms. It is to Edvard Beneš's credit that, although he was in a most precarious position, he did not try to build bridges to the Third Reich. But the kind of temerity he demonstrated in his talk with Eisenlohr could have been sustained only if he had different allies.

An indication of what the Führer had in store came just four days later, on 20 February 1938. Having driven with great pomp through the streets of Berlin, which were lined by units of the SS for the occasion, Hitler delivered a long speech before members of the Reichstag at the Opera House. He dealt with his favorite topic, "the violence done to the map of Europe" by the Paris Peace Conference, and then he dove into his central theme. "Over ten million Germans live in two of the States adjoining our frontiers," he announced, and he claimed that these ten million suffered and were persecuted because they were German. Other powers, like England, looked after their interests on a global scale. Henceforth, said Hitler, Germany would also pursue and defend its interests. Among such interests would be "the protection of those fellow Germans who live beyond our frontiers." Lest there was any doubt that Hitler was speaking of Austria and Czechoslovakia, he singled out Poland for praise. It respected the rights of Germans, and Germany respected the rights of Poles. He also praised Hungary, Bulgaria, and Yugoslavia, Czechoslovakia's partner in the Little Entente, for their "warm friendship" with the Third Reich.[44] There could be no doubt that Hitler had just publicly claimed jurisdiction over Austrians and Czechoslovak Germans.

Many in Prague listened to the speech; most Czechoslovaks, even professional politicians, had never heard the man before. Until then, the Führer appeared to be an unpleasant but mercifully distant crackpot. Now his voice—vulgar, cheap, and revealing a lack of class—cut into the unhurried Sunday afternoon. Among those who listened was Drtina. He recalled that the whole country seemed to shudder after the speech, which seemed to be nothing short of a declaration of war. The mighty Third Reich had delivered an angry kick on Czechoslovakia's gate. Drtina's telephone started ringing off the hook: "Did you hear Hitler?" his friends asked.[45] Only little consolation was obtained from Czechoslovakia's victory (3 to 0) that same afternoon over Germany in ice hockey. Soon Prague received a diplomatic report to the effect that Hitler's occupation of Austria was imminent.[46]

Hitler's performance at the Opera House was discussed immediately by French Prime Minister Camille Chautemps and U.S. Ambassador William C. Bullitt. Chautemps indicated that he was fully aware of the strategic importance of both Austria and Czechoslovakia, but he seemed fatally resigned to the inevitable: the incorporation of the Sudetenland and Austria into the Third Reich. It was "simply a question of time." He predicted with astounding accuracy that Central and Eastern Europe would fall to Hitler, Western Europeans would rally together, and, after years of war, the power of Germany would be broken by Stalin.[47] Foreign Minister Delbos, who had spoken in Prague so eloquently about the sanctity of international agreements only a few months earlier, now merely foresaw that Austria and Czechoslovakia would collapse. He was very critical of Great Britain; its prime minister had apparently decided to surrender the whole of Central and Eastern Europe to the Führer. Under such circumstances, Delbos warned, France could do nothing. In fact, it might simply "retire behind the Maginot line" and watch the rest of Europe fall into Hitler's lap. Only Édouard Daladier, the defense minister, told the American ambassador that if Hitler attacked Czechoslovakia France would immediately mobilize. As far as Austria was concerned, nothing could be done for that country, Daladier sighed.[48]

If possible, signals from London were even more ominous. On the day of Hitler's speech of 20 February 1938, without any previous warning, Anthony Eden announced he would leave the top foreign policy post.[49] His successor was chosen promptly. It was Lord Halifax, the man who had told the Führer as early as November 1937 that the map of Central Europe could be redrawn in Germany's favor. Sir Nevile Henderson, the British ambassador in Berlin, quickly sent the new foreign secretary a warm note of welcome. He regarded Eden's disappearance and Halifax's emergence as his new boss with the greatest relief, Henderson confessed. The reason was quite simple. Henderson explained that Eden could never have come to an agreement with Hitler.[50] President Beneš knew nothing concrete about the growth of French fatalism, and there was so far no real reason for anyone in the Prague Castle to doubt the reliability of the French alliance. But the arrival at this crucial time of Lord Halifax at the Foreign Office could augur nothing good. Even Paris was upset at such changes.[51]

The ground was still trembling from Hitler's speech when Beneš hosted an official dinner for members of the government and foreign diplomats at the Castle on 9 March 1938. All conversation at the table was focused on Austria. Minister Eisenlohr kept hinting to Foreign Minister Krofta that should something happen between Germany and Austria, there was no reason for Prague to be alarmed, but he also wanted to know whether it was true that Czechoslovakia would intervene militarily in case of a German action in Austria. Krofta was quick to assure the German diplomat that such rumors were unfounded. Eisenlohr was very "friendly" and eager to report this to Berlin.[52] Could it be that the Third Reich was concerned lest Czechoslovakia mobilize in response to rumors of a German military invasion of Austria?[53] If so, there was nothing to worry about: Prime Minister Hodža met with the chief of the General Staff, General Ludvík Krejčí, on the afternoon of 11 March 1938 and they agreed that the army would do nothing.[54] By that time, large parts of Vienna were already in the hands of local Nazi mobs and Hitler had drafted an obsequious letter to Mussolini, explaining his decision to occupy Austria. He falsely charged that Austria and Czechoslovakia had been developing intolerable ties and that "the Germans in Austria have been oppressed and mistreated by a regime which lacks any legal basis. The sufferings of innumerable tormented people know no bounds."[55] At 10:25 P.M. on 11 March 1938, Hitler heard from Rome that Mussolini did not object to Germany's take-over of Austria. The Führer was touched. He would never forget the favor. "Never, never, never," he repeated mechanically, mesmerized by the opportunity now open to him. There was no reason to postpone action. Germany invaded at 5:30 A.M. on 12 March 1938.[56] The Czechoslovak police monitored a telephone conversation of Ferdinand Marek, the Austrian minister in Prague, with Vienna. When the envoy learned of the *Anschluß*, he burst into tears.[57] *Finis Austriae.*

From Vienna, Berlin now controlled the greatest Central European crossroads between the Baltic and the Adriatic seas. Germany acquired three new and friendly neighbors (Italy, Yugoslavia, and Hungary), and it lengthened its borders with Czechoslovakia and Switzerland. In only one night, Radio Vienna reported with much glee, sixty Austrian Jews took their lives. A Czech intellectual weekly commented that those sixty were not Viennese, they were not people, they were not even animals, for the protection of whom there is a world famous organization in the Austrian capital. They were simply Jews. "In the soul of Europe a trace of embarrassment will remain forever. It cannot be otherwise, unless there are no people left in Europe."[58] On the day of the *Anschluß*, a German airplane crossed the Czechoslovak border and dropped clouds of leaflets. Each said: "Sagen Sie in Prag, Hitler läßt Sie grüßen." Hitler's regards to the Prague government were duly conveyed.[59]

The *Wehrmacht* showed itself a poor performer on the Austrian "battlefield," where the only obstacles were too-enthusiastic crowds of Austrian Nazis who rushed to the streets to throw flowers in the path of German mechanized columns, thereby slowing their advance. When those same columns broke down near Linz because of a minor snowstorm, Czech diplomats seized on this to portray the *Anschluß* as a failure.[60] The Czechoslovak military attaché in Vienna found that the German action had shown signs of improvisation. He dismissed rumors that the *Anschluß* was a preparation for a German attack on Czechoslovakia on the grounds that the troops showed a lack of training and their junior officers had not mastered basic leadership skills. The officer saw several cases of traffic jams caused by inexperience and indecisiveness. He spoke with German officers and sensed that they were embarrassed by the Wehrmacht's performance. "They are very grateful that their neighbors did not cause any trouble."[61]

Some of this was true: the lack of trained reservists was a serious problem for the German armed forces in early 1938. Nevertheless, it was clear to all people with military knowledge that the new situation was disastrous for Czechoslovakia.[62] Hitler's presence in Austria meant that the country's underbelly was exposed to the *Wehrmacht*. After the *Anschluß*, a Czechoslovak strategist remarked, even a glance at the map of Europe showed that the next target of future German activity would be Czechoslovakia—not immediately, but in a few months.[63] Joseph Paul-Boncour, who briefly held the foreign affairs post in Paris, observed that, with Hitler in Austria, the issue was bigger than the Sudeten German minority, it was bigger than the existence of Czechoslovakia itself.[64] Europe's destiny was now at stake. "Does London think it expedient, fair and clever to abandon to Germany central Europe and the Danubian area," he asked.[65] Of course not, the British would have answered in all likelihood. But the real question would soon be formulated differently: Should one risk a global military conflict in Europe in order to maintain the unhappy Sudeten Germans and the soil of German-speaking districts in Czechoslovakia?

Once Mussolini's assurance that Italy would not interfere with the *Anschluß* had been obtained, Germany was in full control of the situation. No one could stop Hitler. France just happened to be amid one of its frequent political crises: the government of Prime Minister Chautemps fell on the eve of the Austrian *Anschluß*, on 10 March, and it took three days for the new prime minister to form a new cabinet.[66] Hitler's presence in Vienna made the British, of course, even more determined to stay out of the crisis in Central Europe, and Berlin knew it. Tentative French attempts to remain a credible party to the Czechoslovak-German conflict by bringing in the weight of the British were doomed to failure.[67] Shortly after the *Anschluß*, Paris inquired what steps the British would take in case of German aggression against Prague. London's reaction was predictable—And what do *you* intend to do?—which merely returned the ball to France, the country that was, unlike Great Britain, legally bound to stand by Czechoslovakia. After some thought, the French responded that they could help Beneš indirectly. Without much conviction, Foreign Minister Paul-Boncour suggested that a French mobilization would divert large German resources from the Czechoslovak front to the west.[68]

Against this background of Italian acceptance, French impotence, and British apathy, it becomes clear why Hitler and his colleagues were so concerned about the Prague government's reaction to the Wehrmacht's drive into Austria: Czechoslovakia seemed to be the only country that could take action. On the critical *Anschluß* night, 11 March 1938, Hermann Göring sought out Minister Mastný at a reception and assured him ("Ich gebe Ihnen mein Ehrenwort" [I give you my word of honor] Göring had said) that the *Anschluß* had been "nothing more than a family affair" and that "Germany has no hostile designs against Czechoslovakia. On the contrary,

Germany expects an improvement in its relations with Prague, on the condition that there is no mobilization.''[69] Göring even assured the Czechs that the Wehrmacht would not enter a fifteen-kilometer-wide zone adjacent to the Czechoslovak-Austrian border. Mastný drove quickly to the Czechoslovak legation to telephone the news to Prague. He then returned to the official function. And again Göring sought him out and repeated his assurances. This time he could do more than state his own position.

While Mastný had been at the legation, Göring had been on the telephone with Hitler. On the basis of their conversation, he could now assure Prague's envoy also in the name of the Führer himself. Touched by the greatness of this occasion, Göring added: "Mehr können Sie wohl nicht verlangen" (You can't ask for more). Göring subsequently repeated his assurances on 12 March 1938 on the telephone and once again in person the next day.[70] And that was not the end of it. Mastný also received assurances that Germany intended no harm to Czechoslovakia from Baron von Neurath, who spoke "on behalf of Herr Hitler," and from the state secretary in the German Foreign Ministry, Hans Georg von Mackensen, who stated with diplomatic caution that "the clarification of the Austrian situation will tend to improve German-Czechoslovak relations."[71]

Mastný spent the next several weeks telling everyone in Berlin who was ready to listen about the special assurances he had received during the Austrian crisis. He subsequently put them on record during his first meeting with the new German foreign minister, Joachim von Ribbentrop. Mastný also saw the new state secretary, Baron von Weizsäcker, and told him that Prague understood Göring's *Offiziers-ehrenwort* (word of honor of an officer) to be binding and virtually unbreakable. The two diplomats quickly agreed that such was the case.[72] Once again, after the *Anschluß* crisis had fizzled out, the Prague government started to breathe more freely.

Czechoslovakia after the *Anschluß*

Although he tried not to show it, Beneš was nervous after the *Anschluß*. But he was convinced that Czechoslovakia was from Berlin's perspective a serious problem that could not be solved by the method employed against Austria. Essentially, the president believed the German minister in Prague, Eisenlohr, when he told him that Hitler recognized Czechoslovakia as a sovereign state, whereas the relationship between Germany and Austria was to him a *Familienangelegenheit* (family affair). Beneš took additional comfort from his conviction that Hitler's domestic situation was far from stable. He told Colonel František Moravec of the army's Second Bureau that "such regimes as Hitler's, based on violence and oriented toward the lowest human instincts, must fall after the first failure. That is a sociological law."[73] This was all very well, but who was going to bring about Hitler's first failure?

Western democracies had been disoriented before Hitler's triumph in Austria, and they now seemed to be at a loss. Even Beneš, who took pride in his ability to see through the thickest kinds of political fog, could no longer predict how Paris and London would act in the future. For instance, Prague learned that well-informed circles in Geneva had begun to consider Czechoslovakia's position untenable.[74] This did not make much sense to the president because the news he was getting from the Czechoslovak legation in Paris was not bad at all. Minister Štefan Osuský reported that the French had reminded the British Prime Minister Chamberlain that they considered their commitment toward Czechoslovakia "engagement d'honneur."[75] France would fulfill its obligations, Chamberlain was informed, under all circumstances. Better still, right after the *Anschluß*, Prime Minister Léon Blum received Osuský and stated that even if France were to act alone, it would provide Czechoslovakia with *"aide immédiate, efficace et intégrale."*[76] It would have seemed impolite to ask for more, and no one in the Castle pointed out that France did not have any concrete plan for coming to Czechoslovakia's assistance in case of German aggression.

From Prague's point of view, the problem was that the value of French assurances was diminished by the growing hostility of London toward the Czechoslovak cause. When Jan Masaryk saw Lord Halifax in London on the day of the *Anschluß*, he was told that von Ribbentrop had assured the British there was no comparison between Austria and Czechoslovakia, and he cited Göring's similar statements to Mastný in Berlin. What do you think of these assurances? he asked Masaryk with a sense of satisfaction. "Even a boa constrictor needs a few weeks of rest after it has filled its belly. And last night was a Lucullean feast," responded Masaryk, and the foreign secretary stopped smiling. What would you do if Germany attacked? Halifax probed. "We'll shoot," rang the answer.[77] Masaryk was not bluffing. The thought of capitulating had not crossed anyone's mind in Prague. Convinced that their allies had not abandoned them, Czechoslovaks reacted to the *Anschluß* with hard-headed fatalism. Should Hitler attack, he would run into a wall of steel wrote a left-wind intellectual. Knowing that the war could result in the complete destruction of the country would make its defenders all the more desperate and, eventually, a worldwide firestorm would begin. Once the dust settled, the dictators would be defeated.[78]

Later that month, Lord Halifax commented on the *Anschluß* before the House of Lords. Incredibly, he repeated almost word for word what he had told Hitler in November 1937, that no one in Britain intended to maintain the status quo as established by the peace conferences "for all time." The British were merely "concerned to see . . . that no changes should be made in Europe by violence, or by something approaching violence."[79] Prague had hoped that the *Anschluß* would strengthen British resolve to prevent any further German expansion. Alas, it did not happen. On 18 March 1938 President Beneš devoted three and a half hours to attempts at persuading the British minister in Prague, Basil Newton, that the abandonment of Czechoslovakia meant the end of France as a Great Power which, in turn, would result in a direct threat to Great Britain. The Prague government, said Beneš forcefully, had never asked for anything which its allies could not deliver without undermining their own national security. Could not London and Paris declare that a repetition of the *Anschluß* would be intolerable? Newton replied calmly that Britain's sphere of interest traditionally ended on the Rhine, and it was doubtful that Prime Minister Chamberlain would be willing to extend it further east.[80]

Lest there was any doubt whatever regarding London's disinterest in the fate of

Czechoslovakia, Newton went a few days later to see Foreign Minister Krofta. His verbal note underlined that Great Britain had no obligations toward the continued existence of Czechoslovakia. Newton's statement concluded with a touch of Gilbert and Sullivan:

> The Czechoslovak Government will, I am sure, believe it is with greatest regret His Majesty's Government have been forced to the conclusion that they are unable to take any further direct and definitive commitments in respect of Czechoslovakia. They will, however, I hope have confidence that His Majesty's Government, within the limits of their ability, will do everything to assist the Czechoslovak Government, who can be assured of their sympathy and good will towards a solution of their difficulties.[81]

Shortly after Newton had delivered his message, London found out from its military attaché in Prague, Lieutenant Colonel H. C. T. Stronge, that the Nazi elements among Czechoslovakia's Sudeten Germans were no longer prepared to demand merely cultural autonomy. Henceforth, they would insist on nothing short of incorporation in the Third Reich.[82] It seemed to make no impression on the course of British policy.

After the war, Allied authorities found in the Reich Chancellery in Berlin transcripts of important telephone conversations of March 1938 between Berlin and various capitals in Europe. In one, on 13 March 1938, Göring spoke with von Ribbentrop, who was in London during the *Anschluß*. Right after Hitler's invasion of Austria, von Ribbentrop was able to report he had "the very best impression of Chamberlain." Göring and Ribbentrop agreed further that Lord Halifax ("a very reasonable man," said Ribbentrop) and Chamberlain were "really excellent."[83] Could anything shake London's desire for a rapprochement with the Third Reich?

For the British position to prevail, London needed to persuade Paris that British pragmatism regarding Central Europe was superior to all the French talk of "engagement d'honneur." The second Blum government fell on 8 April 1938, and, two days later France had a new prime minister, Édouard Daladier, who had kept the defense portfolio.[84] He and Foreign Minister Georges Bonnet would remain at the helm of France for the next two years.[85] They were invited at the end of the month to London for two days of talks regarding the new situation brought about by the *Anschluß*. To underline the urgency of the moment—air travel was a daring novelty—the French chose to fly. When they landed in England, the visitors were pale and seemed shaken: they had just flown through a heavy storm above the Channel. Their opposite numbers, Neville Chamberlain and Lord Halifax, made quite clear at the beginning of the two-day conference that they considered the Czechoslovak crisis to be an intolerable burden on Franco-British relations.[86] Chamberlain said openly that he knew little about Czechoslovakia or the Sudetenland, but a friend had been there and had told him that the Beneš government "had promised rather more than they had, in fact, carried out." Halifax jumped into the discussion and invited all to review the Czechoslovak issue "in a spirit of complete realism," indicating that the country's disappearance from the map might have to be accepted.

Daladier responded forcefully and with conviction. He had been to Czechoslovakia and its German-speaking districts several times, and he could report that the country had done more for its minorities than other countries in Europe had.[87] But, he asked, were minorities really the issue? In his view, Herr Henlein was not interested in any concessions: he wanted to destroy the country. The French prime minister stressed further that he had been a combat infantryman. He had seen four years of war, the destruction of the richest provinces of his country, and he had seen his best friends die. No one could suggest that he took the thought of another war in Europe lightly. Of course, France and Great Britain should attempt to solve the crisis by negotiations rather than force, but "it was not really at Prague that it was necessary to bring pressure to bear." If the Third Reich were allowed to achieve one success after another, then eventually all the countries in Central and Eastern Europe would have to submit to Hitler's dictatorship. At that point, "As we had been warned in *Mein Kampf,* Germany would turn to the west." If Great Britain and France surrendered Czechoslovakia to Hitler as they had surrendered the Rhineland and Austria, "we should then have prepared the way for the very war we wished to avoid."

Daladier proceeded to challenge the fatalistic view that Czechoslovakia's eventual destruction was inevitable. The country had a strong, well-trained army with excellent equipment, and it was supported enthusiastically by the public. No matter how strong Germany appeared at the moment, France's obligations toward Czechoslovakia were embedded in a treaty that had been signed on its behalf by M. Aristide Briand, a man of peace, not war. Paris "regarded this treaty as vital and considered that it must be respected and executed." Bonnet added that in Great Britain all "school children were taught the importance of honoring their promises [and they] would readily understand the attitude of France."[88] These were powerful words, and the British must have felt uneasy having to listen to such lectures on public morality. Chamberlain even feared that an open conflict might become inevitable.[89] Daladier and Bonnet were invited to Windsor Palace, where they heard from the king that war had to be avoided.

The next day, both sides agreed to continue exploring ways of solving the crisis between Czechoslovakia and Germany without dragging the whole world into another conflagration. Finally—it was getting quite late and the weather was again turning nasty—the British and French agreed that they would simultaneously intervene in Prague and ask President Beneš for further concessions to the Sudeten Germans while the British alone would approach Berlin and express the view that both Germany and Czechoslovakia had to make contributions to peace in Europe. If Germany would continue to threaten the use of force, it would be doing so fully aware of the dangers involved: "France would be compelled to intervene by virtue of her obligations, and . . . His Majesty's Government could not guarantee that they would not do the same."[90]

From Prague's point of view this was not a bad conclusion. Not bad at all. But soon the British began, informally, to interpret the meeting in their own way. Leslie Hore-Belisha, the secretary of state for war, prepared the ground on 27 April 1938 when he said—in strict confidence but to a group of American journalists—that France would eventually not honor its obligations toward Czechoslovakia and Germany would take over the whole of Central Europe. As was to be expected, Hore-Belisha's view became public, and Minister Masaryk reported it to Prague while the

Franco-British meeting was still in progress.[91] The German ambassador in London, Herbert von Dirksen, summed up the signals his embassy was receiving from the British at that time: "Most brutal but also most characteristic is the advice given to a German acquaintance by an influential Englishman: 'Don't shoot Czechoslovakia, strangle her.' Or, in other words: Anything which can be got without a shot being fired can count upon the agreement of the British."[92] This was, of course, contrary to the letter and spirit of the Anglo-French resolution. It was a return to the view presented to Hitler by Halifax in November 1937, the view that had contributed to the *Anschluß* of Austria.

From April to the end of September 1938, London would gradually increase its influence over France, and by the time the four powers had gathered in Munich to sign the final solution of the Czechoslovak crisis Daladier would have become merely a supporting actor, outshone by the new star of European politics, Chamberlain. Moreover, Daladier's strong words sounded empty to the British, who knew that the French had no concrete plans to attack Germany in support of Czechoslovakia. Daladier would eventually accept the British position. This was made easier by the realization in Paris that Chamberlain and Halifax expressed the view acceptable to the majority of the French. The crisis in French society would ultimately make France's retreat and dishonor, against which Daladier had spoken so eloquently in London, the only realistic course of action.[93] Beneš was well informed from Paris and London regarding the struggle between the "pragmatism" of Chamberlain and the view of Daladier that *pacta servanda sunt*. Thanks to Minister Newton, he had few illusions about the British position but he would to the very end expect France to honor its commitment.

Moscow's Reaction to the *Anschluß*

President Beneš had one other remaining ally, the Soviet Union. Relations between Prague and Moscow did not get off to a good start at the beginning of 1938. V. P. Potemkin demanded in January that Czechoslovakia "liquidate" its consulate in Kiev.[94] Prague complied only to find itself under attack because of a New Year's speech by Rudolf Beran of the Czechoslovak Republican party. Beran demanded of the Beneš government more imaginative measures to bring about a decrease in tensions between Prague and the Sudeten Germans, as well as between Prague and Warsaw. Moscow attacked this purely domestic political debate in uncompromising terms.[95]

When this storm passed, and just as Beneš was hoping for an improvement in his relations with Moscow the Kermlin invented yet another crisis. It almost seemed as if the Soviet Union needed something to focus on—something other than the Third Reich and its threats to Czechoslovakia. On 6 February 1938, a Soviet diplomat, Butenko, disappeared from his post at the Soviet legation in Bucharest. For the next several weeks, *Pravda* carried out a campaign against Romania, which stood accused of having murdered the diplomat.[96] Because of the unfortunate tensions between Prague and Warsaw, the Soviet Union could only provide Czechoslovakia with military assistance via Romanian territory, and it was vitally important for

Beneš that the relations between Moscow and Bucharest remain friendly. This was not easy. Under the best of circumstances, Soviet-Romanian relations were marred by the territorial issue of Bessarabia. After Butenko's disappearance, Soviet diplomacy jumped at the opportunity to escalate the already existing tensions. In mid-February 1938 Butenko appeared in Italy, explaining at various press conferences that he had left his post voluntarily because he no longer wanted to serve Stalin's Soviet Union. When the Romanian chargé d'affaires in Moscow, Popescu-Pascani, attempted to explain to Litvinov that Romania was innocent in this affair and that it did not deserve the hostile press it was getting, the Soviet commissar responded that Butenko's letters had been forged and the press conferences had been given by a White Russian impersonator. The real Butenko had been murdered, Litvinov repeated, by Romanian fascists.[97] There was no merit in such a response.

Bucharest asked Prague to emphasize in Moscow that the campaign had caused irreparable harm to Romania's relations with the Soviet Union and that the Kremlin should apologize for the offensive tone of its propaganda.[98] But Potemkin impatiently dismissed a lukewarm attempt by Czechoslovak Minister Zdeněk Fierlinger to mediate the crisis. An apology was out of the question, he said.[99] Butenko was a bona-fide defector, and the Kremlin must have known it. Its continued propaganda war against Romania was not a good sign from President Beneš's perspective. How could Romania allow a transfer of Soviet troops across its territory when Moscow had so dangerously escalated the Butenko episode?

As the Butenko scandal started to fade from the pages of Soviet newspapers in late February 1938, Moscow was getting ready for yet another auto-da-fé, Stalin-style. In early March, Nikolai Bukharin and twenty other defendants were herded into the October Hall to play their final, tragic roles in the case of the "Anti-Soviet Bloc of Rightists and Trotskyists." This fictitious organization, created by Stalin and the NKVD, was charged with a grand-scale conspiracy against the Soviet revolution and the Kremlin tyrant himself. Eighteen death sentences pronounced at the end of the eleven-day trial were hardly enough to shock anyone in Moscow.

Unlike German and British diplomats who attended the trial, Fierlinger was enthusiastically certain that the defendants were guilty as charged. Some, especially the former Soviet ambassador to Germany, N. N. Krestinsky, and Bukharin, openly or in Aesopian language repudiated the confessions they had been tortured to sign.[100] The additional suffering they had to endure for such acts of courage was in vain, as far as Minister Fierlinger was concerned. He found that the confessions made "an immensely powerful impression as a captivating, exhausting, and historically accurate description of the conspiracy and its contacts with Germany, Poland and Japan, culminating in the coup d'état prepared for May 1937." Fierlinger predicted that the trial would prove to be a great moral victory for the Stalin regime.[101] The defendants' confessions gave "a completely persuasive picture of the opposition's terrorist activities." Fierlinger expressed his conviction that no force had been used to produce the confessions.[102] As had been the case in the January 1937 trial, Czechoslovakia was mentioned during the proceedings in March 1938. One of the defendants confessed to having contacts with the Sudeten German party of Konrad Henlein. Prosecutor Andrei Vyshinski asked, What sort of party is it? "It is an agency of German fascism," replied the defendant, repeating a script he had been tortured to follow. Fierlinger, who apparently believed Vyshinski's every word, concluded that the reference to Henlein's party was put into the script in order to prepare Soviet citizens for the future conflict in Central Europe and Soviet participation in it.[103]

The trial ended some twenty-four hours after Hitler had carried out the *Anschluß* of Austria. The timing alone showed that the Soviet Union's value for any anti-Hitler alliance—even assuming the Kremlin's good intentions—had become very limited. While the Third Reich marched from one international success to another, the Soviet Union was busy destroying its own elites. As Hitler imposed his rule over Austria, Stalin was preoccupied with strengthening his totalitarian rule over the Soviet Union. The Kremlin's unpreparedness for the *Anschluß* was best demonstrated by a "top-secret" communication sent to the Czechoslovak Communist party (CPC) from Moscow right after Hitler installed himself as the ruler of Vienna. It consisted of one sentence, which stated that after the *Anschluß* Czechoslovakia had become the main target of Hitler's aggression. It was signed: "With best greetings! K."[104] It is not hard to imagine the face of the communist apparatchik in Prague who opened and read this trivial but still top-secret message. Surely, the CPC leadership did not need to be informed through a secure channel about a development screaming from the front pages of most newspapers in Europe. "I know that, but what are we going to do about it and with what means?" he was likely to think. For such centrally important questions Moscow seemed to have no answers.

But one branch of the Soviet government did not ignore developments in Central Europe: the Soviet propaganda machine. From the beginning of 1938, it dealt with the Hitler phenomenon with a mixture of self-confidence and bemused contempt. For instance, on 22 February *Pravda* reacted indirectly to the Führer's speech of 20 February by saying that it could serve partly as material for humorist magazines and partly as material to be studied by psychiatrists. While Stalin murdered real-life Red Army officers, Moscow movie theaters presented celluloid "evidence" that the Soviet armed forces were second to none. Movies like *Deep Intrusion* and *If There's War Tomorrow* depicted an imaginative Soviet defensive against a German attack followed by an aggressive, overwhelming response.[105] Inasmuch as one could discern any political signals in such movies, it seemed that the main message was one of isolationism: the Soviet Union would defend itself if attacked but would seek no foreign causes for which to fight. This interpretation was confirmed on the most authoritative pages of the Stalinist realm. *Pravda* wrote on 11 February that the Soviet government was committed to a policy of peace, and it "will conduct war only with aggressors, with violators of peace, with violators of Soviet borders." Beneš would have searched in vain for any evidence in the article indicating that the Soviet Union was ready, together with France, to fulfill its obligations toward Czechoslovakia under the terms of the agreement of 1935. Rather than attacking the growth of Nazi power, Soviet propaganda focused its critical energy on Poland, which was depicted as little more than a vassal of the Third Reich.[106]

The *Anschluß* of Austria triggered a barrage of articles in the Soviet press, but their main target was not Hitler, it was Great Britain. After the Hitler-Schuschnigg meeting at the Berghof, Moscow had pointed out that the Führer's heavy-handed treatment of Austria was made possible not so much by the might of the German armed forces but by the British policy of neutrality and capitulationism.[107] Later, on 26 March 1938, the Soviet press attacked the British for their reluctance to guarantee Czechoslovakia's territorial integrity. And *Izvestia* predicted—with astonishing accuracy—developments in Europe from the *Anschluß* to the outbreak of World War II. It warned Great Britain that it was in its own interest to maintain France as a great European power. To do that, Czechoslovakia would have to be defended because its fall would result in the decline of France. When London refused to stand by Czechoslovakia after the *Anschluß*, the very war the prime minister had tried to avoid was made more likely.

Unfortunately, this kind of common-sense talk seemed to be directed only at foreign readers. The Kremlin did not practice what it preached to others. While the *Anschluß* was taking place, Soviet papers ignored it, and officials refused to answer questions regarding Moscow's attitude to Hitler's latest success. Even Fierlinger, who cultivated his image as an envoy "friendly" to the Kremlin, was unable to obtain any assurance during those crucial days of 10–14 March 1938. A Kremlin official dismissed him, saying simply that there was no "Austrian question" for the Soviet government.[108]

Once the immediate crisis was over, President Beneš was exposed to conflicting information from various Soviet sources. In Paris, Soviet diplomats assured the French that the Red Army would immediately join them if they responded to a German attack on Czechoslovakia.[109] In Warsaw, however, Soviet sources were telling a different story. The Soviet Union would go to war if France did, but a corridor would have to be provided for its assistance to Czechoslovakia.[110] In Moscow, Litvinov told U.S. Ambassador Joseph Davies that the Red Army might go to the assistance of Czechoslovakia *even though France did not*.[111] Finally, less than a week after his surprising suggestion of unilateral Soviet assistance, Litvinov told Davies that France had no confidence in the Soviet Union, the Soviet Union had no confidence in France, and Czechoslovakia would surrender voluntarily.[112] Prague picked up most of such reports and found them, of course, confusing and contradictory.

Beneš tried to crack the mystery of the Soviet position in case of a German attack on Czechoslovakia. Some signals seemed almost too good to be true. On 13 March 1938 the Czechoslovak minister reported from Bucharest on a conversation with Aleksandrovsky, who was probably in town to investigate the Butenko case. The Soviet diplomat stated that in case of a German attack on Czechoslovakia the Kremlin would seize any pretext as a *casus foederis,* whereupon it would effectively intervene. It was up to the Prague government to make sure that the conflict would not remain isolated.[113] Beneš was undoubtedly glad to hear this, but the message came to him from, of all places, Bucharest and had no binding force on the Soviet Union. Therefore, the careful president instructed Fierlinger to inquire directly in the Kremlin. Could Stalin be forced to reveal his cards? The president did not want anybody to realize how alarmed he was by the *Anschluß*, and so he asked his minister in Moscow to approach the issue as if on his own initiative, not on instructions from Prague. But he should ask a straightforward question: "What would the Russians do if Czechoslovakia were attacked?"[114]

Fierlinger could report only more of the same: conflicting signals. On 15 March he asked V. P. Potemkin "whether, in light of the French assurances, we can also rely on the Treaty with the Soviet Union. Potemkin's answer was categorically positive. But he added that the French attitude toward the Soviet Union was not quite sincere."[115] On the very same day, Maxim Litvinov sounded positive regarding the Soviet Union's likely response to a German attack on Czechoslovakia. He stated to a group of British and American journalists attending a dinner hosted by the Persian ambassador that the Soviet Union would carry out its treaty obligations toward Czechoslovakia "as a matter of course." In reply to a further question on how the Soviet Union could help, in view of the fact that it did not have common borders with Czechoslovakia, Litvinov stated matter-of-factly that "some sort of corridor was certain to be found."[116] The truth was that Moscow was not interested in finding any such corridor because talking about it allowed Soviet leaders to maintain pressure on Poland and Romania, the two countries through which Soviet troops coming to Czechoslovakia's assistance might have to march. The mysterious corridor was still being discussed in late September 1938 when the German attack was imminent. Even then the Soviet Union neither sought to establish the corridor nor admitted that it did not wish to find one. The appearance of looking for the corridor gave the Kremlin more power than a conclusion of the search and, therefore, the make-believe process of "looking for the corridor" would be prolonged as long as possible.

On 17 March 1938, Litvinov read an official statement in English in which he said a great deal about the League of Nations and Moscow's attitude toward this organization. He stated further that his government was prepared to "join in collective action" against aggression. And what kind of collective action? Litvinov spelled it out: the Soviet government would "proceed immediately to discuss practical measures . . . with other Powers in the League of Nations or outside it." Czechoslovakia was mentioned only twice in the whole statement, in each case in connection with the Franco-Soviet-Czechoslovak pacts. This was not good news. If the Wehrmacht and Luftwaffe pounced on Czech, Moravian, and Slovak cities, Beneš was hoping for meaningful military assistance, not debates in Geneva. Therefore, Litvinov's promise to become involved in a collective action, particularly given the sorry record of the League of Nations with regard to Italian aggression in Ethiopia and the civil war in Spain, not to mention the conflicts in the Far East, was a slap in Beneš's face. Under the terms of the Czechoslovak-Soviet treaty, the parties were bound to come to each other's assistance even if the League of Nations had failed to reach an agreement or had done nothing at all. After all, that was one of the reasons why Germany had so vigorously objected to the treaty, as well as to the Franco-Soviet treaty. It was only at the end of the press conference, in response to a question posed by a Polish journalist, that Litvinov rediscovered his firmness. Asked whether the Soviet Union would fulfill, in cooperation with France, its obligations toward Czechoslovakia in case of an unprovoked attack by Germany, Litvinov answered in English, "Naturally." When asked how and in what form would Soviet assistance be rendered, the Soviet commissar stated, "A method would certainly be found."[117]

President Beneš needed this positive signal. The death of Thomas Masaryk, the executions in Moscow, and the *Anschluß* of Austria were taking place as Hitler's power grew. The optimism Major Winslow noticed in Prague during the summer of 1937 had evaporated, and by the time frenetic crowds of Austrian Nazis were greeting their triumphant Führer in Vienna after the *Anschluß*, the Prague political elite was very concerned. Soon after the *Anschluß*, a well-connected German journalist, Rudolf Herrenstadt, came to Prague with an important message. He had worked as the *Berliner Tagesblatt* correspondent in Moscow and Warsaw before he was fired as a Jew. But he managed to maintain his contacts with German diplomats in the Soviet Union and Warsaw; his main informant seemed to be Hans von Moltke, the German minister in Poland. Herrenstadt came to Prague with an important warning and he begged to be taken seriously. He repeated to a member of Beneš's staff a statement of General Göring's during his February 1938 trip to Poland: Austria, Göring predicted, would be "liquidated" in a matter of weeks. Next in line was Czechoslovakia. Germany would not engage the country in a war but would bring about its internal disintegration. It would be first deprived of its border areas inhabited by the Sudeten Germans and then taken over by Germany. As for Slovakia, the eastern province of Czechoslovakia, a part of it would be maintained as a buffer state under Hitler's protectorate while chunks of its territory would go to Hungary and Poland. When the president received the report, he rejected it out of hand. Herrenstadt, he insisted, was a German agent conducting psychological war against Prague. Others in the Castle, however, were not so sure. They found Herrenstadt to be a trustworthy man.[118]

Beneš received a needed injection of optimism on 14 April 1938. Prague learned via its legation in Moscow that Paris wanted to take part—as soon as possible—in a meeting of military experts from Czechoslovakia, the Soviet Union, and France. Knowing exactly what Moscow intended to do if Germany attacked Czechoslovakia was important for French military planners, stressed Ambassador Robert Coulondre. Specifically, Paris wanted to clarify how the French and Soviet air forces could effectively cooperate in case of a Czechoslovak-German war. The French also wanted to make sure that the Red Army would be able to reach the future battlefield through a corridor going across Romania. Fierlinger demanded prompt instructions from Prague on how to react to this request.[119] As he read this communication from Moscow, Beneš might well have felt a sense of professional and personal satisfaction. The many years of intense diplomatic work had borne fruit. There, on the table before him, was proof of an emerging alliance consisting of France, Czechoslovakia, and the Soviet Union. In that kind of company, President Beneš would be happy to stand up to Adolf Hitler's Third Reich. Of course, it would have been nicer to receive the French request for military consultations directly from Paris, from the recently installed Prime Minister Daladier, rather than from Ambassador Coulondre in Moscow. Nevertheless, the Franco-Soviet-Czechoslovak alliance, which he had done so much to create, existed, and that was what mattered.

Surprisingly, Prague did not fire off an enthusiastically positive response. Beneš and Foreign Minister Krofta held several meetings to determine how to react to Fierlinger's request for instructions. Some of the hesitation was understandable: Prague was presented with the offer to put a military bite on the Franco-Czechoslovak-Soviet alliance only four days after the departure of Léon Blum and Joseph Paul-Boncour and their replacement by Édouard Daladier and Georges Bonnet. Bonnet had to be a particular source of concern because he was slowly developing a reputation for trying to undermine those French commitments that could result in a conflict with Germany.[120] After a full week of deliberations in the Prague Castle, Fierlinger received a carefully formulated response. Thus far, it stated, Prague had never taken the lead in introducing new initiatives in the alliance between Paris, Moscow, and Prague and it would not now organize discussions between the military leaders of the three countries. "We have said several times in Paris that because of our exposed position and out of loyalty to Poland and Romania, we could not do it. We can only join what has been previously negotiated between Paris and Moscow."[121] Just as he had waited for France and the Soviet Union to come to terms politically in 1935, Beneš now hoped to join an already existing military agreement between his two main allies. But it would never materialize.

The president's reference to Poland is intriguing. From the beginning of his diplomatic career, Beneš had not felt comfortable dealing with Warsaw. On occasion, he made harsh, undiplomatic comments regarding the country and its national character, and he remained pointedly silent whenever Czechoslovak generals, especially Ludvík Krejčí, demanded grand gestures of diplomats in Prague in order to secure Poland's friendship.[122] In response to the emergence of Hitler as Germany's Führer, Czechoslovak army leaders tried to increase cooperation with their Polish colleagues. The Poles tended to respond with friendship and sympathy, and then such initiatives died for lack of political support on both sides.[123] Although Czechoslovakia had more to gain from a rapprochement with Poland, it had done little to improve relations—save, perhaps, for a few isolated and random diplomatic probes by Prague's minister in Warsaw, Juraj Slávik. The Polish-German Declaration of Non-Aggression of 1934 made the Czechoslovak political elite so angry that Prague would subsequently fail to exploit opportunities that could have brought a different set of circumstances at the height of the crisis with Germany in September 1938.[124] In retrospect, it seems understandable that Beneš did not jump at the suggestion of military talks between Paris, Prague, and Moscow. If the French had been serious, they should have approached him directly, not via Moscow. But to explain his reluctance to initiate the consultations by bringing up, as he did, his respect for Polish or Romanian sensitivities does not make sense.

Soon, Prague would hear more good news from the Soviet Union. It came directly from the Kremlin and was better than could have been hoped. On 23 April 1938 Fierlinger reported that a high-level meeting took place in the Kremlin and its sole topic was Czechoslovakia's security. Minister Aleksandrovsky was called from Prague to brief a very select group of Soviet politicians: Stalin, Molotov, Voroshilov, Litvinov, and Kaganovich. The resolution was so good that Fierlinger could barely restrain himself from openly boasting that he had been predicting such an outcome all along.[125] On the basis of Aleksandrovsky's report, Stalin determined that if Soviet assistance were requested by the Prague government it would be, in cooperation with France, rendered. The Red Army, stated the resolution, had all the necessary means for such an intervention. The report concluded that as long as Czechoslovakia remained a democratic country, the Soviet Union would provide it with effective military assistance against Germany.[126] Fierlinger reported that Marshal Voroshilov was particularly enthusiastic. President Beneš must have been delighted to read this. In his meeting with Voroshilov in the summer of 1935 the optimism of the first soldier of the Soviet state was infectious. At that time, the German threat to Czechoslovakia was still vague, and Soviet promises came cheaply. But now, after Hitler's speech of 20 February 1938 and the *Anschluß*, Stalin's promise of immediate assistance to Czechoslovakia and Voroshilov's belief that it was technically feasible had much greater value. Having almost given up on the Soviet Union as an ally in late 1937, President Beneš now rediscovered his old conviction that just as Moscow needed Europe to overcome the crisis caused by the Revolution of 1917, so Europe needed Moscow to establish a balance of power that would provide lasting peace.

For some reason, the Kremlin and Sergei Aleksandrovsky did not consider the news regarding the Kremlin meeting to be terribly urgent. Rather than rushing to Prague, the Soviet minister decided to stay in Moscow for May Day celebrations. But Fierlinger was burning with the desire to inform Beneš and Krofta. He fired off his first report on the meeting on 23 April 1938—based on information from an unnamed source in Moscow. When he saw Potemkin four days later, the Czechoslovak minister was delighted to hear the details of the meeting confirmed. He asked for permission to inform Prague instantly. Potemkin told him to do so.[127] That request was somewhat deceptive because Fierlinger had already informed Beneš and Krofta. In contrast to Prague, where the report caused much happiness, Moscow seemed to be rather blasé about the meeting. In fact, Aleksandrovsky would not meet President Beneš until 18 May 1938—twenty-five days after the meeting had taken place.[128]

But if the Soviets were slow in informing Prague regarding the Kremlin meeting of 23 April 1938, they did not mind spreading the news to others. Just five days after the event, the British military attaché in Moscow, Lt. Colonel Firebrace, knew about it. He told Fierlinger that he had been received by Voroshilov, who told him that the Soviet army was ready to intervene on behalf of Czechoslovakia if France would do the same. Firebrace concluded his discussion with Fierlinger by warning that the German embassy in Moscow did not believe that the Kremlin would involve itself in the Czechoslovak crisis.[129]

Fierlinger was unpersuaded by the pessimism of German specialists on Soviet affairs. After all, it was in their interest to put a negative construction on any development in Moscow. The Czechoslovak minister remained optimistic and he did not mind saying so openly. He considered the news regarding the Kremlin meeting on Czechoslovakia of 23 April to be centrally important. Later in the summer of 1938 Fierlinger would attempt to turn Lord Chilston, the British ambassador in Moscow, into a fellow believer. Chilston remained skeptical regarding Soviet commitments toward Czechoslovakia's security. He asked Fierlinger in what form Moscow had committed itself to assisting Prague against a German attack. Fierlinger would put everything on the table: there was a meeting in the Kremlin, and ''Voroshilov himself'' had spoken in an optimistic vein about the Soviet armed forces' ability to intervene on Czechoslovakia's behalf. "I explained to him," Fierlinger wrote to Prague, "how the Soviets gave us assurances at every opportunity that they would stand by their treaty commitments." Assurances of Soviet "allied loyalty were given directly to President Beneš in a very solemn manner by Aleksandrovsky." Unconvinced, Chilston repeated his question: What would the Soviets do specifically on behalf of Czechoslovakia? To this, alas, Fierlinger had no answer.[130] Such conversations tended to confirm the growing suspicion in London that Moscow liked to beat the drums of war without committing itself to any particular course of action once hostilities broke out.

Before he marched into Austria, Hitler had so cleverly isolated the country that he was dealing with an abandoned victim. He achieved this in part by flattering Czechoslovak politicians that their position was incomparably different. Therefore, when Chancellor von Schuschnigg was bullied by the Führer at the Berghof in February 1938, Beneš was convinced it could never happen to him. The *Anschluß* a month later concerned Beneš greatly and he said later to his secretary that during the critical days "everything was at stake." He wondered aloud whether his whole political construct had not been built on mistaken assumptions. But once Prague received strongly supportive assurances from France and the Soviet Union, it could relax. The president sat down and wrote to Minister Masaryk in London: "All of us here are at peace, not afraid of anything in the near future. You in London can also maintain full confidence. Nothing bad will happen in the nearest future."[131] He was just as optimistic in the presence of Prokop Drtina. He predicted that Czechoslovakia's position would improve and concluded, "Let's hope that we've already won." Soon normal life returned to the Castle in Prague.[132] Beneš was not bluffing. Nothing in his papers indicates that he was on the verge of despair at the beginning of May. (He calmly sent a telegram to His Excellency Adolf Hitler congratulating him on the occasion of a German state holiday and the telegram was formally acknowledged by the Führer himself.)

Beneš was not alone in feeling greatly relieved that Czechoslovakia had survived the *Anschluß* of Austria with its territory intact. In fact, most people in Prague believed in early May 1938 that Czechoslovakia's security was adequately provided for by the Czechoslovak army and by the existing treaties with France and the Soviet Union. Newspapers reminded their readers that some twenty years earlier Germany had prepared for the final offensive that ultimately failed because the Allies stood firm. A military writer attempted to use the past event in order to present his view of the present. He stated that, after a period of uncertainty in the West regarding the German danger, the Anglo-French tandem had finally awakened to reality. The result, he argued, was obvious: Great Britain and France had never been so strong.[133] This feeling was shared by President Beneš. Thinking aloud, as was his custom, the president told one of his assistants, "I'm convinced that Hitler doesn't want war with us." The statement that came out of the Anglo-French talks, Beneš claimed, made clear: a German attack on Czechoslovakia would result in a European war. "I don't think the war will break out," the president concluded.[134]

This sense of relief was premature. Having occupied Austria, Hitler no longer needed to maintain good relations with Prague politicians. In fact, it was now Czechoslovakia's turn, and just as Hitler had isolated Vienna before the *Anschluß* he could move to isolate Prague.

Konrad Henlein's Eight Points: Demand the Impossible

Two days before Prague heard from Fierlinger that Stalin and Voroshilov were ready, together with France, to come to its assistance, Hitler was putting the final touches on Operation Green, the code name for Germany's attack on Czechoslovakia, which had been updated intermittently for three years. Focusing first on the political component of the operation, the Führer ruled out the possibility of attacking Czechoslovakia without a pretext. Germany's target was to be invaded at the height of a diplomatic crisis that would gradually escalate to war. Then an incident was to be staged—for instance the murder of the German minister in Prague—to be followed by lightning military action in the form of simultaneous attacks by land and air forces. The first four days, Hitler told General Wilhelm Keitel, would be "decisive." The German military could not falter at this stage because a failure to overwhelm Czechoslovakia's defenses would certainly result in a European crisis. "*Faits accompli* must convince foreign powers," stated Hitler, "of the hopelessness of military intervention; call in allies to the scene (sharing the booty!); demoralize 'Green' [Czechoslovakia]."[135] Beneš and his colleagues in Prague had no information regarding Operation Green, but they knew a great deal about another important event: a congress of the Henlein movement in the Sudetenland. Given Hitler's conviction that a staged incident would have to precede the German military action against Czechoslovakia, it was possible that the two were connected.

While Hitler was instructing General Keitel, Czechoslovakia was gripped by expectations of the annual congress of the Sudetendeutsche Partei (SdP). It opened on Saturday, 23 April 1938, in Carlsbad with the drama and pomposity the world had come to associate with Nazi party events in Germany. National socialist propaganda and the display of fascist symbols had been banned on Czechoslovak territory, but SdP members, all of them citizens of Czechoslovakia, put on their gray uniforms and marched in columns of four from the train station across town. SdP flags, closely resembling those of the Nazi party in Germany, were proudly displayed. The foreign press and Czechoslovak journalists were excluded. Nazi reporters from Germany, ostentatiously giving the Hitler salute, received V.I.P. treatment.[136]

The next day, after the audience had been whipped into a frenzy by professional cheerleaders, the main speaker of the event appeared on the stage. It was the SdP leader (and citizen of Czechoslovakia) Konrad Henlein. When necessary, he could sound like a professor of political science rather than a Nazi, and the introductory part of his oration shows why he had been so successful in building his image abroad, especially in England, as a reasonable man with constructive ideas. But his speech revealed that seeking a political solution to the crisis was not the mission of the Henlein movement in April 1938. Two years before, when a foreign visitor was introduced to Henlein's lieutenants, he noted that they were "the toughest Nazi leaders and embryo concentration camp commandants whom it has ever been my ill luck to shake by the hand." These SdP regional leaders displayed—even in 1936—their "savage racial hatred of Czechs and Jews, adoration of Adolf Hitler and an unconcealed determination to bring the whole area under the rule of German Nazi dictatorship."[137] At that time, all such feelings were to be hidden from the international media so Henlein could posture as a loyal Czechoslovak citizen whose main objective was the improvement of political, economic, and cultural conditions in the Sudetenland.

There was no need for such discretion in late April 1938. The Third Reich had ordered the Henlein movement to escalate the internal crisis in Czechoslovakia. Henlein was to present the Beneš government with demands that could not in good faith be honored. Therefore, after a somewhat theoretical introduction, came the practical list of demands. Henlein presented several requests, one of which was a call for a radical revision of Czechoslovakia's foreign policy: the country was no longer to be in the ranks of Hitler's opponents. In addition, for the first time in the history of the SdP, Henlein openly embraced Nazi ideology. In it, all Germans, Henlein said, wherever they were, found their way of life and morality "realized." The Sudeten Germans "delight to profess . . . the National Socialist fundamental conceptions of life."[138] In conclusion, Henlein summed up his party's position in the so-called Carlsbad program of eight points.

The Nazis in the audience reacted to Henlein's speech with fanatical approval. Without having to analyze each of the eight points, they understood that Henlein was no longer interested in further negotiations with Prague. He appeared before them as a Nazi leader of an open revolt against Czechoslovakia and its democratic institutions. The Führer was apparently satisfied with Henlein's performance because he named him on the spot his viceroy in the Sudetenland. Henceforth, Henlein's instructions were clear: "Demands should be made by the Sudeten German party which are unacceptable to the Czech government." Just to be sure he understood his task correctly, Henlein summed up the order he had received: "We must always demand so much that we can never be satisfied."[139] Clearly, he was supposed to lead a domestic uprising against Czechoslovakia.

That is the way it was understood in Prague. The German legation there reported on 26 April 1938 that the entire Czechoslovak press dealt with Henlein's eight points. The main objections were directed at his demand that Prague change its foreign policy, the granting of a special status to the Sudeten Germans insofar as this would be unconstitutional, and his demand for freedom for Nazi ideology because it was totalitarian, dictatorial, and therefore unacceptable.[140] The semiofficial *Prager Presse* stated on 26 and 27 April 1938 that the Prague government would not even discuss Herr Henlein's demand for a revision of Czechoslovakia's foreign policy. The country could not fulfill his demands because that would mean an abdication of its sovereignty. Prague's response went on to imply that Henlein's speech was deliberately harsh in order to steel the SdP as the first round of communal elections (scheduled for 22 May 1938) approached.

May Day 1938: Gottwald in Moscow, Henlein in the Sudetenland

Just two days before the beginning of May 1938, while the London summit was in progress, the Czechoslovak communist leader Klement Gottwald analyzed the crisis in Central Europe for the benefit of the Comintern's Executive in Moscow.[141] He spoke well, and his speech was free from the ideological clichés that had become commonplace in communist circles at the time. Uncharacteristically making no references to Stalin, Gottwald dealt strictly with Czechoslovakia's position during the most severe crisis of its history. His analysis now offers an interesting view into the thinking of the Czechoslovak government.

The president was determined to maneuver, Gottwald reported, in order to satisfy the demands of Western democracies for a diplomatic solution. The Prague government was even willing to send signals to Henlein that it was open to negotiations. However, Beneš was not prepared to allow the Sudeten Nazis into the government; most important, he would never surrender Czechoslovakia's pacts with France and the Soviet Union. Under this diplomatic umbrella, Beneš wanted to play for time, arm, and build more fortifications. Czechoslovakia would never capitulate:

> Every attempt by Henlein to carry out a coup d'état is to be resisted by armed force. If Hitler interferes, we shall fight. If we hold our ground for three weeks and if France and the Soviet Union get involved we will have won. We might, perhaps, become a second Belgium or Serbia but we shall take part at the peace conference among the victorious parties.[142]

From Beneš's perspective, Gottwald continued, the most challenging political task was to make absolutely sure that Hitler's attack on Czechoslovakia would eventually escalate into a European war. No one should doubt the country's willingness to defend itself against the Third Reich. Although some, even among the left-wing parties, had predicted that Czechoslovakia would remain on its own in case of Hitler's attack, Czechoslovak workers and farmers, as well as urban bourgeoisie and the intelligentsia, stood ready to fight for the country under any circumstances. Gottwald outlined Beneš's strategy with accuracy and insight.

On this occasion Gottwald stayed in Moscow for a long time.[143] He arrived there in late February 1938 and did not return to Prague until 16 May 1938.[144] It seemed strange that he would remain abroad during the developing crisis.[145] Gottwald's long stay in the Soviet Union made it impossible for the Communist party to be represented properly at the May Day celebrations. In fact, the party's behavior in Prague and throughout the country was surprisingly meek. According to the contemporary press, members of the CPC gathered "briefly" in Prague on Republic Square. Then, this time without the insignia of the party, they peacefully moved to nearby Wenceslas Square to join the national demonstration just as it was being addressed by Prague's lord mayor, Petr Zenkl. The speaker's main point was clear: in any kind of emergency the government could count on all its citizens without regard for political affiliations.[146] This was unusual behavior for a party whose leaders had promised on the floor of the Czechoslovak parliament, as well as in writing, to strangle or decapitate the Czechoslovak bourgeoisie.[147] It could well be that the policy of the popular front, advanced by the 7th Congress of the Comintern in 1935, was—albeit for a day—implemented in Prague. Police informers inside the communist apparat reported that as a result of the *Anschluß* Moscow reaffirmed its order to abandon the dictatorship of the proletariat as the CPC's immediate objective. Instead, all of its strength was to be committed against Nazism. The Kremlin's view was that the necessary preconditions for a new communist offensive would exist only after the destruction of the Third Reich and that this could be achieved only through war. Once that had occurred, the dictatorship of the proletariat would be resurrected as the party's main objective. The main task of the CPC was to ensure that the Czechoslovak-German conflict would be fought as an all-out war, whatever the consequences. It was to be a people's antifascist war fought in the Hussite tradition, side by side with the Soviet Union and the progressive elements in France.[148]

Gottwald had not even been in Czechoslovakia during much of the crisis of 1938, but the Henlein party had its leader in full operation on May Day 1938. A visitor to the Sudetenland recalled:

> [I was] facing 43,000 disciplined yet fanaticised men and women, tense with awaiting the deliberately delayed thrill of Konrad Henlein's arrival. The songs they sang and the slogans they roared at the prompting of the trained chorus—from my point of vantage I could pick out the latter very clearly in the right-hand front corner of the gathering—were all familiar to me from Vienna, the new and brutalized Vienna which I had just left behind. "To-day Germany belongs to us, tomorrow we shall rule the world," they sang. Instead of brown shirts and jackboots there were white shirts and jackboots; instead of the Swastika banner the scarlet Henlein banner with the white shield in the center and the monogram "S.d.P." As the loudspeakers announced *"Der Führer kommt"* the roaring of the open exhausts of twenty motor-cycles of Konrad Henlein's motorized bodyguard heralded the arrival of the Führer.[149]

The danger to Czechoslovakia's territorial integrity had become clear and overwhelming on the first day of May 1938.

The prospect of Czechoslovakia's disintegration did not concern the *Times* of London. On 2 May 1938 the paper published an article complaining that Czechoslovakia was but a copy of the Austro-Hungarian empire—with all its faults. Who would have thought twenty years ago, the paper asked, that Great Britain and France now had to consider the possibility of another war only to maintain the Czech rule over Germans and Hungarians? Nevertheless, the French were still firmly on Czechoslovakia's side. In the middle of May 1938, Arnošt Heidrich, a Czechoslovak diplomat and Beneš's confidant, spoke with Georges Bonnet. The French foreign minister stressed that Prague should do everything possible to find a modus vivendi with the Sudeten Germans. At the end, however, Bonnet spelled out his message for Prague: "France will fulfill its obligations under all circumstances."[150] Such assurances were received in Prague with much gratitude.

The Soviet Union's image had improved since the low of January 1938. Even in late February 1938, Beneš told the U.S. minister in Prague that because of the crisis in the Soviet Union the Red Army was no longer a factor as far as he was concerned.[151] By May, however, there was a new sense of optimism regarding the Soviet card in the Czechoslovak foreign affairs community. It was not a coincidence. On 8 May 1938 Mikhail Kalinin, titular head of the Soviet Union, assured a visiting Czechoslovak delegation that Moscow would fulfill its treaty obligations toward Czechoslovakia and France "to the last letter." There may also have been other positive signals to Beneš, because sometime before 13 May 1938 the Czechoslovak Foreign Ministry had indicated to U.S. diplomats its "positive belief" that Moscow would come to the assistance of Czechoslovakia within twenty-four hours.[152] Prague also believed that the recent visits to Bucharest by Minister Aleksandrovsky were attempts to negotiate a Soviet-Romanian understanding regarding the transfer of Soviet troops over Romanian territory to Czechoslovakia in case of war.[153]

The Czechoslovak legation in Bucharest reported to Prague rumors that the Soviet Union, in case of a Czechoslovak-German armed conflict, would render effective assistance to Prague at the first opportunity. It was up to Beneš to make sure the conflict would not remain "localized."[154] Litvinov saw Arnošt Heidrich in Geneva to warn him that Berlin would not be afraid of the mere threat of force from France. A little more would be needed, he implied. What about the Soviet Union? Heidrich asked. Specifically, "What would the Soviet Union do in case of a German attack on Czechoslovakia and if France fulfilled its obligations?" Litvinov quickly responded that Prague had not yet officially approached the Kremlin with such questions. But what about Fierlinger's discussions in Moscow with Potemkin? Litvinov's response was that certain matters could not be discussed among diplomats; only soldiers could hold such talks.[155] This was quite true. A crisis can reach a point at which soldiers dominate the conduct of policy. The Prague government would soon arrive at the conclusion that such a point had been reached.

Czechoslovakia Takes the Initiative: The Partial Mobilization of May 1938

On Friday evening, 20 May 1938, the Prague government responded to reports of German military concentrations along the Czechoslovak border and passed a decree that instructed Minister of National Defense František Machník to call up reservists and preselected military specialists. The so-called partial mobilization provoked a European crisis.[156] How did it come about?

As a military man, Major Lowell M. Riley, the U.S. military attaché in Prague, felt an obligation to maintain himself at a high degree of physical fitness, and because the weather was beautiful he decided that the Czechoslovak-German crisis would have to wait a while.[157] It was a Saturday morning, 21 May 1938, and Riley went to the War College stables for his accustomed ride. Alas, there were neither horses nor troops anywhere in sight. In fact, he seemed to be alone in the spatial palace. The major knew immediately that something was amiss, and he wasted no time in the building. The U.S. legation was already full of rumors. There had been trouble in the Sudetenland on Friday night, Riley heard; there was subsequently a political crisis in Prague and Czechoslovak troops were being called up. He jumped into his car and drove in a westerly direction, where he saw columns of army trucks leaving the city. Riley turned back, returned to his office, and called the liaison officer, Colonel Beneš, at the Ministry of Defense. Czechoslovakia was sending troops to the Sudeten area to increase its security, Beneš told Riley.[158] The American received a full briefing on the same day at 5 P.M. Colonel Beneš was now more specific: there had been a strategic concentration of troops in Germany in the crucially important area of Leipzig, Chemnitz, and Zwickau. Prague, stated Colonel Beneš with a hint of humor, was not proposing to attack the Third Reich but, he continued with complete seriousness, Czechoslovakia "will defend its territory to the best of its ability." Riley concluded his report on that eventful day in May by saying that the Czechoslovaks had made "a wise, though possibly dangerous choice."[159] Major Riley was briefed again on 25 May 1938. A spokesman of the Defense Ministry told him that seven German divisions—the 13th, 14th, 19th, 23d, 24th, 29th, and 31th—had been moved from their peacetime locations and deployed along the Czechoslovak border.[160]

The May crisis started so unexpectedly that it surprised not only Major Riley but also President Beneš. In the morning of 20 May 1938 he met with a journalist from *Life* magazine, to whom he gave a long interview that was followed by a photo session. At 12:30 P.M. he received a writer and a photographer from *Lyon Soir* in yet another effort to counter hostile German propaganda.[161] That session had to be kept short. Only minutes after the French had been asked to leave, at 1:15 P.M., Beneš received Minister Machník and the army chief of staff and top commanding officer, General Ludvík Krejčí, who had requested an emergency meeting.[162] The news they brought shattered the relatively peaceful course of the day.

Machník and Krejčí told the president that they had confirmed reports indicating a strategic concentration of nine to twelve German divisions along the Czechoslovak border.[163] With the Wehrmacht in Austria, the president's guests did not have to waste time explaining the possible significance of this development. Beneš summoned Emil Sobota, a constitutional expert, and asked him what would count, on legal grounds, as an appropriate Czechoslovak response.[164] Although Sobota was assisted by Drtina, it was two hours before the president was able to meet, at 4:30 P.M., with representatives of the main political parties. On this occasion, General Krejčí presented for the second time that day evidence of German military preparations against Czechoslovakia. Not until 6:30 P.M., more than five hours after Beneš had met Machník and Krejčí, did a meeting of the government with the president took place. There was some debate regarding the proper extent of Czechoslovakia's response, but no one doubted that definite military countermeasures would have to be taken.[165] The soldiers were only too happy to oblige. The governmental decree that set the machinery in motion was grounded in law number 22 of the Defense Legal Code of May 1936, the main instrument for regulating Czechoslovak military affairs.

Viewed militarily, the operation was a success. Minister Machník called up one year-class (70,000) of first-line reservists; five classes (114,000) of specialists, highly trained men who had been issued distinct mobilization cards upon being discharged from regular service; and 15,000 men of state defense guard (SOS) units, whose mission was to maintain law and order in the border areas.[166] Altogether, some 199,000 men were called up, and the Czechoslovak army grew to a force of 383,000 determined, well-trained men.[167] The reservists, together with the standing army, marched into the Sudetenland and occupied the front-line fortifications. They could temporarily hold the frontier and prevent a German surprise attack; if Hitler were to move, there would be a shooting war.

The mobilized reservists reported for duty with genuine enthusiasm. Having secured imaginative means of transportation, many had arrived at their regiments hours before they were expected. Once in position, they worked with zeal and discipline. Major Riley noted that "the assembly and movement of Czech troops was smoothly and well conducted."[168] He drove along the strategically important road to Karlovy Vary and watched a battalion of mechanized infantry loaded on modern six-wheel trucks moving swiftly toward the Czechoslovak-German border. Riley was touched by the troops fighting spirit. They seemed cheerful and eager.[169] His impressions were later confirmed by Czechoslovak army officers. They found that the mobilized troops stood ready for a war against Hitler and that the Sudeten German followers of Henlein were taken aback by the army's precision and discipline. Overnight, Nazi symbols disappeared, as did abusive behavior by local leaders of the SdP. Army generals seemed conspicuously proud, and Beneš repeatedly expressed his satisfaction over the operation.[170]

On 21 May 1938 the president traveled to Tábor, a city with a long military tradition, where he delivered one of the best political speeches of his life. Nothing, he told the audience, absolutely nothing could change the democratic character of Czechoslovak political institutions. As for the future, Beneš asserted that there was no reason to be afraid. "We are ready for everything." he concluded.[171] After many months of passivity, uncertainty, and humiliation, the path had now been cleared: Czechoslovakia was not Austria, it was not going to be wiped off the map without an all-out fight. In the Austrian case, Hitler opted for a combination of internal subversion with external pressure. The May partial mobilization demonstrated that the Austrian pattern was inapplicable in Czechoslovakia. The general feeling in Prague was that with the *Anschluß* Hitler had exhausted his reservoir of easy successes. If he wanted to go any further there would definitely be war—first a local one and finally a world war.[172]

German diplomacy, as was to be expected, reacted to the partial mobilization with fury. The German minister in Prague, Ernst Eisenlohr, denied the existence of any military concentrations in an interview with Krofta.[173] When the Czechoslovak foreign minister insisted that German military measures had been detected and verified, Eisenlohr responded that such reports were "grober Unsinn" (vulgar nonsense).[174] This was followed by a number of angry denials to the Czechoslovak minister in Berlin, Mastný. Officials of the foreign policy establishment, such as Ernst von Weizsäcker and Hans Georg von Mackensen, suggested that the rumors regarding German war preparations had been manufactured by those who stood to profit from a war in Central Europe.[175] It was not entirely clear to whom this referred. Mastný also had to endure an unpleasant interview with Joachim von Ribbentrop, who insisted that there was not a word of truth in Prague's assertion that it was reacting to a German mobilization. The German foreign minister warned that

Hitler, in response to this provocation, might order the very measures Prague had invented.[176] The British ambassador in Berlin, Sir Nevile Henderson, saw von Ribbentrop on instructions from London to reassure the German government that the British were doing their best to contain the crisis. Von Ribbentrop talked bitterly about the "großsprecherische Herren in Prag" (the big-mouthed gentlemen from Prague) who tell lies. Sir Nevile agreed that the Czechoslovak partial mobilization was "very foolish," and he pleaded for Berlin to show prudence. He was certain that if Hitler remained patient, "all will work well and Germany will score a sweeping victory." Despite Henderson's conciliatory efforts, von Ribbentrop refused to part on friendly terms. He predicted that, unless satisfied, "the German nation will stand up as one man. Let no one have any illusion."[177] Berlin went so far as to spread the false rumor that the May partial mobilization was carried out by a Czechoslovak military clique that had presented the Prague government with a fait accompli.[178] The German legation took part in this campaign designed to portray Czechoslovakia as a military dictatorship.[179]

Hitler was enraged by the audacity of the Prague government, and the May crisis only strengthened his resolve to destroy Czechoslovakia. He sensed that the swift and enthusiastic strategic concentration on the other side of the border had brought about a loss of German, and his own, prestige. He sat down to rewrite the Operation Green directive, the very first sentence of which now read, "It is my unalterable intention to smash Czechoslovakia by military action in the nearest future.[180] The Führer accused the Prague government of having committed fraud in order to put terrorist pressure upon the course of municipal elections scheduled to take place on 22 May 1938.[181] Actually, even with the Czechoslovak army deployed in the Sudetenland, the majority of the German population was free to vote for the SdP: in some parts, almost 90 percent of Sudeten Germans voted for it. Overall, the party polled 82 to 85 percent of the German vote.[182] In larger cities, however, pro-Czechoslovak parties and German democrats held at least one-third of the vote.[183] The anti-Nazi German Social Democrats had been energized by the May partial mobilization. Wenzel Jaksch, a leading personality among democratically minded Germans in Czechoslovakia, said in early June that Czechoslovakia would fight for its existence and independence to the last man. The military measures taken in May were but the first warning to all those blinded by their love for the Führer.[184]

Poland was also critical of Prague's decision to carry out the partial mobilization. A spokesman for the Warsaw Foreign Ministry stated that Polish intelligence sources had confirmed the absence of any German military concentrations. The military measures taken by Prague were but a skillful maneuver designed to pacify the German minority, he asserted. He predicted that Great Britain and France would continue pressuring Czechoslovakia to make bigger and bigger concessions to Hitler until the state would dissolve.[185] The director of the Eastern Department of the Polish Foreign Ministry, M. Kobylański, received the Czechoslovak minister in Warsaw and protested against the May partial mobilization. It was uncalled-for and justified only by fantasies, he claimed.[186] To make matters worse, the Polish ambassador in London informed the British that "there had not, in fact, been any concentration of German troops on the Czechoslovak frontier ten days ago." Lord Halifax, who tended to blame the Prague government for the Czechoslovak-German crisis, was pleased to hear this, and he promptly passed the information on to British diplomats in Warsaw.[187]

But not everyone in Poland took joy in the prospect of Czechoslovakia's disintegration. Those most unhappy about the growing isolation of the Prague government were officers of the Polish armed forces. Many did not trust the Third Reich. They were convinced that, after Czechoslovakia, Poland would be Hitler's next victim. There were indications that the Polish army leaders wanted to see a renewal of contacts with their Czechoslovak colleagues. As military professionals, they were impressed by the swiftness of the May partial mobilization and the enthusiasm of the Czechoslovak troops. An American specialist on Central Europe, Charles Hodges, who spent time in Poland, spoke subsequently in Prague with Beneš, Krofta, and a lesser official of the Foreign Ministry. He told them that many Polish officers looked on Czechoslovakia as their potential ally against Germany. Hodges's overall impression was that Poland would not march with Hitler against Czechoslovakia; at a minimum, Warsaw would maintain neutrality.[188]

This analysis was confirmed by several reports from the Czechoslovak legation in Warsaw.[189] They indicated that a large segment of the press expressed approval of the partial mobilization. Many in Warsaw understood that the territorial integrity of Poland, a country with a large German minority, was also at stake. *Kurjer Warszawski* published articles on 22 and 23 May by the future Polish prime minister, General Władysław Sikorski, who predicted that Czechoslovakia, with the assistance of its French ally, would offer spirited military resistance against the Third Reich. On 24 May *Kurjer Polski* celebrated the partial mobilization as Germany's first defeat. It stated further that dictators lived by successes and that even a small failure could lead to a quick decline of the whole totalitarian system. It warned that the German dictatorship was capable of anything in the future and concluded by calling for all nations to arm and act in concert against Adolf Hitler. *Nowa Rzeczpospolita,* also on 24 May, saw in the partial mobilization proof that Prague would not retreat without a bitter fight. It predicted that Germany would fail in its effort to localize the conflict with Czechoslovakia because its allies would eventually fulfill their obligations.

Save for a few half-baked efforts, there is no indication that President Beneš's diplomacy vigorously tried to reach beyond the hostile anti-Czechoslovak group around Colonel Józef Beck and exploit the positive signals from Poles who looked on the May partial mobilization with approval.[190] In any case, their friendly attitude toward the Czechoslovak position could not last. By late September 1938 the disputed territory of Těšín had come to dominate Czechoslovak-Polish relations to such an extent that only a few Polish periodicals—suspect because of their ideological bent—dared to express a pro-Czechoslovak attitude.[191] Consequently, like the Austrians before them, Czechoslovaks and Poles would walk toward their private Golgothas on their own, for Hitler's convenience and pleasure.

The partial mobilization in May 1938 played an important role in the development of the Czechoslovak-German crisis, and its accurate analysis is crucial for an understanding of European diplomacy on the eve of World War II. Historians have so far had to rely on generally available Western diplomatic documents and on evidence seized from German officers and presented at Nuremberg.[192] Such sources

of information had been exhausted by the 1960s. The analysis that follows is based
on documents received and produced by the Second Bureau of the Czechoslovak
army's General Staff, that is, the military intelligence service, during the May crisis.
The file consists of reports from Czechoslovak agents in Germany who were controlled by the bureau's operational section. Its chief, Colonel (later General) František Moravec, passed such reports on to the chief of the analytical section of the
service, Colonel František Havel. Unless indicated otherwise, information on the
partial mobilization is derived from this file.[193]

The May Mobilization and Analysts of the Second Bureau

According to documents of the Second Bureau, the Prague government decided to
carry out the partial mobilization on the basis of three sources of information. The
first and most important source has not been identified. It is not surprising because
only case officers of the offensive, operational section of the Second Bureau knew
the real identity of agents who worked for them. Intelligence analysts of the Second
Bureau and various Prague politicians who had access to intelligence reports were
only told whether a particular source was reliable and whether he possessed specialized (for instance, military) knowledge. It has been suggested that the primary
source for Colonel Moravec and the whole operational section during the May crisis
was Paul Thümmel, Czechoslovak agent A-54.[194] It has now been shown that
Thümmel met with his control officers from the Second Bureau on Thursday, 12
May 1938. On that occasion, many aspects of the Czechoslovak-German crisis were
discussed, but a strategic concentration by the Wehrmacht was not mentioned. After
this meeting the agent disappeared for several weeks: he wrote to the Second Bureau
only at the end of June 1938. The message stressed that the May crisis must have
been caused by an error on the part of Czechoslovak authorities, because any
German military action would have had to be preceded by a state of readiness of the
Abwehr—the so-called *Spannung*—and that had not been declared. At the next
meeting after a long hiatus (on Thursday, 11 August 1938) Thümmel told Colonel
Moravec and his colleagues from the Operational Section of the Second Bureau that
there was no immediate danger of German invasion. *Spannung* was not declared,
even in the middle of August, let alone in May.[195] In short, Paul Thümmel had
nothing to do with Prague's decision to carry out the May mobilization.
    A tentative case could be made that the source may have been Willy Lange,
agent D-14, a German social democrat and one-time deputy mayor of Leipzig,
who had built up an information-gathering network among railroad personnel
(mostly former social democrats and communists) in Germany.[196] Lange worked
for the Second Bureau from the beginning of 1933. It is true that on 20 May 1938
Prague received his message written in vague terms, about movements of the
Wehrmacht.[197] However, it will be shown that the first of the reports that caused
Prague to declare the May mobilization came two days before 20 May. This, as well
as the other reports from the source, were detailed, involved specialized military
terminology, and could not have come from a lower-ranking social democratic
politician whose left-wing ideology and political career made him a prime suspect in

the eyes of Heinrich Himmler's Gestapo, which had efficiently flushed out underground communist networks in Germany by 1935.[198]

The Social Democratic party, banned in June 1933, only months after Hitler had outlawed the Communist party, had also collapsed. When the May crisis broke out, most German communists and social democrats were dead, imprisoned, or exiled—or they had accepted the Third Reich. Depending on their personal circumstances, they tried to stay away from politics and remained neutral or they joined the NSDAP. Therefore, likelihood is close to zero that Lange was in 1938 capable of running a vast network of social democratic and communist agents who could supply him and the Second Bureau with sophisticated military intelligence covering at least one-fourth of the German field army and movements of the Luftwaffe along the Czechoslovak-German borders.

Willy Lange could not have been the main trigger of the May crisis. It is important to note that Colonel Havel shared this view; he rejected out of hand the possibility that the crucial information had come from D-14.[199] Havel held a grudge against Colonel Moravec, and his testimony has to be regarded with caution when his rival, Moravec, is involved. But Havel is a scrupulously accurate witness in all other instances, and we can accept his opinion that the information, which caused Prague to carry out the partial mobilization, had come neither from A-54 nor from D-14. Let us call the entity which caused the partial mobilization "source X."

Whoever he was, source X was important enough to trigger the May crisis. The first reports from Germany indicating a strong military concentration in Saxony and in the northeastern corner of Bavaria were received on the evening of 18 May 1938. The analysts in the Second Bureau, who worked with the raw material delivered to them by the operational section, were skeptical at first. Their initial reaction was to write the reports off as politically motivated demonstrations designed psychologically to strengthen the Henlein party for the coming municipal elections and to alarm the democratically minded German minority. However, three and a half hours after midnight on 20 May 1938, more reports from the source operating in Germany were passed on to officers of the Second Bureau stationed in one of the forward intelligence centrals (Předsunuté agenturní ústředny, PAU) established throughout the tense border region during the 1930s.[200] The new reports were immediately passed on to Prague, where Staff Captain (later Major) Kostka of the German Department, Analytical Section of the Second Bureau, received them at 6:15 A.M.

The emerging picture was alarming. The latest intelligence reports stated that hundreds of German reservists had been called up in various locations along the Czechoslovak-German border. Furthermore, whole combat-ready Wehrmacht divisions were said to be leaving their barracks to assume jump-off positions in preparation for offensive action. Unusually heavy activity by the Luftwaffe was reported in various cities along the Czechoslovak borders; several airports were said to have been placed under a special regime. Given the location and pattern of military activities for the past two days, there were similarities with what Czechoslovak military specialists had observed on the eve of the *Anschluß* of Austria. Intelligence analysts in Prague worked feverishly to produce a map capturing the essence of the reports received during the night.

By 8 A.M. on 20 May 1938, the Second Bureau had come up with the following summary of reports received so far. In Saxony, elements of the 4th, 14th, and 24th divisions (IVth) had been concentrated along the Czechoslovak border. In northern Bavaria, units belonging to the 7th (XIth) and 17th divisions (XIIIth) were "alerted." In addition, the 19th and 31st divisions (XIth) and the 23d Division (IIIrd) were reportedly moving toward the Czechoslovak border, together with units of the 22d Division (Xth) from Bremen and the 12th Division (IIth) from Schwerin. The airport at Chemnitz was said to have received 32 fighter planes; Altenburg, 100 fighters; and Plauen, 8 bombers. This looked ominous. Around noon, on 20 May 1938, the document went from the bureau's chief analyst, Colonel Havel, to the bureau's chief, Colonel František Hájek, who quickly passed it to General Bohumil Fiala, deputy chief of General Staff. Fiala gave it to his boss, General Krejčí, who, together with Minister Machník, delivered it to President Beneš at 1:15 P.M.

In addition to source X, Prague also heard from British Intelligence. That was the second source of information. The Second Bureau had approached the British with a request to confirm or deny military activities in Germany.[201] The British complied and communicated with Prague via the Czechoslovak legation in Berlin. Minister Mastný came to the legation early on 20 May 1938 and discovered that Colonel Antonín Hron, the military attaché, had already been in touch with Prague through his own channels. The minister learned only that Hron had passed a message from the British on to his superiors in the Second Bureau.[202] This report, which Mastný never got to see, stated that a good source with no military knowledge had observed German military formations moving toward the Czechoslovak border. The British specifically mentioned a report from an intelligence asset in Dresden regarding possible German military concentrations in southern Silesia and northern Austria. All military leaves in Dresden had been canceled. However, the British were careful enough to state that, in their view, these were probably only demonstrations of military might, not preparations for an all-out aggressive action.[203]

Complementing the two intelligence reports from Germany was information received from a third source, the domestic counterintelligence service. President Beneš found out that Minister Eisenlohr had boasted before a supposedly discrete audience in the German legation on 18 May 1938 that a Wehrmacht offensive was to be expected in the near future. The statement was relayed to the authorities by an agent at the legation.[204]

Having heard from the Second Bureau's source X, from the British, and now from the German legation, Beneš no longer believed that the crisis could be handled exclusively by diplomats. He had to take action because all seemed ominously clear: Hitler had decided to repeat the Austrian scenario. He would invade Czechoslovakia in concert with terrorist actions by the Sudeten German Henleinists, who would cause disturbances in cities and carry out acts of sabotage elsewhere. The latter would make it impossible for the Czechoslovak army to make use of the defensive fortified positions that were being constructed at a feverish pace along the borders. The Wehrmacht would easily cut through the German districts of Czechoslovakia and prevent the army from carrying out a general mobilization. Unopposed, the first German units could reach Prague within hours. This scenario seemed depressingly feasible and, therefore, Prague's decision to declare the partial mobilization made complete sense.

But there was a problem. Having mobilized, Prague began hearing from various quarters that Germany had made no aggressive moves whatsoever. A second message from British Intelligence stated that London had no evidence for reports that the important 19th Division had moved from Hannover to an offensive posture—this was most likely a response to another concrete inquiry from Prague. On 21 May 1938, just hours after the partial mobilization had been declared, Colonel Havel and others in the analytical section began to doubt the whole affair. Havel started to speculate—and he had to speculate because only the Operational Section knew the identity of source X—that all the reports had in fact come from one intelligence-gathering central, possibly one person.

Havel's marginal comments on the materials he received on 21 May 1938 grew more and more critical as the crisis progressed. Specifically, he wondered how one intelligence central could report on an area covering Nuremberg, Würzburg, Augsburg, Zwickau, Aue, Johanngeorgenstadt, Eibenstock, Amberg, Regensburg, Deggendorf, and Straubing. The next day, after source X reported that Germany had mobilized three year-classes and, in areas along the Czechoslovak border, six year-classes, the analysts became convinced that the reports were a hoax. "The whole report, it is immediately obvious, is fantastic," commented Havel in the margin. How could one intelligence center, even with many subagents, have had enough resources to investigate the area of Hof, Berlin, Munich, Kassel, and Hannover? And how did it happen that such large-scale German military measures had not been confirmed from other sources available to the Second Bureau? On 23 May 1938 Colonel Havel made up his mind that the Operational Section was being deceived. He wrote that further analysis of the reports he received from Colonel Moravec was a waste of time. How could one source accurately report on movements of some ten higher units from the areas of all the German *Gruppenkommandos?* That would have amounted to one-fourth of the entire German field army, Havel noted ironically.

Moreover, a Czechoslovak diplomatic courier traveled on 23 May 1938 from Prague to Switzerland via Munich and saw no military concentrations anywhere. Agents of the Second Bureau reported no suspicious movements in Austria, around Chemnitz and Leipzig in Saxony, in Glatz in Prussian Silesia, and in the area of Zittau-Bautzen-Görlitz. The 23d Division stationed in Potsdam was in its barracks and followed a regular, peacetime schedule. By 25 May 1938, Second Bureau analysts noted that source X who confidently claimed until the day before that the Wehrmacht had been on the verge of attacking Czechoslovakia was now forced to report the absence of detectable signs of any strategic concentrations. Finally, five days after the May crisis began, President Beneš was informed by the Second Bureau via his Military Office, headed by General Sylvestr Bláha, that, according to Czechoslovak intelligence assets in Germany and a reliable foreign source, all units of the Wehrmacht were in their peacetime locations.[205] Colonel Havel did not hesitate to express his comtempt for the way in which the Operational Section had relied on its mystery source and allowed itself to be fed disinformation.

Colonel Havel and other skeptics in the Analytical Section of the Second Bureau could cause no harm to Czechoslovakia's reputation because their work was, naturally, top secret. There is, in fact, no indication that President Beneš was informed of the conflict between the operational and analytical sections, and he consequently never doubted the correctness of the decision to carry out the partial mobilization, although he privately admitted that the Second Bureau had exaggerated the danger Czechoslovakia was facing on 20 May 1938. Such a tendency, he observed, was the Second Bureau's "déformation professionelle."[206] Nevertheless, the president was proud of Czechoslovakia's sudden action in May. He told the U.S. military attaché in early July that had it not been for the partial mobilization Czechoslovakia would have been already at war.[207] Along with the president, the whole country lived under the impression that Prague's military measures were in fact a response to an imminent German offensive.

Not only the analysts of the military intelligence under Colonel Havel doubted the veracity of the mystery source; soon, information from all other quarters indicated that Havel's skepticism was justified. The British military attaché, Colonel H. C. T. Stronge, a friend of the democratic cause in Czechoslovakia, was glad that Czechoslovakia had carried out the partial mobilization. His report to London stated that it "had a most salutary effect on the [Sudeten] population, who were becoming very confident and overbearing. . . . The lightning action which had been taken left them dumbfounded and considerable sobered."[208] However he drove all around Saxony and Silesia but found no traces of any German military movements.[209] Similarly, two British military diplomats posted in Berlin were dispatched on an extensive reconnaissance through Saxony and Silesia. Like Stronge, they found no signs of unusual German military activity.[210] On 24 May 1938, French Intelligence, the Deuxième Bureau, told the Second Bureau in Prague that it had no reports of untoward preparations in Germany.[211] On the same day, the Czechoslovak air attaché in Berlin flew back to Prague along a route designed to cover the most militarily sensitive areas; he reported that he had seen no military movements whatever. On 25 May 1938 another Czechoslovak officer flew from Berlin to Prague via Dresden and reported that no military convoys were anywhere in sight. Altogether, Havel noted, four allied military attachés and two Czechoslovak officers were able to deny any noticeable preparations for a German military offensive. He was convinced that the whole affair had been provoked by Czechoslovakia's enemies. He did not speculate any further as to the identity and intentions of the source that had engineered the provocation.

The doubts expressed throughout the May crisis by Second Bureau analysts and the reports of various military specialists and diplomats who denied that the Third Reich was about to attack Czechoslovakia were justified. There was (and is) no evidence of a German strategic concentration against Czechoslovakia in May 1938. Why then did the Prague government, which had so far behaved with characteristic caution, decide to carry out the partial mobilization?

The possibility can be dismissed that source X had made an honest error (caused, perhaps, by lack of experience) during the undoubtedly difficult process of gathering intelligence on behalf of democratic Czechoslovakia in the hostile Third Reich. According to his report, ten Wehrmacht divisions (the 4th, 7th, 12th, 14th, 17th, 19th, 22d, 23d, 24th, and 31st) were alerted and involved in the strategic concentration along the Czechoslovak borders. The plausibility of this report can be checked against a list prepared on 16 May 1938, two days before hostile movements of the Wehrmacht would be reported by source X; the author of the list was Lt. Colonel (later General) Kurt Zeitzler of the German supreme headquarters, the Oberkommando der Wehrmacht. Hitler wanted Zeitzler to name specific divisions that could march against Czechoslovakia within twelve hours. Of the ten divisions identified by the mystery source, five (the 4th, 7th, 14th, 17th, and 24th) were on Zeitzler's list. Those could plausibly have been involved in that alleged concentration against Czechoslovakia, the beginning of which the mystery source reported on 18 May 1938. However, source X had failed to report the state of readiness of five other divisions (the 3d, 8th, 10th, 18th, and 28th) that were on Zeitzler's list, and he fabricated the readiness of five others (the 12th, 19th, 22d, 23d, and 31st). They were not on the reliable list Zeitzler prepared, and they could not have been ready for war forty-eight hours later.[212] If a division is to be capable of marching, visible measures must have been taken that can be detected by any inquisitive layman. For example, every tavern-owner can tell when a division stationed nearby is on that kind of alert, for there are no customers in uniform. All in all, the list of source X was one-third plausible and two-thirds wrong, and this has all the footprints of professional deception. The picture of German military measures that the source delivered to Prague was far too sophisticated to have come from well-meaning but inexperienced German democrats. It could only have come from professionals who knew a great deal about the Wehrmacht and possessed specialized military knowledge.[213]

Rejecting the view that the mystery source had made an honest error leaves only one remaining alternative: the reports that came to the Second Bureau between 18 May and 24 May 1938 were part of a deliberate deception. The offensive section of the Second Bureau had been deceived. Berlin sensed that this was, at least in part, the right explanation. The German minister in Prague told an official of the Czechoslovak Foreign Ministry on 25 May 1938, ''The Czechoslovak General Staff acted *bona fide* but it had been duped by its secret informers.''[214] But who was the source of the disinformation, and what were his objectives?

London and Paris are obviously innocent. They both saw in Prague's decision to call up reservists a dangerous provocation, if not an act of jingoism.[215] Moreover, British intelligence is on record as having told the Second Bureau that whatever measures Berlin may have taken had been intended as a political demonstration, and it subsequently denied any evidence of hostile preparations against Czechoslovak territory. Paris was just as skeptical, and the Deuxième Bureau rejected the possibility of German aggression. It has been speculated that the deception operation had been designed and carried out by the Abwehr.[216] Even now, almost six decades after the crisis, there is no evidence that Admiral Wilhelm Canaris or his colleague Colonel Hans Oster or anybody else in the Abwehr community had planned in May 1938 to scare Hitler from escalating the crisis with Czechoslovakia any further. The Abwehr theory has to be rejected for lack of even the remotest supportive evidence. Application of the principle of cui bono allows us to dismiss other potential candidates, for example, Poland and Hungary. Neither had an interest in the outbreak of hostilities between Czechoslovakia and Germany. In fact, both stood to profit from the continuing crisis because it allowed them to press for their own territorial demands in Prague, weakened yet not destroyed by Hitler. Had war broken out and

Czechoslovakia been occupied by the Wehrmacht, Warsaw and Budapest could have had a hard time reclaiming Těšín and southern Slovakia from Hitler. The Poles and Hungarians wanted Czechoslovakia to be weak so they could take over the disputed territory, but they did not want Hitler's troops deployed in Slovakia. That would have caused a strategic problem to Poland and kept Warsaw and Budapest from becoming neighbors.

A stronger (but far from definite) case could be made to suggest that source X was Soviet. Germany, France, and Great Britain reacted to the partial mobilization in May in a predictable manner. In contrast, the behavior of the Soviet Union was enigmatic. Before the crisis, the Kremlin had strengthened Czechoslovakia's determination to defend itself against the Third Reich by posturing as a reliable ally. Once the crisis started, however, Soviet officials retreated and made themselves unavailable for official business. Paradoxically, after the tensions declined, Moscow emerged to claim that the partial mobilization was a success, at least in part because of the firmness of Soviet foreign policy.

The key to Soviet thinking during the May crisis can be found in a conversation between Maxim Litvinov and the Czechoslovak diplomat Arnošt Heidrich in Geneva on 11 May 1938. The two had known each other since 1925, and Heidrich stated later that Beneš had asked him to see the Soviet commissar because in the past Litvinov had always been frank with him. In their hour-long conversation, Litvinov said without hesitation that war was inevitable. We know, he continued, that the "West wishes Stalin to destroy Hitler and Hitler to destroy Stalin." But Moscow would not oblige its enemies, warned Litvinov. "This time it will be the Soviets who will stand by until near the end when they will be able to step in and bring about a just and permanent peace."[217] One is naturally inclined to be skeptical when important politicians speak with such openness. But Litvinov's summary of Soviet policy in the Czechoslovak-German crisis, as recorded by Heidrich, was authentic and would be, in August 1938, verified by Andrei Zhdanov (chapter 6). Moscow apparently hoped that a collective of states would emerge that would commit itself to an anti-Hitler agenda. The Kremlin intended to strengthen the collective's resolve by its own warlike élan, then drive it into a shooting war with Hitler—and stand aside. The anarchy caused by the war against the Third Reich was to be transformed into a class-minded struggle that would bring about socialist revolutions (chapter 3).

The argument that Czechoslovakia mobilized in May on a false Soviet tip is strengthened when one examines the behavior of Soviet diplomats in Moscow. From late April to mid-May 1938, Moscow expressed great optimism regarding the possibility of containing the German threat, thereby building up Czechoslovakia's self-confidence. However, when Fierlinger tried to see Litvinov in order to discuss the military measures taken by Czechoslovakia on 20 May 1938, he ran into a wall of bureaucratic obstacles. After three tense days of unfulfilled expectations, the Czechoslovak minister was received only by Potemkin, who praised Prague's decision to call up reservists. Litvinov was unavailable, explained his deputy, because he had bronchitis.[218] Having strengthened Czechoslovakia's resolve to resist the Third Reich, Soviet leaders retreated behind the Kremlin wall, apparently waiting for Hitler's reaction to the partial mobilization.

It was not until 25 May 1938, about twenty-four hours after it had become clear that the crisis would be contained, that Litvinov's health allowed him to receive Prague's top diplomat in Moscow. The commissar used the opportunity to congratulate the Czechoslovak government for the energetic measures it had taken to solve the crisis in the Sudetenland. Litvinov stated further that Moscow was ready to discuss military measures with France and Great Britain. He wanted a concrete arrangement with the French army General Staff, not merely talks with the French military attaché in Moscow. Recently, reported Fierlinger, Lord Halifax had asked Litvinov how the Soviet Union intended to assist Czechoslovakia. He had responded by saying that he was ready to discuss it in the spirit of his plan for collective security. He also told Lord Halifax that Moscow was ready to join Great Britain and France to discuss a possible diplomatic intervention in Berlin on Czechoslovakia's behalf. If the British remained unprepared to act collectively with the Soviet Union, warned Litvinov, Moscow might have to seek protection in an agreement with Germany.[219] This made sense, except that the Soviet Union was legally bound to come, together with France, to Czechoslovakia's assistance in case of an unprovoked German attack. And it was about this centrally important aspect that Litvinov was silent. It was well known that Great Britain was unwilling to enter into any collective arrangements, to say nothing of those that would include the Bolshevik regime. Therefore, Litvinov's suggestion that German pressure on Czechoslovakia could be relieved by a collective démarche in Berlin was utterly unrealistic and the Kremlin knew it.

The script played in Moscow by Litvinov during the May crisis was reflected in the behavior of the Soviet press. Having first whipped up an optimistic campaign regarding Czechoslovakia's chances against Hitler, the controlled media retreated, awaiting the outcome of the crisis. The first mention of the partial mobilization was made by TASS on 22 May 1938. The agency simply stated that the Czechoslovak government had called up a class of reservists and sent military units to the German border. No other comment was offered.[220] The next day, Soviet media carried new dispatches under foreign date lines on the situation but refrained from making any editorial comment. The Kremlin must have been waiting for the situation to develop in one way or another while keeping its options open. On 23 May 1938 a Soviet official told the U.S. ambassador that the Czechoslovak government was "thoroughly correct" in mobilizing and that it would be an error to expect a repetition of the Austrian affair, "for Czechoslovakia would fight." On the important topic of Soviet actions in case of a Czechoslovak-German war, the official remained silent.[221] On 24 May, four days after the mobilization, still not a word from the Kremlin regarding its own behavior in case of a German attack had appeared in the official press. The next day, *Pravda* broke its silence and announced that should Hitler choose to attack, "the direct responsibility will rest upon the Governments of England and France." But the paper said nothing about the attitude of the Soviet Union and made no reference to the Czechoslovak-Soviet treaty of 1935.

On 25 May 1938 Czechoslovak General Husák was received by Marshal Voroshilov in the Kremlin. Stalin's top soldier recommended that Prague push France as hard as possible to take a strong stance. Mere declarations by France that it would fulfill its obligations toward Czechoslovakia were not enough. It was necessary to take decisive action, warned Voroshilov. Strangely enough, the Soviet marshal said not a word regarding the May partial mobilization or the Soviet Union's likely course of action in case of a German attack upon its ally. His main concern was that a Czechoslovakia defeated by Germany meant the Wehrmacht on the borders of the Ukraine and, eventually, a war against the Soviet Union. "We all have to take care," stated Voroshilov, "to prevent such an untoward development.[222] On the same day, Minister Fierlinger wrote a personal note to President Beneš suggesting that the Prague government should be magnanimous and offer the Red Army the latest in military technology under the most generous terms.[223]

Finally, on 26 May 1938, the Kremlin made its opinion official. *Izvestia* published an article, "Czechoslovakia: A Bastion of Peace," which declared sympathy with the timely military measures taken by Prague. It was, after all, one reason the Third Reich had to postpone its aggression. The article observed further that "no one doubts the loyalty of the Soviet Union to the obligation which it has assumed and this has played a tremendous role." It was important for the German aggressor to realize that no one in Europe intended to surrender "the last bastion of peace in Western Europe, the independent Czechoslovak Republic."[224] This was quite ironic. Having made no attempt during the crisis to contact President Beneš in Prague via Alexsandrovsky (his first appearance after the partial mobilization of 20 May 1938 at the Castle would not be until 27 June 1938) and having kept Litvinov away from Minister Fierlinger as long as the tension lasted, the Kremlin was now posing as one of the powers that had kept Hitler at bay.

Soviet behavior during the May crisis was well understood by the German embassy in Moscow. Ambassador Count von der Schulenburg found that Soviet officials made every effort in Paris, London, and Prague to influence the respective governments toward taking energetic measures and maintaining a tough stance toward Hitler. The ambassador indicated that throughout the crisis Minister Fierlinger had kept in close touch with Soviet authorities, and he may have received encouragement for Czechoslovakia to escalate the crisis. Nevertheless, von der Schulenburg predicted, the Kremlin would be unwilling to march on behalf of Czechoslovakia. After all, the Red Army existed for the protection of the Stalinist regime and also to further world revolution. Why should it go to war to protect the existence of a bourgeois regime? The Kremlin, wrote the German ambassador, would follow "the proved tactics of mobilizing other powers, particularly France, against foes, of fomenting those conflicts which do break out—as for example in Spain and China—by deliveries of war material, and of extending them as much as possible by political agitation and intrigues of all kinds."[225] The opinion of Ambassador Schulenburg must be taken seriously because it was his embassy that was best informed about the situation in the Kremlin.

In contrast to von der Schulenburg's memoranda, reports from the American embassy to Washington advanced the view that Moscow no longer believed in the possibility of avoiding war. In fact, Ambassador Davies had heard from Minister Fierlinger that the Red Army had already taken "certain military measures."[226] This was untrue, and the diplomatic community in Moscow knew it. Except for Fierlinger, nobody among foreign diplomats in Moscow thought that the Soviet Union would come to assist Czechoslovakia in case of a German attack.

CONSIDER A POSSIBLE EXPLANATION of the evidence before us. The Kremlin's *modus operandi* during the May 1938 crisis was based on the premise that a European war was not to be feared as long as it took place far from Soviet territory. In fact, a war between Germany and Western democracies was desirable because it would channel the destructive energy of the Third Reich away from the Soviet Union. Stalin did not fear war among any combination of European bourgeois states as much as he dreaded being isolated. It was isolation that would sooner or later result in Hitler's attack on the Soviet Union. After the *Anschluß* of Austria, it became possible that London and Paris would attempt to appease Berlin by forcing Czechoslovakia to grant greater and greater concessions to the Sudeten Germans until the whole country would fall apart—with bits and pieces open to German domination or outright conquest.

But if Czechoslovakia were to become Hitler's puppet, who was going to prevent German armed forces from pressing further east? A tentative hypothesis could be proposed to the effect that in May 1938 the Kremlin struggled to accelerate the outbreak of the Czechoslovak-German war. Soviet intelligence sources falsely informed the Second Bureau that Hitler had commenced preparations for an attack against Czechoslovakia. Moscow had an active intelligence central in Prague. It was code named VONAPO 20 and it had been operational since 27 May 1936.[227]

Moscow had a reason to expect that, possibly, the unprovoked Czechoslovak countermeasures would make the impulsive Führer unleash the Wehrmacht and Luftwaffe on Prague, that he would give the Czechoslovaks what they had made up: an all-out German aggression. France, deprived of the diplomatic option, its escape route, would be pressured to go to war against the Third Reich; Great Britain could conceivably be drawn in at some point; and the Soviet Union, as Litvinov told Heidrich in Geneva, would sit, wait, watch, deliberate, and join at the right moment on the right side. Time was on its side because the future war, originally fueled by nationalism, would have gradually become a revolutionary war against the European bourgeoisie.[228] Such a conflict outside the Soviet Union's borders appeared to be a guarantee against a Franco-British-German rapprochement, which would constitute the greatest threat to Soviet security.[229]

At the moment, such speculation is no more than an audacious theory unverifiable by available documents. For now we must be satisfied with the knowledge that Hitler did not intend to attack Czechoslovakia in May 1938 and that Prague had been misled by a professional intelligence organization into believing that he did. The identity of the source of the reports that caused the confusion remains unclear.[230]

Notes

1. AMFA, Bohdan Pavlů, the Czechoslovak Legation, Moscow, to the Ministry of Foreign Affairs, Prague, 2 August 1937. Pavlů heard from the deputy commissar on foreign affairs, Potemkin, that the purge—he called it "measures recently taken"—did not weaken the Soviet Union. The purge had merely "simplified the internal order. . . . Our friends in the West can be sure that the recent events had strengthened the Soviet Union's direction. . . . We don't insist on implementing communism [in the West]. [However we] won't

allow the victory of fascism in the West. We would like to see the strengthening of democracy.''

2. NA 760F.61/67, Wilbur J. Carr, the U.S. Legation, Prague, to the Secretary of State Washington, D.C., 18 February 1938.

3. AMFA, Zdeněk Fierlinger, the Czechoslovak Legation, Moscow, to the Ministry of Foreign Affairs, Prague, 19 December 1937. The greatest pessimists regarding the value of the Red Army among foreign diplomats in Moscow were in the German embassy; their views on the severity of the crisis were shared by others, particularly the Poles and Balts. The British probably also subscribed to the pessimistic view, but they were too cautious to express it openly. There were two notable optimists among diplomats in Moscow: U.S. Ambassador Davies and the new Czechoslovak Minister Zdeněk Fierlinger, who assumed Minister Pavlů's duties in Moscow on 5 October 1937. Ambassador Davies (Fierlinger consistently spelled his name ''Davis'' and Davies misspelled Fierlinger's name in his memoirs as ''Feirlinger'') told Fierlinger that President Beneš and President Roosevelt were the two best politicians in the world. The U.S. ambassador was very supportive of Czechoslovakia's alliance with the Soviet Union. It had a moral as well as real, practical value for Prague because the Soviets, Davies claimed, had a ''vital interest in the security of Czechoslovakia.''

4. PRO FO 408/68.R802/385/12, Mr. Newton to Mr. Eden, Prague, 22 January 1938.

5. AMFA, Zdeněk Fierlinger, the Czechoslovak Legation, Moscow, to the Ministry of Foreign Affairs, secret, 17 January 1938.

6. Ibid., 1 January 1938. Fierlinger quotes from a memorandum by U.S. Ambassador Davies, who had spoken with many European politicians and businessmen and ''failed to find one whose opinion was that in the event of a German *Putsch* against Czechoslovakia, France, despite her offensive and defensive alliance, would come to Czechoslovakia's aid. One Foreign Minister went so far as to say that he had found in England a very substantial group that had expressed the opinion that the one country that could be wiped out without serious consequences in Europe was Czechoslovakia. He stated further that a substantial group in England was making plans on that basis.''

7. Magda Ádám, *Richtung, Selbstvernichtung: Die Kleine Entente 1920–1938* (Budapest: Corvina and Vienna: Österreichischer Bundesverlag, 1988).

8. ANM-M, Mastný, the Manuscript, 46.

9. *Lidové Noviny,* 19 January 1938, showed how the Czechoslovak economy had improved in 1937 (in million crowns, Kc):

	Import	Export
1935	6.743	7.947
1936	7.915	8.036
1937	10.966	11.981

The stock market also started showing signs of life after several lean years.

10. Robert Kvaček et al., *Československý rok 1938* (Prague: Panoráma, 1988), 30. Živnobanka was designed by architect František Roith; see Emanuel Poche, *Praha Krok za Krokem* (Prague: Orbis, 1958), 103.

11. The two principals were so popular that they were granted an audience with President Beneš on 19 May 1937. OP, Book of Presidential Audiences, 1937.

12. This is pointed out in Kvaček et al., *Československý rok 1938,* 9–11.

13. NA, Record Group 165 (Records of the WFGS), Military Intelligence Division, Correspondence, 1917–41 (henceforth NA RG 165) Major J. S. Winslow, U.S. military

attaché, Warsaw, G–2 Report no. 2957, G–2 Report 2657–II–92, box 1704, 29 June 1937. The major, of course, paid special attention to the Czechoslovak armed forces. He found their equipment, leadership, and training to be good. Untested as yet in combat, it was hard to evaluate the army's potential battle morale, he said. But, like the French in 1914, the Czechoslovak army could have combat worthiness "far in excess of any prediction based on its military appearance."

14. AMFA, Bohdan Pavlů, the Czechoslovak Legation, Moscow, to the Ministry of Foreign Affairs, Prague, 23 September 1937.

15. NA RG 165, Major J. S. Winslow, U.S. military attaché, Warsaw, G–2 Report 2657–II–92, box 1704, 28 September 1937.

16. Edward Taborsky, "The Triumph and Disaster of Eduard Beneš," *Foreign Affairs* 36 (July 1958): 669–70.

17. A. J. P. Taylor pointed out that "Beck, Stojadinović, Antonescu and Bonnet despised [Beneš's] integrity and prided themselves on their cunning; but their countries, too, fell before the German aggressor and every step they took has made the resurrection of their countries more difficult. [In contrast] the foreign policy of Dr. Beneš during the present war has won for Czechoslovakia a secure future." See Jan Opočenský (ed.), *Edward Beneš: Essays and Reflections Presented on the Occasion of His Sixtieth Birthday* (London: Allen & Unwin, 1945), 169.

18. Clement Attlee, *As It Happened* (London: W. Heinemann, 1954), 90, 93.

19. Prokop Drtina, *Československo můj osud* (Toronto: Sixty-Eight Publishers, 1982), 42.

20. Beneš and Štrimpl shared the estate in Sezimovo Ústí with Minister Zdeněk Fierlinger. Beneš's house was by far the biggest of the three.

21. For Beneš's views on politics and diplomacy, see Piotr S. Wandycz, "The Foreign Policy of Edvard Beneš, 1918–1938," in *A History of the Czechoslovak Republic 1918–1948,* eds. Victor S. Mamatey and Radomír Luža (Princeton: Princeton University Press, 1973), 218–19.

22. Edvard Beneš, *Problémy nové Evropy a zahraniční politika Československa: Projevy a úvahy r. 1919–1924* (Prague: Melantrich, 1924), 102.

23. PO, Book of Presidential Audiences, 1937. Beneš received Minister Dérer, Minister Girsa, Minister Krofta, and General Syrový.

24. Beneš's mother had hoped that her youngest child would become a priest, and "Edek" was brought up as a strict Catholic. His brothers Václav and Vojta had both become teachers. They were "freethinkers" and inclined toward socialism. There was an intense but brief conflict between them and Beneš's mother regarding little Edek's education. The brothers won, and young Beneš joined them in Prague. That was the end of Beneš's involvement in any organized religion. By the time he entered the *gymnasium,* young Edek was a cool-headed rationalist and "virtually an atheist," as he put it. Later in life, Beneš acknowledged a belief in an "immanent theology." See Antonín Klimek, *Zrození státníka, Edvard Beneš, 28.5. 1884–24.9.1919* (Prague: Melantrich, 1992), 2.

25. Moreover, Beneš also disapproved of vain talk about women. Even as a teenager, he protested when his classmates indulged in stories about their female colleagues. He subsequently recalled that his relations with girls were "platonically pure and beautiful" and that he used the occasions when he spoke with them to propagate his politically "progressive views." See the unpublished manuscript by Ladislav Kunte, "Do třiceti let," no date [probably 1936–37], 3, MHA-B, box: Articles about Beneš, 1. This is all the more interesting because Kunte, who had written about Beneš's platonic attitude toward girls, warned that it was based on hearsay. Beneš, who personally edited the manuscript, energetically crossed out the passage about hearsay and wrote in his own hand: "Beneš recalls that in his youth. . . ."

26. MHA-B, Personalities, box 8, file General Štefánik; quotation is from Lev Sychrava's diary, 1916.

27. Drtina, *Československo*, 44. Drtina worked at the Castle in Prague from December 1929 until his escape from occupied Czechoslovakia in December 1939.

28. Hitler's statement to General Halder in Jeremy Noakes and Geoffrey Pridham, *Documents on Nazism, 1919–1945* (New York: Viking, 1974), 538.

29. MHA-MOP, secret, 1935–39, Air Force, 192/37. The file contains, among other things, a series of articles by Antonín Srba, published in *Právo lidu* on 16 and 17 November 1937, "Potřeby našeho letectví." Srba warned that the achievements of several Czechoslovak flying aces had made the public blind to lack of preparedness of the air force.

30. MHA-MOP, No. 174/33, 1 June 1933.

31. For details, see Jonathan Zorach, "Czechoslovakia's Fortifications: Their Development and Role in the 1938 Munich Crisis," *Militärgeschichtliche Mitteilungen* 2 (1976): 81–94; Jonathan Zorach, "The Czechoslovak Army, 1918–1938," Ph.D. dissertation, Columbia University, 1975; Brian D. Adams, "The Role of Military Considerations in Anglo-French Decision-Making in the Munich Crisis," Ph.D. dissertation, University of Denver, 1970.

32. Zdeněk Procházka et al. (eds.), *Vojenské dějiny Československa, 1918–1939* (Prague: Naše Vojsko, 1987) 3:424–41.

33. The best analysis is in František Havel, "Konflikt s Německem," unpublished MS, the Military Historical Institute of the Czech Army, Prague; see especially 114–25. The most recent analyses can be found in Anthony Adamthwaite, "Le facteur militaire dans la décision franco-britannique avant Munich," and Milan Hauner, "La Tchécoslovaquie en tant que facteur militaire," both in *Revue des Études Slaves*, 1–2 (1979): 59–70 and 179–92; both articles were presented at the conference *"Munich 1938: Mythes et Réalités."* Useful information is also in Václav Hyndrák, "K otázce vojenské hodnoty čs. armády v druhé polovině třicátých let," *Historie a vojenství*, 1 (1964): 63–103; Milan Hauner, "Září 1938: Kapitulovat či bojovat?" *Svědectví*, 49 (1975): 151–63; H. C. T. Stronge, "The Czechoslovak Army and the Munich Crisis: A Personal Memorandum," *War and Society* 1 (1975): 162–77, and "The Military Approach to Munich," *Times*, 29 September 1967; Karel Novotný, "Několik poznámek ze cvičení a manévrů v československé armádě z let 1930–1938," *Historie a vojenství*, 6–7 (1968): 1046–77; Václav Melichar, "Některé otázky obrany Československa v roce 1938," *Československý časopis historický* 22, no. 3 (1974): 321–28; Josef Kalvoda, "Munich: Beneš and the Soldiers," *Ukrainian Quarterly* 47, (summer 1991): 153–214; Alfred Ressel, "Mnichov ve vzpomínkách a v kritice důstojníka generálního štábu československé armády," *Historie a vojenství* 2 (1969): 302–58; Ivan Pfaff, "Mohli jsme se v září 1938 sami bránit?" *Reportér* 41 (1991): 1–4 [see also nos. 42, 43, and 46]. The important Polish perspective is developed in Marian Zgorniak, *Wojskowe aspekty kryzysu czechosłowackiego 1938 roku* (Cracow: Zeszyty Naukowe Uniwersytetu Jagiellonskiego, 1966) and Marian Zgorniak, *Europa w przededniu wojny: Sytuacja militarna w latach 1938–1939* (Cracow: Księgarnia Akademicka, 1993).

34. MHA-MOP, Secret, 1935–39, general, 144/38. These are notes prepared on 31 May 1938 by the army main commander, General Ludvík Krejčí, for his audience with President Beneš on 3 June 1938.

35. According to a German officer, the greatest weakness of the fortified system at the height of the Czechoslovak-German crisis was its unfinished condition. The Czechoslovaks had tried, he said, to build a dam, only the flood had come too soon. Under such circumstances, he felt certain that a breakthrough in a few weak spots would have brought about a collapse of the whole defensive line. However, by the spring or fall of 1939 the fortifications would have provided so much advantage to the defenders that, in his opinion, the Czechoslovak army would have never surrendered. It would have fought, and toughly, with or

even without any allies. See *Royal Engineers Journal* (June 1939): 212–23; the original article was written by Oberst Bierman and appeared in *Vierteljahrshefte für Pioniere* (February 1939).

36. Havel, "Konflikt s Německem," 45.

37. Ibid., 12–14, 45.

38. The conversation is described in Kurt von Schuschnigg, *Austrian Requiem* (New York: Putnam's, 1946), 12–19. Translation slightly altered.

39. Seyss-Inquart's devotion to Nazism would lead him to the defendant's bench at Nuremberg and, finally, the gallows.

40. Von Schuschnigg, *Austrian Requiem*, 24–25.

41. ANM-M, Mastný, the Manuscript, 47.

42. Beneš used the term *Kuh-Handel*, negotiating the price of cattle.

43. AMFA, the Cabinet, no. 827, 16 February 1938.

44. Milan Stojadinović, the Yugoslav prime minister, who had strengthened his country's ties with Mussolini's Italy in 1937, was well received in Berlin by the Führer in January 1938. Norman H. Baynes (ed.), *The Speeches of Adolf Hitler, April 1922–August 1939* (London: Oxford University Press, 1942), 1404–9.

45. Drtina, *Československo*, 45–48.

46. AMFA, telegrams received, Juraj Slávik, the Czechoslovak Legation, Warsaw, to the Ministry of Foreign Affairs, Prague, no. 123/38, 23 February 1938. Minister Slávik reported that Göring, who went to Poland officially on a hunting trip, told Colonel Beck enough about German plans for Austria that the latter "predicted an end to Austrian independence."

47. NA 762.00/164, William C. Bullitt, U.S. Embassy, Paris, to the Secretary of State, Washington, D.C., 21 February 1938.

48. NA 740.00/299, William C. Bullitt, U.S. Embassy, Paris, to the Secretary of State, Washington, D.C., 21 February 1938.

49. Eden devoted chapter 13 of his memoirs [*Facing the Dictators, 1923–1938* (Boston: Houghton Mifflin, 1962)] to this issue. His decision to resign was caused, primarily, by a procedural dispute in the context of Chamberlain's attempts to negotiate with Mussolini.

50. Gerhard L. Weinberg, *The Foreign Policy of Hitler's Germany: Starting World War II, 1937–1939* (Chicago: University of Chicago Press, 1980), 134–35.

51. Telling is the following message from Delbos to Halifax: he, Delbos, also "retained happy memories" of his previous encounters with the new British foreign secretary. "But all personal considerations aside, it is necessary for London to understand that the French government has the right to insist on having the fullest information concerning the objectives of British policy, at a time when it seems to be undergoing, in certain respects a change of direction." See Anthony Adamthwaite, *France and the Coming of the Second World War, 1936–1939* (London: Frank Cass, 1977), 82–83.

52. ANM-S, box 38, entry dated 30 March 1938.

53. See Alfred D. Low, "Edvard Beneš, the Anschluss Movement, 1918–1938, and the Policy of Czechoslovakia," *East Central Europe/L'Europe du Centre-Est* 10, nos. 1–2 (1983): 46–91.

54. ANM-B, Fond Munich, box 8. The meeting took place on 11 March 1938 at 4:30 P.M.

55. The full text is published in Telford Taylor, *Munich: The Price of Peace* (Garden City, N.Y.: Doubleday, 1979), 358–60.

56. The transcript of the telephone conversation between Hitler and Prince Philipp von Hesse, Hitler's special envoy to Italy, is in von Schuschnigg, *Austrian Requiem*, 309–10. He is misrepresented as the German ambassador in Rome; this was—until 4 February 1938—

Ulrich von Hassell, who was in 1944 sentenced to death in connection with the attempt on Hitler's life in July. Von Hassel's successor was Hans Georg von Mackensen, von Neurath's son-in-law. See Weinberg, *Foreign Policy of Hitler's Germany: Starting World War II*, 285–86. MHA-B, Fond Munich, box 7. Colonel Ostřížek, the Czechoslovak military attaché in Vienna, to Prague, 13 March 1938.

57. Ibid., report of the Ministry of Interior to President Beneš, no date, signed by Hamáček.

58. W. S. [Willi Schlamm], "Šedesát za noc," *Přítomnost*, 23 March 1938, 181. The last words of the sixty who took their lives, W. S. wrote, were probably quite plain: "Passport, departure, residence permit, money, hunger, visa, the Nuremberg Laws, and perhaps a few contemptuous curses."

59. ANM-S, box 28, entry dated 12 March 1938.

60. NA 760F.62/212, Wilbur J. Carr, the U.S. Legation, Prague, to the Secretary of State, Washington, D.C., 28 March 1938. Minister Carr met with Dr. Kubka, an official of the Czechoslovak Ministry of Foreign Affairs, who told him shortly after the *Anschluß* that the Czechoslovak General Staff specialists "had been impressed by the ineffective equipment, the papier-mache quality of German arms . . . and by the exhausted condition of the troops."

61. MHA-B, Fond Munich, box 7, the Czechoslovak military attaché, Vienna, no date, no addressee.

62. AMFA, Fond Minister Krofta, box 12. The Czechoslovak chargé d'affaires in Bogota, Colombia, spoke on the *Ile de France* with William Bullitt, who told him that, according to U.S. military specialists, a defense of Czechoslovakia was impossible after the *Anschluß*. Dated May 1938.

63. AMFA, Major Klein, the Czechoslovak military attaché, Budapest, to Prague, 13 March 1938. See also Stanislav Yester, "Voják se dívá na Anschluß," *Přítomnost,* 23 March 1938, 182–85.

64. The second Blum government lasted for only twenty-seven days; Paul-Boncour would be soon (10 April 1938) replaced by Georges Bonnet.

65. Adamthwaite, *France and the Coming of the Second World War,* 85.

66. Hitler's timing of the *Anschluß* during the French interregnum (10 March to 13 March 1938) is analyzed in Kvaček, *Obtížné spojenectví,* 63–97.

67. The French response to the *Anschluß* is in Williamson Murray, *The Change in the European Balance of Power, 1938–1939: The Path to Ruin* (Princeton: Princeton University Press, 1984), 162–66.

68. Adamthwaite, *France and the Coming of the Second World War,* 87.

69. PRO, FO 408/68.R.2524/162/12, M. Masaryk to Viscount Halifax, London, 12 March 1938. Prague had seized on this statement and spread it as wide as it could, hoping that it would become more difficult for Berlin to renege on its assurances.

70. ANM-M, Mastný, the Manuscript, 50.

71. PRO, FO 408/68.R.2524/162/12.

72. ANM-M, Mastný, the Manuscript, 58–59. The meetings took place on 31 March and 2 April 1938.

73. František Moravec, *Špión, jemuž nevěřili* (Prague: Rozmluvy Alexandra Tomského, 1990), 168.

74. MHA-B, Fond Munich, box 8, a report from (signature unclear), Geneva, 18 March 1938.

75. On Osuský, see Bernard Michel, "L'ambassadeur Osuský et son action en France," *Revue des Études Slaves* 1–2 (1979): 125–34.

76. MHA-B, Fond Munich, box 1, Štefan Osuský, the Czechoslovak Legation, Paris, to

the Ministry of Foreign Affairs, Prague, 19 April 1938. Osuský's meeting with Blum took place on 13 March 1938, the day Blum became prime minister.

77. Masaryk could not have known how right he was when he brought up the boa constrictor's need to rest. General Jodl noted in his diary that after the *Anschluß*, Hitler said he was in "no hurry to solve the Czech question because Austria [had] to be digested first." See Noakes and Pridham, *Documents on Nazism, 1919–1945*, 541. MHA-B, box 11, Jan Masaryk, the Czechoslovak Legation, London, to the Ministry of Foreign Affairs, Prague, 12 March 1938.

78. ANM-F, box 5, Břetislav Karel Palkovský to L. W. B. Smith, Prague, 18 March 1938. Palkovský went on to predict that, after the defeat of the dictators, the victorious masses might well impose a new regime, one that would not be far from "a very radical socialism."

79. PRO, FO 408/68. C2261/317/62, statement by Viscount Halifax, Secretary of State for Foreign Affairs, in the House of Lords, 16 March 1938, respecting Austria.

80. AMFA, Kamil Krofta, Prague, to the Czechoslovak Legation, London, telegrams sent, 254–258/1938, 19 March 1938. See also *Documents on British Foreign Policy, 1919–1939* (henceforth *DBFP*), 3d series, vol. 1 (London: Her Majesty's Stationery Office, 1949), document no. 101, 74–76.

81. MHA-B, Fond Munich, box 3, verbal note by Newton to Krofta, 24 March 1938, on orders from H.M.'s government; see also PRO, FO 408/68.C.1933/6, Viscount Halifax to Mr. Newton, Foreign Office, 23 March 1938.

82. PRO, FO 408/68. C2805/1941/18, Mr. Newton to Viscount Halifax, Prague, 6 April 1938. Lt. Colonel Stronge's memorandum is dated 3 April 1938.

83. Von Schuschnigg, *Austrian Requiem*, 312–13.

84. Édouard Daladier, *In Defense of France* (New York: Doubleday, Doran, 1939); Stanton B. Leeds, *These Rule France* (New York: Bobbs-Merrill, 1940); Elisabeth Du Riau, *Édouard Daladier, 1884–1970* (Paris: Fayard, 1993); *Édouard Daladier, chef de gouvernement, Avril 1938–Septembre 1939* (Paris: Presses de la Foundation Nationale des Sciences Politiques, 1977).

85. Georges Bonnet, *La défense de la paix, 1936–1940* (Geneva: Les Editions du Cheval Ailé, 1946, 1948); Adamthwaite, *France and the Coming of the Second World War*, 95–110; Weinberg, *Foreign Policy of Hitler's Germany: Starting World War II*, 350; Kvaček, Obtížné spojenectví, 99, 135–39.

86. Murray, *Change in the European Balance of Power*, 166–70.

87. MHA-B, box 20. Daladier was right in this regard. In 1938 the Czechoslovak National Assembly had 450 members. Among them were 106 Sudeten German deputies (23 percent), 18 Hungarians (4 percent), 9 Ukrainians (2 percent), and 2 Poles (0.5 percent). This division almost perfectly corresponded with the population of Czechoslovakia. As of 31 October 1936, the Sudeten Germans had 3,311 basic schools, 455 junior high schools, 90 high schools, 198 professional schools, and 3 universities. In the Sudeten districts of Czechoslovakia, there was one basic school per 862 citizens. In Prussia, there was one school per 1,112 citizens.

88. PRO, FO 408/68.C 3730/1941/18, extract from Record of Conversations between British and French Ministers on April 28 and 29, 1938.

89. Keith Feiling, *The Life of Neville Chamberlain* (London: Macmillan, 1946), 353.

90. *DBFP*, 3d series, vol. 1 document no. 164, 231–32.

91. AMFA, Jan Masaryk, the Czechoslovak Legation, London, to the Ministry of Foreign Affairs, telegrams received, no. 399/38, 28 April 1938; see also Kvaček, *Obtížné spojenectví*, 135; Weinberg, *Foreign Policy of Hitler's Germany: Starting World War II*, 356.

92. Dr. Herbert von Dirksen, London, to the Foreign Ministry, Berlin, 8 June 1938;

Documents on German Foreign Policy, 1918–1945 (henceforth *DGFP*) Series D, vol. 2 (Washington, D.C.: U.S. Government Printing Office, 1949), document no. 244, 393.

93. As early as 1936, a Czechoslovak journalist wrote from Paris: "Never rely on France. This France has lost all its virtues, this France is broken up inside, this France will betray everyone, this France is not capable of fighting. It is morally fallen." This lament had to be taken all the more seriously because it came from the pen of a great admirer of France and its culture: Richard Weiner, the Paris correspondent for *Lidové noviny*. See Ferdinand Peroutka, *Muž Přítomnosti* (Curych: Konfrontace, 1985), 209.

94. AMFA, Zdeněk Fierlinger, the Czechoslovak Legation, Moscow, to the Ministry of Foreign Affairs, Department B, received no. 17/38, 12 January 1938.

95. Ibid., 14 February 1938, secret. The official critique of Beran's speech appeared in *Pravda* on 4 February 1938.

96. See, for instance, *Pravda* of 10 February, 11 February, and 15 February 1938.

97. AMFA, Fierlinger's reports of 14 February and 19 February 1938.

98. AMFA, Foreign Minister Kamil Krofta, the Ministry of Foreign Affairs, Prague, to Zdeněk Fierlinger, the Czechoslovak Legation, Moscow, Department B, 122/38, 19 February 1938.

99. AMFA, Zdeněk Fierlinger, the Czechoslovak Legation, Moscow, to the Ministry of Foreign Affairs, Prague, received 107/38, 21 February 1938.

100. See especially Krestinsky's statement that his confession was "false from beginning to end." In Robert C. Tucker and Stephen F. Cohen (eds.), *The Great Purge Trail* (New York: Grosset & Dunlap, 1965), 55,656–68 and many other passages.

101. AMFA, Zdeněk Fierlinger, the Czechoslovak Legation, Moscow, to the Ministry of Foreign Affairs, Prague, received 161/38, 5 March 1938.

102. Ibid., received, 166/38, 10 March 1938.

103. Ibid., received, 218/38, 13 March 1938.

104. ACC CPC, Fond 20, signature 81. The whole text reads: "Nach Österreich ist die Tsch.S.R. noch mehr in den Mittelpunkt der Hitlerischen Aggression gerückt."

105. AMFA, Zdeněk Fierlinger, the Czechoslovak Legation, Moscow, to the Ministry of Foreign Affairs, Prague, secret, 13 April 1938.

106. *Pravda,* 12 January 1938, stated that Colonel Józef Beck was "the main exponent of German fascism, the officially recognized commis-voyageur of Berlin." On 17 March 1938 the paper asserted that Beck's foreign policy was a slavish immitation of the methods of aggressive powers.

107. *Izvestia,* 17 February 1938.

108. AMFA, Zdeněk Fierlinger, the Czechoslovak Legation, Moscow, to the Ministry of Foreign Affairs, Prague, secret, 13 April 1938.

109. NA 760F.61/68, Wilson, the U.S. Embassy, Paris, to the Secretary of State, Washington, D.C., 15 March 1938.

110. NA 760F.61/170, Anthony J. Drexel Biddle Jr., the U.S. Legation, Warsaw, to the Secretary of State, Washington, D.C., 16 March 1939.

111. NA 760F.61/163, Joseph E. Davies, the U.S. Embassy, Moscow, to the Secretary of State, Washington, D.C., 17 March 1938.

112. NA 760F.62/213, Joseph E. Davies, the U.S. Embassy, Moscow, to the Secretary of State, Washington, D.C., 26 March 1938.

113. AMFA, Minister Veverka, the Czechoslovak Legation, Bucharest, to Kamil Krofta, the Ministry of Foreign Affairs, Prague, telegrams received, no. 188/1938, 13 March 1938.

114. ANM-S, box 38, entry 12–14 March 1938.

115. AMFA, Zdeněk Fierlinger, the Czechoslovak Legation, Moscow, to the Ministry of Foreign Affairs, Prague, 15 March 1938.

116. Ibid., received 218/38, 13 March 1938.

117. Ibid.

118. ANM-S, box 38, entry 6 April 1938. I am grateful to Professor D. C. Watt for suggesting (in a telephone conversation, July 1995) it might be profitable to take a close look at Rudolf Herrenstadt. There seem to be indications that he played some role in Soviet intelligence. It will be interesting to follow this lead.

119. AMFA, Zdeněk Fierlinger, the Czechoslovak Legation, Moscow, for Minister Kamil Krofta's eyes only, received 350/38, 14 April 1938.

120. In March 1939 a group of prominent Frenchmen would charge Bonnet directly with "undermining French commitments." Adamthwaite, *France and the Coming of the Second World War,* 105.

121. AMFA, Minister Kamil Krofta, Prague, to Zdeněk Fierlinger, the Czechoslovak Legation, Moscow, sent 423/38, 21 April 1938. Although the document was sent under Krofta's signature, its draft is in Beneš's hand; it is in MHA-B. Word for word, the text was written by the president. He even added Krofta's signature.

122. The best analysis of Beneš's attitude toward Poland is in Piotr S. Wandycz, *The Twilight of French Eastern Alliances 1926–36: French-Czechoslovak-Polish Relations from Locarno to the Remilitarization of the Rhineland* (Princeton: Princeton University Press, 1988). Wandycz quotes Sir Joseph Addison, the British minister in Prague, as saying that Beneš's views of Poland were so extremely critical that he thought he was hearing "Dr. Goebbels or General Göring" rather than Minister Beneš. It is not impossible that Beneš was guilty as charged, but it should be pointed out that Sir Joseph disliked Edvard Beneš with considerable passion and took delight in embarrassing him in his reports from Prague (Wandycz, *The Twilight,* 331).

123. MHA-B, box 10, General Jan Syrový, Chief of Staff, to General Janusz Tadeusz Gansiorowski, Chief of Staff, 22 November 1933. Also enclosed is the Polish response of 21 December 1933.

124. AMFA, Second Section, box 470, the Ministry of Interior to the Ministry of Foreign Affairs, 9 November 1937. One such missed gesture is described in a report submitted by the Ministry of Interior. The memorandum reports that the Polish General Bernard Mond (b. 14 November 1887), military commander of Cracow who is described (with some exaggeration) as a personal friend of Generals Józef Piłsudski and Edward Rydz-Śmigły, sought out on 1 November 1937 a Czechoslovak citizen (unidentified in the memorandum). He warned that Germany was likely to cause a military conflagration with Czechoslovakia and suggested a tough Czechoslovak response to threats: Germany was not as strong as it pretended. He stated further that Colonel Józef Beck was much disliked by officers of the Polish army for his Germanophile policy. Because of certain traditions, it was impossible for Polish officers to get rid of Beck. However, it would be welcome if either France or Czechoslovakia could take the initiative in this matter. For instance, said General Mond, if proof were furnished by Prague that Colonel Beck had a bank account in Switzerland, then it would be easy to depose him. Finally, Mond stated that the Těšín territorial dispute was no longer a problem as far as the Polish army was concerned. Borders were simply final. If Czechoslovakia were to be attacked by Germany, the Polish General Staff would consider this a threat to Poland and would not hesitate to help. Prague took no initiative in this matter.

125. Repeated efforts to obtain the Russian original in Moscow have, so far, been in vain. Because the meeting involved Stalin, the document, if it exists, is said to be deposited in the

Presidential Archives which remain closed (as of June 1994) to Western researchers. Therefore, this text relies on Fierlinger's report of the event. Naturally, he did not take part in the Kermlin meeting, and he reports what he was told about it by an unnamed Soviet diplomat and, later, by V. P. Potemkin.

126. AMFA, Zdeněk Fierlinger, the Czechoslovak Legation, Moscow, to the Ministry of Foreign Affairs, Prague, received 380/38, 23 April 1938.

127. AMFA, secret (the Safe) 63.275/1938, Zdeněk Fierlinger, Moscow, to Foreign Minister Kamil Krofta, 28 April 1938.

128. ANM-S. The meeting of 18 May 1938 was recorded by Dr. Jaromír Smutný.

129. AMFA, Zdeněk Fierlinger, Moscow, to the Foreign Ministry, Prague, 29 April 1938, telegrams received 409/38.

130. AMFA, secret, Zdeněk Fierlinger, Moscow, to the Foreign Ministry, Prague, 27 June 1938. According to his own record of the conversation, Fierlinger assured Chilston that there was not one Soviet pilot on Czechoslovak territory.

131. MHA-B, Fond Munich, box 1, from President Edvard Beneš, the Castle, Prague, to the Czechoslovak Legation, London, 19 March 1938.

132. Drtina, *Československo,* 50–52.

133. Stanislav Yester, "Fronta na západě," *Lidové noviny,* 1 May 1938.

134. ANM-S, box 38, Smutný's entry of 29 March 1938.

135. Memorandum on Operation Green of 22 April 1938, initialed by Hitler's adjutant, Major Schmundt, is in *DGFP,* document no. 133, 239–40.

136. The following description of the April 1938 SdP congress in Carlsbad is based on R. G. D. Laffan, *The Crisis over Czechoslovakia* (New York: Oxford University Press, 1951), 94–97 and on George E. R. Gedye, *Betrayal in Central Europe: Austria and Czechoslovakia: The Fallen Bastions* (New York: Harper & Brothers, 1939), 387–89.

137. Gedye, *Betrayal in Central Europe,* 385–86.

138. Laffan, *Crisis over Czechoslovakia,* 96.

139. Noakes and Pridham, *Documents on Nazism,* 539.

140. Ernst Eisenlohr, Prague, to the Wilhelmstraße, 26 April 1938, *DGFP,* document no. 138, 245.

141. ACC CPC, Fond 20, signature 83; Gottwald's report to the EKI of 28 April 1938.

142. ACC CPC, Fond 57, signature 16.

143. ACC CPC, Fond 57, signature 16. Gottwald stayed in Moscow until 11 May 1938; he then treated himself to a bit of sightseeing. Rather than going back directly—via Poland—Gottwald chose to travel through Finland, Sweden, and France, where he stayed for three additional days.

144. SCA, Police Directorate, 1931–1940, box 1532, State Security (StB), 23 February 1938. The report noted that Gottwald had been called to Moscow in order to discuss the Communist International's strategy. He left Czechoslovakia on 19 February 1938.

145. ACC CPC, Fond 57, signature 16. At least some of Gottwald's long absence had not been planned, because his Soviet visa allowing residency in Moscow had to be renewed three times. The first visa, no. 250580, was valid until 13 March 1938; it was renewed on 3 May 1938 for just a few days until 7 May. On 9 May 1938 another renewal was stamped into Gottwald's passport, until 12 May. It would appear that the Comintern's Executive Committee had been fine-tuning its strategy toward the Czechoslovak crisis as it evolved, and that just as Gottwald was supposed to leave on three occasions changes had to be made and he had to stay in Moscow to await new instructions.

146. *Lidové noviny,* Prague, 2 May 1938. A recent source estimates that some 120,000

people had gathered for the demonstration of national unity on Wenceslas Square; see Robert Kvaček et al., *Československý rok 1938*, 75.

147. *Rudé Právo*, 11 March 1931.

148. SCA, Police directorate, 1931–1940, box 1532, State Security (StB), 17 March 1938.

149. Gedye, *Betrayal in Central Europe*, 396.

150. MHA-B, Arnošt Heidrich, Geneva, to the Foreign Ministry, Prague, 14 May 1938, telegrams received 449/38, box 8.

151. NA 760F.61/67, Wilbur J. Carr, the U.S. Legation, Prague, to the Secretary of State, Washington, D.C., 18 February 1938.

152. NA 760F.62/379, Wilbur J. Carr, the U.S. Legation, Prague, to the Secretary of State, Washington, D.C., 13 May 1938.

153. Actually, it is more likely that Aleksandrovsky went to Bucharest to investigate the disappearance of the Soviet diplomat Butenko.

154. AMFA, the Safe, the Czechoslovak Legation, Bucharest, to the Ministry of Foreign Affairs, received 188/38, 13 March 1938.

155. MHA-B, Arnošt Heidrich, Geneva, to the Foreign Ministry, Prague, 14 May 1938, telegrams received 449/38, box 8.

156. AMI, file 12434. Minister Machník, a member of the Republican (Agrarian) party, paid a high personal price for Czechoslovakia's dismemberment in 1938–39. He was arrested by the Gestapo on 12 July 1943 in Klatovy, a town west of Prague, after three members of a resistance organization had named him as an accomplice. The Gestapo gave the former minister a clear choice: betray others, or face the predictable consequences. Machník declined the offer to become an informer and was sentenced to death for treason against the Third Reich on 16 December 1943 by a special court in Dresden. He stayed on death row until 9 September 1944, when his sentence was commuted to ten years in a concentration camp. Machník took part in the infamous death march and was liberated by the U.S. Army on 29 April 1945. He returned to Prague on 22 May 1945.

Military experts like to point out that since no new units had been formed, one should not use the term *mobilization*. Indeed, the official term used by the Czechoslovak army planners was "mimořádná vojenská opatření" (emergency military measures).

157. MOP, 1938, secret, no. 305. Major Lowell M. Riley was received by President Edvard Beneš as the new U.S. military attaché in Czechoslovakia on 25 April 1938.

158. NA RG 165, U.S. Military Attaché Major Lowell M. Riley, report no. P-742, 24 May 1938, G-2/2657-II-95-1.

159. NA RG 165, Major Lowell M. Riley, report no. P-742, 24 May 1938, G-2/2657-II-95-2.

160. NA RG 165, Major Lowell M. Riley, report no. P-745, 25 May 1938, G-2/2657-II-95-3.

161. Office of the President of the Republic of Czechoslovakia, the Castle, Prague, Book of Presidential Audiences for 1938.

162. Drtina recalled that General Jan Syrový had accompanied Machník and Krejčí. See Drtina, *Československo*, 59. But Syrový testified after the war that he had first found out about the partial mobilization on 21 May 1938 while on a tour of inspection in Trutnov. He then quickly returned to Prague. SCA, National Tribunal, TNS 1/47, Jan Syrový.

163. SCA, National Tribunal, NS, interrogation protocol of Army General Ludvík Krejčí (ret.) of 16 April 1946. General Krejčí was the army's chief of staff from 1 December 1933 to 1 March 1939.

164. Drtina, *Československo*, 59.

165. SCA, Ministerial Council, PMR, Government Protocols XVII-29.

166. These units were typically deployed in critical areas along the border, often in front of the fortified line.

167. MHA, Ministry of National Defense, the General Staff, first department, 1938, box 242.

168. NA RG 165, U.S. Military Attaché Major Lowell M. Riley, the U.S. Legation, Prague, 1 June 1938, 2657–II–90, box 1704.

169. Ibid., 24 May 1938, P–742, G–2/2657–II–95–1.

170. MHA-MOP, report by the Second Bureau of the General Staff, 1938, secret, 444, 1 June 1938; ANM-S, box 38, 23 May 1938; ibid., box 38, 24 May 1938: "The President is happy that our military measures worked so smoothly. The soldiers made a good impression. Now it's important not to ruin it politically."

171. *Národní osvobození*, 22 May 1938.

172. Ferdinand Peroutka, "Co bylo, nebude," *Přítomnost*, 23 March 1938.

173. MHA-B, Fond Munich, box 1, documents on the May crisis, no. 2. The meeting took place on 21 May 1938 at 12:52 P.M.

174. Ibid., Eisenlohr's telegram to Berlin, 21 May 1938.

175. Ibid., documents on the May crisis no. 4 and 5.

176. Ibid., document on the May crisis, no. 6.

177. Ibid., document no. 7.

178. *DGFP*, series D, vol. 2, document no. 181, 308–9.

179. MHA-B, Fond Munich, box 8, MOP, 24 May 1938, report of Dr. Passer, a lawyer and a Czechoslovak army reserve officer, who had spoken with Dr. Hoffmann, a secretary of the German legation in Prague.

180. *Trial of the Major War Criminals before the International Military Tribunal (TMWC)*, (Nuremberg: International Military Tribunal, 1947), 25:434–35. The original text was, "Es ist mein unabänderlicher Entschluß, die Tschechoslowakei in absehbarer Zeit durch eine militärische Aktion zu zerschlagen." See also ACC CPC, Fond 100/45, file 8, archival unit 177, *Kniha o přepadení Československa ve světle dokumentů předložených Mezinárodnímu vojenskému soudu v Norimberku* (Prague: Ministry of Interior, no date [probably 1946]).

181. *Speeches of Adolf Hitler*, 2:1494.

182. Dwight E. Lee, *Ten Years: The World on the Way to War, 1930–1940* (Boston: Houghton Mifflin, 1942), 320.

183. ANM-S, box 38. Smutný's entry for 24 May states that such was the case in Česká Lípa, Duchcov, Teplice, and Most.

184. A sympathetic portrait of Jaksch is in Karel Nedvěd, "Němec, který zůstal demokratem: Wenzel Jaksch," *Přítomnost*, 20 July 1938, 454–57; *Lidové noviny*, 10 June 1938.

185. MHA-B, box 470, the Czechoslovak Legation, Warsaw, to the Ministry of Foreign Affairs, Prague, 27 May 1938.

186. MHA-B, box 10, Juraj Slávik, the Czechoslovak Legation, Warsaw, to the Ministry of Foreign Affairs, Prague, 3 June 1938.

187. PRO, FO 404/27.C5335/1941/18, Viscount Halifax to Sir H. Kennard (Warsaw), Foreign Office, 2 June 1938.

188. AMFA, Second Section, box 470, František Kubka's record of his meeting with Professor Charles Hodges, 2 September 1938.

189. AMFA, Second Section, box 470, The Czechoslovak Legation, Warsaw, to the Ministry of Foreign Affairs, Prague, 24 May 1938.

190. AMFA, the Cabinet, no. 1800, records of Václav Fiala's conversations in Poland between 6 and 13 April 1938. In the spring of 1938, Beneš sent his personal emissary, the journalist Fiala, a specialist on Poland, on a fact-finding mission to Warsaw. Fiala was

received neither by Beck nor by others in the official circles; he only managed to speak with leaders of various opposition parties. He returned with a report indicating that, as a precondition for a Czechoslovak-Polish rapprochement, even Beck's opponents demanded not only territorial adjustments but also the annulment of the Czechoslovak-Soviet agreement of 1935. That was obviously unacceptable in Prague. The Fiala mission is described in Anna M. Cienciala, *Poland and the Western Powers, 1938–1939: A Study in the Interdependence of Eastern and Western Europe* (London: Routledge, 1968), 66–69 and in Kvaček, *Obtížné spojenectví*, 112–13. Some of Beneš collaborators (e.g., Jaromír Smutný) were openly anti-Polish. By contrast, the Czechoslovak minister in Warsaw, Juraj Slávik, understood that the position of Warsaw would be crucially important for Prague's ability to stand up to the Third Reich. See Slávik's reports to Beneš in MHA-B, box 10.

191. MHA-B, Second Section, box 470, the Czechoslovak Legation, Warsaw, to the Ministry of Foreign Affairs, Prague, 26 September 1938.

192. The partial mobilization is discussed, for instance, by Gerhard L. Weinberg, "The May Crisis, 1938," *Journal of Modern History* 29 (September 1957): 213–25; W. V. Wallace, "The Making of the May Crisis of 1938," *Slavonic and East European Review* 41 (June 1963): 368–90; D. C. Watt, "The May Crisis of 1938: A Rejoinder to Mr. Wallace," *Slavonic and East European Review,* 44 (July 1966): 475–80; see also W. V. Wallace, "A Reply to Mr. Watt," *Slavonic and East European Review* 44 (July 1966): 481–86; D. C. Watt, "Hitler's Visit to Rome and the May Weekend Crisis: A Study in Hitler's Response to External Stimuli," *Journal of Contemporary History* 9 (January 1974): 23–32. The May crisis is also dealt with in several books: Henderson B. Braddick, *Germany, Czechoslovakia, and the "Grand Alliance" in the May Crisis, 1938* (Denver, Colo.: University of Denver, 1969), passim; Taylor, *Munich: The Price of Peace*, 390–95, 517–20, 654–55; A. J. P. Taylor, *The Origins of the Second World War* (London: Hamilton, 1961), 165; Weinberg, *Foreign Policy of Hitler's Germany: Starting World War II*, 366–77; Murray, *Change in the European Balance of Power*, 171–74; D. C. Watt, *How War Came: The Immediate Origins of the Second World War, 1938–1939* (New York: Pantheon, 1989), 26; Keith Eubank, *Munich* (Norman: University of Oklahoma Press, 1963), 59–73; Robert Kvaček, *Obtížné spojenectví: Politicko-diplomatické vztahy mezi Československem a Francií, 1937–1939* (Prague: Acta Universitatis Carolinae, 1989), 150–54. Often cited was the diary of General Alfred Jodl, covering the period from 4 January 1937 to 25 August 1939 in *TMWC*, 28:345–90.

193. The file is deposited in the MHA, Ministry of National Defense (MNO), additions, box 24. It is also in the Historical Institute of the Czech Army, Prague (HI CR). Finally, it can be found in the archive of (President) Klement Gottwald, who received the document from the minister of defense (and his son-in-law), General Čepička. See ACC CPC, Fond 100/24, file 56, archival unit 905. This file has two parts. The first consists of four pages of Havel's analysis and six appendixes (eight pages) in Czech and German; the second has five pages of Havel's analysis and sixteen appendixes.

194. A flattering portrait of Paul Thümmel is in Moravec, *Špión,* 111–24; a much less optimistic view of A-54 is expressed, in bitter terms, in an unpublished manuscript by Colonel František Havel, "Agent A-54 a Moravcovo zpravodajství bez legend," a manuscript of twenty-eight pages, no date, deposited in the Historical Institute of the Czech Army, Prague. Moravec describes A-54 as one of the aces of international espionage during World War II; Havel pictures him as a German double agent who was able to deceive the Second Bureau because he played on the vanity of Moravec, Havel's rival. A balanced treatment of A-54 is in Colonel Emil Strankmüller, "Čs. ofenzivní zpravodajství od března 1939," *Odboj a revoluce* 8, no. 1 (1970): 189–229. The most recent effort to analyze the case of Thümmel by professional historians with access to archival documents is Jaroslav Kokoška and Stanislav

Kokoška, *Spor o agenta A-54* (Prague: Naše Vojsko, 1994). The authors paint a critical portrait of Thümmel, who comes across as a vain and greedy man and a deceitful double agent whose main loyalty was to the Abwehr.

195. Kokoška and Kokoška, *Spor o agenta A-54,* 80–91.

196. See Kokoška and Kokoška, *Spor o agenta A-54,* 85–86, 325n40.

197. Ibid., 85.

198. After the Munich Agreement, Lange and his wife escaped to Prague and then moved to London. The Second Bureau intervened on Lange's behalf with the British, and D-14 received British passport no. 227 242. He obtained a new identity, becoming Harry Johnston, a businessman from Bristol. During the war Lange-Johnston continued working for the Czechoslovak Second Bureau from Switzerland. Ibid., 155–56; Strankmüller, "Čs. zpravodajství," 193.

199. Havel, "Agent A-54 a Moravcovo zpravodajství bez legend," 6.

200. Jan Gebhart and J. Kuklík, "Zápas o Československo na poli zpravodajství ve druhé polovině 30. let," *Historie a vojenství* 1 (1988): 107–9. The first PAU was established in Liberec in the early 1930s. Others followed in quick succession: Ústí nad Labem, Plzeň, Česká Lípa, Karlovy Vary, Teplice, Litoměřice, Hradec Králové, České Budějovice, Znojmo, Ostrava, Bánská Bystrica, Košice, and Užhorod. Their main mission was to develop intelligence networks in the border areas and penetrate as far as was possible into the heart of Czechoslovakia's main opponent, the Third Reich.

201. Colonel Havel stated that the information from the British came in response to two explicit requests from Prague. The Second Bureau communicated with the British Intelligence Service via Major Harold Charles Gibson, who was posted to Prague (as a passport officer at the British legation) soon after Hitler's *Machtergreifung*. He established solid ties with the Czechoslovak military intelligence and masterminded (on 14 March 1938 at 5 P.M.) the escape from Prague of Moravec and ten of his colleagues in the Second Bureau, only hours before the Wehrmacht occupied the country.

202. ANM-M, Mastný, the Manuscript, 72.

203. The British report stated, "Der Berichterstatter ist der Meinung, daß die Deutschen für die Wahlen in der Tschechoslowakei eine Truppendemonstration an den Grenzen in Absicht haben."

204. MHA-B, box 1, Minister Eisenlohr, the German Legation, Prague, 18 May 1938, 8 P.M., no. 147.

205. MHA-B, box 8, MOP, 25 May 1938.

206. ANM-S, box 38, 23 May 1938: "Well," said the president, "Krejčí had wanted too much. But I stood firm and, as we can see, it has worked very well." Drtina states that Minister Machník and General Krejčí had originally demanded a mobilization of five year-classes and that President Beneš negotiated the request down to one year-class. See Drtina, *Československo,* 61–62.

207. NA RG 165, Major Lowell M. Riley, U.S. military attaché, Prague, report no. P–799, 5 July 1938, G–2/2657–II–90–30. Riley spoke with Beneš on 2 July 1938.

208. PRO, FO 408/68.C5435/4786/18. Newton's report to Halifax of 1 June 1938 includes a report by Lt. Colonel Stronge to Newton on the former's trip to the Sudetenland on 28 and 29 May 1938.

209. H. C. T. Stronge, "The Military Approach to Munich," *Times,* 29 September 1967. Colonel Stronge's reports, often contradicting those of his colleague in Berlin, were mostly ignored by Whitehall, and Stronge's military career after his tour of duty in Prague was short and unillustrious. See Stronge, "The Czechoslovak Army and the Munich Crisis: A Personal Memorandum," in *War and Society,* 1:162–77.

210. Sir Nevile Henderson, *Failure of a Mission, Berlin 1937–1939* (New York: Put-

nam's, 1940), 136–37. Sir Nevile speculated that the Prague government had been misled by "unskilled agents and observers."

211. Colonel Havel, "Zpravodajská činnost 2. oddělení hlavního štábu čs. armády v letech 1936–1939," 50–51; the manuscript has 176 typed pages and is deposited at the H1 CR, Prague.

212. *TMWC*, 25:420. It will be noticed that Zeitzler listed divisions that *could* march within twelve hours, not divisions that had marched against Czechoslovakia.

213. Having written this sentence (in the summer of 1994), I received (in December 1994) a letter from Professor Donald Cameron Watt, who wrote, "The reports reaching the Czechs were far too detailed and far-reaching to be the product of error, or of misinterpretation of the natural regrouping of German forces consequent on the occupation of the Austro-Czech border and the incorporation of the Austrian army in the Reichswehr. They were a deliberate piece of misinformation." I am convinced that Professor Watt is right.

214. *Dokumenty k historii mnichovského diktátu, 1937–1939* (Prague: Svoboda, 1979), document no. 66, 119.

215. ACC CPC, Fond 100/24, file 172, archival unit 1524. Beneš's statement to David, Stašek, Gottwald, Richter, Rašín, Stránský, Klíma, and Tykal on 30 September 1938 at 2 P.M.

216. Gebhart and Kuklík, "Zápas o Československo," 59. This is a manuscript of the article that appeared in *Historie a vojenstvi* 1 (1988): 88–112.

217. ANM-D, box 4. This is the manuscript of a text later published as "International Causes of the Czechoslovak Tragedies" (Washington, D.C.: Czechoslovak Society for Arts and Sciences in America, 1962).

218. AMFA, Zdeněk Fierlinger, the Czechoslovak Legation, Moscow, to the Ministry of Foreign Affairs, telegrams received, 493/38, 23 May 1938.

219. Ibid., telegrams received 501/38, 26 May 1938.

220. NA 760F.62/286, Joseph E. Davies, the U.S. Embassy, Moscow, to the Secretary of State, Washington, D.C., 22 May 1938.

221. NA 760F.62/315, Joseph E. Davies, the U.S. Embassy, Moscow, to the Secretary of State, Washington, D.C., 23 May 1938.

222. ANM-F, box 23, record of General Otakar Husák's trip to the Soviet Union in 1938 (2 May–27 May 1938).

223. Ibid., Zdeněk Fierlinger's note for President Beneš, 25 May 1938.

224. Parts of the article are quoted by Alexander Kirk, the U.S. Embassy, Moscow, to the Secretary of State, Washington, D.C., 28 May 1938 [NA 760F.62/421]. *Izvestia's* statement on Czechoslovakia was prominently reprinted on 27 May 1938 in the daily of the Czechoslovak Communist party, *Rudé Právo*.

225. *DGFP*, series D, vol. 2, document no 261, 423–26.

226. NA 760F.62/287, Joseph E. Davies, the U.S. Embassy, Moscow, to the Secretary of State, Washington, D.C., 22 May 1938.

227. It is said that the acronym stood for *voennyi nabliudatelnyi post* (military observation post, in Russian) and *volající na poušti* (voice in the desert, in Czech). Colonel Moravec claimed that cooperation between Czechoslovak and Soviet intelligence was agreed upon on 16 May 1935 when Prague and Moscow signed the treaty of mutual assistance. See Moravec, *Špión*, 97–110, 154–61; Kokoška and Kokoška, *Spor o agenta A-54*, 53.

228. ACC CPC, Fond 20, signature 83, Klement Gottwald's report to the Communist International, 28 April 1938, Moscow. Gottwald stated that the main objective of his party was to transform the future war into a revolution.

229. Some material on this topic is in Igor Lukes, "Did Stalin Desire War in 1938? A New Look at Soviet Behavior during the May and September Crises," *Diplomacy & State-*

craft 2 (March 1991): 28–30 and Igor Lukes, "Benesch, Stalin und die Comintern: Vom Münchner Abkommen zum Molotow-Ribbentrop Pakt," *Vierteljahrshefte für Zeitgeschichte* 3 (1993): 346–53.

230. Further progress will be achieved when all archives in Moscow become accessible to Western researchers. The most interesting would be the Presidential Archives and the Archives of the GRU (the Soviet military intelligence agency). That the Soviet intelligence was directly responsible in May 1938 for misleading Prague into thinking that a German aggression was imminent is asserted, but without any evidence, by Bohdan Chudoba, "The Pattern of Soviet Foreign Policy: Czechoslovakia, May 1938," *Sudeten Bulletin* 11 (December 1963): 394.

6

Lord Runciman and Comrade Zhdanov: Western and Soviet Policies toward Czechoslovakia from June to Early September 1938

The partial mobilization of the Czechoslovak army in May turned, at least for a fleeting moment, into a near triumph for the Prague government. It seemed that Hitler had lost initiative. Rumors started to circulate in Berlin that the Führer was in one of his "black moods" and that he would try to regain momentum by occupying the Sudetenland before the opening of the Nazi party congress scheduled to take place at Nuremberg in September.[1] The leadership of the Czechoslovak army responded to this threat by requesting that the Prague government pass a law adding another twelve months to the existing two-year military service obligation.[2] Meanwhile, an additional forty thousand reservists were called up, and the Goebbels propaganda machine appeared to have stalled when confronted with units of the Czechoslovak army deployed along the fortified borders.[3] The tension between Prague and Berlin was such that a few cannon shots fired in error could have set in motion what many had come to fear: another war in Europe.

In the early summer of 1938, German diplomacy retreated and eased direct pressure on President Beneš, indicating that there was nothing new to discuss. It preferred to deal primarily with London and, to a lesser extent, Paris. The message Berlin sought to communicate to the British and French could be summed up in three propositions. First, the Sudeten Germans were entitled to raise the principle of self-determination just as Masaryk and Beneš had done during the Great War.[4] Second, despite Hitler's patience and willingness to aim at a political, rather than military, settlement of the crisis, the Beneš government had given no sign of its preparedness to offer a comprehensive solution that would satisfy the Sudeten German party of Konrad Henlein, the SdP. It had only played for time behind the facade of working on a new legal instrument for administration of the Sudetenland. Prague's real intention was to gain time so that the Czechoslovak army could increase it combat readiness. Third, President Beneš had not seen fit to solve the Sudeten crisis because he had reason to believe that he could hide behind the backs of Great Britain and France. But now the Führer's patience had come to an end. If London and Paris desired a peaceful solution, they had to compel Prague to make all the necessary concessions.[5]

Such an analysis could seem persuasive only to those prepared to accept the premise that there was a similarity between democratic Czechoslovakia and the Henlein movement, based as it was on the principles of national socialism. It rested, furthermore, on the assumption that Hitler truly sought to improve the standing of the Sudeten Germans within Czechoslovakia rather than use the issue in order to weaken and ultimately destroy the country. Nevertheless, German diplomacy had successfully made it appear that the key to peace lay in the Franco-British ability to force Beneš to capitulate to Hitler's demands and not in restraining Berlin from aggression against Czechoslovakia. The stratagem had worked. From June to the end of September, Beneš would be subjected to intimidation more by British and French diplomats than by the Führer.

France: Firm Statements of Support on Shaky Foundations

After the May mobilization, the official circles in Paris became fatalistic and re-signed.[6] It was unclear whether the French army could prevail over its historic enemy as it had done with Allied help two decades earlier. But it was certain that even a glorious victory would come at a terrible price. Nevertheless, no Frenchman in an official capacity was willing to state publicly that France would renege on its legal obligation to defend Czechoslovakia in case of an unprovoked German attack. In fact, declarations by French officials could not have been more supportive of the Prague government. In mid-July 1938 France stated that its "solemn engagements undertaken towards Czechoslovakia were indisputable and sacred."[7] Further, when Field Marshal Göring asked visiting French air force general Joseph Vuillemin point-blank what France intended to do in case of a Czechoslovak-German war, he replied, "If you attack Czechoslovakia, we will attack you. Moreover, since the possibility of a German attack on Czechoslovakia exists, my General Staff and myself, in accordance with our duty, have made all our preparations for a war with Germany."[8]

Official circles in Berlin were taken aback by the directness of the statement; the doyen of the diplomatic corps in Germany, French Ambassador André François-Poncet, told Minister Mastný that, in his view, Berlin had been hoping to drive a wedge between France and its Czechoslovak ally, and the ploy did not work.[9] Later, when Lord Halifax lectured the French chargé d'affaires in London about the neces-sity of viewing the Czechoslovak-German crisis with cold realism, the diplomat responded by saying that the official signature of France had been given and it committed his country to stand by its ally, come what may. Ignoring the signature now would depreciate its value "for all time."[10] The line taken by Lord Halifax had remained unacceptable in French government circles for quite a while. On 4 September 1938 Foreign Minister Georges Bonnet reaffirmed his government's pledge to defend Czechoslovakia, and even on 8 September 1938—that is, after the breakdown of negotiations between the Prague government and the SdP, Prime Minister Édouard Daladier stated "most positively" that the moment the first German soldiers crossed the borders of Czechoslovakia, "the French will march to a man."[11] He repeated the same to the British ambassador in Paris (although "with evident lack of enthusiasm") on 13 September 1938.[12] Such declarations, of course, encouraged Beneš, although he had expected nothing less than loyalty from the French government, no matter who happened to be its prime minister.

On 18 July 1938 Minister Mastný spoke with Beneš for five and a half hours at the Prague Castle and analyzed Czechoslovakia's international situation in the most pessimistic terms. One should have no doubts, Mastný warned, about the intentions of Adolf Hitler; he was determined to smash Czechoslovakia by one means or another. Similarly, one should give up illusions about Great Britain because its government had convinced itself that Hitler could be won over to conduct a constructive policy in the West so long as he received freedom of action in Central Europe. And France? Mastný told Beneš that, according to all his sources, the country was so internally rotten that not a single French soldier would obey the order to march against the Third Reich. The president rejected Mastný's analysis, directly referring to assurances he had received from the most authoritative individuals in the French government.[13] Despite Mastný's pessimism, Beneš felt confident that France would remain faithful to its obligations.

After World War II Georges Bonnet succumbed to the temptation to diminish French (and his own) responsibility for Czechoslovakia's abandonment during the crisis of 1938. At a minimum, he distorted the record of his interview with the Czechoslovak minister in Paris, Štefan Osuský, in which he allegedly said on 20 July 1938 that France would not be able to march in support of its Czechoslovak ally.[14] Another possibility is that the whole interview had never taken place. It was invented *post factum* and the record of the purported interview was fabricated.[15] Although a note on this supposed conversation was made part of the official collection of French diplomatic documents and can also be found in the *Papiers de Édouard Daladier* at the Foundation Nationale des Sciences Politiques, there is no trace of it in either the archives of the Quai d'Orsay, the archives of the Prague Foreign Ministry, the office of President Beneš at the Castle, or the archives of President Beneš.[16] In fact, the president registered the first official indication that France would betray its commitments only on 16 September 1938. He noted that the French minister in Prague, Victor de Lacroix, came to him looking embarrassed, and he realized that Foreign Minister Bonnet "was preparing a backdoor to treason."[17] Even if Bonnet had given the Prague government advance warning, it would not have removed the odiousness of France's betrayal of its ally.

But President Beneš did not rely only on diplomatic reports from Paris to discern the intentions of his most important ally. He also followed the French press, and on its pages one found a picture that differed from the noble-sounding declarations made by French government officials. Excepting the communist press, virtually absent were articles stressing that the Prague government was justified in defending Czechoslovakia against the threat of German aggression; even reminders that France was honor-bound to assist its ally were difficult to find. Most French periodicals pointed out in no uncertain terms the absurdity of going to war and risking the slaughter of some estimated three million (Bonnet would raise the number to ten million by the middle of September) Frenchmen on behalf of a country that seemed to be merely an aggregate of several nationalities, some of whom did not wish to live with others. Virtually all Paris-based newspapers shared the view that the Sudeten issue should not be allowed to trigger a general war. *La République* said forcefully on 6 September 1938 that only a peaceful solution of the Sudeten crisis was acceptable; that this would mean ripping up France's treaty of mutual assistance with Czechoslovakia did not need to be spelled out.

The Paris press reflected the views of the general public only to a limited extent. It failed to show fully that French society was divided into ideologically defined camps, unwilling to pull together despite the German threat.[18] Most of the social and economic classes in France were united only by their shared conviction that one world war in a lifetime was enough. For them, the notion of "standing by Czechoslovakia" smacked of a foreign ploy. There was not much of a consensus on other issues.[19] The propertied classes looked on Bolshevism, not the Third Reich, as the main enemy of France. Communists had done their best to support the emergence of the *Front Populaire* which the Communist International prescribed as the right antidote to Nazism. But in order to be palatable to the vigorously anticommunist middle-class, small business owners, and elements left of center, the popular front had to be presented as a tool for improving the French social welfare system. Consequently, the economy and the French armed forces were hurt by socialist legislative measures introduced at the most inappropriate time.[20] For instance, in August 1938, as German and Czechoslovak armament factories worked at a feverish pace, French metallurgical workers spent twenty-five days of paid vacations in the countryside or along the seacoast. Only thirteen airplanes were produced during the month.[21] (Normally, France produced forty-five to fifty planes a month, whereas Germany, it was believed, could turn out ten times that number.)[22] This, of course, was bound to have serious consequences. The French air force reached a point of unprecedented weakness during the crisis of September 1938.[23]

Given that the public was not prepared to press the government to uphold national *honneur* and stand by the country's legal commitments to Czechoslovakia, it is remarkable that French officials had persisted in asserting their loyalty to Czechoslovakia for so long. However, even the most radical among them, the *bellicistes* (those who spoke with the greatest passion about the sacred nature of diplomatic commitments) supported the Prague government not because they believed in the merit of its case against the Third Reich but because they hoped that Hitler was only bluffing. They favored a firm stance toward the Third Reich because they hoped that toughness, not concessions, could avoid war. The most bellicose among the *bellicistes* were committed to maintaining peace under almost any circumstances, and the prospect of German bombs raining on Paris could lead them to reassess the sacred value of an official French signature.[24] From this perspective, it would appear that the *bonnetistes* (those who supported the policy of Minister Bonnet) subscribed to a remarkably similar course of action as their more hawkish colleagues, except they were not willing to march quite as close to the abyss. In the end, neither party was ready to go to war.

Great Britain Takes Charge

The men responsible for formulating British foreign policy, Prime Minister Neville Chamberlain and his foreign minister, Lord Halifax, were also not ready to resign themselves to the prospect of another war.[25] They were determined to prevent the crisis between Czechoslovakia and Germany from dragging France, and possibly also Great Britain, into the second conflagration of the century. That prospect appeared particularly irrational because no British commitments or even interests were involved in what looked—from the isle of Albion—to be no more than a jurisdictional dispute between the likable Sudeten German leader Henlein and the hard-headed President Beneš.[26] In the view of many Britons, the Sudetenland crisis was to be solved by a rational compromise, peacefully executed. Ministers Masaryk and Mastný urged the Prague government from their posts in London and Berlin to make ''magnanimous'' concessions to Henlein, but it is unlikely that—in the summer of 1938—any offer would have been enough to satisfy the Sudeten politicians, and therefore, also the British. On 14 June and again on 7 September 1938, the *Times* suggested with an air of its inimitable authority that Sudeten Germans should be allowed to determine their future.[27] This meant giving freedom of action to the SdP, the very party that had in April embraced Nazism. The paper did not speculate on the consequences this was likely to have for those inhabitants of the Sudetenland who had failed to join the SdP or were deemed ineligible for membership.

The Prague government tried to offer the Sudeten Germans everything short of territorial autonomy and formation of a Sudeten Diet. It was certain that the latter would be dominated by the SdP, which would without hesitation introduce Nazi-style institutions in the region. Such a prospect was unacceptable to all the political parties represented in the Beneš government. After all, how could schools in some districts of the country educate children in the spirit of Masaryk's democracy and toleration while in other parts Nazism would be treated as the official Weltanschauung? And what would happen to Czechs, German socialists, and Jews in the Sudetenland under the heel of the SdP? Therefore, Prague refused to discuss Sudeten autonomy and a separate German legislature. President Beneš tried to explain to Basil Newton that his country could not afford to toy with such experiments.[28] The British minister had little sympathy for Czechoslovakia, but even he began hinting to Lord Halifax in early June 1938 that London should press for more concessions in Prague cautiously without giving offense. After all, if the territorial integrity and independence of Czechoslovakia were endangered, the army—devoted as it was to the principle of democracy—might have to act with or without Beneš's support. The country would not ''submit tamely to foreign threats,'' Newton warned.[29]

Lord Halifax was not impressed with this reasoning. Bring more pressure to bear on Beneš, he ordered. The Prague government was in no position to reject a

Sudeten German Diet, and if the president did not like dealing with the relatively moderate Henlein he might well find himself facing one of the extremists among the SdP's leadership.[30] A paradoxical situation had developed in the summer of 1938: France was Czechoslovakia's primary ally and yet the French were mostly silent and withdrawn. Great Britain, on the other hand, had no bilateral legal ties with Czechoslovakia, and it had stressed publicly its noninvolvement in Central Europe. Nevertheless, British diplomacy had become quite active in the Czechoslovak crisis, not only through its diplomatic posts in Paris, Berlin, Warsaw, and Moscow but also in Prague.

In the summer of 1938 the British legation in Prague sent Major Reginald Sutton-Pratt and Consul Ian Henderson to travel through the tense areas of western Czechoslovakia.[31] Their mission was to examine causes of the crisis on the spot. Anticipating their tour of inspection, the Prague government sent a circular note to local authorities stating that since the policy of Czechoslovak organs in the Sudetenland had been fundamentally correct they should now be "absolutely honest with the British observers." It explicitly prohibited any attempts at deceiving the travelers or masking the reality.[32]

The British covered a lot of territory, not only in the Sudetenland, and soon the Ministry of Foreign Affairs in Prague had to deal with a stream of missives typed by Consul Henderson on the characteristic blue stationery of His Majesty's legation. Using exclusively German names for localities in Czechoslovakia, or mangling those Czech words for which there was no German equivalent, Consul Henderson formulated his petitions in a manner so arrogant that one is hard-pressed to remember that he was a diplomat addressing the Foreign Ministry of a sovereign country. A Sudeten German woman had been dismissed from her factory job and another had been transferred. Consul Henderson was quick to inquire: Was it not because both had taken part in a function organized by the Henlein party?[33] There was a street brawl in the center of Prague between a group of Sudeten Germans illegally wearing Nazi uniforms and marching in military formation and Czechoslovak citizens. Nobody was hurt or injured. Still, Consul Henderson inquired what the Prague government intended to do about it.[34] A rumor reached the British that school children at Benešov and troops at Hradec Králové had sung ribald songs insulting to the Führer. The consul sat down and wrote to the Foreign Ministry, "Could you kindly tell me what significance is attached, in the Czech official view, to these [events]?"[35]

Soon even the British minister became involved in this campaign. During an official audience with Foreign Minister Krofta, Newton complained in all seriousness against a statement in one newspaper to the effect that compromise with Nazism—not the SdP—was no more possible than it would be between fire and water. He was also upset that another newspaper portrayed Konrad Henlein "as a living microphone of Berlin."[36] It so happened that both observations were correct, and one can imagine how Minister Krofta must have felt while having to carry out such a senseless conversation with a representative of a country as important as Great Britain. Finally, Lord Halifax himself sent a personal message to President Beneš stating that he had been very much "disquieted by the attitude of the Czech press."[37] Given that the danger to Czechoslovakia's existence was imminent and overwhelming, the press was, if anything, unnaturally subdued and naively optimistic. It was unpleasant to have to deal with such British interference in Czecho-slovakia's internal affairs. In fact, it was in violation of Newton's self-proclaimed "general policy of avoiding getting drawn into details."[38] One wonders how the British government would have responded had Czechoslovak diplomats submitted questions to the Foreign Office regarding the British treatment of Irish Catholics or if protests had been lodged against anti-Czechoslovak articles in the *Daily Mail.*

Most serious were frequent British hints that the Czechoslovak army should release the reservists and specialists it had mobilized in May. Eventually, General Krejčí on behalf of the Army General Staff asked the British minister in Prague to stop demanding "explanations for every military measure taken in the interests of Czechoslovak security," and Beneš plucked up his courage to complain to Newton about hostile British propaganda.[39]

Although the president and Czechoslovakia's top general could afford to protest against the unfriendly behavior of Great Britain, the lower-ranking officials of the Prague Foreign Ministry were clearly under instructions to deal with Newton's and Henderson's interventions as well as they could. It is hardly surprising that the president and his team had developed a low opinion of Newton. Beneš, who under normal circumstances did not show his emotions before his staff, could not restrain himself when it came to the British minister in Prague. That Newton, he sighed once, he is so *tupý* (dumb); in his private notes he went further and described the diplomat as "a thick-headed ignoramus."[40] The problem was that Newton, whatever his personal qualities, represented the British Foreign Service, and the Czechoslovak president could not dismiss that institution with a single turn of phrase.

The British Intervention: Lord Runciman in Prague

For a long time, the Sudeten German party had demanded that the Prague govern-ment adopt the Nationality Statute, a constitutional amendment redefining the rights of minorities and the administrative pattern in Czechoslovakia. It had intended to use it as a legal tool for turning the Sudetenland into a homogeneously German territory administered by the Henleinists. In spite of a bad premonition, the Prague govern-ment complied. In mid-April 1938 London and Paris were notified that a compre-hensive plan for the solution of the Sudeten German problem was ready for their review.[41] Minister de Lacroix received the text of the statute before the end of April, paradoxically only two days after Henlein's declaration in Karlovy Vary that the SdP was a Nazi organization.[42] Nevertheless, the Prague government guided the Nation-ality Statute through the appropriate political channels, and in the middle of July 1938 a bill had been prepared which parliament was expected to debate later. It did not embody all the Henlein party had desired, but it offered everything that was compatible with the constitution and the sovereign status of the Czechoslovak Re-public. Most important it provided for a significant decentralization of government because it transferred much of Prague's jurisdiction to municipalities and newly formed administrative areas. It was expected that the proposed statute would pass and become law.

As we have seen, the Führer had instructed the SdP to resist any prospect for a political solution of the crisis in Czechoslovakia's Sudetenland. Therefore, the party reversed its position regarding the Nationality Statute. It now launched a campaign to prevent parliament from discussing the bill. Incredibly, the British, who had insisted that the Prague government produce the statute, now accepted Henlein's *volte face;* they assumed the positon that it would be provocative and destabilizing for parliament to pass the new law on nationality maters without prior approval of its proposed text by the SdP.[43] Proceeding in accordance with Henlein's new demand was unconstitutional. The SdP was one of many political parties in Czechoslovakia, it was amply represented in parliament, and its deputies were free to address the merits of the bill during formal debate. They were also free to cast their votes at its conclusion. Giving Henlein the right to determine what bill the Czechoslovak parliament could discuss meant that the SdP had become a state within a state. It was hardly surprising that the Henleinists would present such a demand, but it must have hurt Beneš and his colleagues that this undemocratic measure had won the support of Great Britain, the country whose democratic political tradition Czechoslovakia's founders had so much admired. Eventually, the Beneš government surrendered to the demands of Great Britain and the SdP and withdrew the proposed Nationality Statute.

Parliament's role had been weakened considerably, and this simplified the task of British diplomats in Prague. They did not need to dilute their energy by having to communicate with representatives of various political parties; they could focus pressure on just one person, the president, and he had little room to maneuver. He could not hide behind the normally lengthy decision-making process typical for any functioning democracy. Henceforth, Beneš would appear to be the only obstacle in the way of a compromise in Czechoslovakia, and that did not improve his standing in the eyes of the public in Western Europe. By accepting this arrangement, the president deprived himself of the protection offered by those democratic institutions he had helped to build twenty years before, and he became vulnerable during the crucial moments of the crisis. It is unlikely that the outcome of Czechoslovakia's conflict with the Third Reich would have been different had parliament been allowed to play its role as provided for by the Constitution. But cutting it out altogether was an error, and Beneš would pay for it when the odium for Czechoslovakia's capitulation at the end of September 1938 would be put, exclusively and unfairly, on him alone.

In the middle of July 1938, the British ambassador in Berlin observed that Prague, if a peaceful solution were still deemed desirable in the West, would have to be pressured by Great Britain and France to abandon its hostile attitude toward the Sudeten Nazis.[44] Chamberlain and Halifax understood Henderson's message, and they proceeded to force Czechoslovakia to comply with the demands of the SdP. Once again Minister Newton stepped in to warn against putting too much public pressure on Prague. It caused the Sudeten Germans to resort to more provocations, to which, as had happened in May, the Prague government could respond by force. A better approach, Newton suggested, was to propose an impartial British investigator and mediator who would travel to Czechoslovakia to study the Sudeten problem and offer his independent advice regarding its solution.[45] That seemed to be a more profitable way of putting pressure on Beneš, and doing so behind the facade of mediation. Lord Halifax, who had been toying with such an idea for several weeks, quickly responded to Newton that the mediator chosen for the job was Lord Walter Runciman, a sixty-eight-year-old businessman who had been created First Viscount of Doxford only the previous year for his service in the Baldwin cabinet.

The foreign secretary had thought through the strategy behind the Runciman operation like a chess-player would have. He reasoned that it would be well and good if the British negotiator succeeded in bringing the parties together. On the other hand, if he failed to achieve progress, he might indicate that the blame was with the SdP, express his regret, and leave. Or he could blame Beneš. In that case, once Hitler attacked Czechoslovakia, the British public would most likely say that the Czechs had had their opportunity and had brought the war on themselves.[46] Newton was instructed to approach Beneš without delay and "to press him strongly to declare himself ready to accept . . . the proposal."[47] The British minister's instructions could not have been put more plainly. Henceforth, the British would make little pretense at being concerned but neutral observers of the Czechoslovak-German crisis. They would become enforcers of almost any Sudeten demand that was likely to appease Hitler and make war in Europe, so they hoped, less likely.

The British were not just understandably unwilling to get involved in war, they were also acting on their dislike of President Beneš and his fellow countrymen. In the words of the British ambassador to Berlin, the Czechs were a "pig-headed race," and Beneš was "not the least pig-headed among them." He was "a master of words and formulae, which sound magnificent but are really empty." Sir Nevile implied that the Czechs belonged to the camp that desired war, together with "Jews, communists and doctrinaires in the world for whom Nazism is anathema."[48] Beneš liked to pretend that all difficulties should be attributed to Germans, Sir Nevile wrote on another occasion, but he was not to be trusted, and extremists were not only in Germany. One only had to look at France and "the Jews and communists everywhere."[49]

London's ambassador in Berlin stood out among the British political establishment, but only because he expressed his views on Czechoslovakia with complete freedom. Few among his colleagues in Britain had been won over by Beneš's style of diplomacy. They shared Henderson's conviction that Hitler did not desire war, at least not in 1938.[50] Those among the political class in Great Britian who did not agree with this analysis were intensely unpopular. For instance, Sir Eric Phipps, the British ambassador in Paris, stated flatly that Winston Churchill, one of the most vocal opponents of the policy of maintaining peace through concessions to the Third Reich, was "a fool and his present activities criminal."[51] The Foreign Office had come to the conclusion that Adolf Hitler and the energy he had unleashed in Germany could be contained, but only if one put enough pressure on Czechoslovakia to surrender to the demands of the SdP. The mission of Lord Runciman was a determined step in that direction.[52]

When Newton went to see Beneš on 20 July 1938 to propose that Prague accept the services of the British negotiator he was met with unexpected opposition. As soon as the president heard of the plan he seemed greatly upset and taken aback. Flushing slightly, Beneš warned Newton that the proposal affected Czechoslovakia's sovereignty and could provoke a serious crisis that might even escalate into the fall of the government and his own resignation. Furthermore, the Runciman mission would put the SdP and the Prague government on an equal footing, and this would violate the Czechoslovak consititution. In addition to problems he anticipated on the domestic scene, Beneš told Newton that the plan could cause great problems internationally; for instance, he was bound to consult with his French ally. Beneš stressed also that he would never negotiate with Hitler, and he concluded by expressing his regret that London would make such a farreaching proposal without talking to him first. He dismissed the British minister without accepting the proposal.[53] Throughout the interview, the president made no mention of the Soviet Union.

Perhaps to signal how well he fulfilled the instructions he had received from Halifax, Newton noted in his report on the initial meeting that Beneš "was much shaken by this development and . . . it put him under great pressure."[54] No wonder the president was disturbed. The proposal threatened to reduce the Prague government to but one of two parties to the crisis on the territory over which the government was supposed to have unlimited sovereignty. The SdP and its members were Czechoslovak citizens who had full access to the democratic institutions of the country, and they should have sought change through the ballot, not by violence and threats of an international war against their own state, the state to which most Sudeten German men swore allegiance as soldiers. The involvement of a British mediator would underline the failure of the Czechoslovak political system. The president understood instantly that accepting Lord Runciman was possibly a fatal step, and he declined doing so.

As happened often with Edvard Beneš, no sooner did he take a strong stance than he began to have doubts. After all, he desperately needed to hold onto his French ally, whose availability had come to depend on the attitude of Great Britain. Could he afford to antagonize London? After a brief struggle, the president decided he was in no position to reject the Halifax proposition. It is possible that Beneš, always the optimist, had persuaded himself that the Runciman mission represented a token of British involvement in the Central European crisis. Within an hour of Newton's departure from the Castle, Beneš called the British legation. He was now inclined to believe that an agreement regarding Runciman could be reached. When the French indicated their support for the British proposal, Czechoslovakia formally accepted it with *note verbale* delivered to Newton on 23 July 1938.[55] Prime Minister Chamberlain would soon boast before the House of Commons of his tactical success, although he was less than truthful when he said that the Runciman mission would go to Czechoslovakia "in response to a request from the [Prague] Government."[56] This was at variance with facts. Berlin approved of the British plan with arrogant reluctance.[57] Always ready to offer his advice, Ambassador Henderson wrote to Lord Halifax: "We shall have to at long last put our foot down very firmly and say to Beneš 'You must.'"[58] Because the British were so active, German diplomats in Berlin and Prague were happy to leave the job of putting pressure on Beneš to them.[59]

The Runciman mission is typically treated in history books as a forgettable sideshow, at best a prelude to the real drama. This attitude is understandable. The mission carried out most of its business during the relatively slow month of August

1938 and was subsequently overshadowed by Prime Minister Chamberlain's dramatic trips to Germany and the Munich conference itself. While the negotiations were in progress, the press was discouraged by all parties from publishing more than general information about the movements of the British team rather than details of the various provisional agreements. It is therefore typically assumed that the mission's only significance was in the appearances it created. By dispatching Lord Runciman to Prague, Great Britain had signaled that it was committed to seeking a purely political solution to the crisis. Hitler, by contrast, was ready to go to war if Czechoslovakia's surrender could not be obtained by political pressure, and this alone put him in an advantageous position with respect to Great Britain and France. An examination of available diplomatic documents will show that the Runciman mission was in fact enormously successful in coercing Beneš to concede to the combined forces of Runciman and the SdP almost all that the Henleinists had ever dreamed of demanding. In that regard it set the stage for the final solution of the crisis. One might even say that Runciman probably made it possible by preparing the Prague government in advance for the price the British and the French would insist that Czechoslovakia pay in return for a promise of peace in Europe.

Lord Runciman had only eight days to study the background of the complex Czechoslovak-German crisis, but he was not unduly worried. When his appointment was announced, he went yachting for two days.[60] He was convinced that he could approach the job on the basis of his experience as a business negotiator.

Lord and Lady Runciman arrived at Wilson Station in Prague on 3 August 1938, just before 3 P.M. They were welcomed on behalf of the president by Jaromír Smutný, who acted as the chief of protocol. Beneš's emissary recorded that Lord Runciman looked somewhat like a grandfather. It seemed inconceivable that he was the kind of man who could solve the crisis; Lady Runciman appeared to be more energetic than her husband, and Smutný speculated that she enjoyed the attention the couple was getting. It was a bad omen that Newton insisted on bringing to the station as his personal guests Messrs. Ernst Kundt and Wilhelm Sebekowsky of the SdP.[61] As it turned out, he had invited them in writing to come as his personal guests without informing the Prague government, a serious violation of the basic principles of diplomatic conduct. After a brief confusion on the platform, Smutný introduced the Czechoslovak members of the welcoming party, including the lord mayor of Prague, while Newton introduced the two Sudeten German representatives.[62] The meaning of this episode was lost on no one. Just as Beneš had feared, the self-proclaimed Nazis from the SdP were to be treated as co-equal partners to the Czechoslovak government.

The British negotiators established themselves at the Alcron Hotel in the center of Prague, where, according to the *Times* (4 August 1938), Lord Runciman announced to 150 members of the press assembled there that he had come "as a friend of all and enemy of none." Members of his staff included the economist Frank Ashton-Gwatkin of the Foreign Office, R. J. Stopford, who had had a number official appointments as British representative on international committees; Consul Ian Henderson, whose missives were well known in the Foreign Ministry in Prague; and Geoffrey Peto, a former member of Parliament, who acted as Lord Runciman's secretary. Despite the sweltering heat, the British impressed their hosts by wearing top hats to all official functions. After a visit to the Castle, the delegation received Wenzel Jaksch, the leader of the anti-Nazi minority among the Sudeten Germans. And then the commission members traveled throughout the country, spending weekends at large estates owned by pro-Nazi Sudeten landowners such as Prince Ulrich Kinsky and Max von Hohenlohe-Langenburg. It was worrisome that only three days after Lord Runciman's arrival, Geoffrey Peto told a German diplomat in Prague that he understood why the SdP disliked Jews.[63] Just as disquieting was a report from the Czechoslovak Ministry of Interior that a Miss Miller and others of the Runciman team had developed the habit of returning the Nazi salute and shouting *Heil!* in response to cries of *Sieg Heil!* from the SdP crowds.[64] Even Lady Runciman saw fit to express herself critically on "Bolshevik influence in Czechoslovakia" at a well-attended diplomatic function at the Castle.[65] Czechoslovakia had signed a treaty with Moscow in response to Hitler's *Machtergreifung,* and only then after it had protected the primacy of its alliance with France. It was, therefore, unclear precisely what kind of Bolshevik influence Lady Runciman had detected in Czechoslovakia. But the Prague government did not exaggerate the significance of such episodes, caused, perhaps, by the inexperience and naïveté of Lord Runciman's staff. Or perhaps members of the Beneš team had become realistic enough not to bother with such trifles when the survival of the state was in question. No official protests were lodged.

At the end of the first week, Ashton-Gwatkin noted that the Runciman mission was mediating "on the edge of Niagara," and he was struck by the sense of fatalism on both sides of the dispute. "People are much less squeamish here about war and its terrors than they are in more civilized lands," he wrote.[66] For centuries the English had fought on battlefields around the world whereas the Czechs had been engaged in their last war in 1620.[67] Therefore, the British diplomat's observation was puzzling, but it captured well the superficial attitude of the mission toward the Czechoslovak-German crisis.

Lord Runciman held several meetings with Beneš and officials of the SdP ("I am already tired of the dinners!" he wrote to Halifax), but he had little hope of achieving anything useful. As he observed, accurately, to Lord Halifax, it all depended on whether the Führer wanted war. The Czechoslovak "fabric" was "of sterner stuff than was set up in Austria" but it could not stop the Third Reich. Only a week had passed, and Runciman wanted to know how long he would be expected "to hold the fort." And would London please give him warning if hostilities were about to break out? In that case he could "be of no further use out here."[68] Lord Runciman had no intention of becoming a casualty in the next war.

The mission worked around the clock. In addition to long discussions with Beneš, members of the British team gradually met with representatives of all parties to the conflict. Lord Runciman was briefed by Sudeten German democrats regarding the terroristic methods the SdP had applied to obtain votes among the Sudeten German population. He also received ample testimony from various Jewish organizations on the prospects for Jews in case of the *Anschluß* of the Sudetenland. Both groups stressed that they desired for the Sudetenland to remain within Czechoslovakia. Coming under the jurisdiction of the SdP, or being incorporated in the Third Reich, would mean their "material and moral annihilation."[69]

Such petitions, as it turned out, had little impact on the opinion of the British. Runciman was a man known for his impartiality, but like many British politicians he had come to the conclusion that concern for the democratic cause in Czechoslovakia had to be pushed aside in the interest of peace. Because the mission's main objective in Prague was to force Beneš to accept more or less what the SdP demanded, Runciman had to establish his authority early in the process, and he was successful in this regard. Just two weeks after his arrival in Prague, he could boast in his report to London, "I am something less than a Dictator and more than an Adviser."[70]

For the next two weeks, Beneš was subjected to pressure without many precedents in modern diplomacy. It was all the more painful (and effective) because it came from Czechoslovakia's quasi ally. The president tried to gain time by giving in gradually on lesser points of contention (municipal jobs set aside for the Sudeten Germans, grants for various Sudeten areas, ethnic composition of local police, the presence of the mostly Czechoslovak state police in the Sudetenland, and reparations for German losses caused by land reform), while holding onto his promise that he would not accept territorial autonomy and a separate Sudeten Diet.

In contrast to President Beneš, who had made himself available for consultations with the British mission almost daily, Konrad Henlein had been far too busy to meet with Lord Runciman and his staff for many days.[71] After more than two weeks, he was able to spare just one hour of time. In his conversation with Runciman on 18 August 1938, interpreted by Prince Hohenlohe, Henlein expressed the opinion that a peaceful solution was still possible. However, what the Prague government had offered so far was "contemptible." The British found him to be uncompromising but friendly, courteous, and honest.[72] Coincidentally, just before Runciman's meeting with Henlein, K. H. Frank, a leading strategist of the SdP (who was subsequently hanged in Prague for crimes he committed in occupied Czechoslovakia during World War II) briefed a party delegation on how to deal with the Runciman team:

> It is the duty of the Sudeten German Party to convince His Lordship that the nationality problem in Czechoslovakia cannot be solved within the State, and that the Czechs are in no way prepared to make concessions of a kind that could lead to a real pacification of the State. His Lordship must take away with him the impression that the situation in this State is so confused and difficult that it cannot be cleared up by negotiations or diplomatic action, that the blame for this lies exclusively with the Czechs, and thus that the Czechs are the real disturbers of peace in Europe.[73]

Here, in a nutshell, was the fundamental negotiating position of the SdP. It did not want concessions from the Prague government. It wanted to destroy the country. Had the members of the Runciman team failed to detect it? Unperturbed by such questions, they worked feverishly to force Beneš to give up more and more.

By 24 August 1938 the British had before them the fruits of their pressure on the president, a proposal that redesigned the relationships between the various nationalities of Czechoslovakia. It was described as a plan (a.k.a. the Third Plan) that represented a compromise between the Prague government's memorandum handed to Runciman upon his arrival and the original position of the SdP. In reality, the concessions were exclusively on the Czechoslovak side. The proposal contained several provisions of an economic nature, but the seventh point stated that the country would be divided into new administrative regions, cantons (*Gaue*). These areas, the plan stated, should be as ethnically homogenous as possible, and at least three of them would be German.[74] This came close to violating Beneš's original position that he would never consider any form of territorial autonomy. Upon receiving this plan, there was uneasiness among the Sudeten leaders, whose main mission was to *prevent* an agreement. More disturbances and street unrest were arranged by the SdP. As a result, dozens of Czechoslovak police and custom officers were murdered, typically by gangs who ambushed them at night and then escaped across the border to the Reich, where they were immune to any legal consequences. The disturbances were reported in the Sudeten press and spread by the Goebbels propaganda machine as another wave of "bloody terror" by the Prague government.[75] In reality, the Czechoslovak organs were under the strictest orders against the use of firearms and almost all of the shoot-outs arranged by the SdP's specialists in unconventional warfare were shamefully one-sided.

Meanwhile, objections had been found to the latest plan. The SdP declared it could not accept it because it divided the German *Volksgruppe* into different cantons. In a desperate effort to keep the door open, on 30 August Beneš received again the two Sudeten negotiators, Messrs. Kundt and Sebekowsky, and told them he was ready to accept, de facto, the eight points program presented by Henlein at Carlsbad. He stated further that he would not object if the SdP chose to announce that the program would be gradually fulfilled. Beneš looked the two gentlemen in the eye and asked them to respond with a clear yes or no within three days.[76] This was the foundation of Beneš's latest retreat. Unable to accept on the spot what had been their *pium desiderium* only at the end of April 1938, the negotiators left without a word to consult with their SdP colleagues and Berlin.

On 1 September 1938, in a strange twist in the developing drama, Lord Runciman usurped the role of a virtual sovereign in issuing a safety pass for Henlein's trip to Germany; it stated that he was going to see the Führer at the viscount's request. "I believe," Runciman's letter stated, "in Henlein's genuine desire for peace." (The SdP leader returned the compliment by bringing back Hitler's assurance that Germany had only peaceful intentions. "I do not want war," Henlein quoted the Führer's message for Runciman.)[77] Because the SdP leader traveled—and very extensively—on a valid Czechoslovak passport, there was no reason for this theatrical measure.[78]

The next day, on Friday, 2 September, the Sudeten German negotiators returned to the Prague Castle to reply to President Beneš's offer of 30 August. Although Beneš had asked them for a yes-or-no answer, they presented a lengthy memorandum that failed to take note of the totality of Beneš's surrender and instead addressed the legal concept of Czechoslovakia's administration. The latest missive from the SdP never clearly spelled out an answer to the proposal, but the president had to assume it was negative.[79] Having de facto offered to accept Henlein's eight points as the basis for the solution of the crisis, the Prague government had pretty much run out of positions it could surrender. But Runciman demanded more and more. He arrived at the Castle on the heels of Kundt and Sebekowsky to lecture the president sternly: Beneš should be under no illusion that Great Britain would go to war on behalf of Czechoslovakia.[80]

The next day, Newton stepped in to tell the president almost matter-of-factly that in case of war Czechoslovakia would be overrun and devastated. Moreover, it was doubtful that the country would be reestablished at the end of hostilities. Therefore, "it was vital for Czechoslovakia to accept great sacrifices and even if necessary considerable risks in order to avoid much greater risks leading to disaster." Newton observed that Beneš was "painfully impressed" by what he had heard from him.[81] Given the seriousness of Newton's threats, it was quite understandable that Beneš was shocked. But there was more suffering in store for the embattled president: for the next month, every single appearance of the British minister at the Castle marked another catastrophe.

As before, British interventions produced immediate results. Punchdrunk from his recent encounters with Runciman and Newton, the president decided on a maneuver that is possibly without precedent in the annals of international negotiating. As he recalled after the war, he had invited SdP representatives to meet him at the Castle on Sunday, 4 September 1938. The two had come, most likely, ready to battle Beneš on some fine point of yet another (promptly to be rejected) "plan." But as soon as the audience had started, the two negotiators realized that something was amiss. Under normal circumstances, the president radiated energy, and he tended to wave his arms, almost abnormally, to underline his points.[82] This time, Beneš appeared to be unnaturally withdrawn and blasé. In fact, he seemed almost bored. Without the usual pleasantries required by diplomatic custom, he produced a piece of paper, pushed it toward Sebekowsky and Kundt, and invited them to write down a complete list of their demands. "I promise you in advance to grant them immediately." Shifting uncomfortably in their chairs, the SdP representatives appeared thunderstruck and angry. Neither uttered a word. The scene embodied, in the true Central European tradition, elements both of tragedy and humor. At the time of his surrender, Beneš appeared triumphant and victorious while the SdP negotiators seemed shaken by the prospect of their victory. The president enjoyed every moment of the occasion. When the silence became unbearable, Beneš slowly and deliberately retrieved his large fountain pen, saying, "Very well; if you won't write it down, I will. You tell me what to say." At long last, the SdP representatives had rediscovered their faculty of speech, and they began dictating their demands. President Beneš wrote down every one of their words. When they had finished, he signed the list and bid his guests goodby.[83] This became the foundation of the last plan—so-called Fourth Plan—obtained in Prague by the Runciman mission. With the stipulation that its international commitments remained intact, Czechoslovakia accepted the Carlsbad program.[84]

Only the word consternation adequately describes the SdP's reaction to the piece of paper, with Beneš's signature, which Kundt and Sebekowsky carried with them from the Castle. "My God, they have given us everything!" exclaimed K. H. Frank.[85] When Henlein learned of the latest development, he disappeared in Germany, with other SdP leaders, including Frank, in train. After hurried consultations with the Führer, the SdP leadership received new marching orders. They were simple: cut off negotiations and stage incidents throughout the country. Overnight, clashes took place in many parts of the Sudetenland, and the inevitable happened soon enough. On 7 September 1938, during an attack on police personnel at Moravská Ostrava, an SdP deputy was struck by an officer, and the party rushed to inform the Prague government the same day that it would take no part in further talks.[86] Under these circumstances, there was nothing left for the Runciman team to achieve in Czechoslovakia. On Thursday, 15 September 1938, Prime Minister Chamberlain telephoned Prague and asked members of the Runciman team to return to London.[87] They were, one imagines, happy to leave that sad, doomed country.

Lord Runciman issued his official finding a week after his return to London.[88] It put the blame for the breakdown of the negotiations on the radical elements in the SdP, but it also registered "much sympathy" for the Henleinist point of view. In a blatant disregard for the "fourth plan," Runciman found "no readiness on the part of the Czechoslovak government to remedy [the grievances of the Sudeten Germans] on anything like an adequate scale." Although he had accepted virtually everything the SdP had ever raised, Runciman still portrayed Beneš as the chief obstacle to peace in Central Europe. The president had suffered a defeat. Lord Runciman's mandate amounted to mediating between the Prague government and the SdP in search for a political solution of the crisis within the existing borders of the Czechoslovak Republic. Beneš would not have been legally allowed to accept Runciman's services if Newton had told him openly that the mission's finding could propose the loss of Czechoslovak territory. In violation of this assumption, the Runciman report arrived at the conclusion that parts of Czechoslovak territory should be transferred to Germany "at once," "promptly," and "without procrastination."

In a section dealing with the political aspects of the crisis, Lord Runciman added insult to injury by making the following demands: that Czechoslovak parties and politicians who were critical of the Third Reich should be forbidden to continue in politics; that the Prague government "remodel" its foreign relations and assure its neighbors that it would under no circumstances attack them; and that a special commercial agreement be negotiated between Prague and Berlin. If these demands were fulfilled, Runciman proposed to grant the new entity assurances against an unprovoked aggression. One could argue that the demand for a transfer of SdP-controlled Sudeten territory to Germany may have been motivated by a desire to preserve peace at all costs. But Runciman brought dishonor upon his name by demanding that Czechoslovakia reorient its policy so as to become a political and economic vassal of Nazi Germany. The request that Czechoslovakia, having surrendered its militarily defensible fortified positions along the historical borders, issue a guarantee of nonaggression to the war-crazed party around the Führer revealed that the viscount was either ignorant of the reality of Central Europe in September 1938 or cynical enough to put into his final report almost anything that the SdP had suggested to him.

The timing of the report's release on 21 September 1938 was not coincidental. The text was placed on Beneš's table just after he had surrendered to combined pressure from the French and British ministers in Prague and accepted their ultimatum demanding that Czechoslovakia give up to the Third Reich the areas inhabited by the Sudeten Germans. The events surrounding the Franco-British ultimatum gave Beneš the greatest blow of his political life.[89] As he was trying to recover from it, London dropped Runciman's report on him, which weakened his will even further. Having first pushed and kicked the Prague government toward accepting the eight points of the SdP, the British turned around and declared this total sacrifice, including, as it did, the abandonment of the Czechoslovak constitution, not to be sufficient. Obviously, neither Henlein nor London was interested in improving the Sudeten Germans' position in Czechoslovakia through an equitable distribution of jobs in the German districts or even in political autonomy for the area. Now the issue was sovereignty and surrender of territory. It was one thing for the SdP to bring up grievances regarding, for instance, arrogant Czechoslovak customs and police officers who spoke little German. But a destruction of the country, barely twenty years after it had come to exist under the auspices of the international community, was an entirely new situation.

One could evaluate Lord Runciman's attempt to adjudicate the Czechoslovak crisis by looking at the evidence the British team gathered regarding Prague's treatment of the Sudeten German minority and at the findings it offered on that basis. Viewed thus, the mission was a failure because the final report disregarded or went directly against the available data.[90] One might argue that Runciman's analysis of the Sudeten crisis could have been written in London by any number of individuals who shared the view that it was desirable to appease Hitler and who had never bothered to spend any time researching the conflict in Czechoslovakia. The feverish fact-finding activity of the British diplomats who had come with Runciman had been wasted. Dozens of interviews, position papers, and depositions were all for naught. Although he had arrived, in his words, as ''a friend of all, and enemy of none,'' Runciman was not an impartial judge, and the final report ignored the evidence his staff had gathered.

But the purpose of the Runciman mission was not to get to the bottom of the Czechoslovak-German crisis and render an objective opinion on its solution. Chamberlain and Halifax had dispatched Runciman to the scene in order to pave the way for a settlement of the crisis in disregard of the merit of the case. From this perspective, the British team was successful. One could say that without the concessions Runciman extracted from Beneš in late August and early September 1938 it would have been more difficult to make the president accept the Franco-British ultimatum of 20 September 1938. Although he was to achieve less notoriety than other British appeasers, Lord Runciman had successfully deprived the Prague government of all of its negotiating positions even before the main confrontation took place. Hitler did not even need to open his mouth and an English viscount with no serious understanding of the region's history and politics was able to force the Czechoslovak president to accept the eight points of the Carlsbad program. Lord Runciman had prepared the ground over which the more famous appeaser, Prime Minister Chamberlain, would walk to Munich.[91]

Although the French publicly played no role in the Runciman mission, behind the scenes they helped push President Beneš toward greater concessions to Henlein. On 24 August 1938 the French ambassador, François-Poncet, told Mastný in Berlin that it was vitally important for Prague to accept whatever Lord Runciman would recommend. If Beneš accepted his terms before the Nuremberg Nazi congress in September 1938, then Great Britain would stand by France and Czechoslovakia and Hitler would suffer a defeat. On the other hand, if Prague were to reject the viscount's recommendations, London would definitely abandon Central Europe to Hitler, and France would not be militarily capable of preventing the complete destruction of Czechoslovakia, even if the Third Reich were ultimately defeated.[92] This was an important argument, and it explains why Beneš was prepared to retreat so much in his negotiations with the SdP. He had been led to believe that if only he swallowed the bitter pill and accepted the eight point program, the so-called Fourth Plan, Great Britain and France would protect the status quo in Central Europe. He could not have known that the final report of the British mission would go well beyond the Fourth Plan and prescribe the loss of Czechoslovak territory as the solution of the crisis.

The Runciman mission was a form of political ambush. Once Beneš found himself in it and under the fire of British threats, his retreat was blocked and he could only move forward, prodded by blackmail and promises of peace, further along the path where other disasters were bound to happen. The terminus would be in Munich.

The Three-Pronged Soviet Strategy from June to Early September 1938

In the spring and early summer of 1938, as Great Britain had taken upon itself the responsibility of protecting its French ally from becoming entangled in a conflict between Czechoslovakia and Germany, diplomats around the world produced countless memoranda speculating about the respective positions of governments in Berlin, Paris, London, Rome, and Prague and in other capitals involved in the crisis. They paid much less attention to the Soviet Union. The latest public trial in Moscow and the continuing purge of the Soviet armed forces had contributed to the general feeling among foreign diplomats that Joseph Stalin had driven the Soviet Union into the ground. This was expressed by the German military attaché in Moscow, who claimed that the country, especially its armed forces, had ceased to be a factor of importance in international politics. Others went further to claim that the whole Soviet structure had started to crack.[93]

The Soviet Union's domestic crisis was very real indeed. Yet that did not prevent the Kremlin from following a complex strategy concerning Czechoslovakia during the summer. After the Czechoslovak partial mobilization in May 1938, the policies of Berlin, Paris, and London started to follow predictable patterns. The Führer's lieutenants muttered dark threats implying that, unless the demands of the Sudeten Germans were satisfied—and pronto—the Wehrmacht would march. The French maintained, with diminishing conviction and always with an eye on disapproving London, that France would honorably fulfill its obligations toward the victim of German aggression. Chamberlain and Halifax had apparently made up their minds to manage the crisis in Central Europe by forcing Prague to accept the demands of the SdP and Berlin.

Stalin conducted a less predictable policy, one designed to advance the ambitious objectives harbored by the Soviet system despite its crisis. During the summer of 1938 the Kremlin pursued a three-pronged policy. The first component concerned Moscow's relations with the Prague government. The Kermlin correctly viewed the possibility of an *Anchluß* of Czechoslovakia with the gravest concern because it would result in a military threat to the Soviet Union itself. Therefore, Moscow needed to strengthen Beneš's resolve to resist the Third Reich, with arms if necessary. It tried to achieve this by hinting or stating officially that, in case of need, Czechoslovakia could rely on meaningful military assistance from its Soviet partner. At the same time, the Soviet Union could not allow the Czechoslovak crisis to drag it into a shooting war with Hitler. To avoid that, Moscow would ignore Prague's pleas to enter into bilateral military consultations. During the summer of 1938 the Kremlin would offer Prague only words and neither Red Army soldiers nor military materiel.

The second component of Soviet policy from June to early September of 1938 aimed at preventing Moscow's isolation. For the moment, the Kremlin's relations with Hitler appeared to be beyond repair.[94] There was no hope at all of improving relations with the Chamberlain government, and Soviet relations with France, notwithstanding the 1935 agreement, were less than cordial and marred by mutual suspicion. Still, the Soviet Union needed to be admitted among those states that would eventually design a solution of the Czechoslovak-German conflict. Kremlin leaders were more interested in being accepted as partners by other European powers than in their ability to influence the solution of the crisis in Czechoslovakia's favor. For this reason, the Soviet Union had to signal its constructive desire to join a political front against war.

Finally, Stalin had not forgotten the long-term plan inaugurated at the 7th Congress of the Communist International. He hoped that Europe's struggle against Nazi aggression could provide a catalyst for a wave of socialist revolutions and the growth of the Soviet influence. *This* kind of war, far from Soviet territory, he did not fear. He desired it. For such a war to break out, Czechoslovakia would have to defend itself against the Wehrmacht, with France on its side. To encourage resolute French military action on behalf of Czechoslovakia, Stalin would offer to take part in trilateral military consultations involving Paris, Prague, and Moscow, but he would ignore President Beneš's invitation to hold bilateral military talks. This ambitious political scheme was explained in detail to the leaders of the Communist party of Czechoslovakia (CPC) by Stalin's close collaborator Andrei Zhdanov.

The three components of Soviet foreign policy during the summer of 1938 can be illustrated specifically. As he was pressured by the British to offer bigger and bigger concessions to the SdP, Beneš did not have the luxury—available to London and Paris, for instance—of ignoring the Soviet Union. No matter what the Stalinist regime was doing domestically, it was his ally and, especially once the Runciman mission had gotten under way, a precious one. Moreover, the president had no reason to believe that the Soviet Union was on the verge of collapsing. Quite the contrary, he was one of very few European leaders who was receiving good news from Moscow. Throughout the summer of 1938 Czechoslovak Minister Zdeněk Fierlinger offered a very positive perspective on recent developments in the Soviet Union. Although some have questioned Fierlinger's loyalty, Beneš did not rely only on reports from the legation to learn about the Soviet scene.[95] One of his emissaries,

General Otakar Husák, had spent almost the full month of May 1938 in discussions with leading Soviet military personalities. With evident approval, Marshal Voroshilov told him during a private conversation that Czechoslovakia was a dagger in Germany's back and that the Czechoslovaks were the best among all Slavs. As far as future Soviet policy was concerned, Voroshilov predicted mysteriously that Moscow would be as friendly, or as hostile, as would be called for by the developing situation.

But there was nothing mysterious when Husák and Voroshilov touched on the national security of Czechoslovakia. The marshal stated without hesitation that the Soviet Union would go "to the end" in its support.[96] General Husák reported on his trip to Beneš at the beginning of June. He told him that Red Army officers were determined to find a way to assist Czechoslovakia militarily against Germany, whether or not Poland and Romania offered a corridor for the transfer of Soviet forces.[97] Minister Fierlinger used the opportunity provided by Husák's trip to point out to Beneš that "a very effective Soviet intervention" in Czechoslovakia's conflict with Germany was "likely."[98] On 29 June 1938 Czechoslovakia and the Soviet Union signed an important and potentially far-reaching agreement on technical cooperation, mostly in the area of military hardware. Its importance was underlined by the fact that the two Czechoslovak negotiators, Vilém Hromádko, representing the Škoda industrial concern, and General Karel Husárek, the army deputy chief of staff, had been granted a three-hour-long audience with Stalin and Molotov the day before the signing ceremony.[99]

This was definitely better than the threats and recriminations aimed at the Prague government by Halifax, Runciman, and Newton or the silence of France. It would have been abnormal if President Beneš had not been positively influenced by such Soviet gestures, although so far they were no more than gestures. During a dinner conversation with Mastný in July 1938 at the Prague Castle, Beneš vigorously rejected the minister's pessimism regarding Czechoslovakia's overall situation. He pointed out that he was "certain" he could rely on the promised Soviet military assistance. On the spot Beneš reached for a file containing diplomatic memoranda from Geneva and quoted to Mastný Litvinov's authoritative assurances to the Prague government. Moreover, the president believed he could rely on Soviet assistance on the basis of his own conversations with Marshal Voroshilov and Minister Aleksandrovsky. He then invited Mastný to join him in watching a newly released Soviet military movie depicting the mighty Red Army on the offensive against Germany.[100] Even the stirring images on the screen did not change Mastný's dark mood. Although he stopped short of saying it explicitly, Mastný clearly implied that Beneš—at least that evening —entertained many illusions regarding the value of the Soviet card.

Moscow's policy toward Czechoslovakia was designed privately to boost Prague's willingness to resist the Third Reich. The Kremlin wanted to appear, from the Czechoslovak perspective, to be willing to provide Prague with military assistance which, together with the French army in the West, would cut the string of Hitler's successes. To Beneš, the Soviet Union wanted to appear ready—indeed, eager—to go to war. Toward the West the Soviet Union needed to present itself as a reliable, strong, but prudent partner. On this front, the main objective was to prevent the Soviet Union's isolation by working against a rapprochement between Western democracies and Hitler. At the end of May, Ambassador Troyanovsky stated in the United States that the Soviet Union was not threatened by anyone but that it refused to wash its hands of the crisis in Central Europe. It was ready, with France, to defend Czechoslovakia against a German attack. "We do not want to be isolated in international affairs," Troyanovsky concluded.[101]

A month later, Maxim Litvinov joined in the efforts against the Soviet Union's isolation. He did so by indicating his eagerness for the Kremlin to be invited to assume its share of responsibility for maintaining peace in Europe. It would be impossible, the Soviet commissar warned, to discourage further German aggression unless the Soviet Union were asked to play a role in the alliance against war. Prague's pact with Moscow was, in Litvinov's opinion, "the most important factor improving the atmosphere around Czechoslovakia."[102] At the end of the May crisis, having been silent for five days, Moscow came out of its self-imposed isolation and stated that its steadfast support of Czechoslovakia was, together with the resolute military measures implemented by Prague, the reason Hitler had retreated. A month later it seemed that a similar scheme was attempted. Moscow wanted to strengthen Prague's determination to stand up to the SdP or to those Western politicians who advocated appeasement of the Third Reich, but it did so with speeches only—and words came cheaply in the summer of 1938. What mattered were concrete actions against the aggressiveness of the Third Reich, and in that regard the Soviet Union was as cautious as Great Britain and France. What did Litvinov do in June 1938 to clear away the clouds gathering above Czechoslovakia? Did he raise the issue of the corridor with Bucharest? Did he even talk to Beneš? He did neither. What Litvinov really wanted was to break through the emerging diplomatic blockade around the Soviet Union, and Czechoslovakia's fate was of secondary importance. Still, Litvinov's signs of concern stood in contrast to the hostility of the Western allies. Against this background, Moscow's words of encouragement sounded sweet to Beneš.

About a week after the president had been forced to invite the Runciman mission, on 28 July 1938 *Pravda* published a delightful article that combined common sense with just a touch of political signaling. It charged the British with interfering in Czechoslovakia's domestic affairs and predicted that SdP leaders had been instructed by Berlin not to be satisfied by any consessions. Therefore, Lord Runciman's mediating efforts notwithstanding, any future talks with the SdP were bound to fail. The paper went on to predict that the British would attempt to solve the Czechoslovak-German crisis by means of a four-power conference consisting of Great Britain, France, Germany, and Italy. *Pravda* indicated that this would seem to give the Prague government only two options: either to be at the mercy of the Third Reich or to become subject of trading among four imperialist states. In reality, the paper implied, there was a third option, one tested during the May crisis when Prague's military measures had successfully cooled the hotheads in the SdP. The fate of Austria after the *Anschluß*, the article concluded, should discourage those in Prague who would like to buy domestic peace by coming to an agreement with the SdP of Konrad Henlein. All of this was quite true, as was the prediction that the British would eventually seek to "solve" the Czechoslovak crisis at an international conference that included Chamberlain, Daladier, Hitler, and Mussolini—yet no one to present the Prague government's point of view. The Czechoslovak press reciprocated *Pravda*'s support for the cause of democracy in Central Europe; most newspapers adopted a friendly attitude to the Soviet Union.[103]

On 3 August 1938, just as Lord Runciman's team had begun its mission in Czechoslovakia, *Pravda* posed tongue-in-cheek questions about the latest scheme of Prime Minister Chamberlain and Lord Halifax. So Lord Runciman had come to Prague as a private personality? Why was it that his hotel and meals had been paid for by His Majesty's government? Soon *Pravda* wanted to know what Runciman was doing in Prague when the London government had stated that Great Britain had no commitments in Central Europe. The paper lamented on 5 August that Britain was ready to barter Prague's interests in a business deal with the Führer. Czechoslovak diplomats reported from Moscow that their contacts among Soviet foreign policy specialists spoke in a united voice and declared that it was not possible to come to an agreement with Hitler and that every concession offered him was bound to whet his appetite. In a short time he would come back with new, even more outrageous demands. The only way to deal with the Third Reich was to form a front of states that would confront it from a position of superior strength.[104] That front, of course, was to include the Soviet Union.

This was strong stuff, and the sort of thing that Beneš himself strongly believed although he could not say so openly. In the summer of 1938 he was under such pressure that, had he expressed explicit support for Moscow's hints regarding collective security, he would have given more ammunition to the SdP and its supporters, who liked to advance the view that Czechoslovakia was an outpost for the Soviet Union in the heart of Europe. Worse, had Beneš publicly applauded such Soviet statements, he would have discovered that they were not aimed primarily at him. Moscow was addressing Paris and London. It was with them that the Kremlin wanted to stand in a common front. No one could have known in August 1938 whether the Czechoslovak crisis would be solved through diplomacy or by war. But Stalin knew that he needed to become one of those who would eventually be in a position to decide. The alternative was a rapprochement between Western Europe and Hitler, and that would mean isolation with its consequences. After the Third Reich had come to dominate Central Europe, his next target could be in the East.

In the middle of August the Kremlin brought its campaign on Czechoslovakia's behalf to a new level. The U.S. embassy reported an official statement that the Soviet Union, in case of German attack, would honorably and effectively fulfill its obligations, even if it were compelled simultaneously to wage war in the Far East. Rumors swept Moscow that the Soviet air force had already prepared 350 airplanes, presumably light bombers, to assist the Czechoslovaks. The embassy warned that there was no evidence for such far-reaching measures having been undertaken. But the myth of the Red Air Force coming to Czechoslovakia's assistance had been born and it would preoccupy Europe until the end of the crisis.[105] Just one day later, the Soviet ambassador in London, Ivan Maiski, told the Czechoslovak minister in London, Masaryk, "with the full authority of Stalin . . . that if Czechoslovakia is attacked Russia will fulfill her treaty obligations to the letter the minute that France moves."[106] The next day, speaking with a U.S. diplomat, Maiski repeated his assurance of Soviet action against Germany—side by side with France. Great Britain, Maiski predicted, would also be drawn in. The key to the whole crisis, Maiski stated to a U.S. diplomat, was in London. The Soviet ambassador seemed completely confident that Great Britain and France were facing real danger, while the Soviet Union would be able to take care of itself.[107]

If the Soviet Union had been ignored by the West as a factor in the Czechoslovak-German crisis during the spring and early summer of 1938, by the middle of August the question of what the Kremlin would do on Czechoslovakia's behalf in case of war almost replaced speculation about the behavior of France. Moscow did not mind that the world had to keep guessing. On 22 August Litvinov received von der Schulenburg; during the course of their conversation the German ambassador wanted to know exactly what the Soviet Union planned to do about Czechoslovakia. The Soviet commissar made several important observations, demonstrating that, unlike others in Europe, the Kremlin had not been deprived of common sense. He pointed out that the Third Reich had no interest in the fate of the Sudeten German population in Czechoslovakia; it pretended to be concerned with this issue in order to conquer the whole country. He then spoke at length about the Czechoslovaks' determination to defend themselves against German aggression. Once that happened, France was sure to mobilize, and Great Britain would, willy-nilly, have to march to defend its French ally. Under these circumstances, the Soviet Union would also "keep her word and do her best."

This was a rather cautious interpretation of Moscow's obligations toward Prague, and the experienced von der Schulenburg understood it only too well. He reported to Berlin that Moscow would try to push the British and French into a military conflict with Germany, but "she herself will hold back."[108] As time passed, Litvinov's statement to von der Schulenburg started to appear more and more heroic. The interview was interpreted in London, in Paris, and in the diplomatic circles of Moscow itself in such glowing terms that neither von der Schulenburg nor Litvinov would have recognized it.[109] According to the newly born legend, the Soviet commissar told the German ambassador in no uncertain terms that if Germany moved, the Soviet Union would live up to its commitments toward Czechoslovakia to the utmost. We only happen to know from von der Schulenburg that Litvinov never said anything of this sort.

In late August, while Runciman mercilessly pressured Beneš to surrender, Kremlin dignitaries had a different (but also unhelpful) agenda. At that most critical time they focused their attention on a ceremony, a meeting of the Supreme Soviet. For no less than eleven days the public was saturated by celebrations of Soviet life. At a time when the hungry and frightened multitudes would have liked to escape from the jurisdiction of Joseph Stalin's NKVD, speaker after speaker lauded Soviet citizenship as the most desirable legal status in the world.[110] The meeting paid little attention to the Czechoslovak crisis.

Although Beneš was then working around the clock on his ongoing negotiations with the Sudeten German representatives, he took the time to instruct Fierlinger to solve the puzzle of Moscow's likely behavior in case of war. The minister was instructed to propose military consultations between the Czechoslovak and Soviet General Staffs. It will be recalled that in April 1938 Prague stated that it could join only existing military agreements between Paris and Moscow. Beneš and Krofta had earlier explained they had to respect the views of Poland and Romania;[111] now, four months later, regard for Polish or Romanian concerns had to be pushed aside. Fierlinger saw Litvinov on 26 August and told him that the Czechoslovak General Staff wished to meet with their Soviet opposite numbers in order to discuss "issues of importance." Within days, Prague would surrender to Runciman and Henlein, de facto accepting the Carlsbad program, only to realize that no concessions could appease the SdP. Under such circumstances it is not difficult to guess exactly what "issues of importance" were to be discussed. Beneš had apparently decided to initiate combined military preparations with the Red Army for the defense of Czechoslovakia against Hitler. Litvinov formally "took note" of the request and immediately asked for something in return: information about continuing negotiations among the countries of the Little Entente.[112] As a sign of desperation Prague obsequiously complied, and Minister Krofta briefed Aleksandrovsky the very next day on the topic.[113] Litvinov quickly brought up other demands as a down payment for the promise of Czechoslovak-Soviet military talks. For instance, Moscow insisted that Prague ban several Russian and Ukrainian émigré organizations (this the government found the strength to reject).[114] Yet Litvinov never mentioned Prague's request again; he let it die of official neglect. The Soviet commissar did not return to the topic because the Kremlin had no interest in revealing to Beneš that the Red Army was not prepared to provide Czechoslovakia with military assistance. It was vital for Soviet influence in Prague that no one there knew for certain what Stalin intended to do.

If the Soviet foreign service officers seemed rather standoffish with Fierlinger, they were reportedly open and friendly with diplomatic representatives of Great Britain. Fierlinger informed the Prague government about his conversation with Lord Chilston at the end of August. According to Fierlinger, the ambassador, who had recently spoken with Soviet officials regarding Moscow's likely response to the outbreak of war between Prague and Berlin, received a positive response: the Soviet Union would fulfill its obligations to the letter. Fierlinger stated further that Lord Chilston had spoken quite warmly about Czechoslovakia, and he had supposedly expressed the view that there would be a general conflict in case of German aggression.[115]

But words, no matter how supportive, could not protect Czechoslovakia's existence. And when it came to concrete action, the Soviet Union appeared just as unwilling as France. Eventually, even Fierlinger started losing patience with Moscow's confusing maneuvers. An opportunity to make his frustration known offered itself soon enough. On 1 September the French chargé d'affaires in Moscow, Jean Payart, saw Litvinov on Bonnet's instructions and asked him officially what sort of Soviet assistance could be counted on in case of a Franco-Czechoslovak war against Germany.[116] Paris expected war to break out any moment, and it stood ready to fulfill its allied obligations. What would the Red Army do? If the Kremlin had been serious about its commitment to a united front of states willing to resist Hitler's aggression, by force if necessary, this would have been the moment to act, to put its cards on the table. But Litvinov hid behind legal excuses. France, he said, was obligated to assist Czechoslovakia irrespective of Soviet help, therefore, it was really Litvinov who should pose the question to France. Clearly, this was true, but if Moscow had been committed to living up to its treaty obligations, why would it not have inquired on its own initiative along the lines of the question, which eventually had to come from the French chargé d'affaires?

Litvinov went on to suggest that in case of trouble the League of Nations might be consulted in securing an appropriate corridor for the Red Army through Romania. When Payart showed his skepticism regarding the League's ability to render a swift and unanimous decision at the height of the crisis, Litvinov allowed that even a majority opinion would be helpful. He told Payart it was important to avoid war, and he suggested that a political declaration by Great Britain, France, and the Soviet Union against war was more likely to succeed than military consultations.[117] This was a new theme. Moscow had been telling Beneš since at least 1936 that only force would provide a solution to his dispute with the Third Reich, and it had done a great deal to strengthen Prague's view that in the last analysis there could be no compromise with Hitler. However it responded with silence when Prague proposed bilateral military consultations in late August 1938 and now, when the French suggested trilateral military talks, Moscow signaled that it placed the highest degree of utility on seeking a *political* solution that would have included the Soviet Union and excluded representatives of Czechoslovakia.

Beneš learned of the French initiative in Moscow from Aleksandrovsky on 3 September, just a day before he would, in his own hand, record the complete list of the SdP's demands as dictated to him by Sebekowsky and Kundt. According to the Soviet minister, the president stressed that he was counting on automatic assistance from the Red Army the moment France moved. Aleksandrovsky became enigmatically silent, not indicating whether Beneš's expectations were justified.[118]

This kind of maneuvering was too much even for the docile Fierlinger. On 3 September he went to see Potemkin and told him that he considered Litvinov's response to the French initiative "too theoretical." He would have liked to see the Kremlin play a more active role. Fierlinger reminded him that the Prague government had to be included in any kind of international conference involving the crisis in Czechoslovakia's Sudetenland.[119] Such frank criticism of Soviet foreign policy toward Prague was without precedent for the Czechoslovak minister, but he was not finished yet. On 9 September 1938 he met again with Potemkin. The interview lasted for two hours and was, according to Fierlinger, "very dramatic." Potemkin attempted to criticize a recent speech by a trade union leader in Prague who had expressed skepticism about the value of the Soviet card. Fierlinger responded with scathing passion. He had warned several times before that various Soviet transgressions against Czechoslovakia would have consequences, he stated, and the present distrust of Moscow, which one could detect among officials in Prague, was only natural. It was also the price that had to be paid for Moscow's maneuvering and for various provocations staged by Soviet organs in order to compromise Czechoslovak army officers and industrial experts visiting the Soviet Union.

Potemkin seemed taken aback by Fierlinger's criticism, and he began apologizing for errors and misunderstandings caused by "subordinates." Then abruptly, he expressed the view that France sought to exclude the Soviet Union from any kind of cooperative arrangement and warned that the policy of France amounted to the

betrayal of Czechoslovakia. Fierlinger did not fall for this debating trick and dog-
gedly returned to the question of Soviet behavior. He clearly believed that the
Kremlin bore its share of responsibility for the inability of the European countries to
confront Hitler with a barricade he would dare not charge. From the Czechoslovak
perspective, Fierlinger stated, the real problem was the atmosphere of mutual mis-
trust that tripped up Prague's efforts at the most decisive moment.[120] This was a
powerful statement, especially as it came from Fierlinger. His reference to NKVD
operations targeting Czechoslovak army officers and technical specialists is interesting but remains unexplained on the basis of currently available archival documents.
(Perhaps this is why the last report from the Czechoslovak military attaché in
Moscow available in the Prague archives is dated 10 January 1938.)[121] All one can
conclude from Fierlinger's hint to Potemkin is that Czechoslovak-Soviet relations
were not as smooth and unproblematic as the minister's memoirs sought to prove.[122]

Moscow tailored its policies with respect to the governments in Czechoslovakia
and Western Europe, but it was to the Kermlin's advantage that it commanded a vast
army of communists around the world who were subject, in most cases, to the
discipline of the Communist International. Therefore, it could pursue its objectives
with the aid of the *apparats* of various communist parties. In the spring of 1938
police in Prague intercepted an important missive from the Comintern to the CPC. It
pointed out that the march toward building a communist society would be renewed
only after the defeat of the Third Reich. For the time being, the party should prevent
any kind of compromise as a solution to the crisis in Czechoslovakia's Sudetenland
because only a violent explosion would create the conditions under which a serious
communist offensive in Europe would be possible.[123] This represented the third
dimension of the Soviet strategy for responding to the Czechoslovak-German conflict.[124] The Kremlin hoped that a war would break out outside its borders and the
ruins of the old order would be swept aside by a new wave of revolutions. The
Czechoslovak crisis meant danger for the Soviet Union, but it also offered opportunities.

No one expressed this approach better than a man very close to Stalin at the
time, Andrei Zhdanov, during his visit to Prague in late August 1938. The trip was
arranged under conspiratorial conditions so that even Beneš did not know about his
activities in Czechoslovakia, and they were to remain a well-kept secret for the next
five decades in the Archives of the Central Committee of the CPC.[125] Stalin's
emissary arrived just as Beneš was on the verge of surrendering to Runciman and the
SdP. His main task was to brief a group of party officials of the Central Committee
on the latest strategy of the Communist International. He was joined at the meeting
by Harry Pollitt and Marcel Cachin, who came to represent the British and French
Communist parties and share with the CPC their experiences with the concept of
popular front.

In a three-hour-long analysis of the contemporary situation, Zhdanov stressed
that although fascism was a threat it also played a positive role. He went on to
explain his point. If the war between Czechoslovakia and Germany broke out, the
CPC would have an open field of opportunities. First, it would be the duty of all
party members to fight the fascist aggressor. At the same time, communists would
''have to try with all their might to utilize the economic and political crisis caused by

the war to mobilize the masses and to accelerate the downfall of capitalism in Czechoslovakia.'' In their struggle against Hitler and, subsequently, capitalism, members of the CPC would be assisted by the Red Army, which would "represent a great political factor in this conflict.'' The Communist International would not insist on approving every decision taken by the CPC leaders; they should feel free to design their own policy for the near future. However, any concessions that the party would have to make in order to gain a leading position in the struggle against the Third Reich would be only temporary, "forced upon us by the present situation. . . . They must be purely instrumental.'' The CPC abandonment of the dictatorship of the proletariat would be only tactical.

In conclusion, Zhdanov assured his audience that the concept of "the second wave of proletarian revolutions'' was to be taken seriously and that the current political situation in Czechoslovakia gave the CPC a means with which it could accelerate the wave's arrival. "Hitler's attack upon Czechoslovakia will be the beginning of the end of the fascist rule,'' Zhdanov predicted, "but also of the bourgeois system of exploitation in this country.'' The Czechoslovak people would at first fight side-by-side with the Red Army against the Third Reich. Then, under the leadership of the CPC, they would liberate themselves from their bourgeoisie.

These were very bold words. If viewed in isolation, one could speculate that Zhdanov, Pollitt, and Cachin had come to Prague merely to boost the spirits of their Czechoslovak colleagues and that no such plans had been taken seriously by either the Communist International or the realistic Klement Gottwald. But the message of Zhdanov's speech in Prague acquires clearer contours and a more realistic tone when put within the context of the 7th Congress and the mission it assigned to Czechoslovakia. Furthermore, Soviet planners truly believed in the possibility of a renewed wave of revolutions in Europe following a war against Nazism. The authoritative military journal *Voyennaya Mysl'* analyzed the Central European crisis in September 1938 in much the same way as Zhdanov had done a month earlier in Prague.[126]

Why was it, the journal asked, that Great Britain and France, the two countries whose vital interests were directly threatened by the Third Reich, had done nothing in support of Czechoslovakia? The West was too frightened to stand up to Hitler because a war under the present conditions will unleash wide revolutionary actions of the working masses and, without a doubt, force the ruling classes to surrender their interests. The apparition of revolutionary upheavals triggered by the imperialistic war of 1914–18 in a number of European countries is still fresh in the memory of the bourgeois rulers of England and France.

In the view of Soviet military analysts, Prime Minister Chamberlain tried to avoid the outbreak of war because he feared its socialist consequences. This was why he continued appeasing Hitler, the one man in Europe who was simply unappeasable. Austria and Czechoslovakia were the price Chamberlain was willing to pay to protect the bourgeois status quo in the world. *Voyennaya Mysl'* allowed that it was impossible to foresee exactly the outcome of the crisis although one aspect was clear: by tolerating Hitler's aggression so far (the article had been written before the Munich conference), the French and the British would help produce the very war and the very socialist revolutions they dreaded so much. The journal concluded by predicting that, at some future point, London and Paris would realize the selfdestructivness of their policies and come to seek the aid of the ''most powerful force for peace, the Soviet Union.'' The Kremlin seemed to offer Great Britain and France a choice. They could form a political alliance with the Soviet Union and bring about a negotiated settlement with the Third Reich in which the allies would be in a position to dictate the terms. Or they could insist on keeping the Soviet Union in isolation, which would make them so weak against the Third Reich that they would have to continue retreating. This would have predictable consequences: it would increase Hitler's appetite and his demands. A war would have to be fought eventually. It would start as a struggle against Nazism but would culminate in a series of socialist revolutions.

It appeared that the only country that stood to gain under both scenarios was the Soviet Union. Its prestige and international influence would be greatly increased if the British and French had to go to the Kremlin in search of a partner who would help them neutralize the dynamic might of the Third Reich. On the other hand, the Western democracies could decide to deal with Hitler directly, without any regard for the wishes of the Kremlin. In that case they were bound to discover that they were too weak to win an acceptable bargain for themselves and, ultimately, a war between the British-French alliance and Germany would have to be fought. It would take place outside Soviet territory, and Kremlin leaders could observe it from the sidelines. Once the second wave of socialist revolutions broke out, the Soviet Union would emerge from the safety of its cocoon and give direction to the ongoing upheavals. Not having taken part in the protracted war, Moscow would be in the strongest position to rearrange the bits and pieces of postwar Europe in accordance with its wishes.

The revolutionary component of Soviet strategy in the late 1930s is centrally important. Without it, it could be said that Stalin reacted to the rise of Adolf Hitler much like others in Europe—he hoped that somebody else would stand up to him and that somebody else would eventually come to blows with the Wehrmacht and Luftwaffe. This was dictated by common sense because there was and is no place for self-sacrifice in international relations. But unlike the British and French, who tried to avoid war even if it resulted in the growth of German might and the devaluation of their moral and physical capital, the Kremlin had no illusion that Hitler was appeasable. War to him was an end in and of itself, and negotiations as well as concessions only postponed the explosion. Soviet leaders calculated that a war would break out, and this was no catastrophe. They subscribed to the Marxist view that nationalism was not part of ''the base'' but belonged in ''the superstructure.'' Therefore, it was within the ideological framework of the Soviet state for the Kremlin to assume that, although powerful, nationalism could be replaced in the minds of suffering Europeans by the more rational sense of class solidarity, that cut across state borders. Hence the belief that, after a global war against Hitler, Europe could be ready to witness proletarian upheavals, the outcome of which would be directed by the worker's most legitimate representative, Moscow. This happened to be Beneš's reading of the situation. During an informal dinner at the Castle on 30 March 1938, the president told his guests, mostly government ministers, that, unlike the British and French, the Soviet Union wanted a war against the Third Reich. The reason was simple. After the war, Beneš predicted, ''communist infiltration'' of Europe would increase manifold.[127]

OBVIOUSLY, NOT ALL SOVIET expectations were accurate. For instance, the Kremlin must have watched with a mixture of awe and horror as the Blitzkrieg swept through Western Europe and brought the Swastika all the way to Paris and to the English Channel. Yes, Stalin wanted a war of Hitler against Great Britain and France, but not such a quick one. Germany's swift and militarily brilliant victory in Western Europe was bound to strengthen the Führer's conviction that he was invincible and chosen by fate to rid the world of Bolshevism, his next target. Hitler's turn eastward meant that Stalin failed in his effort to stay out of the war, and the German military would come dangerously close to breaking the back of the Stalinist system. None of this was predictable. Even during the last days of September 1938 the Kremlin could not have foreseen future developments in highly volatile Central Europe with any degree of certainty. A year later it was still not clear what Great Britain would do or how well the French would fight should it come to a shooting war with Germany.

However, it is impossible to overlook the fact that the most accurate analysis of the European scene in the summer of 1938 had been made in the Kremlin. Great Britain stooped to coercing President Beneš and to designing such clumsy measures as the Runciman mission, which were unworthy of its democratic tradition. France dug a hole for itself by declaring its "solemn," "indisputable," and "sacred" obligations toward Czechoslovakia. In a matter of just a few weeks it would climb out of the hole on the ladder of betrayal. Eventually, just as Moscow had predicted, both countries would within a year get into the war they had hoped to avoid.

What happened to the second wave of socialist revolutions anticipated by the 7th Congress of the Communist International in 1935 and by Zhdanov in Prague three years later? It did not take place quite the way Moscow had hoped; in fact, World War II failed to fragment European societies into hostile classes, but instead bonded most nations involved in the fighting, on both sides. Therefore, the second wave of revolutions was actually launched in 1944 by the Red Army when it entered Eastern and Central Europe. Imposing communism with troops and secret policemen lacked elegance. It would have been nicer if Soviet-style regimes had grown organically from the suffering and upheavals caused by the latest capitalist war. They would have been more legitimate and therefore also more self-reliant and stable. This technique had furthermore important geographic limitations because the Red Army's presence was a necessary (though not sufficient) precondition for the emergence of communist elites. Nevertheless, the second wave of proletarian revolutions would take place, if only in the portion of Europe under Stalin's control. It would come to a successful conclusion in February 1948 with the communist coup d'état in Prague, as Zhdanov had predicted in the same city a decade before. Into the ruins fertilized by Europe's war against Nazism Stalin would plant seeds that would yield his East European empire.

Notes

1. *Documents on British Foreign Policy, 1919–1939* (henceforth *DBFP*), 3d series. vol. 1 (London: Her Majesty's Stationery Office, 1949), document no. 494, 569.

2. MHA-MOP, secret, 1935–39, general, 144/38. This is a memorandum from General Ludvík Krejčí to President Beneš, 31 May 1938.

3. *DBFP*, 3d series, vol. 1, document no. 393, 463.

4. *DBFP*, 3d series, vol. 2, document no. 590, 59. The view was embraced by Sir

Nevile Henderson: "We cannot honourably go back on the principle of self-determination, or one day Germany will swallow the Czechs also. That principle is the main safeguard of the Czechs themselves. If they deny it to the Sudeten, it will one day be denied to them."

5. *DBFP*, 3d series, vol. 1, document no. 378, 447.

6. This topic is covered extensively elsewhere. For instance see Antoine Marés, "La question tchéchoslovaque devant l'opinion francaise en 1938," *Revue des Études Slaves* 1–2 (1979): 109–24; Williamson Murray, *The Change in the European Balance of Power, 1938–1939* (Princeton: Princeton University Press, 1984), 190–94; Keith Eubank, *Munich* (Norman: University of Oklahoma Press, 1963), 74–81; Telford Taylor, *Munich: The Price of Peace* (Garden City, N.Y.: Doubleday), 504–34; Robert Kvaček. *Obtížné spojenectví: Politicko-diplomatické vztahy mezi Československem a Francií, 1937–1938* (Prague: Univerzita Karlova, 1989), 175–88.

7. Royal Institute of International Affairs, *Documents on International Affairs, 1938* (London: Oxford University Press, 1939), 1:216.

8. *Documents on German Foreign Policy, 1918–1945* (henceforth *DGFP*), series D, vol. 2 (Washington, D.C.: U.S. Government Printing Office, 1949), 612–13. Schmidt recalled that General Vuillemin's answer was: "France will keep her word." Paul Otto Schmidt, *Hitler's Interpreter* (London: Macmillian, 1951), 88.

9. ANM-M, Mastný, the Manuscript, 112.

10. PRO, FO 408/68.C8727/1941/18. Viscount Halifax to Mr. Campbell (Paris), Foreign Office, 25 August 1938.

11. *Documents on International Affairs, 1938*, 2:178; *DBFP*, 3d series, vol. 2, document no. 807, 269.

12. *DBFP*, 3d series, vol. 2, document no. 857, 312.

13. ANM-M, Mastný, the Manuscript, 97–98.

14. Léon Noël, *La Guerre de 39 a commencé quatre ans plutôt* (Paris: Editions France-Empire, 1979), 83–85; Noël suspects the veracity of Bonnet's story.

15. J. W. Bruegel, "Remarks on the Roundtable 'Munich from the Czech Perspective,'" *East Central Europe/L'Europe du Centre-Est* 10, nos. 1–2 (1983): 158–60. Bruegel calls Bonnet's record of his alleged conversation with Osuský on 20 July 1938 an outright fabrication.

16. *Documents diplomatiques français, 1932–1939*, vol. 10 (Paris: Imprimerie Nationale, 1976), document no. 238, 437; Bonnet's record of his meeting with Osuský on 20 July 1938. On the occasion Bonnet claims to have told Osuský that France would not go to war in support of Czechoslovakia. Its continued affirmations of solidarity with Prague should be understood as being made for public consumption only. Czechoslovakia should obtain the best possible solution for itself, but neither London nor Paris would intervene in case of German aggression. Bruegel, "Remarks on the Roundtable 'Munich from the Czech Perspective,'" 158.

17. MHA-B, box 6, Beneš's notes on his meeting with de Lacroix on 16 September 1938.

18. See the essay by Jean-Baptiste Duroselle in *Munich 1938: Mythes et réalités* (Paris: Institut National d'Études Slaves, 1979).

19. For a study of such themes, see Nicole Jordan, *The Popular Front and Central Europe: The Dilemmas of French Impotence, 1918–1949* (Cambridge: Cambridge University Press, 1992).

20. See Élisabeth du Réau, "Édouard Daladier et les problèmes de mobilisation industrielle au moment de Munich," *Revue des Études Slaves* 1–2 (1979): 71–98.

21. French metal workers started their paid vacations on 5 August and returned to work on 29 August 1938. R. G. D. Laffan, *Survey of International Affairs, 1938* (London: Oxford

University Press, 1951), 2:172–73. The number of airplanes is quoted from John Wheeler-Bennett, *Munich: Prologue to Tragedy* (New York: Viking, 1964), 99. See also Anthony Adamthwaite, *France and the Coming of the Second World War, 1936–1939* (London: Frank Cass, 1977), 159–72.

22. Wheeler-Bennett, *Munich,* 99.

23. Henry Dutailly, *Les Problèmes de l'armée de terre française, 1935–1939* (Paris: Imprimerie Nationale, 1976); Milan Hauner in "Round Table," *East Central Europe/L'Europe du Centre Est* 8, nos. 1–2 (1981): 89.

24. Laffan, *Survey of International Affairs, 1938,* 2:172–76.

25. British policy toward Czechoslovakia during the summer of 1938 is analyzed in many volumes. See, for instance, Gerhard L. Weinberg, *The Foreign Policy of Hitler's Germany: Diplomatic Revolution in Europe, 1933–36* (Chicago: University of Chicago Press, 1970), 378–442, and Taylor, *Munich: The Price of Peace,* 457–503.

26. Even Sir Robert Vansittart, who had developed a fairly realistic view of Nazism, opined three months after Henlein had publicly declared himself a Nazi that neither Great Britain nor France could be expected to go to war in defense of the Prague government's "foolishly stiff and imprudent policy."

27. The paper noted that more than 90 percent of Sudeten Germans had voted for the SdP. Therefore, "What remains to be done is to rectify the error of 1919, and to allow the Sudeten Germans peacefully to express their own views as to their future. Self-determination was a principle upheld by the makers of the Peace Treaties, by the League of Nations, and now by the Germans of the Reich, who ask it on behalf of their kinsmen in Czechoslovakia."

28. *DBFP,* 3d series, vol. 1, document no. 373, 443.

29. Ibid., document no. 368, 439.

30. Ibid., document no. 384, 454.

31. AMFA, Second Section, box 458a. The British legation informed the Czechoslovak Ministry of Foreign Affairs on 9 June 1938 that Major Reginald Sutton-Pratt was appointed assistant military attaché to His Majesty's legation in Prague.

32. Ibid. The circular note warned against any attempts to cover up errors and failings because such efforts "would make a far worse impression on the British observers."

33. Ibid., Henderson's note of 2 July 1938.

34. Ibid., Henderson's note of 5 July 1938.

35. Ibid., Henderson's note of 28 July 1938.

36. *DBFP,* 3d series, vol. 1, document no. 434, 508.

37. Ibid., document no. 449, 526.

38. Ibid., document no. 496, 573.

39. Ibid., document no. 398, 462, document no. 402, 473.

40. ANM-S, the diary, box 38, Beneš's statement of 30 March 1938; MHA-B, box 6.

41. *DBFP,* 3d series, vol. 1, document no. 147, 160–61.

42. *Documentes diplomatiques français,* 2, 10, no. 245, 511–18.

43. *DBFP,* 3d series, vol. 1, document no. 508, 582.

44. Ibid., document no. 494, 568.

45. Ibid., document no. 497, 574–75.

46. Ibid., vol. 2, document no. 587, 55.

47. Ibid., vol. 1, document no. 508, 583.

48. Ibid., vol. 2, document no. 551, 11.

49. Ibid., vol. 1, document no. 534, 617.

50. Ibid., vol. 2, document no. 590, 60. Henderson wrote to Halifax on 6 August 1938: "Germany does not want war this year; that is my definite opinion, for what it is worth, and we should treat with them on that basis and not on that of the fear that they may want it."

51. NA 760F.62/353, George S. Messersmith, the U.S. Legation, Vienna, to the Secretary of State, Washington, D.C., 4 June 1938.

52. The Runciman mission is discussed, for instance, in Weinberg, *Foreign Policy of Hitler's Germany*, 430–38; Adamthwaite, *France and the Coming of the Second World War*, 202; Taylor, *Munich: The Price of Peace*, 734–98; and Eubank, *Munich*, 101–2.

53. *DBFP*, 3d series, vol. 1, document no. 525, 605.

54. Ibid., document no. 521, 600.

55. PRO, FO 408/68.C7320/1941/18, Sir E. Phipps to the Foreign Office, Paris, 20 July 1938. Phipps had seen Daladier and Bonnet, and the "French ministers expressed their agreement with the action we had taken." *DBFP*, 3d series, vol. 2, document no. 550, 10.

56. *Documents on International Affairs, 1938,* 2:148.

57. PRO, FO 408/68.C8711/1941/18. Ribbentrop said to Halifax that Germany would not participate in the Runciman mission. He complained that it had only strengthened Czech aggressiveness. "In fact, there can be no doubt that the attitude of the Prague Government, which is strongly influenced by Bolshevik ideas, represents the only real obstacle to a settlement and pacification of Europe."

58. *DBFP*, 3d series, vol. 2, document no. 551, 11.

59. ANM-M, Mastný, the Manuscript, 124; *DGFP,* series D, vol. 2, document no. 344, 544–46.

60. Vaughan Burdin Baker, "Selective Inattention: The Runciman Mission to Czechoslovakia, 1938," *East European Quarterly* 24 (January 1991): 427.

61. ANM-S, the Diary, Smutný's entry on 3 August 1938.

62. *DGFP*, series D, vol. 2, document no. 335, 534.

63. Ibid., document no. 339, 539.

64. AMFA, The Ministry of Interior to the Ministry of Foreign Affair, box 458a, 23 August 1938.

65. *DGFP*, series D, vol. 2, document no. 373, 593.

66. *DBFP*, 3d series, vol. 2, document no. 598, 70.

67. The Czechs, of course, had fought after 1620 and before 1938, but not on their own behalf.

68. *DBFP*, 3d series, vol. 2, document no. 602, 74.

69. Baker, "Selective Inattention," 435.

70. *DBFP*, 3d series, vol. 2, document no. 644, 115.

71. There is a special folder listing all the audiences of Runciman with Beneš in the Office of the President, the Castle, Prague.

72. *DBFP*, 3d series, vol. 2, document no. 652, 122, document no. 731, 200.

73. *DGFP*, series D, vol. 2, document no. 366, 578.

74. Laffan, *Survey of International Affairs, 1938* 2:225–26.

75. Ibid., 2:231.

76. *DGFP*, series D, vol. 2, document no. 407, 660–61.

77. *DBFP*, 3d series, vol. 2, document no. 765, 231.

78. MHA-B, box 255. Lord Runciman saw fit to conclude his safety pass for Henlein with this sentence: [Runciman] "trusts that his [Henlein's] journey will not be misinterpreted [by the Prague government] . . . so that no ill consequences may come upon him therefrom."

79. *DBFP*, 3d series, vol. 2, document no. 746, 215.

80. Ibid., document no. 753, 221.

81. Ibid., document no. 758, 226–27.

82. Andrei Gromyko, *Memoirs* (New York: Doubleday, 1989), 57. Gromyko wrote

that during one of his encounters with Beneš "there was barely enough room for his gestures."

83. The episode was told directly by President Beneš to Wheeler-Bennett during their interview in July 1946 at the Castle. See *Munich: Prologue to Tragedy* (New York: Duell, Sloan and Pearce, n.d.), 90–91.

84. Technically, Henlein's demand that Czechoslovakia no longer placed itself "in the ranks of the enemies of the German people," that is, a demand for a revision of the country's foreign policy, was not one of the eight points; it was one of "three preliminary requests." Therefore, it could be said that on 4 September 1938 President Beneš accepted the complete Carlsbad program, the eight points.

85. Wheeler-Bennett, *Munich*, 92.

86. *DBFP*, 3d series, vol. 2, document no. 801, 265.

87. Ibid., footnote to document no. 882, 329.

88. MHA-B, Fond Munich. The full text was published in the *Times*, 29 September 1938, and in *DBFP*, 3d series, 2:675–79.

89. After Beneš had accepted the Franco-British ultimatum, delivered on 20 September 1938 at 2 A.M., he had an accurate indication of what the Munich agreement would be like.

90. Such is the conclusion of Baker in "Selective Inattention."

91. It must be stressed again that, in accepting the Runciman mission, Beneš acted on the assumption that it would merely mediate between himself and the SdP. Neither he nor anybody else in Prague had an inkling that Runciman would eventually propose that Czechoslovakia be deprived of its historical borders in Bohemia.

92. ANM-M, Mastný, the Manuscript, 115–16.

93. *DBFP*, 3d series, vol. 1, enclosure to document no. 355, 422. The German attaché, General Ernst Köstring, who had been born in Russia, was one of the best informed experts on the Soviet military. *DBFP*, 3d series, vol. 1, enclosure to document no. 411, 483.

94. Symbolic was Hitler's terse, one-sentence speech at the reception, on 13 July 1938, given to welcome the new Soviet Ambassador in Berlin. See Norman H. Baynes (ed.), *The Speeches of Adolf Hitler* (London: Oxford University Press, 1942), 2:1464.

95. Some of Beneš's colleagues and collaborators speculated that Fierlinger might have been disloyal to Czechoslovakia during his diplomatic career in the Soviet Union. For instance, General Sergej Ingr, one of Beneš's chief military aides in London, complained that "Fierlinger acts primarily with an eye on Moscow and the Comintern. He pays more attention to their viewpoint than to the position of our government." ANM-F, box 5, Prokop Maxa's record of 10 September 1942. And even Polish Prime Minister Sikorski came to warn Beneš that "Fierlinger is completely owned by the Soviets." ACC CPC, Fond 100/24, file 175, archival unit 1566. It seems obvious that his sympathy for the Stalinist system overshadowed Fierlinger's ability to think critically enough to remain a reliable analyst of the Soviet scene. But Fierlinger was not alone among the staff of the Czechoslovak legation in Moscow to express one-sided views. The reports and analyses of the Czechoslovak military attaché in Moscow, Colonel František Dastich, were at least as starry-eyed as those of Fierlinger; some of Dastich's observations were completely Stalinist. Was Fierlinger of a fellow-traveler? At a minimum, he was a spineless opportunist. See the testimony of the communist leader Antonín Novotný, who stated in 1968, "There was a time when he [Fierlinger] was more Bolshevik than the whole [Communist party] politburo put together. He used to give us lessons on how to be revolutionaries. I hardly know a greater opportunist than Fierlinger. Once in a conversation, Edvard Beneš was brought up and Fierlinger started bad-mouthing him so much that I felt embarrassed. He talked about Beneš's millions in foreign banks, how servile he used to be toward the French; he even talked about various intimate details from the former president's

private life." See Rudolf Černý, *Antonín Novotný: Pozdní obhajoba* (Prague: Kiezler, 1992), 79.

96. ANM-F, box 23, Record of General Otakar Husák's Trip to the Soviet Union in 1938 (2 May–27 May 1938).

97. Ibid., General Husák's audience with Beneš, 1 June 1938. In his written record, Husák offered a very pro-Soviet analysis of the situation. He had noticed no weaknesses of the system, everything was good and getting better. He concluded, "One day, as a democratic state, we will become a bridge for all other states, especially Poland, into the world of the Soviets."

98. ANM-F, box 23, Zdeněk Fierlinger's statement to President Beneš regarding General Husák's visit to the Soviet Union, 24 May 1938.

99. AMFA, Zdeněk Fierlinger, the Czechoslovak Legation, Moscow, to the Ministry of Foreign Affairs, telegrams received, 578/78, 30 June 1938; same in ANM-F, box 23, Fierlinger for Beneš and Krofta only, 586/secret/38, same date.

100. ANM-M, Mastný, the Manuscript, 98.

101. *Documents on International Affairs, 1938*, 1:315. Aleksandr A. Troyanovsky spoke on 25 May 1938.

102. AMFA, Zdeněk Fierlinger, the Czechoslovak Legation, Moscow, to the Ministry of Foreign Affairs, secret, 29 June 1938. Litvinov's speech was delivered on 23 June 1938; it appeared in toto in *Journal de Moscou* on 5 July 1938.

103. Articles expressing a friendly perspective on Soviet affairs could be found not only in the Communist *Rudé Právo* but in other newspapers as well; for instance see *České slovo, Lidové noviny, Právo lidu,* and *Prager Presse* (August–September 1938).

104. AMFA, Josef Šust, the Czechoslovak Legation, Moscow, to the Ministry of Foreign Affairs, Prague, secret, 5 August 1938.

105. NA 760F.62/569, Alexander Kirk, U.S. Embassy, Moscow, to the Secretary of State, Washington, D.C., 15 August 1938.

106. NA 760F.62/571 and NA 760F.6111/38, Chargé d' Affaires Johnson, U.S. Embassy, London, to the Secretary of State, Washington, D.C., 16 August 1938.

107. NA 760F.62/575, Chargé d' Affaires Johnson, U.S. Embassy, London, to the Secretary of State, Washington, D.C., 17 August 1938.

108. *DGFP*, series D, vol. 2, document no. 396, 630-31.

109. NA 760F.62/615, Chargé d' Affaires Johnson, U.S. Embassy, London, to the Secretary of State, Washington, D.C., 29 August 1938; NA 760F.62/625, William C. Bullitt, U.S. Embassy, Paris, to the Secretary of State, Washington, D.C., 16 August 1938, NA 760F.62/631, Alexander Kirk, U.S. Embassy, Moscow, to Secretary of State, Washington, D.C., 31 August 1938.

110. AMFA, Zdeněk Fierlinger, the Czechoslovak Legation, Moscow, to the Ministry of Foreign Affairs, secret, 25 August 1938. The Supreme Soviet meeting lasted from 10 August to 21 August 1938.

111. AMFA, Kamil Krofta, the Czechoslovak Ministry of Foreign Affairs, Prague, to Zdeněk Fierlinger, the Czechoslovak Legation, Prague, telegrams sent 423/38, 21 April 1938.

112. AMFA, Zdeněk Fierlinger, the Czechoslovak Legation, Moscow, to the Ministry of Foreign Affairs, Prague, telegrams received 694/38, 26 August 1938.

113. AMFA, Kamil Krofta, the Czechoslovak Ministry of Foreign Affairs, Prague, to Zdeněk Fierlinger, the Czechoslovak Legation, Prague, telegrams sent 893/38, 27 April 1938.

114. AMFA, Zdeněk Fierlinger, the Czechoslovak Legation, Moscow, to the Ministry of Foreign Affairs, Prague, telegrams received 715/38, 1 September 1938; AMFA, Kamil

Krofta, the Czechoslovak Ministry of Foreign Affairs, Prague, to Zdeněk Fierlinger, the Czechoslovak Legation, Prague, telegrams sent 918/38, 3 September 1938.

115. AMFA, Zdeněk Fierlinger, the Czechoslovak Legation, Moscow, to the Ministry of Foreign Affairs, Prague, telegrams received 704/38, 29 August 1938. Unfortunately, Fierlinger's report to Beneš was significantly at variance with Lord Chilston's own record of the converstation. *DBFP*, 3d series, vol. 2, document no. 761, 230–31. The British ambassador noted that he attached little "importance to the somewhat half-hearted assurances which my Czech and French colleagues from time to time extract from M. Litvinov." He also put on record his inability to share Fierlinger's optimism regarding the willingness and ability of the Soviet Union to render effective assistance to Czechoslovakia in case of war. One wonders to what extent Fierlinger may have deliberately exaggerated Chilston's optimism and to what extent the British ambassador had tried to please his colleague by appearing more supportive of the Czechoslovak cause than he really was. Given the accuracy of Chilston's other reports, one is inclined to place the greater burden of responsibility for the discrepancy on Prague's minister.

116. According to Litvinov, the meeting took place on 2 September; see Federální Ministerstvo zahraničních věcí ČSSR a Ministerstvo zahraničních věcí SSSR, *Dokumenty k historii mnichovského diktátu, 1937–1939*, ed. Dušan Spáčil et al. (Prague: Nakladatelství Svoboda, 1979), 183. According to Aleksandrovsky's statement to Beneš it took place on 1 September 1938, AMFA, second section, box 564. It seems that Payart met Litvinov on 1 September and that the conversation continued the next day in the presence of Potemkin. At the end of the second meeting, Litvinov sent its record to the Soviet embassy in Paris and asked that Minister Bonnet be briefed directly by Soviet Ambassador Suric. See *Dokumenty k historii mnichovského diktátu*, 184–85.

117. Ibid., 183–84.

118. Ibid., 185.

119. AMFA, Zdeněk Fierlinger, the Czechoslovak Legation, Moscow, to the Ministry of Foreign Affairs, Prague, telegrams received 725/38, 3 September 1938. Beneš also learned about Payart's interview with Litvinov from Aleksandrovsky. He came to see Beneš on 3 September 1938.

120. Ibid., telegrams received 746/38, 9 September 1938.

121. MHA-MOP. Dastich's reports from Moscow during the cruicial months of 1938 had been removed from the archives before their opening to Western researchers in 1990. Because General Dastich (he was promoted after World War II) left his last diplomatic post at the end of 1948 in protest against the communist coup d'état in February 1948 and sought political asylum in the United States, it is likely that the files containing his reports were removed from the record during the late 1940s or early 1950s.

122. Zdeněk Fierlinger, *Ve službách ČSR: Paměti z druhého zahraničního odboje* (Prague: Práce, 1947).

123. SCA, the Police Directorate, a report by the State Security (StB), 29 March 1938.

124. One must be careful, of course, not to assume that Comintern policies were always identical with those of the Kremlin. The Communist International was an organization devoted to world revolution, and its officers could hardly have ignored that fact in their public statements. By contrast, those speaking for the Kremlin had to project a considerably more constructive image. Nevertheless, in the view of Lars T. Lih, Stalin remained dedicated to the cause of world revolution even at a time when he seemingly focused exclusively on building up the Soviet state. In fact, as Robert Tucker summed it up, "in Stalin's mind the Soviet state and international revolution coalesced." See Lih's "Introduction" in *Stalin's Letters to Molotov* (New Haven: Yale University Press, 1995), 1–63, and Tucker's "Foreword," ibid,

ix; see also Robert C. Tucker, *Stalin in Power: The Revolution from Above, 1928–1941* (New York: Norton, 1990), 45–50 and passim.

125. ACC CPC, Fond 100/45, vol. 10, archival unit 184. The meeting took place on 20–21 August 1938; Zhdanov's speech was interpreted by a Comrade Hájek.

126. V. Pavlov and I. Petrov, "The Military-Political Situation in Central Europe," *Voyennaya mysl'* 9 (1938); the article was noticed by the U.S. military attaché in Moscow, Lt. Colonel Philip R. Faymonville, U.S. Embassy, Moscow, to Washington, D.C., 20 October 1938, report no. 1361, box 1800, G–2 report 657–D–1054.

127. František Ježek, "Z pamětí o mnichovské krizi roku 1938," *Historie a vojenství* 4 (1969):680.

7

September 1938

The first operational study of a German military offensive against Czechoslovakia, code-named "Schulung," was prepared in May 1935.[1] On this foundation was built the original study's more advanced version, Operation Green.[2] This plan acquired realistic dimensions by late June 1937 and was redrawn in April 1938 to reflect the new situation brought about by the annexation of Austria. On 30 May 1938 the Führer signed yet another version of the plan: German armed forces had to smash Czechoslovakia "in the near future." They were specifically instructed to carry out "a thrust into the heart of Czechoslovakia . . . with the strongest possible" force.[3] An attached cover letter stipulated that the day of execution for Operation Green was 1 October 1938 "at the latest."[4] A number of meetings between Hitler and Germany's top military commanders followed, but not all were amiable. Many officers were unable to have faith in the Führer's military genius; some told him openly that Germany's western defenses could be held against a French attack for only three weeks. In that case, Hitler replied during a meeting on 10 August 1938, the whole Wehrmacht "would not be good for anything." There was open talk about defeatism and opposition among the generals.[5]

The German public, just like many German officers, felt no enthusiasm for the next war. The British embassy in Berlin noted that the country was against war but "helpless in the grip of the Nazi system." At the height of the hysteria whipped up by the Nazis, the British found no animosity toward the Czechs among Germans, who were "like sheep being led to the slaughter."[6] Unpersuaded by the warnings from his generals, Hitler refused to discuss the deadline for Operation Green, and it remained unchanged.

Hitler at Nuremberg and a State of Emergency in the Sudetenland

Nuremberg, the city closely tied to the fate of the Holy Roman Empire, had become early on a place of pilgrimage for the Nazis. And it was there that the NSDAP, amid much pomp, held its congress in September 1938. Hitler arrived unexpectedly early, on 6 September 1938, and he was followed by a surprising number of foreign observers accredited in Berlin. Together with other diplomats, Vojtěch Mastný was invited to attend a small reception at the Deutscher Hof Hotel. Speaking on behalf of all his colleagues, the French ambassador, André François-Poncet, delivered impromptu remarks reminding Hitler that the best laurels of victory were those untouched by a mother's tears.[7] The Führer's pale face remained drawn and cold.

It was for a good reason that Hitler did not betray his thoughts. On 9 September 1938 he presided over another meeting with some of his top military advisors. Their discussion lasted until 3:30 A.M. the next day, and its sole topic was Operation Green.[8] General Franz Halder opened the meeting by describing how the Wehrmacht's 2d and 14th armies would carry out a pincer attack in the direction of Olomouc and Brno to cut Czechoslovakia in half. The enemy would be unable to mobilize, and the whole defensive effort would collapse within days.

Unlike on previous occasions, when he was bursting with martial optimism, this time Hitler seemed worried, and he played the devil's advocate throughout the meeting. The plan did not strike him as being safe enough. He reminded the soldiers that one should prepare one's action based on the probable behavior of the enemy, not on wishful thinking. True, he said, the planned pincer movement that would cut "Green" in half was clearly the most advantageous opening gambit for the Wehrmacht. But the enemy must have anticipated such a maneuver, and after the *Anschluß* the Czechoslovak-Austrian border had been fortified and was manned by the best regiments of the enemy. The pincer movement was too uncertain, he warned, and the plan could not depend solely on its success.

The Führer proposed changes in Operation Green and also brought up his experience in France, at Verdun, during the Great War. He specifically warned against throwing troops into half-developed breaches in the enemy's front. He did not want any kind of "bleeding-to-death" approach. Only a swift victory was acceptable from a political point of view. The record of the meeting is brief, but a great deal must have transpired during the five-and-a-half-hour discussion. Although Hitler seemed nervous about the plan, he no longer had to debate its desirability with his generals. Despite their serious misgivings, German military leaders had finally accepted the inevitability of war.

On Saturday, a few hours after the conference on Operation Green had ended and under the threatening clouds gathering at Nuremberg, Beneš took to the microphone in Prague. Speaking in Czech, Slovak, and German, he attempted to explain to the public the so-far secretive negotiations with the SdP that had resulted in the Fourth Plan. He tried to present the plan—rendered irrelevant by the SdP's and Lord Runciman's demand for territorial changes—as one which, for all the sacrifices it entailed, upheld the democratic tradition of Czechoslovakia. He urged all the citizens of Czechoslovakia to remain calm and reasonable. "Let us be prepared," Beneš concluded, "for every sacrifice, but let us also be optimists through the darkest days."[9] Those were, undoubtedly, noble ideas, but the occasion only showed Beneš's shortcomings as an orator. His high-pitched voice and pedantic style would have been tolerable in a professor whose captive audience of students was eager to learn about the laws of physics or the Mayan civilization. But the president was addressing a country on the verge of war, a people anxious to receive inspiration. Still, his was a voice of reason and civilization. By contrast, Hermann Göring, who spoke before members of the NSDAP at Nuremberg while Beneš was delivering his address in Prague, felt no obligation to uphold a civilized standard in politics. He could not restrain himself on the subject of Czechoslovakia: "We know how intolerable it is that that little fragment of a nation down there—goodness knows where it hails from—should persistently oppress and interfere with a highly civilized people. But we know that it is not these absurd pygmies who are responsible. Moscow and the eternal Jewish-Bolshevist rabble are behind it."[10]

The Soviet Union had so far provided Czechoslovakia with no assistance whatever. It would have been one thing to suffer Nazi insults in return for Soviet fighter planes or antiaircraft artillery. But the Prague government had been almost excluded from civilized Europe as a result of a chimera created by the Goebbels propaganda machine, that Czechoslovakia was Stalin's puppet. Both Paris and London knew that the Kremlin had done nothing to assist the Prague government, but it made little difference. Even Göring's language, hitherto unheard of in diplomacy, did not seem to shock anyone, and there were no protests. The British embassy in Berlin calmly concluded that he was bluffing.[11]

Hermann Göring was not allowed to outshine Adolf Hitler, whose speech was scheduled for Monday, 12 September 1938, two days after Beneš and Göring had spoken.[12] The pomposity of the introduction to the Führer's appearance surpassed all previous occasions. He first reviewed and personally gave commands to an impressive military parade, and only later in the evening was it his turn to discuss the topic of Czechoslovakia.[13] He charged that the Prague government had systematically tried to "annihilate" the Sudeten Germans; it hunted them "like helpless wild-fowl for every expression of their national sentiment." He brought up the humiliation he had suffered at the time of the Czechoslovak partial mobilization in May 1938 and revealed that it only strengthened his determination to increase Germany's armed might. He was now in a position to demand that the suffering of the Sudeten Germans cease: they had to be given the right to self-determination. The Führer cautiously signaled that France and Great Britain should not interfere with his aggression against Czechoslovakia. But if his action on behalf of the Sudeten Germans were to cause war with other European states, it would not be his fault. Under no circumstances was he prepared to see a second Palestine emerging in Central Europe. "The poor Arabs are defenseless and perhaps deserted," said Hitler, but the Sudeten Germans were not. One of the greatest atheists of the century concluded his speech with a pious demand: "So help us God."

Although it had been built up as a seminal statement on German foreign policy that would determine the future course of European politics, Hitler's speech at Nuremberg took the diplomatic corps by surprise. The Führer did not declare war on Czechoslovakia, and he did not even set a deadline by which the crisis would have to be solved. He was vulgar and aggressive, but when the dust settled he had only insisted on the right to self-determination for the Sudeten German population of Czechoslovakia. This demand left many questions wide open. Did he want an immediate transfer of territory? If so, then exactly which part of Czechoslovakia did he expect to get? What about communities in which the population was evenly divided? What about Czech-speaking islands within the Sudetenland or German villages scattered throughout Bohemia, Moravia, and even Slovakia? Did he expect that plebiscites would solve such questions? Was the whole speech merely a camouflage for Operation Green? The possibility exists that as late as the evening of 12 September 1938 Adolf Hitler was not quite sure whether he was ready to start a war.

The Führer's admirers in the SdP had no such uncertainty, however. As far as they were concerned, the Nuremberg address was a signal for an SdP uprising against the Czechoslovak authorities. The party's specialists in low-level warfare, the Sudetendeutsches Freikorps, were among those who eagerly awaited an opportunity to attack.[14] They had been trained in the art of terrorism by Wehrmacht, SS, and SA instructors on the German side of the border; they were armed with rifles and machine guns; and they were divided into four sections, each consisting of some ten thousand men. Their headquarters were at the Castle Dondorf near Bayreuth in Bavaria.[15] The *Freikorps* were determined to use Hitler's speech at Nuremberg to commence an open rebellion. It is possible that the SdP's leaders had gotten ahead of Berlin in this instance in part because they had hoped that a successful action by the party's paramilitary units would increase their prestige in Berlin and expand their future influence over the Sudetenland.

The SdP's offices in Prague closed down while Hitler spoke at Nuremberg; only a small staff stayed behind to burn all sensitive documents during the night. Ablebodied men were ordered to report for duty in the Sudetenland. The official explanation for their departure was that a German air raid on Prague was expected within forty-eight hours.[16] All of the party's newspapers published in the capital appeared the next day only to announce that they had ceased publication.[17] The Henleinists in the Sudetenland had prepared to hear the speech collectively in many communities, mostly in local beer-halls. By 9 P.M., barely a quarter of an hour after the Führer had concluded his speech and asked God to help him in his future endeavors, crowds of Sudeten Nazis took to the streets.

The omnipresent British assistant military attaché, Major Reginald Sutton-Pratt, had traveled to the heart of the Sudetenland to listen to the speech as a guest of Dr. Kriegensteiner, an SdP member in Cheb. The major's account of events that followed the speech may serve as a *pars pro toto* in depicting the atmosphere in the Sudeten region. Right after the Führer finished, a sympathetic crowd of paramilitary Sudeten Germans gathered outside the house where Sutton-Pratt was staying. They demanded a speech. As a foreign diplomat accredited to the Prague government, the major tried to be prudent. Speaking from an open window, he told the crowd that he had come to their community to investigate incidents in the region and was confident that, eventually, "truth will out." He personally would do all in his power to see to it that justice was done. The crowd instantly interpreted the major's speech as being supportive of the SdP:

> There was enormous enthusiasm, and they cheered me and nearly pulled me out of the window shaking hands, and then sang *Deutschland über Alles* and *Horst Wessel Lied*. The *Bezirksleiter* then requested the people to go home, and they formed into a column of eight abreast, and marched round the town. I can confirm that they were in a frenzy of joy and not in any way ill-natured, for I walked around the town for half an hour, except that all Jewish shops had their windows shattered.[18]

On his jaunt, Sutton-Pratt ran into the town's Czechoslovak police chief. The major found him to be "a blustering, irresponsible fool, for he announced his intention of having every *Hakenkreuz* flag removed," whereas Sutton-Pratt had told him that he thought it "wiser to turn a blind eye." They failed to reach an agreement, and the major moved on. Just around a corner, he came across a mob of two or three hundred Henleinists armed with laths and bricks. Before the major's eyes, twelve of them broke ranks, ran after a young man who happened to be on the street, and started to beat him. The victim "looked like a prosperous Jew: they were hitting and kicking him, and he was streaming with blood and rocking dazedly." At first Major Sutton-Pratt approached the scene, but his SdP "companion, perhaps wisely, prevented me from intervening, and drew me away." Although he had witnessed this scene, the only person for whom the British observer had any critical words in his report to Lord Halifax was the Czechoslovak policeman who stood alone, or with a handful of his colleagues, against this sea of madness.[19]

At night the unrest spread throughout the Sudetenland, and by the morning of 13 September 1938 at least four Czechoslovak police officers had been murdered and twenty-six kidnapped to Germany. Those in the latter category were never heard from again.[20] The streets of large towns in the Sudetenland were covered with broken glass from the shop windows of stores owned by Czechs, Jews, or German democrats. As always, the authorities were under strict orders not to fire unless fired upon, and this put them in an impossible situation, especially in darkness or when they had to patrol an open space like a town square, fully exposed to Freikorps snipers. Consequently, the area of Aš, an enclave almost encircled by the German border, had to be abandoned to the Henleinists. However, everywhere else steps were taken to restore order. On 13 and 14 September in several German districts *stanné právo* (a state of emergency) was declared, providing the police and courts with additional powers.[21] Reinforcements of police officers as well as troops calmly marched into areas that had been captured by the SdP paramilitary units. When the shooting stopped, the final tally was twenty-seven dead (sixteen Czechs, eleven Sudeten Germans).[22] This was testimony to the discipline and self-restraint of the authorities, especially if one considers that the Freikorps were merely groups of illicitly armed civilians who enjoyed no legal standing under Czechoslovak or international law and had no protection as combatants under the law of war.

As had happened in May, resolute measures produced results, and by 15 September 1938 complete order had been restored throughout the Sudeten region. The SdP was declared illegal—its senators and deputies were not deprived of immunity—and a warrant was issued for Konrad Henlein's arrest. He called on his followers to fight "Czech tyranny" with any means available and escaped to Germany.[23] He was joined by scores of other SdP bosses. The pent-up energy released throughout the Sudetenland by Hitler's speech at Nuremberg quickly died out; the SdP uprising against the democratic government in Prague had failed after a mere forty-eight hours.

A new situation developed in German districts. The long column of cars packed with SdP officials escaping to safety over the border, after they had told their followers to fight to the end, was a sight to behold. The convoy could not be concealed from Czechoslovak authorities: some policemen and soldiers actually cheered as the cars, packed with nervous Nazi apparatchiks, sped in the direction of the Third Reich.[24] The scene had the opposite effect on the Sudeten German population. As long as party bosses were around to keep an eye on rank-and-file members, few Sudeten Germans chose to go against the current, and they took part in demonstrations and other party activities when so ordered. It was dangerous not to participate. However, they went home as soon as they could without gaining the stigma of being lukewarm about the Nazi ideology. And this is what they did on 12 September 1938. They marched, sang songs, beat up an innocent or two, broke Jewish windows, and went to bed.[25] The Freikorps had shown enthusiasm for action, but that changed with Henlein's speedy departure. Who could expect the Sudeten Germans to rise against the legal authorities and "fight to the end" while their officers fled to safety across the border? The German military attaché in Prague reported to Berlin that Henlein's flight had a "crushing effect" on the local population and that the Prague government was master of the situation.[26] Radio Berlin broadcasts aimed at Czechoslovak Germans lied so openly that its credibility declined sharply.[27] The mood among the population was, according to the German legation in Prague, "extraordinarily depressed."[28] It was also notable that a state of emergency had to be declared in only sixteen of the forty-nine districts of the Sudetenland.

This made sense. Many had joined the SdP because it was dangerous not to do so and because the organization embraced some popular causes, such as those involving distribution of government jobs with pensions. But it now seemed that there would be a shooting war, a war fought in the Sudentenland. And who would fight it? Obviously not Herr Henlein and his friends who had run away before the first shots had been fired. The overwhelming majority had accepted the SdP's authority as long as the party was powerful and proposed to increase their economic security and national pride. But a bloody war in their own backyard was likely to take away the little that most of them had. Why should they support it? In a number of communities, including Mariánské Lázně, leading members of the former SdP publicly welcomed the restoration of order by the authorities and proposed to cooperate with the Prague government. Prominent Sudeten personalities began suggesting that a new political party could be formed, consisting of German agrarians, Catholics, and a section of the more reasonable members of the SdP. The new party would without delay renew negotiations with the Beneš government on the basis of the Fourth Plan.[29] After all, it gave Sudeten Germans outside the fanatical core of SdP leaders more than they had ever intended to demand. The tide seemed to have turned in the Sudetenland.

Berchtesgaden: A Step to Munich

Hitler's concern that his troops might end up "bleeding to death" after they had hit the steel and concrete of Czechoslovak fortifications, his worries about causing another Verdun, and the surprising vagueness of his speech at Nuremberg showed that the Führer's steely appearance may have been only a mask. And now the routing of the Freikorps in a low-key action by the Czechoslovak police and the sudden collapse of the SdP in the middle of September 1938, when Berlin needed it most, must have increased his doubts. Hitler's domestic position, of course, had remained strong, but only as long as he marched from one success to another. One setback—and who knew what would have happened. The question was whether President Beneš, his allies, and the rest of democratic Europe would be able to sustain the tide's new, favorable direction. For the second time during the course of the Czechoslovak-German crisis—the first occasion had been in May—there was an opportunity to restrain the further growth of the Third Reich.

The Czechoslovak army understood that the crisis had reached a crucially important point. On 9 September 1938, while Hitler was discussing Operation Green at Nuremberg, General Ludvík Krejčí addressed President Beneš and the government with a memorandum. This in itself was an unusual step because a separation of the military profession from all political deliberations had been always strictly observed. Czechoslovakia's top general warned against any compromise and pointed out that the army stood ready to do its duty. It was well armed and eager to fight, and the Wehrmacht should not be overestimated. "This is a decisive moment in our nation's history and it calls for resolute decisions. . . . If we do not defend ourselves there will be no mercy for us. We would be annihilated in the most barbaric manner. If we must die let us do so honorably."[30]

Without waiting for the government's response, the army took a series of steps to increase combat readiness. By the evening of 12 September 1938, in anticipation of Hitler's speech at Nuremberg, officers and the mobilization apparatus were put on full alert. All leaves were canceled, and troops were restricted to the barracks. At 11 P.M. next day, as the Freikorps went into action in the Sudetenland, the government accepted General Krejčí's request to carry out another partial mobilization. Within hours, reservists and selected specialists flooded mobilization centers, and regiments all along the Czechoslovak-German borders were brought up to half a million men under arms. They were optimistic and cocky. It was these men who later watched and mockingly cheered the column of cars carrying Henlein and SdP officials escaping *"Heim ins Reich,"* running from the fight they had declared.[31] On 13 September, although it had been weakened by the concessions extracted by Lord Runciman, the Prague government was in full control of the domestic situation. When the British, finally, took certain "naval measures" by putting the fleet on partial alert, it seemed that the tide had really turned, not only in the Sudetenland, but in Europe.[32]

Inexplicably, it was at this time, on 14 September, that Neville Chamberlain announced his intention to meet with Hitler.[33] As it turned out, the prime minister had conceived of the idea of visiting the Führer as early as 30 August 1938.[34] This visit, perhaps, would have been a plausible maneuver for averting an explosion of violence in late August when Czechoslovakia had been weakened under the blows of the SdP, but it was inappropriate two weeks later, after the Prague government had reestablished control over its territory.[35] It seems that pressure from France was one of the factors that had led to Chamberlain's decision to meet Hitler.[36]

On 13 September, at 8:30 P.M., London learned that Prime Minister Daladier was ready, albeit with reluctance, for France to fulfill its obligations and assist Czechoslovakia against Hitler, but less than two hours later it heard from him that Hitler's aggression had to be prevented "at all costs."[37] One way, Daladier suggested, was to propose a conference of Germany, Great Britain, and France that would result in "that pacific settlement" suggested by the Führer in his speech of 12 September.[38] Chamberlain had probably believed for some time in his ability to solve the crisis through personal contact with Hitler, but Daladier had few illusions about the Third Reich. What had happened? It was the report of the uprising in the Sudetenland, following Hitler's speech, that reduced him to "begging" the British ambassador in Paris to urge Chamberlain into action. Although the Freikorps had been beaten within forty-eight hours, Paris had concluded that the Sudetenland was in flames and that the Henleinists had formed a carpet on which Hitler would march into Czechoslovakia.

When Prague found out that the British prime minister was ready to fly to Germany for consultations with Hitler, Beneš immediately perceived the danger this development embodied. Yet neither the president nor any of his colleagues despaired, not because they had faith in Chamberlain's ability to restrain the Führer, but because they believed, paradoxically, that Hitler would not let them down.[39] They hoped that Hitler would reveal his vulgar, aggressive self and that the prime minister, the product of English public schools, would know how to deal with a bully.

The news of Chamberlain's visit to Germany was greeted with great relief especially in Great Britian, France, and Germany.[40] The German military attaché in Rome told his British colleague that he was "expressing the views of the whole German army when he said the last thing in the world they wanted was war and particularly war with Great Britain."[41] The Führer was also delighted. Could not the prime minister bring Mrs. Chamberlain along, inquired the charming Austrian, and, perhaps, given the prime minister's age, he, Hitler, should fly to London?[42] No, that did not suit Chamberlain, who felt he needed to protect the "dramatic force" of his peace mission.[43]

In the end, it was the Führer who set up the scene. The prime minister flew in the morning of 15 September to Munich, where he arrived in the middle of the day. He then had to take the train to Berchtesgaden. For no less than three hours, Chamberlain sat in his compartment and watched passing military trains moving in the direction of the Czechoslovak border, carrying guns and shock troops in brand-new uniforms. It began to rain.[44] From the train station, a column of Mercedes cars, especially designed for the steep drive, took the British guests to the Berghof. Soon the Prime Minister found himself in the same austere, almost unfurnished room where Lord Halifax (in November 1937) and Chancellor von Schuschnigg (in February 1938) had been before him. Chamberlain recalled a few days later that the atmosphere surrounding Hitler was one of extraordinary excitement. "The wildest and most fantastic stories were coming in every moment from Czechoslovakia and were greedily swallowed."[45] Remarkably, the prime minister did not seem to realize that such background developments had been engineered for his benefit because the situation in Czechoslovakia was calm at the moment.

What was there for Chamberlain to discuss with Hitler? As we have seen, Daladier had made clear on 13 September that war had to be avoided "at all costs." Bonnet said the next day that he could not sacrifice ten million French soldiers only to keep the Sudeten Germans in Czechoslovakia.[46] And on 15 September the French foreign minister, having thanked Chamberlain for his "magnificent gesture" in going to see Hitler, assured London that he would "strongly advise" that France accept whatever the prime minister would propose, "whether it were accepted by the Czechs or not."[47] If these were the views of France, the country that had a legal obligation to defend Czechoslovakia against German aggression, what was there to be expected from Great Britain, which was free from any such responsibility? After all, Lord Runciman had already demonstrated in Prague what the British regarded to be an honorable solution to the crisis.

It was clear throughout their one-on-one discussion that both Hitler and Chamberlain took the secession of the Sudetenland for granted.[48] The rest of the country, Hitler asserted, was of no interest to him. But the status quo was intolerable because Czechoslovakia was a spearhead in the side of Germany, and it had killed three hundred Sudeten Germans. This had to end. Chamberlain had failed to challenge Hitler on this or on any other point so far, but the Führer was already working himself into a frenzy. He did not care whether there would be a world war; he would settle the crisis *so oder so,* by one means or another, and soon. He could not allow Czechoslovakia, "a small subordinate country, to treat the great German Reich, with its thousand years of history, as something inferior."[49] Chamberlain as a good negotiator patiently inquired, Why, then, did you let me come here? What is there for us to discuss? Hitler had an answer for that question. If Great Britain publicly embraced the idea of the *Anschluß* of the Sudetenland, their talks could continue. Speaking for himself, the English guest immediately accepted the proposition but said he would have to consult his colleagues in London. It did not occur to him that he should also ask what Prague thought of the idea. Could Herr Hitler give him his word that there would be no aggression in the meantime? The Führer immediately found difficulties with making such a promise. The German military machine was enormous and once it moved, it would be impossible to stop it. But, yes, he conceded, he would be willing to assure his guest that, if he could help it, he would not order the machine to move. Just do your best, pleaded Chamberlain. He must have felt tired after such long day, his first flight in an airplane, hours on the train, and now talking to the impulsive Hitler. On these terms, the two parted. The final communiqué merely acknowledged that the meeting took place and that the prime minister would return the next day to London for consultations.[50]

Although he had no mandate to dispose of the Sudetenland, let alone to redraw the historical borders of Czechoslovakia, the British prime minister opened his negotiations with Hitler by conceding the ultimate prize. He did not bother proposing cultural or even political autonomy for the Sudeten Germans within the democratic Republic of Czechoslovakia; he did not mention the Fourth Plan, which his own emissary, Lord Runciman, had extracted from the desperate President Beneš. He made clear that as far as he was concerned the Third Reich could take the Sudentenland. No wonder Hitler let it be known that Chamberlain had made a good impression on him. The Führer especially liked the prime minister's forthrightness. He "felt he was speaking to a man."[51] Like the Runciman mission, Chamberlain's conversation with Hitler at Berchtesgaden had been regarded in the shadow, as it were, of the more spectacular event, the Four Power conference at Munich. This is not justified, for the Four Power Act signed at the end of September would contain only marginal additions to what had been already agreed on two weeks earlier.

It should not be forgotten that Chamberlain found himself in the summer and fall of 1938 in an extraordinarily difficult situation. Through no fault of British diplomacy, France had taken upon itself, in 1925, an obligation to protect Czechoslovakia against Germany; it did so in the belief that it had gained an ally who would help protect France against any future German threats. In that sense, Germany was justifed when it complained against French efforts to encircle it by French allies. But by the time Hitler came to power, France found that Czechoslovakia had become a liability. After several high-sounding official declarations that French national *honneur* would be upheld under any circumstances, the Paris government finally admitted on 13 September 1938 that it would welcome a negotiated settlement. Under those circumstances, the British prime minister could not have been expected to step into the breach to make up for the failure of his French ally, especially after Hitler had successfully persuaded the West that, unless completely satisfied in his demands, he would go to war. Chamberlain arrived at the conclusion that he had no alternative but to concede a chunk of Czechoslovak territory in exchange for a promise of peace.

But this interpretation covers up an ugly side of the British political strategy in September 1938. The diplomatic record indicates that Great Britain did not need to be forced by Berlin's threats to accept Hitler's demands. Without prodding from Hitler, the British doubted Czechoslovakia's viability as a state, and they disliked President Beneš. How else is one to understand that the British prime minister surrendered the Sudentenland at the beginning of the negotiations? Once the principle of the transfer of territory had been conceded, the next two meetings between Chamberlain and Hitler would involve much drama but little that had not already been accepted on 15 September. This was a strange manner of negotiating: the prime minister would not have employed it if he had been arranging the purchase of a horse.

The Franco-British Proposal

After he had safely returned to London, the British prime minister had to meet with his government, summon the French for consultations, and prevent the increasingly nervous government in Prague from mobilizing. He performed all three tasks like a virtuoso. It helped, of course, that he enjoyed the support of his colleagues and that he was ably assisted by Lord Runciman, who was invited to 10 Downing Street to brief the government right after his return from Prague. The French were a different sort of problem altogether. Daladier was embarrassed by what was about to happen and would need encouragement to accept the view that there was no alternative but to abandon the Czechoslovak Sudentenland to the Third Reich.

And the Czechoslovaks? They had been watching the growing German military concentrations along their borders with great alarm. General Krejčí warned the British military attaché in Prague that no one could deny the Prague government the right to self-defense, and Krofta told Newton that, according to his information, Hitler would complete military preparations for an attack on Czechoslovakia by 22 or 23 September.[52] The British minister responded by advising the Prague government against mobilization. The French minister, Victor de Lacroix, followed his British colleague with a similar message. He warned Prague against taking any measures that could serve as a pretext for German aggression. Especially, pleaded de Lacroix, do not mobilize (*ne pas prendre mesures de mobilisation*) so as not to disturb the effort to safeguard peace and to secure the vital interests of Czechoslovakia (*la sauvegarde des intérêts vitaux de la Tchécoslovaquie*).[53]

Hoping that the problem posed by the Czechoslovak desire to mobilize had been taken care of by this pressure, Chamberlain could focus on the French delegation, due to arrive on Sunday, 18 September 1938.[54] The Czechoslovak minister in Paris, Osuský, had tried and failed to speak with Daladier or at least with Bonnet before their departure for England. He immediately called Minister Masaryk in London and asked him to try to meet with the French once they arrived on the other side of the Channel. Although he had done his best, Masaryk also failed to secure an interview with the French delegation. He rushed to the Foreign Office to find out what the Franco-British summit was all about, but even the lower-ranking bureaucrats refused to enlighten him. Masaryk returned to the legation and called the Castle in Prague. Because Beneš was out walking, Masaryk could only speak to his secretary, Prokop Drtina. Masaryk sounded like a broken, depressed man. He was full of bad omen: the British and the French were "talking about us without us."[55] This would be subsequently transformed into a slogan by Europeans who found the Munich "solution" of the Czechoslovak-German crisis distasteful.

At 10 Downing Street, speaking quite matter-of-factly, Chamberlain summed up to his French guests his conversation with Hitler.[56] Only if Great Britain and France agreed to sanction Hitler's *Anschluß* of the Sudetenland, Chamberlain concluded, could a German attack on Czechoslovakia and its unpredictable consequences be avoided. At this point, he proposed to hear what the French had to say. One senses from the record that Daladier responded with reluctance. He seemed to have recognized that the Führer had successfully manipulated the British prime minister, perhaps even impressed him. Yes, Daladier acknowledged, it must have been difficult to negotiate with Hitler, "but mysticism did not exclude skill," he warned, pointing out that some of Hitler's arguments against Czechoslovakia smacked of "Nazi propaganda." He reminded his hosts that "not so very long ago" Göring had assured the allies that Germany had no desire to annex the Sudetenland. What would Hitler demand next, after he annexed the German districts of Czechoslovakia?

Chamberlain did not like the direction in which the meeting was moving and he took action to rectify it. Lord Runciman had spoken with Beneš just before his departure from Prague, Chamberlain announced, and the president indicated he was worried lest Czechoslovak interests be betrayed during the meeting at Berchtesgaden. "Lord Runciman had replied that any sacrifice of Czechoslovak interests could only be laid at Dr. Beneš's door. He had throughout been dilatory and had delayed putting forward the necessary proposals until the time when they might be accepted had long passed." Chamberlain went on to defend Hitler's point of view. There had been a time when Germany had no interest in seizing the German districts of Czechoslovakia, he said, but Beneš had not been "prompt" enough in accommodating German demands. Now, as Lord Runciman's fact-finding mission had discovered, nothing short of the *Anschluß* would solve the crisis. That was the naked reality, Chamberlain suggested.

It was absurd to blame Beneš for the escalation of Hitler's demands. The Führer had increased his pressure on the Prague government after the *Anschluß* of Austria because he no longer needed Czechoslovakia's neutrality. And it was outrageous for Chamberlain to suggest that Beneš should have "promptly" accepted the eight points of the SdP when they were in violation of the Czechoslovak constitution and were, moreover, presented by Henlein on the same day he declared himself a Nazi. It is to Beneš's credit that he found the pill of Nazism so hard to swallow. Daladier sensed that Chamberlain had set the ship of Western democracies on the wrong course. German propaganda was already working elsewhere, he observed. Soon, despite Polish illusions, there would be trouble regarding the Polish corridor. The position of France, Daladier stated powerfully, was defined with perfect accuracy. Its treaty with Czechoslovakia was binding, and "in all honour and morality" France had no right to ignore it. Speaking on behalf of his government and the French people, Daladier told the meeting that he could not desert his ally: "No Frenchman would be capable of committing such a crime." The Third Reich, Daladier continued, would not stop after the *Anschluß* of the Sudetenland. Its aim was to wipe out Czechoslovakia and move further east.

Once Eastern Europe had been brought under German domination, Hitler would attack in the West:

> Within one year we might expect [Germany] to turn back against France and Great Britain, who would then have to meet her in much more difficult circumstances than those existing to-day. . . . If we were to accept the German ultimatum by conceding all her demands, we should have created a very serious precedent. Further German demands would follow in due course and Germany would conclude that we should again give way.[57]

The practical-minded British must have found Daladier's statements puzzling. If this was the official view of Paris, then why had the French foreign minister stated before the Berchtesgaden meeting took place that he would support "any proposal Mr. Chamberlain might make, whether it were accepted by the Czechs or not?"[58] And if Daladier took his own words seriously, why was he at 10 Downing Street? He was not only the French prime minister but also the minister of national defense, and if he believed what he had just said, he should have been at a command post, preparing an attack on the Siegfried Line, because unless the Führer got what he had asked there would be war. Was France ready to fight? Despite his rhetoric, Daladier was not convinced.

After a lunch break, finally, the British heard the first words from Daladier that made sense to them: "If friendly pressure were brought to bear on Prague . . . stressing the necessity of giving up some portion of Sudeten territory, the Czechoslovak Government might agree to such a proposal." From this point on, Daladier spoke like a different man, as if a burden had been lifted from his shoulders. He had made his statements about French honor, he had tasted the bitter medicine prescribed by Chamberlain and became—from the British perspective—reasonable. The two sides quickly agreed to present President Beneš with strongly formulated statements demanding territorial concessions to Hitler. But, Chamberlain inquired, what if Beneš rejected their propositions? The "new Daladier" agreed that would have to be avoided. On this note the meeting ended. It was already past midnight. Hitler had won yet another round without firing a shot.

As the heads of the French and British delegations retired for the night, their ministers continued working. On Monday, 19 September 1938, just before 3 A.M., a text was dispatched from London to the French and British legations in Prague. The memorandum was long, but it was possible to sum up its message in one sentence: "The point has been reached where the further maintenance within the boundaries of the Czechoslovak State of the districts mainly inhabited by Sudeten-Deutsch [*sic*] cannot in fact continue any longer without imperiling the interests of Czechoslovakia herself and of European peace." Lord Halifax, who seems to have been one of the drafters of the text, acknowledged that in accepting the present proposition the Prague government would be making a great sacrifice. To make it more palatable, the memorandum promised that Great Britain would be ready to "join in an international guarantee of the new boundaries" of Czechoslovakia.[59] Both the French and British agreed to demand an answer from Beneš, "tonight" hopefully but no later than Wednesday, before Chamberlain's second trip to Germany.

On Monday morning, 19 September 1938, Beneš had not yet seen the memorandum, but the quarantine imposed on Czechoslovak diplomats in Great Britain and France contributed to a dark, depressed atmosphere at the Castle.[60] The president met at 1:45 P.M. with Minister Jaromír Nečas, his confidant, who had just returned from France, where Beneš had sent him on 15 September 1938 to see Léon Blum with an important message for Prime Minister Daladier.[61] There were no witnesses at the meeting, but a document in the president's archive indicates that the two met in order to compare notes on Beneš's desperate last-minute plan, developed after the breakdown of negotiations with the SdP.

In anticipation of the demand that Czechoslovakia surrender parts of its territory to the Third Reich, Beneš proposed to give up 2,600 to 3,900 square miles of the Sudeten territory and with it one and a half to two million SdP activists. At the same time, he would maintain Czechoslovak jurisdiction over large parts of the Sudetenland, where he could protect those Sudeten Germans most likely to suffer under the Nazi rule. In making the unofficial offer, informally known as the Nečas, or fifth, plan, Beneš was hoping to inform the French about the ultimate limit beyond which no concessions should be demanded of Czechoslovakia. The president had resorted to a highly unconstitutional action and he knew it. He stated at the beginning of his discussion with Nečas: "Never allow that the plan could be said to have come from Czechoslovakia." He also asked that his name never be connected with the proposal and that all notes be destroyed.[62] He hoped that if the proposal came from France it would be possible to exercise some control over its implementation, thus protecting all those inhabitants of the Sudetenland who were loyal to the republic.

As was to be expected, the news regarding the plan—thanks to Daladier's indiscretion—found its way to British diplomatic communications as early as on 16 September, that is, before the Franco-British consultations at Downing Street.[63] During his meeting with Nečas on 19 September Beneš complained that Great

Britain, France, and Germany—yes, in that order—wanted to force him to surrender thousands of democrats, socialists, and Jews to Hitler. It would be "a massacre . . . [and] barbarian anti-Semitic murder. . . . This he would not do."[64]

Just as Beneš had uttered these words, at 2 P.M., Ministers Newton and de Lacroix, like two angels of death, arrived at the Castle to present to the Prague government the results of the Franco-British conversations at Downing Street. Drtina came to tell Beneš, who was in the middle of his conversation with Nečas, that the two envoys had come. Under normal circumstances the president liked to keep his visitors waiting, but this was no time to play diplomatic power games. Beneš quickly led Nečas into another room adjacent to his office and asked Drtina to usher in the envoys.[65] The meeting lasted for three quarters of an hour. When the president read the document that had been drafted in London his face turned red.[66] He was abandoned, France had betrayed him.

His first reaction was that, because his government had not been consulted and because he was a president of a democratic state, he would not be able to give an immediate reply. The two cut in to point out that a response was expected without delay, and they began pressuring the president. Their proposition had seductive packaging: give up some unspecified piece of territory inhabited by a people who have caused you nothing but trouble, and we will guarantee that no one will threaten you ever again. When Beneš expressed doubts about the value of such a guarantee, he received explicit assurances that "His Majesty's Government" would take upon itself the responsibility of maintaining Czechoslovak national security against any further demands by the Third Reich. On occasion, Newton sounded like a salesman peddling a product; he knew that the Czechs were a brave people and going to war would not greatly weigh with them, he said, but they should think of their future, "backed by a British guarantee of nearly everything which they had gained" in 1918. Should you reject our proposal, the document implied, you would be alone in a state of war with the Third Reich. Without a simultaneous French military action against Germany, your organized resistance would collapse in a matter of days, but a great percentage of your people would be slaughtered, your ancient capital would be destroyed, and the whole international community will label *you* as the warmonger. Make your choice. With this, the two envoys bid the president a good day. Newton cabled Lord Halifax that he expected the president to accept the proposal.[67]

Beneš quickly called in Drtina and without any comment handed him the English version of the text, asked him to translate it as soon as possible, and returned to continue his conversation with Nečas, which the two envoys had interrupted.[68] Drtina, glancing nervously at the blue stationary from the British legation, found a typist, but as he started dictating the Czech version of the cruel text, he noticed that her tears were dropping onto the paper. The document was translated and brought to the presidential suite, where Beneš was already presiding over a meeting with ministers and representatives of the major political parties. The news of the Franco-British proposal was received as a shock by those who assembled at the Castle. Before the president could make up his mind, he would need to consult his Soviet ally. He had taken the trouble to develop the Soviet connection; now was the time to exploit it.

Prague's Response to the Proposal and the Soviet Union

While President Beneš and the ministers were discussing the Franco-British proposal (some copies of which had been marked by the typist's tears), Aleksandrovsky was drafting a report to Moscow. It was based on what he had learned from Gottwald, who had seen the president two days earlier. Beneš was said to have stated to the CPC leader that his government was "ready for everything" and would defend the country's sovereignty even if abandoned by Great Britain and France. As far as the Soviet Union was concerned, the president observed with satisfaction that on that front at least all was clear. Unfortunately—because all was clear—the Soviet minister had failed to elaborate on this point, and it remains a mystery what Beneš meant. Aleksandrovsky was also able to report (with complete accuracy) on the nature of the proposal that Newton and de Lacroix had delivered a few hours before. He knew that "political circles close to the Government" were sharply critical of it.[69] Aleksandrovsky was obviously well informed: the Soviet legation had its sources at the Castle, possibly among the highest-ranking assistants to President Beneš. Even Drtina had been in the dark on the issue for a long time; he did not find out what the government had decided until 20 September, and then from a friendly minister.[70]

The meeting was still in progress when the Castle called the Soviet legation and arranged a meeting between the president and Aleksandrovsky for 7 P.M. Beneš, who had no idea that his guest had his own sources of information in the Castle, outlined the proposal he had received from Newton and de Lacroix. Then Aleksandrovsky learned something new: the Czechoslovak government had just decided to reject the proposal. The president was in a bellicose mood. He had a half-million men under arms, and he was determined to resist Hitler's aggression with all his might. He expected, moreover, that Czechoslovakia might have to declare a general mobilization the next day in anticipation of a breakdown in the Chamberlain diplomatic initiative. The prime minister's second trip to Germany either would not take place or would collapse once it became clear that the combined pressure from Great Britain and France had failed to bring Czechoslovakia to its knees.

Under these circumstances, Beneš posed two questions, which Aleksandrovsky was to relay to Moscow as soon as possible. The first question was simple: if Paris, despite the Franco-British proposal, were to remain faithful to its obligation toward Czechoslovakia after all, would the Soviet Union also provide the Prague government with assistance against the Third Reich? The second, and crucial, question was recorded by Beneš as follows: "What will the attitude of the Soviet Union be if France refuses to fulfill her obligations?"[71] However Aleksandrovsky recorded the second question differently. His version inquired whether the Soviet Union would assist Czechoslovakia as a member of the League of Nations on the basis of Articles 16 and 17 of the League's Covenant.[72] It does not take much intelligence to see that Aleksandrovsky's version is less plausible than Beneš's. Czechoslovakia needed from its Soviet ally usable military assistance, not procedural interventions in the notoriously slow legislative mechanisms of the League. We will see shortly that once the Soviet legation transmitted Aleksandrovsky's version of Beneš's second question, an already complicated situation became opaque.

Unlike Newton, who was too much of a snob ever to engage Beneš's staff in small talk, Minister Aleksandrovsky liked to do just that. As he was leaving the president's suite around 8 P.M., he stopped at Drtina's desk. It was important, he told Beneš's secretary, for Czechoslovakia to remain firm. The two would have continued their conversation, but Beneš was nervously pressing the buzzer; he needed his secretary immediately. When he heard that Aleksandrovsky had warned Drtina against capitulating, Beneš waved his arm, "I know," he said. "They naturally play their own game. We cannot trust them completely either. If they get us into it," Beneš warned, referring to a war against Germany, "they will leave us twisting in the air."[73] This, of course, gives the president's assertion to Gottwald that "all was clear" regarding the Soviet Union's position an unexpected twist. It also shows that Beneš had, at least at that moment, a realistic view of Moscow's *modus operandi*.

Still, the president could not simply give up the Soviet card he had gained at a considerable price in 1935. He again invited Klement Gottwald to come to see him, and the meeting took place shortly after Aleksandrovsky had left. As always, the CPC boss subsequently briefed the Soviet legation, which passed the information on to the Kremlin. According to this record, Beneš was probing regarding Moscow's intentions. He inquired whether Gottwald could tell him anything specific about the Soviet Union's attitude at this stage of the crisis. He was probably hoping to learn what instructions the CPC had received via the Comintern or directly from the Kremlin. But Gottwald was a man of Bolshevik discipline, and indiscretion was not tolerated in his circles. He responded that he was not authorized to speak on Moscow's behalf, but that the Soviet Union always fulfilled its commitments. If Beneš wanted something that went beyond Soviet legal obligations, he should formulate his questions in precise terms and submit them via the proper channels to Moscow.[74] Gottwald was apparently referring to what had become the central question: Would Stalin provide Czechoslovakia with military assistance unilaterally, that is, without France? In that case, this confirms that Beneš's version of the second question was the accurate one.

The next day, on Tuesday, 20 September 1938, the president continued meeting with ministers, representatives of political parties, and top army officers. Throughout the day Prague waited to hear the Kremlin's response to the two questions submitted to Aleksandrovsky. Its answer was crucially important: Abandoned by France, could Czechoslovakia rely on military assistance from the Soviet Union? Stalin chose silence. The tension in London and Paris had risen to an unprecedented height. After all, the British prime minister was scheduled to see the Führer, and no one knew whether Europe would celebrate peace, that is, Czechoslovakia's capitulation, or resign itself to an armed conflict at its center. When evening came Beneš could no longer postpone. At 7:45 P.M., Krofta handed Newton and de Lacroix a statement in French. It thanked Great Britain and France for their efforts and rejected the Franco-British proposal.[75] It would not achieve peace, Krofta stressed; it would mutilate the state, and the Prague government had not been consulted. In any case, only the parliament could decide a question pertaining to national borders. Prague's response pointedly warned that a realization of the proposal would have seriously disrupted the balance of power throughout Europe, and the consequences would be felt in every state, especially in France. Krofta did not encourage discussion. He made his points briefly. The two envoys were taken by surprise. Newton had confidently predicted that Prague would accept the proposal, and now this.[76] He chillingly warned that this refusal "meant the destruction of [Krofta's] beautiful country." Hitler would never accept arbitration, and only the Franco-British proposal could save Czechoslovakia. But Krofta stood his ground. The proposal was not acceptable. He was resigned to the idea of a war.[77] It was 20 September 1938, 8 P.M.

Just twenty minutes later the Foreign Ministry decoded a telegram from the Czechoslovak legation in Moscow. Fierlinger reported that the Kremlin had met to consider Beneš's two questions. Would the Soviet Union provide military assistance to Czechoslovakia if France remained loyal to its obligations? "Yes, immediately and effectively," cabled Fierlinger. The second answer was also positive, only the question was distorted: it had to do with Soviet actions as a member of the League of Nations under Articles 16 and 17.[78]

The Czechoslovak government had announced its decision to reject the Franco-British proposal half an hour before it heard from Moscow, and its position had, therefore, played no role in Beneš's decision making.[79] When Beneš realized that Aleksandrovsky had misrepresented his second question he was reaffirmed in the view he had expressed to Drtina: the Kremlin could not be trusted. It was also notable that the Soviet response came via Fierlinger and not Aleksandrovsky. The Czechoslovak minister only relayed information between Prague and Moscow, but what he said did not bind the Kremlin. The offical answer could come only from Aleksandrovsky, who was nowhere to be seen.

The Franco-British Ultimatum and Its Consequences

After the Prague government took the crucial step and rejected the proposal to surrender the Sudeten territory to Hitler, members of the president's staff felt as if a boulder had been lifted from their shoulders. Most of them, Drtina recalled, thought that Czechoslovakia should fight against the Third Reich under any circumstances. They believed that the whole world viewed the Czechoslovak-German crisis as a test of the ability of democracies to resist totalitarian manipulation. If the country were to allow itself to be pushed into the Führer's jaws, Nazism would score yet another victory. How could the world not credit the growth of German power to the totalitarian Weltanschauung? But now the decision had been made to fight, alone if necessary, and the general feeling was one of relief. Drtina went home, and President Beneš, whose reservoir of energy seemed to have no limit, had another meeting to attend.[80]

Eventually, even Beneš went to bed and fell asleep. Just before 1 A.M. on 21 September 1938, the French legation called the castle and demanded an audience with the president for 2 A.M.[81] The British minister would come along as well. Beneš was awakened, and he asked his staff to call a meeting with the ministers to be convened after the envoys had left. Newton and de Lacroix arrived fifteen minutes late (the British legation had a hard time decoding Newton's instructions from Lord Halifax), but they wore top hats.[82]

Darkness provided an appropriate background for their arrival. From a distance they could be mistaken for seconds who were to officiate a duel between gentlemen. But the president was more likely to see them as executioner's helpers who had come to make preliminary arrangements in his cell before he would be taken out at dawn. As soon as they entered, Beneš noticed that they seemed unspeakably sad, almost fearful, studiously avoiding his eyes.[83] Newton was more decisive than de Lacroix, and he delivered his message first. London and Paris refused to accept Prague's rejection of the Anglo-French proposal and threatened that Hitler's attack was imminent. Beneš now had one more chance, Newton stressed, to save his country from disaster.[84] De Lacroix had begun weeping even before he delivered his lines. Crying, he stumbled over the first sentences, but he gradually rediscovered his courage and his voice finally acquired a steely undertone. When he read the crucial sentence, that France would break its legal obligations to Czechoslovakia and would not go to war against the Third Reich (''la France ne s'y associera pas''), it sounded merciless. Ignoring Newton, Beneš asked for a written statement from de Lacroix, which he was unwilling to provide. (Later, after a telephone call to Paris, a text was made available, a watered-down version of what de Lacroix had stated verbally.[85]) Beneš inquired: Is this ''une sorte d'ultimatum''? Newton and de Lacroix confirmed it by repeating they had nothing else to add.[86]

While the meeting was in progess, Drtina knocked on the door. Although he had left the Castle after the government had rejected the proposal, he found it difficult to stay at home. At 2:35 A.M. he called the operator on duty and learned that the ''two top hats'' were with Beneš.[87] A car was dispatched to his house, and in half an hour Drtina stood outside the study where the drama was taking place. He had heard from a colleague that Fierlinger had cabled very good news from Moscow. On the basis of that information, it seemed to Drtina that Stalin was ready to provide Czechoslovakia with military assistance even without France (which is not what Fierlinger's cable said). Drtina became agitated. He felt he had to see the president immediately. In violation of protocol, he interrupted the meeting and asked the president to step outside. His premise, Drtina said when Beneš came out, was that the Franco-British pressure was driving Czechoslovakia into Stalin's arms. If the West and the Third Reich wished to keep Bolshevism out of Central Europe, they had to allow an honorable solution to the Sudeten crisis. A capitulation to Hitler would only strengthen Stalin. Beneš's reply made no mention of Moscow; it focused only on France and Great Britain. Their behavior, the president briefly argued, was determined by two factors: they were not ready to fight, and they feared that a war in Europe could turn into a large-scale socialist revolution. Yet accepting the Franco-British proposal, Drtina exclaimed, would mean revolution in Czechoslovakia. ''Perhaps,'' Beneš responded laconically, ''but we'll have to suppress it.'' With this the president turned and went back to Newton and de Lacroix.

Because the two envoys were unable to say anything in addition to reading the texts they had already communicated, it was only Beneš who spoke. Neither Great Britain nor France knew what they were doing, he said, and their policy would have grave consequences for Czechoslovakia, Central Europe, and Europe in general.

The consequences would be dreadful, he repeated. De Lacroix began to weep again, and the meeting was over. Now the government had to meet to make a decision. It was 4:20 A.M.[88]

Beneš went to discuss the ultimatum with the ministers in a different part of the Castle. They had to face a hideous dilemma. Leaving, Newton walked by Drtina's desk without noticing him, but the French minister stopped in the middle of the room and offered a handshake. Drtina reluctantly accepted. He felt there was nothing he could do.[89] The government pondered the ultimatum to 1 P.M. and again from 3:30 to 5 P.M. Several ministers broke down and wept.[90]

When Newton returned to the British legation, he predicted that Beneš would cave in.[91] But the president continued to have doubts. At noon on 21 September 1938, Newton and de Lacroix came back to demand an answer to the ultimatum they had left in Beneš's hands some eight hours ago.[92] They repeated that unless an official acceptance was forthcoming immediately, neither London nor Paris would have any responsibility for the consequences. The president asked what guarantees he would have against being attacked by Hitler after he had accepted the ultimatum and withdrawn the Czechoslovak army from the fortresses. Newton said he did not know, but he thought that Great Britain had no obligation toward Czechoslovakia. The President turned to de Lacroix: "We are allies, after all, we have a treaty and that treaty is valid, is it not?" The French minister, terrified of making an irreparable error, refused to answer. When Beneš kept pressing, de Lacroix said he was not certain whether the ultimatum had altered or voided the treaty. It was, paradoxically, Newton who tried to end the conversation by observing that, in his opinion, old treaties were valid. Unpersuaded, de Lacroix said he would have to contact Paris.

The whole discussion, Beneš noted, was extremely embarrassing:

> Standing in the door of my Library, upstairs at the Castle, the English Minister displayed the sad audacity to tell me he could not understand what sort of government we had that it was unable to make up its mind. I was furious, seeing that while the existence of the state was at risk this ignoramus and imbecile complained that the government was unable to decide within a few hours to take the step which the two had simply dictated.[93]

During the dark years of World War II, and again during the postwar period until the communist coup d'etat in February 1948, President Beneš and other Czechoslovak politicians would appear to have less sympathy for the West and more understanding for Stalin's Soviet Union than others in Central Europe. Inasmuch as this appearance had some substance, its roots could be traced to scenes like the one described here.

Minister Štefan Osuský cabled from Paris that neither Paris nor London sought to find an honorable solution to the crisis because their intention was to gain time for themselves by feeding Hitler chunks of Czechoslovak territory. "Judge the situation calmly and objectively," Osuský urged the Prague government, 'without regard to what you hear from Great Britain and France.''[94] This did not change the direction of the tide, and on 21 September 1938, just before 5 P.M., Krofta officially informed Newton and de Lacroix that "under pressure of urgent insistence" the Prague government "sadly accepts the French and British proposals." Krofta went on to state that this decision was made on the assumption that the allies would protect the remaining Czechoslovak territory against a German invasion and that details for the execution of the proposal would be worked out "in agreement with" Prague.[95]

Only twelve hours had passed since the proposal that Czechoslovakia surrender the Sudetenland had been communicated to Beneš. Yet he had already been denounced as a warmonger for taking so long to decide. It should be noted that the Hapsburg emperor Franz Joseph was magnanimous enough to have given Serbia forty-eight hours to ponder his ultimatum in the summer of 1914.

As soon as the president had stopped agonizing over the Franco-British ultimatum and accepted it, he had to deal with other crises. Polish Minister Kazimierz Papée and his Hungarian colleague Jean Wettstein de Westersheimb chose this occasion to present their demands on Czechoslovakia.[96] These interventions did not come out of the blue: Warsaw and Budapest had always suggested they would demand for their minorities in Czechoslovakia the same concessions that Prague would grant to others. Now was the time to put such demands on the table; Beneš's attention was guaranteed. In the evening on 21 September, the Polish minister brought up the painful and divisive issue of Těšín with an official at the Foreign Ministry. Prague's position was that it had been already settled by international arbitration. At that time, the Polish minister responded, Bolshevik troops were outside Warsaw, and Poland was weak and had to take any decision. If we employ this logic, Minister Krno of the Czechoslovak Foreign Ministry replied, then the Těšín issue should not be dealt with at the moment because Czechoslovakia in 1938 was in the same position as Poland had been in 1920. On instructions from Minister Beck, Papée could only repeat: give us the disputed area in the Těšín region, and Czechoslovak-Polish relations would be cleared *via facti*.

The Polish envoy explicitly demanded that Prague grant to the Polish minority what it was about to grant the Sudeten Germans.[97] The Polish position was not as bellicose as might have been feared, but it caused Prague's position to become more precarious. Although the Hungarian minister presented his demands on behalf of Budapest with equal firmness, Prague was less concerned about a possible military clash with Hungary.[98] But if Czechoslovakia were to fight alone, army planners considered the benevolent neutrality of Poland to be the minimal condition for a plausible military defense against the Third Reich. No sooner had the Polish and Hungarian ministers departed than envoys from Belgium, Greece, Bulgaria, Italy, and the United States requested audiences at the Foreign Ministry. Each came to express his conviction that further coexistence between Czechoslovaks and Sudeten Germans was impossible. Although it would undoubtedly be painful, Prague, in their opinion, could not but accept the ultimatum.[99] Like Austria a few months earlier, Czechoslovakia was now completely isolated.

Did Stalin play a role in these dramatic events? Because Beneš's second question had been distorted, the Kremlin's promise to come, together with France, to Czechoslovakia's assistance would have had little practical value for the Prague government, even if it had reached the Castle in time.[100] De Lacroix had made unmistakably clear that Paris would not abide by its legal commitments to Czechoslovakia; therefore, Stalin had nothing to lose by responding positively to both questions. Not everyone was taken in by this tactic. An unidentified member of the

Prague government went to see Aleksandrovsky on 21 September and inquired about the Kremlin's position on the ultimatum. The Soviet minister was outraged. He rushed to the Foreign Ministry and complained that Beneš's "questions were clear and Moscow answered them clearly." His behavior was almost imperial.[101] Eventually, the Kremlin was able to create the appearance of being supportive of the Prague government but without accepting any responsibility. Some did not fall for this trick but others did, and the Soviet Union would repeat the same maneuver a few days later.[102]

While the drama involving the Franco-British proposal and the subsequent ultimatum was taking place in Prague, Litvinov was busy in Geneva. But he carefully waited for Beneš to surrender before he said publicly that Moscow had given an affirmative answer to the president's question about whether it would stand by Czechoslovakia, together with France, in case of German aggression.[103] The perceptive German ambassador in Moscow saw through Litvinov's posturing. He informed Berlin that the Kremlin had made its support to Czechoslovakia "absolutely dependent" on France moving first.[104] Because France had already made clear that it was not prepared to live up to its obligations, Moscow's promises of support had purely cosmetic value.

What the Soviet Union really wanted was to secure for itself a seat at the international conference that would eventually deal with the crisis. Litvinov told Lord De La Warr in Geneva that Great Britain, France, and the Soviet Union should meet in Paris to discuss the crisis.[105] Certainly the Kremlin dreaded its increasing isolation, and wanted to avoid the possibility that the Sudetenland issue should be solved by an international conference among Great Britain, France, and Germany, but excluding the Soviet Union. Note that Litvinov's suggestion to Lord De La Warr did not mention the participation of Czechoslovakia.

President Beneš followed Litvinov's speeches at Geneva, but his main focus, of course, was on the scene at home. No one in Prague seems to have thought that accepting the Franco-British ultimatum meant that a solution had been found and that the crisis had ended. Soon after he had received the ultimatum from Newton and de Lacroix, Beneš spoke with Drtina. The president seemed strong, determined, and even optimistic. He was convinced that the Czechoslovak cause, in contrast to that of the Third Reich, was just and that it would eventually be victorious. The president expressed the view that a war was bound to break out, and Drtina fully agreed. He went home, sent his family to the countryside, dismissed the maid, and locked his recently refurbished apartment. He feared that his family would never live there; from then on, the president's secretary would work and sleep only at the Castle.[106]

It was a beautiful fall afternoon on Wednesday, 21 September 1938. As soon as the news had spread that Czechoslovakia had surrendered to the Franco-British pressure, crowds began to gather around the Castle.[107] One of the few visitors who had made his way through the crowds to the president was Soviet Minister Aleksandrovsky. In a memorandum written shortly after the crisis was over, he reported that Beneš was in a good mood. The president was convinced that a war against the Third Reich was bound to break out eventually. He expressed his conviction that in that case the Soviet Union would "fight its way through Poland and Romania" to help Czechoslovakia in its war against the Third Reich. Aleksandrovsky listened with polite interest but said as little as possible.[108]

President Beneš's optimism is not explainable by the archival evidence now available. After all, even Fierlinger had complained that Soviet support to Czechoslovakia was only theoretical in early September, and little had happened since then. After Prague had accepted the ultimatum, the Czechoslovak legation cabled from Moscow that no one in the Kremlin was prepared to advise Beneš about the most appropriate course of action; but it went on to express the Soviet hope that Czechoslovakia would withstand the pressure to surrender and force France to live up to its obligations by steadfastly rejecting any negotiated settlement. In that case, the whole Soviet army would march "with enthusiasm."[109] This was fine, but since France had made clear it would ignore its treaty with Czechoslovakia and Prague had accepted the ultimatum, this was just another theoretical promise.

Why was Beneš so optimistic? One could speculate that the president's good mood was explainable by his expectation of concrete military steps to be taken by the Soviet Union and positive political changes in France. Regarding the former, an intriguing hint can be found in Fierlinger's telegram to Prague received on 21 September. It demanded that an airplane for two Soviet officers be dispatched to Kiev without delay. Travel through Poland would be too dangerous, the telegram warned.[110] Nothing is known about the nature of this particular mission.[111] It is also likely that Beneš may have derived his optimism from rumors that had been brought to Prague from France by Jaromír Nečas. The minister claimed that the Daladier-Bonnet government in Paris was weak and collapsing. Édouard Herriot, president of the Chamber, was said to be in line to take over, and Prague believed that the new prime minister would abide by the terms of French obligations toward Czechoslovakia.[112]

While Aleksandrovsky was speaking with Beneš, one could see groups of men around the Castle, passionately discussing the situation. Then suddenly, just after 10 P.M., without any warning from the guards or the police on duty, a large crowd appeared under the windows of the presidential suite. It seemed to be a well-organized, professional operation. The demonstrators were led by people who knew what they were doing. When the small police unit responsible for maintaining law and order at the Castle attempted to push the crowd out of the area, the organizers started singing the national anthem and were soon joined by the crowd. The moment that happened, the police ceased all activity and stood at rigid attention, saluting. While the officers were immobilized by the old trick that had been developed in the late nineteenth century when Bohemia was part of the Hapsburg Empire, additional demonstrators poured into the area. It now seemed perfectly plausible that they could break into the building, cause panic, and maybe even use violence against the president. The crowd thundered over and over again: "Give us weapons! Give us weapons!" When those in the front lines tried to break down the door leading to the presidential suite and Beneš's apartment, the commander of the small palace guard told Drtina he would have to open fire. Since this could have triggered off a civil war, a potential catastrophe was brewing. "These are your just deserts," remarked Gottwald matter-of-factly to a group of stunned politicians at the Castle.[113] Even an improvised speech by the popular General Jan Syrový had failed to dissipate the tension. It was past midnight on 22 September 1938 when the state police went into action and swept the whole area clean, arresting only a few participants. Among them, however, was a surprising collection of various nationalities. There was an Italian, an Austrian, a Pole, and a Hungarian. Was this what Zhdanov had in mind when he spoke exactly a month earlier in Prague about "the second wave of proletarian revolutions"?

Beneš and Klement Gottwald approached this very question after the end of World War II. Gottwald confessed to the president that Soviet leaders had severely criticized him for his failure to carry out a communist coup d'état in Prague during the September 1938 crisis. Beneš, of course, listened with interest and, as always, he scribbled notes for his own record as the conversation progressed. After Gottwald had left, the president summed up the meaning of his talk with the communist leader: "Fundamentally important was for me Gottwald's confession that [leaders of the Communist party of Czechoslovakia] were reprimanded in Moscow for their failure to carry out a revolution, and that they defended themselves by using virtually the same arguments which I used to use."[114]

As it turned out, Beneš was blissfully unaware of the demonstration in his own backyard. When Drtina went to the president's apartment, he saw Mrs. Beneš tiptoeing out of the bedroom. "Forgive me, gentlemen," she said to a small group that had gathered in the drawing room, "but I really cannot wake up my husband."[115] The president, who must have been exhausted, had slept through what may have been a tentative attempt at a revolution.

As soon as Beneš awoke early on 22 September 1938, he had to focus his attention on the domestic crisis that had started while he was asleep. Although the state police had suppressed the demonstration at the Castle, it was impossible to do the same elsewhere in Prague. In the morning the city overflowed with energy that had been pent up during the long, humiliating months. The masses in the street had gathered to demand weapons and mobilization; they rallied around the call that the government that had accepted the ultimatum had to go. Incidentally, not even the greatest radicals among the demonstrators dared to call for Beneš's resignation. The street's anger was directed only against Prime Minister Milan Hodža.[116] Beneš had become irreplaceable.

All Czechoslovaks identified with the slogans against the Franco-British proposal and in favor of their country's defense. The CPC leader Gottwald was the most visible among the personalities who appeared before the crowd, but no one would have called the events a communist plot. The party merely guided existing trends when it called for a general strike. Most factories came to a halt, and a major demonstration was arranged in front of the parliament, where Gottwald appeared side by side with democratic politicians. Among those present were the conservative Ladislav Rašín and Lord Mayor of Prague Petr Zenkl. The U.S. military attaché described the events as a natural reaction to the "cavalier treatment accorded" to Czechoslovakia by France and Great Britain.[117] This was the situation that had been outlined by the 7th Congress of the Comintern, and these were the conditions predicted in Zhdanov's speech delivered in Prague in late August 1938.

But it was also the kind of crisis in which Beneš could show that he was a master politician. He brought the domestic upheavals to an end within a few hours.

He met briefly with the prime minister and asked for his resignation. Hodža obliged on the spot and went looking, on Beneš's instructions, for Jan Syrový, the one-eyed army general who had been at the castle since the evening of 21 September. Hodža found him, took his arm, and told him that he would have to become the next prime minister.[118] Syrový was an honest man who had displayed considerable courage in his youth. By now he was most remarkable for his lack of brilliance. His army career had advanced effortlessly to the post of inspector general because he had come to symbolize the mystical heroism of the Masaryk legions in Russia, whose endeavors were given considerable credit for the emergence of the Czechoslovak Republic. Confronted with this unusual offer, Syrový responded frankly that he did not feel adequately qualified for such a responsible role at the height of the crisis. "Hodža told me," Syrový testified after the war, "that I was a soldier and that when I receive an order I have to obey. . . . Shortly thereafter, I had an audience with the president of the Republic who invited me to assume the office of prime minister."

The appointment of General Syrový as prime minister and minister of defense turned out to be a clever political maneuver. The masses received the news with jubilation. The popular war hero was precisely the kind of man they wanted. After the demonstrators had taken a public oath to fight the Third Reich to the death and sang the national anthem, they returned to their factories. The country had been stabilized. Beneš solved the brief crisis masterfully. He had no idea how closely the CPC followed the spontaneous developments on the streets of Prague.

When Syrový became prime minister, the mechanism of power in Czechoslovakia was simplified even further. Although Beneš had often presented Prime Minister Hodža with faits accompli, he did not dare bypass him. Hodža was a serious politician with his own agenda and contacts in international diplomacy. Syrový, however, could make no such claims. Beneš now stood alone: he was a democratically elected president, but both the parliament and the government would at best only affirm his decisions. He never discredited himself by abusing his absolute power, but with absolute power came absolute responsibility.

At 7 P.M. the president was scheduled to deliver a radio address from his office at the Castle, an event awaited with much anxiety by the whole country. Drtina saw him furiously scribbling the text of the speech as the radio announcer began reading an introduction. Even after he had been formally introduced, Beneš continued writing. Drtina estimated that the pause lasted for some five very tense minutes. Most Czechoslovaks were glued to their radios, and tensions rose with every inexplicable moment of silence. Finally, Beneš took the microphone and declared: "I have said before that I have never in my life been afraid, and even today I have no fear for our State. I have a plan for all eventualities, and will not let myself be thwarted of my purpose. . . . If it should be necessary to fight we will know how to do so to the last breath. If it is necessary and possible to negotiate, we will negotiate."[119]

The president's assertion that he had a plan which would allow him to respond to all the dangers lurking in the jungle of European politics was a bold one. Cynics would later lampoon him: "He said 'I have a plan' but what he meant to say was 'I have an airplane.'" Should this speech by Beneš be taken seriously, or was it an act of deception by a desperate man? Research in the Beneš archives indicates that there was in fact a plan. Some have speculated that Beneš was referring to the Nečas plan.

The so-called Fifth Plan undoubtedly existed, but on this occasion the president had yet another proposition in mind. He had hoped at the last moment to internationalize Czechoslovakia's problem with the Sudeten German minority by initiating an all-European reexamination of the status of all minorities. "If the gentlemen want to play up the minority question here [in Czechoslovakia] I will give it to them in the whole of Europe—and then we cannot lose."[120] (It is ironic that the Czechoslovak crisis would in fact be "solved" by an international conference, but Beneš would not be invited to attend and its agenda and final communiqué would be dictated by Hitler.)[121] This is an indication that even Beneš, who understood the Führer better than most politicians at the time, had failed to appreciate to what extent the Sudeten issue was in the fall of 1938 nothing more than a tool for the destruction of Czechoslovakia.

Godesberg: The Last Missed Opportunity

Czechoslovakia formally accepted the Franco-British ultimatum on 21 September at 5 P.M. But Chamberlain and Hitler had already agreed several hours earlier that they would meet the next day at Godesberg, a scenic German city on the Rhine. The Führer was fond of a local hotel, the Dreesen, owned by an old war comrade and fellow Nazi, whence he had launched the bloody purge of his rivals during the Night of the Long Knives in June 1934. No one on the British side seemed to be bothered by the symbolism of Hitler's residence. The prime minister was to stay across the river at the Petersberg Hotel. On 22 September, before his departure for Germany, Chamberlain read a short statement. A peaceful solution of the Czechoslovak-German conflict, he said, would provide for a better understanding between the British and German peoples, and this in turn would form a foundation for peace in Europe.[122] Yet, what kind of partner had Chamberlain expected to find in the Führer if his cooperation, not to say friendship, were obtainable only after the British and French had transferred the Czechoslovak Sudetenland to him? The British took off from the Heston airport, where some in the crowd booed the departing prime minister. After landing at Cologne, Chamberlain reviewed an SS guard of honor and drove through the streets of Godesberg, lavishly decorated by the Swastika and the Union Jack, to his hotel.

When the two politicians met at 4 P.M. at the Dreesen Hotel, Chamberlain felt he had all the trumps in his hand. After all, he had promised to force the Prague government to surrender the Sudetenland and he had succeeded. The prime minister confidently opened the meeting by summing up his recent achievements.[123] Czechoslovakia would be deprived of the Sudetenland and neutralized, and its new borders would be guaranteed against any unprovoked aggression although they could be again altered by negotiation. When he finished, Chamberlain made himself comfortable in his chair; he felt satisfied. The expression on his face seemed to say, "Haven't I worked splendidly during these five days?"[124]

Then came the shock. The Führer's very first words signaled a crisis: "Es tut mir sehr leid" (I'm very sorry), he said, but the proposed solution would no longer do. Czechoslovakia was an artificial construction; it had no history, no tradition, and no right to exist. Hitler focused on fantastic stories of suffering caused by the Prague government in the Sudetenland and then introduced a new theme: Poland and Hungary also had legitimate claims on Czechoslovak territory, and the Slovaks yearned to free themselves from the rule of the Prague government. Moreover, the present government crisis and street demonstrations in Prague showed that the Bolsheviks could "take the rudder." The only solution was for the Third Reich to seize the Sudeten territory immediately by armed force.

Chamberlain knew next to nothing about the actual situation in Czechoslovakia, and so he was not in a position to challenge Hitler's analysis of the country's domestic situation. But he was appalled by the manner in which the Führer had dismissed his achievements. His face flushed with anger at the Führer's ingratitude.[125] After all, the prime minister protested, he had accepted all German claims and "induced" the French and the Prague government to accept them as well. He "had got exactly what the Führer wanted and without the expenditure of a drop of German blood." Moreover, his political life was on the line, warned Chamberlain. He had already been accused of selling Czechoslovakia to Hitler and yielding to dictators. Chamberlain demanded: Why should Hitler resort to war when he could get everything in a peaceful manner? The meeting was often interrupted by messengers who came with urgent dispatches for the Führer about the continued Czechoslovak terror against the Sudeten Germans. On one occasion, Hitler jumped up and shouted: "The Czechs must be annihilated." When the British guests made ready to leave it was 7 P.M. They were very tired and deeply disappointed. Chamberlain described the meeting as "most unsatisfactory."[126] He left, his mind full of "foreboding."[127]

The next day, 23 September 1938, began with an exchange of letters initiated by Chamberlain early in the morning. Already his first missive made clear that Hitler's temper tantrums had won him another victory: the British now proposed that the Sudeten Germans could immediately police themselves. This meant, of course, that the Czechoslovak authorities would have to withdraw. Chamberlain's latest offer went beyond the Franco-British proposal Prague had accepted on the assumption that the new frontier would be established by an international commission, not by the SdP or Hitler. Although the two delegations had been scheduled to resume their talks at 11:30 A.M., the meeting was postponed as Hitler and von Ribbentrop worked on their written reply until half-past three.

While the drama was unfolding at Godesberg, President Beneš had apparently managed to recover from the depressing scenes surrounding the Franco-British ultimatum. One reason for this was that he had had a few good signals from Moscow. On 22 September Potemkin had asked Fierlinger why Prague had not brought up the question of "Soviet unconditional [i.e., unilateral] assistance."[128] Beneš, as we know, had done so, but his question had ended up being distorted into an inquiry involving the League of Nations. Nevertheless, Potemkin's interest was welcomed. The next day, at 4 A.M., the Kremlin issued a formal warning to the Polish chargé d'affaires in Moscow, Tadeusz Jankowski, against military concentrations on the Czechoslovak border in the Těšín area.[129] Should Poland commit aggression against Czechoslovakia, the Soviet Union would consider itself released from the Soviet-Polish nonaggression agreement of 1932.[130] This, too, was helpful.

The problem was that Warsaw immediately suspected that the Soviet intervention had been requested by Czechoslovakia. The suspicion was apparently justified, Warsaw rejected the Soviet warning, and Prague's relations with Poland degenerated even further.[131] Beneš boldly tried to improve the state of affairs by writing directly to Polish President Ignacy Mościcki. In the letter, he accepted in principle that the Czechoslovak-Polish border could be rectified, but only as a result of negotiations not force. This, he hoped, might open a new chapter in the troubled history of the two countries.[132] But such last-minute diplomatic gestures could not make up for two decades of neglect, suspicion, and arrogance on both sides, and the initiative had failed to clear the dark clouds above Prague and Warsaw.

While Chamberlain and Hitler continued corresponding across the Rhine at Godesberg, on 23 September 1938 Aleksandrovsky came to the Castle in Prague at 6 P.M. He requested an audience with Beneš in order to protest a police action involving *Rudé Právo*, the communist daily. This bit of official business was a simple matter.[133] When Beneš and Aleksandrovsky met, the president seemed even more optimistic than he had during their last meeting two days earlier. He felt he had succeeded "in forming a worldwide coalition against the onslaught of fascism."[134] In the context of Aleksandrovsky's visit on 21 September, it is impossible to explain Beneš's optimism on the basis of evidence currently available. Even if Chamberlain's meeting with the Führer had failed, Beneš could not have known about it in the early evening of 23 September. Had the president received reports—undiscovered as yet—indicating that a new, radically anti-Hitler government was about to emerge in Paris? In the absence of archival evidence, we must assume that Beneš's talk was an effort to cover up Czechoslovakia's desperate situation, thus maintaining the country's position of a worthy partner for the Kremlin.

While Beneš was still with Aleksandrovsky, a message came regarding the Soviet warning to Poland, and shortly thereafter Drtina heard for the first time that the meeting at Godesberg was not going well.[135] Then, Counselor Tomeš from the Ministry of Foreign Affairs came and delivered to Drtina a sealed envelope, which he asked be given to the president as soon as possible, unopened. As he was saying this, the door opened; Aleksandrovsky was leaving. He seemed to be in a good mood. He shook Drtina's hand and said, "Stand firm! Now it's up to you!" Drtina did not want to prolong the conversation because of the strange envelope and because Beneš was pressing the buzzer nervously, demanding that his next visitor be ushered in. That audience would not take place. "Mr. President, there is an important message from Minister Krofta," said Drtina, opening the envelope before Beneš's eyes. It was 7 P.M. on 23 September 1938. Although the letter was short, the president read it for a long time. Absentmindedly, he began repeating "yes, yes, yes" as if Drtina had not been there, and he started pacing around the room. He appeared excited beyond anything Drtina had ever seen. Finally, when the tension had become unbearable, the president stopped, looked at his secretary, and asked, "Do you know what this is?" Drtina could only indicate he did not. "Read it! This means war!" The statement from London suggested that the British and French had withdrawn their objection against Czechoslovak mobilization. Without waiting for Drtina's reaction, Beneš rushed to the telephone.

The president must have felt triumphant. Czechoslovakia had been warning both the British and the French for several days that German military concentrations along its borders could be interpreted only as preparations for an attack. Its most recent warning had been dispatched to London via the British legation at 4:45 P.M. on the same day, 23 September.[136] The Second Bureau had definite information about movements of Wehrmacht divisions east of Dresden, in the area of Zwickau, around Passau, and in other strategically vital locations. Consequently, Czechoslovakia had intended to carry out a general mobilization on 17 and again on 21 September.[137] Each time, the British and the French had argued strongly against doing so because they feared the disruption of Chamberlain's second trip to Germany.[138] Therefore, the message from Newton to Beneš that His Majesty's government and the French government could no longer "take the responsibility of advising [Prague] not to mobilize" was very welcome.[139]

More important was a similar statement made almost simultaneously by de Lacroix at the Foreign Ministry.[140] France, after all, was Czechoslovakia's primary ally, and its encouragement for Prague to mobilize could only mean, Beneš must have thought, that Paris had thereby reaffirmed its obligations under the terms of the treaty of 1925. The president now had real grounds for believing that the tide had turned in his favor. Hitler, he reasoned, had been finally unmasked by Chamberlain. No more retreating, not one inch! So far, Hitler had managed to isolate Czechoslovakia by misrepresenting it as a collection of unhappy minorities, all brutalized by the Prague government. Now the deception had been revealed. The Führer would be neutralized.

These were not merely fantasies of an anxious mind. In anticipation of a final break in Chamberlain's talks with Hitler, Lord Halifax inquired by cable with the British delegation at Godesberg whether some "precautionary" military steps should be taken at home.[141] He also fired off a request asking the French to determine the extent and manner of Soviet military assistance to Czechoslovakia, and he wrote to Chamberlain to inform him that British public opinion "seems to be hardening."[142] The public, he went on to say, felt that the British had gone to the limit of concessions.[143] Yes, this could be seen as signs of a new, positive trend.

The presidential suite at the Castle came alive. Scores of officials and military officers began carrying out tasks well thought out in advance and required by law.[144] The government met with President Beneš, and the meeting continued into the night, but the decision to carry out a general mobilization was made at its beginning. By 8 P.M. General Krejčí was on his way to carry out the complex operation. Everyone seemed reinvigorated. Even years later, Drtina and many of his contemporaries could still remember "that beautiful evening of 23 September."[145] At 10:30 P.M. the whole country was notified by radio of the mobilization order. All reservists who were forty years old or younger were to report to the colors immediately.[146]

The first trains packed with reservists began leaving the Prague train stations at 1:30 A.M. on 24 September. In anticipation of German bombing attacks or airborne assaults targeting Czechoslovak army command posts, General Krejčí and his staff relocated during the night to Klánovice outside Prague, whence they continued unharassed to Brno in Moravia and finally to Vyškov nearby.[147] A blackout was enforced in Prague and other large cities. Shortly after midnight, as the ministers of General Syrový's government began leaving the Castle, the city before them was completely dark. It was a powerful moment, especially because no one knew whether the Luftwaffe would attack that very night or only under the cover of the morning gray. Would they ever see their shrine of architectural beauty again? U.S. Military Attaché Major Riley reported that the mobilization was proceeding "with haste but without disorder and showing fine organization. Boy scouts and civil guards used largely to replace police." Many men, he found, had reported to their regiments within six hours. "They are a fine type of soldier, strong, obedient, ready to fight."[148] There was a practice air-raid alarm at 3 A.M. which was conducted calmly and in good order. Wilbur J. Carr, the U.S. minister in Prague, described railroad stations full of "cheering, laughing [reservists] packed into trains. . . . There was no confusion, but everyone fell into places with utmost promptitude."[149]

Gradually, Czechoslovakia mobilized 1,250,000 men, which meant that, together with the standing army, it had more than 1,500,000 soldiers. About 10 percent of all Czechoslovak citizens were in uniform.[150] As had to have been expected, some 50 percent of Sudeten German men had deserted to Germany. A smaller percentage of Czechoslovak Hungarians had failed to show up, as did a fraction of reservists of Polish extraction. Nevertheless, the Czechoslovak army was ready to do the utmost in defense of the republic.

Just after midnight, on 24 September, Beneš drafted in his own hand a statement to be distributed by the Ministry of Foreign Affairs to all Czechoslovak legations. The mobilization, it stated, was being carried out flawlessly, the public was absolutely firm, and the government was in complete control. Czechoslovakia could now calmly await Hitler's next step.[151] Throughout the day, the Ministry of the Interior kept the Castle informed about the course of mobilization. In the Czech part of the country, all went well and in complete order. Czechs and democratic Germans joined with enthusiasm, reacting to the first radio announcement without waiting for the order to be posted. People who had heard the news quickly woke their neighbors, especially those subject to mobilization. Members of the outlawed SdP appeared depressed and afraid. In Moravia, the ministry reported, mobilization was greeted with joy. Men rushing to train stations and marching soldiers were cheered by crowds of Czechs and democratic Germans. Frequently, however, members of the Henlein movement avoided duty. German villages from Frývaldov to Krnov, the report stated, were "half deserted." In Czechoslovakia's east, according to the reports reaching the Castle, mobilization was greeted with great enthusiasm by all Czechoslovaks.[152] Because the Third Reich enjoyed massive air superiority, it was feared that the Luftwaffe could severely disrupt Czechoslovak mobilization. Army officers looked from the clock to the sky and back again at the clock, wondering how much more time they would have free of German interference. But nothing happened, nothing at all. And so the mobilization continued successfully until the army achieved full combat readiness.

On 21 May 1938 the Führer had briefly lost the initiative after Czechoslovakia unexpectedly called up some reservists and specialists. He was similarly taken aback on 13 September after the Prague government declared a state of emergency, secured the Sudetenland, and caused Henlein to desert his SdP comrades. Now, on 24 September 1938, for the third time in four months, Hitler's "dynamism" suffered a setback when the mobilized Czechoslovak army established and secured positions along the borders. One and a half million men under arms, disciplined and eager to fight for a just cause, were aided by 9,632 light and medium reinforced ferroconcrete bunkers, 227 larger fortified posts, and 38 fortresses.[153] The question was whether the politicians' performance could live up to what the soldiers had achieved.

We left the British team at Godesberg at 3:30 P.M. on 23 September 1938. Chamberlain had been deeply disappointed by Hitler during their meeting the day before. Now, as he read the latest missive from the Führer, he had every reason to be outraged by its terms and harsh tone. The prime minister wrote again, this time merely asking for a memorandum he could take with him and pass on to Prague. He did not expect to meet Hitler again. However, further contacts among lesser members of the two delegations resulted in an agreement that the British and the Germans would meet again, at 10:30 P.M. Exactly as Radio Prague was declaring a general mobilization Chamberlain walked into Hitler's suite and was handed the very memorandum for which he had asked. He could scarcely believe his eyes. Germany demanded that Czechoslovakia surrender the Sudetenland by 28 September with all commercial, military, and agricultural infrastructure untouched; no military hardware, raw materials, food, or farm animals were to be removed.

Chamberlain found the *style* of the memorandum unacceptable, and the deadline seemed equally impossible. "But this is an ultimatum," protested the prime minister when he heard the translation. It is "ein Diktat" chimed in Henderson who liked to show off his German.[154] Chamberlain later boasted before the House of Commons that on that occasion he "bitterly reproached the Chancellor for his failure to respond in any way to the efforts which I had made to secure peace."[155] Hitler seemed to have mellowed somewhat and agreed to remove from the text the date the British found so offensive (28 September) and proposed to replace it with 1 October. This was not a concession of any real value, of course, because the directive for an attack on Czechoslovakia, Operation Green, had already set 1 October as the deadline.

While the haggling continued, the interpreter, Dr. Schmidt, read to the whole group a telegram that had arrived from the German legation in Prague: Czechoslovakia had declared a general mobilization. After a long pause, Hitler quietly said that he would not attack his opponent as long as negotiations were in progress. As he stood up to leave around 2 A.M., Chamberlain told Hitler that he was merely an intermediary, and he would see to it that the Beneš government receive the memorandum. He could not guarantee anything. He did not seem to be optimistic. But before all departed, Hitler reassured the prime minister that the Sudetenland was his last territorial demand in Europe and that he was interested only in having jurisdiction over the Sudeten Germans. "There need be no differences between us," Hitler said seductively. "We shall not get in the way of the exercise of your extra-European interests, while you can leave us a free hand in Central and South-Eastern Europe without harm."[156]

As the column of cars with the British delegation was on its way across the Rhine early in the morning on 24 September, the memorandum's translation was being telegraphed to Newton in Prague. British and French correspondents who had come to Godesberg to cover the meeting scurried off at its conclusion to France or

Belgium. They expected the war to break out and did not wish to spend it interned as enemy aliens.[157]

Hitler's memorandum from Godesberg reached the Czechoslovak Foreign Ministry at 6:30 P.M. on Saturday, 24 September. For the first time, Krofta had the sense that Newton was embarrassed, at least briefly, by the role he had to play. As he handed over the harsh document, the British minister stressed that his mission was only to deliver the text; he was not in a position to advise how Czechoslovakia should react. But this was the Führer's last word.[158] While President Beneš and military specialists started studying the Godesberg memorandum, news reached Prague that the French government had finally called up reservists, bringing up its armed forces to one million men.[159] Reports from the Soviet Union were also encouraging. Fierlinger went so far as to suggest that Prague and Moscow should immediately set up a "coordinating body to deal with questions of common defense." Potemkin promised to report the Kremlin's reaction as soon as possible. The Czechoslovak minister was optimistic that the response would be positive.[160]

Meanwhile, the commission Beneš had chosen to analyze the Godesberg memorandum produced its report. It warned that the proposed borders had been drawn deliberately in such a manner that Czechoslovakia would not be able to defend itself in the future.[161] No one thought that the proposal had any merit. On Sunday Minister Masaryk delivered Prague's response to the Foreign Office. It was short but to the point. His government had had a chance to study the document from Godesberg, Masaryk wrote:

> It is a *de facto* ultimatum of the sort usually presented to a vanquished nation and not a proposition to a sovereign state which has shown the greatest possible readiness to make sacrifices for the appeasement of Europe. . . . My Government is amazed at the contents of the memorandum. The proposals go far beyond what we agreed to in the so-called Franco-British plan. . . . My Government wish me to declare in all solemnity that Herr Hitler's demands in their present form are absolutely and unconditionally unacceptable. . . . Against these new and cruel demands my Government feel bound to make their utmost resistance and we shall do so, God helping. The nation of St. Wenceslas, John Hus, and Thomas Masaryk will not be a nation of slaves.[162]

Beneš instructed Krofta to inform Newton and de Lacroix there would be no further explanations and additions to it. The statement was now the official and final reply of the Prague government.[163]

The first news from London was good. Duff Cooper, a minister in the Chamberlain government, later described his reaction to Godesberg in a speech before the House of Commons. Although the prime minister had shown "sweet reasonableness" in his talks at the Dreesen Hotel, it won him "nothing except terms which a cruel and revengeful enemy would have dictated to a beaten foe after a long war. Crueler terms could hardly be devised than those of the Godesberg ultimatum." Once he had understood the terms of the ultimatum, Cooper thought, "If these are accepted it will be the end of all decency in the conduct of public affairs in the world." His colleagues agreed with him, and the British government rejected the Godesberg proposal.[164] Even Lord Halifax joined those who found it unworthy.

The French again agreed to fly to London for urgent discussions regarding the new developments. But before he left Paris, Prime Minister Daladier made clear that the territorial demands embedded in the Godesberg ultimatum were unacceptable. When asked how France would react if Hitler attacked Czechoslovakia without provocation, Daladier said he would go to war.[165] The mood in French political circles and the press turned against further concessions to the Third Reich. Godesberg, the German embassy wrote from Paris, was found to be "quite unacceptable."[166]

All of these signs were good. But, inexplicably, Chamberlain chose this occasion to ask the British ambassador in Berlin to tell the Führer that he should not be disturbed by Prague's rejection of the Godesberg document or by the reports of another round of Franco-British talks in Berlin.[167] This blunted the edge of the allied sword significantly, and Hitler could relax. One can sympathize with Chamberlain as a man so appalled by the immorality of war that he put his political life on the line to seek a negotiated settlement. But the ease with which he capitulated at Berchtesgaden and again right after Godesberg, at a time when his side enjoyed the advantage of opportune winds, was an altogether different matter. He seemed to be ready to accept almost any solution, as long as his peace mission was crowned with success.

Beneš in Prague did not know about Chamberlain's back-channel message to Hitler, and he was therefore riding high on the waves of hope. The Castle seemed to have been taken over by military personnel. Army cots littered the normally empty corridors, and in the morning Drtina was shocked by the sight of officers shaving in rooms never intended for such purposes. The president's staff felt that war was preferable to peace dictated by Hitler and the majority hoped that the Third Reich would start a shooting war.[168] Beneš also held this view. On Sunday, 25 September, having rejected the Godesberg ultimatum, the president received Aleksandrovsky.[169] The Soviet minister was amazed how much had changed since his visit on 23 September. At that time, Beneš was full of fighting spirit, but he had looked like a democratically elected civilian president. The Castle now reminded Aleksandrovsky of a military encampment, and Beneš was at the center of feverish activities. He was proud and cocky. There was a gas mask on his desk, and determined-looking military personnel kept entering and leaving the presidential suite without regard for protocol. Beneš spoke with confidence about his French ally. Unlike 23 September, on this occasion he did not want to treat Aleksandrovsky to yet another of his pedantic monologues. The president had many "practical questions" for the Soviet minister: How many thousands of airborne Soviet troops would be deployed to Czechoslovakia? With what equipment? What means of technical support would they have when they engaged the enemy? And what was Aleksandrovsky's reaction? "I confess," he wrote, "to having a heavy feeling because I could tell Beneš nothing, especially regarding his 'practical questions.' "

If one relies exclusively on Aleksandrovsky's version of the meeting, as we must for lack of other sources, the president's optimism makes no sense. It seemed irrational for Beneš to expect a deployment of Soviet paratroopers. But the president was not an irrational man. There is an intriguing indication of behind-the-scenes developments, probably a continuation of what Fierlinger had already mentioned on

21 September. There was an urgent telegram from Fierlinger to Prague on 26 September: "Immediately return a new airplane to Kiev since the [Soviet] Government is sending new military representatives. The president will receive answers to his concrete questions on the spot." Fierlinger also reported that the Soviet Union was about to come to an agreement with Romania regarding the disputed Bessarabian territory.[170] This could only mean that a corridor would be provided for Soviet troops coming to Czechoslovakia's assistance against Hitler. Prague, of course, welcomed the news and instantly cabled back to its legation in Moscow that an airplane was on its way.[171] Who was behind this operation and what it was meant to achieve remains a mystery to this day.

While Beneš, energized by the warlike atmosphere at the Castle, talked to Aleksandrovsky about Soviet airborne units, and while mysterious Soviet military emissaries were supposed to be flown from Kiev to Prague to respond to the president's "practical questions," the British and the French met again in London to discuss the results of Godesberg.[172] To a great extent, the talks followed a familiar pattern. Chamberlain urged that they had to face reality, warts and all, while the French prime minister was unwilling to accept the British view without some resistance, at least at the beginning. As before, Daladier brought up the value of French commitments. Then what did Paris propose to do if Hitler invaded Czechoslovakia? asked the British prime minister. "In that case France will come to the assistance of the Czechs," Daladier responded. But Chamberlain wanted to know more: If German bombs were to rain upon Paris, would France be in a position to defend itself? Could the French strike back effectively against the Third Reich? Could the allies count on Russian intervention on their side? Daladier tried to escape this kind of discussion by suggesting that it was too technical. He wanted to speak of "the moral obligations of France," not of "war and strategy."

Daladier reminded the meeting that "a week ago he had agreed . . . to dismember a friendly country bound to France not only by treaties but also by ties centuries old." In doing so he acted "like a barbarian," he confessed, and he posed a question of his own: Was Great Britain prepared to give in and accept Hitler's new ultimatum? After Czechoslovakia, Hitler's conquests would continue until he attacked France and took Boulogne and Calais. Why, he might even occupy Ireland. Of course, France was prepared to accept "certain measures of conciliation," but at some point the allies would have to stand up to Hitler. Daladier warned that the Sudeten area that the Third Reich demanded was inhabited by many democrats. "Were they to be left to the axe and the executioners of Herr Hitler?" he asked. If Minister Masaryk, or any other Czechoslovak diplomat, had been in the room, he would not have been able to put it better. Chamberlain could only sum up the situation as it stood on 26 September. Europe, he said, was moving toward a crisis: Czechoslovakia was going to resist the German aggression, the French had said "plainly" that they "would fulfill their treaty obligations," and Great Britain would not allow France to be defeated by Germany.[173]

Undoubtedly, to most Europeans this seemed like a cruel, vicious repetition of the madness of August 1914. Did the crisis over the Sudetenland represent a *casus belli* that was in any way more legitimate than Franz Joseph's dispute with Serbia? Would Europe never jump over the shadow of its self-destructive impulses? Was there no space left for a rational accommodation of the crisis? While others in Europe despaired at the prospect of domino-style mobilizations in Europe, the Prague government could not complain about the outcome of Godesberg and the Franco-British discussions that followed. The danger to Czechoslovakia had not disappeared, but from President Beneš's perspective, the situation on 26 September represented a miraculous recovery from the depth of that horrible night just six days ago when the arrogant Newton and weeping de Lacroix had awakened him only to announce that the Czechoslovak foreign policy for which he had been responsible for two decades had crumbled in ruins. That Monday afternoon was very tense in all European capitals. Hitler was scheduled to deliver a speech at the Sportpalast in Berlin at 8 P.M., and it was not entirely unreasonable to fear that Operation Green would be unleashed at that time so he could announce it. At 4 P.M., Carr, the U.S. minister in Prague, warned Washington that according to the opinion of various military specialists, a German attack on Czechoslovakia was "probable."[174] This would have been welcome by many in Czechoslovakia, especially by those who were unhappy about Beneš's capitulation to the Franco-British ultimatum. Although the Prague government rejected the Godesberg memorandum, its acceptance of the conditions agreed on at Berchtesgaden remained on record. A war, however, would have erased all agreements with Hitler because they had been entered into on the condition that a solution would be reached peacefully by negotiations. All politically minded people in Europe awaited Hitler's speech with great anxiety.

Folding the Flag: From the Sportpalast to Munich

In anticipation of the imminent German offensive, rooms had been quietly reserved for President Beneš in a private villa in Zátiší on the outskirts of Prague, and throughout the afternoon of 26 September 1938 members of Beneš's staff at the Castle kept checking the quickest way of getting the president into his air-raid bunker at the Castle.[175] It was estimated that the Luftwaffe would take no more than twenty-five to thirty minutes to reach Prague after crossing the border, and the Castle would be in all likelihood one of its main targets. Beneš's military uniform was kept within reach at all times.

Amid all the nervous anticipation, the president calmly worked on his response to a letter Franklin D. Roosevelt had sent to him and the Führer. He needed to hurry because he was supposed to leave the Castle in the evening for Zátiší, hopefully before Hitler's speech at 8 P.M. Beneš was disappointed that Roosevelt had sent identical texts to Prague and Berlin, thus implying moral equivalence between the respective causes of the Third Reich and Czechoslovakia. Roosevelt's plea that the conflict should not be solved by force was fine, but Czechoslovakia was not proposing to attack Germany. It was the Führer who threatened to use violence to seize the Sudetenland and maybe more. Beneš felt bitter about being put on the same level with Hitler. Later, he would describe Roosevelt's intervention in the crisis as a stab in the back and the "last heavy blow."[176] But he was a statesman, and he was able to suppress personal feelings when politics was at stake. His response to Roosevelt—written as it was in that nervous time when German bombers could come at any moment and when his offices were filled with dozens of noisy guests—was a masterpiece. Once the letter had been drafted, it was dictated to London and cabled to Washington. As they were leaving the Castle, Beneš told Drtina that things were going well: Hitler had isolated himself. For some time, he continued thinking aloud, it had seemed that Czechoslovakia had been isolated, but the situation was now reversed.[177] The president and his entourage stood outside the Castle, and they were ready to go. It was 8 P.M.

Just when the column of seven presidential cars left the Castle—the journey was long because a complete black-out was in force and the streets of Prague were full of slowly moving military convoys—Adolf Hitler approached the microphone at the Berlin Sportpalast. He was in a particularly vile and aggressive mood. Only three hours before he had received Sir Horace Wilson, Chamberlain's emissary, who brought a letter from the prime minister. When the interpreter came upon the point that Czechoslovakia had found the Godesberg memorandum unacceptable, the Führer leaped to his feet screaming, "Es hat keinen Sinn weiter zu verhandeln" (there is no sense at all in negotiating further) and ran to the door.[178] Although he returned to his chair, he was extremely excited. "Germans were being treated like niggers; one would not dare to treat even the Turks like that," he screamed. "On 1 October I shall have Czechoslovakia where I want her. If France and England decide to strike, let them strike." It was this kind of behavior that justified his reputation as being a *Teppichfresser* (carpet-chewer.)[179]

Sir Horace did his best to ignore Hitler's explosions, and he repeated that the British government would see to it that "the Czechs did hand over the territory." But Hitler responded with dismissive gestures. The Sudetenland would be his by 1 October 1938. If the Czechoslovak government wished to avoid war, it had to accept the Godesberg memorandum by 2 P.M. on 28 September 1938 the Führer concluded.[180] Negotiating with Hitler had to have been difficult. But with the benefit of hindsight it is hard to believe that the British, who were all experienced diplomats, did not see the pattern evident in all their encounters with him: first, violent threats and claims that only force would do; then, British concessions and promises to bring pressure to bear on Prague; finally, Hitler's grudging promise to keep the dogs of war leashed for another day or two on the condition that all his demands were satisfied and *blitzschnell* (quick as lightning).

Much of the violent emotion that Hitler had shown to Sir Horace was reflected also in his speech at the Sportpalast three hours later. The main theme of this harangue was a vulgar personal attack on President Beneš. It was Beneš who had lied Czechoslovakia into being, and it was Beneš's terror that had virtually depopulated the Sudetenland. Tens, hundreds of thousands of German refugees escaped daily from the Czechoslovak hell, Hitler shouted, and this had to end:

> Now two men stand arrayed one against the other. There is Mr. Beneš and here stand I. We are two men of a different make-up. In the great struggle of the peoples while Mr. Beneš was sneaking about through the world, I as a decent German soldier did my duty. . . . I desire to state before the German people that with regard to the problem of the Sudeten Germans my patience is now at an end! . . . The world must take note that in four and a half years of war and through the long years of my political life there is one thing which no one could ever cast in my

teeth: I have never been a coward! . . . We are determined! Now let Mr. Beneš
make his choice![181]

The speech was not quite as irrational as it may have appeared. While he
attacked Beneš, Hitler was careful to flatter the British prime minister and to signal
that the Prague government had tried to play for time in the hope that both Chamberlain and Daladier would be overthrown and replaced by their domestic political
rivals. Thanks to the wireless, Hitler's voice thundered throughout Europe. As soon
as the Führer spat out the last sentences of his diatribe, politicians and diplomats,
who had been glued to their shortwave radios, began to analyze it: Did he slam the
door on further negotiations? Was it a declaration of war?

There was only one man among the actors in the crisis who was not disturbed
by the Führer's fury. President Beneš, the main target of Hitler's threats, slept
through the whole performance at the Sportpalast. Immediately after the column of
presidential cars arrived at Zátiší, the president, too tired to walk to the bedroom,
found the first chair in the downstairs lounge, sat down, and fell asleep. He woke up
around 10:30 P.M. and joined members of his secretariat engaged in a slow-moving
political debate. Beneš inquired: What did Hitler have to say? As it happened, only
General Sylvestr Bláha, the chief of the presidential military office, had heard the
speech, and Beneš asked him to summarize it. It appeared that the Führer had
described the whole situation as a duel between himself and the president, stam-
mered Bláha. ''Well, I am much honored,'' replied Beneš with a smile.

He was in an excellent mood and immediately launched into a political lecture.
Czechoslovakia was on its way to victory, the president predicted, but there would
be war. Despite Hitler's threats in the Sportpalast, which reduced General Bláha to a
nervous wreck, the president saw that there was no immediate danger, and therefore
he decided to return to the Castle around 11 P.M.[182] Clumsily, the column started the
long trek back across the dark city.

During the night, Beneš received Aleksandrovsky, who had come to hear his
reflections on Hitler's performance in Berlin. (Neither the British nor the French
minister ever seemed to be interested in what the president thought; they only went
to see him when London or Paris needed another concession.) The Soviet minister,
who had no idea that Beneš had slept through the Sportpalast drama noted that he
seemed to be in a good mood. It was an error, Beneš argued, for Hitler to believe that
the crisis could be reduced to a confrontation between the German Führer and the
Czechoslovak president. In reality, Beneš sought to persuade Aleksandrovsky,
Hitler stood alone against a coalition consisting of France, Great Britain, the Soviet
Union, and Czechoslovakia, with the United States ready to support the coalition
morally and materially. The president ventured to predict that Hitler was going to be
forced to resign.[183]

In retrospect, his analysis was wrong. But it should not be forgotten that late at
night on 26 September 1938 the Prague government knew only that both Great
Britain and France had joined Czechoslovakia in rejecting the Godesberg memorandum. Beneš had reason to believe either that there would be an all-out war in which
Great Britain, France, and Czechoslovakia (and maybe even the Soviet Union)
would fight the isolated Third Reich or that a settlement would be achieved,

as a result of which Czechoslovakia would give up no more than those parts of the Sudeten territory, such as the Cheb area, which it had been prepared to give up already during the peace conferences at the end of the Great War.

While Beneš was talking to Aleksandrovsky about the alliance against the Third Reich, Chamberlain was in the process of destroying it. Early in the morning of 27 September, he drafted yet another letter to the Führer, saying that efforts to secure peace could not be abandoned. The Berchtesgaden proposal, Chamberlain pleaded, would provide all that Hitler desired without causing bloodshed.[184] Chamberlain's messenger, Sir Horace Wilson, presented the latest British plea in the morning.[185] He began by flattering the scowling dictator. Hitler hardly bothered to respond. The British emissary took extra care to remind the Führer that Great Britain would see to it that the Prague government fully obliged with any negotiated political settlement of the crisis. But Hitler had learned too well how to treat British diplomats, and he proceeded to threaten Sir Horace. There were only two options, he stated. Either Czechoslovakia would accept the Godesberg memorandum (which even the British and French governments had rejected) or there would be war. "Ich werde die Tschechen zerschlagen," Hitler shouted several times with savage fury (the interpreter rendered the sentence as "I will smash-sh-sh the Czechs.")[186] If you attack Czechoslovakia, responded Sir Horace, France would fulfill its obligations, and the British would feel obliged to support its ally. "So in six days we should all be at war," responded Hitler with a show of indifference, and ended the interview.

The Führer knew exactly what he was doing. By focusing on the seeming irrationality of a war breaking out as a result of treaty obligations entered into long ago and under different circumstances, he was twisting the knife in Chamberlain's back. Even the most dedicated appeasers in London and Paris were not pacifists of the Tolstoyan variety. They would not have hesitated to fight for their countries. What they sought to avoid was a war breaking out for a marginal cause and domino-style. They remembered August 1914, when armies had been mobilized because of conditions built into semisecret (and sometimes mutually exclusive) diplomatic agreements. As soon as the British had left, at 1 P.M., Hitler ordered German assault units—seven divisions—to move to their jump-off stations. Operation Green would be launched on 30 September 1938.[187]

To calm his nerves, Hitler had arranged for a motorized division to drive by the Chancellery; he intended to review it from the balcony. Possibly, he had expected a repetition of the scenes that had shaken up Berlin and other European capitals in 1914 on the eve of the Great War, when cheering crowds showered troops marching to the Front with love and flowers. This time no more than two hundred people gathered to watch the spectacle, and they stood motionless, in utter silence.[188] Hitler soon went inside, remarking grimly, "I can't lead a war with such a people."[189] This was not new. As early as the Berchtesgaden meeting, formations of Sudeten Germans in white stockings had marched through Berlin in order to whip up public support for the SdP, but there was no cheering or support. Only cutting, ironic remarks could be heard from Berliners. The Germans, the Czechoslovak legation reported, had nothing but fear and loathing for the prospect of another war.[190] It was precisely such sentiments that Sir Horace Wilson and his colleagues had failed to exploit or even to take into account.

On the afternoon of 27 September, Beneš in Prague had no idea that the emissary of Prime Minister Chamberlain offered to make him "sensible."[191] He was still under the impression that the rejection of Godesberg united him with France and Great Britain. At the same time, he kept his Soviet card constantly at the ready, and his meetings with the Soviet minister were frequent. The two saw each other again while Hitler was trying to absorb the antiwar lesson he had just received from the Berliners. Beneš told Aleksandrovsky that he no longer believed war was avoidable. He pretended to be calm, but Aleksandrovsky understood that Beneš feared a German attack on Czechoslovakia at any moment. "I sensed clearly," wrote Aleksandrovsky, "that with much nervous tension, and with the ultimate seriousness, Beneš wanted to hear from us when and how we would help." But, again, Aleksandrovsky did not respond. He later expressed the view that Beneš had attempted to deceive the Soviet Union. The president, according to Aleksandrovsky, sought to drag the Soviet Union "into war against Western Europe so that Czechoslovakia's fate would not be decided by some [international conference], but by a large-scale European war." The Soviet minister reflected that Beneš was at that moment ready to provoke the Soviet Union into a "war against the whole world" only to prevent a localized, isolated conflict between Czechoslovakia and the Third Reich.[192] (This portrait of Beneš is dramatically at variance with later sketches of the president by Gottwald, his colleagues, and scores of Marxist historians who insisted that throughout the crisis Beneš looked for excuses to capitulate.) On 27 September Aleksandrovsky left the Castle. He and Beneš would never see each other again, although they did speak on the telephone.[193]

It is not a mystery why President Beneš seemed to be expecting a German attack any moment in the evening of 27 September. The British had either misunderstood or misinterpreted Hitler's demand for Czechoslovakia's acceptance of the Godesberg platform by 2 P.M. on 28 September to mean that, in the absence of such communication from Prague, he would initiate hostilities.[194] In fact, Hitler had not said that, and the Wehrmacht was not ready. Nevertheless, Newton came at 7 P.M. on the 27th to deliver a panicky note from Lord Halifax, stating that a German offensive would be launched "almost immediately" unless Czechoslovakia surrendered and accepted Hitler's demands.[195] Prague took the warning seriously, especially so because it had been led to think that it had come from a British intelligence source inside Germany. Beneš believed that, and so did others around him. Drtina had dinner at the Castle with Minister Smutný and Counselor Klubíčko, a foreign service officer. They laughed about Hitler choosing the wrong date for his aggression: 28 September was St. Wenceslas Day, the patron saint of Bohemia. Beneš's collaborators felt reasonably optimistic. They did not know what Sir Horace had been doing in Berlin. Like the president, they knew only that Chamberlain had denounced Godesberg and that France continued to mobilize.[196]

In the evening, while Drtina and his friends were jesting about the legendary Blaník knights who were said to intervene on the side of the Czechs whenever the nation was threatened by a foreign invader, the British had put the final touches on yet another proposal to be delivered immediately to the Führer and the French.[197] It offered to accept German occupation of the Cheb and Aš areas in western Bohemia (outside the fortified line) by 1 October and then to preside over meetings of

Czechoslovak and German plenipotentiaries two days later. The Franco-British plan, which Beneš, prodded by the ultimatum, had accepted, was to provide a foundation on which the international commission would gradually finalize the new border, and British observers would see to it that the agreement was implemented. At the end, all parties would demobilize, and the new Czechoslovakia would receive joint guarantees. Under the horrible circumstances of late September 1938 this plan had potential. But it would have required a degree of reasonableness on Hitler's part, and that condition was no longer obtainable. His interest in the fate of the Sudeten Germans, or even in the Sudeten territory, was purely instrumental. He was a warlord yearning for action.

Chamberlain refused to be deterred by recent setbacks. Having received a report from Sir Horace on the disastrous second interview with Hitler, the prime minister brought the crisis before the British people and the whole world. At 8 P.M. on 27 September he tried to strengthen the forces of reason with a speech broadcast around the world. "How horrible, fantastic," he said famously, "that we should be digging trenches and trying on gas masks here because of a quarrel in a far-away country between people of whom we know nothing."[198] One can appreciate Chamberlain's desire to stay out of war over an issue in which his country had no legal obligations. One must also admire his dogged search for peace: he described himself, with justice, as a man of peace to the depths of his soul. But how had he missed the demonic aspects of Nazism, of Hitler's personality, and the deviousness of the Third Reich's policy since 1933?

In contrast to Chamberlain, Beneš knew that a lasting, honorable agreement with Hitler was impossible. In the evening of 27 September, soon after the prime minister's speech ended, he chaired a meeting of the government.[199] The situation, he said, was serious. He had received a note from Newton that the Third Reich would attack the next day at 2 P.M. But there were also some good signs. Beneš reported Masaryk's view that Great Britain was getting ready for war, and Krofta offered Litvinov's opinion that war was inevitable: Russia, England, and France would come to an agreement against Hitler. The president agreed with this analysis. The Kremlin, he said, could see that Hitler's demands were unacceptable, and it would carry out its duty. "A superhuman effort," Beneš announced, was being made to form a defensive front in Czechoslovakia. Should Hitler attack, the country would defend itself. The meeting ended at 10:30 P.M.

In view of the likelihood that war could break out within hours, the Foreign Ministry produced a note that was cabled after midnight to the Czechoslovak minister Arnošt Heidrich, who was in Geneva.[200] He was instructed to submit the enclosed statement to the secretary general the moment Germany unleashed its aggression. It requested that the League of Nations move swiftly to identify Germany as the aggressor. Measures were taken at the same time to prepare the transfer abroad of intelligence officers who worked for the Foreign Ministry and had been selected to leave immediately upon the commencement of hostilities.[201] Jan Hájek, the chief of the ministry's Third Section (intelligence and propaganda) had been issued an official safety pass that authorized him to travel without interference from Czechoslovak authorities through army road blocks and across the border in his car (license plate P 23.871). He and his deputy Dr. Oskar Butter were supposed to prepare the ground for the activities of a Czechoslovak government-in-exile. Their destination was either Paris or Toulouse.[202]

Czechoslovakia was on the verge of war. As of 28 September, the Prague government was committed to defending the country by all military means under its command. The British military attaché, who traveled the border area where the mobilized Czechoslovak army was deployed, found that the troops had confidence, good leadership, and equipment. They would "render a good account of themselves," he predicted.[203] The mobilization declared in the evening of 23 September had been completed. Now the question was whether Czechoslovakia had any allies left. Given the sentiments expressed by Chamberlain in his recent speech, and the almost complete absence of contacts with Paris, Beneš had to turn again to the Soviet Union. During 27 and 28 September Prague had set up various additional communication links with Moscow, and on the 28th Beneš requested direct Soviet help in case of war.[204] Fierlinger cabled from Moscow at 4:10 P.M.: "The president's request for immediate air support has been submitted." Fierlinger expressed hope that it would be dealt with favorably.[205] Beneš had decided to ask the Kremlin, for the second time, for unilateral support, at least in the air. The telegram shows that Beneš was determined to defend Czechoslovakia militarily and that, moreover, he sought to obtain military support from the Soviet Union. This realization goes directly against one of the major arguments of Czechoslovak communists who claimed that the president was unwilling to accept Soviet military assistance because he consistently put his "class interests" above Czechoslovakia's "national interest."[206]

In his speech on Tuesday, 27 September 1938, Chamberlain indicated his willingness to return to Germany for the third time if there were any hope left for a peaceful solution. The next day, early in the morning, the French ambassador, François-Poncet, came to plead with Hitler not to start the war. He stressed that Germany could get everything it desired by peaceful means.[207] Just before noon on 28 September in front of various foreign envoys—Prague was still awaiting Moscow's response to its request for military support—Hitler made a great show of postponing a general mobilization in Germany for twenty-four hours at Mussolini's suggestion. No sooner did François-Poncet leave than his British colleague, Henderson, arrived. He kept appealing, as he put it, to "Herr Hitler's humanity" and pleaded against war.[208] The Führer complained that Czechoslovakia wanted war, but after a conversation with the Duce, he agreed that pursuing a negotiated settlement would not be such a bad idea.[209] After all, he had been assured several times that he could get anything he wanted, and London and Paris were ready to assume the role of his enforcers in Prague. He would not have to move a finger, and hog-tied Czechoslovakia would be brought to his door by French and British deliverymen, gratis. In late afternoon on the day of St. Wenceslas, while the Blaník knights slept, Beneš was informed by a beaming Newton that Chamberlain, Daladier, and Mussolini had accepted Hitler's invitation to meet the next day, 29 September, in Munich. London assured Beneš that Chamberlain "shall have the interests of Czechoslovakia fully in mind."[210] The Prague government responded immediately by asking that nothing should be agreed upon in Munich without consideration being given to the Czechoslovak opinion.[211] But no one took the trouble to respond. The very thought that a war would be avoided at the last moment gave most Europeans a shot of powerful euphoria.

The Yawning Affair at Munich

The atmosphere at the Castle in the evening of 28 September, on the eve of the Munich conference, was heavy, almost suffocating. The first signs of domestic attacks on Beneš's foreign policy appeared. General Krejčí and other army leaders were outraged that, having been deprived of the centrally important French military assistance and having seen no signs of Soviet willingness to provide military aid, the Czechoslovak military was now expected to resist Germany, Poland, and possibly even Hungary at the same time. The president's old political opponents, as well as his recent sycophants, started second-guessing his past policy decisions and pointing out errors. All eyes turned toward Edvard Beneš. His loyal friends still nursed the hope that he might come up with a last-minute solution, others indicated that they had always predicted this would happen. The man who had guided, indeed, determined, Czechoslovak foreign policy for two decades stood alone amid his collaborators. Beneš's health declined sharply, and he had to be treated for blood-pressure problems. He had expected to be in his uniform, waging a war against Hitler as of 2 P.M. Instead, he heard from Chamberlain of the proposed conference. It was a serious blow. No one knows how he would have behaved had a shooting war broken out. But the prospect of Czechoslovakia's fate being determined by a gathering of Chamberlain and Daladier with Hitler and Mussolini, a conference to which the Czechoslovak president was not even invited, was cruel and humiliating.

Next to Czechoslovakia, one other state received the news of Munich with horror—the Soviet Union. Moscow was greatly concerned that Hitler's *Anschluß* of the Sudetenland could cause the collapse of the whole country, and this would bring Germany's armed might close to the Soviet Union. Stalin was equally worried about his diplomatic isolation. Any conference involving Great Britain, France, Germany, and Italy represented a threat to the Soviet Union because an agreement among the four could mean only one thing: Hitler had accepted the status quo in the West and would direct his aggression toward the East. The conference at Munich meant that the Soviet Union would be isolated, and in the future possibly sacrificed to the Third Reich. When it became clear that Chamberlain, Daladier, Mussolini, and Hitler would meet, Soviet diplomacy made a last attempt to win a seat for itself. On 28 September, Litvinov spoke in Moscow with U.S. Chargé d'Affaires Kirk about President Roosevelt's intervention in the Czechoslovak-German crisis—that is, about his letter to Beneš and Hitler of 27 September. The Soviet commissar stated that Moscow accepted the American proposal to assist in the prevention of war. The Soviet Union, Litvinov said, was ready to support the U.S. proposal "for the calling of an international conference and to take active part therein." Kirk was confused: his Soviet colleague was thanking him for an invitation that had never been extended in the first place, and he said so. There were obstacles in the Franco-British mediation of the Czechoslovak crisis, Litvinov responded, indicating to Kirk that he, Litvinov, could do a better job. The American viewed the scene as surreal.[212] The British ambassador in Moscow, Chilston, also learned that the Kremlin had expressed its readiness to take part in a conference on Czechoslovakia.[213]

No tricks could change the fact that the Soviet Union was not wanted at Munich, and despite their desire to participate at the conference Soviet diplomats were left out. Ironically, this is what would give the Kremlin ammunition for propaganda when the word *Munich* had acquired its unpleasant connotation. Yet had Litvinov attended the Munich conference there is no telling how he would have behaved on the issue of Czechoslovakia's territorial integrity.

On Thursday, 29 September, at 2 P.M., representatives of the four powers sat down in front of a large fireplace at the Führerhaus in Munich. The British were on the left, their French colleagues were on the right, and Hitler and Mussolini were in the middle. The conference had begun. It was a strange affair. It had no prepared agenda, no one chaired it, and there were no official note-takers. The conversation preceded only slowly because everything had to be translated three times.[214] Soon, an atmosphere of general goodwill had been established because all the participants spoke in favor of a peaceful solution. Only occasionally, whenever Hitler launched into a violent attack on President Beneš, Daladier felt honor-bound to stand up for the ally whom he was going to betray.[215] Otherwise, there was little that was unexpected. The conference was the culmination of a series of British diplomatic initiatives that began with Lord Halifax's visit to Berchtesgaden in November 1937 and went through the Runciman mission in the summer of 1938 and Chamberlain's two trips to Germany in September. It was quite clear that Hitler would get anything he chose to demand. The very presence of British and French negotiators indicated that the allies would not resist German claims to the Sudeten territory. After a lunch break at 3 P.M., the conference continued; gradually, the ranks of participants were increased by numerous ambassadors, diplomats, generals, legal advisors, and secretaries.

When Hitler invited his guests to lunch, two Czechoslovak emissaries, Hubert Masařík and Vojtěch Mastný, left Prague and flew to Munich.[216] They arrived at 4:20 P.M. and were driven by Gestapo agents to the Regina Hotel, where the British delegation was staying; the French had taken ten rooms in the Vierjahreszeiten Hotel. And there they sat, closely watched by the Gestapo, waiting. Only at 7 P.M. did the two Czechoslovak emissaries see someone who could give them at least a hint of what was going on at the Führerhaus. Counselor Frank Ashton-Gwatkin of the British Foreign Office, well known in Prague from the days of the Runciman mission, came, but he merely implied that the outcome would be worse than Hitler's demands at Godesberg. Then he hurried away to rejoin the conference. Meanwhile in Prague, at 7:25 P.M. Beneš, Prime Minister General Syrový, eighteen ministers, and eleven representatives of various political parties met at the Castle. Deputy Rudolf Beran of the Republican party asked Syrový whether the Czechoslovak army had an "agreement with the Russian army" and, if so, with "what force and when would it intervene."[217] Syrový replied that there was "no concrete agreement with Russia; we only talked about their air assistance, effective quickly. The infantry would take a long time; therefore we have always counted on swift intervention by France and England."[218] The meeting ended inconclusively at 9:45 P.M. amid general depression.

Ashton-Gwatkin and Sir Horace Wilson came to see Mastný and Masařík at 10 P.M. to explain the basic points of the agreement. When the Czechoslovaks tried to interrupt and object to what was about to be signed, Sir Horace merely repeated that he had nothing to add. "You have no idea how hard it is to negotiate with Hitler," sighed Ashton-Gwatkin several times. Masařík responded by saying the allies should stand up to the Nazis, but Ashton-Gwatkin declared in a theatrically officious voice: "Should you reject this plan you'll be dealing with Germany completely on your own. The French will put it to you more elegantly, but believe me, they are in complete agreement with us. They will be disinterested."

At about this time, Beneš received a note from Fierlinger, who wrote that, according to Potemkin, if Czechoslovakia were attacked by Hitler "the procedure in Geneva could be short as soon as one found powers that would be ready really to stand up to the aggressor." This was the Kremlin's response to Beneš's request for "immediate air cover," which he had submitted in the morning of the 28th: go and find someone who would petition the League on your behalf. Where was the president supposed to have found statesmen who would stand up to Hitler? The only powers that mattered were at Munich, and they looked forward to celebrating the imminent victory of reason over violence. It was understandable, added Fierlinger, that "the Soviet government hesitated and hesitates to enter the conflict without the Western Powers." Unilateral Soviet intervention in Czechoslovakia's war with the Third Reich would create another Spain, "with all the horrible consequences for all of Europe and especially Czechoslovakia."[219] Is it farfetched to imagine that Beneš, as he read these lines, thought of the explicit promises he had received from Voroshilov in the summer of 1935? Now, when he needed the Soviet alliance most, he found that the Red Army would not march against the Wehrmacht. Instead, the Kremlin advised him to bring his case up with the League of Nations.

While the conference at Munich was still in progress the president had to endure another ordeal. Four of the top generals of the Czechoslovak army came to see him at the Castle after they held informal meetings on 28–29 September at Kroměříž in central Moravia.[220] According to Beneš's notes, taken during the event, their argument consisted of four points.[221] First, Czechoslovakia should go to war under any circumstances. Second, the Allies would eventually be forced to fight. Third, the nation was united and the army wanted to fight. Fourth, even if the country were to remain isolated, the army should fight. Although the president described the event as "moving" (he noticed tears in the eyes of some generals), his response was crisp. He was well aware that the Czechoslovak nation and the army wanted to fight come what may and against whatever combination of aggressors. But the generals, Beneš stressed, were mistaken. France and Great Britain would not follow. Nothing whatsoever could make them go to war against the Third Reich, and he, Beneš, was not prepared to lead the country into a slaughterhouse for some empty gesture. Munich, Beneš continued, was the beginning of a great European tragedy. It would be followed by war and revolution. The allies "do not want to fight with us, and it would have been easier now, so they will have to fight the hard way and on our behalf when we are no longer able to fight. They will pay a heavy price. I must act to save the nation." For all their desire to fight, the generals were part of a democratic political system, and they obeyed the president's command. They nodded and left, expecting the worst, which for them was not death, but surrender.

The meeting was brief, but it summed up well the devilish dilemma that the president had to face. Although he had never been a soldier, Beneš had an excellent understanding of modern warfare. He knew that the kind of war Hitler was about to force on Europe—strained, diplomatic smiles at Munich notwithstanding—was going to be qualitatively different from the more or less static warfare of organized armies of twenty years earlier.[222] The Nazi assault on Poland eleven months later and Hitler's subsequent attempts to exterminate every trace of Polish existence showed quite well what the president felt obligated to avoid. At the same time, the wounds (physical and psychological) caused by the Czechoslovak army's failure to resist were as deep as and maybe more treacherous than whatever injuries Czechoslovakia would have sustained in war against Germany.

The conference at Munich continued past midnight, and the final document, dated 29 September, was actually signed only the next day. The terms the Führer extracted from Chamberlain and Daladier for a promise not to go to war were high. No one took issue with Hitler's frivolously exaggerated geographic definition of the Sudeten territory, the first zone of which was to be occupied by the Third Reich on 1 October. The allies, moreover, gave Hitler Czech territory that had not been included in the Godesberg memorandum, which the prime minister had indignantly rejected as unacceptable. For instance, the Third Reich gained under the terms of the Four Power Act the following cities: Polička and environs (11,739 Czechs and 503 Germans), Svinov (4,319 and 722), Třebovice (1,751 and 71), Klimkovice (2,934 and 229), Kopřivnice (3,968 and 622), Štramberk (3,497 and 46), and Krumlov (3,047 and 749).[223] In addition to handing to Hitler some eleven thousand square miles of Czechoslovak territory, the Munich Agreement also gave the Third Reich jurisdiction over more than eight hundred thousand Czechoslovaks. Ultimately, the country lost 86 percent of its chemical industry, 86 percent of its glass industry, 80 percent of its textile industry, and 70 percent of its iron and steel enterprises. This was the outcome of Newton's promise to Beneš that, if only he accepted the Franco-British plan, London would guarantee "nearly everything" that Masaryk and Beneš had gained in 1918.

The British and French were neither informed enough nor willing to discuss territorial issues at Munich. On that question they surrendered unconditionally. Only Chamberlain challenged one of the least important stipulations—that Czechoslovak farmers could leave the territory marked to become part of the German Reich but could not take their livestock. Chamberlain, who had expressed no interest in the fate of Czechs, Jews, and Sudeten German democrats, raised *this* issue repeatedly. Finally, Hitler exploded, "Our time is too valuable to be wasted on such trivialities!" The matter was dropped, and the conference came to an end.[224] Before the participants broke up, the French ambassador in Berlin tried to joke: "I am going to a dying man to give him supreme unction," he said about the prospect of having to meet the two Czechoslovak emissaries, "but I do not have oil with me to pour on his wounds."[225]

At 1:30 A.M., Mastný and Masařík finally met Chamberlain, Daladier, and others at the British prime minister's hotel suite. Chamberlain looked tired after some nine hours with Hitler. But he was, as he put it, *pleasantly* tired.[226] He told the Czechoslovaks that this was the best achievable outcome. Daladier, who knew what he had done, seemed deeply ashamed. He looked broken and defeated.[227] He was mostly silent throughout the meeting, his head was bowed, and his eyes were focused on his fingernails, not daring to look at the Czechoslovak representatives. Chamberlain gave a copy of the agreement to Mastný and asked him to read it aloud, but as soon as the reading had started he began yawning, discretely at first, then without any scruples. He deluded himself into thinking he had won. There would be no war, and that was what mattered the most to him. Whether a city with an unpronounceable name would be on this or another side of the new border was irrelevant. The emissaries attempted to object to specific conditions but without success. After Mastný had finished reading the final Munich document, the Czechoslovaks were informed that no response was expected from Prague, and they were asked to leave. That was the end of the democratic experiment in Central Europe.

Agony in Prague

The president's office learned the terms of the Munich agreement on 30 September at 2 A.M. from the German radio station DNB. Beneš was asleep, and the chief of protocol and Beneš's main secretary, Jaromír Smutný, decided to let him rest. At 5 A.M., the German legation in Prague called the Foreign Ministry and requested an interview for Chargé d'Affaires Hencke with Krofta.[228] The German diplomat came at 6:15 A.M. and gave the Czechoslovak foreign minister the text of the Munich Agreement; the map, he said, would be supplied by the British legation later. Beneš woke up and, looking groggy, stumbled into his study dressed only in his pajamas and a gown. When Smutný outlined the terms of the agreement, Beneš buried his head in both his hands and repeated over and over: "Unbelievable, unbelievable. . . . Horror. Such French treason. They betrayed us completely."[229]

Although Beneš focused his sentiment on Paris, he felt equally betrayed by London. Within the space of some ten days he had received no less than four knockout blows from the British and French: the Franco-British plan of 19 September, the joint Franco-British ultimatum of 21 September, the Runciman report of 21 September, and now the demand that Prague accept the terms of the Munich Agreement—and in just a few hours. When the president recovered somewhat, he asked Smutný to arrange a meeting of the governing coalition parties at the Castle.[230] Meanwhile, at about 7 A.M., Beneš dictated a short statement, his abdication, and put it in his pocket.

Just before the meeting was to take place, at 9:30 A.M., Beneš tried one last option. He called Aleksandrovsky and told him that Great Britain and France had sacrificed Czechoslovakia to Hitler.[231] The country now had to choose between a war with Germany (in which case the Western Allies would identify the Prague government as the warmonger and culprit) or capitulation. Under these circumstances, Beneš asked the Soviet minister to inquire as quickly as possible in Moscow regarding the Soviet view of the situation. Should Czechoslovakia fight or should it capitulate? For the time being, Aleksandrovsky did not cable the question to Moscow and later characterized this episode as Beneš's "agonized cry."[232] The question submitted, Beneš had to return to his domestic problems, and he went to meet with leading Czechoslovak politicians.

When Drtina opened the door of the Blue Salon at the Castle to announce the president, no one rose. This had never happened before. Some looked at Beneš with barely concealed hatred.[233] Many would soon blame him for the national catastrophe. While the meeting was in progress, Mrs. Hana Beneš rang Drtina and asked him to come to the presidential apartment, where she was talking with Alice Masaryk, the daughter of former President Masaryk. The two ladies asked Drtina plainly whether, in his opinion, Czechoslovakia should surrender or fight to the bitter end. No nation, he said, could lose its liberty without a struggle, unless it was ready to accept moral disintegration. The ladies shared his view and urged him to talk with Beneš in the same vein without delay. But the meeting was already in progress, protested Drtina. Then interrupt it and talk to the president immediately, they demanded. The secretary hesitantly agreed. He sensed that Mrs. Beneš was concerned that her husband would surrender simply because he had run out of physical and nervous strength to continue. Beneš came out, listened to Drtina's message, nodded "yes, yes, yes" and never once registered his disagreement. Then he returned to the meeting.

While the governing coalition was with the president, the Czechoslovak government held a meeting at the Kolowrat Palace, not far from the Castle. Prime Minister Syrový opened it by saying that the four powers had given Czechoslovakia a choice between being murdered and committing suicide. Krofta followed. This report was the most dreadful duty of his life he said before he began to outline the events at Munich as described by Mastný and Masařík, who had returned to Prague at eight in the morning. Theoretically, he said, it was possible to reject the Four Power Act. This would be followed by German aggression and war in which Czechoslovakia would be completely isolated. It was doubtful that the Soviet Union would come to the country's assistance or that its military aid would be effective. Although several ministers made emotional and patriotic declarations, the transcript indicates clearly that the majority was more inclined to follow reason, not their hearts.[234]

At 10 A.M., the Czechoslovak legation in Moscow telephoned Fierlinger's message: "Don't let them get us, and stay the course!"[235] Unfortunately, this was not followed by any information regarding Soviet response to the Munich Agreement or to President Beneš's urgent question submitted half an hour earlier. In fact, Aleksandrovsky had not even cabled it to Moscow. At 10:30 A.M., having apparently done nothing for an hour, the Soviet minister drove to the Castle in his black Packard limousine to ascertain for himself what was going on. He did not meet Beneš but picked up bits of information from his staff, primarily from Smutný, probably his best source of information.

The government's meeting ended inconclusively at the Kolowrat Palace at 11:30 A.M., and then the ministers drove up the steep hill to the Castle to meet with the president. The next meeting started fifteen minutes later. Beneš, Prime Minister Syrový, seventeen ministers (all but Petr Zenkl), and General Krejčí were present. The president stated at the beginning that Czechoslovakia could go against the wishes of all the European powers and fight on its own. But the result would be an end of independence and a massacre of the nation. Under these circumstances, he could not but "suggest the acceptance" of the Munich Agreement. There was little debate.[236]

The meeting ended at noon, and Aleksandrovsky learned from Smutný that it was no longer necessary for Moscow to reply to the original inquiry. As it happened, only fifteen minutes earlier the Soviet legation finally cabled the crucially important question to Moscow, which it had received at 9:30 A.M. At noon, Aleksandrovsky was still at the Castle.[237] At 12:20 P.M., the Czechoslovak legation in Moscow telephoned that it had "nothing new to report," and ten minutes later Minister Krofta formally announced to Newton and de Lacroix that Czechoslovakia accepted the Munich *Diktat.*[238]

The Soviet legation cabled the second telegram of the day to Moscow at 1:40 P.M. to inform the Kremlin that Beneš had accepted the Munich Agreement and that a Soviet reply was no longer expected.[239]

Prime Minister Syrový addressed the country at 5 P.M. This was the saddest and worst moment of his life, he said. "I would prefer to be dead rather than to have to tell you" that Czechoslovakia had been "deserted by all its allies and friends." Consequently, it had to accept "the most ruthless and unfair terms ever forced on anybody in history."[240] As the prime minister stumbled over his words, Moscow started to receive Beneš's urgent questions posed at 9:30 A.M. The delay in transmission has never been explained. Forty-five minutes later, it received the second telegram.[241] The first telegram was finally decoded at 6 P.M.

That evening, crowds on the streets of Prague thundered with anger and frustration. As had occurred a week before, the main target of the protesters was the Castle. Gottwald and the Communist party leadership had prepared for this eventuality. Their intention was to overthrow the government that had accepted the Munich *Diktat,* to mobilize the masses, and to coordinate the party's policy with the anticapitulationist elements in the Army's General Staff. The party, Gottwald claimed later, was ready to use force.[242] This time, however, the state police were ready. All government buildings had been cordoned off and were protected by sand bags and military obstacles. When a large crowd attempted to break through, it was pushed back and scattered in a swift and energetically executed police action.

Although the government had lost the Sudetenland, it was in complete control everywhere else. During the day, the president and Prime Minister Syrový received telegrams from deputies representing various political parties.[243] They warned that to surrender Czechoslovak territory was tantamount to high treason, they demanded that the fortresses remain under Czechoslovak control, and they predicted that capitulation would turn the nation and the army into a desperate but determined crowd. As it happened, it was Beneš who proved to be more in touch with the feelings of Czechoslovak citizens. Although all were angry, although many cried, ultimately, the government's decision to bow to the *Diktat* from Munich was accepted. Even Gottwald admitted that the revolutionary potential that had existed in Prague a week earlier declined noticeably.[244] By nightfall, the demonstrators went home, and the army, its raison d'être trampled into the dust, began its painful retreat from the fortresses. Deprived of the chance to fight, and perhaps die, on the battlefield in the fall of 1938, many officers found a way to resist the Third Reich nevertheless. For instance, at the time of the September crisis, the Czechoslovak army had 114 generals.[245] Of those, twenty-nine perished during the war, primarily for their participation in the resistance on the home front.[246] Such losses would hardly have been higher had the Army fought.

The next day, 1 October 1938, the whole Sudetenland seemed to be covered with the Swastika. *Es kommt der Tag* (the day will come) Henlein used to say, and here it was. This was the time to put on white stockings and greet the German troops. They entered the former Czechoslovak territory at 2 P.M. During the day, Czechoslovak Foreign Ministry technicians tried unsuccessfully to reestablish the temporary radiotelephone connection between Prague and Moscow. They did not succeed that day "since Moscow did not broadcast anything in open language."[247] This was strange because the connection had been initially established at the request of the Soviet legation in Prague. As radio technicians from the Foreign Ministry combed the ether for signals from Moscow, they could not help but feel deep frustration at hearing over and over again the joyful roar of crowds in London and Paris. No such celebrations could be detected in Berlin. German stations had a simpler message for their audiences: Beneš had failed to drag the world into war. Ominously, the stations claimed that Czechoslovakia continued to be governed by a "military dictatorship with a Jewish-Bolshevik background."[248] Soon, Göring would present to Mastný the Third Reich's first demand: President Beneš's immediate abdication. Berlin would not deal with him (*Mit Beneš werden wir nicht verhandeln*).[249]

As the Wehrmacht continued to pour into the remaining zones of the Sudetenland on 2 October 1938, the corridors of the Castle were ringing with discussions about whether the president should resign. Although he had already prepared a written announcement of his abdication, it had remained undisturbed in his pocket. "As always," Smutný wrote, "his tendency to deliberate won over his desire to act."[250] (Beneš would resign on 5 October.) Thus, it was still President Beneš who received on 3 October a cable from Fierlinger in Moscow.[251] It stated that the Kremlin was critical of the Prague government's decision to capitulate and that it would have come to Czechoslovakia's assistance "under any circumstances." The message was received and decoded at the Foreign Ministry at 2 A.M. This was exactly sixty-one and a half hours after Prague had accepted the Munich *Diktat* and at least thirty-six hours after the Czechoslovak army had withdrawn from the fortified, defensible perimeter. Under these circumstances, the Kremlin's answer to Beneš's inquiry played no role in the decision-making process that had taken place before noon on 30 September 1938. When all was said and done, Prague received from Moscow only carefully timed platonic expressions of sympathy.

The Man Who Won at Munich:
Stalin and the Four Power Act

Soon after the Prague government accepted the Munich *Diktat,* Gottwald and other members of the CPC leadership began spreading the view that the Soviet Union, alone among the world powers, had stood by Czechoslovakia throughout the crisis.[252] They were joined by others, including the president himself. But it was Gottwald who was most determined to turn the alleged willingness of Moscow to assist Czechoslovakia in 1938 into a tool of political struggle. He dealt with this topic briefly after the war.[253] Then he addressed the issue with full force after the February 1948 communist coup d'état. In a speech celebrating J. V. Stalin, Gottwald asserted that he had met the Kremlin leader specifically to discuss the Czechoslovak-German crisis. Stalin had supposedly told him that "the Soviet Union was ready to assist Czechoslovakia unilaterally even if France did not do so . . . and even if Poland and Romania refused to allow a transfer of Soviet troops." Gottwald claimed that when he asked Stalin whether he could relay this assurance to Beneš, Stalin authorized him to do so, and he passed the news to the Czechoslovak president.[254] This assertion was uncritically accepted by historians who, unable to gain access to archives, had to rely on the word of the founding father of Czechoslovak communism.

It is notoriously difficult to prove that an event did not happen, and we do not know what Stalin may have said to Gottwald, or whether the two ever met to discuss the Czechoslovak crisis.[255] But we do know what the CPC leader said to the president in Prague. There is evidence of only three meetings between Beneš and Gottwald during the fateful year 1938. They met for the first time on 17 September, as recorded in the Book of Presidential Audiences. On that occasion, the alleged offer of Soviet unilateral assistance was not mentioned. When they met again on 19 September, Beneš inquired whether Gottwald could tell him anything specific regarding the Soviet Union's attitude toward the crisis, whereupon the CPC boss told the president that the Prague government should submit its questions directly to the Kremlin.[256] When Beneš and Gottwald met again, on 30 September 1938, it was 2 P.M. Czechoslovakia had accepted the Munich *Diktat* an hour and a half earlier and all was lost. On that occasion, Gottwald saw the president with a group of seven other people.[257] According to the written record of the meeting, Gottwald spoke twice.[258] On each occasion, he eloquently reminded President Beneš that capitulation was unacceptable, as did the others who came with him. However, he did not bring up the alleged offer of Stalin to defend Czechoslovakia unilaterally. In fact, he did not mention the Soviet Union. At no point during the crisis did Gottwald tell President Beneš that Stalin was willing to provide Czechoslovakia with unilateral assistance. One tends to suspect that Gottwald invented his meeting with Beneš in order to increase the president's burden of responsibility for Czechoslovakia's capitulation to the Munich *Diktat*. Whether Gottwald ever met Stalin to discuss the Czechoslovak crisis, and who said what, has to remain unsolved until the opening of the Presidential Archives in Moscow.

Luckily, we know what President Beneš thought of Stalin's involvement in the Czechoslovak-German crisis of 1938. During World War II and even later, Beneš would make a number of flattering statements about the Kremlin and its role in the Munich affair. But he saw through the Soviet charade. In the fall of 1947 Beneš pointed out that Fierlinger's claims about Soviet readiness to assist the Prague government in 1938 and the official Czechoslovak propaganda were "utterly false." "The truth is that the Soviets did not want to help us," said Beneš, and he added that Moscow "acted deceitfully." The president then returned to the questions he had presented at the height of the crisis to Minister Aleksandrovsky: "I asked him three questions, whether the Soviets would help us, and I repeated them. He did not answer, he never answered. That was the main reason why I capitulated."[259] This recently uncovered document answers once and for all the riddle of Moscow's treatment of Czechoslovakia on the eve of the Munich conference. It also exposes Beneš's own politically motivated assertions that the Soviet Union was his sole ally.[260]

How did the Kremlin look upon the Four Power Act? The Munich Agreement represented the worst possible development from the Soviet Union's perspective. Moscow felt it had been set up. Two days after the conference, Georgi Dimitrov, the Comintern chief, expressed the opinion that the Munich Agreement was directed against the Soviet Union.[261] He said nothing of Czechoslovakia. But only three weeks later, as if the Kremlin had reminded itself of the platform adopted by the 7th Congress of the Comintern, this pessimistic view was abandoned. Dimitrov now set a different tone: Munich was a Pyrrhic victory of fascism. There was no force in the world that could "turn back the wheel of historical progress. The near future does not belong to dying capitalism, but to rising socialism."[262] Dimitrov maintained this optimistic position even during a Comintern meeting that dealt specifically with the Munich defeat and judged the leadership of the Czechoslovak Communist party.[263]

There is further evidence that the Soviet leaders saw in the European political scene, scarred as it was by the Munich Agreement, not just a threat of isolation, but also an opportunity. A document obtained by the U.S. consul in Prague in 1939 described a trip by a group of Czechoslovak communists to Moscow after the outbreak of World War II. (At the time, Czechoslovakia no longer existed; the country created at Munich was destroyed by Hitler on 14–15 March 1939.) They had gone there demanding an explanation of the astounding friendship between Stalin and Hitler. Their comrades suffered in Gestapo jails for their love of the Soviet Union, and Stalin was seen beaming with joy as the pact with Nazi Germany was being signed. How was this possible?

The delegation was received by an official of the Commissariat for Foreign Affairs. The Molotov-Ribbentrop pact was justified, he said:

> If the USSR had concluded a treaty with the Western powers, Germany would never have unleashed a war from which will develop world revolution which we have been preparing for a long time. . . . A surrounded Germany would never have entered into war. . . . We cannot afford Germany to lose because if she should come under the control of the West and Poland [were to be] reestablished, we would be cut off from the rest of Europe. The present war must last as long as we want. . . . Keep calm because never was the time more favorable for our interests than at present.[264]

The long-term Soviet strategy outlined in the document obtained by the U.S. consul in Prague was in harmony not only with the 7th Congress but also with the ideas laid down by Zhdanov in his August 1938 speech before the Czechoslovak Communist party's Central Committee.

On 29 November 1938 a group of communist leaders from the Sudetenland came to see Minister Aleksandrovsky to request Soviet visas. But instead of providing them with travel permits, Aleksandrovsky—speaking in flawless German—offered his opinion. We are standing on the threshold of great events; I cannot tell you exactly what is going to happen, but now every fighter is needed here, not in the

Soviet Union. "Cheer up," he concluded, "you haven't been forgotten."[265] Aleksandrovsky continued developing this theme a few days later. This time, however, he was not speaking with a group of communists without a country or legal protection. He encountered Minister Smutný at a well-attended soirée at the Soviet legation. Aleksandrovsky remarked that Moscow now saw there would have to be a war against Germany one day. "But eventually the two countries will probably divide Poland between themselves," he continued, "and it will become the next theater of war."[266] On this occasion, Aleksandrovsky was not just unusually frank; as the future was to show, he was also right.

Although Soviet diplomacy suffered a defeat when it was excluded from the Munich conference it recovered itself quickly. Stalin saw the need to take aggressive action to break through his isolation, hence the immediate Soviet effort to make Hitler's war against Poland possible and a German conflict with the West inevitable. For the time being, a war over Poland would mean that the British and the French would be the first to absorb Germany's deadly blows. By late August 1939, Germany, Great Britain, and France were committed to fighting a war at a place and time of Hitler's choosing. But Stalin, as Litvinov had predicted in his discussion with Arnošt Heidrich in Geneva, could wait and deliberate. Having been shut out of the Munich conference in 1938, he was the only European leader who had managed to reserve considerable freedom of action for himself a year later.

Throughout his career, Joseph Stalin had suffered many tactical defeats, and Munich was one of them. But he crowned his tactical failures with impressive strategic victories. By the end of World War II, the Munich solution of the Sudeten crisis had been shattered and none of the four powers who had designed it was in a position to dictate the course of events in the reestablished Czechoslovakia. Only Stalin, who had been excluded from the 1938 meeting at the Führerhaus, was on his way toward the creation of a powerful empire. And Czechoslovakia, the apple of discord in 1938, would soon become one of the empire's crown jewels. The man who profited from the legacy of the Munich charade the most was Stalin.

The Munich affair proved to be a godsend also for the Communist party of Czechoslovakia.[267] Klement Gottwald noted in late December 1938 before the Presidium of the Communist International's Executive Committee in Moscow that, despite its defeat, the CPC had succeeded in drilling into the minds of Czechoslovak citizens the link between the security of their country and the security of the Soviet Union. During the crisis, Gottwald observed, anticommunism had for the first time become unfashionable and unpatriotic. Party propaganda had managed to form the public view that hostility toward the CPC meant endangering Czechoslovakia's national security and that hostility toward the Soviet Union weakened Czechoslovakia.[268] It is possible that Gottwald was exaggerating. After all, he was speaking in Stalin's Soviet Union, the year was 1938, and the purge was devouring foreign communists in large numbers.[269] Moreover, he did confess to Beneš after the war that he had been ordered to carry out a revolution in Prague at the height of the crisis of 1938 and that, except for one or two public demonstrations, he had done nothing concrete to bring about the "second wave" of proletarian revolutions in Europe.[270] In short, Gottwald had reasons to be nervous. But there was much that was authentic in his report: pro-Soviet sentiment in Prague during September 1938 was certainly evident.

As a result of the West's abandonment of Czechoslovakia in the fall of 1938, many Czechoslovaks started to rethink their country's position. Hitler and the behavior of French and British diplomats enhanced the appeal of the Soviet Union and its main advocate in Czechoslovakia, the CPC. The Munich Agreement legitimized the view that "old Europe" was unable to deal with "dynamic" political ideologies, such as Nazism. A young American diplomat who served in Prague observed in late 1938 that, as a result of the deal in Munich, liberalism in general, and democracy in particular, were discredited.[271] The Franco-British agreement with Hitler allowed for a connection to be formed between Czechoslovak patriotism and sympathy for Stalin. It set in motion processes that slowly gained momentum and culminated in the electoral victory of the CPC in 1946. This victory, too, would serve the interests of Stalin.

The Victims of the Munich Agreement

Stalin was in fact the only winner. All others lost.[272] The agreement which Chamberlain brought from Munich threw many defenseless Czechoslovaks, Czechoslovak Jews, and Sudeten German democrats to the Gestapo. True, it contained a right of option into and out of the Sudetenland that had been put into the text to silence Chamberlain's and Daladier's domestic critics. But, as could have been easily predicted by anyone familiar with Nazi methods, this was never observed. With the new rulers of the Sudetenland came the Gestapo, which mercilessly pounced on Hitler's opponents and shipped them to various concentration camps.[273]

The Sudeten Germans who had supported the Henlein movement even as it degenerated into a conduit of Nazism had little to celebrate. After the first few heady weeks in the fall of 1938, the rejoicing was over. The Sudeten Germans became citizens of the Third Reich, and that had serious consequences. Once the war broke out, the men were impressed into Wehrmacht and SS units and sent to fight on behalf of the Führer. They suffered enormous losses, especially as part of the Sixth Army at Stalingrad, as well as on other battlefields of World War II. Not many Sudeten German men of military age lived to experience the freedom that returned to Europe in the spring of 1945. Fate was unkind also to civilians in the Sudetenland. In the spring of 1945 they found themselves under the jurisdiction of liberated Czechoslovakia once again. This time, Prague's rule was less benign than it had been in the 1930s. On the basis of internationally sanctioned agreements, the government expelled most Sudeten Germans to Germany proper. They became refugees, uprooted from the territory on which their ancestors had lived and worked in peace for generations.

Initially, of course, there was much celebrating in Great Britain. Chamberlain was welcomed with the same pomp as a conqueror returning from a victorious campaign. The public's naïveté is easy to understand and can be readily forgiven.[274] Similarly, it is not difficult to forgive Prime Minister Chamberlain, a sincere, tragic figure. "It has been my fate to see the failure of all my efforts," he had to conclude in his letter of resignation.[275] It is considerably more difficult to be as understanding of those British diplomats who unabashedly displayed their prejudice against democratic Czechoslovakia and its president and who showed off their sympathy for Henlein. But these were extreme cases. For the majority in Great Britain, Munich was a deal, a good deal in fact. It was in this spirit that London approached the Prague government with a business proposition shortly after the Four Power Act had been signed. The British Defense Ministry was interested in buying up Czechoslovak military hardware, rendered redundant by the Munich Agreement.[276] Undoubtedly, it was expected that weapons could be had in Czechoslovakia for a good price.

The cheering was no less sincere and intense in France, where a movement was set afoot to rename one of the main streets "Rue du 30 September."[277] That idea was quickly abandoned as the public absorbed the consequences of France's betrayal of its Czechoslovak ally. It would be only a slight exaggeration to suggest that the greatness of France for years ahead came to an end in September 1938. Daladier was as tragic a figure as the British prime minister, but he was considerably more tortured by the legacy of Munich. Chamberlain died in the fall of 1940, but Daladier had to endure many more years of reflection about 1938. He died in 1970, at the age of eighty-six.

It should not be forgotten that among the victims of the Munich Agreement also stands Germany. Although the country was swept off its feet by the Führer, few Germans took joy in the prospect of war. The Four Power Act made Hitler appear to be the genius he had claimed to be. His victory at Munich disarmed German domestic opposition because its main argument—that Hitler would drag Germany into a devastating war—proved to be wrong, at least in 1938. But in order to succeed in Munich, Hitler had to lie quite openly. When he violated his solemn commitment that the Sudeten territory was his last demand, Chamberlain and Daladier simply had to confront him. Great Britain and France, under whatever government, could tolerate such a humiliation only once. Henceforth, there would have to be war, a war in which the German people would suffer enormously. It could be that the Munich Agreement marked the beginning of the end of the Third Reich.[278]

No one was as touched by the horror of Munich as President Beneš. The September drama, the gathering of Western democracies with the Nazis, and the imminent death of the Republic of Czechoslovakia were agonizing for him. The allies, he said shortly after the crisis, were "cowards." Out of fear of communism, the French and the English joined the Nazis. Just look at it, the president said to a small audience, the Munich Agreement was signed by four powers—and two of them were Czechoslovakia's "friends."[279] This had a profound impact on Beneš's psychology. The "repudiation of that despicable Munich" and the reconstitution of Czechoslovakia became his idée fixe.[280] And Beneš was a man of limitless energy. He felt vindicated as he watched the world slide closer and closer to the abyss of war. In his view, an all-out war would undo the horror of Munich and its consequences: the imposition of the German protectorate over Bohemia and Moravia and the anti-Semitic Slovak state in March 1939. "Europe must go to war," said Beneš firmly, "and all those responsible [for the Munich *Diktat* and the policy of appeasement] must be punished." Beneš found the Molotov-Ribbentrop pact of August 1939 morally appalling. But he knew that it would enable Germany to attack Poland, and that was good because it meant war. He believed that Europe was responsible for the rise of Hitlerism between 1933 and 1939; only war would wash away its sins.[281] Even the Franco-British declaration of war on Germany in September 1939 did not satisfy the exiled president. He was convinced that the anti-Hitler alliance would have to include the Soviet Union to be complete. He saw it fulfilled in June 1941. Hitler's attack on the Soviet Union, he said, "gave him great satisfaction." Finally, an alliance was formed which he had hoped for two years before.[282] That alliance included Czechoslovakia, and in it Beneš eventually found his reparation for Munich.

THE PRESIDENT CHOSE NOT TO fight on 30 September 1938 because he had been abandoned by his French ally and by the Soviet Union. At the same time, he was under great pressure from Great Britain, and many other countries to accept the view that the Sudetenland was Hitler's last demand. Surrendering its historical borders, Beneš was told, had to be Czechoslovakia's contribution to European peace.[283] The president hoped that the Munich Agreement would not mark the end of his country but the beginning of a large conflict between Hitler and the democracies. At the end, Czechoslovakia would reemerge. He anticipated that the Third Reich would be defeated by a large coalition in which he would play a role.[284]

Although he continued to be haunted by his acceptance of the Munich *Diktat* until the end of his life, Beneš thought that he had made the right decision. Many disagree. They blame his capitulation in September 1938 for the destruction of the moral principles on which the state had been founded in 1918.[285] They argue that Beneš's acceptance of Munich had created a precedent to which other Czechoslovak crises and capitulations can be attributed. But if his behavior in September 1938 is destined to remain controversial, it should not be overlooked that Beneš showed considerable greatness immediately afterward. Others in his place would have stumbled from the horror of Munich into depression, political oblivion, and physical decline. Beneš recovered from his defeat. After a brief pause, he returned to active politics and established himself in Great Britain, the country where he had been belittled by so many. There, on the home turf of Chamberlain, Halifax, and Runciman, he worked ceaselessly to liberate Czechoslovakia from the consequences of Hitler's aggression and the Franco-British policy of appeasement. In that regard, he was as successful as he had been in Paris during the Great War. Hitler's behavior after the Munich conference caused the political decline of Chamberlain, Daladier, and many of their collaborators. But it rehabilitated Edvard Beneš. In the spring of 1945, the president returned in triumph from exile to the Prague Castle and a new, so he hoped, political life.

Alas, happy endings are rare in Central Europe. If Stalin's tactical defeats resulted in strategic victories, Beneš's tactical successes (the undoing of Munich and the reconstitution of Czechoslovakia were prominent among them) crumbled in the strategic, and final, defeat he suffered at the hands of Stalin ten years after the Four Power Act. The Soviet Union, which had been excluded from the Führerhaus in Munich, came to extract its pound of Czechoslovak flesh in February 1948.[286] But

Stalin's conquest of the heart of Europe was a consequence of Hitler's assault on the established order, and not many politicians in the 1930s, the decade of swine, could say that they saw the emerging Nazi threat with the same clarity as did Edvard Beneš.

Notes

1. Robert Kvaček et al., *Československý rok 1938* (Prague: Panoráma, 1988), 11.

2. Gelford Taylor, *Munich: The Price of Peace* (Garden City, N.Y.: Doubleday, 1979), 681–99, 706–9, and *passim*.

3. *Documents on German Foreign Policy, 1918–1945* (henceforth *DGFP*), series D, vol. 2 (Washington: U.S. Government Printing Office, 1949), document no. 221, 360–61.

4. *Survey of International Affairs, 1938*, 2:143.

5. General Jodl's diary presented before the International Military Tribunal at Nuremberg, in *Trial of the Major War Criminals before the International Military Tribunal* (*TMWC*) (Nuremberg: International Military Tribunal, 1947), 28: 345–90.

6. *Documents on British Foreign Policy, 1919–1939* (henceforth *DBFP*), 3d series, vol. 2 (London: Her Majesty's Stationery Office, 1949), document no. 830, 289.

7. Paul Schmidt, *Hitler's Interpreter* (New York: Macmillan, 1951), 69.

8. *DGFP*, series D, vol. 2, document no. 448, 727–30.

9. Royal Institute of International Affairs, *Documents on International Affairs, 1938* (London: Oxford University Press, 1939), 2:184–88.

10. *Survey of International Affairs, 1938*, 2:302.

11. *DBFP*, 3d series, vol. 2, document no. 830, 289.

12. Gerhard L. Weinberg, *The Foreign Policy of Hitler's Germany: Starting World War II, 1937–1939* (Chicago: University of Chicago Press, 1980), 423–25.

13. Norman H. Baynes (ed.), *The Speeches of Adolf Hitler: April 1922–August 1939* (London: Oxford University Press, 1942), 2:1487–99.

14. See especially, Martin Broszat, "Das Sudetendeutsche Freikorps," *Vierteljahrshefte für Zeitgeschichte* 9 (January 1961): 30–49 and many other authors, e.g., Taylor, *Munich: The Price of Peace*, 798–99.

15. Zdeněk Procházka, et al. *Vojenské dějiny Československa*, (Prague: Naše Vojsko, 1987) 3:496.

16. *DGFP*, series D, vol. 2, document no. 481, 764.

17. R. G. D. Laffan, *Survey of International Affairs, 1938* (New York: Oxford University Press, 1951), 2:311.

18. PRO, FO 408/68. C 9800/4839/18, Major R. Sutton-Pratt to Viscount Halifax, the British Legation, Prague, 13 September 1938.

19. British Minister Newton recommended Sutton-Pratt's analyses of the Czechoslovak-German crisis as "careful and unbiased observations and enquiries." *DBFP*, 3d series, vol. 2, document no. 916, 367.

20. *Survey of International Affairs, 1938*, 2:311.

21. This is not to be confused with martial law because there was a significant legal difference between *stanné právo* (*Standrecht*) and martial law. Those arrested under *stanné právo* were tried by civilian, not military, courts although the procedure was accelerated.

22. *DGFP*, series D, vol. 2, document no. 502, 812.

23. *Times*, 16 September 1938.

24. Interview with Z. L., a Czechoslovak army reserve officer, stationed in the Sudetenland in 1938.

25. This is stated or implied in *DGFP*, series D, vol. 2, document no. 481, 764.

26. Ibid., document no. 515, 824.

27. Ibid., document no. 516, 825.

28. Ibid., document no. 520, 828.

29. *Survey of International Affairs, 1938,* 2:316.

30. *Vojenské dějiny Československa,* 3:498.

31. "Home to the Reich" was one of the most frequently used slogans of the SdP.

32. *DBFP,* 3d series, vol. 2, document no. 827, 286. The military dimension is analyzed by Williamson Murray, *The Change in the European Balance of Power, 1938–39* (Princeton: Princeton University Press, 1984), 217–63, and David Vital, "Czechoslovakia and the Powers, September 1938," *Journal of Contemporary History* 1 (October 1966): 37–67.

33. *DBFP,* 3d series, vol. 2, document no. 873, 322.

34. Ibid., note 2, 314.

35. Weinberg, *Foreign Policy of Hitler's Germany,* 425–32.

36. Anthony Adamthwaite, *France and the Coming of the Second World War, 1936–1939* (London: Frank Cass, 1977), 211–12.

37. *DBFP,* 3d series, vol. 2, document no. 857, 312.

38. Ibid., document no. 861, 314.

39. Prokop Drtina, *Československo můj osud* (Toronto: Sixty-Eight Publishers, 1982), 83–84.

40. *DBFP,* 3d series, vol. 2, document no. 890, 334.

41. Ibid., document no. 899, 356.

42. Ibid., document no. 897, 353.

43. Keith Feiling, *The Life of Neville Chamberlain* (London: Macmillan, 1946), 363.

44. Schmidt, *Hitler's Interpreter,* 91.

45. *DBFP,* 3d series, vol. 2, document no. 928, 374.

46. Ibid., document no. 874, 323.

47. Ibid., document no. 894, 337.

48. Ibid., document no. 895, 338–41.

49. Ibid., document no. 896, 342–51.

50. Ibid., 351.

51. Ibid., document no. 897, 353.

52. Ibid., document no. 922, 370, document no. 924, 372.

53. MHA-B, Fond Munich, box 3. De Lacroix saw Minister Krofta on 19 September 1938 at 10 A.M.

54. See, for instance, Adamthwaite, *France,* 213–14 and Weinberg, *Foreign Policy of Hitler's Germany,* 439–44.

55. Drtina, *Československo,* 101.

56. *DBFP,* 3d series, vol. 2, document no. 928, 373–99.

57. Ibid.

58. Ibid., document no. 894, 337.

59. Ibid., document no. 937, 404–6.

60. Drtina, *Československo,* 102.

61. On the Nečas mission, see "Dosseir Nečas," *Revue des Études Slaves* 1–2 (1979): 135–40; Vladimir Soják (ed.), *Mnichov v dokumentech* (Prague: Orbis, 1958), 2:209–10; Jonathan Zorach, "The Nečas Mission during the Munich Crisis," *East Central Europe* 16, nos. 1–2 (1989): 53–70; Josef Kalvoda, "Munich: Beneš and the Soldiers," *Ukrainian Quarterly* 47 (summer 1991): 153–214; Joel Colton, *Léon Blum: Hunanist in Politics* (New York: Knopf, 1966), 315; Adamthwaite, *France,* 213; Weinberg, *Foreign Policy of Hitler's Germany,* 441–42; Nicole Jordan, *The Popular Front and Central Europe: The Dilemmas of*

French Impotence, 1918–1940 (Cambridge: Cambridge University Press, 1992), 319–22; Taylor, *Munich: The Price of Peace,* 777–78.

62. Nečas obviously decided it was safer, for his own protection, to maintain a record of Beneš's plan. Thus, although Beneš's instruction state clearly "destroy these papers," they exist in Beneš's archives.

63. Colton, *Léon Blum,* 316; *DBFP,* 3d series, vol. 2, document no. 902, 358 and document no. 913, 364.

64. MHA-B, box 1a. There is no date on the document itself. One of the meetings between Beneš and Nečas took place on 19 September 1938; see Drtina, *Československo,* 103.

65. Details of the audience on 19 September 1938 are from Drtina, *Československo,* 103–6.

66. *DBFP,* 3d series, vol. 2, document no. 961, 416–17. Although the document was sent from the Foreign Office on 19 September 1938 at 2:45 A.M., it was dated 18 September 1938. Was it an effort to lessen the appearance that the president was exposed to an impossible time pressure?

67. *DBFP,* 3d series, vol. 2, document no. 961, 417.

68. Drtina, *Československo,* 105–6.

69. *Dokumenty k historii Mnichovského diktátu, 1937–1939* (henceforth *Dokumenty*) edited by Dušan Spáčil et al. (Prague: Svoboda, 1979), no. 139, 224–25.

70. Drtina, *Československo,* 107.

71. Edvard Beneš, *Mnichovské dny* (Prague: Svoboda, 1968), 316.

72. *Dokumenty,* no. 140, 226.

73. Drtina, *Československo,* 106.

74. *Dokumenty,* no. 147, 233.

75. *DBFP,* 3d series, vol. 2, document no. 986, 431–34.

76. Ibid., document no. 961, 416.

77. Ibid., document no. 981, 426–27.

78. AMFA, Zdeněk Fierlinger, the Czechoslovak Legation, Moscow, to the Ministry of Foreign Affairs, Prague, telegrams received 857/38, 20 September 1938, decoded at 8:20 P.M.

79. Aleksandrovsky claimed subsequently that he had telephoned Moscow's response to Beneš's questions at 7 P.M. on 20 September 1938, that is, after the president had received the proposal and before he was presented with the ultimatum. *Dokumenty,* no. 151, 237–38. Alas, there is no evidence in the Beneš archives that such a communication reached the president. In any case, because the second question had been distorted, the answer did not matter.

80. Drtina, *Československo,* 110; ANM-S, box 38. Smutný's entry for 20–21 September 1938 indicates that Beneš met from 8:30 to 10 P.M. with Jozef Tiso, the Slovak leader hanged for war crimes after World War II.

81. Taylor, *Munich: The Price of Peace,* 788–93; Keith Weaver Eubank, *Munich* (Norman: University of Oklahoma Press, 1963), 144–54; Adamthwaite, *France,* 216–18. Standard Czechoslovak accounts of this episode can be found in Václav Král, *Dny, které otřásly Československem* (Prague: Naše Vojsko, 1975), 75–99, and Král, *Zářijové dny 1938* (Prague: Svoboda, 1971), 86–92.

82. ANM-S, box 38, Smutný's entry for 20–21 September 1938.

83. MHA-B, Fond Munich, box 6. These are Beneš's own notes, taken in the special shorthand he had partly invented. Some were transcribed during the war in England, others by Lev Sychrava in the early 1950s.

84. MHA-B, box 6. The English ultimatum is dated 18 September, the French version

has the date of 19 September 1938. But both were delivered only on 21 September 1938. *DBFP*, 3d series, vol. 2, document no. 991, 438.

85. ANM-S, box 38, Smutný's entry for 22 September 1938; it contains Beneš's note, a personal record of the meeting, he made for the Ministry of Foreign Affairs.

86. There has been speculation that on 20 September 1938 Beneš had indicated to the British and French envoys in Prague his willingness to accept even a harsh solution of the Czechoslovak crisis as long as it appeared that it been forced on him as an ultimatum. Minister Newton wrote to Viscount Halifax from Prague: "If I can deliver a kind of ultimatum to President Beneš, Wednesday, he and his Government will feel able to bow to *force majeure*." *DBFP*, 3d series, 2:425. This was only Newton's speculation. Beneš truly despised the British minister, and there is every reason to doubt that he would have entrusted him with such a sensitive diplomatic operation. It has also been claimed that Czechoslovak Prime Minister Milan Hodža asked the French to present Prague with an ultimatum. This assertion was made publicly on 29 October 1938 by H. Beuve-Méry, who published in *L'Europe Nouvelle* and article "La vérité sur la pression franco-britannique exercée a Prague le 20 Septembre." The author argued that Hodža told de Lacroix on 20 September 1938 that a firm ultimatum from the Allies would make Beneš's position (and capitulation) easier. This was not news to Beneš. He had already heard the allegation on 3 October 1938 from the Czechoslovak minister in Paris, Štefan Osuský, who twice called Beneš and angrily demanded an explanation for the rumor started, apparently, by Bonnet. MHA-B, Fond Munich, box 1b; Beneš's own record of his conversation with Osuský in Paris.

Hodža addressed this assertion in a written statement for Beneš, dated 17 February 1941, in London. He vigorously denied having made such a request. When he saw de Lacroix on 20 September 1938, the French minister wept: "Quel sale métier, quel sale métier, Mon Président." There had been no talk along the lines alleged by Bonnet, stated Hodža. Beneš and Hodža discussed this question during a personal meeting on 17 February 1941. The president told the former prime minister that he collapsed when he had learned from Paris the allegation that Hodža had requested the ultimatum. He felt as if he had been stabbed in the back and fell onto his fauteil. Hodža stood his ground and repeated what he had stated in writing: the French allegation was untrue. Beneš apparently believed him, because he wrote on 17 July 1943 to Hodža that he met a Frenchman in Washington who had held an important position at the Quai d'Orsay in September 1938. Beneš learned from him that Bonnet had instructed de Lacroix to provoke Prime Minister Hodža into making a statement that Paris would subsequently use to argue that the Czechoslovak-French agreement had been abandoned by Czechoslovakia, not France. "And Berlin was listening in on this conversation," sighed Beneš. MHA-B, Fond Munich, box 1b, Beneš to Hodža.

87. Drtina, *Československo*, 112–13.

88. The timing is based on Smutný's record. Newton indicated that the meeting had ended at 3:45 A.M. See *DBFP*, 3d series, vol. 2, document no. 992, 438.

89. Drtina, *Československo*, 114.

90. František Ježek, "Z pamětí o mnichovské krizi roku 1938," *Historie a vojenství* 4 (1969): 674–701. Time references are on page 684.

91. *DBFP*, 3d series, vol. 2, document no. 992, 438.

92. MHA-B, box 6. This is Beneš's own record of the meeting of 21 September 1938 at 12 o'clock.

93. Ibid.

94. MHA-B, Fond Munich, box 1b, Štefan Osuský, the Czechoslovak Legation, Paris, to the Ministry of Foreign Affairs, Prague, 21 September 1938. The content of Osuský's message to Beneš was leaked. The reaction of the British ambassador in Paris was "I have

consulted [French] Minister for Foreign Affairs and suggested that he should give Czech Minister in Paris piece of his mind. M. Bonnet promised to do so at once and to warn Czech Government." *DBFP,* 3d series, vol. 2, document no. 1001, 444.

95. Ibid., document no. 1002, 444–45.

96. Henryk Batowski, "La politique polonaise et la Tchécoslovaquie," *Revue des Études Slaves* 1–2 (1979): 51–58; see also Jaroslav Valenta, "Cesta k Mnichovu a k válce (1938–1939)," in *Češi a Poláci v minulosti* (Prague: Academia, 1967), 600–15; Anna M. Cienciala, *Poland and the Western Powers, 1938–1939* (London: Routledge, 1968); Henryk Batowski, *Rok 1938: Dwie agresje hitlerowskie* (Poznań: Wydawnictwo Poznańskie, 1985); Henryk Batowski, *Europa zmierza ku przepasci* (Poznań: Wydawnictwo Poznańskie, 1977); Henryk Batowski, *Zrada monachijska: Sprawa Czechosłowacji i dyplomacja europejska w roku 1938* (Poznań: Wydawnictwo Poznańskie, 1973); and Henryk Batowski, *Kryzys dyplomatyczny w Europie: Jesien 1938–wiosna 1939* (Warsaw: Wydawnictwo Ministerstwa Obrony Narodowej, 1962).

Diplomatic documents on Czechoslovak-Hungarian relations are in Francis Deák and Dezsö Ujváry, *Papers and Documents Relating to the Foreign Relations of Hungary* (Budapest: Royal Hungarian Ministry for Foreign Affairs, 1939–48); Edward Chászár, *Decision in Vienna: The Czechoslovak-Hungarian Border Dispute of 1938* (Astor, Fla.: Danubian Press, 1978); Ivan Volgyes, *Hungary: A Nation of Contradictions* (Boulder: Westview Press, 1982); Yvon Lacaze, *De l'Anschluß a la crise de Mai 1938: Contribution des documents diplomatique français a l'étude du probléme tchécoslovaque* (Paris: manuscript, 1976); Magda Ádám (ed.), "Documents relatifs à la politique étrangère de la Hongrie dans la période de la crise tchécoslovaque (1938–1939)," *Acta Historica* 10 (1963–64).

MHA-B, Fond Munich, box 1b. This is Minister Krno's record of his conversation with Minister Papée on 21 September 1938.

97. Kazimierz Papée, the Polish Legation, Prague, to the Ministry of Foreign Affairs, Warsaw, 21 September 1938; in Zbigniew Landau and Jerzy Tomaszewski, *Monachium 1938: Polskie dokumenty dyplomatyczne* (Warsaw: Państwowe Wydawnictwo Naukowe, 1985), document no. 253, 345. "Le Gouvernement Polonais attend une décision du Gouvernement Tchécoslovaque au sujet des territoires habités par la population polonaise, décision immédiate et analogue à celle que le Gouvernement Tchécoslovaque a prise à l'égard du problème allemand." The Polish text is in document no. 252, 344.

98. Magda Ádám, "La Hongrie et la Tchécoslovaquie," *Revue des Études Slaves* 1–2 (1979): 41–50; Batowski, *Kryzys,* 73–98.

99. MHA-B, box 6.

100. Czechoslovak historians who published before November 1989 fully accepted the Aleksandrovsky version of the second question and ignored President Beneš's rendition of it. See, for instance, *Vojenské dějiny Československa,* 3:503.

101. AMFA. A record of Aleksandrovsky's protest against accusations of Soviet betrayal of 21 September 1938, 10:15 A.M., document no. 3290. The Soviet minister spoke with Dr. Jína, a foreign service officer.

102. See Rudolf Halík, "Zrazeni," *Venkov,* 21 September 1938. Expressing the view of the Republican party, Halík stated that Czechoslovakia had been betrayed by both its allies, (France and the Soviet Union) and also by Great Britain. Aleksandrovsky expressly demanded of Dr. Jína that the record be set straight. Moscow's behavior was flawless, he claimed.

103. *Documents on International Affairs, 1938,* 2:224–25.

104. *DGFP,* series D, vol. 2, document 620, 947.

105. *DBFP,* 3d series, vol. 2, document no. 1071, 498.

106. Drtina, *Československo,* 114–17.

107. Ibid., 118–28.

108. "Miunkhen: Sviditel'stvo ochevidtsa," *Mezhdunarodnaia zhizn'* 11 (1988): 128–42.

109. AMFA, Zdeněk Fierlinger, the Czechoslovak Legation, Moscow, to the Ministry of Foreign Affairs, Prague, telegrams received, 866/38, 21 September 1938.

110. AMFA, Zdeněk Fierlinger, the Czechoslovak Legation, Moscow, to the Ministry of Foreign Affairs, Prague, telegrams received, 870/38, 21 September 1938.

111. Soviet authors have argued repeatedly that large units of the Red Army were "alerted" in preparation for Soviet intervention on Czechoslovakia's side in the war against the Third Reich. See Matvei Vasil'evich Zakharov, *General'nyi shtab v predvoyennye gody* (Moscow: Voenizdat, 1989); V. K. Volkov et al., *1939 god: Uroki istorii* (Moscow: Mysl', 1990); Oleg Aleksandrovich Rzheshevskii, *Europe 1939: Was War Inevitable?* (Moscow: Progress Publishers, 1989); A. S. Stepanov, "Pered Miunkhenom," *Voenno-istoricheskii zhurnal* 4–5 (1992): 4–9; S. I. Prasolov, "Sovietskii soyuz i Chekhoslovakia v 1938 g.," in *Miunkhen: Preddverie voiny*, ed. V. K. Volkov (Moscow: Nauka, 1988); D. A. Volkogonov, "Drama reshenii 1939 goda," *Novaia i noveishaia istoriia* 4 (1989): 3–27. The most current collection of Soviet documents is *God krizisa, 1938–1939: Dokumenty i materialy* (Moscow: Politizdat, 1990).

Some authors have accepted the claim that the Red Army was put on alert to assist Czechoslovakia. See G. Jukes, "The Red Army and the Munich Crisis," *Journal of Contemporary History* 26 (April 1991): 195–214. The author seems to trust Zakharov's account of large-scale military measures allegedly taken by the Red Army during the Czechoslovak crisis. It is possible that some measures were taken in the Kiev district in response to the tensions on the international scene in the late summer of 1938, yet this leaves room to doubt their extent and whether they were really meant as a prelude to a Soviet military intervention on Czechoslovakia's behalf. It has not even been established that they were related to the Munich crisis at all. The well-informed German embassy in Moscow consistently denied that the Soviets had taken military measures in support of the Beneš government: "No one in the Embassy thought the Russians would go to war over Czechoslovakia, or that they were in a position to wage an aggressive war of any sort." This view was fully shared by the German attaché, General Ernst Köstring, perhaps the best expert on the Red Army at the time. A German diplomat, highly knowledgable about the affairs of Stalinist Russia in the 1930s, drove in late July 1938 from Moscow to Odessa. He got much information on the stationing of Soviet troops, "but found no indications that they were preparing to move." Hans von Herwarth, *Against Two Evils* (New York: Rawson, Wade, 1981), 123. This is an important source.

112. František Ježek, "Z pamětí o mnichovské krizi roku 1938," *Historie a vojenství* 4 (1969): 684.

113. ACC CPC, Fond KI 20, Gottwald statement before the Executive of the Communist International, 26 December 1938.

114. MHA-B, notes for manuscripts, box 10a. The conversation took place in September 1945.

115. Drtina, *Československo*, 126.

116. Prime Minister Milan Hodža (1878–1943) was a prominent Slovak politician and one of the leaders of the Republican (Agrarian) party. Before World War I, he had become known for his critical views regarding Hungary's treatement of minorities, and he found his way to the circles around the Archduke Franz Ferdinand in Vienna. After the emergence of Czechoslovakia, Hodža fully embraced the position of "Czechoslovakism"— that is, the view that there was one Czechoslovak nation. He forcefully rejected Slovak separatism. During World War II, however, he gradually accepted the position that the Slovak nation had acquired a separate personality.

117. NA RG 165, G-2 Report 2657–II–90–80 to the Chief of Staff, 22 September 1938.

118. SCA, National Tribunal, NS, TNS 1/47, protocol of Syrový's interrogation of 26 March 1946.

119. *Survey of International Affairs, 1938,* 2:368.

120. MHA-B, World War II, box 95, Vasil Škrach to Edvard Beneš, 6 November 1938.

121. This is noted in Antonín Klimek, "Edvard Beneš: postava v mlhách," *Historie a vojenství* 4 (1991): 149–50.

122. *Survey of International Affairs, 1938,* 2:376.

123. *DBFP,* 3d series, vol. 2, document no. 1033, 463–73; *Survey of International Affairs, 1938,* 2:376–95.

124. Schmidt, *Hitler's Interpreter,* 96.

125. Ibid.

126. *DBFP,* 3d series, vol. 2, document no. 1038, 477.

127. *Parliamentary Debates, House of Commons,* 5th series (London: His Majesty's Stationery Office, 1937–38), 339:20.

128. AMFA, Zdeněk Fierlinger, the Czechoslovak Legation, Moscow, to the Ministry of Foreign Affairs, Prague, telegrams received, 876/38, 22 September 1938.

129. Landau and Tomaszewski, *Monachium 1938,* document no. 282, 371–72.

130. AMFA, Zdeněk Fierlinger, the Czechoslovak Legation, Moscow, to the Ministry of Foreign Affairs, Prague, telegrams received, 889/38, 23 September 1938.

131. Ministerstvo inostrannykh del CCCP, *Dokumenty vneshnei politiki SSSR* (Moscow: Izdatel'stvo Politicheskoi Literatury, 1977), vol. 21, document no. 365. This shows that Moscow's intervention had been requested by Czechoslovak Foreign Minister Krofta. Landau and Tomaszewski, *Monachium 1938,* document nos. 289, 293, 376, 379.

132. Ibid., document no. 360, 425–26. The Beneš letter was dated 22 September but was only delivered on 26 September 1938. See also Edvard Beneš, *Mnichovské dny* (Prague: Svoboda, 1968), 304–5.

133. Drtina, *Československo,* 145.

134. "Miunkhen: Sviditel'stvo ochevidtsa," 128–42.

135. Drtina, *Československo,* 145–53.

136. *DBFP,* 3d series, vol. 2, document no. 1059, 490–91.

137. HI ČA, František Havel, "Vzpomínky," 95.

138. MHA-B, Fond Munich, box 3. See, for instance, a statement by de Lacroix to Minister Krofta on 19 September 1938 at 10 A.M.

139. *DBFP,* 3d series, vol. 2, document no. 1027, 461.

140. MHA-B, Fond Munich, box 3; De Lacroix spoke with Minister Krno.

141. *DBFP,* 3d series, vol. 2, document no. 1050, 483.

142. Ibid., document no. 1051, 484.

143. Ibid., document no. 1058, 490.

144. MHA-MOP. The formal statement of the declared mobilization is in MOP, secret, 1935–1939, general, 261/38.

145. Drtina, *Československo,* 148.

146. *Vojenské dějiny Československa,* 3:511.

147. HI ČA, Havel, "Vzpomínky," 95–96.

148. NA RG 165, G-2 Report 2657–II–90–84, 24 September 1938, Major Riley, the U.S. Legation, Prague, to the Chief of Staff, Washington, D.C.

149. NA 760F. 62/1079, Wilbur J. Carr, the U.S. Legation, Prague, to the Secretary of State, Washington, D.C., 24 September 1938.

150. *Vojenské dějiny Československa,* 3:517.

151. ANM-S, box 38, Smutný's entry for 24 September 1938, Beneš's draft dispatched at 00:35 A.M.

152. AMFA, Second Section, box 502, the Ministry of Interior to the Czechoslovak government, 24 September 1938.

153. *Vojenské dějiny Československa*, 3:517. This source fails to make clear whether it lists only those bunkers, fortified posts, and fortresses that were fully equipped and operational at the time of the September 1938 mobilization or whether it counts also those fortifications that were still under construction. It would be only prudent to suspect the latter case.

154. Schmidt, *Hitler's Interpreter*, 100.

155. *Survey of International Affairs, 1938*, 2:389.

156. Schmidt, *Hitler's Interpreter*, 102.

157. William Shirer, *The Rise and Fall of the Third Reich* (New York: Simon & Schuster, 1960), 397n.

158. MHA-B, Fond Munich, box 1b.

159. *Survey of International Affairs, 1938*, 2:392.

160. AMFA, Zdeněk Fierlinger, the Czechoslovak Legation, Moscow, to the Ministry of Foreign Affairs, Prague, telegrams received, 904/38, 24 September 1938.

161. MHA-B, Fond Munich, box 1a. The commission consisted of Minister Künzel-Jizerský, Colonel Štepánský, and Colonel Pták.

162. *DBFP*, 3d series, vol. 2, document no. 1092, 519–20.

163. ANM-S, box 38, Smutný's entry for 26 September 1938.

164. *Parliamentary Debates, House of Commons*, 36.

165. *Survey of International Affairs, 1938*, 2:394–95.

166. *DGFP*, series D, vol. 2, document no. 613, 938.

167. Ibid., document no. 610, 936–37.

168. Drtina, *Československo*, 155, 165–66.

169. "Miunkhen," 128–42.

170. AMFA, Zdeněk Fierlinger, the Czechoslovak Legation, Moscow, to the Ministry of Foreign Affairs, Prague, telegrams received, 937/38, 26 September 1938.

171. Ibid., telegrams sent, 1364/38, 26 September 1938.

172. *DBFP*, 3d series, vol. 2, document no. 1093, 520–35.

173. Ibid., document no. 1096, 536–41.

174. NA, Wilbur J. Carr, the U.S. Legation, Prague, to the War Department, Washington, D.C., 2657–II–90–143, box 1704, 26 September 1938.

175. MHA-MOP, 1939, general, 2964. In addition to the villa, three rooms were also reserved at a nearby pension for the president's staff. Ironically, the owner of "By the Golden Pheasant" did not get paid by the presidential office, and he had to petition Beneš's successor, President Hácha, to be reimbursed. The bill was paid in full.

176. ACC CPC, Fond 100/24, a record of President Beneš's discussion with General Sikorski in London, 20 May 1942. The president also complained that Roosevelt "even ordered for himself [similar] statements from twenty-one South American republics." There are additional records (MHA-B, Fond Munich, box 8) of interventions by diplomatic representatives of Argentina, Bolivia, Chile, Colombia, Cuba, the Dominican Republic, Ecuador, El Salvador, Guatemala, Haiti, Honduras, Iraq, Nicaragua, Panama, Peru, and Venezuela. They contained the same message for President Beneš: Mr. President, please find a *peaceful* solution.

177. Drtina, *Československo*, 171.

178. Nevile Henderson, *Failure of a Mission, Berlin 1937–1939* (New York: Putnam, 1940), 163.

179. John Wheeler-Bennett, *Munich: Prologue to Tragedy* (New York: Viking, 1964), 135.

180. *DBFP*, 3d series, vol. 2, document no. 1118, 555.

181. Baynes, *Speeches of Adolf Hitler*, 1508–27.

182. Drtina, *Československo*, 169–70.

183. "Miunkhen," *Mezhdunarodnaya Zhizn* 11 (1988), 128–42.

184. *DBFP*, 3d series, vol. 2, document no. 1121, 559.

185. Ibid., document no. 1129, 564–67.

186. Henderson, *Failure of a Mission*, 164.

187. *Survey of International Affairs, 1938*, 2:415.

188. Shirer, *Rise and Fall*, 399.

189. Klemens von Klemperer, *German Resistance against Hitler: The Search for Allies Abroad* (New York: Oxford University Press, 1992), 106.

190. MHA-B, Fond Munich, Colonel Antonín Hron, Czechoslovak military attaché, Berlin, to the Military Office of the President, Prague, 20 September 1938.

191. *DGFP*, series D, vol. 2, document no. 634, 965.

192. "Miunkhen," 140.

193. MHA-B, notes for manuscripts, box 10a. In September 1945, in a conversation with Gottwald, Beneš expressed the view that he had disliked Aleksandrovsky. The president also discussed Aleksandrovsky with Fierlinger on 7 October 1945. The two agreed that Aleksandrovsky had performed poorly during the Czechoslovak crisis of 1938 and that was supposedly the reason he had been executed on Stalin's orders.

194. *DBFP*, 3d series, vol. 2, document no. 1118, 556–57, document no. 1126, 562, document no. 1142, 574.

195. Ibid., document no. 1136, 570.

196. Drtina, *Československo*, 171.

197. *DBFP*, 3d series, vol. 2, document no. 1140, 572–73.

198. *Survey of International Affairs, 1938*, 2:416–17.

199. SCA, Protocols of the 18th Czechoslovak government.

200. MHA-B, Fond Munich, box 8, Minister Kamil Krofta, Prague, to Minister Arnošt Heidrich, Geneva, telegrams sent 1376/1938, 28 September 1938.

201. MHA-B, Fond Munich, box 8, Organization of the Intelligence and Propaganda Service in Time of War, 31 May 1938. Among those selected to leave was Karel Čapek, the famous writer, who was to work on behalf of Czechoslovak interests in Great Britain.

202. Rudolf Urban, *Tajné fondy III. sekce: Z archivů MZ Republiky Česko-Slovenské* (Prague: Orbis, 1943), 9. Given the geographic realities, it is not entirely clear through which country Section Chief Hájek intended to travel on his way from Czechoslovakia. Through Romania? It would have been a long and perilous journey at a time of war. Hungary? Hardly. Poland would be the most likely point of Hájek's departure.

203. *DBFP*, 3d series, vol. 2, document no. 1148, 582.

204. AMFA, Zdeněk Fierlinger, the Czechoslovak Legation, Moscow, to the Ministry of Foreign Affairs, Prague, telegrams received, 968/38, 27 September 1938 and 1378/38, 28 September 1938.

205. Ibid., telegrams received, 980/38, 28 September 1938. Fierlinger suggested in the late 1960s that possibly the telegram had been falsified. But even communist historians had to state firmly that an error, deliberate or innocent, could be ruled out. The existence of this telegram in the AMFA signed by Fierlinger, and its timing, cannot be questioned. Fierlinger's opportunism is shown in Věra Olivová, "Československo-sovětské vztahy mezi oběma vál-

kami,'' *50. výročí Československé republiky: Materiály z vědecké konference* (Prague: Ústav Dějin KSČ, 1968), 2:183–84.

206. For example, before Communist party officials in Prague on 24 September 1948: Václav Kopecký said "It has been shown perfectly clearly . . . that the capitulation of our Munichites [i.e., Beneš and his colleagues] was deliberate, that it was dictated by class interests, by the bourgeois fear of the forces of socialism. . . . It is linked with class fear and class hatred of the Soviet Union and socialism." A copy of the speech is in ACC CPC, file 2, archival unit 75. See also Zdeněk Fierlinger, *Zrada československé buržoazie a jejích spojenců* (Prague: Nakladatelství Mír, 1951).

207. Schmidt, *Hitler's Interpreter*, 106.

208. *DBFP*, 3d series, vol. 2, document no. 1180, 597.

209. Ibid., document no. 1181, 598.

210. Ibid., document no. 1184, 599.

211. Ibid., document no. 1194, 604 and document no. 1198, 606–7.

212. NA 760F.62/1268, Alexander Kirk, the U.S. Embassy, Moscow, to the Secretary of State, Washington, D.C., 28 September 1938.

213. *DBFP*, 3d series, vol. 2, document no. 1214, 617.

214. Kvaček et al., *Československý rok*, 219.

215. Schmidt, *Hitler's Interpreter*, 109.

216. Dr. Hubert Masařík, a Czechoslovak Foreign Ministry official, served as Foreign Minister Kamil Krofta's *chef de cabinet*. Description of the Munich conference, as perceived by the two Czechoslovak emissaries, is based, unless indicated otherwise, on Hubert Masařík's notes taken at the Regina Hotel around 4 A.M. on 30 September 1938 (MHA-B, box 1) and on his, "Hrstka dojmů z konference mnichovské" broadcast on Radio Prague, 29 September 1943. Its text is in MHA-B, box 266. Another source is Vojtěch Mastný, "Vzpomínka na Mnichov," 26 September 1943, MHA-B, box 266. Because they were not invited to take part in the conference itself, Masařík and Mastný could report only on developments outside the Führerhaus. Although their recollections had to pass Nazi censors in 1943, they are remarkably balanced and, it would seem, accurate.

217. SCA, the protocols of the 18th Czechoslovak government, 23 September–4 October 1938. Beran was secretary general of the Republican party and prime minister from November 1938 to March 1939.

218. Ibid.

219. AMFA, Fierlinger to Krofta, secret, 29 September 1938.

220. Radomír Luža, the son of a senior Czechoslovak general, in "Munich 1938," *East Central Europe*, parts 1–2, vol. 8 (1981): 77; also MHA-B, Fond Palkovský, "Pro memoria."

221. MHA-B, Fond Munich, box 1. Beneš listed the following generals as the participants in the meeting that took place on 29 September 1938: Luža, Prchala, Vojcechovský, and Krejčí. The encounter between Beneš and the four generals is assumed to have taken place around noon on 30 September 1938; see, for instance, Drtina, *Československo*, 182. But Beneš's own record of the meeting clearly states that the meeting was on 29 September 1938.

222. For Beneš's keen interest in modern warfare, see Drtina, *Československo*, 37–38.

223. R. W. Seton-Watson, "Godesberg and Munich" (London: Favil Press, n.d.), in MHA-B, box 9.

224. Schmidt, *Hitler's Interpreter*, 110.

225. Ibid., 114–15.

226. Wheeler-Bennett, *Munich*, 174.

227. Shirer, *Rise and Fall*, 418.

228. SCA, the protocols of the 18th Czechoslovak government.

229. Kvaček, *Československý rok,* 225.

230. Included were Milan Hodža, Rudolf Beran, and Josef Černý for the Republican (Agrarian) party; František Ježek for the National unity; Antonín Hampl, Rudolf Bechyně, and Ivan Dérer for the Social Democratic party; Jan Šrámek for the People's party; Emil Franke for the Czechoslovak National Socialist party; Rudolf Mlčoch for the Small Businessmen party; and František Hodač for the National Democratic party.

231. The timing of this call is from Aleksandrovsky's "Miunkhen," 128–42.

232. Ibid., 142.

233. Drtina, *Československo,* 181–82.

234. SCA, the protocols of the 18th Czechoslovak government.

235. AMFA, the Safe, secret, 138.589/1938.

236. SCA, the protocols of the 18th Czechoslovak government.

237. *Dokumenty k historii mnichovského diktátu,* 328.

238. AMFA, the Safe, secret, 138.589/1938; MHA-B, Fond Munich, box 1b. In contrast to Newton, de Lacroix seemed to have some sympathy for the Czechoslovak cause and the position of Beneš. Although he always behaved strictly in accordance with instructions from Quai d'Orsay, de Lacroix's wife told Smutný that her husband hated his job and felt ashamed of having to represent French policy to Prague. After he had retired from the post in Prague, de Lacroix told Smutný that Bonnet was "deceitful."

239. *Dokumenty k historii mnichovského diktátu,* 328.

240. *Lidové noviny,* 1 October 1938.

241. *Dokumenty k historii mnichovského diktátu,* 325.

242. ACC CPC, Fond KI 20, file 85, Gottwald's statement before the Executive Committee of the Communist International of 26 December 1938.

243. MHA-B, box 6, 30 September, 10:00 A.M., telephonogram from deputies Josef David, Vlastimil Klíma, Ladislav Rašín, Ferdinand Richter, Monsignor Stašek, Jaroslav Stránský, Deputy Toušek, and Josef Tykal.

244. ACC CPC, Fond KI 20, file 85, Gottwald's statement before the Executive Committee of the Communist International of 26 December 1938.

245. Alfred Ressel, "Mnichov ve vzpomínkách a v kritice důstojníka generálního štábu československé armády," *Historie a vojenství* 2 (1969): 323.

246. Havel, the Manuscript, 174.

247. AMFA, the Safe, secret, 138.589/1938.

248. MHA-B, box 13, the "O" Service, that is, *odposlechová služba* (monitoring service).

249. ANM-M, record "pro domo" of Mastný's conversation with Göring on 3 October. The marshal added that Berlin would like to see Mastný as the next Czechoslovak president: "Sie müssen die Regierung in der Tschechei übernehmen" (You must take over the Czechoslovak government).

250. ANM-S, box 38, Smutný's entry for 2 October 1938.

251. AMFA, Zdeněk Fierlinger, the Czechoslovak Legation, Moscow, to the Ministry of Foreign Affairs, Prague, telegrams received 1037/38, 3 October 1938.

252. *Rudé Právo,* 6 October 1938.

253. *Rudé Právo,* 11 September 1945.

254. ACC CPC, Fond 100/24, archival unit 729. The speech appeared in Russian as "J. V. Stalin i chekhoslovatskii narod," in *Za prochnyi mir, za narodnuyu demokratsiyu,* 21 December 1949, 5. On the timing of the Gottwald-Stalin and Gottwald-Beneš interviews, see Igor Lukes, "Stalin and Beneš at the End of September 1938: New Evidence from the Prague Archives," *Slavic Review* 52 (spring 1993): 31–34.

255. Efforts to gain access to the so-called Presidential Archives in Moscow have been in vain.

256. *Dokumenty k historii mnichovského diktátu*, 233.

257. In addition to Gottwald, the group received by Beneš included Dr. Stránský, Josef David, Msgre Stašek, Josef Tykal, Deputy Richter, Dr. Rašín, and Dr. Klíma.

258. ACC CPC, Fond 57, signature 329. The record was prepared by Josef David because Beneš was not taking notes on this occasion.

259. MHA-B, notes for manuscripts, box 10a. Record of Beneš's conversation (probably with Smutný) of 21 October 1947. The record was typed the next day.

260. Beneš, *Memoirs of Dr. Eduard Beneš* (Boston: Houghton Mifflin, 1954), 42: *"In September . . . we were left in military, as well as in political, isolation with the Soviet Union to prepare our defence against a Nazi attack."* [Emphasis is in the original.]

261. Dimitrov to Manuilski, Moskvin, Kuusinen on 2 October 1938. See Dimitrov, *Georgi Dimitrov. Pisma, 1905–1949* (Sofia: Izd. na BKP, 1962); telegrams nos. 6, 9, 10, 11, 14, 17, and 18 cover the period from 14 September through 26 October 1938. They were published in "Pokyny Jiřího Dimitrova k činnosti komunistické Internacionály na pomoc ČSR proti fašismu" *Příspěvky k dějinám KSČ* 6 (December 1963), 860–82; the statement is on p. 869.

262. "Pokyny Jiřího Dimitrova," 880.

263. ACC CPC, Fond 100/45, vol. 15, archival unit 263. The handwritten notes were taken by Václav Kopecký, no date. The Munich conference was a serious setback for the Comintern, Dimitrov admitted, but it would be only a temporary one. In the future Dimitrov perceived great difficulties, but also much promise.

264. NA 860F.001/106, Irving N. Linnell, U.S. Consul in Prague, to the Secretary of State, the Protectorate of Bohemia and Moravia, 20 November 1939.

265. SCA, the Interior Ministry, 1936–40, X/K/26, 225–1056, the Police Directorate to the Ministry, 9 December 1938.

266. ANM-S, box 8, 14 December 1938.

267. See Jacques Rupnik, "Le parti communiste de Tchécoslovaquie face à Munich," *Revue des Études Slaves* 1–2 (1979): 193–202.

268. ACC CPC, Fond KI 20, file 85. The copy is marked "Presidium of the Executive, Communist International," 9516/4. It seems to be a transcript, not the full text, of Gottwald's speech.

269. B. Lazitch, "Stalin's Massacre of the Foreign Communist Leaders," in *The Comintern: Historical Highlights, Essays, Recollections, Documents*, ed. M. M. Drachkovitch and B. Lazitch (New York: Praeger, 1966).

270. MHA-B, notes for manuscripts, box 10a. Beneš's record of his conversation with Gottwald in September 1945.

271. George Kennan, *From Prague after Munich* (Princeton: Princeton University Press, 1968), 7.

272. Without doubt, the Munich Agreement discredited the West and enhanced the standing of the Soviet Union. This helped the Communist party of Czechoslovakia gain power between 1945 and 1948. But the brutal purges of the party leadership in the early 1950s allow the argument that, ultimately, the CPC also failed to profit from the imposition of Stalin's control over Central Europe. Although Gottwald survived the purge, he was scarred by it for the rest of his life.

273. Seton-Watson, "Godesberg and Munich."

274. MHA-B, box 1, contains a thick file of letters mailed to Beneš from Great Britain, urging him to fight the Third Reich and alleging that the British public was on his side. They seem hardly representative. The supportive resolutions were issued by the "Ethical Union,"

"World League against Vivisection," "Communist Party of Great Britain," "Spanish Medical Aid Committee," "National Clarion Cycling Club," "National Union of Clerks and Administrative Workers" (this one in Esperanto), and "The Young Communist League."

275. Feiling, *Life of Neville Chamberlain*, 452.

276. MHA-B, box 13. Jan Masaryk, the Czechoslovak Legation, London, to the Ministry of Foreign Affairs, Prague, telegrams received 1190/38, 20 October 1938.

277. Wheeler-Bennett, *Munich*, 179.

278. Weinberg has made the argument that even Hitler believed the Munich Agreement was a failure. See *The Foreign Policy of Hitler's Germany*, 463. "We ought to have gone to war in 1938," he said. See Hugh R. Trevor-Roper (ed.), *The Testament of Adolf Hitler: The Hitler: Bormann Documents* (London: Cassell, 1961), 84–85.

279. ACC CPC, Fond 100, inventory number 24, file 172, archival unit 1524.

280. Compton Mackenzie, *Dr. Beneš* (London: G. G. Harrap, 1946), 322.

281. Beneš to Smutný, Aston Abbots, 23 June 1941; in *Dokumenty z historie československé republiky, 1939–1945*, ed. Libuše Otáhalová and Milada Červinková (Prague: Academia, 1936), 2:235.

282. Beneš to Smutný, Aston Abbots, 23 June 1941, ibid., 234.

283. MHA-B, box 6, Minister Krno's notes of 20 September 1938 on his meetings with the ministers of Belgium, Greece, Bulgaria, Italy, and the United States.

284. ANM-D, box 4. Beneš summed up his reasons for accepting the Munich *Diktat* in thirteen points.

285. This is forcefully argued by Jan Patočka in *Was sind die Tschechen: Kleiner Tatsachenbericht und Erklärungsversuch* (Prague: Panoráma, 1992).

286. See, for instance, the testimony of Václav Černý, who spoke with Beneš at Sezimovo Ústí on 12 March 1948, in *Vývoj a zločiny panslavismu* (Prague: Institut pro středoevropskou Kulturu a Politiku, 1995), 128–31.

SOURCES AND
BIBLIOGRAPHY

Research for this book was conducted mainly in various archives in Prague and in the National Archives, Washington, D.C., as well as in Suitland, Maryland. The Prague archives contain primary evidence on Czechoslovak diplomatic activities during the interwar period; they also allow insight into the workings of the Soviet foreign affairs establishment before World War II. This is not a coincidence. As a result of World War I, the Bolshevik revolution, and the activities of the Czechoslovak legions in Russia, tens of thousands of Czechoslovak citizens came into direct contact with Soviet Russia. Officers and soldiers of the legions were being repatriated for years after the Great War had ended. Therefore, even before Czechoslovakia and the Soviet Union had recognized each other, the two countries had to negotiate. Under one cover or another, Prague and Moscow maintained channels of communication from the moment the Bolsheviks seized power. It is a testament to such contacts that the State Central Archives in Prague now have remarkable collections of important documents on Soviet Russia and the Soviet Union before World War II.

The growth of Prague into a major center for Russian and Soviet studies was also enabled by President Thomas G. Masaryk. He was perhaps the best informed among world-class politicians when it came to matters Russian and Soviet. He had traveled in Russia both under the Old Regime and during the Civil War, and he had personally dealt with leading Russian and Soviet politicians. In the 1920s, the president's Russian library was among the best resources of its kind in the world. And Masaryk's interest in Russian and Soviet affairs set the tone for other politicians, intellectuals, and journalists in Czechoslovakia before World War II.

In the aftermath of the Russian revolution in 1917, Prague became a way-station for tens of thousands of Russian refugees escaping from the Bolsheviks. Some chose to stay in Czechoslovakia, but others moved on to Paris and other destinations in the West. Those who settled in Prague left behind documents and manuscripts and formed organizations which published newspapers and journals. In 1922 the Czechoslovak parliament had decreed the creation of the Slavic Institute in Prague. Although its collections were looted by the NKVD at the end of World War II, the institute survived all the upheavals of Czechoslovak history, and it remains now a rich resource on Soviet affairs before the war. Some of the evidence on the Tukhachevsky affair (chapter 4) is derived from the institute's library.

Furthermore, soon after the emergence of independent Czechoslovakia, Deputy Foreign Minister Václav Girsa invited the historian Jan Slavík, a specialist in Russian and Soviet affairs, to build up the Russian historical archive within the organizational structure of the Foreign Ministry. Slavík accepted the invitation and went on to fulfill Girsa's wish that whoever "wanted to study the Russian revolution would have to come to Prague." Professor Slavík traveled to Russia as frequently as possible and became one of the most perceptive commentators on Soviet affairs. The materials he collected at the Foreign Ministry in Prague are another important source for scholars dealing with Soviet history.

Finally, the draconian anti-Comintern and anti-Communist measures in the Third Reich made Czechoslovakia an attractive base for Comintern and Soviet intelligence operations in Central Europe. This resulted in frequent attacks on Czechoslovakia by its neighbors for being tolerant of Bolshevik plotting. To take the sting out of this charge, the Prague government attempted to run counterintelligence operations against the Communist party of Czechoslovakia, against the Comintern activities within its jurisdiction, and against any organization that could be considered sympathetic to Moscow. Historians can now learn from all the materials gathered by the responsible agencies of the Czechoslovak government in pursuit of their tasks.

Following is a list of archives in which I started working soon after the fall of the old regime in Prague.

Archives of the Central Committee of the Communist Party of Czechoslovakia
Fond 19/5, Presidium and Secretariat
Fond 20, Comintern Materials from the Soviet Union
Fond 54, Jan Šverma Archive
Fond 55, Bohumír Šmeral Archive
Fond 56, Antonín Zápotocký Archive
Fond 56/2, Marie Zápotocká Archive
Fond 57, "The Young Gottwald" Archive
Fond 60, Václav Nosek Archive
Fond 93, André Simone Archive
Fond 100/24, Klement Gottwald Archive
Fond 100/45, Václav Kopecký Archive
Fond 115, CPC Leadership in Moscow during World War II

Archives of the Ministry of Foreign Affairs
AMFA, 1935–1938
The 'O' Service (Telephone tapping service)
Records of the Russian Red Cross Mission
The Safe (sensitive political reports)
Second Section Archive

Archives of the Ministry of Interior
Various numbered files

Archives of the National Museum
Prokop Drtina Archive
Zdeněk Fierlinger Archive
Jaromír Smutný Archive

Military Historical Archives, Invalidovna
The Beneš Archive
The Military Office of the President of the Republic

Office of the President of the Republic of Czechoslovakia
Record of Presidential Audiences for 1936, 1937, 1938, 1939
Reports from the Czechoslovak Legation in Bucharest
Reports from the Czechoslovak Legation in Moscow
Reports from the Czechoslovak Legation in Vienna
Reports from the Czechoslovak Legation in Washington

State Central Archives at Loreta
Archive of Newspaper Clippings
Ministry of the Interior, Presidium
Ministry of National Security
Police Directorate
Postal and Experimental Institute (Telephone tapping service)

Published Documents

Most of the evidence offered in this book comes from various Czechoslovak and American archives. In addition, references can also be found to some published collections of diplomatic documents, mostly German and British. The following is a list of relevant sources in this category.

Das Abkommen von München: Tschechoslowakische diplomatische Dokumente 1937–1939, edited by Václav Král. Prague: Academia, 1968.
The Communist International, edited by Jane Degras. London: F. Cass, 1971.
Documents diplomatiques français, 1932–1939, 2d series. Paris: Imprimerie Nationale, 1963.
Documents on British Foreign Policy, 1919–1939, 2d and 3d series. London: Her Majesty's Stationery Office, 1949–.
Documents on German Foreign Policy, 1918–1945, series D (1937–1945). Washington, D.C.: United States Government Printing Office, 1949.
Documents on International Affairs, 1938, edited by the Royal Institute of International Affairs. London: Oxford University Press, 1939.
Dokumenty a materiály k dějinám československo-sovětských vztahů [Documents and materials on Czechoslovak-Soviet relations], edited by Čestmír Amort et al. Prague: Academia, 1975–79.
Dokumenty i materiali po istorii sovietsko-chekhoslovatskikh otnoshenii, edited by P. N. Pospelov et al. Moscow: Nauka, 1973–78.
Dokumenty k historii Mnichovského diktátu, 1937–1939 [Documents on the history of the Munich Diktat], edited by Dušan Spáčil et al. Prague: Svoboda, 1979.
Dokumenty k otázce spojenectví s SSSR [Documents regarding the alliance with the

Soviet Union]. Prague: Společnost Pro Kulturní a Hospodářské Styky se SSSR, 1938.

Dokumenty po istorii Miunkhenskogo sgovora: 1937–1939, edited by V. F. Maltsev. Moscow: Izdatelstvo Politicheskoi Literatury, 1979.

Dokumenty vneshnei politiky SSSR, edited by Komisia po Izdaniiu Diplomaticheskikh Dokumentov. Moscow: Izdatelstvo Politicheskoi Literatury, 1977.

Dokumenty z historie československé republiky, 1939–1943 [Documents on Czechoslovak history, 1939–1943], edited by Libuše Otáhalová and Milada Červinková. Prague: Academia, 1966.

Dokumenty: Depeše mezi Prahou a Moskvou 1939–1941 [Radio messages between Prague and Moscow, 1939–1941], edited by Gustav Bareš. *Příspěvky k Dějinám KSČ* 7, 3, (1967): 375–433.

Foreign Relations of the United States: Diplomatic Papers. Washington, D.C.: U.S. Government Printing Office, 1922–.

Germany and Czechoslovakia, 1918–1945: Documents on German Policies, edited by Koloman Gajan and Robert Kvaček. Prague: Orbis, 1965.

Monachium 1938: Polskie dokumenty dyplomatyczne [Munich 1938: Polish diplomatic documents], edited by Zbigniew Landau and Jerzy Tomaszewski. Warsaw: Państwowe Wydawnictwo Naukowe, 1985.

New Documents on the History of Munich, edited by V. F. Klochko et al. Prague: Orbis, 1958.

Nové dokumenty k historii Mnichova [New documents on the history of Munich], edited by V. F. Klochko et al. Prague: Státní Nakladatelství Politické Literatury, 1958.

Parliamentary Debates, House of Commons. London: His Majesty's Stationery Office, 1937–38.

Protifašistický a národně osvobozenecký boj českého a slovenského lidu 1938–1945 [The anti-fascist and national liberation struggle of Czech and Slovak people, 1938–1945]. Prague: Ústav Marxismu-Leninismu ÚV KSČ, 1979.

Soviet Documents on Foreign Policy, 1917–1941, edited by Jane Degras. London: Oxford University Press, 1951–53.

SSSR v borbe za mir na kanune vtoroi mirovoi voiny, edited by A. A. Gromyko. Moscow: Politizdat, 1971.

Trial of the Major War Criminals before the International Military Tribunal, Nuremberg, 1945–46. Nuremberg: International Military Tribunal, 1947–49.

Září 1938: Dokumenty k událostem v západočeském a jihočeském pohraničí [September 1938: Documents regarding the situation in western and southern Bohemian borderlands]. *Historie a vojenství* 2 (1967): 303–50.

Selected Periodicals

Čas
České Slovo
Československá republika
Deutsche Zeitung Bohemia
Deutsche Zentral-Zeitung
Důstojnické listy
Frankfurter Allgemeine
Gazeta Polska
Izvestia

Journal de Moscou
Krasnaya Zvezda
Kurjer Polski
Kurjer Warszawski
Lidové noviny
Národní listy
Národní osvobození
Národní politika
New Times
Nowa Rzeczpospolita
Prager Tagblatt
Prager Presse
Pravda
Právo lidu
Přítomnost
Reportér
Rudé právo
Rudý večerník
Sborník zahraniční politiky
The Evening Standard
The New York Times
The Times
Venkov
Voyennaya Mysl'
Znamia Rossii

Selected Literature

The following is a selection of sources used in this book, as well as those that might be relevant for further research.

Abramov, Nikolai. "Případ Tuchačevskij: Nová verze" [The Tukhachevsky case: A new interpretation]. *Nová doba* 13 (1989): 37–39.

Ádám, Magda. "La Hongrie et la Tchécoslovaquie." *Revue des Études Slaves* 1–2 (1979): 41–50.

Ádám, Magda. *The Little Entente and Europe, 1920–1929.* Budapest: Akadémiai Kiadó, 1993.

Ádám, Magda. "Maďarsko a Malá dohoda v údobí před druhou světovou válkou (1937–1938)" [Hungary and the Little Entente before World War II]. *Československý časopis historický* 11 (1963): 742–58.

Ádám, Magda. *Richtung, Selbstvernichtung: Die kleine Entente 1920–1938.* Budapest: Corvina, 1988.

Ádám, Magda (ed.). "Documents relatifs à la politique étrangère de la Hongrie dans la péroide de la crise tchécoslovaque (1938–1939)." *Acta Historica* 10, 1–2 (1963): 89–116 and 11, 3–4 (1964): 373–91.

Adamthwaite, Anthony P. "Le facteur militaire dans la decision franco-britannique avant Munich." *Revue des Études Slaves* 1–2 (1979): 51–58.

Adamthwaite, Anthony P. *France and the Coming of the Second World War, 1936–1939.* London: Frank Cass, 1977.

Adamthwaite, Anthony P. *Grandeur and Decline: France, 1914–1940.* Sevenoaks: E. Arnold, 1992.

Alexander, Martin S. *The Republic in Danger: General Maurice Gamelin and the Politics of French Defense.* New York: Cambridge University Press, 1992.

Alexandrov, Victor. *Les jours de la trahison: L'Histoire secrète de Munich.* Paris: Denoel, 1975.

Amerling, Karel. "Vzpomínka z gymnásia" [A high-school recollection]. In *50 let Dra Edvarda Beneše* [50 years of Edvard Beneš]. Prague: Pokrok—Čs. Obec Legionářská, 1934.

Amort, Čestmír, et al. *Přehled československo-sovětských vztahů v údobí 1917–1939* [A review of Czechoslovak-Soviet relations, 1917–1939]. Prague: Academia, 1975.

Andrew, Christopher and Oleg Gordievsky. *KGB: The Inside Story.* New York: Harper-Collins, 1990.

Anger, Jan. *Mnichov 1938.* Prague: Svoboda, 1988.

Armstrong, Hamilton Fish. *La fausse paix: L'Armistice de Munich.* Paris: Jouve, 1939.

Atlee, Clement. *As It Happened.* London: W. Heinemann, 1954.

Azema, Jean-Pierre. *From Munich to the Liberation, 1938–1944.* New York: Cambridge University Press, 1984.

Baker, Vaughan Burdin. "Selective Inattention: The Runciman Mission to Czechoslovakia, 1938." *East European Quarterly* 24 (January 1990): 425–45.

Bartel, Heinrich. *Frankreich und die Sowjetunion 1938–1940: Ein Beitrag zur französischen Ostpolitik zwischen dem Münchner Abkommen und dem Ende der Dritten Republik.* Stuttgart: F. Steiner, 1986.

Batowski, Henryk. *Austria i Sudety, 1919–1938: Zabor Austrii i przygotowanie agresji na Czechoslowacje* [Austria and the Sudetenland, 1919–1939: The *Anschluß* of Austria and preparations for aggression against Czechoslovakia]. Poznań: Wydawnictwo Poznańskie, 1968.

Batowski, Henryk. *Europa zmierza ku przepaści* [Europe moves toward the abyss]. Poznań: Wydawnictwo Poznańskie, 1977.

Batowski, Henryk. *Kryzys dyplomatyczny w Europie: Jesien 1938–wiosna 1939* [The diplomatic crisis in Europe from the spring of 1938 to the fall of 1939]. Warsaw: Wydawnictwo Ministerstwa Obrony Narodowej, 1962.

Batowski, Henryk. *Rok 1938: Dwie agresje Hitlerowskie* [The year 1938: Two aggressions by Hitler]. Poznań: Wydawnictwo Poznańskie, 1985.

Batowski, Henryk. *Z polityky międzynarodowej XX. wieku: Wybor studiów z lat 1930–1975* [International politics of the twentieth century: A selection of studies]. Cracow: Wydawnictwo Literackie, 1979.

Batowski, Henryk. *Zrada Monachijska: Sprawa Czechoslowacji i diplomacja europejska w roku 1938* [The Munich betrayal: Czechoslovakia and European diplomacy in 1938]. Poznań: Wydawnictwo Poznańskie, 1973.

Batowski, Henryk (ed.). *Irredenta Niemecka w Europie Śródkowej i Poludniowo-Wschodniej przed II Wojną Światową* [The German irredenta in Central and South-East Europe prior to World War II]. Katowice and Cracow: Państwowe Wydawnictwo Naukowe, 1971.

Baturin, M. *SShA i Miunkhen; iz istorii amerikanskoi vneshnei politiki 1937–1939 gg.* Moscow: Izdatelstvo Mezhdunarodnykh Otnoshenii, 1961.

Bavendamm, Dirk. *Roosevelts Weg zum Krieg: Amerikanische Politik, 1914–1939.* Munich: Herbig, 1983.

Baynes, Norman H. (ed.) *The Speeches of Adolf Hitler, April 1922–August 1939*. London: Oxford University Press, 1942.

Bechyně, Rudolf. *Pero mi zůstalo, 1938–1945* [I still have my pen]. Prague: Dělnické Nakladatelství, 1948.

Beck, Józef. *Dernier report: Politique polonaise 1926–1939*. Neuchatel: Éditions de Baconnerie, 1951.

Beck, Józef. "Příčiny války 1939" [Causes of war, 1939]. *Reportér* 6 (1991): 1–4.

Beck, Robert J. "Munich's Lessons Reconsidered." *International Security* 14 (fall 1989): 161–92.

Beer, Siegfried. *Der "unmoralische" Anschluß: Britische Österreichpolitik zwischen Containment und Appeasement, 1931–1934*. Vienna: Bohlau, 1988.

Bellstedt, Hans F. *"Apaisement" oder Krieg: Frankreichs Außenminister Georges Bonnet und die deutsch-französische Erklärung vom 6. Dezember 1938*. Bonn: Bouvier, 1993.

Beloff, Max. *The Foreign Policy of Soviet Russia, 1929–1941*. London: Oxford University Press, 1947.

Ben-Arie, Katriel. "Czechoslovakia at the Time of 'Munich': The Military Situation." *Journal of Contemporary History* 25 (October 1990): 431–47.

Beneš, Bohumil, and Janko Šuhaj (eds.). *Bitva o Československo v britském veřejném mínění: K třetímu výročí mnichovské dohody* [The battle for Czechoslovakia in the British public opinion: The third anniversary of the Munich agreement]. London: Čechoslovák, 1941.

Beneš, Edvard. *Anšlus nebo nová Evropa? Výklad čsl. ministra zahraničních věcí Edvarda Beneše v zahraničním výboru poslanecké sněmovny a senátu dne 23. dubna 1931* [Anschluß or a new Europe? A speech by the Czechoslovak foreign minister Edvard Beneš before the foreign committee of the House and Senate of 23 April 1931]. Prague: Orbis, 1931.

Beneš, Edvard. *Armáda, brannost národa a obrana státu* [The army, national preparedness and the defense of the state]. Prague: Svaz Důstojnictva, n.d., probably 1937.

Beneš, Edvard. *Der Aufstand der Nationen: der Weltkrieg und die tschechoslowakische Revolution*. Berlin: B. Cassirer, 1928.

Beneš, Edvard. *Boj za mír a bezpečnost státu* [The struggle for peace and national security]. Prague: Orbis, 1934.

Beneš, Edvard. *Building a New Europe*. London: Peace Book Co., 1939.

Beneš, Edvard. *Demokratická armáda, pacifism a zahraniční politika* [Democratic army, pacifism, and foreign policy]. Prague: Orbis, 1932.

Beneš, Edvard. *The Diplomatic Struggle for European Security and the Stabilization of Peace*. Prague: Orbis, 1925.

Beneš, Edvard. *Je možný trvalý mír?* [Is permanent peace possible?] Prague: No publisher, 1931.

Beneš, Edvard. *Masaryk's Path and Legacy: Funeral Oration*. Prague: No publisher, 1937.

Beneš, Edvard. *Memoirs: From Munich to New War and New Victory*. Boston: Houghton Mifflin, 1954.

Beneš, Edvard. *Mnichovské dny* [Memoirs of the Munich era]. Prague: Svoboda, 1968.

Beneš, Edvard. *Nesnáze demokracie* [Problems of democracy]. Prague: Nákladem Svazu Národního Osvobození, 1924.

Beneš, Edvard. *Práce za československou samostatnost* [Working for Czechoslovakia's independence]. Prague: Státní Nakladatelství, 1928.

Beneš, Edvard. *The Problem of Central Europe and the Austrian Question*. Prague: Orbis, 1934.

Beneš, Edvard. *Problémy nové Evropy a zahraniční politika Československá: Projevy a úvahy z r. 1919–1924* [The Problems of new Europe and Czechoslovak foreign policy: speeches and commentaries, 1919–1924]. Prague: Melantrich, 1924.

Beneš, Edvard. *Rede an die Deutschen in der ČSR.* Prague: E. Franzel, 1935.

Beneš, Edvard. *La revolution allemande et la nouvelle phase de la politique europeene. Les questions économiques de l'Europe centrale.* Prague: Orbis, 1933.

Beneš, Edvard. *La situation de l'Europe, la Société des nations et la Tchécoslovaquie.* Prague: Orbis, 1930.

Beneš, Edvard. *The Struggle for Collective Security in Europe and the Italo-Abyssinian War.* Prague: Orbis, 1935.

Beneš, Edvard. "Vánoční projev presidenta republiky" [Christmas message by the president of the republic]. *Zahraniční politika* 16, 10–11 (1937): 553–57.

Ben-Villada, Gene H. "No More Munichs! What the Media Won't Tell." *Monthly Review* 39 (April 1988): 9–22.

Berber, Friedrich. *Europhäische Politik 1933–1938 im Spiegel der Prager Akten.* Essen: Essener Verlagsanstalt, 1942.

Bernas, Franciszek. *Fall Grün.* Warsaw: Krajowa Agencja Wydawnictwa, 1984.

Bittman, Ladislav. *Špionážní oprátky* [The noose of espionage]. Prague: Mladá Fronta, 1992.

Bláha, Sylvestr. *Branná politika a demokracie* [Defense policy and democracy]. Prague: Svaz Československého Důstojnictva, 1933.

Bláha, Sylvestr. *Co dal Masaryk armádě a brannosti národa* [What Masaryk bequeathed the army and the military preparedness of the nation]. Prague: Naše Vojsko, 1990.

Bláha, Sylvestr (ed.). *Dvacet let čs. armády* [Twenty years of the Czechoslovak army]. Prague: Svaz Československého Důstojnictva, 1938.

Blodig, Vojtěch. *Boj proti fašismu a na obranu republiky, 1933–1938* [The struggle against fascism and in defense of the republic, 1933–1938]. Prague: FÚV Československého Svazu Protifašistických Bojovníků, 1982.

Blodig, Vojtěch et al. *Mnichov 1938.* Prague: Svaz Protifašistických Bojovníků, 1988.

Boháč, Antonín. *Obyvatelstvo v Československé republice* [Population in Czechoslovakia]. Prague: Čs. Vlastivěda, 1936.

Bolen, Václav. "Gottwald kopíruje Ercoliho" [Gottwald imitates Ercolli]. *Sobota* 7 (February 1936): 176.

Bonnet, Georges. *De Munich à la guerre.* Paris: Plon, 1967.

Bonnet, Georges. *La Défense de la Paix, 1936–1940.* Geneva: Les Éditions du Cheval Ailé, 1946.

Borek, Vladimír. "Dvacet let Rudé armády" [Twenty years of the Red Army]. *Praha-Moskva* 3 (February 1938): 5–8.

Borsody, Stephen. *Beneš.* Budapest: Athenaeum, 193?.

Borsody, Stephen. *The Tragedy of Central Europe: Nazi and Soviet Conquest and Aftermath.* New Haven: Yale Russian and East European Publications, 1980.

Bosl, Karl. *Die erste tschechoslowakische Republik als multinationaler Parteienstaat.* Munich: Oldenbourg, 1979.

Bosl, Karl (ed.). *Die deutsch-tschechoslowakischen Beziehungen von ihren Anfängen bis zum Ausgang der Ära Stresemann, 1918–1929.* Munich: Oldenbourg, 1975.

Bouček, Jaroslav. "Josef Guttmann, Záviš Kalandra, Odhalené tajemství moskevského procesu" [The truth regarding the trial in Moscow]. *Slovanský přehled* 78, 1 (1992): 61–66.

Břach, Radko. "Edvard Beneš, ministr zahraničí" [Edvard Beneš: Minister of Foreign Affairs]. *Historické studie* 12 (January 1989): 3–26.

Břach, Radko. "Francouzský alianční systém" [The French alliance system]. *Historie a vojenství* 1 (1968): 1–21.

Břach, Radko. "Locarno a československá diplomacie" [Locarno and the Czechoslovak diplomacy]. *Československý časopis historický* 8 (1960): 662–95.

Břach, Radko. "'Ruský problém' v čs. zahraniční politice na počátku roku 1924" ['The Russian problem' in the Czechoslovak foreign policy at the beginning of 1924]. *Československý časopis historický* 15, 1 (1968).

Břachová, Věra. "Francouzská mise v Československu" [The French mission in Czechoslovakia]. *Historie a vojenství* 6 (1967): 883–910.

Braddick, Henderson B. *Germany, Czechoslovakia, and the "Grand Alliance" in the May Crisis, 1938.* Denver: University of Denver Press, 1969.

Brandejs, Stanislav. "Význam československo-sovětské obchodní smlouvy" [The importance of the Czechoslovak-Soviet commercial agreement]. *Zahraniční politika* 14, 3 (1935).

Brisch, Hans, and Ivan Volgyes. *Czechoslovakia: The Heritage of Ages Past.* Boulder: East European Quarterly, 1979.

Brod, Toman, and Jiří Doležal. *Nastal čas boje* [It's time to fight]. Prague: Naše Vojsko, 1965.

Broszat, Martin. "Das sudetendeutsche Freikorps." *Vierteljahrshefte für Zeitgeschichte* 9 (January 1961): 30–49.

Brügel, Johann W. *Czechoslovakia before Munich: The German Minority Problem and British Appeasement Policy.* Cambridge: Cambridge University Press, 1973.

Brügel, Johann W. "Der Runciman Bericht." *Vierteljahrshefte für Zeitgeschichte* 26, 4 (1978): 652–59.

Brügel, Johann W. "Dr. Beneš on the Soviet 'Offer of Help' in 1938." *East Central Europe* 4, 1 (1977): 56–59.

Brügel, Johann W. "Remarks on the Roundtable 'Munich from the Czech Perspective.'" *East Central Europe* 10, 1–2 (1983): 158–64.

Brügel, Johann W. *Tschechen und Deutsche, 1918–1938.* Munich: Nymphenburger Verlagshandlung, 1967.

Brügel, Johann W. (comp.). *Stalin und Hitler: Pakt gegen Europa.* Vienna: Europaverlag, 1973.

Butler, J. R. M. *Lord Lothian, 1882–1940.* London: Macmillan, 1960.

Čada, Václav. *Stratégia a taktika KSČ v rokoch 1921–1938* [Strategy and tactics of the Communist party of Czechoslovakia]. Bratislava: Pravda, 1982.

Cameron, Ronald. *Appeasement and the Road to War.* Glasgow: Pulse, 1991.

Campbell, F. Gregory. "Central Europe's Bastion of Democracy." *East European Quarterly* 11 (summer 1977): 155–76.

Campbell, F. Gregory. *Confrontation in Central Europe: Weimar Germany and Czechoslovakia.* Chicago: University of Chicago Press, 1975.

Carsten, F. L. "Munich and After: New Documents from Prague." *Slavonic and East European Review* 47, 109 (1969): 524–27.

Cattell, David. *Communism and the Spanish Civil War.* Berkeley: University of California Press, 1955.

Celovsky, Boris. *Das münchener Abkommen 1938.* Stuttgart: Deutsche Verlagsanstalt, 1958.

Ceplair, Larry. *Under the Shadow of War.* New York: Columbia University Press, 1987.

Černý, Rudolf. *Antonín Novotný: pozdní obhajoba.* Prague: Kiezler, 1992.

Černý, Václav. *Pláč koruny české* [The Lament of the Crown of Bohemia]. Toronto: Sixty-Eight Publishers, 1977.

Černý, Václav. *Vývoj a zločiny panslavismu* [The evolution and crimes of panslavism]. Prague: Institut pro Středoevropskou Kulturu a Politiku, 1995.

César, Jaroslav. *Mnichov 1938*. Prague: Melantrich, 1978.

César, Jaroslav, and Bohumil Černý. "Německá irredenta a henleinovci v ČSR v létech 1930–1938" [The German irredenta and the Henleinists in Czechoslovakia, 1930–1938]. *Československý časopis historický* 10 (1962): 1–17.

César, Jaroslav, and Bohumil Černý. *Politika německých buržoazních stran v létech 1918– 1938* [The policy of German bourgeois parties, 1918–1938]. Prague: Nakladatelství Československé Akademie Věd, 1962.

Chászár, Edward. *Decision in Vienna: The Czechoslovak-Hungarian Border Dispute of 1938*. Astor, Fla: Danubian Press, 1978.

Chudoba, Bohdan. "The Pattern of Soviet Foreign Policy: Czechoslovakia, May 1938." *Sudeten Bulletin: A Central European Review* 11 (December 1963): 388–96.

Churchill, Winston. *The Gathering Storm*. Boston: Houghton Mifflin, 1948.

Cienciala, Anna M. "Poland and the Munich Crisis, 1938: A Reappraisal." *East European Quarterly* 3 (June 1969): 201–19.

Cienciala, Anna M. *Poland and the Western Powers, 1938–1939: A Study of the Interdependence of Eastern and Western Europe*. London: Routledge, 1968.

Cienciala, Anna M. *Polska polityka zagraniczna w latach 1926–1932* [Polish foreign policy, 1926–1932]. Paris: Instytut Literacki, 1980.

Cienciala, Anna M., and Titus Komarnicki. *From Versailles to Locarno: Keys to Polish Foreign Policy, 1919–25*. Lawrence: University Press of Kansas, 1984.

Čierný, Jan. *Mnichov 1938 a rozbití Československa* [Munich 1938 and the destruction of Czechoslovakia]. Prague: Svaz Protifašistických Bojovníků, 1982.

Císařová, Blanka. "Vznik Československa a Rusko" [The emergence of Czechoslovakia and Russia]. *Historické studie* 24 (January 1989): 4–11.

Cockett, Richard. *Twilight of Truth: Chamberlain, Appeasement, and the Manipulation of the Press*. New York: St. Martin's Press, 1989.

Cohen, Barry Mendel. "Moscow at Munich: Did the Soviet Union Offer Unilateral Aid to Czechoslovakia?" *East European Quarterly* 12 (fall 1978): 341–48.

Colquhoun, James. *Chamberlain Averts Armageddon*. Victoria, B.C.: Colonist Printing, 1938.

Colton, Joel. *Léon Blum: Humanist in Politics*. New York: Knopf, 1966.

Communist International. *Thesen und Beschlüsse*. Basel: Prometheus, 1933.

Cot, Pierre. *L'Armée de l'air 1936–1938*. Paris: Editions Gasset, 1939.

Crabites, Pierre. *Beneš: Statesman of Central Europe*. London: Routledge, 1935.

Craig, Gordon A., and Felix Gilbert. *The Diplomats, 1919–1939*. Princeton: Princeton University Press, 1953.

Crossland, John. "Britain's Air Defenses and the Munich Crisis." *History Today* 38 (March 1988): 40–46.

Daladier, Édouard. *In Defense of France*. New York: Doubleday, 1939.

Daridan, Jean. *Le chemin de la defaite: 1938–1940*. Paris: Plon, 1980.

Dastich, František. "Armáda čekala na rozkaz?" [Was the army ready to march when ordered?]. *Čas* 4 (January 1958).

Davies, Joseph E. *Mission to Moscow*. New York: Simon & Schuster, 1941.

Davies, Norman. *God's Playground*. New York: Columbia University Press, 1982.

De Bedts, Ralph F. *Ambassador Joseph Kennedy, 1938–1940: An Anatomy of Appeasement*. New York: P. Lang, 1985.

Deedes, William. "My Munich." *Spectator*, 4 June 1988, 23–26.

Deml, Ferdinand (ed.). *München 29. September 1938; vorher und nachher.* Bonn: Edition Atlantic-Forum, 1969.

Dennis, Alfred L. P. *The Foreign Policies of Soviet Russia.* New York: Dutton, 1924.

Deutscher, Issac. *Stalin: A Political Biography.* New York: Oxford University Press, 1949.

Dimitrov, Georgi. *Georgi Dimitrov. Pisma, 1905–1949.* Sofia: Izd. na BKP, 1962.

"Dokumenty k otázce spojenectví s SSSR" [Documents on the alliance with the Soviet Union]. *Praha-Moskva* 3 (November 1938): 259–68.

Douděra, Karel. *Jak se rozhoupával zrady zvon* [How the bell of treason was rung]. Prague: Nakladatelství Novinář, 1983.

Douglas, Roy. *In the Year of Munich.* New York: St. Martin's Press, 1977.

Doussy de Sales, Raoul (ed.). *Adolf Hitler: My New Order.* New York: Reynal & Hitchcock, 1941.

Dreifort, John D. *Yvon Delbos at the Quai d'Orsay: French Foreign Policy During the Popular Front, 1936–1938.* Lawrence: University Press of Kansas, 1973.

Drtina, Prokop. *Československo: můj osud* [Czechoslovakia: My fate]. Toronto: Sixty-eight Publishers, 1982.

Duclos, Jacques. "The Soviet Union Defends Peace." *World News and Views,* 13 August 1938, 907–8.

Duda, Petr. "Vzpomínky na události za mobilizace 1938: válečné události na hranicích československo-polských" [Memories regarding the 1938 mobilization: military developments on the Czechoslovak-Polish border]. *Historie a vojenství* 5 (1969): 903–7.

Dunn, David. "Maksim Litvinov: Commissar of Contradiction." *Journal of Contemporary History* 23 (1988): 221–43.

Duroselle, Jean-Baptiste. *La décadence 1932–1939.* Paris: Imprimerie Nationale, 1979.

Dutailly, Henry. *Les Problèmes de l'armée de terre française (1935–1939).* Paris: Imprimerie Nationale, 1980.

Dyck, Harvey L. "German-Soviet Relations and the Anglo-Soviet Break." *Slavic Review* 25 (March 1966).

Dziewanowski, M. K. "Polish-Czechoslovak Confederation (A Polish View)." *Polish Western Association of America* 26, 1–2 (1984): 4–10.

Einstein, Lewis. *A Diplomat Looks Back.* New Haven: Yale University Press, 1968.

Eisenmann, Louis. *Un grand européen: Édouard Beneš.* Paris: P. Hartmann, 1934.

Eisler, Pavel. *Munich: A Retrospect.* Prague: Orbis, 1958.

Erickson, John. *The Soviet High Command.* London: Macmillan, 1962.

Essen, Andrzej. *Polska a Mała Ententa, 1920–1934* [Poland and the Little Entente]. Kracow: Wydawnictwo Naukowe PWN, 1992.

Eubank, Weaver Keith. *Munich.* Norman: University Press of Oklahoma, 1963.

Fabre-Luce, Alfred. *Histoire secrète de la conciliation de Munich.* Paris: B. Grasset, 1938.

Feiling, Keith. *The Life of Neville Chamberlain.* London: Macmillan, 1946.

Fič, Victor. *Revolutionary War for Independence and the Russian Question.* New Dehli: Abhinav Publications, 1977.

Fič, Vladimír. *Národní sjednocení v politickém systému Československa, 1930–1938* [National union in the Czechoslovak political system, 1930–1938]. Prague: Academia, 1983.

Fierlinger, Zdeněk. *Ve službách ČSR: paměti z druhého odboje* [In the service of Czechoslovakia: A memoir]. Prague: Práce, 1947.

Fierlinger, Zdeněk. *Zrada československé buržoazie a jejích spojenců* [The betrayal by the Czechoslovak bourgeoisie and its allies]. Prague: Nakladatelství Mír, 1951.

Fisher, Louis. *Russia's Road from Peace to War.* New York: Harper & Row, 1969.

Franzel, Emil. *München 1938: Nie gewesen?* Vienna: Österr. Landsmannschaft, 1971.

Friedrich, G. "The Munich Betrayal." *World News and Views,* 8 October 1938, 1111–12.

Friedrich, Otto. "Appeasement at Munich—and the Way to War." *Smithsonian* 19 (October 1988): 162–83.

Fuchser, Larry William. *Neville Chamberlain and Appeasement: A Study in the Politics of History.* New York: Norton, 1982.

Gajan, Koloman. *Německý imperialismus a československo-německé vztahy* [German imperialism and the Czechoslovak-German relations]. Prague: ČSAV, 1962.

Gajanová, A. *ČSR a středoevropská politika velmocí, 1918–1938* [Czechoslovakia and the Central European policy of the great powers, 1918–1938]. Prague: Svoboda, 1967.

Gannes, Harry. *The Munich Betrayal.* New York: Workers Library, 1938.

Gebhart, Jan, and J. Kuklík. "Zapas o Československo na poli zpravodajství ve druhé polovině 30 let" [Struggle for Czechoslovakia in the field of intelligence in the second half of the thirties]. *Historie a vojenství* 1 (1988): 88–112.

Gedye, George E. R. *Betrayal in Central Europe. Austria and Czechoslovakia: The Fallen Bastions.* New York: Harper, 1939.

George, G. J. *They Betrayed Czechoslovakia.* Harmondsworth: Penguin, 1938.

Gerstl, Josef. "Hospodářské styky výmarského Německa se SSSR od rapallské smlouvy do r. 1929" [Commercial relations of Weimar Germany with the Soviet Union from Rapallo to 1929]. *Historické studie* 12 (June 1989): 21–52.

Gilbert, Martin. "Horace Wilson: Man of Munich?" *History Today* 32 (October 1982).

Gilbert, Martin. *The Roots of Appeasement.* New York: New American Library, 1967.

Gilbert, Martin, and Richard Gott. *The Appeasers.* Boston: Houghton Mifflin, 1963.

Glotz, P. et al. (eds.). *München 1938: Das Ende des alten Europas.* Essen: Reimar Hobbing, 1990.

God krizisa, 1938–1939: Dokumenty i materialy. Moscow: Politizdat, 1990.

Gottwald, Klement. *O československé zahraniční politice* [On Czechoslovak foreign policy]. Prague: Svoboda, 1950.

Gottwald, Klement. *Selected Speeches and Articles.* Prague: Orbis, 1954.

Gottwald, Klement. "The Struggle between War and Peace." *International Press Correspondence* 18 (January 1938): 1–2.

Goyet, Pierre le. *Le Mystère Gamelin.* Paris: Presses de la Cité, 1975.

Grachev, S. *Pomoshch SSSR narodam Chekhoslovakii v ikh borbe za svobodu i nezavisimost'.* Moscow: No publisher, 1953.

Gray, Edmund. *The Road to War, 1918–1939.* London: Chatto & Windus, 1970.

Gromyko, A. A. *Diplomaticheskii slovar'.* Moscow: Izdatel'stvo Nauka, 1985.

Gromyko, A. A. *Memoirs.* New York: Doubleday, 1989.

Hadley, William. *Munich: Before and After.* London: Cassell, 1944.

Haigh, R. H. et al. (eds.). *The Guardian Book of Munich.* Aldershot: Wildwood House, 1988.

Hájek, Jiří. *Mnichov.* Prague: Státní Nakladatelství Politické Literatury, 1958.

Hájek, Miloš. *Od Mnichova k 15. březnu* [From Munich to 15 March 1939]. Prague: Státní Nakladatelství Politické Literatury, 1959.

Hajsman, Jan. *Beneš: státník, člověk* [Beneš: A statesman and man]. Prague: Nákladem Mladých Proti Proudu, 1934.

Halifax, Earl of. *Fullness of Days.* London: Collins, 1957.

Halík, Rudolf. "Zrazeni" [Betrayed]. *Venkov,* 21 September 1938.

Hanak, Harry. "The Visit of the Czechoslovak Foreign Minister Dr. Edvard Beneš to Moscow in 1935 as Seen by the British Minister in Prague, Sir Joseph Addison." *Slavonic and East European Review* 54 (October 1976).

"Hands Off Czechoslovakia!" *International Press Correspondence* 18 (May 1938): 647–48.

Harna, Josef. "Českoslovenští národní socialisté v mnichovské krizi" [Czechoslovak national socialists during the Munich crisis]. *Československý časopis historický* 12 (1974): 57–80.

Haslam, Jonathan. "The Soviet Union and the Czechoslovakian Crisis of 1938." *Journal of Contemporary History* 14, 3 (1979): 441–61.

Haslam, Jonathan. *The Soviet Union and the Struggle for Collective Security in Europe, 1933–1939.* New York: St. Martin's Press, 1984.

Hass, Gerhart. *Münchner Diktat 1938—Komplott zum Krieg.* Berlin: Dietz Verlag, 1988.

Hass, Gerhart. "The 1938 Munich Crisis." *Zeitschrift für Geschichtswissenschaft* 37 (1989): 1105–6.

Hauner, Milan. "Czechoslovakia as a Military Factor in British Considerations of 1938." *Journal of Strategic Studies* 1 (September 1978): 194–222.

Hauner, Milan. "La Tchécoslovaquie en tant que facteur militaire." *Revue des Études Slaves* 1–2 (1979): 179–92.

Hauner, Milan. "Září 1938: Kapitulovat či bojovat?" [September 1938: To fight, or to surrender?]. *Svědectví* (Paris) 49 (1975): 151–63.

Havel, František. "Agent A-54 a Moravcovo zpravodajství bez legend" [Agent A-54: The truth about Colonel Moravec's work]. Unpublished manuscript, Military Historical Institute of the Czech Army, Prague.

Havel, František. "Konflikt s Německem" [Conflict with Germany]. Unpublished manuscript, Military Historical Institute of the Czech Army, Prague.

Havel, František. "Zpravodajská činnost 2. oddělení hlavního štábu čs. armády v letech 1936–1939" [Intelligence work of the 2nd bureau in 1936–39]. Unpublished manuscript, Military Historical Institute of the Czech Army, Prague.

Havlíček, František. *Eduard Beneš: člověk—sociolog—politik* [Eduard Beneš: Man, sociologist, politician]. Prague: Prospektrum, 1991.

Heidrich, Arnošt. *International Political Causes of the Czechoslovak Tragedies.* Washington, D.C.: Czechoslovak Society for Arts and Sciences in America, 1962.

Hencke, Andor. *Augenzeuge einer Tragödie: Diplomatenjahre in Prag 1936–1939.* Munich: Fides-Verlagsgesellschaft, 1977.

Henderson, Alexander. *Eyewitness in Czecho-Slovakia.* London: G. G. Harrap, 1939.

Henderson, Sir Nevile. *Failure of a Mission, Berlin 1937–1939.* New York: Putnam, 1940.

Herman, John. "Soviet Peace Efforts on the Eve of World War Two: A Review of the Soviet Documents." *Journal of Contemporary History* 13 (1984): 577–602.

Herman, Victor. *Coming out of the Ice: An Unexpected Life.* New York: Harcourt Brace Jovanovich, 1979.

Herwarth, Hans von. *Against Two Evils.* New York: Rawson, Wade, 1981.

Heumos, Peter. "Struktura první Československé republiky v poměru k základní ideji západní demokracie" [The structure of the First Czechoslovak republic as related to the concept of Western democracy]. *Historické studie* 12 (June 1989): 3–21.

Hilger, Gustav, and Alfred G. Meyer. *The Incompatible Allies: A Memoir-History of German-Soviet Relations, 1919–1941.* New York: Macmillan, 1953.

Hill, Leonidas. "Three Crises, 1938–39." *Journal of Contemporary History* 3 (January 1968): 113–44.

Hitchcock, Edward B. *"I Built a Temple for Peace."* London: Harper, 1940.

Hochman, Jiří. *The Soviet Union and the Failure of Collective Security, 1934–1938.* Ithaca: Cornell University Press, 1984.

Hodža, Milan. *Federation in Central Europe.* London: Jerrolds, 1942.

Hoensch, Jörg K. *Der ungarische Revisionismus und die Zerschlagung der Tschecho-slowakei*. Tübingen: J. C. B. Mohr, 1967.

Holub, Ota. *A věže mlčí . . .* [And the fortresses are silent]. Prague: Pressfoto, 1973.

Holub, Ota. *Pět minut před půlnocí* [Five minutes to midnight]. Prague: Československý Spisovatel, 1977.

Holub, Ota. *Rovnice řešená zradou* [An equation solved by treason]. Prague: Naše Vojsko, 1979.

Holub, Ota. *Smrt ze zálohy* [A death in an ambush]. Prague: Panoráma, 1979.

Holub, Ota. *Souboj s Abwehrem* [A duel with the *Abwehr*]. Prague: Orbis, 1975.

Holub, Ota. *Třicátá pátá hraniční oblast* [The thirty-fifth border region]. Hradec Králové: Kruh, 1983.

Holub, Ota. *Vlčí komando* [Commando of wolves]. Prague: Naše Vojsko, 1981.

Holub, Ota. *Zrazené pevnosti* [The betrayed fortresses]. Prague: Naše Vojsko, 1982.

Holub, Ota, and Václav Kaplan. *Opevnění 1935–1938: Náchodsko* [The fortifications in the Náchod region]. Náchod: Okresní Muzeum, 1986.

Honzík, Miroslav, Oldřich Mahler, and Miroslav Broft. *Zněl zrady zvon* [The bell of treason could be heard]. Prague: Naše Vojsko, 1988.

Horák, Bohumil. *The Czechoslovak Republic*. Prague: Orbis, 1929.

Hory, Andres. *Behind the Scenes of World War II*. Astor Park, Fla: Danubian Press, 1968.

Hossbach, Friedrich. *Zwischen Wehrmacht und Hitler, 1934–1938*. Göttingen: Vandenhoeck & Ruprecht, 1965.

Höttl, Wilhelm. *The Secret Front: The Story of Nazi Political Espionage*. New York: Praeger, 1954.

Hrubý, Jan. *Munich 1938: An Analysis of Betrayal*. Prague: Orbis, 1987.

Hyndrák, Václav. "K otázce vojenské hodnoty čs. armády v druhé polovině třicátých let" [Regarding the Czechoslovak army's value in the second half of the thirties]. *Historie a vojenství* 1 (1964): 63–103.

Hyndrák, Václav. "K otázce vojenské připravenosti Československa v roce 1938" [Regarding Czechoslovak military preparedness in 1938]. In *Severní Čechy a Mnichov: Sborník statí k 30. výročí Mnichova*. Liberec: Vysoká Škola Strojní a Textilní, 1969.

Hyndrák, Václav. "Polsko a československá krize na podzim 1938" [Poland and the Czechoslovak crisis in the fall of 1938]. *Historie a vojenství* 1 (1968): 84–98.

Hyndrák, Václav. "Vyvrcholení boje na obranu republiky v roce 1938" [The culmination of the struggle to defend Czechoslovakia in 1938]. *Historie a vojenství* 1 (1961): 78–110.

Hyršová, Květa. *Česká inteligence a protifašistická fronta* [The Czechoslovak intelligentsia and the antifascist front]. Prague: Melantrich, 1985.

Institute of International Politics and Economics. *Lectures on the History of Munich*. Prague: Orbis, 1959.

Jackson, Peter. "French Military Intelligence and Czechoslovakia, 1938." *Diplomacy & Statecraft* 5 (March 1994).

"Jak to bylo s pomocí SSSR?" [How was it with Soviet help?] *Praha-Moskva* 3 (September 1938): 217–18.

Jaksch, Wenzel. "The Czech-Sudeten German Dilemma." *Sudeten Bulletin* 13 (April 1965): 119–24.

Jaksch, Wenzel. *Europe's Road to Potsdam*. New York: Praeger, 1963.

Janeček, O. "Pokyny Jiřího Dimitrova k činnosti komunistické Internacionály na pomoc ČSR proti fašismu" [Georgi Dimitrov's instructions regarding the Communist International's assistance to Czechoslovakia against fascism]. *Příspěvky k dějinám KSČ* 6 (December 1963): 880–82.

Jászi, Oszkár. *The Dissolution of the Habsburg Monarchy.* Chicago: University of Chicago Press, 1929.

Jászi, Oszkár. "War Germs in the Danube Basin." *Nation* 139 (1934).

Jaworski, Rudolf. *Vorspoten oder Minderheit? Der sudetendeutsche Volksstumskampf in den Beziehungen zwischen der Weimar Republik und der CSR.* Stuttgart: Deutsche Verlagsanstalt, 1977.

Jensen, Kenneth M. and David Wurmser (eds.). *The Meaning of Munich Fifty Years Later.* Washington: United States Institute of Peace, 1990.

Ježek, František. "Z pamětí o mnichovské krizi roku 1938" [Regarding the 1938 Munich crisis]. *Historie a vojenství* 4 (1969): 674–701.

Jones, Kenneth Paul (ed.). *U.S. Diplomats in Europe, 1919–1941.* Santa Barbara: ABC-Clio, 1981.

Jones, Thomas Brooks. *Munich: A Tale of Two Myths.* Philadelphia: Dorrance, 1977.

Jordan, Nicole. "Maurice Gamelin, Italy, and the Eastern Alliances." *Journal of Strategic Studies* 14 (1991): 428–41.

Jordan, Nicole. *The Popular Front and Central Europe: The Dilemmas of French Impotence, 1918–1940.* Cambridge: Cambridge University Press, 1992.

Jukes, G. "The Red Army and the Munich Crisis." *Journal of Contemporary History* 26 (April 1991): 195–215.

Kahánek, Ferdinand. *Beneš contra Beck: Reportáže a dokumenty* [Beneš vs. Beck: Reports and Documents]. Prague: No publisher, 1938.

Kalašnikovová, Světlana. *Otázka uznání SSSR de jure v politice Československa v letech 1924–1926* [The de jure recognition of the Soviet Union in Czechoslovak politics, 1924–1926]. Prague: Academia, 1983.

Kalvoda, Josef. *Czechoslovakia's Role in Soviet Strategy.* Washington, D.C.: University Press of America, 1978.

Kalvoda, Josef. "Munich: Beneš and the Soldiers." *Ukrainian Quarterly* 47 (summer 1991): 153–69.

Kaplan, Karel. *Mocní a bezmocní* [The powerful and the powerless]. Toronto: Sixty-Eight Publishers, 1989.

Kárný, Miroslav. "Logika Mnichova" [The logic of Munich]. *Československý časopis historický* 35, 2–3 (1987): 371–403.

Kee, Robert. *Munich: The Eleventh Hour.* London: Hamish Hamilton, 1988.

Kennan, George F. *From Prague after Munich: Diplomatic Papers, 1938–1940.* Princeton: Princeton University Press, 1968.

Kennan, George F. *Russia and the West under Lenin and Stalin.* Boston: Little, Brown, 1961.

Kennedy, John F. *Why England Slept.* London: Wilfred Funk, 1964.

Kern, Karl. "The Development of the Czech Nation." *Central European Journal* 15 (December 1967): 333–36.

Kerner, Robert J. (ed.). *Czechoslovakia, Twenty Years of Independence.* Berkeley: University of California Press, 1940.

Kesselring, Albert. *Kesselring: A Soldier's Report.* New York: William Morrow, 1954.

Kleine-Ahlbrandt, W. Laird (ed.). *Appeasement of the Dictators: Crisis Diplomacy?* New York: Holt, Rinehart and Winston, 1970.

Klemperer, Klemens von. *German Resistance against Hitler: The Search for Allies Abroad.* New York: Clarendon Press, 1992.

Klepetar, Harry. *Der Sprachenkampf in den Sudetenländern.* Prague: Strache Verlag, 1930.

Klíma, Vlastimil. "Skupina opozičních poslanců vládních stran v období mnichovské krize roku 1938" [Deputies of ruling parties in opposition during the Munich crisis of 1938]. *Československý časopis historický* 12 (1964): 274–80.

Klimek, Antonín. "Edvard Beneš od abdikace z funkce prezidenta ČSR (5. října 1938) do zkázy Československa (15. března 1939): aneb skon státníka?" [Edvard Beneš from his abdication (5 October 1938) to the demise of Czechoslovakia (15 March 1939): A statesman's death?]. Manuscript, 1992.

Klimek, Antonín. "Edvard Beneš: Postava v mlhách" [Edvard Beneš: The elusive man]. *Historie a vojenství* 4 (1991): 142–52.

Klimek, Antonín. "Janovská konference roku 1922 očima Edvarda Beneše" [The Genoa conference of 1922 as seen by Edvard Beneš]. *Historie a vojenství* 1 (1994): 77–103.

Klimek, Antonín. "Plány Edvarda Beneše na poválečný vývoj Československa" [Edvard Beneš's plans for postwar Czechoslovakia]. *Střední Evropa* 9 (May 1993): 25–31.

Klimek, Antonín. *Zrození státníka, Edvard Beneš, 28.5.1884–24.9.1919* [The birth of a statesman: Edvard Beneš, 28 May 1884 to 24 September 1919]. Prague: Melantrich, 1992.

Klimek, Antonín, and Petr Hofman. "Vítěz, který prohrál" [The defeated victor: General Radola Gajda]. Manuscript, 1995.

Klimek, Antonín, and Eduard Kubů. *Československá zahraniční politika, 1918–1938: Kapitoly z dějin mezinárodních vztahů*. Prague: Institut pro Středoevropskou Kulturu a Politiku, 1995.

Kocman, A. (ed). *Prameny k ohlasu VŘSR a vzniku ČSR: Boj o směr vývoje čs. státu. 1. říjen 1918–červen 1919* [Sources on the impact of the Great October Revolution and the emergence of Czechoslovakia: Struggles regarding the state's political orientation from 1 October 1918 to June 1919]. Prague: Academia, 1965.

Koeppl, E. C. "Byl Dr. Beneš vinen smrtí maršála Tuchačevského?" [Did Beneš cause the death of Marshal Tukhachevsky?]. *Proměny* 13, 2 (1976).

Kokoška, Stanislav. "Poznámky dr. Jaroslava Drábka o jeho rozmluvě s Edvardem Benešem v lednu 1939" [Jaroslav Drábek's notes on his conversation with Edvard Beneš in January 1939]. Manuscript, 1993.

Kokoška, Jaroslav, and Stanislav Kokoška. *Spor o agenta A-54: Kapitoly z dějin československé zpravodajské služby* [Regarding Agent A-54: Chapters from the history of Czechoslovak intelligence]. Prague: Naše Vojsko, 1994.

Kokoška-Malíř, Jaroslav. "Organizace československého vojenského ofenzivního zpravodajství v letech 1934–39" [Organization of the offensive section of Czechoslovak military intelligence in 1934–1939]. *Historie a vojenství* 6 (1989).

Komjathy, Anthony Tihamer. *The Crises of France's East Central European Diplomacy, 1933–1938*. Boulder: East European Monographs, 1976.

Komjathy, Anthony Tihamer. *German Minorities and the Third Reich: Ethnic Germans of East Central Europe between the Wars*. New York: Holmes & Meier, 1980.

Kopecký, Václav. "The Communist Victory at the Prague Elections." *International Press Correspondence* 18 (May 1938): 648–49.

Korbel, Josef. *Communist Subversion of Czechoslovakia, 1938–1948*. Princeton: Princeton University Press, 1959.

Koučka, I., and F. Svátek. *Dějiny ministerstva zahraničních věcí Československa v létech 1918–1938* [History of the Czechoslovak Ministry of Foreign Affairs, 1918–1938]. Prague: Ústav pro Soudobé Dějiny, 1995.

Král, Václav. *Beneš a obrana státu* [Beneš and the defense of the state]. Bratislava: Tatran, 1952.

Král, Václav. *Die Deutschen in der Tschechoslowakei, 1933–1947*. Prague: Nakladatelství Československé Akademie Věd, 1964.

Král, Václav. *Dny, které otřásly Československem* [The days that shook Czechoslovakia]. Prague: Naše Vojsko, 1975.

Král, Václav. *Plán Zet* [Plan Z]. Prague: Naše Vojsko, 1973.

Král, Václav. "Rumunsko a průchod Rudé Armády na pomoc Československu v roce 1938" [The transfer of the Red Army through Romania to assist Czechoslovakia in 1938]. *Slovanský přehled* 52, 6 (1966): 330–38.

Král, Václav. *Spojenectví československo-sovětské v evropské politice 1935–1939* [The Czechoslovak-Soviet alliance in European politics, 1935–1939]. Prague: Academia, 1970.

Král, Václav. *Zářijové dny 1938* [September days 1938]. Prague: Svoboda, 1971.

Kratochvíl, Jaroslav. "Bohdan Pavlů a ruská revoluce" [Bohdan Pavlů and the Russian revolution]. *Praha-Moskva* 3 (May 1938): 109–12.

Krausnick, Helmut et al. (eds.). *Helmuth Groscurth: Tagesbücher eines Abwehroffiziers, 1939–1940*. Stuttgart: Deutsche Verlagsanstalt, 1970.

Krejčí, Ludvík. "Obranyschopnost ČSR v r. 1938" [Defensibility of Czechoslovakia]. *Odboj a revoluce* 6, 2 (1968): 14–41.

Křen, Jan. *Mnichovská zrada* [The Munich treason]. Prague: Nakladatelství Politické Literatury, 1958.

Krivitsky, Walter G. *In Stalin's Secret Service: An Exposé of Russia's Secret Policies by the Former Chief of the Soviet Intelligence in Western Europe*. 1940. Reprint. Frederick, Md.: University Publications of America, 1985.

Kubal, Jan. "Czechoslovakia: Focal Point." *International Press Correspondence* 18 (March 1938): 175–76.

Kubal, Jan. "Czechoslovakia Is Fighting and Expects the Assistance of the Democratic World." *World News and Views* 18 (1 October 1938): 1091–92.

Kubal, Jan. "Decisive Days for Czechoslovakia." *International Press Correspondence* 18 (April 1938): 407–8.

Kubal, Jan, and Jan Šverma. "Political Situation in Czechoslovakia." *International Press Correspondence* 18 (April 1938): 479–80.

Kubů, Eduard. *Německo: Zahraničně politické dilema Edvarda Beneše; hospodářské vztahy s Německem v československé zahraniční politice let 1918–1924* [Germany: Edvard Beneš's foreign policy dilemma; economic relations with Germany in Czechoslovak foreign policy, 1918–1924]. Prague: Univerzita Karlova, 1994.

Kuhn, Heinrich. "The Czech Communist Party and the Sudeten Question." *Sudeten Bulletin* 13, 1 (January 1965): 9–14.

Kural, Václav. "Poznámky na okraj pamětí gen. Františka Moravce" [Notes regarding the memoirs of General Moravec]. *Historie a vojenství* 2 (1990): 128–50.

Kvaček, Robert. "Československo-německá jednání v roce 1936" [The Czechoslovak-German negotiations in 1936]. *Historie a vojenství* (1965): 721–54.

Kvaček, Robert. *Diplomaté a ti druzí: K dějinám diplomacie za druhé světové války* [Diplomats and others: On the history of diplomacy during World War II]. Prague: Panoráma, 1988.

Kvaček, Robert. *Historie jednoho roku* [A history of one year]. Prague: Mladá Fronta, 1976.

Kvaček, Robert. *Nad Evropou zataženo: Československo a Evropa, 1933–1937* [Clouds above Europe: Czechoslovakia and Europe, 1933–1937]. Prague: Svoboda, 1966.

Kvaček, Robert. *Obtížné spojenectví: Politicko-diplomatické vztahy mezi Československem a Francií 1937–1938* [The difficult alliance: politico-diplomatic relations between Czechoslovakia and France, 1937–1938]. Prague: Acta Universitatis Carolinae, 1989.

Kvaček, Robert. *Osudná mise* [The fateful mission]. Prague: Naše Vojsko, 1958.

Kvaček, Robert. "Polsko a Mnichov" [Poland and Munich]. *Historie a vojenství* 1 (1968): 105–111.

Kvaček, Robert. *Poslední den* [The last day]. Prague: Melantrich, 1989.

Kvaček, Robert. "Zur Beziehung zwischen der Tschechoslowakei und den Westmächten vor dem Münchener Diktat." *Acta Universitatis Carolinae* (1968): 209–33.

Kvaček, Robert et al. *Československý rok 1938* [The Czechoslovak year 1938]. Prague: Panoráma, 1988.

Lacaze, Yvon. "De l'anschluß à la crise de Mai 1938: Contribution des documents diplomatique français a l'étude des problèmes tchécoslovaques." Manuscript, 1976.

Lacaze, Yvon. *L'Opinion publique française et la crise de Munich*. Berne: P. Lang, 1991.

Lacaze, Yvon. *La France et Munich: Étude d'un processus décisionnel en matière de relations internationales*. Berne: P. Lang, 1992.

Laffan, R. G. D. *Survey of International Affairs, 1938: The Crisis over Czechoslovakia*. New York: Oxford University Press, 1951.

Lammers, Donald N. *Explaining Munich: The Search for Motive in British Policy*. Stanford: Hoover Institution Press, 1966.

Laqueur, Walter. *Russia and Germany: A Century of Conflict*. London: Weidenfield & Nicolson, 1965.

Laqueur, Walter. *Stalin: The Glasnost Revelations*. New York: Scribner's, 1990.

Laqueur, Walter. "The Strange Lives of Nikolai Skoblin." *Encounter* 72 (March 1989): 11–20.

Latynski, Maya (ed.). *Reappraising the Munich Pact: Continental Perspectives*. Washington: Woodrow Wilson Center and Johns Hopkins University Press, 1992.

Le Goyet, Pierre. *15 Mars 1939, le premier "coup de Prague."* Paris: Éditions France-Empire, 1989.

Le Goyet, Pierre. *Munich, "un traquenard".* Paris: Editions France-Empire, 1988.

Lee, Dwight E. *Ten Years: The World on the Way to War, 1930–1940*. Boston: Houghton Mifflin, 1942.

Leeds, Stanton B. *These Rule France*. New York: Bobbs-Merrill, 1940.

Leoncini, Francesco. *I Sudeti e l'autodeterminazione, 1919–1919: Aspetti Internazionali*. Padova: Centro Studi Europe Orientale, 1973.

Lewis, Terrance L. *A Climate for Appeasement*. New York: P. Lang, 1991.

Lih, Lars T., Oleg V. Naumov, and Oleg V. Khlevniuk (eds.). *Stalin's Letters to Molotov*. New Haven: Yale University Press, 1995.

Lisický, Karel. *Československá cesta k Mnichovu* [The Czechoslovak path to Munich]. Prague: Orbis, 1956.

Litvinov, Maxim. *Against Aggression: Speeches by Maxim Litvinov*. New York: International Publisher, 1939.

Lockhart, R. H. Bruce. *My Europe*. London: Putnam, 1952.

Loewenheim, Francis L. (ed.). *Peace or Appeasement? Hitler, Chamberlain, and the Munich Crisis*. Boston: Houghton Mifflin, 1965.

Lothian, Lord. *The American Speeches of Lord Lothian, July 1939 to December 1940*. London: Oxford University Press, 1941.

Low, Alfred D. "Edvard Beneš, the Anschluß Movement, 1918–1938, and the Policy of Czechoslovakia." *East Central Europe/L'Europe du Centre-Est* 10, 1–2 (1983): 46–91.

Lukeš, František. "Beneš a SSSR" [Beneš and the Soviet Union]. *Sešity pro mladou literaturu* 21 (1968).

Lukeš, František. *Podivný mír* [A strange kind of peace]. Prague: Svoboda, 1968.

Lukeš, František. "Poznámky k čs.- sovětským stykům v září 1938" [Notes on Czechoslovak-Soviet relations in September 1938]. *Československý časopis historický* 5 (1963): 703–31.

Lukes, Igor. "Benesch, Stalin und die Comintern: Vom Münchner Abkommen zum Molotow-Ribbentrop Pakt." *Vierteljahrshefte für Zeitgeschichte* 3 (1993): 325–53.

Lukes, Igor. "Did Stalin Desire War in 1938? A New Look at Soviet Behavior during the May and September Crises." *Diplomacy & Statecraft* 2 (March 1991): 3–53.

Lukes, Igor. "The GPU and GRU in Pre–World War II Czechoslovakia." *International Journal of Intelligence and Counterintelligence* 8 (spring 1995): 91–104.

Lukes, Igor. "Stalin and Beneš at the End of September 1938: New Evidence from the Prague Archives." *Slavic Review* 52 (spring 1993): 28–48.

Luža, Radomír. *Austro-German Relations in the Anschluss Era.* Princeton: Princeton University Press, 1975.

Luža, Radomír. "The Czechoslovak Ground Forces in the Munich Crisis: General Hasal's Notes of May, 1958." *East Central Europe* 8, 1–2 (1981): 97–102.

Luža, Radomír. *The Resistance in Austria, 1938–1945.* Minneapolis: University of Minnesota Press, 1984.

Luža, Radomír. *The Transfer of the Sudeten Germans: A Study of Czech-German Relations, 1933–1962.* New York: New York University Press, 1964.

Lvová, Míla. "Dvacet let o Mnichovu v naší ideologii a vědě" [Twenty years about Munich in our ideology and scholarship]. *Revue dějin socialismu* 9, 3 (1969): 323–61.

Lvová, Míla. "Lid chtěl bojovat" [People wanted to fight]. *Příspěvky k dějinám KSČ* 3 (1963): 542–56.

Lvová, Míla. *Mnichov a Edvard Beneš* [Munich and Edvard Beneš]. Prague: Svoboda, 1968.

Mackenzie, Sir Compton. *Dr. Beneš.* London: G. G. Harrap, 1946.

Maiski, Ivan. *The Munich Drama.* Moscow: Novosti Press, 1972.

Maiski, Ivan. *Who Helped Hitler?* London: Hutchinson, 1964.

Mamatey, Victor S. *The United States and East Central Europe 1914–1918: A Study in Wilsonian Diplomacy and Propaganda.* Princeton: Princeton University Press, 1957.

Mamatey, Victor S., and Radomír Luža (eds.). *A History of the Czechoslovak Republic, 1918–1948.* Princeton: Princeton University Press, 1973.

Marek, Z. "SSSR: silný obránce míru" [The Soviet Union: a powerful defender of peace]. *Praha-Moskva* 3 (August 1938): 181–82.

Mareš, Antoine. "La question tchéchoslovaque devant l'opinion française en 1938." *Revue des Études Slaves* 1–2 (1979): 109–24.

Mareš, Antoine. "La faillite des rélations franco-tchécoslovaques: la Mission militaire française à Prague (1926–1938)." *Revue d'Histoire de la Deuxième Guerre Mondiale* 111 (1978): 45–70.

Marks, Sally. "Mussolini and Locarno: Fascist Foreign Policy in Microcosm." *Journal of Contemporary History* 14 (July 1979): 423–39.

Masaryk, Thomas G. *Česká otázka: Snahy a tužby národního obrození* [The Czech question: Efforts and aspirations of national awakening]. Prague: Nakladatelství Čas, 1895.

Masaryk, Thomas G. *The Making of a State: Memories and Observations, 1914–1918.* New York: Frederick A. Stokes, 1923.

Masaryk, Thomas G. *Natsionalizm i internatsionalizm sotsial' demokratii.* Moskva: Izd. Viktora Kugel', 1906?

Masaryk, Thomas G. *Neznámý Masaryk* [The unknown Masaryk]. Prague: Nakladatelství Riopress, 1994.

Masaryk, Thomas G. *O bolševictví: Československému dělnictvu* [On bolshevism: A message to Czechoslovak workers]. Prague: Evropský Kulturní Klub, 1990.

Masaryk, Thomas G. *Otevřít Rusko Evropě: Dvě stati k ruské otázce v roce 1922* [Open

Russia to Europe: Two essays on the Russian question in 1922]. Prague: H & H, 1992.

Masaryk, Thomas G. *Pomoc Rusku Evropou a Amerikou* [European and American assistance to Russia]. Prague: H & H, 1992.

Masaryk, Thomas G. *The Problem of Small Nations in the European Crisis*. London: Council for the Study of International Relations, 1916.

Masaryk, Thomas G. *The Spirit of Russia: Studies in History, Literature and Philosophy*. New York: Macmillan, 1919. Reprint. London: Allen & Unwin, 1961.

Mastný, Vojtěch. *The Czechs under Nazi Rule: The Failure of National Resistance, 1939–1942*. New York: Columbia University Press, 1971.

Matějka, Jároslav. *Gottwald*. Prague: Svoboda, 1971.

Maugham, Viscount. *The Truth about the Munich Crisis*. London: Heinemann, 1944.

McDermott, Kevin. "Stalinist Terror in the Comintern: New Perspectives." *Journal of Contemporary History* 30 (1995): 111–30.

Melichar, Václav. "Některé otázky obrany Československa v roce 1938" [Some questions regarding Czechoslovakia's defense in 1938]. *Československý časopis historický* 22, 3 (1979): 125–34.

Mencl, Vojtěch, and Jarmila Menclová. "Náčrt podstaty a vývoje vrcholné sféry předmnichovské československé mocensko-politické struktury" [The essence and development of the Czechoslovak power and political structures before Munich]. *Československý časopis historický* 16 (1968): 341–64.

Menclová, Jarmila. "VI. Kongres Komunistické Internacionály v roce 1928" [The 7th Congress of the Communist International in 1928]. *Příspěvky k dějinám KSČ* 3 (December 1983): 803–23.

Mertsalov, Andrei N. *Munich: Mistake or Cynical Calculation?* Moscow: Novosti, 1988.

"Mezinárodní síla Sovětského Svazu ve světě" [Soviet might in the world]. *Praha-Moskva* 3 (June 1938): 145–51.

Michel, Barnard. "L'Ambassadeur Osuský et son action en France." *Revue des Études Slaves* 1–2 (1979): 125–34.

Middlemas, Keith. *The Strategy of Appeasement: The British Government and Germany, 1937–1939*. Chicago: Quadrangle Books, 1972.

Mihalka, Michael. "German Strategic Deception in the 1930s." *Rand Note*, N-1557-NA, July 1980.

Miksche, Ferdinand O. "Masaryk's Role in Central Europe." *Sudeten Bulletin* 8 (April 1960): 95–98.

Miksche, Ferdinand O. "Minorities in Pre-war Czechoslovakia." *Sudeten Bulletin* 10 (February 1962): 29–36.

Miksche, Ferdinand O. *Paratroops*. New York: Random House, 1943.

Ministerstvo Národní Obrany. *Dvacet let československé armády* [Twenty years of the Czechoslovak army]. Prague: Ministerstvo Národní Obrany, 1938.

Ministry of Foreign Affairs. "Memorandum Spojenců Rusku" [The allies' memorandum to Russia]. *Zahraniční politika* 1, 11–12 (1922): 898–903.

Ministry of Foreign Affairs. "Naše prozatimní smlouvy s RSFSR a USSR" [Our provisional agreements with the RSFSR and the USSR]. *Zahraniční politika* 1, 13 (1922): 928–29.

Ministry of Foreign Affairs. "Prohlášení ministra dra Beneše z 2. července o politice Malé dohody a normalisaci styků s Ruskem" [Statement by Minister Beneš of 2 July regarding the Little Entente's policy and the normalization of relations with Russia]. *Zahraniční politika* 13, 7 (1934): 413.

Ministry of Foreign Affairs. "Prozatimní smlouva mezi Československou republikou a RSFSR" [Provisional agreement between Czechoslovakia and the RSFSR]. *Zahraniční politika* 1, 13 (1922): 1010–13.

Ministry of Foreign Affairs. "Ruská odpověd na memorandum Spojenců" [Russia's response to the allies' memorandum]. *Zahraniční politika* 1, 11–12 (1922): 903–908.

Ministry of Foreign Affairs. "Zpráva o rozmluvách dra Edvarda Beneše se soudruhy J. V. Stalinem, V. M. Molotovem a M. M. Litvinovem z 10. června 1935" [Report on talks of Edvard Beneš with Stalin, Molotov, and Litvinov of 10 June 1935]. *Zahraniční politika* 14, 4–5 (1935): 334–35.

Les minorités dans la République Tchécoslovaque. Paris: Bureau d'Informations Politiques et Économiques du Ministère des Affaires Étrangères, 1921.

Mitchell, B. R. *European Historical Statistics, 1750–1970.* New York: Columbia University Press, 1975.

Mlechin, Leonid. "A Minister in Emigration: Hitherto Unknown Pages from the History of the Soviet Intelligence Service." *New Times* 18, 19, and 20 (1990): 37–40, 40–43, 36–39.

"Molotov o posledních událostech v Evropě" [Molotov on the latest events in Europe]. *Praha-Moskva* 3 (December 1938): 292–98.

Moravec, Emanuel. *Das Ende der Benesch-Republik; die tschechoslowakische Krise 1938.* Prague: Orbis, 1941. Note that Emanuel Moravec often wrote under the name "Stanislav Yester."

Moravec, Emanuel. *Jak dochází k veliké válce. Zrání prvé a co bude s druhou* [How big wars happen: Roots of the first war and what will happen with the next one]. Prague: MNO, Kancelář Československých Legií, n.d.

Moravec, Emanuel. "Jak se státy opevňují" [Military fortifications in other countries]. *Přítomnost* (1936): 199.

Moravec, Emanuel. "Kdyby Sovětské Rusko válčilo s Japonskem" [If Soviet Russia were to fight with Japan]. *Přítomnost* (1936): 117.

Moravec, Emanuel. "Občanská válka ve Španělsku" [The Civil war in Spain]. *Přítomnost* (1936): 517.

Moravec, Emanuel. *Obrana státu* [Defense of the state]. Prague: Svaz Československého Důstojnictva, 1936.

Moravec, Emanuel. *Operace na Slovensku 1919* [Military operations in Slovakia, 1919]. Prague: VOK, 1934.

Moravec, Emanuel. "Poučení o manévrech pro laiky" [What laymen should know about army maneuvers]. *Přítomnost* 11, 40 (1934): 637–39.

Moravec, Emanuel. *Příprava na těžké doby. Úvaha o obraně našeho státu* [Preparing for a difficult time: Reflections on the defense of our state]. Prague: František Borový, 1935.

Moravec, Emanuel. *The Strategic Importance of Czechoslovakia.* Prague: Orbis, 1936.

Moravec, Emanuel. "Strategie a psychologie vzniku války" [The strategy and psychology of the outbreak of war]. *Vojenské rozhledy: Revue Militaire Tchécoslovaque* 10, 3 (1929): 223–30.

Moravec, Emanuel. *Třetí říše nastupuje!* [The Third Reich rises!]. Prague:: Svaz Československého Důstojnictva, 1937.

Moravec, Emanuel. *Úkoly naší obrany. Politik a armáda* [The tasks of our military defense: the politician and the army]. Prague: Svaz Československého Důstojnictva, 1936.

Moravec, Emanuel. *V úloze mouřenína: Československá tragédie r. 1938* [In the moor's role: The Czechoslovak tragedy, 1938]. Prague: Orbis, 1940.

Moravec, Emanuel. *Válka a vojáci. Otázky—názory—osoby a události* [War and soldiers: Questions, opinions, personalities]. Prague: Svaz Československých Rotmistrů, 1930.

Moravec, Emanuel. *Vojáci a doba: Důstojnický staz kdysi a dnes* [Soldiers and time: Officers in the past and today]. Prague: Svaz Československého Důstojnictva, 1934.

Moravec, Emanuel. "Voják se dívá na Anschluß." [A soldier's view of the *Anschluß*] *Přítomnost* 15 (23 March 1938): 182–85.

Moravec, František. *Špión, jemuž nevěřili* [The spy whom nobody believed]. Prague: Rozmluvy Alexandra Tomského, 1990.

Morrell, Sydney. *I Saw the Crucifixion*. London: Peter Davies, 1939.

Munich 1938: Mythes et Réalitiés. In *Revue des Études Slaves*, vols. 15–20. Paris: Institut National D'Études Slaves, 1979.

Münzer, Jan. "Ovzduší otrávené reakcí" [The air poisoned by the reactionaries]. *Sobota* 7, 41 (November 1936): 841–43.

Münzer, Jan. "Za pevnou zahraniční politiku" [Toward a firm foreign policy]. *Sobota* 8 (1937): 388–89.

Murray, Williamson. "German Air Power and the Munich Crisis." *War and Society: A Yearbook of Military History* 2 (1977): 107–18.

Murray, Williamson. *The Change in the European Balance of Power, 1938–1939*. Princeton: Princeton University Press, 1984.

Murray, Williamson. "Munich at Fifty." *Commentary* 86 (July 1988): 25–30.

Murray, Williamson. "Munich, 1938: The Military Confrontation." *The Journal of Strategic Studies* (December 1979): 282–302.

Murray, Williamson, and Allan R. Millett. *Calculations: Net Assessment and the Coming of World War II*. New York: Free Press, 1992.

Navrozov, Lev. *The Education of Lev Navrozov*. New York: Harper's Magazine, 1975.

Nedvěd, Karel. "Němec, který zůstal demokratem: Wenzel Jaksch" [A German who remained a democrat: Wenzel Jaksch]. *Přítomnost* 15 (20 July 1938): 454–57.

Nejedlý, Zdeněk. "Česko-Slovensko a cizina" [Czecho-Slovakia and the world]. *Praha-Moskva* 3 (December 1938): 289–90.

Nejedlý, Zdeněk. "O Stalinův projev" [Regarding Stalin's speech]. *Praha-Moskva* 3 (February 1938): 1–2.

Nesvadba, František. *Proč nezahřměla děla* [Why the guns failed to thunder]. Prague: Naše Vojsko, 1986.

Nikonov, A. D. *The Origin of World War II and the Prewar European Political Crisis of 1939*. Moscow: Publishing House of USSR Academy of Sciences, 1955.

Noakes, Jeremy, and Geoffry Pridham. *Documents on Nazism, 1919–1945*. New York: Viking Press, 1974.

Noël, Léon. *La guerre de 39 a commencé quatre ans plus tôt*. Paris: Éditions France-Empire, 1979.

Noguères, Henri. *Munich: "Peace for Our Time."* New York: McGraw-Hill, 1965.

Norton, Donald H. "Karl Haushofer and the German Academy, 1925–1945." *Central European History* 1 (March 1968): 80–97.

Novotný, Karel. "Několik poznatků ze cvičení a manévrů v československé armádě z let 1930–1938" [Some lessons from maneuvers of the Czechoslovak army, 1930–1938]. *Historie a vojenství* 6–7 (1968): 1046–77.

Nurek, M. "Great Britain and the Scandinavian Countries before and after the Signing of the Munich Agreement." *Acta Poloniae Historica* 59 (1989): 109–27.

"Odložte brýle mámení" [Stop fooling yourself]. *Důstojnické listy* (31 January 1935).

Olivová, Věra. "Československo-sovětská smlouva z roku 1935" [The Czechoslovak-Soviet agreement of 1935]. *Československý časopis historický* 13 (1965): 477–500.

Olivová, Věra. *Edvard Beneš proti nacismu* [Beneš against Nazism]. Prague: H & H, 1993.

Olivová, Věra. *The Doomed Democracy.* Montreal: McGill University Press, 1972.

Olivová, Věra. *Politika Československa v ruské krizi roku 1921 a 1922* [Czechoslovak approach to the Russian crisis of 1921–22]. Prague: H & H, 1992.

Olivová, Věra. "Postoj československé buržoazie k Sovětskému svazu v době jednání o prozatimní smlouvu z roku 1922" [Czechoslovak bourgeoisie and the Soviet Union at the time of negotiations of the provisional agreement of 1922] *Československý časopis historický* 1, 3 (1953): 294–323.

Olivová, Věra. *Zápas o Československo: říjen 1937–září 1938* [Struggle for Czechoslovakia: October 1937–September 1938]. Prague: H & H, 1992.

Olivová, Věra (ed.). *Edvard Beneš, 1884–1948: Životopisný medailon* [Edvard Beneš, 1884–1948: A portrait]. Prague: Společnost Edvarda Beneše, 1994.

Olivová, Věra (ed.). *Pocta Edvardu Benešovi* [Homage to Edvard Beneš]. Prague: Společnost Edvarda Beneše, 1994.

Opečenský, Jan (ed.). *Edward Beneš: Essays and Reflections presented on the occasion of his Sixtieth Birthday.* London: Allen & Unwin, 1945.

Orlov, Alexander. *The Secret History of Stalin's Crimes.* London: Jarrolds, 1954.

Ort, Alexandr. *Dr. Edvard Beneš: Evropský politik* [Edvard Beneš: A European politician]. Prague: Vysoká Škola Ekonomická, 1993.

Osuský, Samuel Štefan. *Malá dohoda.* Prague: No publisher, 1933.

Ovendale, Ritchie. *"Appeasement" and the English-Speaking World.* Cardiff: University of Wales Press, 1975.

Papen, Franz von. *Memoirs.* London: Andre Deutsch, 1952.

Papoušek, Jaroslav. *Československo, SSSR a Německo* [Czechoslovakia, the USSR and Germany]. Prague: Pokrok, 1936.

Parker, Robert Alexander Clarke. *Chamberlain and Appeasement: British Policy and the Coming of the Second World War.* New York: St. Martin's Press, 1993.

Patočka, Jan. "České myšlení v meziválečném období" [Czech thinking between the wars]. *Proměny* 25, 1 (1988): 72–81.

Patočka, Jan. "Co jsou Češi?" [What kind of people are the Czechs?] *150 000 slov* 12, 4 (1988): 5–32.

Patočka, Jan. *Was sind die Tschechen: Kleiner Tatsachenbericht und Erklärungsversuch.* Prague: Panoráma, 1992.

Paulhac, François. *Les accords de Munich et les origines de la guerre de 1939.* Paris: J. Vrin, 1988.

Pavlov, V., and I. Petrov. "The Military-Political Situation in Central Europe." *Voyennaya mysl'* 9 (1938).

Pecháček, Jaroslav. *Masaryk, Beneš, Hrad: Masarykovy dopisy Benešovi* [Masaryk, Beneš, and the Castle: Masaryk's letters to Beneš]. Munich: České Slovo, 1984.

Perman, Dagmar Horna. *The Shaping of the Czechoslovak State.* Leiden: E. J. Brill, 1962.

Peroutka, Ferdinand. *Budování státu* [The building of a state]. Prague: Lidové Noviny, 1991.

Peroutka, Ferdinand. *Byl Beneš vinen?* [Was Beneš guilty?]. Perth Amboy: Universum Sokol Publications, 1973.

Peroutka, Ferdinand. "Co bylo, nebude" [What has been, won't]. *Přítomnost* 15 (23 March 1938).

Peroutka, Ferdinand. *Muž Přítomnosti* [The man from the *Pritomnost* magazine]. Curych: Konfrontace, 1985.

Peroutka, Ferdinand. *O věcech všeobecných* [Regarding general topics]. Prague: Státní Pedagogické Nakladatelství, 1991.

Peška, Zdeněk. *Národnostní menšiny a Československo* [Minorities and Czechoslovakia]. Bratislava: Komenského Universita, 1932.

Peters, Ihor. *SSSR, Chekhoslovakia i evropeiskaia politika nakanune Miunkhena*. Kiev: Naukova Dumka, 1971.

Peterson, James W. "Representation of Ethnic Groups within the Czechoslovak Political System, 1918–82." *East Central Europe/L'Europe du Centre-Est* 10, 1–2 (1983): 92–114.

Pfaff, Ivan. "Jak tomu opravdu bylo se sovětskou pomocí v mnichovské krizi?" [How was it really with the Soviet assistance during the Munich crisis?] *Svědectví* (Paris) 56–57 (1978).

Pfaff, Ivan. "Mohli jsme se v září 1938 sami bránit?" [Was it possible for Czechoslovakia to defend itself in September 1938?] *Reportér* 41 (1991): 1–4.

Pfaff, Ivan. "Prag und der Fall Tuchatschewski." *Vierteljahrshefte für Zeitgeschichte* 35, 1 (1987): 95–134.

Pfaff, Ivan. *Ruská zrada: 1938* [Russian treason: 1938]. Prague: BEA, 1993.

Pfaff, Ivan. "Tragédie plná omylů: Kritický portrét Edvarda Beneše" [A tragedy filled with errors: A critical portrait of Edvard Beneš]. *Reportér* 9 (1990): 1–12.

Pieck, Wilhelm. "The Munich Agreement Means War." *World News and Views* 18 (8 October 1938): 1128–30.

Pitt-Rivers, George Lane-Fox. *The Czech Conspiracy: A Phase in the World-War Plot*. London: Boswell, 1938.

Pleský, Metoděj. *Bratr Generál: Památce Stanislava Čečka* [In memorian General Stanislav Čeček]. Prague: Vydavatelství 'Za svobodu,' 1931.

Polichev, V. G. *Anglia i miunkhenskii sgovor*. Moscow: 1960.

Polišenská, Milada, and R. Kvaček. "Beneš a 'případ Tuchačevskij'" [Beneš and the Tukhachevsky affair]. *Mezinárodní politika* 8 (1991): 28–30.

Ponomaryov, Boris, and Andrei Gromyko (eds.). *History of Soviet Foreign Policy*. Moscow: Progress, 1969.

Ponomaryov, Boris, et al. (eds.). *Istoria vneshnei politiki SSSR*. Moscow: Nauka, 1966.

Post, Gaines. *The Civil-Military Fabric of Weimar Foreign Policy*. Princeton: Princeton University Press, 1973.

Post, Gaines. *Dilemmas of Appeasement: British Deterrence and Defense, 1934–1937*. Ithaca: Cornell University Press, 1993.

Potemkin, V. P. (ed.). *Istoria diplomatii, 1919–1939*. Moscow: OGIZ, 1945.

Prasolov, Sergei I. "Československo-sovětská smlouva o vzájemné pomoci z roku 1935" [The Czechoslovak-Soviet agreement on mutual assistance of 1935]. *Studie z dějin československo-sovětských vztahů 1917–1938*. Prague: Academia, 1967.

Prasolov, Sergei I. "Chekhoslovakia v period ugrozy fashizma i gilterovskoy agressii (1933–1937gg)." *Uchenye Zapiski Instituta Slavianovedenia AN SSSR* 7 (1953).

Prasolov, Sergei I. "Sovetskii soiuz i chekhoslovakia v 1938 g." In *Miunkhen: preddverie voiny*, V. K. Volkov (ed). Moscow: Nauka, 1988.

Pražák, H. "Varšava a Moskva" [Warsaw and Moscow]. *Praha-Moskva* 3 (December 1938): 290–92.

Presseisen, Ernst Leopold. *Amiens and Munich: Comparisons in Appeasement*. The Hague: Martinus Nijhoff, 1978.

Price, Ward G. *Year of Reckoning*. London: Cassell, 1939.

Prinz, Friedrich. *Beneš, Jaksch und die Sudetendeutschen*. Munich: Verlag die Brucke in Komm., 1975.

Prinz, Friedrich. "The USA and the Foundation of Czechoslovakia." *Central Europe Journal* 20, 15 (May 1972): 171–85.

Prinz, Friedrich (ed.). *Wenzel Jaksch—Edvard Beneš: Briefe und Dokumente aus dem Londoner Exil, 1939–1943.* Cologne: Verlag Wissenschaft und Politik, 1973.

Procházka, Theodor. *The Second Republic: The Disintegration of post-Munich Czechoslovakia, October 1938–March 1939.* Boulder: East European Monographs, 1981.

Procházka, Zdeněk, et al. (eds.). *Vojenské dějiny Československa, 1918–1939* [Military history of Czechoslovakia, 1918–1939]. Prague: Naše Vojsko, 1987.

Pronay, Nicholas, and Philip M. Taylor. "An Improper Use of Broadcasting . . . The British Government and Clandestine Radio Propaganda Operations against Germany during the Munich crisis and After." *Journal of Contemporary History* 19 (July 1984): 357–84.

Proti fašistické diktatuře, za diktaturu proletariátu [Against fascist dictatorship, for the dictatorship of the proletariat]. Prague: Max Forejt, 1933.

Raack, Richard C. *Stalin's Drive to the West, 1938–1945: The Origins of the Cold War.* Stanford: Stanford University Press, 1995.

Radice, Lisanne. *Prelude to Appeasement: East Central European Diplomacy in the Early 1930's.* Boulder: East European Monographs, 1981.

Radl, Emanuel. *Der Kampf zwischen Tschechen und Deutschen.* Reichenberg: G. Stiepel, 1928.

Ranson, Edward. *British Defense Policy and Appeasement between the Wars, 1919–1939.* London: Historical Association, 1993.

Raschhofer, Hermann. *Völkerbund und Münchener Abkommen.* Munich: Olzog, 1976.

Reichert, Günter. *Das Scheitern der Kleinen Entente.* Munich: Fides-Verlagsgesellschaft, 1971.

Reiman, Michael, and Ingmar Sütterlin. "Sowjetische 'Politbüro-Beschlüße' der Jahre 1931–1937 in staatlichen deutschen Archiven." *Jahrbücher für Geschichtes Osteuropas* 37 (1989): 196–216.

Ressel, Alfréd. "Mnichov ve vzpomínkách a v kritice důstojníka generálního štábu československé armády" [Critical reflections on Munich by a general staff officer of the Czechoslovak army]. *Historie a vojenství* 2 (1969): 302–58.

Rhode, Gotthold. "La situation en Allemagne en 1938 et la question des nationalités en Tchéchoslovaquie." *Revue des Études Slaves* 1–2 (1979): 99–108.

Ripka, Hubert. "Českoslovenští novináři v Sovětském svazu" [Czechoslovak journalists in the Soviet Union]. *Zahraniční politika* 14, 1 (1935): 14–17.

Ripka, Hubert. *East and West.* London: V. Gollanz, 1944.

Ripka, Hubert. *Munich: Before and After.* New York: Howard Fertig, 1969.

Ripka, Hubert. "Přátelství se SSSR státní naší potřebou" [Friendship with the Soviet Union: A necessity for Czechoslovakia]. *Praha-Moskva* 3 (May 1938): 73–75.

Ripka, Hubert. *The Repudiation of Munich.* London: Czechoslovak Ministry of Foreign Affairs Information Service, 1943.

Ripka, Hubert. "Vývoj československo-sovětského přátelství" [The development of Czechoslovak-Soviet friendship]. *Zahraniční politika* 14, 9–10 (1935): 504–11.

Robbins, Keith. *Appeasement.* New York: Blackwell, 1988.

Robbins, Keith. *Munich 1938.* London: Cassell, 1968.

Roberts, Andrew. *The Holy Fox: A Biography of Lord Halifax.* London: Weidenfeld & Nicolson, 1991.

Roberts, Geoffrey. *The Unholy Alliance.* Bloomington: Indiana University Press, 1989.

Rock, William R. *British Appeasement in the 1930s.* New York: Norton, 1977.

Rock, William R. *Chamberlain and Roosevelt: British Foreign Policy and the United States, 1937–1940.* Columbus: Ohio State University Press, 1988.

Roman, Eric. "Munich and Hungary: An Overview of Hungarian Diplomacy during the Sudeten Crisis." *East European Quarterly* 8 (March 1974): 71–97.

Rönnefarth, Helmuth K. *Die Sudetenkrise in der internationalen Politik: Entstehung, Verlauf, Auswirkung.* Wiesbaden: F. Steiner, 1961.

Rosenfeld, Günter. *Sowjetrußland und Deutschland 1917–1922.* Berlin: Akademie-Verlag, 1960.

Rouček, Joseph S. "Europe after Munich." *Social Science* 14 (January 1939): 17–22.

Rouček, Joseph S., and Jiří Škvor. "Beneš and Munich: A Reappraisal." *East European Quarterly* 10, 3 (1976): 375–85.

Rowse, A. L. *Appeasement: A Study in Political Decline, 1933–1939.* New York: Norton, 1961.

Rozviňme veliký zápas za sjednocení dělnictva proti hladu, fašismu a válce [For the unity of the proletariat against hunger and war]. Prague: Nakladatelství Senátora J. Hakena, 1933.

Rupnik, Jacques. *Historie du partii communiste tchécoslovaque.* Paris: Presses de la Fondation Nationale des Sciences Politiques, 1981.

Rupnik, Jacques. "Le parti communiste de Tchéchoslovaquie face à Munich." *Revue des Études Slaves* 1–2 (1979): 193–202.

"Rychlé jednotky u moderní armády, zejména u armády československé" [Modern rapid deployment units, especially those in the Czechoslovak army]. *Sobota* 7 (September 1936): 685–87.

Rychnowsky, Ernst. *Masaryk.* Prague: Staatliche Verlagsanstalt, 1930.

Rýzner, František. "Obrana Československé republiky v období Mnichova" [The defense of Czechoslovakia during the Munich crisis]. *Historie a vojenství* 4 (1956): 451–509.

Rzheshevskii, Oleg A. *Europe 1939: Was War Inevitable?* Moscow: Progress Publishers, 1989.

Šafář, Bohumil. "Co se děje v komunistické straně: Energie marně vyplýtvaná" [What is happening inside the Communist party: Wasted energy]. *Sobota* 7 (February 1936): 173–75.

Sakmyster, Thomas L. "Army Officer and Foreign Policy in Interwar Hungary, 1938–1941." *Journal of Contemporary History* 10 (January 1975): 19–40.

Sakmyster, Thomas L. "The Hungarian State Visit to Germany of August 1938: Some New Evidence on Hungary in Hitler's Pre-Munich Policy." *Canadian Slavic Studies* 3 (winter 1969): 677–91.

Sakmyster, Thomas L. "Hungary and the Munich Crisis: The Revisionist Dilemma." *Slavic Review* 32 (December 1973): 725–40.

Sakmyster, Thomas L. *Hungary's Admiral on Horseback: Miklos Horthy, 1918–1944.* Boulder: East European Monographs, 1994.

Sakmyster, Thomas L. *Hungary, the Great Powers, and the Danubian Crisis 1936–1939.* Athens: University of Georgia Press, 1980.

Sander, Rudolf. "Přehled vývoje československé vojenské správy v létech 1918–1939" [The development of the Czechoslovak army's command, 1918–1939]. *Historie a vojenství* 3 (1965): 359–404.

Saturník, T. et al. (eds.). *Pocta k šedesátým narozeninám Univ. Prof. Dr. Ant. Hobzy* [Festschrift for Professor Hobza]. Prague: Bursík & Kohout, 1936.

Schapiro, Leonard. *The Communist Party of the Soviet Union.* New York: Random House, 1971.

Schellenberg, Walter. *The Schellenberg Memoirs.* London: Andre Deutsch, 1956.

Schi, Li-so. *Das Komplott von München 1938 und die Beschwichtigungspolitik.* Cologne: Rote Fahne, 1978.

Schicktanz-Bor, R. "Základní myšlenky návrhu sudetoněmecké strany" [Fundamental ideas of the proposal of the Sudeten German party]. *Naše doba* 45 (October 1938): 267–74.

Schlamm, Willi. "Šedesát za noc" [Sixty within one night]. *Přítomnost* 15 (23 March 1938).

Schmidt, Gustav. *England in der Krise: Grundzüge und Grundlage der britischen Appeasement-Politik (1930–1937).* Opladen: Westdeutscher Verlag, 1981.

Schmidt, Paul Otto. *Hitler's Interpreter.* London: Macmillan, 1951.

Schuschnigg, Kurt von. *Austrian Requiem.* New York: Putnam's, 1947.

Schwarzenbeck, Engelbert. *Nationalsocialistische Pressenpolitik und die Sudetenkrise 1938.* Munich: Minerva-Publikation, 1979.

Scott, William Evans. *Alliance against Hitler: The Origins of the Franco-Soviet Pact.* Durham: Duke University Press, 1962.

Šeba, Jan. "Naše obchodní posice v Rusku" [Our commercial position in Russia]. *Zahraniční politika* 1, 2 (1922): 10–18.

Sebekowsky, Wilhelm. *The Expansion of the Czechs—Its Psychology, History, Methods, and Results.* Karlsbad: K. H. Frank, 1938.

Seebohm, Hans-Christoph. "Political Aspects of the Munich Agreement." *Central Europe Journal* 14 (October 1966): 295–300.

Seibt, Ferdinand (ed.). *Die böhmischen Länder zwischen Ost und West: Festschrift für Karl Bosl zum 75. Geburstag.* Munich: Oldenbourg, 1983.

Severní Čechy a Mnichov: Sborník statí k 30. výročí Mnichova. Liberec: Vysoká Škola Strojní a Textilní, 1969.

Sevostianov, Grigorii Nikolaevich. *Evropeiskii krizis i pozitsiia SShA, 1938–1939.* Moscow: Nauka, 1992.

Shepherd, Robert. *A Class Divided: Appeasement and the Road to Munich, 1938.* London: Macmillan, 1988.

Shirer, William L. *Berlin Diary.* New York: Knopf, 1941.

Shirer, William L. *The Rise and Fall of the Third Reich.* New York: Simon & Schuster, 1960.

Singbartl, Hartmut. *Die Durchführung der deutsch-tschechoslowakischen Grenzregelung von 1938 in völkerrechtlicher und staatsrechtlicher Sicht.* Munich: Fides-Verlagsgesellschaft, 1971.

Sládek, Zdeněk. "Akce československých a polských vládních kruhů proti sovětskoněmecké neutralitní smlouvě v dubnu 1926" [Czechoslovak and Polish governments' action against the Soviet-German neutrality agreement in April 1926]. *Slovanský přehled* 61 (1975): 255–64.

Sládek, Zdeněk. "Československá politika a Rusko 1918–1920" [Czechoslovak policy and Russia, 1918–1920]. *Československý časopis historický* 16, 6 (1968).

Slavík, Jan. "Aktivita ruské revoluce" [The developing Russian revolution]. *Sobota* 7 (April 1936): 301–2.

Slavík, Jan. *Bolševismus v přerodu* [Bolshevism in transition]. Prague: Melantrich, 1932.

Slavík, Jan. *Co jsem viděl v sovětském Rusku?* [What did I see in Soviet Russia?]. Prague: SNO, 1926.

Slavík, Jan. "Co se děje v Rusku?" [What is happening in Russia?]. *Sobota* 8 (July 1937): 733–35.

Slavík, Jan. "Co se splnilo z předpovědí o létech 1926 až 1936?" [What predictions have been fulfilled regarding the years 1926–1939?]. *Sobota* 7 (November–December 1936).

Slavík, Jan. "Dr. V. Girsa a studium sovětského Ruska" [Girsa and the study of Soviet Russia]. *Národní osvobození,* 1 December 1945.

Slavík, Jan. "Dvacet let sporu o bolševickou revoluci" [Twenty years of debates regarding the Bolshevik revolution]. *Sobota* 8 (October–November 1937): 768–69, 801–3.

Slavík, Jan. *Lenin.* Prague: Melantrich, 1934.

Slavík, Jan. *Leninova vláda* [Lenin's regime]. Prague: Melantrich, 1935.

Slavík, Jan. "Moskevský proces a spisovatelé" [The Moscow trial and writers]. *Sobota* 7 (September 1936): 702–4.

Slavík, Jan. "Na adresu přátel sovětského Ruska" [Addressing the friends of Soviet Russia]. *Sobota* 7 (February–March 1936): 96–99, 117–20, 134–36, 160–62, 201–5.

Slavík, Jan. *Německý postup proti Slovanům a jeho Sudetský agent* [The German anti-Slavic policy and the role of the Sudeten Germans]. Prague: Melantrich, 1938.

Slavík, Jan. "Pád starých bolševiků jako etapa ruské revoluce" [The fall of the old Bolsheviks: A phase in the Russian revolution]. *Národní osvobození,* 4 February 1937.

Slavík, Jan. *Po druhé v sovětském Rusku* [In Soviet Russia for the second time]. Prague, SNO, 1927.

Slavík, Jan. *Po třetí v sovětském Rusku* [In Soviet Russia for the third time]. Prague: SNO, 1932.

Slavík, Jan. "Pól země a pól revoluce" [Focus of the earth and the revolution]. *Sobota* 8 (July 1937): 461–62.

Slavík, Jan. "Sovětská diplomacie" [Soviet diplomacy]. *Národní osvobození,* 20, 21, 23 September 1934.

Slavík, Jan. *Smysl ruské revoluce* [The meaning of Russian revolution]. Prague: SNO, 1927.

Slavík, Jan et al. (eds.). *Russkii zagranichnii istoricheskii arkhiv v Prage.* Prague: R. Z. I. Arkhiv, 1938.

Small, Melvin, and Otto Feinstein (eds.). *Appeasing Fascism: Articles from the Wayne State University Conference on Munich after Fifty Years.* Lanham, Md.: University Press of America, 1991.

Smelser, Ronald M. *The Sudeten Problem, 1933–1939: Volkstumspolitik and the Formulation of Nazi Foreign Policy.* Middletown: Wesleyan University Press, 1975.

Smith, Adrian. "Macmillan and Munich: The Open Conspirator." *Dalhousie Review* 68 (fall 1989): 235–47.

"Smlouva o vzájemné pomoci mezi ČSR a SSSR" [The treaty on mutual assistance between Czechoslovakia and the Soviet Union]. *Praha-Moskva* 3 (March 1938): 37–39.

Šmoldas, Zdeněk. *Českoslovenští letci v boji proti fašismu* [Czechoslovak pilots in the war against fascism]. Prague: Naše Vojsko, 1987.

Šnejdárek, A. "Tajné rozhovory Beneše s Německem v létech 1936/37" [Secret talks between Beneš and Germany in 1936–37]. *Československý časopis historický* 9, 1 (1961): 112–16.

Sobota, Emil. "K diskusi o zákonodárných návrzích sudetoněmecké strany: odpověď panu dru Schickentanzovi" [Regarding the legal proposals of the Sudeten German party: a response to Mr. Schickentanz]. *Naše doba* 45 (October 1938): 337–40.

Sobota, Emil. *Národnostní autonomie v Československu?* [Autonomy for nationalities in Czechoslovakia?] Prague: Orbis, 1938.

Sobota, Emil. *Das tschechoslowakische Nationalitätenrecht.* Prague: Orbis, 1931.

Sobota, Emil. "Zákonodárné návrhy Sudetoněmecké strany z hlediska demokracie" [The legal proposals of the Sudeten German party from the perspective of democracy]. *Naše doba* 45 (October 1938): 67–74.

Soják, Vladimír. *O čs. zahraniční politice 1918–1939* [Regarding Czechoslovak foreign policy 1918–1939]. Prague: SNPL, 1956.

Soukup, František. *Říjen 1918: Předpoklady a vývoj našeho odboje domácího v čes-koslovenské revoluci za státní samostatnost národa* [October 1918: conditions and development of our home resistance; the Czechoslovak revolution for an independent state]. Prague: Ústřední Dělnické Knihkupectví a Nakladatelství Antonín Zasvěcený a Orbis, 1928.

"Sovětský autor o útočných plánech Německa proti Československu" [Soviet author on German aggressive designs on Czechoslovakia]. *Sobota* 7 (October 1936): 826–27.

"Srovnání dvou armád" [A comparison of two armies]. *Sobota* 7 (February 1936): 100–3.

Stanisławska, Stefania. "Korespondence mezi E. Benešem a I. Mościckým v září 1938" [The Beneš-Mościcky correspondence]. *Slezský sborník* 3 (1963).

Stanisławska, Stefania. *Polska i Monachium* [Poland and Munich]. Warsaw: Książka i Widza, 1967.

Stanisławska, Stefania. *Wielka i mała politika J. Becka (marec–maj 1938)* [The politics of Jozef Beck: Big and small]. Warsaw: Polski Institut Spraw Międzynarodowych, 1962.

Starobin, Joseph. "Czechoslovakia and World Peace." *Young Communist Review* (October 1938): 18–19.

Státní Úřad Statistický. *Annuaire statistique de la République Tchéchoslovaque.* Prague: Státní Úřad Statistický, 1934.

Štěpán, František, and J. Soukup. *Měli jsme bojovat: zápisy z jednání politického byra ÚV KSČ v září 1938* [We should have fought: minutes from the meetings of the politburo of the Central Committee of the Communist party of Czechoslovakia in September 1938]. Prague: Ústav Marxismu-Leninismu, 1978.

Stepanov, A. S. "Pered Miunkhenom." *Voenno-istoricheskii zhurnal* 4–5 (1992): 4–9.

Stern, V. "Only the Soviet Union Stood by Its Word." *World News and Views* 18 (29 October 1938): 1180–81.

Stern-Rubarth, Edgar. *Drei Männer suchen Europa; Briand, Chamberlain, Stresemann.* Munich: W. Weimann, 1947.

Stone, Norman, and Eduard Strouhal (eds.). *Czechoslovakia: Crossroads and Crises, 1918–88.* Basingstoke: Macmillan in association with the BBC, 1989.

Strankmüller, Emil. "Československé ofenzivní zpravodajství v létech 1937 do 15. března 1939" [The offensive section of Czechoslovak intelligence, 1937–15 March 1939]. *Odboj a revoluce* 6, 2 (1968): 65–67.

Strankmüller, Emil. "Čs. ofenzivní zpravodajství od března 1939" [The offensive section of Czechoslovak intelligence after March 1939]. *Odboj a revoluce* 8, 1 (1970): 189–229.

Stronge, H. C. T, "The Czechoslovak Army and the Munich Crisis: A Personal Memorandum." *War and Society: A Yearbook of Military History* 1 (1975): 162–77.

Stronge, H. C. T. "The Military Approach to Munich." *Times,* 29 September 1967.

Sturdza, Michel. *The Suicide of Europe: Memoirs of Prince Michel Sturdza, Former Foreign Minister of Rumania.* Boston: Western Islands, 1968.

Sutton, Eric. *Gustav Stresemann: His Diaries, Letters and Papers.* New York, Macmillan, 1935–1940.

Suvorov, Viktor. *Icebreaker: Who Started the Second World War?* London: Hamish Hamilton, 1990.

Sychrava, Lev. "Materiály: z úvah o přípravě mnichovské dohody r. 1938" [Thoughts regarding the preparations of the Munich agreement of 1938]. *Československý časopis historický* 17, 4 (1969): 598–618.

Szklarska-Lohmannowa, Alina. *Polsko-czechoslowackie stosunki dyplomatyczne w latach 1918–1925* [Polish-Czechoslovak diplomatic relations, 1918–1925]. Wrocław: Wydawnictwo Polskiej Akademii Nauk, 1967.

Taborsky, Edward. "Beneš a náš osud" [Beneš and our fate]. *Svědectví* (Paris), 15, 57 (1978): 17–50.

Taborsky, Edward. "Beneš and the Soviets." *Foreign Affairs* 27 (January 1949): 304–20.

Taborsky, Edward. *President Beneš and the Crises of 1938 and 1948.* Phoenix: Arizona State University Press, 1978.

Taborsky, Edward. "President Beneš and the Crises of 1938 and 1948." *East Central Europe* 5, 2 (1978): 203–14.

Taborsky, Edward. *Presidentův sekretář vypovídá: deník druhého zahraničního odboje* [The report of the president's secretary: World War II diary]. Curych: Konfrontace, 1978.

Taborsky, Edward. "The Triumph and Disaster of Eduard Beneš." *Foreign Affairs* 36, 4 (July 1958): 669–84.

Tardieu, André. *Notes de semaine 1938: L'Année de Munich.* Paris: Flammarion, 1939.

Taylor, A. J. P. *The Origins of the Second World War.* London: Hamilton, 1961.

Taylor, Telford. *Munich: The Price of Peace.* Garden City: Doubleday, 1979.

Teichova, Alice. *An Economic Background to Munich: International Business and Czechoslovakia 1918–1938.* Cambridge: Cambridge University Press, 1974.

Teichova, Alice. *Kleinstaaten im Spannungsfeld der Grossmächte: Wirtschaft und Politik in Mittel und Südosteuropa in der Zwischenkriegszeit.* Munich: Oldenburg, 1988.

Teichova, Alice. *Wirtschaftsgeschichte der Tschoslowakei, 1918–1980.* Vienna: Böhlau, 1989.

Thompson, Laurence. *The Greatest Treason: The Untold Story of Munich.* New York: William Morrow, 1968.

Thompson, Neville. *The Anti-Appeasers; Conservative Opposition to Appeasement in the 30s.* Oxford: Clarendon Press, 1971.

Thorne, Christopher. *The Approach to War, 1938–1939.* New York: St. Martin's Press, 1967.

Thyssen, Fritz. *I Paid Hitler.* New York: Farrar & Rinehart, 1941.

Toepfer, Marcia Lynn. "American Governmental Attitudes towards the Soviet Union during the Czechoslovak Crisis of 1938." *East European Quarterly* 14, 1 (1980): 93–108.

Toepfer, Marcia Lynn. "The Soviet Role in the Munich Crisis: An Historiographical Debate." *Diplomatic History* 1 (fall 1977).

Tomáš, Peter. "Kapitoly z české geopolitiky" [Chapters from Czech geopolitics]. *Svědectví* (Paris) 11, 45 (1973).

Tomášek, Dušan. *Deník druhé republiky* [A diary of the second republic]. Prague: Naše Vojsko, 1988.

Trauttmansdorff, Graf zu. "Die Mission des Grafen Trauttmansdorff." *Frankfurter Allgemeine,* 15 January 1962.

Trevor-Roper, High. "The Munich Illusion." *Spectator,* 24 September 1988, 17–18.

Trhlík, Zdeněk. *Jawaharlal Nehru and the Munich Betrayal of Czechoslovakia.* Prague: Orbis, 1989.

Trukhanovsky, V. G. (ed.). *Istoria mezhdunarodnykh otnoshenii i vneshnei politiki CCCP, 1917–1939.* Moscow: Institut Mezhdunarodnykh Otnoshenii, 1967.

Tucker, Robert C. "The Emergence of Stalin's Foreing Policy." *Slavic Review* 36 (1977): 563–89.

Tucker, Robert C. *Stalin in Power: The Revolution from Above, 1928–1941.* New York: Norton, 1990.

Tucker, Robert C., and Stephen F. Cohen (eds.). *The Great Purge Trial.* New York: Grosset & Dunlap, 1965.

Überschär, Gerd R. "General Halder and the Resistance to Hitler in the German High Command 1938–40." *European History Quarterly* 18 (July 1988): 321–47.

Ulam, Adam B. *Expansion and Coexistence: The History of Soviet Foreign Policy 1917–1967*. New York: Praeger, 1968.

Ulam, Adam B. *Stalin: The Man and His Era*. New York: Viking, 1973.

Urban, Rudolf. *Tajné fondy III. sekce. Z archívů MZ Republiky Československé* [Secret funds of the third section: From the archives of the Czechoslovak foreign ministry]. Prague: Orbis, 1943.

Ústav marxismu-leninismu ÚV KSČ. *Protifašistický a národně osvobozenecký boj českého a slovenského lidu, 1938–1945* [The antifascist and national liberation struggle of Czech and Slovak people]. Prague: ÚML, 1979.

Ústav pro mezinárodní politiku a ekonomii. *Kdo zavinil Mnichov: Sborník z mezinárodního vědeckého zasedání k 20. výročí Mnichova* [Who caused Munich: Papers from an international conference on the twentieth anniversary of the Munich agreement]. Prague: SNPL, 1959.

ÚV KSČ. *30. let od Mnichova, 1938–1968; Kořeny, příčiny a důsledky* [Munich: Thirty years later, 1938–1968; Roots, causes and consequences]. Prague: Ideologické Oddělení ÚV KSČ, 1968.

Valenta, Jaroslav. "Addenda et Corrigenda: Zur Rolle Prags im Falle Tuchatschewski." *Vierteljahrshefte für Zeitgeschichte* 3 (1991): 437–45.

Valenta, Jaroslav. "Praha ve zpravodajské hře o M. N. Tuchačevského na jaře 1937" [Prague's role in the intelligence game involving the fate of Tukhachevsky in the spring 1937]. *Studie Muzea Kroměřížska* (1990): 155–72.

Valenta, Jaroslav. "Vyvrcholení národně osvobozeneckého hnutí a utvoření samostatných států (1918–1920)," and "Pokusy o československo-polské sblížení a spolupráci (1921–1925)" [The culmination of Czech and Polish national liberation movements and the formation of independent states, 1918–1920 and Attempts at Czech-Polish friendship and cooperation]. In *Češi a Poláci v minulosti: Období kapitalismu a imperialismu*. Prague: Academia, 1967.

Verstat, Jaroslav. "Životní dílo Dra Ed. Beneše" [Edvard Beneš's lifelong achievements]. *Zahraniční politika* 13 (July 1934): 373–77.

Veselý, Jiří. "Ein Deutscher unter uns: Fritz Walter Nielsen in der Tschechoslowakei, 1933–1939." *Philologica Pragensia* 59, 3 (1977): 138–48.

Vital, David. "Czechoslovakia and the Powers, September 1938." *Journal of Contemporary History* 1, 4 (1966): 37–67.

Vital, David. *The Inequality of States: A Study of the Small Power in International Relations*. Oxford: Clarendon Press, 1967.

Vnuk, František. "Munich and the Soviet Union." *Journal of Central European Affairs* 21 (October 1961): 285–304.

Vojan, K. "Německo a propaganda proti Československu" [Germany and its propaganda against Czechoslovakia]. *Sobota* 8 (February 1937): 121–23.

"Vojenská situace ČSR ve světle Třetí Říše" [Czechoslovakia's military position and the Third Reich]. *Sobota* 8 (July 1937): 568–71.

Volkogonov, D. A. "Drama reshenii 1939 goda." *Novaia i noveishaia istoria* 4 (1989): 3–27.

Volkogonov, D. A. *Stalin: Triumph and Tragedy*. New York: Grove Weidenfeld, 1991.

Volkogonov, D., M. Semiriaga, and I. Pop. "Předehra války . . . Stalin . . . Vlasovci . . . [The approach of war . . . Stalin . . . the Vlasov units . . .]. *Rudé Právo*, 8 May 1991.

Volkov, V. K. et al. *1939 god: Uroki istorii*. Moscow: Mysl', 1990.

Volkov, V. K. *Miunkhen—Preddverie vojny: Istoricheskie ocherki*. Moscow: Nauka, 1988.

Volkov, V. K. *Miunkhenskii sgovor i Balkanskie strany*. Moscow: Nauka, 1978.

Vondráček, Felix J. *The Foreign Policy of Czechoslovakia.* New York: Columbia University Press, 1937.

"Vorošilov o nebezpečí světové války" [Voroshilov on the danger of war]. *Praha-Moskva* 3 (December 1938): 298–301.

Wágnerová, Jarmila. *Protifašistický boj a Mnichov* [Struggle against fascism and Munich]. Prague: Universita Karlova, 1979.

Wallace, William V. "The Making of the May Crisis of 1938." *The Slavonic and East European Review* 41 (June 1963): 368–90.

Wallace, William V. "New Documents on the History of Munich: A Selection from the Soviet and Czechoslovak Archives." *International Affairs* 35 (October 1959): 447–54.

Wallace, William V. "A Reply to Mr. Watt." *The Slavonic and East European Review* 44, 103 (1966): 481–86.

Wandycz, Piotr S. "L'Alliance franco-tchécoslovaque de 1924: Un échange de lettres Poincaré-Beneš." *Revue d'Histoire Diplomatique* 3–4 (1984): 328–33.

Wandycz, Piotr S. "The Foreign Policy of Edvard Beneš, 1918–1938." In *A History of the Czechoslovak Republic, 1918–1949,* ed. Victor S. Mamatey and Radomír Luža. Princeton: Princeton University Press, 1973.

Wandyzc, Piotr S. *France and Her Eastern Allies, 1919–1925.* Minneapolis: University of Minnesota Press, 1962.

Wandycz, Piotr S. *Polish Diplomacy 1914–1945: Aims and Achievements.* London: Orbis, 1988.

Wandycz, Piotr S. *Soviet-Polish Relations, 1917–1921.* Cambridge: Harvard University Press, 1969.

Wandycz, Piotr S. *The Twilight of French Eastern Alliances 1926–36: French-Czechoslovak-Polish Relations from Locarno to the Remilitarization of the Rhineland.* Princeton: Princeton University Press, 1988.

Wark, Wesley K. "British Intelligence on the German Air Force and Aircraft Industry, 1933–1939." *Historical Journal* 25, 3 (1982): 627–48.

Watt, Donald Cameron. "Hitler's Visit to Rome and the May Weekend Crisis: A Study in Hitler's Response to External Stimuli." *Journal of Contemporary History* 9 (January 1974): 23–32.

Watt, Donald Cameron. *How War Came: The Immediate Origins of the Second World War, 1938–1939.* New York: Pantheon, 1989.

Watt, Donald Cameron. "The May Crisis of 1938: A Rejoinder to Mr. Wallace." *The Slavonic and East European Review* 44 (July 1966): 475–80.

Watt, Donald Cameron. *Too Serious a Business: European Armed Forces and the Approach to the Second World War.* Berkeley: University of California Press, 1975.

Weinberg, Gerhard L. *The Foreign Policy of Hitler's Germany: Diplomatic Revolution in Europe, 1933–36.* Chicago: University of Chicago Press, 1970.

Weinberg, Gerhard L. *The Foreign Policy of Hitler's Germany: Starting World War II, 1937–1939.* Chicago: University of Chicago Press, 1980.

Weinberg, Gerhard L. *Germany and the Soviet Union, 1939–1941.* Leiden: E. J. Brill, 1954.

Weinberg, Gerhard L. *Der gewaltsame Anschluß 1938: Die deutsche Aussenpolitik und Österreich.* Vienna: Bundespressedienst, 1988.

Weinberg, Gerhard L. "The May Crisis 1938." *Journal of Modern History* 29, 3 (September 1957): 213–25.

Weinberg, Gerhard L. "Secret Hitler-Beneš Negotiations in 1936–37." *Journal of Central European Affairs* 19 (1961): 366–74.

Wendt, Bernd-Jürgen. *München 1938: England zwischen Hitler und Preussen.* Frankfurt: Europäische Verlagsanstalt, 1965.

Werner, Arthur. *Eduard Beneš: Der Mensch und der Staatsmann.* Prague: Verlag Roland Morawitz, n.d. [1935?].

Werth, Alexander. *France and Munich: Before and After the Surrender.* New York: H. Fertig, 1969.

Wheeler-Bennett, Sir John. *Knaves, Fools and Heroes.* London: Macmillan, 1974.

Wheeler-Bennett, Sir John. *Munich: Prologue to Tragedy.* New York: Viking, 1964.

Whitney, Craig R. "Rudolf Hess's Daring Flight: K.G.B. Files Tell New Tales," *New York Times,* 8 June 1991.

Williams, Rowan A. "The Czech Legion Revisited." *East Central Europe* 6, 1 (1979): 20–39.

Wiskemann, Elizabeth. *Czechs and Germans: A Study of the Struggle in the Historic Provinces of Bohemia and Moravia.* London: Oxford University Press, 1938.

Wolfers, Arnold. *Britain and France between Two Wars.* New York: Norton, 1940.

Wollenberg, Erich. *The Red Army.* London: Secker & Warburg, 1940.

Wolmot, Chester. *The Struggle for Europe.* New York: Harper, 1952.

Wright, Jonathan, and Paul Stafford. "Hitler and the Hossbach Memorandum." *History Today* (March 1988): 11–17.

Wuschek, Anton F. "In Memoriam Wenzel Jaksch." *Central Europe Journal* 15 (January 1967): 13–14.

Young, Edgar P. *Czechoslovakia: Keystone of Peace and Democracy.* London: Victor Gollancz, 1938.

Young, Robert J. *In Command of France: French Foreign Policy and Military Planning, 1933–1940.* Cambridge: Harvard University Press, 1978.

Young, Robert J. "Le Haut Commandement français au moment de Munich." *Revue d'Histoire Moderne et Contemporaine* 24 (1977): 110–29.

Zakharov, Matvei V. *General'nyi shtab v predvoennye gody.* Moscow: Voenizdat, 1989.

Zgorniak, Marian. *Europa w przededniu wojny: Sytuacja militarna w latach 1938–1939* [Europe on the Eve of the War: Military Situation in 1938–1939]. Cracow: Księgarnia Akademicka, 1993.

Zgorniak, Marian. *Sytuacja militarna w Europe w okresie kryzysu politycznego 1938 r.* [The military situation in Europe during the 1938 political crisis]. Warsaw, PWN, 1979.

Zgorniak, Marian. *Wojskowe aspekty kryzysu czechosłowackiego 1938 roku* [The military dimensions of the Czechoslovak crisis of 1938]. Cracow: Zeszyty Naukowe Uniwersytetu Jagiollonskiego, 123, Prace historyczne, 1966.

Zhilin, P. *They Sealed Their Own Doom.* Moscow: Progress Publishers, 1970.

Zimmern, Alfred. "Czechoslovakia To-day." *International Affairs* 17 (July–August 1938): 465–92.

Zorach, Jonathan. "The British View of the Czechs in the Era before the Munich Crisis." *Slavonic and East European Review* 57 (January 1979): 56–70.

Zorach, Jonathan. "Czechoslovakia's Fortifications: Their Development and Role in the Munich Crisis." *Militärgeschichtliche Mitteilungen* 17, 2 (1976): 81–94.

Zorach, Jonathan. "The Nationality Problem in the Czechoslovak Army between the Two World Wars." *East Central Europe* 5, 2 (1978): 169–85.

Zorach, Jonathan. "The Nečas Mission during the Munich Crisis." *East Central Europe* 16, 1–2 (1989): 53–70.

Zsigmond, László (ed.). "Ungarn und das Münchener Abkommen." *Acta Historica* 6, 3–4 (1959): 251–85.

Index

A-54. *See* Paul Thümmel
Abovich, Miron Yakovlevich, 20
Abwehr, 148, 153
Addison, Sir Joseph, 55–57, 165
Aleksandrovsky, Sergei S., 30, 36–37, 40, 46, 48–50, 60, 76, 99–100, 102–104, 118, 136–138, 143, 156, 192, 196–197, 223–225, 229–230, 235, 240–241, 244–246, 253–259, 265, 271
Alksnis, Y. I., 54
Anschluß. See Austria
Antonov-Ovseenko, Vladimir A., 15, 30, 60
Arosev, Aleksandr Yakovlevich, 36, 60
Aroseva, Gertruda, 36, 60
Ashton-Gwatkin, Frank, 183–184, 250–251
Attlee, Clement, 117
Austria, 10, 16, 20, 31, 37, 46, 56, 74, 80–92, 114, 119–129, 130, 132–133, 135, 137–139, 144–145, 149–150, 157, 184, 191, 193, 199, 209–210, 217, 220, 228, 231

Baltic countries, 44–45
Bartík, Josef, 100, 110
Barthou, Louis, 37, 43–44
Baxa, Karel, 16
Beau-Rivage Hotel, 4, 23
Beck, Józef, 45, 147, 164–165, 168, 228
Belgium, 4, 34, 61, 228, 239
Beneš, Edvard: goes abroad, 3, 23; and the *Anschluß*, 124–126; and army generals, 215, 251–252; and authoritarian states, 83–84, 126; his character, 5, 23–24, 56–57, 83, 114, 118–119, 177, 181–182, 262–263; and democracy, 6, 180, 232; and egalitarianism, 68; returns from exile, 5; and France, 33–35, 40, 43–44, 84, 123, 127, 142, 174–77, 189, 192, 201, 222, 248, 253, 262; and the Franco-British proposal, 218–225, 234, 252–253; and the Franco-British ultimatum, 189, 225–234, 253, 266; and the Franco-Soviet pact, 45–46; and Great Britain, 117, 127, 180–182, 185, 189, 201, 262 (*see also* Beneš and Addison, Beneš and Newton, and Czechoslovakia and Great Britain); did not lack greatness, 119, 262; his health, 118, 231, 249, 262; views on history, 117–118; at Locarno, 34; his marriage, 118; and Munich, 249–256, 261–262; after Munich, 262–263; his optimism, 118, 138, 143, 192, 210, 229–230, 232–233, 235–237, 240–241, 243–245; as orator, 145, 210–211, 232; at the Paris Peace Conference, 4–5, 222, 252; and Poland, 9–10, 12–13, 25–28, 45, 57, 66, 130–131, 136, 146–147, 165, 168–169, 228, 234–235; becomes president, 58, 116–117; and religion, 159; dictates resignation statement, 253; Berlin demands his resignation, 256; resigns, 256; and the Rhineland crisis, 75; and Russia, 11–12, 22–23, 41; and the Second Bureau, 151–152, 170; and "secret negotiations" with Berlin, 96–107; his villa in Sezimovo Ústí, 117–118; and socialism, 11; and Soviet assistance, 38–39, 54–55, 85–86, 132–138, 154–157, 190–201, 211, 223–225, 228–231, 235–236, 239–241, 244, 246–248, 251, 253–260, 262,